T0388917

Palgrave Handbooks in German Idealism

Series Editor
Matthew C. Altman, Philosophy and Religious Studies,
Central Washington University, Ellensburg, WA, USA

Palgrave Handbooks in German Idealism is a series of comprehensive and authoritative edited volumes on the major German Idealist philosophers and their critics. Underpinning the series is the successful *Palgrave Handbook of German Idealism* (2014), edited by Matthew C. Altman, which provides an overview of the period, its greatest philosophers, and its historical and philosophical importance.

Individual volumes focus on specific philosophers and major themes, offering a more detailed treatment of the many facets of their work in metaphysics, epistemology, logic, ethics, aesthetics, political philosophy, and several other areas. Each volume is edited by one or more internationally recognized experts in the subject, and contributors include both established figures and younger scholars with innovative readings. The series offers a wide-ranging and authoritative insight into German Idealism, appropriate for both students and specialists.

More information about this series at
http://www.palgrave.com/gp/series/14696

Cynthia D. Coe
Editor

The Palgrave Handbook of German Idealism and Phenomenology

palgrave
macmillan

Editor
Cynthia D. Coe
Philosophy and Religious Studies
Central Washington University
Ellensburg, WA, USA

ISSN 2634-6230   ISSN 2634-6249   (electronic)
Palgrave Handbooks in German Idealism
ISBN 978-3-030-66856-3   ISBN 978-3-030-66857-0   (eBook)
https://doi.org/10.1007/978-3-030-66857-0

This Palgrave Macmillan imprint is published by the registered company Springer Nature Switzerland AG
The registered company address is: Gewerbestrasse 11, 6330 Cham, Switzerland

Series Editor's Preface

The era of German Idealism stands alongside ancient Greece and the French Enlightenment as one of the most fruitful and influential periods in the history of philosophy. Beginning with the publication of Kant's *Critique of Pure Reason* in 1781 and ending about ten years after Hegel's death in 1831, the period of "classical German philosophy" transformed whole fields of philosophical endeavor. The intellectual energy of this movement is still very much alive in contemporary philosophy; the philosophers of that period continue to inform our thinking and spark debates of interpretation.

After a period of neglect as a result of the early analytic philosophers' rejection of idealism, interest in the field has grown exponentially in recent years. Indeed, the study of German Idealism has perhaps never been more active in the English-speaking world than it is today. Many books appear every year that offer historical/interpretive approaches to understanding the work of the German Idealists, and many others adopt and develop their insights and apply them to contemporary issues in epistemology, metaphysics, ethics, politics, and aesthetics, among other fields. In addition, a number of international journals are devoted to idealism as a whole and to specific idealist philosophers, and journals in both the history of philosophy and contemporary philosophies have regular contributions to the German Idealists. In numerous countries, there are regular conferences and study groups run by philosophical associations that focus on this period and its key figures, especially Kant, Fichte, Schelling, Hegel, and Schopenhauer.

As part of this growing discussion, the volumes in the *Palgrave Handbooks in German Idealism* series are designed to provide overviews of the major figures and movements in German Idealism, with a breadth and depth of coverage that distinguishes them from other anthologies. Chapters have been specially commissioned for this series, and they are written by established and emerging scholars from throughout the world. Contributors not only provide overviews of their subject matter but also explore the cutting edge of the field by advancing original theses. Some authors develop or revise positions that they have taken in their other publications, and some take novel approaches that challenge existing paradigms. The *Palgrave Handbooks in German Idealism* thus give students a natural starting point from which to begin their study of German Idealism, and they serve as a resource for advanced scholars to engage in meaningful discussions about the movement's philosophical and historical importance.

In short, the *Palgrave Handbooks in German Idealism* have comprehensiveness, accessibility, depth, and philosophical rigor as their overriding goals. These are challenging aims, to be sure, especially when held simultaneously, but that is the task that the excellent scholars who are editing and contributing to these volumes have set for themselves.

Matthew C. Altman

Contents

Notes on Contributors

Sorin Baiasu is Professor of Philosophy at Keele University and Distinguished Research Fellow at the Oxford Uehiro Centre for Practical Ethics. He has published extensively in his research areas, including *Kant and Sartre: Re-discovering Critical Ethics*. His work is supported by the British Academy, the European Commission, and the ERC.

David Batho is a Postdoctoral Scholar at the Humanities and Social Change Center at Santa Barbara, University of California. He has previously taught at the University of Oxford and the University of Essex, where he received his Ph.D.

M. Jorge de Carvalho is Associate Professor of Philosophy at the New University of Lisbon and Member of the IEF Research Unit (University of Coimbra). He has authored books and articles on Sophocles, Plato, Aristotle, the Stoics, Augustine, Sextus Empiricus, Swift, Kant, Fichte, Schelling, Hegel, Kierkegaard, Husserl, Heidegger, and Wittgenstein.

Cynthia D. Coe is Professor of Philosophy at Central Washington University. She specializes in contemporary Continental ethics, feminist theory, and critical race theory. She has previously published *Levinas and the Trauma of Responsibility* (Indiana, 2018) and *The Fractured Self in Freud and German Philosophy*, co-authored with Matthew Altman (Palgrave, 2013).

Zachary Davis is Associate Professor of Philosophy at St. John's University in Queens, NY. His most recent research project is the forthcoming English translation of Max Scheler's *Cognition and Work*. He is also the President of the Max Scheler Society of North America.

Federico Ferraguto is Professor at the Pontifícia Universidade Católica do Paraná in Curitiba (Brazil). He researches classical German philosophy, has published several articles on the thought of Fichte and Reinhold, and collaborated on Reinhold's *Gesammelte Schriften*.

Markus Gabriel is Professor and Chair in Epistemology, Modern, and Contemporary Philosophy, at the University of Bonn. He is the author of more than twenty books and a hundred articles, including *Transcendental Ontology* (2013); *Fields of Sense* (2015); and *I am Not a Brain* (2017).

Theodore George is Professor of Philosophy at Texas A&M University. His research and teaching interests include continental European philosophy since Kant, with emphasis on Gadamer, contemporary hermeneutics, contemporary continental ethics, philosophy of art and aesthetics, Hegel, and German Idealism and Romanticism.

Azzedine Haddour is Professor of Francophone and Comparative Literature at University College London. He is the co-translator of Sartre's essays, *Colonialism and Neo-colonialism* (2001), editor of *The Fanon Reader* (2006), and author of *Colonial Myths: History and Narrative* (2001) and *Frantz Fanon, Postcolonialism and the Ethics of Difference* (2019).

Jill Hernandez is Professor of Philosophy and Dean of the College of Arts & Humanities at Central Washington University. She publishes on issues intersecting ethics, existentialism, and philosophy of religion, and her works include *Gabriel Marcel's Ethics of Hope* (Bloomsbury).

Mette Lebech is Lecturer in Philosophy at the University of Maynooth, Ireland. She holds degrees from Copenhagen, Louvain-la-neuve, and Leuven. She has published widely on human dignity and Edith Stein, and is founding President of the International Association for the Study of the Philosophy of Edith Stein (IASPES).

Elisa Magrì is Assistant Professor of Philosophy at Boston College. Among other works, she authored *Hegel e la genesi del concetto. Auto-riferimento, memoria, incarnazione* (Padua, 2017) and co-edited *Hegel and Phenomenology* (Springer, 2019).

Dermot Moran holds the Joseph Chair in Catholic Philosophy, Boston College. He was previously Professor at University College Dublin. His publications include *Introduction to Phenomenology* (2000), *Edmund Husserl: Founder of Phenomenology* (2005), and *Husserl's Crisis of the European Sciences and Transcendental Phenomenology* (2012).

Shannon M. Mussett is Professor of Philosophy at Utah Valley University. She publishes on Simone de Beauvoir, French Existentialism, and Hegelian philosophy. She is currently completing her manuscript, *Entropic Philosophy: Chaos, Breakdown, Creation* with Rowman and Littlefield Press.

Robert Piercey is Professor of Philosophy at the University of Regina, Canada, and works on contemporary continental philosophy, metaphilosophy, and the philosophy of history. He is the author of *Reading as a Philosophical Practice*, *The Uses of the Past from Heidegger to Rorty*, and *The Crisis in Continental Philosophy*.

María-Luz Pintos-Peñaranda is Professor in the Faculty of Philosophy at the University of Santiago de Compostela (Spain). After earning a doctoral degree in philosophy with a dissertation on Merleau-Ponty, all her research has been focused on phenomenology.

Frank Schalow is University Research Professor at the University of New Orleans. His books include *The Renewal of the Heidegger-Kant Dialogue* (1992), *The Incarnality of Being* (2006), *Departures: At the Crossroads Between Heidegger and Kant* (2013), and *Toward a Phenomenology of Addiction* (2017). He is co-editor of *Heidegger Studies*.

Claudia Serban is Assistant Professor (maîtresse de conférences) at the Toulouse Jean Jaurès University in France, having completed a Ph.D. at the Sorbonne (2013). She has published several papers on German and French phenomenology and Kantian idealism, as well as *Phénoménologie de la possibilité: Husserl et Heidegger* (2016).

Jon Stewart is a researcher at the Institute of Philosophy at the Slovak Academy of Sciences. He is the general editor of *Kierkegaard Research: Sources, Reception and Resources*, *Texts from Golden Age Denmark*, and *Danish Golden Age Studies*. He is the co-editor of the *Kierkegaard Studies Yearbook* and *Monograph Series*.

Jan Strassheim is a DFG-funded Researcher at the University of Hildesheim, where he is developing a philosophical anthropology, referring to Alfred Schutz and Kitarō Nishida, around the phenomenological concept of "relevance." His publications include *Sinn und Relevanz* (2015), *Relevance and Irrelevance* (2019, co-edited with Hisashi Nasu), and several articles on Schutz.

Íngrid Vendrell Ferran is a Heisenberg Fellow at the Goethe University Frankfurt. Her research interests are phenomenology, philosophy of mind, epistemology, and aesthetics. Some of her publications include: *Die Emotionen. Gefühle in der realistischen Phänomenologie* (Akademie, 2008) and *Die Vielfalt der Erkenntnis. Eine Analyse des kognitiven Werts der Literatur* (Mentis, 2018).

Stephen H. Watson is Professor of Philosophy at the University of Notre Dame and has published ten books and over sixty articles on figures and topics in Kant and post-Kantian European philosophy. He has written on aesthetics, the history of philosophy, phenomenology, and recent Continental philosophy more generally.

Jason M. Wirth is Professor of Philosophy at Seattle University. His recent books include *Schelling's Practice of the Wild* (SUNY), *Nietzsche and Other Buddhas* (Indiana), and *Mountains, Rivers, and the Great Earth: Reading Gary Snyder and Dogen in an Age of Ecological Crisis* (SUNY).

Takashi Yoshikawa is Associate Professor at the University of Kochi. His main interests are in Husserl's phenomenology, phenomenological ethics, and contemporary ethics. Among his publications is "Akrasia and Practical Rationality: A Phenomenological Approach" in *New Phenomenological Studies in Japan* (Springer, 2019).

Note on Sources and Key to Abbreviations

The following major works are referenced in the text parenthetically, using the abbreviations listed below. When available, authors have used the standard English translations. Works cited only in endnotes are given with their full publication information.

Kant

CPR   *Critique of Pure Reason* (1781, 1787). Trans. and ed. Paul Guyer and Allen W. Wood. Cambridge: Cambridge University Press, 1998.

CJ   *Critique of the Power of Judgment* (1790). Trans. Paul Guyer and Eric Matthews. Ed. Paul Guyer. Cambridge: Cambridge University Press, 2000.

CPrR *Critique of Practical Reason* (1788). In *Practical Philosophy*, trans. and ed. Mary J. Gregor, 137–271. Cambridge: Cambridge University Press, 1996.

G   *Groundwork of the Metaphysics of Morals* (1785). In *Practical Philosophy*, trans. and ed. Mary J. Gregor, 41–108. Cambridge: Cambridge University Press, 1996.

MM   *The Metaphysics of Morals* (1797). In *Practical Philosophy*, trans. and ed. Mary J. Gregor, 363–602. Cambridge: Cambridge University Press, 1996.

Pro   *Prolegomena to Any Future Metaphysics That Will Be Able to Come Forward as a Science* (1783). Trans. Gary Hatfield. In *Theoretical Philosophy After 1781*, ed. Henry Allison and Peter Heath, 49–169. Cambridge: Cambridge University Press, 2002.

Hegel

EL   *The Encyclopedia Logic: Part I of the Encyclopedia of the Philosophical Sciences with the Zusätze*. Trans. T. F. Geraets, W. A. Suchting, and H. S. Harris. Indianapolis: Hackett, 1991.

EPN   *Philosophy of Nature: Being Part Two of the Encyclopedia of the Philosophical Sciences* (1830). Trans. A. V. Miller. Oxford: Clarendon, 1970.

PhG   *Phenomenology of Spirit* (1807). Trans. A. V. Miller. Oxford: Oxford University Press, 1977.

SL   *The Science of Logic* (1812, 1813, 1816). Trans. and ed. George di Giovanni. Cambridge: Cambridge University Press, 2010.

Husserl

CM   *Cartesian Meditations*. Trans. D. Cairns. Dordrecht: Kluwer, 1988.

C   The Crisis of European Sciences and Transcendental Phenomenology. Trans. D. Carr. Evanston: Northwestern University Press, 1954.

Ideas I   *Ideas Pertaining to a Pure Phenomenology and to a Phenomenological Philosophy—First Book: General Introduction to a Pure Phenomenology*. Trans. F. Kersten. The Hague: Nijhoff, 1982.

Ideas II   *Ideas Pertaining to a Pure Phenomenology and to a Phenomenological Philosophy—Third Book: Phenomenology and the Foundations of the Sciences*. Trans. T. E. Klein and W. E. Pohl. Dordrecht: Kluwer, 1980.

Ideas III   *Ideas Pertaining to a Pure Phenomenology and to a Phenomenological Philosophy—Second Book: Studies in the Phenomenology of Constitution*. Trans. R. Rojcewicz and A. Schuwer. Dordrecht: Kluwer, 1989.

LI   *Logical Investigations*. Trans. J. N. Findlay. London: Routledge, 1973.

Heidegger

BPP   *The Basic Problems of Phenomenology.* Trans. A. Hofstadter. Bloomington: Indiana University Press, 1982.

BT   *Being and Time.* Trans. J. Macquarrie and E. Robinson. Oxford: Basil Blackwell, 1962.

KPM   *Kant and the Problem of Metaphysics.* Trans. R. Taft. Bloomington: Indiana University Press, 1929.

Merleau-Ponty

PP   *Phenomenology of Perception.* Trans. Donald Landes. London: Routledge, 2012.

VI   *The Visible and the Invisible.* Trans. Alphonso Lingis. Evanston: Northwestern University Press, 1968.

1

Introduction

Cynthia D. Coe

German Idealism and phenomenology are two of the most important traditions in Western philosophy in the last two hundred and fifty years. They largely define the trajectory of post-Kantian Continental philosophy and jointly provide a counterpoint to the veneration of a materialist worldview and empirical methods of investigating reality that have dominated not only the natural and social sciences but also analytic philosophy. Fundamentally, these two philosophical movements are concerned with describing human subjectivity in its specificity and uniqueness, and charting the many implications of understanding the subject as a self-conscious and free being—with the caveat that there are serious internal contestations about the nature of subjectivity, consciousness, and freedom. These ideas continue to inform contemporary philosophy and have extended their discursive reach to engage with psychology, history, cognitive science, and literary theory.

There are a number of crucial convergences between German Idealism and phenomenology, which explains why many classical phenomenologists drew upon the work of Kant, Fichte, Schelling, and Hegel in formulating their own positions. Both traditions resist the idea that the subject can be

C. D. Coe (✉)
Philosophy & Religious Studies, Central Washington University,
Ellensburg, WA, USA
e-mail: cynthia.coe@cwu.edu

© The Author(s), under exclusive license to Springer Nature
Switzerland AG 2021
C. D. Coe (eds.), *The Palgrave Handbook of German Idealism and Phenomenology*,
Palgrave Handbooks in German Idealism,
https://doi.org/10.1007/978-3-030-66857-0_1

adequately understood as a physical object to be studied from the outside. Instead, both German Idealism and phenomenology emphasize the activity of consciousness that undergirds all possible experience. In this sense, these traditions rehabilitate the subjective standpoint in an intellectual culture that has increasingly looked to objective investigation as the source of truth. They thus grapple with questions around how we represent the world, how we experience time, and how we relate to others.

Phenomenologists intentionally interpret and draw upon the work of the German Idealists—for instance, Heidegger's readings of Kant and Hegel—but the earlier tradition also serves as a foil against which they define themselves. Phenomenologists tend to emphasize how the subject is immersed in an intersubjective, temporal, and material world, as opposed to what they claim is an isolated, disembodied consciousness at the core of German Idealism. This understanding then leads to a revised account of how philosophy should proceed, in answering its fundamental questions. Idealist philosophers stand in the position of intellectual forebears whose assumptions need to be challenged in order to establish a more legitimate method, including Husserl's *epoché*, Heidegger's fundamental ontology, and Merleau-Ponty's engagement with the social sciences (primarily psychology and linguistics). This emphasis on lived subjectivity leads to a certain hesitation in phenomenology about system-building, or the exhaustive mapping of the foundations of knowledge or morality. In this sense, phenomenologists intensify Kant's caution about the limits of knowledge, by describing the irreducibly historical nature of interpretation, or the entangling of transcendence (freedom) with immanence. Phenomenologists particularly highlight and try to capture aspects of human experience that cannot be isolated from their first-person significance. For instance, Husserl and Heidegger—among others—argue that the understanding of time as a succession of present moments (a public or "clock" time that undergirds causal explanations) is abstracted from a more subjective, primordial experience of time, in which past, present, and future overlap and become meaningful through our ordinary engagements with the world. In this sense, temporality becomes intrinsic to all experience, in a way that highlights the finitude and mortality of the human subject. Similarly, phenomenologists emphasize the irreducibly social nature of subjectivity. We do not exist as atomistic individuals, but find ourselves in a thoroughly interpersonal, humanly mediated environment, which itself needs to be understood as part of the lived world (or lifeworld).

More recently, phenomenologists have explored the implications of our conceptions of the subject, freedom, and embodiment for questions of racial, gender, and postcolonial justice. They have contested the notion of a generic or universal subject, and asked how one's social location shapes experience and possibilities of self-determination, for instance. How do socially learned habits of perception provide frameworks of meaning that both allow and limit our interactions with the world? How is one's own bodily experience shaped by social discourses of normalcy and deviance? Recent phenomenologists have also applied those insights to our relation to environmental concerns, including challenges to anthropocentric assumptions that have been naturalized by both German Idealism and classical phenomenology, an expanded sense of nonhuman sensibility, and explorations of how a sense of place constitutes the lifeworld. In what follows, I discuss some broad themes of German Idealism and how they have been inherited by phenomenologists in the last century, and then outline the structure of this volume.

German Idealism and the Centrality of Consciousness

The period of classical German Idealism was an unusually intense and influential time in intellectual history, beginning with Kant's critical philosophy and the many, varied reactions to it. Kant's transcendental idealism famously attempts to overcome the epistemic limitations inherent in rationalism and empiricism by synthesizing insights from both approaches. In order for us to have experiences at all, information that is given to us through the senses must conform to *a priori* structures of our thought: the pure forms of sensible intuition (space and time) and the categories of the understanding. Experience is impossible without the conditioning activity of consciousness. For this reason, we can only experience the world as it appears to us, not as it is in itself. But Kant also calls himself an empirical realist (unlike Berkeley), meaning that we receive sense impressions from mind-independent sources, as empiricists claim. The work of consciousness introduces a subjective element into experience, but also (for Kant) a universal, objective quality— namely, that we can justify beliefs about phenomena using our shared concepts. We make true claims about the (apparent) world when we use our pure concepts to make sense of what is given to us through the senses in the right way.

Kant explicitly compares his epistemic innovation to Copernicus's overthrow of the Ptolemaic, geocentric model of the universe for a heliocentric one, in which the movement of the earth is both imperceptible and structures all experience. Kant argues that objects must conform to thought, rather than thought merely reflecting and receiving information about objects (CPR

Bxvi). Kant's Copernican turn is thus a re-centering of experience in the activity of consciousness. This recognition of how all our experience is conditioned by consciousness entails a certain humility about the boundaries of knowledge. We cannot step outside of the activity of thinking in order to see the world, or even ourselves, as we are in ourselves. We therefore in principle cannot have knowledge of what is unconditioned by the subjective conditions of knowing—paradigmatically, God, immortality, and freedom.

Kant's crucial move, to identify the conditioning that makes all experience possible, sets up later phenomenological investigations into the irreducibly subjective quality of all experience. It also prefigures—in ways that Kant would have disavowed—an attention to human finitude and the necessarily incomplete attempt to reach epistemic certainty, moral clarity, or existential equilibrium.

German Idealism originates in transcendental idealism, with various philosophers claiming to take up the Kantian mantle, but also with the ambition of resolving conflicts that readers found in the Kantian system. Karl Reinhold attempts to unify the two elements of experience, sensibility and the understanding, under the faculty of representation or the principle of consciousness. But Johann Gottlieb Fichte claims that this overlooks Kant's key insight: namely, the fact that subjective activity makes objective representations possible. According to Fichte, there are two stark alternatives for philosophy: we subscribe either to dogmatism, in which matter is primordial and causality determines all events, or to idealism, in which the activity of the free, undetermined, conscious subject is primordial and constitutes the world that forms the horizon for that activity. According to Fichte's idealism, consciousness itself generates the distinction between the knowing subject and the objects of knowledge, or the I and the not-I. Fichte's extension of that core insight into questions of intersubjectivity, knowledge of a shared world, and temporality shapes later phenomenological readings of those issues.

Schelling's wide-ranging interests expand the focus of German Idealism to interrogate the relationship between consciousness, the natural world, and artistic creation. His work is particularly fascinating for twentieth-century phenomenologists because he brings a Romantic challenge to the hegemony of reason. That challenge targets both a Cartesian vision of a thinking subject who knows itself completely and the scientific ambition to describe the natural world exhaustively. This critique also offers a counterpoint to Hegel's dialectical approach, in which the oppositions within consciousness must eventually be overcome and subsumed within a systematic, totalized narrative—a critique that resounds in the work of Rosenzweig and Levinas.

Schelling's interest in the dynamic potential of nature leads him to the philosophical significance of art, in a way that links German Idealism to the contemporary Romantic movements in painting and poetry. In his view, art reveals the original unities that are split apart in philosophical reflection, in the natural world, and in human action. This interest in artistic creation prefigures Schopenhauer's and Nietzsche's analyses of the philosophical significance of artistic contemplation and activity, which then influence Heidegger and José Ortega y Gasset, among others.

Like Kant and Fichte before him, Hegel seeks to overcome the opposition of phenomena and noumena, subject and object, but he does so by historicizing the work of consciousness. The I should be understood not as a single conscious mind but as the universal activity of thought that struggles to surmount obstacles and comprehend the world. Through that activity, *Geist* (mind or spirit) comes to comprehend itself. Religion, art, political institutions, and philosophy itself all express various accounts of self and world, and attempt to reconcile the contradictions within the ideas inherited from previous accounts. Rather than identifying an ahistorical foundation of all experience, then, Hegel says that absolute knowing arises out of a long process of development during which *Geist* dynamically works out its innermost potential. Hegel's consideration of diverse aspects of philosophy gives rise to a range of responses among twentieth-century phenomenologists: for instance, Sartre largely incorporates Hegel's understanding of intersubjectivity and recognition in his discussion of the look, and Gadamer and Merleau-Ponty develop the idea of conscious activity shaped by and embedded in a historical context.

Starting from the basic question of the relation between subjectivity and the objects of thought and action, the German Idealists discuss a vast range of issues—the nature of freedom, the significance of art, the authority of moral judgments, and the role of religious faith. As the chapters in this volume demonstrate, German Idealism remains a powerful intellectual influence and legacy for twentieth-century phenomenologists, even as they revise some of the key elements and assumptions of the earlier movement and extend its insights into unforeseen directions.

Phenomenology's Focus on Lived Experience

As a concept, phenomenology has a long history. The Latin word *phenomenologia* was used to describe sense impressions as early as 1736. The word itself comes from the Greek *phainomenon*, derived from the verb *phainesthai*, to appear, to show, to bring to light, or to shine forth. The most famous pre-twentieth-century use of the term is Hegel's *Phenomenology of Spirit* (1807). At the end of the nineteenth century, Franz Brentano uses the word as a synonym for descriptive psychology, the description of mental activities, but it is in the work of Edmund Husserl that the term acquires its contemporary philosophical significance, as the methodical study of consciousness. For Husserl, that means how consciousness relates to its intentional objects, the objects toward which it is directed. Two aspects of consciousness are crucial here: that consciousness is an activity that is directed toward objects, and that it is through such intending or taking up of objects that our experience gets content and meaning.

For Husserl, phenomenology proceeds by bracketing the skeptical question of whether our perceptions correspond to a mind-independent reality—whether they represent it accurately, or whether it exists at all. In this way, phenomenology departs from the "natural attitude" that undergirds both common-sense and scientific approaches to experience, which assumes that the world exists more or less as we perceive it. The natural attitude skips over the unique qualities of first-person experience and treats consciousness as transparently representing the world that surrounds it. It is this assumption that opens up an unresolvable epistemic skepticism (one which Kant was attempting to address in formulating transcendental idealism). Although Husserl himself emphasizes the continuities between his work and Descartes's project, this is a transcendental move on Husserl's part—what are the conditions for the possibility of experience? How can we account for the first-person quality of consciousness without collapsing into a description of the "merely subjective," what a singular person perceives through her own idiosyncratic worldview? What are the shared activities through which consciousness constitutes meaning in experience? Thus, Kant stands as an important predecessor of Husserl's project, even if Husserl himself largely sought to distance himself from German Idealism.

Heidegger critically transforms Husserl's phenomenological method to challenge the distinction between subject and object that, on Heidegger's view, has dominated Western philosophy. In this sense, Heidegger departs from some of the foundational concepts of German Idealism, by criticizing them as perpetuating these metaphysical assumptions. For Heidegger, phenomenology is not the study of the subject as consciousness or intentionality, but the examination of our own activity as a way of illuminating the event of Being, or letting beings show themselves as themselves. In Heidegger's terms, this philosophical project should be understood as fundamental ontology. Our investigation into ourselves, as *Dasein*, is only a preliminary project that allows us insight into the originary conditions for the possibility of experience. And we practice phenomenology not by bracketing ordinary experience to grasp the essence of things, but by analyzing how we are immersed in a world of meaning and how we act within this world. Despite his critique of metaphysics, Heidegger devotes a significant number of published books and lecture courses to Kant, Fichte, Schelling, and Hegel—on topics as varied as apperception, the imagination, negativity, and self-positing. In that sense, Heidegger is committed to recovering and re-interpreting elements of German Idealism in his transformation of phenomenology's aim and methods.

Sartre gives Heidegger's analysis of *Dasein* an existential interpretation (or metaphysical misinterpretation, according to Heidegger), in the sense that his primary interest lies in investigating the nature of the free, conscious subject. Phenomenological description allows us to capture the nature of consciousness as "nothingness" or "for-itself," consciousness that is not a thing but reaches out to comprehend or interact with things around it. Unlike things, which have a determinate essence, subjects remain undefined, a space where spontaneous decision-making and self-creation happen—even if subjects often disavow the burden of responsibility generated by that freedom. Like Fichte, Sartre reaffirms the centrality of self-determination, against the threat of being determined by external or pre-given forces.

Of all the classical phenomenologists, Merleau-Ponty most explicitly studies the significance of embodied experience, by drawing on work from psychology and linguistics to untether consciousness from the Cartesian concept of the isolated, rational mind. Experience testifies to how subjects are immersed in a world, so that sensation should be understood as dynamic interplay between the embodied subject and its environment, a world to which we respond but also continually invest with meaning. Merleau-Ponty thus systematically challenges a dualism at the core of modern Western philosophy, between conscious, free, rational subjects and an external, determined, material set of objects. Instead, he describes a "body-subject" engaged in myriad ways with an intersubjective, historically grounded situation.

Even from these brief descriptions, it is clear that phenomenologists were deeply ambivalent about their inheritance of German Idealism. There is a shared rejection of the scientific worldview as offering an exhaustive picture of human reality, a focus on lived experience, and an interest in the temporal and historical quality of experience. The crucial theme of subjectivity—or, even more broadly, how we are engaged in the world—and the many ramifications of how we understand that theme are carried forward. At the same time, many phenomenologists—including Husserl, Gabriel Marcel, Edith Stein, and Max Scheler—wrestle with how to distance themselves from what was seen as the excesses of idealism: for instance, a relative lack of attention to social experience and an overconfidence about our ability to create systematic accounts of reality, without tracking the forms of epistemic finitude that complicate that ambition.

The Structure of the Book

This volume elaborates on the various dimensions of this ongoing conversation between German Idealist thought and phenomenology. The authors of these chapters represent a diverse range of perspectives and interests, and their work engages the iconic figures of the two movements, as well as lesser-known philosophers and texts. These authors are a notably international group of philosophers examining issues that emerge from the intersections of German Idealism and phenomenology, including embodiment, animality, religious faith, memory, imagination, ethics, and intersubjectivity. The book is organized into six main themes that unite these two traditions: starting with the nature of subjectivity and then exploring the broader implications of how we understand the subject—intersubjectivity and the other; our lives as ethical and aesthetic beings; the significance of time, memory, and history; what the world is and what we can know of it; and finally, the work of interpretation and meaning-making.

The six chapters in Part I focus on the core concept of subjectivity, as discussed by a range of figures in German Idealism and phenomenology. Dermot Moran explores Husserl's account of transcendental subjectivity as immersed in the world without being reducible to an objective piece of it. Moran also considers the inherently intersubjective nature of transcendental subjectivity, which will be taken up in the chapters in Part II. Claudia Serban's chapter then raises the question of the connection between the transcendental subject and the "outer man," the subject who can be studied by psychology and anthropology, in both Kant and Husserl. Federico Ferraguto examines Husserl's interpretation of Fichte, specifically on the topic of the I's activity in knowledge and the possibilities for cultural renewal. Jill Hernandez's chapter analyzes Gabriel Marcel's concept of the authentic, ethical self, the subject capable of seeing herself as free, and how this concept evolves in relation to idealist notions of subjectivity. Finally in this section, Sorin Baiasu discusses how Sartre radicalizes Kant's account of freedom, unconditioned by causal and material forces; despite the fact that Sartre rejects Kant's rule-based moral system, he generates a structurally similar purpose-centered practical philosophy.

Although some of the chapters in Part I have already forecast the constitutive role that intersubjectivity plays in phenomenological conceptions of subjectivity, Part II examines this theme in more detail, by applying the core ideas of German Idealism and phenomenology to concrete questions of how we relate to others. These chapters thus engage with the disciplines of anthropology, critical race theory, postcolonial theory, and feminist theory. Jan Strassheim describes Alfred Schutz's anthropological account of intersubjectivity—in which "transcendence" refers to how the subject is open to an Other—in relation to Husserl's transcendental subject and argues that Schutz's unfinished project can be usefully supplemented by a reading of Kant's distinction between phenomena and noumena. In keeping with the focus on situated, lived experience, Shannon Mussett discusses Beauvoir's revision of the Hegelian account of freedom, a revision that challenges the optimistic claim that the oppressed will overcome the state of "ineffectual freedom." Instead, Beauvoir describes complaint and resignation as expressions of profoundly limited freedom—particularly in the lives of women—that do not generate social transformation. She thus challenges the teleological, optimistic register of the Hegelian dialectic. Azzedine Haddour's chapter is also concerned with the ways in which the freedom of human beings is curtailed and undermined, in investigating Frantz Fanon's critique of Hegel's master/slave dialectic and its implicit rationalization of colonial violence. As Haddour argues, Fanon's work examines the limitations that racism and colonialism place upon lived freedom and the claiming of subjectivity in the creative work of decolonization.

Part III explores the conjunction of German Idealism and phenomenology as they relate to value theory, specifically ethics and aesthetics. David Batho analyzes what it means to act "in the light of norms," norms that have authority over us while simultaneously being self-posited. He traces the connections between Hegelian self-legislation and Heidegger's account of death, in which authentically acknowledging mortality sharpens how we live out possibilities, which sets up our ability to act in the light of norms. Takashi Yoshikawa interprets the evolution of Husserl's transcendental idealism in the historical context of his thought: the influence of Kant in *Ideas I* (1913), the dialogue sustained with Fichte's ideas about human progress in the Japanese journal *Kaizo* (1922–1924), and the connections between Husserl's ethical focus and contemporary accounts of moral perfectionism. María-Luz Pintos-Peñaranda's chapter engages the specific ethical question of how we relate to nonhuman animals, and how differently Husserl and Kant understand the transcendental subject. Husserl's focus on how subjectivity is embodied and immersed in a lifeworld allows us to see stronger connections between human and nonhuman species, and thus to begin to overcome the anthropocentrism that has pervaded modern Western thought. In my own chapter, I take up a related issue: how Kant and Levinas discuss the possibility of human morality by contrasting human possibilities with a Hobbesian-Darwinian interpretation of the natural world. However, within that convergence, Levinas rejects Kant's appeal to rational law, in favor of an ethical phenomenology that emphasizes anarchical responsibility. The last chapter in Part III discusses phenomenological aesthetics and our proper comportment toward works of art. Íngrid Vendrell Ferran reads Moritz Geiger's and José Ortega y Gasset's rejection of sentimentalism as a complex inheritance of Kant's claim that the pleasure we take in observing the beautiful should be disinterested. For Geiger and Ortega y Gasset, the ideal aesthetic attention would focus on the values within a work of art, rather than mere pleasure.

Part IV concerns the themes of time, memory, and history, as dimensions of subjectivity that figure prominently both in German Idealism and in phenomenology, but in quite different ways. Kantian and Hegelian notions of time and history repeatedly appear in these chapters as precursors of or foils for phenomenological discussions of temporality. Jason Wirth argues that Schelling's account of time, through his positive philosophy in *The Ages of the World* (1811), is completed by Franz Rosenzweig's work a century later in *The Star of Redemption* (1921). Like Schelling, Rosenzweig is concerned with the barbarian "outside" of reason, that which disrupts attempts at totalizing knowledge but opens the possibility of existential transformation. Markus Gabriel's chapter responds to Heidegger's critique of Hegel's account of time, an analysis that reveals Hegel's distance from a "vulgar" conception of time as a series of present moments and instead emphasizes the irreducibly subjective quality of time for *Geist*. Elisa Magrì continues this discussion of Hegel's understanding of time by considering absolute knowing as the outcome of a process of sedimentation, as Merleau-Ponty describes it—how embodied subjects retain and appropriate past experience. This appropriation can then give rise to what contemporary theorists have named ethical memory, in the reflective, critical, and social transmission of the past. Finally, Zachary Davis provides a reading of Max Scheler's account of history, in a critical inheritance of Schelling, Hegel, and Marx. Influenced by his experiences during World War I, Scheler describes a vision of cultural renewal based on a cosmopolitan ideal of human freedom, an account that is shaped by his response to German Idealism.

The authors in Part V examine the ontological and epistemological ideas and methods that arise in the conversation between German Idealism and phenomenology. Mette Lebech discusses Edith Stein's engagement with Kant, in her developing critique of Husserl's idealism, to stake out a phenomenological stance that overcomes the uncritical assumptions of transcendental idealism. Jorge de Carvalho traces Heidegger's reading of Fichte's "first principles" and describes the connections between Fichte's investigation of the conditions for the possibility of knowledge and Heidegger's phenomenological project. His chapter illuminates Heidegger's greater emphasis on finitude and the impossibility of any exhaustive knowledge of the *a priori*. Jon Stewart considers the meaning of the term "phenomenology" in Hegel, Husserl, and the French phenomenologists and argues that, despite Husserl's neglect of Hegel, there are significant connections between Hegel's approach and phenomenology as Husserl conceives of it. Stephen Watson's chapter describes the influence of Hegel in Merleau-Ponty's work—particularly the role of the dialectic in his later work, and his response to existentialist objections to Hegel. In so doing, Watson argues, we can better appreciate Merleau-Ponty's contributions to the phenomenological movement as a whole.

The sixth and final part of the volume centers on the theme of hermeneutics—a fitting end to a book concerned with interpreting and critically inheriting ideas within an intellectual tradition. Frank Schalow examines Heidegger's reading of Kant on the work of imagination, a reading that both criticizes Kant's participation in metaphysics and reworks his insights into finitude and freedom. Schalow thus draws out the contrasts between a hermeneutical approach and the dialectical method developed out of Kant's thought in German Idealism. Theodore George extends this focus on interpretation by considering Gadamer's "hermeneutics of facticity" and his engagement with Hegel to examine the significance of history and language in our self-understanding. This analysis highlights Gadamer's divergence from the early Heidegger's phenomenological approach. Finally, Robert Piercey considers the various ways in which Ricoeur interprets Hegel's project and the tensions between these registers. Recognizing what Ricoeur rejects in Hegel, and where his project aligns more closely with Hegel's, exemplifies the complexity with which German Idealism was received and transformed by the movement of phenomenology.

Conclusion

The diverse facets of the dialogue between German Idealism and phenomenology reveal the contemporary relevance of these movements and the wide-ranging connections to areas of philosophy that have not traditionally been associated with them, such as environmental philosophy and critical race theory. The issue of how to understand the nature of subjectivity remains a central question in philosophy, and the implications of how we answer or complicate this question resonate not only within philosophy but in our way of life—our political institutions, economic structures, religious traditions, education, our relation to nonhuman animals and the natural world, and the ideals that guide all of those activities. Not only contemporary philosophy but the wider culture has inherited ideas from both German Idealism and phenomenology—at times implicitly or unquestioningly. Investigating these ideas more fully, as we attempt to do in this book, will help us to understand ourselves and critically reflect upon some of our foundational intellectual commitments.

Part I

Subjectivity

2

Husserl's Idealism Revisited

Dermot Moran

In this chapter, I argue that Husserl's deepening understanding of his fundamental thesis of the intentionality of consciousness (every experience is
object-directed) eventually led him to prioritize consciousness and embrace
transcendental idealism, albeit of a fundamentally new kind,[1] one built on
the primacy of *intersubjectivity*. Husserl's transcendental idealism has interesting allegiances with—and deviations from—traditional German Idealism,
although Husserl was not particularly interested in pursuing these relations;
he did not want to simply add a new theory to the history of philosophical
positions. His transcendental idealism has an entirely new sense, as he writes
in the *Crisis of European Sciences*[2]:

> I ask only one thing here at the outset, that in reference to these prejudices,
> one's intentional presupposing [*vermeintliches Im-voraus-Wissen*], one keeps
> whatever is meant by the words 'phenomenology', 'transcendental', 'idealism'
> (as transcendental-phenomenological idealism, etc.), locked tightly in one's
> breast, as I have fitted them out with completely new meanings. (*Crisis*, Hua
> VI 440, my translation)

D. Moran (✉)
Philosophy Department, Boston College, Chestnut Hill, MA, USA
e-mail: morandg@bc.edu

© The Author(s), under exclusive license to Springer Nature
Switzerland AG 2021
C. D. Coe (eds.), *The Palgrave Handbook of German Idealism and Phenomenology*,
Palgrave Handbooks in German Idealism,
https://doi.org/10.1007/978-3-030-66857-0_2

One must put to one side all previous conceptions of transcendental idealism as found within the European philosophical tradition and rethink the concept anew (Hua VI 440). Husserl is not even happy with the term "idealism" *tout court*, preferring "transcendental-phenomenological idealism" or "phenomenological idealism" (FTL, §66, 170; Hua XVII 152),[3] in contrast to "argumentative idealism," based on speculative philosophy (FTL §42g, 119; Hua XVII 105), or "psychological idealism." Husserl could never accept traditional "psychological" idealism (*Ideas* II, 417; Hua V 150).[4] He consistently rejects the "bad idealism" of Berkeley or Hume as "psychologistic" (FTL §66). Husserl partly praises the German Idealist tradition (Fichte, Schelling, Hegel), but also criticizes it for being seduced by speculative concepts, no matter how it was committed to absolutely grounded science. Additionally, Husserl always rejected the Hegelian "dialectic" and thought that Schelling and Hegel employed unclear concepts. However, as we shall see, Husserl's construal of egoic subjectivity as always implicated in intersubjectivity (in what he calls the "we-world" [*Wir-Welt*] of "absolute spirit") brings him closest to Hegel.

The first major publication in his lifetime (most of his works were published posthumously in the Husserliana series)[5] to announce this turn to idealism is *Ideas* I (1913),[6] although, strictly speaking, he did not use the term "idealism" there.[7] The term "transcendental idealism" (*transzendentaler Idealismus*) begins to appear from around 1915[8] and is omnipresent after 1916.[9] Thus, Husserl proudly proclaimed his idealism in his *Fichte Lectures* of 1917/1918 (where he treats Fichte's transcendental ego as activity),[10] *Encyclopedia Britannica* article (1928),[11] *Formal and Transcendental Logic* (1929), especially §§94–100, and perhaps gave his strongest articulation in *Cartesian Meditations* (1931, especially §§11, 34, 40, 41)[12] and *Crisis of the European Sciences* (1936/1954). Moreover, his transcendental idealism deepened as he expanded his focus to transcendental intersubjectivity and the constitution of the world as such.

Intentionality as Starting Point

Intentionality as sense-making is Husserl's bedrock philosophical starting point. Every conscious experience is directed to an object. Intentionality involves an *a priori* correlation between subject and object that can be mapped. Indeed, Husserl claims he had this insight concerning *a priori* correlation already in 1898 (*Crisis*, 165; Hua VI 168) while writing his *Logical*

Investigations. Phenomenology seeks "clarification of sense" through intentional analysis, i.e., clarifying the sense of both act and object, but the source of all sense-making is precisely subjectivity.[13] Subjectivity has the overall constituting function in the correlation; therefore, subjectivity has ultimate ontological priority.[14] Subjectivity, furthermore, is always first-personal, or, as Husserl puts it "egoic" (*ichlich*). For Husserl, the first and foremost starting point is "I am." As he puts it in *Formal and Transcendental Logic* (1929), I am the "primitive ground [*Urgrund*]" (FTL 237) for my world. Husserl states that for "children in philosophy" this claim is haunted by fear of solipsism and psychologism, but he aims to fill this "dark corner with light" (FTL §95).

Beginning with the transcendental ego as the source of all "meaning and being" undoubtedly makes Husserl an idealist in some Cartesian sense. But Husserl rejects the claim that all of the world can be anchored in the ego understood as some "bit of the world" (*Endchen der Welt*, Hua I 9). Traditional idealism (e.g., Berkeley) was misled, according to Husserl, because the transcendental (i.e., sense-giving) ego was mistakenly confused with the empirical ego: "the confounding of the ego with the reality of the I as a human psyche" (FTL 230; Hua XVII 238).[15] As he put it later, the countersense was to assume the relation between world and ego to be a natural, causal relation, whereas, in fact, it is a correlation inside of transcendental subjectivity (FTL 252; Hua XVII 223).

Husserl himself also offers a re-interpretation of the history of the idealist tradition (which for him begins with Descartes' turn to the *cogito*) in several texts, including a detailed critical engagement with Kant, a shorter one with Fichte, and the brief expression of some qualified sympathy for Hegel (in *Crisis*). In *Formal and Transcendental Logic* (1929) §100, he embarks on a "historico-critical digression [*nach diesem historisch-kritischen Exkurs*]" (FTL 266; Hua XVII 235), offering a short history of the development of transcendental philosophy, especially in relation to its treatment of formal logic and the *a priori* analytic. Here, he briefly discusses Descartes, Locke, Hume, and Kant (with a brief mention of Brentano). Husserl appreciates Hume for taking Descartes seriously to reduce everything to inwardness but he criticizes him for overlooking the essential element of intentionality. Kant also failed to set up a "genuine intentional psychology" (FTL 257; Hua XVII 227). Even Brentano did not grasp the essence of intentionality as a transcendental problem. Husserl is the first to put intentionality on a new footing. For Husserl, Kant's failure, furthermore, was to assume that the purely concrete ego was just a "senseless bundle or collection of data—which come and perish … according to a senselessly accidental regularity" (FTL 255; Hua XVII

226). Kant assumed that what was given empirically was a flow of sensations, whereas Husserl understands givenness as a meaningfully structured flow of subjective experiences directed to their objects in horizonal contexts.[16]

Husserl's Transcendental-Phenomenological Idealism (1908–1938)

Husserl's transcendental idealism is complex, and the scholarship on it is immense.[17] To a large extent, Husserl's idealism was resisted by the realist phenomenologists of the Göttingen school (e.g., Reinach, Stein, Ingarden). Husserl himself could not understand the "scandal" generated among his followers by his embrace of idealism and dismissed the battle between realism and idealism as "sterile [unfruchtbar] and unphilosophical" ("Epilogue," Ideas II, 421; Hua V 154). As he states in 1930, he does not deny the existence of the world or reduce its status to mere semblance ("Epilogue," Ideas II 420; Hua V 152). Rather, he is, in contemporary parlance, a kind of Putnamian internal realist avant la lettre, who maintains that the very concepts of "being," "reality," and so on are constituted in consciousness and to think of them as "things-in-themselves" is countersensical.[18] He also thinks being must be correlated to mind, either actual or possible mind.[19] But his idealism contains more complex strands, as I shall argue, and can only be grasped from within the transcendental attitude. It is not a philosophical "theory" as such, not merely one philosophical position among others. It is not a bald ontological assertion about subjectivity. Rather, Husserl's idealism is an ultimate science that encompasses "the universal horizon of the problems of philosophy" (Ideas II, 408; Hua V 141).

Husserl continued to refine his idealism between 1913 and 1937. For Husserl, transcendental phenomenology is a "radical and genuine" and indeed the "final form" (Endform) of transcendental philosophy as inaugurated by Descartes (Crisis §14). Classical Greek philosophy was world-oriented and naively objectivist. Although a first breakthrough was made by the ancient Sophists (Protagoras, Gorgias) who introduced a new distinction between how things appear to the subject and how they are in reality, the truly radical turn to subjectivity was first made by Descartes, who also inaugurated the transcendental turn by seeking the "ultimate foundations in the subjective" (Crisis §19, 81; Hua VI 83) of all being.

The Starting Point: Intentionality and the Ontological Priority of Subjectivity

In *Logical Investigations* (1901), Husserl states that the central feature of consciousness is *intending* (*Vermeinen, Intention*),[20] and in *Ideas* I (1913), he calls intentionality the "main theme" (*Hauptthema*) of phenomenology (Husserl, *Ideas* I, §91, 161; Hua III/1 168). In *Formal and Transcendental Logic* (1929), similarly, he speaks of intentionality as "the own-essentiality of the life of consciousness [*das Eigenwesentliche des Bewußtseinslebens*]" (FTL §97, 245; Hua XVII 216). Phenomenology, then, becomes the "uncovering of the constitution of consciousness [*Enthüllung der Bewußtseinskonstitution*]" (FTL §97).

From *Ideas* I onward, constituting consciousness is located by Husserl in the transcendental ego. In the *Cartesian Meditations*, Husserl says, therefore, that the "self-explication [*Selbstauslegung*]" (Hua I 97, 116, 118) of the transcendental ego presents a set of "great tasks" (CM §29) for transcendental philosophy. Similarly, in the *Crisis*, Husserl proposes a "critical reinterpretation and correction of the Cartesian concept of the ego" (*Crisis* 184; Hua VI 188), as the task of transcendental philosophy. It seems therefore that the exploration of the transcendental ego is the primary focus of his transcendental idealism. But this is only part of the story. There is also the puzzle of the constitution of world-consciousness and intersubjective community of egos.

For Husserl, all meaning and being (*Sinn und Sein*)—sometimes he speaks contractedly of the "being-sense [*Seinssinn*]"—arise out of the "achievements" or "accomplishments" (*Leistungen*) of this intentional, egoic consciousness, including the very sense of "being-in" and belonging to a *world* with others (a conception that Husserl developed quite independently of Heidegger). The very *sense* of both the natural and the cultural worlds (as well as all ideal and possible worlds) is produced in this way. The transcendental ego is even responsible for constituting the basic sense of being and non-being. For Husserl, intentionality involves a correlation; it is simply impossible to think of being without consciousness, unless one is objectifying for a particular goal, e.g., to establish the laws of nature in itself.[21] As he summarizes in his *Amsterdam Lectures* (1928), true being is an accomplishment of knowing consciousness:

> Every real thing, and ultimately the whole world as it exists for us in such and such a way, only exists as an actual or possible *cogitatum* of our own *cogitatio*, as a possible experiential content of our own experience; and in dealing with the content of our own life of thought and knowing, the best case being in

myself, one may assume our own (intersubjective) operations for testing and proving as the pre-eminent form of evidentially grounded truth. Thus, for us, true being is a name for products of actual and possible cognitive operations, an accomplishment of cognition [*Erkenntnisleistung*]. (*Trans. Phen.*, 236; Hua IX 329)

True being is an achievement or accomplishment of the subject's knowing. This is a striking formulation. The essence of transcendental idealism, for Husserl, then, involves acceptance not just of the *a priori* correlation between objectivity and subjectivity, but the ontological primacy of subjectivity (or "consciousness"), although that is not meant in the sense of simply positing subjects as things-in-themselves. Thus, in *Ideas* I and in *Cartesian Meditations*, he asserts the absolute being of consciousness over and against the relative being of all other entities. According to Husserl, transcendentalism overcomes objectivism in knowledge and maintains that "the ontic meaning [*der Seinssinn*] of the pregiven life-world is a subjective structure [*subjektives Gebilde*], it is the achievement [*Leistung*] of experiencing, prescientific life" (*Crisis* §14, 69; Hua VI 70). Roman Ingarden summarizes Husserl's position very well:

> Thus the fundamental thesis of "transcendental idealism" is obtained: what is real is nothing but a constituted noematic unity (individual) of a special kind of sense which in its being and quality [*Sosein*] results from a set of experiences of a special kind and is quite impossible without them. Entities of this kind exist only for the pure transcendental ego which experiences such a set of perceptions. The existence of what is perceived (of the perceived as such) is nothing "in itself" [*an sich*] but only something "for somebody," for the experiencing ego. "*Streichen wir das reine Bewusstsein, so streichen wir die Welt*" ("If we exclude pure consciousness then we exclude the world") is the famous thesis of Husserlian transcendental idealism which he was already constantly repeating in lectures during his Göttingen period.[22]

All being is dependent on consciousness. As Husserl writes in *Ideas* I: "the world itself has its entire being as a certain 'sense' that presupposes absolute consciousness as a field affording sense" (*Ideas* I, 103; Hua III/1 107). Furthermore, the terms "reality" and "world" are "just headings for certain valid unities of 'sense' related to certain connections of the absolute pure consciousness" (*Ideas* I, 102; Hua III/1 107). Similarly, in *Cartesian Meditations*, Husserl speaks of "the essential rootedness [*Verwurzelung*] of any Objective world in transcendental subjectivity" (CM §59, 137; Hua I 164).

The Sense of the World—Horizon-Intentionality

In his mature years, moreover, Husserl expands his account of intentionality to include not just intended objects (and "objectivities," i.e., states of affairs) but also their contexts and *horizons*. For Husserl, things are always encountered within the *background* (*Hintergrund*) of the "surrounding world" (*Umwelt*, *Ideas* II § 51). The "horizon of all horizons" is the world (*Ideas* I § 27), which is infinite and unbounded temporally, spatially, and in terms of unfolding possibilities. Intentionality takes place within the "world-horizon" (*Welthorizont*). Husserl now realizes "horizon-intentionality" (*Horizont-Intentionalität*) must complement object-intentionality. Furthermore, he construes the "world" as the horizon of horizons and, thus, the constitution *of the world as such* becomes the key problem for his mature transcendental phenomenology. Husserl's transcendental idealism therefore addresses world-constitution. As he puts it in his 1930 "Epilogue" (*Nachwort*) to *Ideas* I[23]: "Its [phenomenological idealism's] sole task and accomplishment is to clarify the sense of this world, precisely the sense in which everyone accepts it—and rightly so—as actually existing" (*Ideas* II, 420; Hua V 152). Husserl's transcendental philosophy, then, investigates the *phenomenon of worldhood*, how a world is presumed in all our experiencing, providing its horizon. Moreover, the world is experienced as the one-world-for-all, the *same* world for every subject. Intersubjectivity provides the basis for this experiencing of one, harmonious world.

Husserl claimed that transcendental subjectivity (or intersubjectivity), understood as constituting the world, was unknown in previous philosophy, which was primarily objectivist. Thus, in a draft paper written in 1935 entitled "Antiquity did recognize the correlation between subjectivity and world" (Hua XXVII 228–31), he maintains that the ancient world has no knowledge of functioning, constituting subjectivity:

> Even the teleological worldview of Aristotle is objectivist. Antiquity did not yet behold the great problem of subjectivity as functioning, achieving consciousness-subjectivity [*als fungierend leistender Bewusstseinssubjektivität*], as world- and being-in-the-world human subjectivity [*als Welt und in der Welt seiender menschlicher Subjektivität*] … (Hua XXVII 228, my translation)

It is because of this focus on *world-constituting subjectivity* that, for Husserl, the real breakthrough to transcendental philosophy was brought about not by Immanuel Kant (who is rightfully associated with the explicit terminology of "transcendental" inquiry), but by Descartes, whose radical exclusion of the world led to his discovery of the apodictic *cogito ergo sum* and its life of experiences. Descartes re-oriented the pole of philosophy from being to consciousness. Thus, in the *Crisis of European Sciences*, Husserl applies the term "transcendental" to the "regressive inquiry" (*Rückfragen*) of Descartes:

> I myself use the word "transcendental" *in the broadest sense* for the original motif … which through Descartes confers meaning on all modern philosophies. … It is the motif of inquiring back [*Motiv des Rückfragens*] into the ultimate source of all the formations of knowledge, the motif of the knower's reflecting upon himself [or herself] and his [or her] knowing life in which all the scientific structures that are valid for him [or her] occur purposefully, are stored up as acquisitions, and have become and continue to become freely available. … it is the motif of a universal philosophy which is grounded purely in this source and thus ultimately grounded [*letztbegründeten Universalphiloso-phie*]. This source bears the title *I-myself*, with all of my actual and possible knowing life and, ultimately, my concrete life in general. (*Crisis* 97–98, trans. modified; Hua VI 100–1)

Husserl had already made a similar articulation in his 1924 lecture to the Kant Society:

> In fact, my adoption of the Kantian word "transcendental," despite all remoteness from the basic presuppositions, guiding problems, and methods of Kant, was based from the beginning on the well-founded conviction that all senseful problems which Kant and his successors had treated theoretically under the heading of transcendental problems could, at least in their finally clarified formulation, be redirected to this new basic science. ("Kant and the Idea of Transcendental Philosophy," 9–10; Hua VII 230)[24]

Husserl's Engagement with Kant and Transcendental Idealism

Husserl began a serious re-reading of Kant around 1905.[25] His most explicit engagement with Kant was in his 1924 lecture to the Kant *Gesellschaft* (Hua VII) and in the *Crisis*. He was always critical of Kant's "mythical constructions." Thus, in the *Crisis*, he expresses his unhappiness with the German Idealists for mixing their will to system with purely speculative metaphysical ideas:

> All the transcendental concepts of Kant—those of the "I" of transcendental apperception, of the different transcendental faculties, that of the "thing in itself" (which underlies souls as well as bodies)—are constructive concepts

which resist in principle an ultimate clarification. This is even more true in the later idealistic systems. (*Crisis* 199; Hua VI 203)

Husserl regarded his transcendental idealism as an advancement over Kant. He summarizes Kant's idealism in his *Fichte Lectures* as follows: "Space and time, the great forms of the presentation of natural reality, have, according to Kant, no transcendent-real meaning whatsoever. They originate purely out of the knowing subjectivity as the 'forms of intuition' produced (*beigestellten*) by and in subjectivity" (*Fichte Lectures* 115; Hua XXV 272). After Kant, German Idealism, specifically Fichte, Schelling, and Hegel, sought to overcome the residual dualism in Kant and especially the dualism between appearances and the unknowable thing-in-itself. Eventually, it evolved into the Absolute Idealism of Hegel where the infinite realization of the identity of subjectivity and objectivity is seen as the self-realization of Absolute Spirit.

Schelling especially regarded transcendental philosophy, the attempt to explain how knowledge is possible, as a way of identifying and seeking the grounds for the "prejudice" *that there are things outside us*. Indeed, he regards as one of the great achievements of modern philosophy that it has succeeded in uncoupling the conviction that objects exist outside us from the conviction *that I exist*. According to Schelling, idealism results from thinking of the self as the fundamental principle of all knowledge, whereas realism consists of thinking of the object without the self. His claim is that it is necessary to think the two together, leading to what he calls "ideal-realism" or "transcendental idealism" (*System of Transcendental Idealism*, 1800).[26] This bears a resemblance to Husserl's correlationism; there is, however, no evidence that Husserl ever read Schelling.

Husserl thought of Fichte's work as obscure: "Someone raised as a theoretician in the spirit of rigorous science will find almost unendurable the many demanding acrobatics of thought [*Denkkünsteleien*] of his *Wissenschaftslehren*."[27] But he credits Fichte with overcoming Kant's dualism by positing the self as action. Unlike Kant, the ego does not act on the basis of a prior passivity but is always active, in development, and goal-directed, and Husserl sees merit in this approach in his *Fichte Lectures*. Husserl appears never to have read Hegel in any serious way.

Consciousness as an Original Region of Being

In his mature works, Husserl consistently posits consciousness as a distinct and ontologically prior realm or "region" of being. Thus, *Ideas* I introduces pure consciousness as "*a new region of being never before delimited in its own peculiarity*" (*Ideas* I §33, 63; Hua III/1 58), and as "the all of absolute being [*das All des absoluten Seins*]" (*Ideas* I §51). In *Ideas* I, Husserl speaks, furthermore, of the "intrinsic detachability [*prinzipielle Ablösbarkeit*] of the entire natural world from the domain of consciousness" (*Ideas* I §46, 84; Hua III/1 87), which he presents as an insight implicit, but unexplored, in the Cartesian *cogito*. The transcendent world has "meaning and being" (*Sinn und Sein*) *only in essential interconnection* with consciousness.

In *Ideas* I, §49 Husserl introduces a notorious thought experiment in which he imagines the "annihilation of the world" (*Weltvernichtung*), according to which the entire world is thought of as losing all sense and coherence. But even if all experience is reduced to pure chaos, according to Husserl constituting consciousness cannot be done away with.

In his *Kant Lecture* (1924, reprinted in Hua VII), Husserl explains the new approach of *Ideas* I as a discovery of phenomenology as the eidetic science of *pure* consciousness itself that is the culmination of the Cartesian turn to subjectivity:

> With the *Ideas* the deepest sense of the Cartesian turn of modern philosophy is, I dare to say, revealed, and the necessity of an absolute self-contained eidetic science of pure consciousness in general is cogently demonstrated—this, however, in relation to all correlations [*Korrelationen*] grounded in the essence of consciousness, to its possible really immanent moments and to its noemata and objectivities intentionally-ideally determined therein. ("Kant and the Idea," 12; Hua VII 234)

Similarly, in his 1930 "Epilogue" to *Ideas* I, Husserl conceded that his rather bold Cartesian-inspired claim in *Ideas* I was "incomplete" and "suffered from imperfections" (*Ideas* II, 417; Hua V 150), primarily because it left out of consideration the nature of *transcendental intersubjectivity*, of subjects operating together in the co-constitution of a harmonious world of possible experience. In *Formal and Transcendental Logic*, Husserl insists on the priority of constituting consciousness as productive of all sense and being—including the divine being. He writes:

> The relation of my consciousness to a *world* [*Bewußtseinsbeziehung auf eine Welt*] is not a matter of fact imposed on me either by a God, who adventitiously decides it thus, or by a world accidentally existing beforehand, and a causal regularity belonging thereto. On the contrary, the subjective Apriori precedes the being of God and world, the being of everything, individually and collectively, for me, the thinking subject. Even God is for me what He is, in consequence of my own productivity of consciousness … (FTL 251; Hua XVII 221–22)

Husserl's radical idealism inverts that of Berkeley. Even the being of God is constituted by transcendental subjectivity. One cannot stop, however, with the assertion of the priority of consciousness; one must now clarify this claim through the transcendental reduction. Otherwise idealism, too, would remain in the grip of naturalism.

The Ontology of the Natural Attitude: Naïve Realism and Naturalism

Although *Logical Investigations* gave birth to a movement known as Realist phenomenology,[28] Husserl himself rejected this "realism," because of its naïve acceptance of the ready-made world of our everyday objectivist attitude. For Husserl, the natural attitude could easily give rise to "naturalism" or "naturalistic objectivism" that thought of the world as detached from consciousness. Already, in his 1906/1907 *Lectures on Logic and Epistemology*,[29] Husserl refers to naturalism (and psychologism) as the "original sin" (Hua XXIV 176), as the "sin against the Holy Spirit of philosophy" (Hua XXIV 177). Beginning with "Philosophy as Rigorous Science" (1910/1911),[30] naturalism is portrayed as an inevitable consequence of a certain rigidification of the "natural attitude" (*die natürliche Einstellung, Ideas* I §27) into the "naturalistic attitude" of scientific objectivism (see, for instance, *Ideas* II §49). He writes: "It is not easy for us to overcome the primeval habit [*die urwüchsige Gewohnheit*] of living and thinking in the naturalistic attitude and thus of naturalistically falsifying the psychical" (PRS 271; Hua XXV 31).

Husserl's move to idealism—in part a rejection of the earlier phenomenological realism of the Munich school—was partly an attempt to overcome *naturalism* and *objectivism* and partly a way to explore the realm of consciousness as a sphere of absolute being.[31] From *Ideas* I (1913) onward, he became more sympathetic to the Neo-Kantians, Rickert and Natorp. Thus, in a letter to Heinrich Rickert, December 20, 1915, Husserl allies himself with German Idealism against "our common enemy" (*als unseren gemeinsamen Feind*)—the "naturalism of our time."[32] For Husserl, all forms of naturalism—or what he sometimes calls "naturalistic objectivism"—harbor an inbuilt "absurdity" or "countersense" (*Widersinn*). This absurdity consists in the attempt to *naturalize* consciousness:

> What characterizes all forms of extreme and consistent naturalism … is, on the one hand, the *naturalization of consciousness* [*Naturalisierung des Bewußtseins*], including all intentionally immanent givens of consciousness, and, on the other hand, the *naturalization of ideas*, and thus of all absolute ideals and norms. (PRS 254; Hua XXV 9)

One of Husserl's unique contributions to his transcendental idealism in a new key is his identification of objectivism as the outlook of a specific attitude—the natural attitude. The natural attitude is the everyday outlook of humanity from its earliest stages. In this sense, the attitude itself is "prior to all theory" (*Ideas* I §30) but it can lead to "naturalism" in philosophy because it is seduced by the spirit of unquestioning ("naïve") acceptance of the world that permeates the natural attitude. Naturalism leads to the "reification" (*Verdinglichung*) of the world and its "philosophical absolutizing [*Verabsolutierun*]" (*Ideas* I, §55, 129; Hua III/1 107).[33]

For the mature Husserl, the natural attitude, despite its indispensability in everyday human life, is essentially "naïve," "one-side" (*einseitig*), "close"' (*geschlossen, Crisis* Hua VI 209), and "blind," because it fails to recognize its own outlook as an "attitude" (*Einstellung*). To be in the natural attitude means precisely not to recognize it as such—hence it is an attitude lived in ignorance of its own nature and thereby it assumes it is not an attitude but a transparent access to its objectual domain. In fact, as Husserl's transcendental-phenomenological analysis purports to disclose, the natural attitude itself is, despite its omnipresence and everydayness, relative to the "absolute" transcendental attitude.

The Centrality of the Epochē to the Transcendental Outlook

Husserl's transcendental idealism seeks to overcome naturalism by suspending its "belief-in-being" (*Seinsglaube*) through the reduction, thus making the *epochē* and transcendental-phenomenological reduction central to his idealism. As Husserl writes in his *Encyclopedia Britannica* article (Draft A):

> The transcendental reduction opens up, in fact, a completely new kind of experience that can be systematically pursued: transcendental experience. Through the transcendental reduction, *absolute* subjectivity, which functions everywhere in hiddenness [*in Verborgenheit fungierende absolute Subjektivität*], is brought to light along with its whole transcendental life [*mit all ihrem transzendentalen Leben*] … (*Trans. Phen.*, 98; Hua IX 250)

In *Ideas* II, he says that the reduction frees us "from the sense restrictions of the natural attitude [*Sinnesschranken der natürlichen Einstellung*] and of every relative attitude" (*Ideas* II §49(d), 189; Hua IV 179). He writes:

What is *educational* in the phenomenological reduction, however, is also this: it henceforth makes us sensitive to grasping other attitudes, whose rank is equal to that of the natural attitude (or as we can say more clearly now, the nature attitude) and which therefore, just like the latter, constitute only relative and restricted correlates of being and sense. (*Ideas* II §49(d), 189; Hua IV 179)

The reduction allows us to see our naïve everyday outlook precisely *as an attitude* and furthermore an attitude that can be suspended or altered at will. Furthermore, only phenomenology allows us to investigate *attitudes* and understand also "the correlates constituted by them" "through the relation of the ontological distinctions of the constituted objects to the correlative essential nexuses of the corresponding constituting manifolds" (*Ideas* II §49(d), 190; Hua IV 180).

In his 1928 *Amsterdam Lectures*, Husserl makes clear that the function of the "transcendental phenomenological *epochē*" is to expose the naiveté of the natural attitude and all thinking based on the assumption of the world. Husserl writes there:

The transcendental problem arises from a general turning around of the natural attitude [*aus seiner allgemeinen Umwendung der natürlichen Einstellung*], in which the whole of daily life flows along [*das gesamte alltägliche Leben verläuft*]; in which also the positive sciences continue operating. In this attitude the *real* world [*die reale Welt*] is pregiven to us, on the basis of ongoing experience, as the self-evidently existing, always present to be learned about world to be explored theoretically on the basis of the always onward movement of experience. (*Trans. Phen.*, 238 [translation modified]; Hua IX 331–32)

Husserl elaborates in a quasi-Biblical "expulsion from the Garden of Eden" rhetoric about what happens under the universal *epochē*:

We have been driven out, expelled, from the naivete of natural living-along [*aus der Naivität des natürlichen Dahinlebens herausgedrängt*]; we have become aware of a peculiar split or cleavage [*Spaltung*], so we may call it, which runs through all our life; namely, that between the anonymously functioning subjectivity [*zwischen der anonym fungierenden*], which is continuously constructing objectivity for us, and the always, by virtue of the functioning [*dieses Fungierens*] of anonymous subjectivity, pregiven objectivity, the world. (*Trans. Phen.*, 243 [translation modified]; Hua IX 336)

The *epochē* of the natural attitude lays bare the transcendental insight that all being is correlated with consciousness and even splits the ego itself between natural and transcendental.

Ontologies are revealed under standpoints through transcendental phenomenology. Each material ontology is relative to an "attitude" (*Einstellung*) or "standpoint" (albeit not in the sense employed by the Neo-Kantians).[34] There are different constituting accomplishments correlated with different objectivities. The everyday life-world ontology is made visible through the natural-personalistic attitude attuned to life-world. Genuine phenomenological ontology, for Husserl, requires the clarification of the constitutive conditions that make these ontologies possible. Husserl's "fundamental ontology"—a term he never uses—is a transcendental inquiry into the intersubjective preconditions for the possibility of both a subjective and an objective world.

The Enigma of Subjectivity as Both "in the World" and "for the World"

As we have seen, the discovery of transcendental, world-constituting subjectivity is the first "Cartesian" step in Husserl's transcendental idealism. Subjectivity is not a mere piece of the world (Descartes' mistake) but transcends the world or is "for the world," in Husserl's terms, i.e., *world-constituting*. In the *Crisis*, Husserl presents transcendental idealism as a response to "the paradox of human subjectivity" (*Crisis* §53), namely how it is possible that human beings are both subjects "for the world" and also objects "in the world."[35] Husserl presents this paradox as a serious difficulty and challenge to his investigation of what he calls the "pure problems of correlation" (*Crisis* 174; Hua VI 178) opened up by the phenomenological-transcendental *epochē*, and what he elsewhere calls the "full transcendental *epochē*" (*Crisis* 263; Hua VI 267). Subjectivity is bifurcated between its transcendental and its natural dimension. Husserl writes:

> Only a radical inquiry back into subjectivity—and specifically the subjectivity which *ultimately* brings about all world-validity [*Weltgeltung*], with its content and in all its prescientific and scientific modes, and into the "what" and the "how" [*das Was und Wie*] of the rational accomplishments—can make objective truth comprehensible and arrive at the ultimate ontic meaning [*Seinssinn*] of the world. Thus it is not the being of the world [*Sein der Welt*] as unquestioned, taken for granted, which is primary in itself; ... rather what is primary in itself is subjectivity, understood as that which naïvely pregives the being of the world and then rationalizes or (what is the same thing) objectifies it. (*Crisis* 69; Hua VI 70)

In *Crisis* Part Three—as elsewhere—Husserl makes a distinction between "psychological," "natural or mundane" subjectivity and transcendental subjectivity—that is designated as "absolute." For Husserl, "achieving subjectivity [*die leistende Subjektivität*]," or as Carr translates it "functioning subjectivity" (*Crisis* 67; Hua VI 68)—that is, the intentionality that constitutes the sense of the world itself and which will later be distinguished from active intentionality—is transcendental and cannot be adequately understood by the naturalized science of psychology, as early modern philosophy (Locke) had attempted to do. Husserl begins from the ego as a "concrete world-phenomenon" (*Crisis* 187; Hua VI 191) and inquires back to the transcendental ego in its "concreteness" also.

> At the onset of the *epochē* the ego is given apodictically but as a "mute concreteness." It must be brought to exposition, to expression, through systematic intentional "analysis" which inquires back from the world-phenomenon. In this systematic procedure one at first attains the correlation between the world and transcendental subjectivity as objectified in humankind. (*Crisis* 187, trans. modified; Hua VI 191)

There is a mutual interdependence between the natural and transcendental ego in both directions. Both natural and transcendental egos are singular and concrete, and both are wrapped up in nexuses of intentional implication. But only the natural or "mundane" ego is an extant being in the world. It is "in the world," Husserl repeatedly says, embodied, embedded, acting, and suffering. The transcendental ego cannot be thought of as a real being in the same sense. Husserl often talks of the *self-objectification* of the transcendental ego as a mundane worldly ego. There is a sense (expressed by Sartre as *le néant*) of the transcendental ego being a kind of "pre-being" or a source of meaning that cannot itself be objectified since its objectification is precisely its mundanization as the natural, psychological ego. Hence, Husserl insists on the difficulty of maintaining the transcendental stance. In his posthumous *Phenomenology of Intersubjectivity* volume, Hua XV, he writes:

> But the Eidos "transcendental ego" is unthinkable without a transcendental ego as factual. As long as, based on the fact of my transcendental subjectivity and on the world that is valid for me, I modify and research systematically into the Eidos, I stand in the absolute ontology and correlatively in the mundane ontology. (Hua XV 385, my translation)[36]

We inhabit two worlds, as it were—transcendental and mundane. We live naively in the constituted world, but subjectivity also lives a world-constituting life (entangled with an open-ended stream of other egos, as we shall now discuss).

Transcendental Intersubjectivity (Transzendentale Intersubjektivität) as Monadology

I have been arguing in support of Husserl's own claim that he was a transcendental idealist in a radically new, post-Kantian sense. There is one ego that is bifurcated between natural and transcendental dimensions. Another novelty is his account of transcendental intersubjectivity—the key to his later phenomenology. The ego constitutes itself as an ego that has other egos (*Crisis*, Hua VI 417). There is not just one transcendental ego; rather, there is an open plurality of transcendental egos, extending into the past and open to an indefinite future of possible transcendental egos, constituting "humanity" (*Menschheit*) as such. As Eugen Fink puts it: "Transcendental egology becomes transcendental 'monadology.'"[37]

In articulating his vision of transcendental intersubjectivity, Husserl turns not to Hegel's concept of absolute spirit (with which Husserl was profoundly unfamiliar and indeed to which he had an antipathy inherited from both Brentano and his Neo-Kantian colleagues, Rickert and Natorp), but turns instead to Leibniz's monadology. Thus, in *Cartesian Meditations*, he characterizes intersubjectivity as a *community of monads* acting harmoniously. Although monads are "absolutely separate unities" (CM 129; Hua I 157), nevertheless they are communalized in a "harmony of monads" (CM 108; Hua I 138), in a transcendental "universe of monads" (*Allheit der Monaden, Monadenall*, Hua XV 609); a "transcendental 'we'" (CM 107; Hua I 137). Unlike Leibniz's monads, however, Husserl's monads have "windows" and communicate with one another and indeed form a "communicative community."

What is this transcendental intersubjectivity and indeed what is his concept of "spirit" [*Geist*] that Husserl invokes in late texts? Husserl speaks generally of "intersubjectivity" (*Intersubjektivität*),[38] "all-subjectivity" (*Allsubjektivität*, Hua VI 468, 506, 530; *transzendentale Allsubjektivität*, Hua VIII 482), or "we-subjectivity" (*Wir-Subjektivität*, *Crisis* 109; Hua VI 111).[39] Husserl employs the term already in his Göttingen lectures of 1910–1911 (*Basic Problems of Phenomenology*) and discusses it in depth in his *Cartesian*

Meditations, and of course in *Phänomenologie der Intersubjektivität* (1973).[40]
In order for there to be an experience of a common shared world of publicly
available objects as well as the realm of culture and language, there must be a
transcendental structure of intercommunicating subjects. There could be no
sense of one world, one space, one time, unless all subjectivities united to
constitute it *as one*. In this sense, Husserl speaks of the world as the "achievement" (*Leistung*) of transcendental intersubjectivity (CM §49). In his 1928
Amsterdam Lectures, Husserl similarly proclaims that the ultimate ground is
not the isolated transcendental ego but transcendental intersubjectivity:

> Transcendental intersubjectivity is the absolute and only self-sufficient founda-
> tion [*der absolute, der allein eigenständige Seinsboden*]. Out of it are created the
> meaning and validity [*seinen Sinn und seine Geltung*] of everything objective,
> the totality of objectively real existent entities, but also every ideal world as
> well. An objectively existent thing is from first to last an existent thing only in
> a peculiar, relative and incomplete sense. It is an existent thing, so to speak,
> only on the basis of a cover-up of its transcendental constitution that goes
> unnoticed in the natural attitude. (*Trans. Phen.* 249; Hua IX 344)

Indeed, for Husserl, the great challenge of phenomenology is to grasp the
deepest meaning of the transcendental subject *as* interwoven with transcendental intersubjectivity (see *Crisis* §73).[41] Husserl writes in the *Crisis*—in
a passage that Merleau-Ponty famously highlights in his Preface to the
Phenomenology of Perception—that subjectivity can only function within a
nexus of intersubjectivity: "Now everything becomes complicated as soon as
we consider that subjectivity is what it is—an ego functioning constitutively
[*konstitutiv fungierendes Ich*]—only within intersubjectivity" (*Crisis* §50, 172;
Hua VI 175). Each transcendental ego, for Husserl, as for Hegel, is a "for
itself" (*für sich*), as we have seen. At the same time, transcendental egos are
not just "for themselves" constituting the world, they are also "for each other
[*füreinander*]" (Hua VIII 505), cooperating sense-constituting subjects, who
generate their own sense of the world and their sense of my subjectivity (CM
V §43). Husserl is insistent that the world as the ultimate context and horizon
of human experience cannot be conceived solipsistically as just *my* world but
must be thought of as an inherently *communal* world, world "for others," a
world potentially available "for everyone [*für jedermann*]" (*Crisis* 296; Hua
VI 343; 358; Hua VI 369), or just, in short, *the one* world. Human subjects
exist for-each-other in what he calls *Ineinanderleben* or *Ineinandersein*.[42] As
he writes in the *Crisis*:

> But in *living with one another* [*Miteinanderleben*] each can take part in the
> life of others. Thus, in general, the world exists not only for isolated humans
> but for the human community; and this is due to the communalization [*Verge-
> meinschaftung*] of even what is straightforwardly perceived. (*Crisis* 163; Hua
> VI 166, trans. modified)

As subjects, we are always already caught up in the intersubjective domain.
For example, we speak a language and practice culture inherited from
others—anonymous others whom we do not know personally. But we also
constitute ourselves in meaningful interactions with other subjects apper-
ceived as *persons*. Intersubjectivity has to be understood in terms of each
ego having its other, its "you," its "we," its "they." There can be no "you"
or "we" except from the standpoint of an ego and this, for Husserl, always
gives the first-person ego a certain primacy. But as Husserl constantly points
out this is also true for other egos which also have their own "you's" and
"we's." Although the factual number of egos is indefinite, Husserl emphasizes the *closed* nexus of intersubjectivity: "But each soul also stands in
community [*Vergemeinschaftung*] with others which are intentionally interrelated, that is, in a purely intentional, internally and essentially closed nexus
[*Zusammenhang*], that of intersubjectivity" (Husserl, *Crisis* §69, 238; VI
241). Husserl, then, conceives of the true domain of intersubjectivity as
including all subjects in the past and future, not just all actual subjects but all
possible subjects, functioning together to generate the entire world including
its historical development. Husserl writes:

> Each human being as a person stands in his or her generative interconnec-
> tivities [*Zusammenhängen*], which, understood in a personal spiritual manner,
> stand in the unity of a historicity; this is not just a sequence of past factuali-
> ties, but it is implicated in each present, in its factuality, as a hidden spiritual
> acquisition, as the past, which has formed that specific person, and as such
> is intentionally implicated in him as his formation or upbringing [*Bildung*].
> (*Crisis* VI 488, my translation)

Thus, in 1934, for instance, Husserl had written in a fragment entitled
"Human Life in Historicity" (*Menschlichesleben in der Geschichtlichkeit*, Hua
XXIX):

> The human being [*der Mensch*] lives his [or her] spiritual life not in a spiritless
> world, in a world [understood] as matter, but rather as a spirit among spirits,
> among human and super-human, and this world-totality [*Weltall*] is, for him
> [or her], the totality of existing living, in the way of spirit, of the I-being, of the

I-living among others as I-subjects, life in the form of a universal I-community. (*Ich-Gemeinschaft*, Hua XXIX 3, my translation)[43]

Similarly, in his 1935 *Vienna Lecture*, Husserl articulates a Hegelian-sounding conception of absolute spirit; one, however, that can only be explored by phenomenology:

> It is my conviction that intentional phenomenology has made of the spirit qua spirit for the first time a field of systematic experience and science and has thus brought about the total reorientation of the task of knowledge. The universality of the absolute spirit [*Universalität des absoluten Geistes*] surrounds everything that exists with an absolute historicity, to which nature is subordinated as a spiritual structure [*als Geistesgebilde*]. (*Crisis* 298; Hua VI 347).

Husserl insists on the final interconnecting unity of absolute spirit (*absoluter Geist*). In fact, in line with his anti-naturalism, it is the world of spirit (as the nexus of cooperating intersubjectivity) that has primacy. "Nature" as an independent realm governed by causality is achieved by subtracting the intentional activity of spirit. In the end, absolute spirit alone is "self-sufficient" (*eigenständig*), as he writes in the *Vienna Lecture*:

> The spirit, and indeed only the spirit, exists in itself and for itself, is self-sufficient [*Der Geist und sogar nur der Geist ist in sich selbst und für sich selbst seiend, ist eigenständig*]; and in its self-sufficiency, and only in this way, it can be treated truly rationally, truly and from the ground up scientifically. As for nature, however, in its natural-scientific truth, it is only apparently self-sufficient and can only apparently be brought by itself to rational knowledge in the natural sciences. (*Crisis* 297; Hua VI 345)

Once subjectivity is considered a part of transcendental intersubjectivity, then, the question of absolute priority is displaced. What is absolutely prior is subjectivity operating within the nexus of intersubjectivity, just like each speaker depends upon the network of language meanings and structures that are sustained by the ongoing community of those language speakers.

Conclusion

For Husserl, all consciousness is "egoic" (*ichlich*) or, as we would say, first-personal. Consciousness is always distributed to subjects each of whom experiences it as mine. There is an essentially irreducible first-person access to meaningful experience. Moreover, this ego or I is not static but is dynamic and multi-layered and developing. As Husserl says in *Cartesian Meditations*, the ego unfolds in a unified history, and its experiences become sedimented to it through habit.[44] For Husserl, this egoic subjectivity is a temporal, synthesizing, flowing life that first has to constitute itself as a self and then constitutes everything it encounters in the world. Somehow, the ego *passively* assembles itself as an enduring presence, a "living present" (*lebedige Gegen-wart*), out of its deepest layer of flowing time consciousness and primitive association, to concretize eventually as the full person or monad which encap-sulates a set of capacities and dispositions. This transcendental ego, then, also, has a history and a set of sedimentations and habitualities that accrue to it. In this sense, the transcendental ego is dynamic and unfolds in history.

In Husserl's scheme, the transcendental ego is the counterpart of the empirical ego, providing the framework and enabling conditions to give the empirical ego its sense of worldliness. The ego is always mirrored and encapsulated in the "nexus" (*Zusammenhang*) of intersubjectivity. Husserl opposes all previous idealisms—Platonic, psychological (Berkeleyan, Humean), Kantian, Fichtean, or Hegelian (these devolved into speculative mysticism). As Sidney Hook put it perceptively in 1930:

> the only difficulty we are faced with is to find out what kind of an idealist Husserl is. This is not a difficulty to be sneered at, for all of philosophic Germany has been trying for the last twenty-five years to make it out. It is not Platonic idealism, since Plato's Ideas were stored up in heaven and were the models, not the instruments, of demiurgic creation. It is not Berkeleyan idealism, since that is a theory of mentalism which denies on principle the objectivity of non-mental ideal meanings. It is not Kantian idealism, for Kant stopped where he should have begun; instead of asking how logic itself was possible and submitting the ideal laws of logic to transcendental analysis … he accepted the Aristotelian logics as something finished and self-justifying. As distinct from all these Husserl's idealism is phenomenological idealism. It asks for the certification of everything found in consciousness—even the objective meanings. It asks how are meanings in general possible?[45]

Husserl's path to idealism comes through his conception of intentionality that led him to assert the absolute priority of constituting subjectivity as the source of all meaning and being. Furthermore, this constituting subjectivity is accessible only through the reduction that strips away all naturalization. It seems, however, that the mundane ego is responsible for discovering the tran-scendental ego but the transcendental ego in its essence enfolds all actual and possible egos. Somehow (and Husserl never succeeded in solving this issue) the ego not just constitutes *itself* but also all other egos as alien to it and

themselves having constitutive power within the overall nexus of intersubjectivity. One has to wonder whether Husserl's continued insistence on the strict
parallelism between the transcendental and the "mundane" (Husserl rarely
speaks of the "empirical" ego) does not create an indissoluble problem (that
Michel Foucault has referred to the "transcendental doublet").[46]

Husserl thought that life lived in naiveté was natural, worldly, mundane
life, *Dahinleben*. But he also thought that the transcendental reduction leads
us back into a new domain and a new kind of life, namely transcendental
life. Transcendental life, for Husserl, expresses the idea that human subjects
can come to self-consciousness of their functioning in the overall network of
rationality itself. The self is essentially split or doubled in what Husserl calls
"*Ichspaltung*." I contemplate myself as part of the nexus of infinite, cooperative, intentional agency. Furthermore, this egoic transcendental life is always
in progress and evolves in the form of history. Transcendental intersubjectivity
is essentially embodied, incarnate subjectivities, embedded in the historical
and cultural life-world. As Merleau-Ponty, in his magisterial commemorative
essay on Husserl, "The Philosopher and His Shadow" (1959), puts it:

> One of its [the reduction's] "results" is the realization that the movement of
> return to ourselves—of 're-entering' ourselves, St. Augustine said—is as if rent
> by an inverse movement which it elicits. Husserl rediscovers that identity of "re-
> entering self" and "going-outside self" which, for Hegel, defined the absolute.
> To reflect (Husserl said in *Ideen* l) is to unveil an unreflected dimension which
> is at a distance because we are no longer it in a naive way, yet which we cannot
> doubt that reflection attains, since it is through reflection itself that we have an
> idea of it. So it is not the unreflected which challenges reflection; it is reflection
> which challenges itself.[47]

Notes

1. Vittorio DePalma questions why Husserl should even call it transcendental
   idealism, if it is really a new doctrine, see his "Eine peinliche Verwechslung. Zu
   Husserl Transzendentalismus," *Metodo. International Studies in Phenomenology
   and Philosophy*, Special Issue, no. 1, ch. 1 (2015): 13–45. Husserl, however,
   often employed traditional concepts imbued with new meanings.
2. Edmund Husserl, *Die Krisis der europäischen Wissenschaften und die transzendentale Phänomenologie. Eine Einleitung in die phänomenologische Philosophie*, hrsg. W. Biemel, Husserliana [=Hua] VI (The Hague: Nijhoff, 1962);
   partially trans. David Carr, *The Crisis of European Sciences and Transcendental
   Phenomenology. An Introduction to Phenomenological Philosophy* (Evanston:
   Northwestern University Press, 1970). Hereafter *Crisis* followed by the English

page number; and Husserliana volume and page number of the German edition.

3. Edmund Husserl, *Formale und transzendentale Logik. Versuch einer Kritik der logischen Vernunft. Mit ergänzenden Texten*, ed. Paul Janssen, Hua XVII (The Hague: Nijhoff, 1974); trans. Dorion Cairns, *Formal and Transcendental Logic* (The Hague: Nijhoff, 1969). Hereafter FTL. For the early reception of Husserl's idealism in his *Formal and Transcendental Logic*, see Sidney Hook, "Husserl's Phenomenological Idealism," *Journal of Philosophy* 27, no. 14 (1930): 365–80. Hook sees Husserl as coming close to Hegel's version of idealism.

4. Edmund Husserl, *Ideen zur einer reinen Phänomenologie und phänomenologischen Philosophie, Zweites Buch: Phänomenologische Untersuchungen zur Konstitution*, ed. Marly Biemel, Hua IV (The Hague: Martinus Nijhoff, 1952), trans. R. Rojcewicz and A. Schuwer as *Ideas Pertaining to a Pure Phenomenology and to a Phenomenological Philosophy, Second Book: Studies in the Phenomenology of Constitution* (Dordrecht: Kluwer, 1989); hereafter *Ideas II*, followed by English pagination and Husserliana volume and page number.

5. Edmund Husserl, *Gesammelte Werke*, Husserliana, ed. Ullrich Melle (Dordrecht: Springer, 1956–). Forty-three volumes to date. The English translations are ongoing in Husserl, *Collected Works*, ed. Julia Jansen (Dordrecht: Springer). Husserliana will be abbreviated to 'Hua.'

6. Edmund Husserl, *Ideen zu einer reinen Phänomenologie und phänomenologischen Philosophie. Erstes Buch: Allgemeine Einführung in die reine Phänomenologie 1. Halbband: Text der 1-3. Auflage*, ed. K. Schuhmann, Hua III/1 (The Hague: Nijhoff, 1977); trans. Daniel O. Dahlstrom, *Ideas for a Pure Phenomenology and Phenomenological Philosophy. First Book: General Introduction to Pure Phenomenology* (Indianapolis: Hackett Publishing Company, 2014). Hereafter the work will be cited as *Ideas* I followed by the paragraph number (§), page number of the English translation, and then the Hua volume number and page.

7. Strictly speaking, Husserl does not use the word 'idealism' to apply to his outlook in his *Ideas* I, but his student Gerda Walther added it to the Index of the 1921 edition. He does refer to "subjective idealism" or "Berkeleyan idealism" in *Ideas* I §55 (sometimes, he will call this "psychological idealism").

8. On the evolution of Husserl's transcendental idealism, see the Editors' Introduction to Edmund Husserl, *Transzendentaler Idealismus. Texte aus dem Nachlass (1908–1921)*, ed. Robin Rollinger and Rochus Sowa, Hua XXXVI (Dordrecht: Kluwer, 2003), ix–xxxvii. See also Dermot Moran, *Edmund Husserl. Founder of Phenomenology* (Cambridge: Polity, 2005), 174–201; and idem, *Husserl's Crisis of the European Sciences and Transcendental Phenomenology. An Introduction* (Cambridge: Cambridge University Press, 2012).

9. See Edmund Husserl, *Transzendentaler Idealismus. Texte aus dem Nachlass (1908–1921)*, op. cit. Husserl uses the term to refer to the thesis that the existence of real objects is dependent on an actually existing consciousness.

10. Edmund Husserl, "Fichtes Menschenheits Ideal: Drei Vorlesungen," in *Aufsätze und Vorträge 1911–1921*, ed. Hans Rainer Sepp, Thomas Nenon, Husserliana XXV (Dordrecht: Kluwer, 1986), 267–93; trans. James Hart, "Fichte's Ideal of Humanity: Three Lectures," *Husserl Studies* 12 (1995): 111–33. See Denis Fisette, "Husserl et Fichte: Remarques sur l'apport de l'idéalisme dans le développement de la phénoménologie," *Symposium* 3, no. 2 (Fall 1999): 185–207.

11. Edmund Husserl, "Der Encyclopaedia Brittannica Artikel," in *Phänomenologische Psychologie. Vorlesungen Sommersemester 1925*, ed. W. Biemel. Hua IX (The Hague: Nijhoff, 1968), 237–301; trans. T. Sheehan and R. E. Palmer, in E. Husserl, *Psychological and Transcendental Phenomenology and the Confrontation with Heidegger (1927–31), the Encyclopaedia Britannica Article, the Amsterdam Lectures "Phenomenology and Anthropology" and Husserl's Marginal Note in Being and Time, and Kant on the Problem of Metaphysics.* Husserl Collected Works VI (Dordrecht: Kluwer, 1997), 80–196. Hereafter *Trans. Phen.*

12. Edmund Husserl, *Cartesianische Meditationen und Pariser Vorträge*, ed. S. Strasser, Hua I (The Hague: Martinus Nijhoff, 1973); trans. Dorion Cairns as *Cartesian Meditations: An Introduction to Phenomenology* (The Hague: Martinus Nijhoff, 1973). Hereafter CM, followed by English pagination and Husserliana volume and page number.

13. Dermot Moran, "Making Sense: Husserl's Phenomenology as Transcendental Idealism," in *From Kant to Davidson: Philosophy and the Idea of the Transcendental*, ed. J. Malpas (London: Routledge, 2003), 48–74.

14. Sophie Loidolt argues that Husserl's idealism in fact stems from an ontological presupposition, i.e., the absolute priority of consciousness over being ("Transzendentalphilosophie und Idealismus in der Phänomenologie," *Metodo. International Studies in Phenomenology and Philosophy*, Special Issue, no. 1, ch. 1 [2015]: 103–35). See Julia Jansen, "On Transcendental and Non-Transcendental Idealism in Husserl: A Response to De Palma and Loidolt," *Metodo. International Studies in Phenomenology and Philosophy* (2017): 27–39.

15. Husserl uses the term "the ego'" (*das Ego*) or the "I" (*Ich*) for the "empirical ego" (*Logical Investigations*), "psychological" ego (CM § 11), or "mundane" ego, that is the subject of experiences, and provides identity across experiences, and for what he terms the "pure" (*rein, Ideas* I § 57, § 80) or "transcendental" ego (*das transzendentale Ego*). The transcendental ego is not just the formal condition for the possibility of the empirical ego but actually is an intentional center of sense-giving (*Sinngebung*), giving the empirical ego its concrete sense and capacities. See David Carr, *The Paradox of Subjectivity: The Self in the Transcendental Tradition* (Oxford: Oxford University Press, 1999). Husserl's transcendental ego is not the essence (*eidos*) ego. Husserl's transcendental ego is the ego which relates to the transcendence of the world.

16. See Sebastian Luft, "From Being to Givenness and Back: Some Remarks on the Meaning of Transcendental Idealism in Kant and Husserl," *International Journal of Philosophical Studies* 15, no. 3 (2007): 367–94.

17. For recent discussions, see Dominique Pradelle, "Husserl's Criticism of Kant's Transcendental Idealism: A Clarification of Phenomenological Idealism," *Horizon. Studies in Phenomenology* 4, no. 2 (2015): 25–53; and Rudolf Bernet, "Transcendental Phenomenology?" in *Phenomenology in a New Key: Between Analysis and History*, ed. Nicholas de Warren and Jeffrey Bloechl (Dordrecht: Springer, 2015), 115–33.

18. See Dan Zahavi, "Internalism, Externalism, and Transcendental Idealism," *Synthese* 160, no. 3 (2008): 355–74; and Uwe Meixner, "Husserls transzendentaler Idealismus als Supervenienzthese. Ein interner Realismus," in *Husserl und die Philosophie des Geistes*, ed. Manfred Frank and Niels Weidtmann (Frankfurt: Suhrkamp, 2010), 178–208.

19. See Rudolf Bernet, "Husserl's Transcendental Idealism Revisited," *New Yearbook for Phenomenology and Phenomenological Philosophy* 4 (2004): 1–20; and Ullrich Melle, "Husserl's Beweis für den transzendentalen Idealismus," in *Philosophy, Phenomenology, Sciences*, ed. Carlo Ierna et al. (Dordrecht: Springer, 2010), 93–106.

20. Edmund Husserl, *Logische Untersuchungen. Erster Band: Prolegomena zur reinen Logik*. Text der 1. und der 2. Auflage, hrsg. Elmar Holenstein, Hua XVIII (The Hague: Nijhoff, 1975), and *Logische Untersuchungen. Zweiter Band: Untersuchungen zur Phänomenologie und Theorie der Erkenntnis*, in zwei Bänden, hrsg. Ursula Panzer, Hua XIX 1 and 2 (Dordrecht: Kluwer, 1984); trans. J. N. Findlay, *Logical Investigations*, edited with a new introduction by Dermot Moran (London: Routledge, 2001). Hereafter LU. The reference here is LU, vol. 1, 384–85.

21. Quentin Meillassoux is therefore correct to call Husserl (and Kant) a "correlationist," see his *After Finitude: An Essay on the Necessity of Contingency*, trans. Ray Brassier (London: Continuum, 2008). However, Meillassoux's own attempt to get to the "Great Outdoors" beyond consciousness through mathematical science precisely re-introduces the correlationism he is trying to overcome.

22. Roman Ingarden, *On the Motives That Let Husserl to Transcendental Idealism* (Dordrecht: Springer, 1975), 21.

23. Edmund Husserl, *Ideas: A General Introduction to Pure Phenomenology*, ed. Dermot Moran, trans. W. R. Boyce Gibson (London: Routledge Classics, 2012).

24. Edmund Husserl, "Kant und die Idee der transzendentalphilosophie," *Erste Philosophie (1923/24). Erster Teil: Kritische Ideengeschichte*, hrsg. R. Boehm. Hua VII (The Hague: Nijhoff, 1965), 230–87; trans. Ted E. Klein and William E. Pohl, "Kant and the Idea of Transcendental Philosophy," *Southwestern Journal of Philosophy* 5 (Fall 1974): 9–56.

25. Iso Kern, *Husserl und Kant. Eine Untersuchung über Husserls Verhältnis zu Kant und zum Neukantianismus* (Dordrecht: Nijhoff, 1964).

26. Rather it was Eugen Fink and Martin Heidegger in Freiburg, from 1928 onward, who were discussing German Idealism.
27. Edmund Husserl, "Fichte's Ideal of Humanity," 113.
28. See Alessandro Salice, "The Phenomenology of the Munich and Göttingen Circles," *The Stanford Encyclopedia of Philosophy* (Winter 2019 Edition), ed. Edward N. Zalta. https://plato.stanford.edu/archives/win2019/entries/phenomenology-mg/.
29. Edmund Husserl, *Einleitung in die Logik und Erkenntnistheorie. Vorlesungen 1906/07*, hrsg. Ullrich Melle, Hua XXIV (Dordrecht: Kluwer, 1985).
30. Edmund Husserl, *Philosophie als strenge Wissenschaft*, in *Aufsätze und Vorträge 1911–1921*, ed. H. R. Sepp and Thomas Nenon, Hua XXV (Dordrecht: Kluwer, 1986), 3–62; trans. by Marcus Brainard as "Philosophy as Rigorous Science," *The New Yearbook for Phenomenology and Phenomenological Philosophy* vol. II (2002): 249–95.
31. See Dermot Moran, "Husserl's Transcendental Philosophy and the Critique of Naturalism," *Continental Philosophy Review* 41, no. 4 (December 2008): 401–25.
32. Edmund Husserl, letter to Rickert, 20 December 1915, in *Briefwechsel*, 5:178. See Iso Kern, *Husserl und Kant*, 35.
33. See later Hua XXXIV 258, where Husserl accuses anthropologism of "falsely absolutizing a positivistic world."
34. See Andrea Staiti, *Husserl's Transcendental Phenomenology. Nature, Spirit, and Life* (New York: Cambridge University Press, 2014).
35. Ernest Wolfgang Orth has pointed out that this paradox, whereby the transcendental ego both constitutes the world and is itself constituted as an entity within the world, was raised as a problem for Fichte's transcendental idealism by Herbart (*Edmund Husserls "Krisis der europäischen Wissenschaften und die transzendentale Phänomenologie": Vernunft und Kultur* [Darmstadt: WBG Wissenschaftliche Buchgesellschaft, 1999], 93).
36. "Aber das Eidos transzendentales Ich ist undenkbar ohne transzendentales Ich als faktisches. Solange ich, im Faktum meiner transzendentalen Subjektivität und der mir geltenden Welt stehend, abwandle und zum Eidos übergehend systematisch forsche, stehe ich in der absoluten Ontologie und korrelativ in der mundanen Ontologie."
37. Eugen Fink, "The Phenomenological Philosophy of Edmund Husserl and Contemporary Criticism," in *The Phenomenology of Husserl. Selected Critical and Contemporary Readings*, ed. Roy Elveton (London: Routledge, 2003), 121.
38. According to Zahavi, the German term *Intersubjektivität* was first used by Johannes Volkelt in 1885 and then by James Ward in English in 1896. See Dan Zahavi, *Self and Other: Exploring Subjectivity, Empathy, and Shame* (Oxford: Oxford University Press, 2014), 97.
39. Although Husserl did not invent the term 'intersubjectivity,' he gives the most extensive philosophical conception of it. Iso Kern points to the years 1913–1914 when Husserl wrote a group of 16 texts amounting to 80 pages on

intersubjectivity, part of which was included in *Ideas* II, see Iso Kern, "Husserl's Phenomenology of Intersubjectivity," in *Husserl's Phenomenology of Intersubjectivity: Historical Interpretations and Contemporary Applications*, ed. Frode Kjosavik, Christian Beyer, and Christel Fricke (London: Routledge, 2019), 11.

40. Edmund Husserl, *Zur Phänomenologie der Intersubjektivität. Texte aus dem Nachlass. Erster Teil. 1905–1920*, ed. Iso Kern, Husserliana XIII (The Hague: Nijhoff, 1973); *Zur Phänomenologie der Intersubjektivität. Texte Aus Dem Nachlass. Zweiter Teil. 1921–1928*, ed. Iso Kern, Husserliana XIV (The Hague: Nijhoff, 1973); and *Zur Phänomenologie der Intersubjektivität. Texte aus dem Nachlass. Dritter Teil. 1929–1935*, ed. Iso Kern, Husserliana XV (The Hague: Nijhoff, 1973).

41. See Arun Iyer, "Transcendental Subjectivity, Embodied subjectivity and Intersubjectivity in Husserl's Transcendental Idealism," in *Epistemology, Archaeology, Ethics: Current Investigations of Husserl's Corpus*, ed. Pol Vandevelde and Sebastian Luft (London: Continuum, 2010).

42. Dermot Moran, "The Phenomenology of the Social World: Husserl on *Mitsein as Ineinandersein and Füreinandersein*," *Metodo*, ed. Elisa Magrì and Danielle Petherbridge, 5, no. 1 (2017): 99–142.

43. Edmund Husserl, *Die Krisis der europäischen Wissenschaften und die transzendentale Phänomenologie. Ergänzungsband. Texte aus dem Nachlaß 1934–1937*. Hrsg. Reinhold N. Smid, Husserliana Volume XXIX (Dordrecht: Kluwer, 1992).

44. See Dermot Moran, "'The Ego as Substrate of Habitualities': Edmund Husserl's Phenomenology of the Habitual Self," *Phenomenology and Mind* 6 (July 2014): 27–47.

45. Sidney Hook, "Husserl's Phenomenological Idealism," 367.

46. See Dermot Moran, "*Sinnboden der Geschichte*: Husserl's Mature Reflections on the Structural A Priori of History," *Continental Philosophy Review* 49, no. 1 (2016): 13–27.

47. Maurice Merleau-Ponty, *Signs*, trans. Richard C. McCleary (Evanston: Northwestern University Press, 1964), 161.

3

Transcendental Philosophy, Psychology, and Anthropology: Kant and Husserl on the "Inner Man" and the Human Being

Claudia Serban

Insofar as it values a pure, non-empirical dimension of knowledge whose origin is ultimately subjective, transcendental philosophy, when defined by such an idealist orientation, cannot avoid being confronted by the relationship between the transcendental I and empirical subjectivity, considered in its dual psychological and anthropological dimension. If Kant and Husserl both elaborate a form of transcendental idealism, they assign a quite different function and status to internal (or inner) experience in relation to external (or outer) experience. This chapter will examine their understanding of the nature and content of internal experience and their comprehension of what the "outer man,"[1] or the human being as being-in-the-world, is with respect to transcendental subjectivity, in order to highlight the position of their transcendental philosophy toward psychology and anthropology. More precisely, my thesis is that the way the question of subjectivity and that of inner experience (or of the "inner man") are dealt with not only differently connects psychology and anthropology to transcendental philosophy, but also, by revealing the gap between Husserl's and Kant's transcendental project, allows us to grasp the specific meaning of their idealism.

C. Serban (✉)
Toulouse Jean Jaurès University, Toulouse, France
e-mail: claudia_serban@hotmail.fr

C. D. Coe (eds.), *The Palgrave Handbook of German Idealism and Phenomenology*,
Palgrave Handbooks in German Idealism,
https://doi.org/10.1007/978-3-030-66857-0_3

41

First of all, in order to contrast Husserl's and Kant's stance toward psychology, I shall examine Kant's critique of the fourth Paralogism (the Paralogism of ideality) and his 1787 Refutation of Idealism. While evaluating the consequences of Kant's radically new manner of articulating internal and external experience, I will show that it is possible to reply to some of Husserl's objections to critical philosophy by questioning his own excessive trust in inner experience and his plea for a transcendental psychology. In effect, the way that Kant conceives of the mutual dependency between internal and external experience allows us to measure the distance that separates him from Cartesian (or Husserlian) idealism. It also counts among the reasons for which, transgressing Husserl's expectation to renew psychology on the ground of critical philosophy, Kant will elaborate (and eventually publish) a "pragmatic" anthropology for which the "inner man" is inseparable from "outer man." Yet Husserl's phenomenology itself, far from thoroughly manifesting an "anthropological prohibition," will eventually attempt to reconquer the field of anthropology without abandoning the transcendental phenomenological perspective. In the end, in spite of their radically divergent views on psychology, the anthropological continuation of transcendental philosophy has been regarded as a necessity by both Kant and Husserl.

The Faith of Psychology and the Role of Internal Experience

From the *Logical Investigations* to the *Crisis of European Sciences*, Husserl raised some important objections to Kant: in his view, the author of the three *Critiques* remained imprisoned by numerous dogmatic (either rationalist or empiricist) presuppositions. Kant's decision to restrain the validity of the categories as pure concepts of our intellect both by limiting their application to phenomena and by attributing them only to "finite reasonable beings" (i.e., to us humans) is considered to be the effect of such presuppositions. But there is another critique, more discrete and nevertheless as powerful, that Husserl addressed to Kant, for instance in his *Crisis of European Sciences*, §57: that of establishing a "fatal separation (*verhängnisvolle Trennung*)" between transcendental philosophy and psychology. To begin with, Husserl expresses his astonishment that critical philosophy "did . . . not work out a better psychology" (C 201).[2] At the same time, he confesses his ambition of transforming psychology into a universal transcendental philosophy (C 203),[3] thus maintaining the possibility of a pure, *a priori* psychology. Moreover, he even envisages a "transcendental psychology," related to transcendental philosophy like a sister, "in virtue of the alliance (*Verschwisterung*) of difference and identity . . . between the psychological I . . . and the transcendental I" (C 205).[4]

The founder of phenomenology is undoubtedly conscious of transgressing a Kantian prohibition when he aims to restore in this fashion the connection between transcendental philosophy and psychology. For Kant, in effect, the transcendental and the psychological approach of subjectivity is to be carefully separated, and therefore, psychology could not contribute or belong to a transcendental theory of understanding and knowledge. But Husserl considers that his own project of an eidetic and ultimately transcendental psychology does not demand to take such precautions, as did, in Kant's view, the dogmatic, rational psychology of old-time metaphysicians. The Introduction to Husserl's 1925 lecture on *Phenomenological Psychology* stresses this point:

> In previous times admittedly, *a priori* psychology was much discussed, namely, in the Leibnitzian-Wolffean school of the eighteenth century. Kant's critique put an end to that. But this psychology was ontological-metaphysical. It was not a psychology which like this new one was purely intuitive and descriptive and yet at the same time *a priori*, which therefore, beginning with intuitive concrete instances ascended to intuitive necessities and universalities.[5]

Phenomenological psychology is thus considered to be immune to any Kant-inspired criticism. But is the possibility and legitimacy of such an *a priori* or even transcendental psychology that obvious? That is, was Kant thoroughly mistaken and excessively overcautious when refraining to renew psychology on the ground of critical philosophy? Instead of following Husserl when he condemns the faith that Kant assigned to psychology (by limiting it to be only empirical, and unable to be pure or *a priori* without relapsing into the transcendental illusion depicted by the four Paralogisms at the beginning of the Transcendental Dialectic), one could also wonder to what extent the author of the *Crisis* took into consideration Kant's critique of Cartesian idealism. In this respect, I would agree with Blumenberg when he writes the following:

> In his *pathos* of a new beginning of philosophy directed against its decay into psychologism, Husserl disdained the historical results as being that which had made this decay possible. This concerns first of all his relation to Kant. Had he not done so, he could not have entrusted to self-experience all the profit that phenomenology has to rely on. One has to admit that phenomenology would have paid a high price for being lectured by Kant.[6]

It is indeed true and surprising that, while criticizing Kant's psychologizing of the faculties of the mind, Husserl paradoxically maintains the alliance between transcendental philosophy and psychology that Kant had proclaimed impossible.

Kant, the Interior, and the Exterior

In order to clarify Kant's controversial relationship to psychology, I will now examine the deconstruction of the fourth Paralogism and the Refutation of Idealism where, through the firm rejection of the supposed primacy of inner experience over outer experience, the specific profile of critical idealism is drawn.[7] To begin with, it might be useful to recall the fact that while rewriting the Paralogisms for the second edition of the *Critique of Pure Reason*, Kant makes a significant architectonic change in the structure of his work: the main condemnation of idealism, that the 1781 edition entrusted to the discussion of the fourth Paralogism, is now transferred from the Transcendental Dialectic to the Transcendental Analytic (to the Analytic of Principles, to be more precise), where it follows the exposition of the Postulate of actuality. This important modification suggests that Kant was far from being pleased with the manner in which he had initially solved the problem of idealism, and felt the need to propose, in 1787, a genuine and plain "Refutation of Idealism."

In 1781, the critique of the fourth Paralogism discusses the claim that "the existence of all objects of outer sense is doubtful." But curiously, Kant is relatively moderate toward the idealist position, as he admits that "we can rightly assert that only what is in ourselves can be immediately perceived" (CPR A367). Indeed, the idealist against whom he is arguing is "not someone who denies the existence of external objects of sense, but rather someone who only does not admit that it is cognized through immediate perception" (CPR A368). Otherwise said, this subtle idealism does not state the non-existence of the outer world, but only the fact that its experience or perception is inescapably mediate or indirect. Thus, idealism does not necessarily entail acosmism, but can also take the shape of a potential and always imminent skepticism concerning outer experience and the outer world. The Paralogism of ideality asserts the indirect and inferential character of our experience of exteriority and concludes that the existence of anything exterior to us is uncertain. This being said, Kant's resolution sounds as follows:

external objects (bodies) are merely appearances, hence also nothing other than a species of my representations, whose objects are something only through these representations, but are nothing separated from them. Thus external things exist as well as my self, and indeed both exist on the immediate testimony of my self-consciousness, only with this difference: the representation of my Self, as the thinking subject, is related merely to inner sense, but the representations that designate extended beings are also related to outer sense. I am no more necessitated to draw inferences in respect of the reality of external objects than I am in regard to the reality of the objects of my inner sense (my thoughts), for in both cases they are nothing but representations, the immediate perception (consciousness) of which is at the same time a sufficient proof of their actuality (*Wirklichkeit*). (CPR A370–71)

In order to deactivate the idealist claim of our mediate and always indirect access to exteriority, Kant insists here on the fact that the objects of our outer sense are mere appearances and eventually, mere representations. For this reason, external experience is not more indirect or more mediate than internal experience, insofar as in both cases we have to do with representations which are just as immediately present in me.

Thus, the 1781 resolution of the fourth Paralogism asserts that internal and external experiences are equally immediate and certain. But this equivalency is defended by dissolving exterior objects within the immanent sphere of representation. Through outer sense, I represent to myself objects that are outside me, and yet their representation is *in* me. This argument, however, seems to involve the failure of any attempt to leave the sphere of interiority: as long as the object of the external sense is only regarded as my representation, the reality of the outer world taken as existing outside me will always ineluctably escape me. The appearance, or phenomenon—the *Erscheinung*—fully merges here into the representation: "in our system, on the contrary," writes Kant in his polemics against idealism, "these external things . . . are nothing but mere representations, i.e., representations in us, of whose reality [*Wirklichkeit*] we are immediately conscious" (CPR A371–72). From this perspective, that of which we are immediately conscious is always a representation, be it internal or external. This is how the undoubted existence of the outer world is finally dissolved in the undisputed and immediate presence of its representation within me. The actuality that is proved in this manner is not that of the outer world or of the exterior object, but only that of the representation of exteriority which is in me; in more Cartesian terms, it is only the *formal reality* of the idea or the representation of the world that becomes indisputable. But what about its *objective reality*, that is, what about the existence of the object of this representation?

It is highly significant that Kant will adopt this Cartesian vocabulary (which, as a matter of fact, is rather familiar to him) in the long footnote at the end of the 1787 Preface, where he confesses that the Refutation of Idealism is in fact the only true supplement[8] of the second edition of the *Critique*. Its purpose is to provide "a strict proof (the only possible one . . .) of the objective reality of outer intuition" (CPR Bxxxix note). Undoubtedly, the 1781 resolution of the fourth Paralogism has mainly focused on the formal reality of my representation of exteriority, by asserting that "every outer perception therefore immediately proves something actual [*wirklich*] in space, or rather is itself the actuality [*das Wirkliche selbst*]" (CPR A375, translation modified). The actuality of exteriority was then mainly understood as the actuality of my representation of it: the 1781 resolution of the Paralogism of ideality evolved entirely within the sphere of representation.

By contrast, the 1787 Refutation of Idealism, instead of being satisfied with this first solution, attempts to make a step forward. As the footnote of the second Preface quoted above indicates, the ground of the Refutation is not the field of appearances understood as representations, but that of the consciousness of existence, insofar as the goal is now to show that "the *empirical consciousness of my existence* . . . is only determinable through a relation to something that, while being bound up with my existence, is outside me" (CPR Bxl note). Having this in mind, it is easier to understand why the Refutation is placed, in the second edition of the *Critique*, after the presentation of the Postulate of actuality (*Wirklichkeit*); and also why Kant insists on distinguishing, in the same footnote of the 1787 Preface, "the representation of something persisting in existence" from "a persisting representation": there should indeed be no confusion between that which concerns the objective reality of a representation and that which simply pertains to its formal reality. Only the consideration of the objective reality of representations allows reaching their (outer) correlate and stating something about its existence.[9] This is why the argument of the Refutation of Idealism will so emphasize the actuality of that which is exterior to me.

This argument goes even further insofar as it claims that, without outer correlates, or without an object exterior to me and yet given to me in space, inner sense itself could not properly function: that which is given through this sense would then be evanescent and remain inconsistent. The Transcendental Aesthetic already noticed that internal experience seems to embrace external experience. The novel contribution of the second edition Analytic with respect to the relation between inner and outer sense is to show that internal experience, far from being self-sufficient, is always associated with external intuitions: "the reality of outer sense is necessarily bound up with that of inner sense, i.e., I am just as certainly conscious that there are things outside me to which my sensibility relates, as I am conscious that I myself exist determined in time" (CPR Bxl note). And ultimately, going even further than this acknowledgment of the equal certainty and immediacy of the representations provided by inner and outer sense, the 1787 edition of the *Critique* subordinates internal experience to external experience. The mechanism of the Refutation of Idealism consists indeed in proving not only that the two are equally certain but also that, in the end, the presumed priority and superiority of internal experience needs to be reversed. For it is only then that the idealist who considers all exteriority as intrinsically doubtful is completely defeated.[10]

The crucial argument of the Refutation of Idealism is the fact that only external objects can provide us with a representation of permanence and that "consequently, the determination of my existence in time is possible only by means of the existence of actual [*wirklich*] things that I perceive outside myself" (CPR B275–76). It is in this manner that Kant intends to "turn against it" the "the game that idealism plays," according to which, as seen previously, "the only immediate experience is inner experience" (CPR B276). Kant can speak here of a reversal (*Umkehrung*), insofar as his goal is precisely to prove that only "outer experience is really immediate" and is the condition, "not . . . [of] the consciousness of our own existence, but [of] its determination in time, i.e., [of] inner experience" (CPR B276–77). Quite significantly, there is a resurfacing of the distinction between a consciousness "able to accompany all my representations" (CPR B131) or pure apperception that defines, for Kant, transcendental subjectivity, on the one hand, and internal experience, which adds an intuitive dimension to the subject of thought (which, therefore, is no longer transcendental, but empirical), on the other hand.

The dependence upon external intuitions does not concern the "I think" as a mere logical function, but only the temporal experience and existence of the I that presupposes a "change in outer relations" (CPR B 277): insofar as inner sense cannot provide any representation of permanence, only the matter of external experience can possibly deliver anything that could correspond to the representation of a *substance*. Therefore, it is also the problematic status of the matter given through internal experience, or of its specific content, that is here at stake. In this respect, the second edition of the *Critique* will even claim that it is from "the existence of things outside us" that "we after all get the whole matter for our cognitions, even for our inner sense" (CPR Bxxxix note). Otherwise said, I cannot cognize myself as an existing subject in a purely immanent way.

The Inconsistency of Interiority: A Critical Objection to Husserlian Idealism

Thus, strictly speaking, for Kant, there are no "immediate data of consciousness," understood as genuine contents of a purely internal intuition. The paradox of inner sense is that it cannot really give anything; or rather, that which is given through it is not really *something* (or *someone*), for it is only a perpetual evanescent flow of representations. Consequently, for Kant, that which Husserl calls the "originarily giving (*originär gebende*)" (or "originary presentive," *Ideas I*, 44)[11] intuition is rather external intuition. This view results mostly from the second edition of the *Critique*, for in 1781, Kant would still assert that "the thinking I is given to inner sense, likewise as substance in appearance" (CPR A379). But such a generous interpretation of the giving capacities of internal intuition will not prevail for long: on the contrary, the 1787 edition insists on the extreme poverty of inner sense and, by doing so, reveals the indigence of internal experience itself.

It is for this very reason that the Refutation of Idealism has the ultimate significance of an even more radical refutation of the substantiality of the soul, suggesting, once again, to what extent the destiny of idealism and that of psychology are intimately connected. The argument that the *Critique* uses against the idealism—the fact that internal experience has no autonomous persistence—is indeed the very same that grounds the impossibility of a pure, rational psychology granting an *a priori* access to the soul. The lack of permanence in internal experience was already encountered within the 1781 resolution of the Paralogisms, when stating that "in that which we call the soul, everything is in continual flux" (CPR A381). In this respect, a proximity to Husserl's approach of consciousness as a temporal stream might be hastily deduced. Yet it seems more accurate to think that the Kantian perspective could only lead to rejecting what will be Husserl's solution aiming to prove that the stream of consciousness is not a Heraclitean evanescent flow. For Kant refuses to give a specific content or substantiality to the stream itself (i.e., to the streaming interiority), or to treat it like an autonomous reality, as the founder of phenomenology will in his 1905 *Inner Time-Consciousness Lectures*. On the contrary, Kant's claim is that, in its very flowing, the temporal inner flux itself cannot be perceived, for time does not have the consistency of something permanent. As the pure form of inner sense, time has a content which constantly varies and can never be grasped in itself: for this reason, self-intuition, through which the subject apprehends his or her own interior life (the flow of his or her representations—perceptions, thoughts, memories, or even feelings) can never become a genuine self-cognition: the fact that inner sense provides me with a glimpse of my inner life does not mean that I truly cognize myself as I really am.

Thus, the profound and irreducible divergence between Kant's critical idealism and Husserl's transcendental idealism is tightly dependent on their treatment of temporal inner experience. When Husserl states (in the *Ideen* I §46) that "immanent perception guarantees the existence of its object," he does not transgress any Kantian prohibition yet (*Ideas* I, 100).[12] But when, maintaining that external perception is doubtful in principle, he also claims that "*the immanent being is . . . undoubtedly, an absolute being, as far as nulla 're' indiget ad existendum*," he encounters the danger of relapsing, not only into the Paralogism of ideality, but also, to a certain extent, into that of substantiality (*Ideas* I, 110).[13] It is well known that the Latin expression chosen by the phenomenologist for characterizing the immanent being (i.e., consciousness) is the one used by Descartes in the first part of the *Principles of Philosophy* (article 51) to define substance; Descartes even explains that, strictly speaking, this definition is only verified by God. Of course, in his *Ideas* I, Husserl has no intention to reactivate a metaphysics of substance; but still, in accordance with the orientation of his transcendental idealism, he indisputably emphasizes the absoluteness and the radical independence of the immanent being.

The gap between Kant's and Husserl's idealism becomes even more visible if we pay attention to the terms in which the Paralogism of the substantiality of the soul is refuted by the first edition of the *Critique*: "in that which we call the soul, everything is in continual flux, and it has nothing abiding, except perhaps (if one insists) the I. . . . Yet this I is no more an intuition than it is a concept of any object; rather, it is the mere form of consciousness" (CPR A381–82). By stressing the fact that the formal (logical or transcendental) I is nothing that could be grasped in an intuition, the confusion between the unity of thought and the object of inner sense is diluted. Consequently, "the whole of rational psychology, as a science transcending all the powers of human reason, collapses," and so does the attempt to ground self-cognition on internal intuition (CPR A382). It is, in particular, the very project of a psychology pretending to be *a priori*—that is, claiming to be something more than an empirical description of the soul—that becomes illegitimate.

The irreversible bankruptcy of rational psychology is even more virulently stated by Kant in the 1787 version of the Paralogisms: since I do not cognize myself "by being conscious of myself as thinking," therefore, "through the analysis of the consciousness of myself in thinking in general not the least is won in regard to the cognition of myself as object" (CPR B406, B409). Given that all knowledge rests on intuition, the mirage of a sheer reflexive self-cognition, obtained solely through thinking, needs to be dissipated. Furthermore, that which is given through inner sense—if there is anything given—does not have the autonomy of a proper content when isolated from the representation of external objects: that is, it grants no access (as Husserl questionably assumes) to a phenomenological sphere of the absolute distinguished from that of the world (or of outer objects) as merely relative and doubtful.

Therefore, it is somewhat ironical that Husserl accused Kant of psychologizing the transcendental while he himself was restoring the view according to which internal intuition grants access to an absolute. On the contrary, Kant's concern, in his critique of the Paralogisms and in the Refutation of Idealism, was to carefully separate the transcendental and the psychological. Furthermore, some passages of the second edition of the *Critique*, like the following, even allow speculation about how Kant would reply to Husserl's recourse to Descartes's "*nulla 're' indiget ad existendum*" to characterize egological immanence:

> Thus if that concept, by means of the term "substance," is to indicate an object that can be given, and if it is to become a cognition, then it must be grounded on a persisting intuition as the indispensable condition of the objective reality of a concept, namely, that through which alone an object is given. But now we have in inner intuition nothing at all that persists, for the I is only the consciousness of my thinking; thus if we stay merely with thinking, we also lack the necessary condition for applying the concept of substance, i.e., of a subject subsisting for itself, to itself as a thinking being. (CPR B412–13)

Kant denounces here the excessive empowerment of internal intuition and the confusion between the consciousness that I have of myself while thinking and an intuitive self-cognition.[14] For the concept of substance to apply to the data of inner sense, internal intuition would have to be an *intuitus intellectualis*, or an intuitive self-consciousness in which I am genuinely given to myself. But this case has to be rejected, for "in the consciousness of myself . . . nothing yet is thereby given to me for thinking": the purely intellectual or reflexive consciousness of my existence is irremediably void, without any specific content (CPR B429). In return, "inner empirical intuition is sensible, and makes available nothing but data of appearance" which are inconsistent and void when no outer intuition is associated with them (CPR B430).

This is how the specific relationship that Kant acknowledges between internal and external experience stands at a considerable distance from Cartesian (or Husserlian) idealism. If there is, as Husserl puts it, an "abyss of meaning (*Abgrund des Sinnes*)" (*Ideas* I, 111, translation modified)[15] between immanent self-consciousness and consciousness of exteriority, for Kant, this is the case insofar as only external experience can provide access to a stable and permanent being. In itself, interiority is evanescent and inconsistent, and for this reason, that which is interior to me always sends me back to something exterior.

In turn, if Husserl deplores Kant's empiricist conception of internal perception, he also maintains, at the same time, the Cartesian privileges and rights of inner experience. By doing so, he neglects to fully consider the Kantian critique of Descartes and of rational psychology. Of course, the founder of phenomenology has every right to regret, in the *Crisis*, that "Kant never permitted himself to enter the vast depths of the Cartesian fundamental investigation," or that he did not contribute to the renewal of psychology; but it is crucial to understand that Kant's reluctance and omission are entirely deliberate (C 99).[16] For in his view, the "self-intuition of the mind (*Selbstanschauung des Gemüts*)" (CPR B69) can never mean the self-givenness of the I as an absolute: Kant's critical endeavor implies "keeping as close as possible to the transcendental and setting aside entirely what might here be psychological, i.e., empirical" (CPR A801/B829). On the contrary, in spite of his early critique of psychologism, Husserl does not put aside the project of a phenomenological psychology and pleads for a new perennial alliance between psychology and transcendental philosophy. And while, at the very end of the *Cartesian Meditations*, the founder of phenomenology can significantly relaunch Augustine's famous invitation to explore interiority: "Do not wish to go out; go back into yourself: truth dwells in the inner man [*Noli foras ire, in te redi, in interiore hominis habitat veritas*]" (*De vera religione*, 39, 72; CM 157)[17] by following Kant, one would rather have to praise the richness and resources of exteriority, as the 1798 *Anthropology from a Pragmatic Point of View* (§24) does: "The tendency to retire into oneself, together with the resulting illusions of inner sense, can only be corrected if we are led back into the external world and so into the order of things present to the outer senses."[18] Let us now attempt to evaluate the full significance of the fact that, instead of a transcendental psychology, Kant will only elaborate (and eventually publish) a "pragmatic" anthropology.

From Psychology to Anthropology: The "Inner" and the "Outer Man"

As seen above, according to the first *Critique*, when the surreptitious identification of the unity of thought with the object of inner intuition (i.e., myself as given in time) is overcome, "the whole of rational psychology, as a science transcending all the powers of human reason, collapses" (CPR A382). The Preface to the *Metaphysical Principles of the Science of Nature*, published by Kant between the 1781 and the 1787 editions, is equally severe toward empirical psychology, stating that it "can never become anything more than an historical doctrine of nature, and, as such, a natural doctrine of inner sense which is as systematic as possible, that is, a natural description of the soul, but never a science of the soul, nor even, indeed, an experimental psychological doctrine," given that "mathematics is not applicable to the phenomena of inner sense and their laws."[19] This firm rejection of any form of scientific psychology (*a priori* or empirical), combined with the new way of understanding the relationship between internal and external experience, is reflected in Kant's alternative proposal of a pragmatic (or post-critical) anthropology[20] which brings together the "inner" and the "outer man."

But what is, then, the relation between critical philosophy and pragmatic anthropology? In the Introduction he wrote for his French translation, Foucault advanced the hypothesis of an "anthropologico-critical repetition,"[21] suggesting that the *Anthropology from a Pragmatic Point of View* is in fact, and in spite of appearances, deeply connected to the critical project. I will follow this line of interpretation by stating that the relationship between inner and outer sense that resulted from the Refutation of Idealism determines the distinction that Kant's *Anthropology* establishes between the "inner man" and the "outer man." Indeed, the point of the 1798 work consists precisely in revealing the conditioning of the "inner man" by the "outer man," and this also accounts for Kant's strong reticence toward a rehabilitation of psychology within transcendental philosophy. Shifting from psychology to anthropology means acknowledging and accepting that inner experience (or self-experience) is always conditioned by outer experience (by the experience of the world and of humans as beings-in-the-world).

In effect, far from proposing a description of interiority, the *Anthropology* places the inner man and the outer man on the same level and categorically refuses any privilege to internal self-experience. Furthermore, on more than one occasion, Kant expresses his reticence toward the presumed richness of introspection or superiority of inner experience: such is the case, for instance, with §4, in which he deals with self-observation (*Selbstbeobachtung*) and confesses that "the real purpose of this section concerns the warning mentioned above, namely not to concern oneself in the least with spying and, as it were, the affected composition of an inner history of the involuntary course of one's thoughts and feelings." And a bit further on, he explains as follows: "For the situation with these inner experiences is not as it is with external experiences or objects in space, where the objects appear next to each other and *permanently* fixed. Inner sense sees the relations or its determinations only in time, hence in flux, where the stability of observation necessary for experience does not occur."[22] It is the very argument of the Refutation of Idealism that Kant recalls here: inner experience cannot provide us with the representation of permanence, and therefore is profoundly dependent upon outer experience.

But then why does the 1798 *Anthropology* inaugurates the approach of the human with the description of the "I"—as according to §1, the dignity of the human being is rooted in the fact of having "the I in its representation"? Let us not forget that this egological starting point is immediately amended by considering the potential deviations implied within this very capacity of saying "I," namely, the different forms of egoism exposed in §2 (logical, aesthetic, and moral). And even if, according to the "Remark" of §7,[23] the egological problematic as such "does not really belong to anthropology," questioning the status and the value of the "I" is an efficient means for delimiting the domain of anthropology with respect to both psychology and that which, within transcendental philosophy, pertains to logic. Thus, while recalling the fundamental division of apperception into pure and empirical (in order similarly to divide self-consciousness into intuiting and reflecting consciousness), Kant draws a clear line of demarcation: "In psychology we investigate ourselves according to our ideas of inner sense; in logic, according to what intellectual consciousness suggests."[24] The error and the intrinsic insufficiency of psychology arise from its failure to maintain a distinction between pure apperception and inner sense. If Kant insists upon the necessity of separating them with such vehemence, he does so in order to delimit transcendental philosophy (and transcendental logic, in particular) from the psychological approach (that Husserl will later denounce under the name of psychologism) that fails to distinguish inner sense as "psychological (applied) consciousness" from "pure, logical consciousness."[25]

Nevertheless, this demarcation will not suffice to dissipate the difficulties of self-knowledge. As an important passage of Kant's *Anthropology* (§7) puts it, knowledge of the human being through inner experience, because to a large extent one also judges others according to it, is more important than correct judgment of others, but nevertheless at the same time perhaps more difficult. For he who investigates his interior easily *carries* many things into self-consciousness instead of merely observing.[26]

In other words, even when restrained in its pretensions and carefully distinguished from pure apperception, inner sense remains unable to fulfill the promise of self-knowledge. This is the ultimate reason why the consideration of the "inner man" has to be complemented by that of the "outer man," in order to refrain from the propensity "to accept the play of ideas of inner sense as experiential cognition, although it is only a fiction."[27] Nonetheless, Kant's pragmatic anthropology will not discredit that which is given through inner experience, but will approach it with a new attitude: while from the point of view of (rational) psychology, "the mind, which is represented as a mere faculty of feeling and thinking, is regarded as a special substance dwelling in the human being," the anthropological approach "abstract[s] from the question of whether the human being has a soul or not (as a special incorporeal substance)."[28] The *Gemüt*, or human mind, that the *Anthropology* deals with, just like the *Gemüt* of transcendental philosophy, does not belong to the domain of psychology, whether rational or empirical, for it is neither identical to the soul nor confined in interiority. This accounts for Kant's intention, expressed within the first *Critique*, to transform empirical psychology into a "complete anthropology," insofar as the anthropological approach refuses to objectify the data of internal experience and remains equally distant from the metaphysical, rational psychology, and empirical psychology (CPR A849/B877).

Husserl and the Hesitating Project of a Transcendental Anthropology

Was Husserl more willing to approve Kant's turn to anthropology than he was to follow him in his condemnation of psychology? As recalled above, the phenomenologist considered that the author of the *Critiques* not only failed to reform psychology in accordance with transcendental philosophy, but also maintained a significant residue of former, pre-critical psychology within transcendental philosophy itself, by submitting it to the anthropological restriction expressed by the clause "for us humans." Indeed, this clause unavoidably weakens the status of the *a priori* (of the universal, non-empirical features of our knowledge and experience), by entailing what

Husserl denounces as its illegitimate anthropologization. For the author of the *Logical Investigations*, such an anthropologization is unfounded and misleading, insofar as the true *a priori* does not pertain to the form that the cognizing subject prescribes to the object, but is grounded in the essential features of the object itself. Thus, the *a priori* is valid for any kind of subjectivity, be it human or not, finite or not: this is the meaning of the clause "also for God" (*Ideas* I, 362)[29] that Husserl substitutes for the Kantian clause "for finite rational beings like us" or "for us humans." It is only on this condition that the *a priori* can be regarded as truly necessary, in the sense of a necessity that does not depend upon any facticity. Accordingly, Husserl firmly rejects the hypothesis of an intellect with logical laws other than our own, for such a hypothesis would inevitably lead to assigning a mere anthropological validity to the form of our knowledge. In a 1908 research manuscript that bears the title "Against Kant's Anthropological Theory" (where the target, though, is not the pragmatic anthropology subsequently developed by the author of the *Critiques*, but the anthropological restriction that weighs upon his transcendental philosophy), Husserl denounces the fact that Kant "confounds the necessity and generality of the human fact with the necessity and generality pertaining to the content of the evidence and which is the opposite of any fact;" more precisely, "he confounds the general constraint derived from the human specificity (from a fact) . . . with the necessity apprehended in the evidence of 'it cannot be otherwise.'"[30] In short, Husserl holds the critical enterprise responsible for a genuine "shift to relativism and anthropologism (*Wendung zum Relativismus und Anthropologismus*)."[31]

Furthermore, Husserl deplores the ambiguous status of the Kantian faculties, which he considers to be merely psychological powers whose transcendental genesis remains unclear, and this constitutes in his view an irrefutable proof of Kant's affiliation with a subtle form of psychologism.[32] While limiting the necessity of that which pertains to the subjective faculties—to their structures and accomplishments—Kant presumably amalgamated, in his transcendental considerations, "the factual and the apriorical," and in doing so, he illegitimately disregarded the true nature of the "phenomenological *a priori*."[33] The ultimate reason for this confusion is promptly revealed by Husserl in plain terms: "Because he understands inner perception in this empiricist, psychological sense, . . . Kant gets involved in his mythical concept-formation" (C 115).[34] Significantly, it is the all-too-narrow scope that the author of the *Critiques* assigns to internal experience that is supposed to keep him imprisoned by the psychology of his time and condemns him to endorse its shortcomings.

One might consider, however, that when criticizing Kant's transcendental philosophy for its anthropological concessions, Husserl only rejects a certain kind of recourse to anthropology: namely, the one that dissolves the *a priori* into the empirical and, in doing so, fully naturalizes subjectivity by identifying it with the concrete human being. Yet the 1930 *Nachwort* to *Ideas* I dismissed just as firmly the "transcendental anthropologism" that leads to attribute a transcendental or *a priori* significance to the forms of human knowledge, considering it to be a harmful avatar of psychologism.[35] Such a transcendental anthropologism, which Husserl found in Kant, was held to be a fallacy even more serious than any concession to the empirical, insofar as it threatened the objective and universal grounding of knowledge in general. It is precisely here that ultimately originates, for Husserl, the necessity of a "fundamental decision between anthropologism and transcendentalism" expressed by his 1931 lecture on "Phenomenology and Anthropology."

Nevertheless, if the aim of this famous lecture is to distinguish and separate carefully the two disciplines that its title brings together, Husserl's research manuscripts from the 1930s will rather explore and elaborate what the conference already designated as their "intrinsic affinity."[36] For, as a manuscript from 1936 eloquently puts it, "transcendental philosophy is necessarily related to me and thus to a humanity, to my humanity."[37] There is indeed, in spite of what the Husserlian critique of Kant assumed, a necessity of the "human fact," understood as the irreducible facticity of any transcendental subjectivity or activity. As another 1933 research manuscript states while considering the functioning of transcendental subjective life: "It all eventually depends on my facticity (*Faktizität*)."[38] For this reason, in the end, Husserl no longer hesitates to admit a certainty or even a primacy of the anthropological fact with respect to the transcendental ego, in the sense that the latter is grounded in the former, while Kant never developed such a plain connection between transcendental subjectivity and the human being.

The project of a genuinely phenomenological anthropology will progressively emerge for Husserl insofar as, in spite of any previous reluctance, the task remains to "understand, on ultimate transcendental grounds, why . . . anthropology . . . is in fact not just a positive science along with the natural sciences, but rather has an intrinsic affinity with philosophy, with transcendental philosophy."[39] Therefore, in contrast to transcendental anthropologism, which is the plain negation of the epistemological ambitions of phenomenology, not only a transcendental psychology, but also a phenomenological anthropology can and must be envisioned. Such a legitimate phenomenological anthropology could even deserve to be called "transcendental" insofar as it would aim to mutually reshape the transcendental and the anthropological dimension of subjectivity. And by doing this, it would also importantly provide us with an anthropological continuation of transcendental phenomenology, just as the 1798 *Anthropology* did for Kant's *Critique*.

Nonetheless, if it is not unwarranted to attribute to Husserl the project of a phenomenological anthropology, does this give us the right to speak of a "transcendental anthropology?"[40] This expression, already a unique occurrence in the Kantian context,[41] designates, in Husserl, a group of research manuscripts (E III),[42] but is not easy to find as such in his writings themselves.[43] To give it both consistency and legitimacy, one must think anew the connection between the anthropological and the transcendental dimension of subjective and intersubjective life.[44] But then, a sharp paradox might rapidly emerge, like in this 1933 research manuscript where Husserl states that the phenomenological "I" is "the same as an I and as a human person," and "yet I am not the same" insofar as "the egological human life within the world is . . . my transcendental configuration."[45] But this does not automatically mean that the anthropological dimension of subjectivity is an epiphenomenon of transcendental life: on the contrary, transcendental meaning-giving activity is always rooted in human life, even if it transfigures it in return.

Increasingly emphasizing this point, Husserl's late research shows that transcendental phenomenology can neither ignore nor exclude that which pertains to the anthropological concreteness of the I as a human being. Eventually, "the human I and the transcendental I must coincide (*sich decken*),"[46] and thus, a renewed, phenomenological gaze upon both subjectivity and humanity can be obtained. Several texts from the 1930s, including the *Crisis* (§54) itself, describe the relationship between transcendental subjectivity and the human person as a necessary "self-objectification" (*Selbstobjektivation* or *Selbstobjektivierung*): "each human being 'bears within himself a transcendental I' . . . insofar as he is the self-objectification, as exhibited through phenomenological self-reflection, of the corresponding transcendental 'I'" (C 186).[47] There is, so to speak, an identity without coincidence between the transcendental and the anthropological dimensions of subjectivity, and this is valid not only at an individual level, but also at the intersubjective level of community. Following this train of thought, as Husserl points out, the history of humanity "becomes the history of the total transcendental subjectivity"; what is more, "the articulation (*Gliederung*) of humanity in families, lineages, nations . . . becomes the articulation of transcendental subjectivity."[48] And given that human history comprises "the growth of the born ones . . ., the disappearing of the dying ones"—in short, the "generative cohesion (*generative Zusammenhang*)" of humanity in its specific historicity, this generative dimension itself "has a transcendental meaning."[49] This invitation to pursue and elaborate such a transcendental understanding of the anthropological structures of our lives is perhaps one of the most challenging research horizons opened by the late Husserl.

Thus, not only Husserl's phenomenology has not submitted itself to an "anthropological prohibition," as Blumenberg famously suspected, but it can also hardly be accused of an "anthropological indifference."[50] Rather, Husserl's steadfast intention is to reconquer the anthropological ground of subjective and intersubjective life without abandoning the transcendental phenomenological perspective. By doing so, he brings together transcendental philosophy and anthropology in a much more direct and perhaps even much more radical manner than Kant did.

Conclusion

At the end of this inquiry, the gap between Kant's and Husserl's idealism can be depicted in several ways. It has been shown, firstly, that the specific relationship that Kant acknowledges between internal and external experiences considerably separates him from any Cartesian-style idealism, like that of Husserl. For in accordance with the orientation of his transcendental phenomenology, the 1913 Husserl emphasizes the absoluteness and the radical independence of the subjective immanent being. An *a priori* or even transcendental psychology is then possible and legitimate, in spite of Kant's thorough effort to condemn any attempt to elaborate a scientific psychology, be it pure or empirical. Maintaining this reticence toward the psychological approach of the human, Kant's *Anthropology* insists on the conditioning of the "inner man" (and of inner experience) by the "outer man" (by the experience of the world and of humans as beings-in-the-world). Likewise, Husserl's late thought will progressively admit the necessity of an anthropological continuation of transcendental philosophy, with the ambitious purpose of revealing the transcendental hidden meaning of all the manifestations of human life.

Notes

1. This Kantian language has in English gendered implications of which the German term (*inner Mensch*) is fortunately deprived. Therefore, "man" should not be understood here as opposed to "woman," but as a general denomination for the human being, male and female.

2. See also Edmund Husserl, "Die Krisis der europäischen Wissenschaften und die transzendentale Phänomenologie. Eine Einleitung in die phänomenologische Philosophie," in *Edmund Husserl Gesammelte Werke: Husserliana*, vol. VI, ed. Walter Biemel (The Hague: Martinus Nijhoff, 1954), 205. Hereafter: Hua VI.
3. Ibid., 207.
4. Ibid., 209, translation modified.
5. Edmund Husserl, "Phänomenologische Psychologie. Vorlesungen Sommersemester 1925," in *Edmund Husserl Gesammelte Werke: Husserliana*, vol. IX, ed. Walter Biemel (The Hague: Martinus Nijhoff, 1962), 39; *Phenomenological Psychology*, trans. John Scanlon (The Hague: Martinus Nijhoff, 1977), 28.
6. Hans Blumenberg, *Beschreibung des Menschen* (Frankfurt am Main: Suhrkamp Verlag, 2006), 162. It is well known that the heritage of Brentano played an important role both in Husserl's lack of sympathy for Kant and in his generous vision of internal experience.
7. A more developed version of this analysis is to be found in my paper "Internal and External Experience. From Husserl to Kant," *Meta: Research in Hermeneutics, Phenomenology, and Practical Philosophy* 8, no. 2 (2016): 396–18.
8. See CPR Bxxxix. Paul Guyer and Allen W. Wood are manifestly sensitive to this declaration when they write, in the Introduction to their translation: "The argument that while time is the form of all sense, the representation of space is itself the necessary condition for the representation of determinate order in time, which continues Kant's rebuttal of the charge of Berkeleian idealism, is the chief theme of all of the revisions in the Analytic of Principles" (CPR 71).
9. This emphasis on the fact that the Refutation of Idealism intends to prove something else than the mere existence of an undoubted representation of exteriority is already present in the 1783 Prolegomena, §49 (Pro, AK. IV, 336/trans. 88).
10. See CPR B291.
11. Edmund Husserl, "Ideen zu einer reinen Phänomenologie und phänomenologischen Philosophie," First Book: Allgemeine Einführung in die Phänomenologie, in *Edmund Husserl Gesammelte Werke: Husserliana*, vol. III/1, ed. Karl Schuhmann (The Hague: Martinus Nijhoff, 1976), 51. Hereafter: Hua III/1.
12. Ibid., 96.
13. Ibid., 104.
14. See also CPR B421–22: "The unity of consciousness, which lies at the ground of the categories, is taken here for an intuition of the subject as an object, and the category of substance is then applied to it. But this unity is nothing but a unity of thought, through which no object is given, and consequently, to which the category of substance, which always implies that an intuition is given, cannot be applied."
15. Hua III/1, 105.
16. Hua VI, 102.

17. Edmund Husserl, "Cartesianische Meditationen und Pariser Vorträge," *Gesammelte Werke: Husserliana*, vol. I, ed. Stephan Strasser (The Hague: Martinus Nijhoff, 1950), 51.

18. Immanuel Kant, "Der Streit der Fakultäten; Anthropologie in pragmatischer Hinsicht," in *Kants Gesammelte Schriften*, vol. VII, ed. the Royal Prussian Academy of Sciences (Berlin: G. Reimer, 1907, hereafter: AK. VII), 162; Immanuel Kant, *Anthropology from a Pragmatic Point of View*, trans. Robert Louden (Cambridge: Cambridge University Press, 2006), 164, translation modified. See also the English translation by Mary J. Gregor: Immanuel Kant, *Anthropology from a Pragmatic Point of View* (The Hague: Martinus Nijhoff, 1974), 40.

19. Immanuel Kant, *Metaphysical Foundations of Natural Science*, trans. Michael Friedman (Cambridge: Cambridge University Press, 2004), 7 (AK. IV, 471).

20. The sharp separation between pragmatic anthropology and psychology is also stressed by Kant in a Reflection from the 1780s: "Pragmatic anthropology should not be psychology" ("Reflection on Anthropology" no. 1502a, in Immanuel Kant, *Anthropologie*, in *Kants Gesammelte Schriften*, vol. XV, ed. the Royal Prussian Academy of Sciences, (Berlin: G. Reimer, 1913), 801. Hereafter: AK. XV. On this point, see Holly L. Wilson, *Kant's Pragmatic Anthropology: Its Origin, Meaning, and Critical Significance* (Albany, NY: State University of New York Press, 2006), 20–3; Robert Louden, *Kant's Impure Ethics: From Rational Beings to Human Beings* (Oxford: Oxford University Press, 2000), 63–6.

21. Michel Foucault, "Introduction à l'*Anthropologie*," in Immanuel Kant, *Anthropologie du point de vue pragmatique* (Paris: Vrin, 2008), 52; Michel Foucault, *Introduction to Kant's* Anthropology, trans. Robert Nigro and Kate Briggs (Los Angeles, CA: Semiotext(e), 2008), 83.

22. AK. VII, 133 and 134; *Anthropology from a Pragmatic Point of View*, 22 and 22–3.

23. AK. VII, 142; *Anthropology from a Pragmatic Point of View*, 33.

24. AK. VII, 134; *Anthropology from a Pragmatic Point of View*, 23.

25. AK. VII, 142; *Anthropology from a Pragmatic Point of View*, 33.

26. AK. VII, 143; *Anthropology from a Pragmatic Point of View*, 34.

27. AK. VII, 161; *Anthropology from a Pragmatic Point of View*, 54.

28. AK. VII, 161; *Anthropology from a Pragmatic Point of View*, 53.

29. Hua III/1, 350–51.

30. Edmund Husserl, "Erste Philosophie (1923–1924), Part I: Kritische Ideengeschichte," in *Edmund Husserl Gesammelte Werke: Husserliana*, vol. VII, ed. Rudolf Boehm (The Hague: Martinus Nijhoff, 1956), 358–59. Hereafter: Hua VII.

31. Ibid., 354.

32. According to the *Crisis of European Sciences*, the "faculties," "functions," or transcendental-subjective "formations" of the *Critique* are only "mythical constructions" that reveal the "obscurities of the Kantian philosophy" (C 114; Hua VI, 116).

33. Hua VII, 390.
34. Hua VI, 117.
35. Edmund Husserl, "Ideen zu einer reinen Phänomenologie und phänomenologischen Philosophie, Third Book: Die Phänomenologie und die Fundamente der Wissenschaften," in *Edmund Husserl Gesammelte Werke: Husserliana*, vol. V, ed. Marly Biemel (The Hague: Martinus Nijhoff, 1952), 39.
36. Edmund Husserl, "Phänomenologie und Anthropologie," in *Aufsätze und Vorträge (1922–1937)*, in *Edmund Husserl Gesammelte Werke: Husserliana*, vol. XXVII, ed. Thomas Nenon and Hans Rainer Sepp (Dordrecht: Kluwer Academic Publishers, 1989), 181 [hereafter: Hua XXVII]; Edmund Husserl, "Phenomenology and Anthropology", in *Psychological and Transcendental Phenomenology and Confrontation with Heidegger (1927–1931)*, trans. Thomas Sheehan and Richard E. Palmer (Dordrecht: Kluwer Academic Publishers, 1997), 500.
37. Edmund Husserl, "Die Krisis der europäischen Wissenschaften und die transzendentale Phänomenologie. Ergänzungsband: Texte aus dem Nachlass (1934–1937)," in *Edmund Husserl Gesammelte Werke: Husserliana*, vol. XXIX, ed. Reinhold N. Smid (Dordrecht: Kluwer Academic Publishers, 1993), 332. This quote comes from a research manuscript whose title is "The Anthropological World."
38. Edmund Husserl, "Zur Phänomenologie der Intersubjektivität. Texte aus dem Nachlass. Dritter Teil: 1929–1935," in *Edmund Husserl Gesammelte Werke: Husserliana*, vol. XV, ed. Iso Kern (The Hague: Martinus Nijhoff, 1973), 518–19. Hereafter: Hua XV.
39. Hua XXVII, 181; "Phenomenology and Anthropology," 500. In this quote, it is first and foremost the proximity between psychology and transcendental philosophy that Husserl intends to emphasize. Nevertheless, the contemporary research manuscripts display a specific interest in the idea of a phenomenological anthropology: see, for instance, Hua XV, texts nos. 29 and 30.
40. A longer treatment of this issue is to be found in my "Kant, Husserl, and the Aim of a Transcendental Anthropology," in *Husserl, Kant, and Transcendental Phenomenology*, ed. Iulian Apostolescu and Claudia Serban (Berlin: Walter de Gruyter, 2020), 101–24.
41. In the famous "Reflection on Anthropology" no. 903, stemming from 1776 to 78 (AK. XV, 394–95). Among the attempts to make sense of this unique mention of an *anthropologia transcendentalis*, see Claudia M. Schmidt, "Kant's Transcendental, Empirical, Pragmatic, and Moral Anthropology," *Kant-Studien* 98, no. 2 (2007): 156–82.
42. Cf. Edmund Husserl, "Grenzprobleme der Phänomenologie: Analysen des Unbewusstseins und der Instinkte, Metaphysik, späte Ethik: Texte aus dem Nachlass (1908–1937)," in *Edmund Husserl Gesammelte Werke: Husserliana*, vol. XLII, ed. Rochus Sowa and Thomas Vongehr (Dordrecht: Springer, 2014), 531.
43. Whereas a 1929 text belonging to the C-Manuscripts refers plainly to a "transcendental sociology" and defines it with reference to "the community of human

beings and its world" (Edmund Husserl, "Späte Texte über Zeitkonstitution (1929–1934)," in *Die C-Manuskripte. Husserliana Materialien*, vol. VIII, ed. Dieter Lohmar [Dordrecht: Springer, 2006], 165). Nonetheless, in other texts from 1930, Husserl speaks of a "transcendental person" and even of a "transcendental humanity (*transzendentales Menschentum*)" (Edmund Husserl, "Zur phänomenologischen Reduktion. Texte aus dem Nachlass (1926–1935)," in Edmund *Husserl Gesammelte Werke: Husserliana*, vol. XXXIV, ed. Sebastian Luft [Dordrecht: Kluwer Academic Publishers, 2002], 153 and 201).

44. See, for instance, the recent attempt of Bence Péter Marosán, "Transzendentale Anthropologie. Sinnbildung, Persönliches Ich und Selbstidentität bei Edmund Husserl und ihre Rezeption in László Tengelyis Phänomenologischer Metaphysik," *Horizon: Studies in Phenomenology* 5, no. 1 (2016): 150–70.

45. Hua XV, 540–41.

46. Ibid., 542.

47. Hua VI, 190. See also Hua XV, 388; Hua XV, 549–50.

48. Hua XV, 391. This quote and the following come from a 1931 research manuscript.

49. Ibid.

50. Hans Blumenberg, *Beschreibung des Menschen*, 814.

4

Fichte and Husserl: Rigorous Science and the Renewal of Humankind

Federico Ferraguto

Starting from a reconstruction of Husserl's reception of Fichtean philosophy and from a reconstruction of the reception of Fichte's philosophy in Husserl's lectures on "Fichte's Ideal of Humanity," the chapter aims to describe the themes that characterize a possible phenomenological interpretation of Fichte's doctrine of science (*Wissenschaftslehre*), such as the role of the I in the constitution of knowing and the significance of tendency as drive and striving (*Trieb, Streben*) in both Fichte's practical foundation of transcendental philosophy and Husserl's transition from a static to a genetic phenomenology. In particular this chapter intends to discuss the relationship between renewal and the construction of a philosophy as rigorous science. Both in Fichte and in Husserl these two elements are not separated but define a reciprocal relationship implicit in the very concept of phenomenology elaborated by the two authors.

The reciprocal assimilation of the Husserlian transcendental phenomenological project and that of Fichte has been made possible by two fundamental assumptions: (1) the fact that the context of German neo-Kantianism is characterized by a massive reception of Fichte's thought[1]; and (2) the fact that from the textual point of view there is an explicit confrontation of Husserl with Fichte that, after an initial skepticism, scholars have effectively affirmed.

F. Ferraguto (✉)
Pontifícia Universidade Católica Do Paraná—PUCPR, Curitiba, Brazil

C. D. Coe (eds.), *The Palgrave Handbook of German Idealism and Phenomenology*,
Palgrave Handbooks in German Idealism,
https://doi.org/10.1007/978-3-030-66857-0_4

This comparison made it possible to understand Fichte's doctrine of science no longer as the object of a historical study, but as a philosophical model that originally developed the subject-subject correlation, both in a theoretical sense and in a practical dimension.[2] From another point of view, the interpretation of the Husserlian phenomenology starting from a possible comparison with the doctrine of science of Fichte has allowed to transcendental phenomenology to be located in the great tradition of classical German philosophy and to understand it as a fundamental moment for the construction of a "critique of reason"[3] aimed at clarifying the relationship between science, the theory of objectivity, and "theory of theory in general" thanks to a shift of the plane of philosophical inquiry from the mere object to the construction of science itself, understood "as function, as a knowing activity of the subject."[4] This represents, both in Husserl and in Fichte, the first step in reconfiguring philosophy as a rigorous science in a theory of the renewal of humankind. But on what basis is this reconfiguration possible? Starting from Husserl's lectures on Fichte by 1917–1918, in this chapter I would like to highlight how in Husserl and Fichte this restructuring is based on a deepening of the "per-formative" dimension of consciousness.

Acting to Act

The most significant and systematic treatment that Husserl gives of Fichtean thought consists in the three lectures, presented between 8 and 17 November 1917 and repeated in 1918, entitled *Fichtes Menscheitsideal* ("Fichte's Ideal of Humanity"). The lectures on Fichte's ideal of humanity are above all an important document of the political and cultural ferment that had developed in Germany at the time of the "Great War." But beyond this, in these lectures Husserl provides a considerable number of ideas to determine the meaning of some aspects of the Fichtean vision in the theoretical maturation of the phenomenological-transcendental enterprise, as much with respect to its theoretical approaches, as for its political and ethical implications. Indeed, beyond a consolidated view that considers Husserl's interpretation as motivated by ideology and political convictions,[5] certainly attributable to a debate that involved, among others, Treitschke, Meinecke, Windelband, and Rickert,[6] it is possible to see in these Husserlian lectures important elements both to measure the role of reflection on Fichte with respect to the theoretical developments of phenomenology, and to configure remarkable interpretative perspectives for research on Fichte's philosophy. Significant in this perspective are two important steps that Husserl makes in these lectures: the connection of the notions of drive (*Trieb*) and fact/act (*Tathandlung*, Lecture 1) and the problem of renewal (Lecture 3).

Beyond the emphasis Husserl places on Fichte's vision for the regeneration of Germany after the humiliation suffered in Jena, Lecture 1 of "Fichte's Ideal of Humanity" clarifies Fichte's rethinking of Kantian criticism. Like Kant, Fichte would, according to Husserl, pose the question "of the existence or mode of existence of space-time reality, of the world in the natural sense of the word."[7] But unlike Kant, Fichte would be more inclined to exhaust the question in the immanent sphere of consciousness understood as a space free of dogmatic elements such as sensations, sense data, or hyletic materials.[8] The peculiar position of Fichte is then explained by Husserl through an original interpretation of the fact/act (*Tathandlung*) that defines the first principle of the doctrine of science as an *acting to act* (*Handeln zu Handeln*).[9] It is precisely in a reconfiguration of the *to* (*zu*) contained in this last expression that Husserl finds the fundamental meaning of the passage from Kant to Fichte. According to Husserl, the latter is in fact able to think of the "passivity" of the I not as being affected by an external object but as a pulsional self-determination of the I itself.[10] On the other hand, the clarification of the most elementary levels of conscious activity (such as affection, perception, or thetic consciousness in general) in relation to the project of a phenomenology of instincts allows Husserl to explain the whole sphere of the I's action in light of a *telos*—that is to say, in function of a rational instance or the fulfillment of a task.[11] It is not difficult to find in these few traits the germs of the general development that leads Husserl, just before the 1920s, to give a "genetic" turn to transcendental phenomenology—that is, to think the consciousness not only by reference to its activity, but starting from its unconscious tendencies and habits. This turning point consists substantially in a deepening of the semantics of *drive* (*Trieb*), that is, the set of instincts and tendencies that define the pre-discursive life of consciousness, of the notion of passive synthesis, that is, of the unconscious constitution of an object starting from the habits and tendencies of consciousness, and, more generally, of all those themes that, in the introduction to the *Analyses concerning the Passive and Active Synthesis*, Husserl specifies as belonging to the "universal genesis of consciousness."[12]

The interpretative perspective that Husserl takes on Fichte's philosophy allows him, on the other hand, to deepen the reflection on the transcendental status of the doctrine of science. Indeed, the latter presents itself as a philosophical program in which the I-world dynamic is reduced to dynamic relations of forces, impulses, and tendencies without, however, sinking into a metaphysics of bodies. In fact, Fichte's goal is not to find in the I's spontaneity a metaphysical principle capable of explaining the object opposed to the I as its product. Rather, from his earliest writings Fichte poses the problem of understanding the modalities according to which the relationship between I and object can be understood as an intentional activity of the I itself. Thus, the integration in the transcendental weaving of the doctrine of science of themes inherent in the instinctive nature of the I (*drive*, as specific psycho-physical tendency of concrete subjectivity, and *striving*, as general spontaneity of consciousness) is seen as an attempt to understand the conditions of possibility to attribute the character of the *I-hood* (*Ichlichkeit*) to the representational synthesis. The consequence of this path is the practical foundation of theoretical knowledge in light of the notion of *striving*, which is progressively deepened during the Jena phase of the doctrine of science (1794–1799) as the condition of the possibility of the concept of task (*Zweckbegriff*) in the complete realization of the transcendental research. Freeing itself from any ideological and propagandistic pre-comprehension, Husserl therefore sees one of the fundamental points, and the richest of consequences, of all of Fichte's philosophical program.

In fact, one of the most important elements of "Fichte's Ideal of Humanity" is the characterization of the practical-theoretical unity of Fichte's transcendental vision: his philosophy is a "philosophizing"—that is, not an unproblematic definition of notions, as in Kant or Reinhold, but a self-reflective practice that finds its support in an essential theoretical discourse.[13] According to Husserl, the real merit of Fichte's philosophizing consists precisely in this full unity of theoretical inquiry and practical realization,[14] where the "new philosophy shows the way, the only way, to liberation in rising to the authentic ideal of humanity represented by true morality."[15] It is difficult to distinguish, in these words, how much Husserl is describing the outcomes of the doctrine of science and how much instead he is trying to inscribe the phenomenological-transcendental enterprise in a tradition previously opened by Fichte. Leaving aside the declared profession of patriotism that Husserl incarnates in "Fichte's Ideal of Humanity," it is possible to trace, also at this level, a certain continuity between the Husserlian statements about Fichte and the theoretical outcomes of transcendental phenomenology.

Renewal and Life of Method

The link established between the problems connected to a phenomenology of instincts, the questions inherent to the teleology of reason, and the definition of an absolute science capable of establishing right at the top of its theoretical rigor an ethical renewal of Europe, which Husserl sketches in the lectures on

Fichte, represent the basis of the development of one of the main themes of the articles published by Husserl in the Japanese magazine *Kaizo* between 1923 and 1924. In a letter to W. Hocking of July 1920, Husserl writes about the need for a "universal clarification" and a "transformation of the whole humanity" of which the "war has revealed the inexpressible misery not only moral and religious, but also philosophical."[16] The renewal, writes Husserl to W. Bell a month later, needs an "art, supported by supreme and clearly established ethical ideals" which is also capable of "a universal education of humanity."[17]

These statements seem far from the appeal that Husserl addressed to his students during the lectures on Fichte in 1917, to see in the war "the great and severe destiny … of our German nation" and the "occasion of an era of renewal of the whole Europe."[18] On the other hand, however, the common element in the lectures on Fichte, in the contents of the letters cited, and in the articles of 1923–1924, consists in finding, as Husserl already does in 1917, that "the pure theoretical questioning can and must be decisive for life."[19] Indeed, precisely in the articles on renewal, Husserl describes the problem of renewal (*Erneuerung*) as a possibility to see in the senselessness of European culture the "fact" that must determine "our practical conduct."[20]

However, "seeing the nonsense" does not mean for Husserl devoting himself to an annihilation of the entire cultural tradition of Europe. Rather, it is a matter of giving meaning to the latter, taking on and re-actualizing the most authentic tasks it poses. To give substance to this need implies becoming aware of the incompleteness of European culture—that is to say, translating this awareness into a "rationally evident" thought, which offers a justification of itself, of its purpose and "of the method to achieve it."[21] This means giving a complete definition of the idea of humanity and, in particular, formulating a definition that does not constitute the product of a science of mere facts, but of a science that inscribes this definition in the context of the questions that concern practical reason, that is, "in a generality that transcends all empirical faculties and all contingent concepts."[22] The science to which Husserl refers must therefore "establish a rationality of action" and lead the actual practice of the individual in light of the definition of the ethical ideal of humanity. The formation of such a science, as the first response to the call for renewal, and as a fundamentally ethical issue, constitutes first of all a preliminary work. Nevertheless, it also represents a beginning of renewal because it conceives the idea of it as belonging in a constitutive way to the essence of the human being.[23] In particular, the science demanded by Husserl shows how renewal cannot be founded otherwise than "on an original will … which must always be reactivated again."[24]

The ethical life therefore coincides with a perpetual renewal as an incessant becoming toward the infinite teleological idea. But this life must also be aware; that is, it must be dominated by a constant self-discipline, by constant vigilance over oneself, or by an infinite education. In a word, this ethical life must be a methodological life (*Leben der Methode*). With this expression Husserl indicates an individual living subjected to a "criticism of principle, as well as to an ultimate reflection on the ultimate principles, including those that make criticism possible": a life in which the subject can justify the reason for his allegedly rational life.[25]

The exercise of thought to which the idea of renewal appeals therefore consists in a redefinition of the concept of humanity. However, the essential definition of the human being must also be a deduction—that is, an exposition of conditions for the definition of the human being and a description of the conditions of possibility of the act of formulation of the definition, and of its claim to "universality." To better understand this passage it is necessary to refer to the theoretical results achieved by Husserl in the years we are examining. The definition of the ideas of renewal and life of method proceeds together with a redefinition of the phenomenological research, which coincides with a substantial re-evaluation of the post-Kantian outcomes of transcendentalism. I am referring not only to the famous letter to Rickert of 1917.[26] I refer rather to specific passages of the text *Phenomenology and Theory of Knowledge*. In this text, conceived, like the lectures on Fichte, as the inaugural address in Freiburg, Husserl writes that the most significant progress of post-Kantian philosophy has consisted in overcoming the problem of transcendence, as it was configured by Kant, without, however, losing the fundamental significance of the achievements of Kantian transcendentalism.[27] In the lectures on Fichte, this rethinking of the problem of transcendence coincides precisely with the passage from Kant to Fichte.[28] It must also have as its main place a "critique of reason."[29] This critique of reason concerns thought as thinking. It is therefore an epistemology that conceives objectivity, as constituted in the realm of sciences of facts, and the sciences themselves as functions of constituent subjectivity.[30] Describing the constitution of objectivity and of the sciences, intended "as a theme of the history of culture,"[31] for Husserl, as a function of constituting subjectivity, means understanding them in light of the "ideal system of the ideal functions of consciousness in its unitary connection."[32] More precisely, this means to bring the facts back to possibilities of consciousness that can be thematized through the "freedom of pure fantasy."[33] The work of the pure fantasy, which identifies the specificity of the procedures of transcendental phenomenology as a search for essence, constitutes, in fact, the authentic way to attribute reality to data by virtue of an idea.[34]

Related to the conceptual constitution of facts, the pure fantasy shows the possibility of a negation of the relativity of the perceptive data in order to understand the universality of the real. Compared to the single perceptual moment, on the other hand, the work of the imagination allows us to show the sphere of possibilities of which the single perception represents a specific implementation, contextualizes the real, and contributes to accounting for the complexity of the experience. The work of the imagination, therefore, inscribes the sedimentation of the activity of consciousness in actual positions, both in the context of a reference to a *plus ultra*, understood as the horizon of the infinite possibilities that represents the background for the realization of perception, and in the horizon of a *non plus ultra*, because it constrains the free fiction to specific possibilities motivated by the contact of the consciousness with the factual data. The attribution of reality to things flows, in the development of phenomenological research, not so much into a *stricto sensu* deduction of the individual datum, but into the production of a rule, of patterns of understanding the correlation of consciousness with the data, which are not definitively fixed but which, in part, are updated from time to time and, in part, refer to a reconfiguration that consciousness itself must perform on itself.[35] The freedom of the pure fantasy, in fact, is not indifferent arbitrariness, but it is a freedom whose field is progressively restricted every time to a certain possibility is actualized rather than another.[36] The choice for the possibilities of consciousness is not made by a totally free supreme subject, but by a constituent activity that defines, in the course of experience, a "passage to the act"—that is, as a passage to the implementation of possibilities that are legitimized based on the course of the experience itself.[37]

In the terms that the Husserlian phenomenology develops close to the 1920s, the question of the "passage to the act" is specified in relation to the problem of the connection between the instinctive life of the I and its reflexive operations.[38] In the context of the development of the *Analyses concerning Passive and Active Synthesis* this connection can be seen as the double movement of the awakening of intentional consciousness in relation to the concrete materiality of life and of the concretization of life that is aroused in the sense of theoretical-practical stances of the I. The analysis of this point focuses the investigation on the connection between internal teleology, which identifies the horizon of the spontaneity of the subject, and external teleology, which concerns the connection of the subject to the community in which it lives.

The analysis of the awakening (*Erweckung*) occupies in this complex a fundamental position, since it reveals the "context" in which the modalities of the
constitution of a reflexive consciousness of the I in relation to the world
mature. In fact, reflexive activity is exercised in a context that Husserl calls
"tendentious" which, however, can be understood recursively, that is, related
to the reflective gaze. The possibility of reawakening therefore finds its original source in the enhancement of reflexivity through its affective encounter
with the world, understood as causality of motivation. The explication of
the relationship between internal and external teleology, as an explanation
of the motivational structure of the single subject, is therefore not reflected
in a search for motivations outside the subject but in a conscious investigation of "the whole range of typicality of the singular operations and of
its intersubjective forms"[39] "which has as its instrument, but also as a goal,
the self-consciousness (*Selbstbesinnung*), the apodictic knowledge of itself and
therefore of the world."[40] The reconstruction of these theoretical passages
allows, in my opinion, for a better understanding of the meaning of the
notions of renewal and the life of method in the Husserlian thought.

The redefinition of the ethics that must lead to the renewal of Europe is,
in fact, superimposed on the redefinition of philosophical discourse in terms
of self-consciousness (*Selbstbesinnung*). This redefinition coincides, precisely,
with a reference to what is the authentic *ethos*, i.e., the fundamental disposition, of philosophical discourse itself: the method. However, the method
does not represent only a preliminary exercise for the implementation of a
specific mode of philosophical understanding. Rather, it exhibits the nature
of thinking as consciousness of its integral historicity.[41] Through the reference to the passive constitution of the reflexive activity, in fact, Husserl can
thematize the whole sphere of expectations and implicit motivations in every
determined understanding of the world affirmed in the course of history
and, therefore, make explicit the overall sense of the cultural heritage of the
Europe. In this way Husserl also manages to highlight the reasons for the
"failure" and "misery" of those conceptions and of the cultural tradition that
identify European humanity.[42] The presentation of the problem of renewal
implies, in fact, the need for phenomenological self-consciousness to also
be translated into a historical consciousness (*historische Besinnung*) capable
of determining the teleological idea that allows us to understand the whole
history of philosophy as a liberation movement: the historical world discloses
in the awareness of the ethical idea, of which the request for renewal is a
concrete expression. Conversely, however, the investigation of the origin of
meaning requires tracing back the paths of the transcendental constitution,
up to the final layers of passivity and of the living present, which permits

that apodictic critique of transcendental experience capable of justifying its founding claim. In this way the phenomenological enterprise, in addition to explaining the cultural origins of Europe, implements and justifies itself as a critical and radical methodological disposition. In doing this, it performs its self-reflexive process, clarifies itself in its factual conditions of possibility, and justifies its historical function as an individual reactivation of the awareness and will implicit in the idea of renewal:

> Knowledge, which becomes conscious in individual cases, of the possibility of obvious justifications, as well as that of the possibility of preparing one's own action and being able to give it form so that it is not justified only a posteriori and as a matter of chance, but, as founded by rational considerations, bring with it in advance the guarantee of their own legitimacy, they create the awareness of the responsibility of reason or the ethical conscience.[43]

As a universal science, philosophy must be traced back to itself by simultaneously dealing with the question of its own legitimacy. In this inevitable circularity, philosophy can take charge of all the individual disciplines and, above all, of the "responsibility of oneself in the most radical and absolute sense."[44] This circularity exhibits the ethical side implicit in the phenomenological reduction, which makes transcendental phenomenology a critical, self-reflexive, and immanent science, but which is also presented as an "ethical conversion and formation of a universal ethical culture" and as "the birth and the beginning of a new era for humanity."[45] The philosopher, who comes to lead a methodological life, becomes so responsible for a cultural need, that is not an expression of a mere geographical determination, but is an universal and rational form. The interesting aspect of this complex theoretical movement consists in the continuous overlapping and mutual implication of the planes on which Husserl's investigation takes place. Only through the complete phenomenological self-reflection—which also includes the legitimacy of the historicity of its own existence—is it possible to define a universal ethics as a reminder of absolute responsibility, capable of instituting renewal and capable of posing the question "to a humanity essentially inherent in approaching the ideal of an ethical community of will based on free reason solely through and through an empire, a state."[46]

In this sense, phenomenological research takes shape not only as an epistemological inquiry, but primarily as a habit, that is, an individual disposition, capable of legitimizing a political dynamic. The latter, in turn, represents the preliminary historical condition through which phenomenological research can realize its own self-consciousness and design, on this basis, possible models of rational action: "man as an *animal rationale*, acts rationally: in all his actions there is the intention towards rationality, the intention to be able to respond critically to his goals and his works."[47]

On the basis of these considerations we can also understand the complex movement with which Husserl concludes his lectures on Fichte, where, mentioning the ethical-political developments of the latter's thought, he states:

> In no way does the personality of Fichte show itself more splendidly than in the way in which, in the years of Germany's most profound humiliation, he put his national idea in front of the German people in noble form and in the same way that at the same time he combined it with ideal of a true and authentic people; and also in the way in which it awakened in the people the faith in the fact that, in the event that it freely fulfills its highest destination, with this it must reach liberation even for the whole of humanity. The Fichte of the wars of liberation also speaks to us.[48]

The formulation of a new concept of humanity, to which Husserl dedicates himself and which is implicitly found also in some outcomes of the Fichtean reflection, therefore expresses the intention to make the whole of humanity participate in the instruments to conceive on the basis of it, what it defines also as the end or the "meaning" of the same thought that produced it. The historical-geographical expression from which the idea of humanity emerges can thus be rearticulated on the basis of the task configured in the free self-reflexive practice of thought. It is interesting to note at this level the way in which Husserl succeeds in capturing one of the characteristic traits of the doctrine of science in the analysis of Fichte's philosophy, namely the relationship between transcendental self-reflection and the renewal of humankind as ethical-political reform of the latter. It therefore becomes interesting to show how this device is concretely activated during the Fichtean reflection.

Fichte: Philosophy as Fact-Foundation (Tatbegründung)

The problem of an ethical-cultural reform of Europe, to be implemented through a redefinition of the latter's history, is one of the main driving forces of Fichte's thought, starting from the *Random Thoughts of a Sleepless Night* (1788). In a more mature phase of his reflection, Fichte condenses these themes first of all in the "popular" writings, in which the justification of the cultural and historical structures that define the human meets with the need for the philosopher to account "of the conditions of his factual existence inasmuch as precisely exceeding every factual existence and every empiricism."[49] However, this explanation must also be accompanied by a determination of empirical existence as that which must be presupposed for the possibility of history.[50]

This procedure also involves the problem of the concrete self-collocation of the doctrine of science in the historical development of humankind and that of the definition of the conditions of possibility for its being included in the historical-cultural framework of the era in which it appears.[51] The understanding of the doctrine of science must, in fact, bring about a transformation (*Umschaffung*), a conversion (*Umwandlung*), and finally a renewal (*Erneuerung*) of humankind as a whole.[52] In its historical-cultural dimension, moreover, the renewal promised by the *Wissenschaftslehre* must be translated into the extension (*Erweiterung*) of a "philosophical symbol," which has materialized in Christian Europe, but which must not simply be passed down passively but be "renewed," that is, constantly translated into something new.[53]

The connection of these elements takes place, for Fichte, in the systematic field between "pure science and mere experience," that is, in history (*Historie*).[54] This field is that of applied philosophy (*angewandte Philosophie*), whose most complex expression can be found in the named *Theory of State* (*Staatslehre*) of 1813. It is precisely in the position of the concrete practice of the doctrine of science, which Fichte discusses in this series of lectures, that it is possible to clarify from a systematic point of view the link that identifies the historical-political definition of the present in light of the renewal of humanity and the recursive self-understanding of the doctrine of science, which in turn makes renewal itself possible.[55]

The exposition of lectures on applied philosophy, in a general sense, aims at presenting knowledge in an image, that is, in a form that does not posit its being but only requires it. This level of exposition of the transcendental philosophy is, in the first instance, completely praxeological: the lectures on applied philosophy, held from the point of view of the doctrine of science, offer a "training for the scientific use of the intellect."[56] As we have seen when reading Husserl, however, the transcendental delimitation of the praxeological realm of the concrete subject is relevant for the self-reflexive unfolding of transcendental knowledge, insofar as it allows us to outline the historical meaning of philosophy itself and, in so doing, it allows us to clarify and apply the methods by which self-reflexive knowledge can affect life.

These problematic connections allow us to isolate at least three meanings of application (*Anwendung*) in Fichte's lectures. First, the return of philosophy to life through application coincides with the coming of philosophical consciousness to true wisdom. The latter consists in the creative production of a free act following the clarity of the transcendental vision. In fact, it is a question of knowledge that is fully exhausted in action, which dies as knowledge and lives as the creation of a living being, in the sense that it understands it as necessary for the concrete manifestation of freedom.[57] Second, "applying" philosophy means making it a guide for life, and therefore understanding it in the most traditional sense of practical philosophy.[58] Third, applied philosophy means a "representation of the external conditions, given in the world, of ethical freedom."[59] In this representation, philosophy is a fact-foundation (*Tatbegründung*): it assumes something previously given, shows how it can be deduced from the self-identification of knowledge and, on this basis, indirectly establishes effective actions. This third possible specification of the application sheds light on the relationship between the factual exposition of the applied philosophy, the factual conditions from which this exposition comes to life, and the doctrine of science as a self-reflexive and genetic exposition of the laws and the essence of knowledge. In this way, the doctrine of science unifies theory and practice, becomes capable of founding a rational action, and grounds itself as a rational action.[60] More precisely, the doctrine of science, in its application, is clarified as the "drive (*Trieb*) and determination of a life that creates the world," in relation to the "external circumstances" that allow the realization of freedom. The application must therefore make mere speculation become practical by transfiguring its explanation in the form of an "appeal to" and "showing" a practice of thought that allows an independent standpoint in the ethical-political concreteness represented by the life of the state.[61] Nevertheless, the concrete opening of the doctrine of science to the world cannot be effectively practical if it is not clarified in its character of event[62]—Fichte speaks more properly of phenomenon (*Erscheinung*),[63] that is, as a factual and non-deducible element of history, which however the doctrine of science itself legitimates starting from a concept that it deduces in its necessity: the meta-historical purpose is inscribed in the very structure of reason and gives its meaning to the whole historical process.[64]

Fichte's Phenomenology

As is the case with Husserl, the practical and praxeological dimension of Fichte's philosophizing does not represent an addition to theoretical reflection but is the correlative of a path of the self-reflection and transcendental self-legitimization of philosophy itself. In Fichte this self-legitimization passes through a phenomenology, which in this sense is not intended as a philosophy *tout court*, but as a tool for philosophy to develop and be fulfilled as a complete justification of knowledge. Knowing, in fact, does not only mean knowing theoretically an object, but inserting it in the context of a broad rationality determined both under the practical and the theoretical profile. In this sense Fichtean phenomenology meets the Kantian need related to the fact that the formation of a justified and rigorous knowledge must have a clear awareness of the separation between the principles proper to knowledge and the field of intellectual things.[65] This requirement implies a clear differentiation between appearance (*Schein*) and phenomenon (*Erscheinung, Phänomenon*), which Kant records in the *Critique of Pure Reason* as propaedeutic to metaphysics.[66] However, according to Kant, phenomenology would not only have the task of showing how the phenomenon turns into appearance due to an incorrect use of reason, but rather to establish the conditions of possibility to show how the phenomenon "becomes experience … in all philosophy."[67]

Since its first occurrence in the thirteenth lesson of the second exposition of the doctrine of science of 1804,[68] the phenomenology elaborated by Fichte reflects these requirements and differentiates them throughout the construction of the doctrine of science as specific philosophy (*Wissenschaftslehre in specie*).[69] In general, phenomenology identifies the course by which philosophy exhibits consciousness as a tool for the manifestation of a superior principle, the absolute. This display leads to a clear and rigorous differentiation between what manifests itself through consciousness and consciousness itself. The latter, in turn, can never be taken as the absolute starting point for the description of the structures of the real.[70] Phenomenology, therefore, has to show to what extent the dynamics of appearing, which Fichte identifies with the structure of consciousness, is necessary to reach truth, namely the principle that allows us to legitimize and determine our entire relationship with the world.[71] The difference between phenomenon (*Erscheinung*) and appearance (*Schein*) would be that phenomenon presupposes an accomplished foundation. The phenomenon is a manifestation of something and reveals the difference between what appears and what happens and, at the same time, hides through the appearing itself.

The appearance, on the contrary, only shows in a superficial sense the characteristic dynamics of the phenomenon. In fact, in the appearance nothing real appears. It is the simple product of a psychological illusion.[72] In this context, phenomenology has to explain consciousness as something that should be subtracted from the truth for the truth to appear in all its integrity; but at the same time as the place where this manifestation can only happen concretely. Consciousness is only its phenomenon, and as it were, the device that makes possible an effective and original manifestation of it. Precisely because of this, consciousness is only a fact and, in particular, "the source of all facticity."[73] And as it is a fact, consciousness is never pure: "Whoever finds it pure is in a psychological illusion."[74] The doctrine of science can therefore correct the first lie (*proton pseudos*) typical of philosophical systems that exchange fact and principle—that is, place consciousness as a principle rather than a phenomenon of the absolute. It is a peculiar gesture of supposed idealism, which coincides with the ordinary interpretation of the doctrine of science, which had led Jacobi to identify the doctrine of science with an absolute subjectivism and a form of nihilism. But it can also correct the realism of Reinhold and Bardili, who intended to found the reality of consciousness above something whose existence no one can doubt, namely thought. In the doctrine of science, idealism and realism represent both sides of the same thing. Idealism makes knowledge the generating principle of being, and the latter a mere projection of knowledge. Realism, on the other hand, states that knowledge is generated from being. However, Fichte also states that this generation is possible only on the horizon of knowledge and, in particular, within the sphere of thought as (*als*) thought. Idealism immediately identifies knowledge and truth. Realism identifies them only indirectly, that is, by subordinating the manifestation of being to the self-reflection of thought *als* thought. But in Fichte's opinion, neither realism nor idealism can fully account for the function of this *als* and the sense in which we have to understand it.

In fact, for Fichte phenomenology does not consist only in the description of the acts of consciousness, but in the deduction of the performances of the consciousness itself as a reflection, or phenomenon, of a wider dynamic, which for Fichte is the appearance of reason.

Phenomenology and the Theory of the I

This position could represent an indirect response to the consideration formulated by Husserl in the *Crisis of the European Sciences*, as: "I, myself, as a transcendental I constitute the world and, at the same time, as a soul, I am a human I in the world.... Can the self-positing I of which Fichte speaks be anyone other than Fichte himself?"[75] Despite the Husserlian question having a marked rhetorical content, the answer could be yes and no at the same time. Yes, insofar as Fichtean phenomenology shows that there is no possibility of philosophizing happening outside of a mediation represented by the I or concrete consciousness. No, for in the sense of Fichtean phenomenology, the fundamental mediation of consciousness is a general structure in which a principle is manifested that is not produced and/or constituted by a personal being. This conclusion can be clarified by a brief analysis of the other three occurrences of the term "phenomenology" in the 1812 *Theory of Ethics* (*Sittenlehre*).[76] In this series of lectures Fichte draws the consequences of the fundamental vision matured within the framework of the first philosophy, in the context of a special philosophical science, namely ethics. Once the factual point of ethics is determined, as "the concept (*Begriff*) is the cause of the world," Fichte goes on to clarify how the concept is defined by the unity of life and seeing. The concept is seeing, for in itself it is a figurative capacity and not simply passive reproduction.[77] The concept is an image that anticipates and re-elaborates figuring what it has to (*Soll*) be.[78] In this perspective the concept "is absolutely creative for objectivity, as the founder of the new, that which never existed before."[79] And in its anticipatory and creative character, the concept is life, the "absolute creative power (*Schöpferkraft*) of consciousness."[80] But for Fichte the identity of life and seeing is the self, which permits a transformation of the concept in a causal force.[81] This transformation is understood as an action, i.e., as moral action, that the self performs and that concretizes the virtuality of the concept. This action, seen as an individual response to a task opened by the idea that correlates with the concept itself, is unique and irreplaceable: the result of a human, empirical personality, and the index of a particular specification of the ethical idea at a self-conscious point of activity. Since it moves from the deduction of the principle of ethics to the explanation of the way in which the self can be the vehicle of the concept, the analytic path must confront the emergence of an element not analytically deducible by the principle and, therefore, reconfigure itself into reason for the emergence of radical freedom. It is at this point that phenomenology comes into play, as it seeks to find in the freedom of self the traces, or rather the visibility, of the concept.

In other words, the I appears as an analytical implication of the concept only in a first moment, but in a second moment it needs to be viewed as a fact and described as life's own manifestation of the concept. Phenomenology has a dual function here. On the one hand, it has to confirm what is exposed in the plan of deduction of the principle and to show to what extent the concept is the cause of the world. On the other hand, the analysis of the concept has to be continued until the criteria are displayed according to which it is possible to recognize how the causality of the concept is realized in the world, understood as the sphere for effective action of the self and a community of selves. Phenomenology, therefore, appears as the doctrine of the manifestation of truth (the I) in relation to the truth itself (the concept), in the same sense as the second exposition of the *Wissenschaftslehre* of 1804. The phenomenon (*Erscheinung*) has to be understood as essentially linked to the truth (or concept) of which it is the image. On the basis of this, the distinction between *Erscheinung* and *Schein* may occur, that is, between the legitimate phenomenon of truth and the exchange between manifestation and truth, in which manifestation itself is taken as truth. And only in this speculative profile does phenomenology become *Ichlehre*. Within the framework of the theory of ethics, this *Ichlehre* is based on two fundamental assumptions. The first has to do with the fact that even though phenomenology that presents the criteria for the self to become a moral being, it cannot be reduced to a theory of art (*Kunstlehre*), that is, to a doctrine that speaks how an individual self can become moral. More than that, phenomenology has to show how the whole of the I as such, that is, as an authentic phenomenon of the absolute and as unity of life and seeing, is moral in itself.[82] The second has to do with the fundamental criterion of morality presented by phenomenology: "The self must immediately appear as willing."[83] But in this self-understanding and as determined by the will, the self "has to manifest itself only as manifestation, for it does not have to be the very life of the concept, but the life of something else, which is far from itself, of the concept."[84]

A detailed analysis of the other criteria arising from the phenomenology of moral theory is beyond the scope of this chapter. This general analysis of the position of phenomenology in the *Theory of Ethics* of 1812 makes it possible to clarify that the material dimension of the I represents an element that can neither be deduced nor postulated. Furthermore, Fichte's analysis shows that the manifestation actually happens as an active signification of a higher principle, that is, in the form of a practical action determined and justified by a principle. In this sense, as Fichte argues in the XVII and XVIII lectures of the *Theory of Ethics*, phenomenology opens the space for personal responsibility and intersubjectivity as a field in which the latter can be explained. In this view, a broader contextualization of the meaning and extension of the Fichtean concept of phenomenology, understood as the construction of a doctrine of phenomena as a manifestation of the absolute, would confirm the connection between Fichte and Husserl established by Theodor Celms already in 1928. According to Celms, the Husserlian transcendental phenomenology would represent, above all, a philosophical, metaphysical, and spiritualist development, rooted in Leibnizian thought and, especially, in the idealism of the Fichtean doctrine of science.[85] Intentionally linked to a *Selbsverantwortung* of philosophy before itself, Husserl seems close to Fichte.[86] This approach takes place especially with regard to the definition of the practical horizon in which the self-justification of phenomenology happens. But, on the other hand, the contextualization of Fichtean phenomenology, as a problematization of the supposed naturalism of ordinary consciousness, would confirm Stumpf's interpretation, which greatly influenced the Husserlian conception.[87] According to Stumpf, the doctrine of science is merely an expression of a form of mysticism, or of a philosophy that refuses all empirical observation, which is very far from phenomenology as preliminary science (*Vorwissenschaft*) that finds in the empirical and psychological description of the acts of the I its appropriate starting point.[88] It is an ambiguity that, far from being eliminated, can represent a starting point for identifying tensions that define the relationship between Fichte and Husserl.

Notes

1. On this topic see Denis Fisette, "Phénomenologie et/ou idéalisme? Réflexions critiques sur l'attribution d'une forme ou d'une outre d'idéalisme à la phénomenologie," in *Idéalisme et phénomenologie*, ed. Marc Maesschalck (Hildesheim: Olms, 2010): 25–55; Olivier Lahbib, "Husserl lecteur de Fichte," *Archives de Philosophie* (2004): 421–43; and Klaus Christian Koenke, *The Rise of Neo-Kantianism: German Academic Philosophy between Idealism and Positivism* (Cambridge: Cambridge University Press, 1991).
2. The panorama of the critical literature on Fichte and Husserl is, in this sense, very wide. I will mention just a few recent and significant contributions on this topic: Daniel Breazeale, "Fichte's Nova metodo phenomenologica. On the methodological role of intellectual intuition in the later Jena Wissenschaftslehre," *Revue Internationale de Philosophie* (1998): 587–616; Günther Zöller, "An Eye for an I: Fichte's Transcendental Experiment," in *Figuring the Self: Subject, Absolute, and Others in Classical German Philosophy*, ed. Günther Zöller and August Kemm (Albany: State University of New York Press, 1997), 73–95;

and Günther Zöller, *Fichte's Transcendental Philosophy: The Original Duplicity of Intelligence and Will* (Cambridge: Cambridge University Press, 1998).

3. Edmund Husserl, *Gesammelte Werke*, ed. Hermann Leo van Breda (Den Haag: Nijhoff, 1950), vol. XXV, 189.
4. Ibid., 206.
5. This interpretative perspective is consistent with what the editors of the edition of the *Fichtes Menscheitsideal* in Vol. XXV of *Husserliana* claim: Husserl is simply speaking *pro domo sua* (Husserl, *Gesammelte Werke*, vol. XXV, XXVIII–XXXIII). It is therefore difficult not to give into the temptation to understand Husserl's Fichte as a sort of avatar for political and ideological needs extraneous to the specific point of view of the *Wissenschaftslehre*.
6. On this topic see Pietro Marino, "Edmund Husserl e la Grande Guerra," *Atti dell'accademia di scienze morali e politiche* (2009): 52–66.
7. Husserl, *Gesammelte Werke*, vol. XXV, 271.
8. Ibid., 274.
9. Ibid., 275.
10. Ibid., 276.
11. Ibid., 274.
12. Ibid., vol. XI, 24.
13. Ibid., vol. XXV, 270.
14. Ibid., 276.
15. Ibid., 274.
16. Edmund Husserl, *Briefwechsel* (Dordecht: Springer, 1994), vol. III, I, 163.
17. Ibid., 12.
18. Husserl, *Gesammelte Werke*, vol. XXV, 271.
19. Ibid.
20. Ibid., vol. XXVII, 4.
21. Ibid., 5.
22. Ibid., 10.
23. Ibid., 21.
24. Ibid., 42.
25. Ibid., 107.
26. Husserl, *Briefwechsel*, vol. V, 178.
27. Husserl, *Gesammelte Werke*, vol. XXV, 141.
28. Ibid., 271.
29. Ibid., 234.
30. Ibid., 279.
31. Ibid.
32. Ibid.
33. Ibid., 179.
34. Ibid., vol. XXVII, 13.
35. Ibid., vol. XXXVI, 171 and 173.
36. See for a clearer exposition Husserl's *Analyses concerning Passive and Active Synthesis*: "Such an object emerges, we follow the affection, *we turn toward*

it, we grasp it. In a special way, we now live through the continual unity of the objective sense, that is, the continuity of the streaming and varying consciousness, a continuity in which the continually unitary self is constituted. We are continually directed to this self, to the object of experience; we actively carry out the continual consciousness of the experiencing: The consciousness of existence is hereby a *living awareness, a living belief. But in this firm directedness toward the object,* in the continuity of its experiencing, there is an *intention* that *intends beyond* what is given and beyond its momentary mode of givenness toward a progressing *plus ultra.* It is not only a progressive conscious-having in general, but a *striving onward* to a new consciousness. This striving is founded in an *interest* in the enrichment of the self [of the object] that is *eo ipso* being augmented with the grasping, according to its content streaming toward the ego. Interest is a feeling and a positive feeling, but only apparently is this feeling a sense of well-being with respect to the object" ([Dordecht: Kluwer, 2001], 289).

37. See Rudolph Bernet, *Conscience et existence. Perspectives phénoménologiques* (Paris: PUF, 2004).

38. On the concept of *Trieb* in Husserl see Erich Holenstein, *Phänomenologie der Assoziation* (Den Haag: Nijhoff, 1972); Bernard Rang, *Kausalität und Motivation. Untersuchungen zum verhältnis von Perspektivität und Objektivität in der Phänomenologie Edmund Husserls* (Den Haag: Nijhoff, 1973); and Ichiro Yamaguchi, *Passive Synthesis und Intersubjektivität bei E. Husserl* (Den Haag: Nijhoff, 1982). For a deeper and specific account of Husserl's theory of drive see Nam-In, Lee, *Edmund Husserls Phänomenologie der Instinkte* (Dordecht: Nijhoff, 1993). On the relationship between passive synthesis and self-reflection see Tom Dedeurwaerdere, *Action et contexte. Du tournant cognitiviste à la Phénoménologie transcendentale* (Hildesheim: Olms, 2002), 198–210; Ulrich Keinser, *Das Motiv der Hemmung in Husserls Phänomenologie* (München: Piper, 1997); and Rolph Kühn, "Besoin Nature et animalité," *Annales de Philosophie* (1996): 65–79.

39. Husserl, *Gesammelte Werke*, vol. VI, 204.

40. Ibid., 430.

41. See on this topic Corrado Sinigaglia, "Presentazione," in Edmund Husserl, *L'idea di Europa. Cinque saggi sul rinnovamento* (Milano: Cortina, 1999), ix–xxxv.

42. See the writings on the history of philosophy in Husserl, *Gesammelte Werke*, vol. XXIX, 371–72.

43. Ibid., vol. XXVII, 36.

44. Ibid., 58.

45. Ibid.

46. Ibid.

47. Ibid., vol. XXIX, 282.

48. Ibid., vol. XXV, 292.

49. Johann Gottlieb Fichte, *Gesamtausgabe der Bayerischen Akademie der Wissenschaften*, ed. Reinhard Lauth, Hans Gliwitzky, Erich Fuchs, and Peter Karl Schneider (Stuttgart: Fromman Holzboog, 1962–2013), vol. I, 8, 298.
50. Ibid., vol. I, 8, 299.
51. See the *Einleitungsvorlesungen in die Wissenschaftslehre 1813*, in Reinhard Lauth, *J.G. Fichtes Ultima inquirenda* (Stuttgart: Frommann-Holzboog, 2000), 3.
52. Lauth, *Fichtes Ultima inquirenda*, 10.
53. Johann Gottlieb Fichte, *Sämtliche Werke*, ed. Immanuel Hermann Fichte (Berlin: De Gruyter, 1845), vol. IV, 34.
54. Fichte, *Gesamtausgabe*, vol. II, 5, 60.
55. Fichte, *Sämtliche Werke*, vol. IV, 390.
56. Ibid., 394.
57. Ibid., 389: "Diese angewendete lebt man nur; sie trägt man nicht vor in Reden als in einem neuen Bilde."
58. Ibid. For an account on the concept of application see Gaetano Rametta, "Libertà, scienza e saggezza nel secondo Fichte," in *La libertà nella filosofia classica tedesca. Politica e filosofia tra Kant, Fichte, Schelling e Hegel*, ed. Giuseppe Duso and Gaetano Rametta (Milano: Franco Angeli, 2000), 87–115; and "Gaetano Rametta, Doctrine de la Science et Doctrine e l'état. La dissolution de la théologie politique chez le dernier Fichte," in *Fichte. La Philosophie de la maturité*, ed. Jean Christoph Goddard (Paris: Vrin, 2003), 143–58.
59. Fichte, *Sämtliche Werke*, vol. IV, 390.
60. Ibid., 29.
61. Ives Radrizzani, "La Doctrine de la Science et l'engagement historique," *Archives de Philosophie* (1997): 36 and 43–44.
62. Fichte, *Sämtliche Werke*, vol. IV, 570.
63. See on this topic Jean Christoph Goddard, "Le Christ et l'histoire dans la Staatslehre de 1813," *Revue de Métaphysique et de Morale* (1996): 71–83.
64. Fichte, *Sämtliche Werke*, vol. IV, 529–30.
65. Immanuel Kant, *Theoretical Philosophy 1755–1770*, ed. David Walford (Cambridge: Cambridge University Press, 1992), 384; and Marco Ivaldo, *I principi del sapere* (Napoli: Bibliopolis, 1987).
66. Immanuel Kant, *Gesammelte Schriften*, ed. Preusslichen Akademie der Wissenschften (Berlin: De Gruyter, 1902–), vol. X, 96.
67. Ibid., vol. IV, 554.
68. Fichte, *Gesamtausgabe*, vol. II, 8, p. 138.
69. A discussion of this construction is given by Ivaldo, *I principi del sapere*, 333–48.
70. Fichte, *Gesamtausgabe*, vol. II, 8, 214.
71. Ibid., 220.
72. Ibid., 213.
73. Ibid.
74. Ibid.
75. Husserl, *Gesammelte Werke*, vol. VI, 205.

76. For a detailed description of this theme see Federico Ferraguto, "Fenomenologia tra etica e ontologia. Sulla *Sittenlehre* 1812 di J.G. Fichte," in *Etica e ontologia*, ed. Francesca Bonincalzi (Soveria Mannelli: Rubettino, 2009), 99–126; Marco Ivaldo, "Fichte: l'orizzonte comunitario dell'etica (le lezioni del 1812)," *Teoria* (2006): 37–54; Giovanni Cogliandro, *La dottrina morale superiore di Fichte* (Milano: Guerini, 2005); and Marco Ivaldo, *Libertà e ragione* (Milano: Mursia, 1992).
77. Fichte, *Gesamtausgabe*, vol. II, XIII, 308.
78. Ibid., 316–17.
79. Ibid., 312.
80. Ibid.
81. Ibid., 317.
82. Ibid., 337.
83. Ibid., 343.
84. Ibid., 339.
85. Husserl, *Gesammelte Werke*, vol. I, 182.
86. Ibid., vol. VI, 5–6.
87. Ibid.
88. On this topic see Stefano Poggi, "Husserl und die klassische deutsche Philosophie: eine Leidenschaft im reifen Alter?" in *Husserl und die Klassische Deutsche Philosophie*, ed. Faustino Fabbianelli and Sebastian Luft (New York: Springer, 2014), 65–78.

5

Bodies, Authenticity, and Marcelian Problematicity

Jill Hernandez

For those who know a little about Gabriel Marcel (1889–1973), the first French existentialist, it might at first glance seem odious to consider that his thought was significantly influenced by German Idealism, given that he repudiates idealism in his more important, later works. Yet those who are deeply familiar with his philosophy recognize the impact Hegel and Fichte (specifically) had on it. It is true that, even during the time Marcel was attracted to idealism early in his career, he was skeptical of any philosophical method which was teleologically constructed toward building a unified system of thought. However, it is equally true that near the end of his career and life, Marcel was keen to identify the points of contact and departure of idealism with his scholarship, and always acknowledged that he owed a debt to the German Idealists for a substantive portion of his thought (whether for content he engaged, or for the response it elicited). This chapter will explore Marcel's relationship with German Idealism, the impact idealism had on his existentialism, his philosophical evolution beyond idealist conceptions of objectivity and consciousness, and his own move toward the authentic "ethical self," whose goal is a reciprocal, intersubjective relationship with others

J. Hernandez (✉)
College of Arts & Humanities, Central Washington University,
Ellensburg, WA, USA
e-mail: jill.hernandez2@cwu.edu

C. D. Coe (eds.), *The Palgrave Handbook of German Idealism and Phenomenology*,
Palgrave Handbooks in German Idealism,
https://doi.org/10.1007/978-3-030-66857-0_5

85

who are freely seeking the inner meaning of experience. It will argue that the authentic self is fundamentally personal because it is embodied, non-objective, and creates opportunities for others to existentially flourish. The continuing progress of the ethical, authentic self in a world that threatens it establishes Marcel's existentialism as a way to flourish in the midst of absurdity, and so establishes it as more than a mere reaction to German Idealism.

Marcel's Early Relationship with German Idealism

Marcel came to the German Idealists by way of Samuel Taylor Coleridge, the nineteenth-century English poet whose "social self" was cast as a relational being thrown into a world in which others reflect the self's projections. Marcel saw the social self as a way to "hit back at the practical world which at every step proved to me my ineptitude and my awkwardness."[1] We might today say that imposter syndrome led Marcel to idealism, because he was profoundly skeptical of concrete experience and his own ability to philosophically navigate it. He subsequently was drawn to abstraction, prior to his service in World War I (after which he published *The Metaphysical Journal*). He was attracted early on to Hegel, Schelling, and Fichte (and, especially, the neo-Hegelian Francis Herbert Bradley), for their dialectical process, which Marcel believed provided an "ability to surpass and transcend everyday life and all its monotonous round of trivial and exacting concerns."[2] Idealism also gave Marcel an alternative methodology to engage the world other than through science, which he criticized because it reduced the body to its functions and could not provide valuable solutions to the human questions of existential significance. Idealism's marriage of epistemology and ontology—that being and thought are inseparable—proved important to Marcel: to understand the self, we must understand the activity of self-consciousness.

As a youth and emerging adult, Marcel was compelled by Hegel's views about the constitution of real objects, and bought into the truth of idealism as a process to understand the relationship between thinking and being. Marcel agreed with Hegel that, if every object is understood corporately as thought and being, and an individual object cannot be separated ontologically in thought and being, then thinking is prior to the metaphysical composition of objects and the structure of their behavior. In Marcel's essay "Existence and Objectivity" (part of the *Journal*, and written beginning in 1914), he conceived of the object as "the rationally articulated spectacle" which thought sets against itself.[3] Consciousness deliberately sets aside "the mode in which the object is present to the person who considers it . . . the mysterious power of self-affirmation by which it confronts a spectator."[4] There is little distinction, then, in the meaning of "existence" and "objectivity" in Marcel's early scholarship (although his later emergence as an existentialist provides meaning to the distinction). Further, although the relationship between the object and the self (and the role of self-affirmation through objects) remained a thematic concern throughout his life (and represents a view about which Marcel reversed himself), even in his early thought Marcel took refuge in the metaphysical primacy of thought. He attributed his appropriation of this priority to Hegel's influence, rather than to the "sense presence of the thing."[5] Indeed, Marcel went to great lengths in the *Journal* to explore the inadequacy of the sense presence of objects and empiricism generally. Later, Marcel would write that he could "see the reason why abstraction was the keynote of my early philosophical thoughts and why I was almost contemptuously hostile towards empiricism . . . Experience, as it is mostly conceived by philosophers, was to me impure and profoundly suspect."[6] A main reason he was enamored with Hegel and rejected empiricism during those early years is that he saw idealism as a way to better respond to the phenomenal problems generated by *das Ding-an-sich* (the thing in itself). If thought is prior to the sense presence of objects, we can have a platform to reject any reduction of humanity to material objects, and to understand thought in relationship to the self, to freedom, and to God.

The value of Fichte's idealism for Marcel was its aesthetic, creative principle, which Marcel saw as a way to "transcendentalize" the self, or "to substitute for the empirical self a unifying, universal principle."[7] This view, coupled with the time in which Marcel discovered it, proved to be a guiding influence on Marcel's emerging metaphysics. Fichte's spontaneous act, which posited that the "I" has existence (and so introduced a subject/object opposition within the I),[8] allowed Marcel "to extract the empirical self from the absolute or merely transcendental self," and so to bring "to light the opposition between the two principles which cannot be designated by the same word, *moi* (self), without creating the most dangerous confusion."[9] Identifying the *moi* with a mind that exists by itself with no particular space/time location allows existence to be a function of the self. If existence is a function of the self, the world is objectively given, and thought is ideal. In Fichte's idealism, Marcel saw an opportunity to make the individual central to philosophical inquiry, which would later become a cornerstone of Marcel's existentialism. In Fichte's principles, Marcel "was impelled by that same sense of the concrete and that awareness of irreconcilable differences which lay at the origin of my need to create."[10] Those differences were revealed to Marcel through his participation in World War I, during which Marcel confronted the moral ambiguities of peace through conflict, and artistic expression despite atrocities of war. His own creative impulse could only be realized through writing (and not through musical composition), and the result was the *Journal* and Marcel's first inquiry into the concrete as a way of explaining existential meaning and the self, thrown into a world that it did not create. At that time, Marcel saw idealism as a way to imagine a world grounded in humanistic values, with a sustained pattern of normalcy that projected the inevitability of the progress of humanity because idealism provided a way to abstract away from life's irreconcilable differences.[11] Marcel commented, "I think that not one of us could suspect the fragility, the precariousness, of the civilization which enveloped us like a tegument; a civilization on which the wealth of centuries seemed to have conferred a solidity we would have thought it madness to question."[12]

Marcel recorded existential and ethical tensions throughout the war. The abstract could no longer adequately explain experience. Humanistic values are sacrificed to utility in a state of war. Marcel could rationally explain the individual, as an epistemic and ontological point of departure prior to his experiences at war, but the ethical questions demanded by war compelled him to evolve out of idealism and toward existentialism. There were, ultimately, two main reasons Marcel grew to move away from idealism, and, in his mature work, repudiate it altogether: First, he believed that idealism could only derive existence from objectivity and could not account for true being—one whose fact provides "existential assurance whose pure immediacy is incapable of being mediated" and "is incapable of specifications (it is not this or that)."[13] If idealism cannot account for true being, it is insufficient to explain meaning for the individual. Second, idealism required a unified system of thought which set existence over a subject. He always considered Hegel and Schelling to be creative, decisive metaphysicians, but came to doubt views that he thought were meant to serve as "imperfect substitutes" for "true experience."[14] The War gave Marcel a deep interest in the concrete—not just the relation between the self and the situation, but the unity of sensing, thinking, and feeling within a single self. But it also gave him a curiosity about whether there could be a transcendent unity to relationships and experience. Idealism, until then, had provided Marcel with an (albeit complicated) approach to the lived experiences of suffering that he encountered as a medic. Prior to 1925, Marcel still was wedded to making idealism compatible with "an attempt to reinstate existence" as metaphysically prior.[15] The publication of the *Journal* (which had dominated his philosophical life for nearly a decade) represented Marcel's own transition out of idealism. In Part I, Marcel accepted idealism over empiricism as a means to understand thought, objects, and individuals; by Part II, Marcel mused, "It is private life that holds out the mirror to infinity; personal intercourse, and that alone, that ever hints at a personality beyond our daily vision."[16] Idealist tenets, such as the need for knowledge claims to be substantiated against tangible, physical objects in the world and the need to deconstruct philosophical systems, were juxtaposed against the concrete and a communal self in Marcel's thought, and he followed an inquiry into the concrete.[17]

Interestingly, Marcel initially thought Hegel's idealism was mostly consistent with an inquiry into the concrete. "For, in spite of appearances to the contrary," Marcel wrote, "Hegel did make a very splendid effort to preserve the primacy of the concrete; and no philosopher has protested more strongly against the confusion of the concrete with the immediately given."[18] Rather than providing clarity for Marcel, however, the problem of the nature of reality,

> obsessed me throughout those years of blind groping. What I wanted to know was not so much what reality is, as what we mean when we assert its existence, and when we say that it cannot be reduced to its outward appearances, or that these appearances probably conceal more than they disclose.[19]

He assessed other forms of idealism as less ready to tackle the challenge of engaging with the concrete. What he found compelling in Hegel, Fichte, and Bradley were their similar views about the relationship between knowledge, existence, and self-consciousness. Knowledge is about what can be substantiated in the world, including the self as an object of which true things can be asserted and verified.[20] However, Marcel came to believe that none of their varieties of idealism could respond to the question of being in the world, because they, at root, established a philosophical system whose success depended upon the total objectification of being. Being is not a spectacle, however, and so the illusion that idealism built of a successful total objectification was exactly what vitiated idealism, in his opinion.[21]

However, Marcel's realization that idealism could not account for concrete experience led him to critique idealism for (what he termed) its *spirit of abstraction*. Although abstraction is necessary to reason at the level of the problematic, Marcel came to believe that abstraction should not be used to conceptualize the self, but should remain limited to the objectified realms of things.[22] Whereas abstraction focuses on solving problems (an important function of the mind), the spirit of abstraction is a feeling of contempt for "the concrete conditions for abstract thinking," and so can result in "the most dangerous abstractions" through which, Marcel suggested, the mind "deceives itself about the nature of what is, in itself, nothing more than a method, one might almost say nothing more than an expedient."[23]

As much as he was drawn to Hegel and Schelling, then, for their insistence on the primacy of thought over object, Marcel as a mature philosopher took on the task of showing the primacy of the concrete, and especially the metaphysical priority of the concrete human person. Rather than cast skepticism on experience, as he did in Part I of the *Journal*, in Part II, Marcel embraced a metaphysics in which, "the theory of sensation and of the body leads us to a positive conception of existence, the theory of value and of love leads us to a positive conception of being, and the theories sketched at the start of the *Journal* find a new signification."[24] To pivot to an existentialism rooted in the self, Marcel had to come to a point in which he rejected the Hegelian Absolute, his emphasis on mediation, and the synthesis of opposites. Metaphysically, the result for Marcel is that, except for the question, "'What am I?' there are no other metaphysical problems, since in one way or another they all lead back to it."[25] Whereas Hegel explained existence from objectivity, Marcel's foray into existentialism motivated him to explain being from existence, and to do that, he needed to shift even more toward the concrete, and to the lived experiences of the body.

It should not surprise us that, as a philosopher who was also famous as a concert pianist and playwright, some of the best examples of Marcel's tenets (including his criticisms of idealism) come from his elucidation of musical and theatrical principles. Marcel himself recognized that there are dangers implicit in attempting to understand the "direction of Being" by "referring to a concrete totality," and he compared such an endeavor to an orchestra performing a polyphonic work.[26] Marcel explained that within such a performance, each musician plays a unique part within the ensemble, but that the ensemble would be completely misrepresented if someone identified the group by the arithmetical sum of juxtaposed elements. Each performer might only initially be conscious of the part entrusted to him or her, but must become consciously aware of the ensemble as the piece emerges. The conductor, as well, understands each part is constructed as a function of the whole. The whole precedes the parts in an orchestra, and the same can be said for being. The self is more than an amalgamation of its experiences. The risk is that we might fall "again into a precritical dogmatism to claim from my experience alone, with its gaps and its insufficiencies, that I am obliged to go back to the existence of an all-inclusive thought which controls it."[27]

Idealists would be right, here, to push back against Marcel's about-face on systematization, at least. There is a need for corporeal and corporal unity, after all, in Marcel's later work, including bodily unity, as well as a heterogeneity of subjects who are available to each other and receptive to the needs of those who are hurting (particularly). Thought's role in Marcel also remained important as a conduit of, about, and for, being. Without unity and a system for explaining the interface between thought and objects, it seems that, under Marcel's view, to have an experience of the self and objects in the world, the mind must abstract from a multiplicity of sources. But this seems at least as problematic as the pitfalls Marcel identified in idealism. Perhaps Marcel would reject equivocating between reality and the abstractions (and a *system for unification*) required to understand it, but he then would still have to have a way to help the individual use sense, experience, and thought to mediate what is not immediately given in experience. To resolve this tension, Marcel came to believe that the first-person standpoint can be a point of departure to understand what he called the human experience of the immediate, through concrete, lived experience of the body.

The Self as Body

Emerging out of idealism gave Marcel an opportunity to explore what he saw as a distinction between existence and objectivity. The experience of the immediate does not require philosophy to question the reality of things, but "to specify that their existence is apprehended by incarnate beings like you and me and by virtue of being incarnate."[28] Marcel's use of "incarnate" is quite masterful here: He both stripped the word of any of its theological connotations by applying it directly to the fact that I am my body (so constrained by the limits of my physicality and my experiences of living in time), and in equal parts, imbued the term with a secular sacredness. The everyday concrete becomes, for Marcel's readers, the launching point for existential meaning, and prepares the reader to grasp an existential truth that gives hope: I am my body but am not reduced to it.[29] An upshot is that "a philosophy that gives a central importance to incarnation will lead to quite a different ethic from that proposed by a rationalistic idealism which tends to make the most complete abstraction possible from the concrete rootedness of human beings."[30]

Secular incarnation (*être incarné*) refers to the concrete physical, inextricable tie between the self and the body. When I think about the facticity of my body, I recognize that I am this specific body, and that my body experiences others in the world, typically without the mediation of any other thing. Rather than the self as a Cartesian cogito, whose essence is bound by its rational function, Marcel's self understands the body independent of its instrumentality, "To presuppose that the body is an instrument of the self is to assume a bodily power already possessed by the self of which the instrumental body is an extension, which is to say that it is effectively impossible to conceive the body as an instrumental extension of the self."[31]

Marcel's reconception of the self is such that, thought is understood in relation to the body, rather than either as a primary representation of the self, an unmediated essential self, or a property of some (more basic, formal) self. Body is a necessary condition for the interpretation of the object by the subject, and of the self as an experience, and so becomes a mediator in cognition.[32] Thomas C. Anderson's *Commentary* is helpful, here:

> To claim, then, that my felt embodied self, "the existential immediate that . . . I am," is not a "thought-content" means not only that it is not a conclusion reached by a thought process but also that it is not known by means of other concepts of thought. Rather, the most fundamental datum of my existence, my body as me, is at bottom not a thought or concept at all but a felt experience for Marcel, an experience which is the underlying basis of all my activity of thought—even though it "transcends every thought content . . . inserted into it."[33]

This reconception of the self, which eliminates equivocating the self with the functionality of thought or body, required Marcel to come back to the concrete experiences of the self as body, and to understand thought in relation to the body.

Marcel's reconceptualization also required him to abandon an essentialist conception of the self. The self starts as body, but is not limited to the body. The analogy used by Marcel to explain the self as a body was as "a moving and vulnerable enclave: an enclosure which is alive."[34] The image is one that has an outline, but the content contained within it is mobile, receptive, and evolving. The self, then, is in process even as it undergoes concrete experiences. Thought is, then, in relation to experiences of the self as a lived body. For Marcel, the possibility that the self is vulnerable was significant, because the results include that a sense experience cannot encapsulate the self, the self is not encapsulated by a totality of experience, and that the self can be jeopardized by harmful interactions with the world. The ability to cognize, ruminate, imagine, or reason in and through experiences cannot inoculate the self from harm that can threaten the self's ability to interact with others, or to reflect on the self. To help understand the relationship between thought and this evolving self (and its experiences), Marcel turned toward the concept of "reflection." One of the major contributions Marcel made in philosophy was his post-idealist distinction between primary and secondary reflection. As will be shown below, the distinction maps onto two different aspects of humanity—the problematic and the mysterious.

Primary reflection is the reflection we use when we directly relate to scientific or objective problems. It takes as its starting point what is given in experience, distinct from the self, so includes causal thinking, scientific ordering, and abstraction. Peter McNelis explains that at the level of the problematic,

> nothing about it is explained or understood; it is "out-thereness," pure given-ness. This is the level of immediate, unreflective awareness of empirical data. As one begins to analyze the empirical data, to mull it over, and abstract from its essential nature, one progresses to the second level of intelligibility—the level of primary or first reflection.[35]

Primary reflection's goal is to break down issues into their verifiable aspects so that they are easier to grasp, and to objectify as many characteristics of a problem as possible.[36] We are trained at an early age to rely on primary reflection to navigate the world, because it is necessary to identify and solve problems: "a problem is something which I meet, which I find complete before me, but which I can therefore lay siege to and reduce,"[37] and the results are positive. We can solve, conquer, create, and reconceptualize the world we navigate through primary reflection. To identify, reduce, and solve objects as problems, primary reflection also problematizes the self and its relation to the world—and this can be an appropriate function of primary reflection. There are times at which I have to characterize myself according to the duties I perform, what I make or create, and sometimes just based on my brute physical attributes (whether a certain age, height, weight, skin/eye/hair color, etc.).

However, primary reflection seems inadequate to explain or motivate personal or ontological growth, and frustrates the ability to think of the self as anything beyond a set of functions: one who sleeps, eats, procreates, reflects, creates. The body itself seems to be more than its functions—more than a casing for the self, and more than a machine for some res cogitans. Rudolf Gerber explains that

> For Marcel's purpose in the discussion of the personal body, the method and results of primary or scientific reflection are not only undesirable but also inap-plicable. In a scientific analysis body and soul become abstract things, logical terms which are imagined as a strictly defined and linked to each other by some determinate relation. This abstractive approach entirely misses the issue

at hand, the incommunicable experience of the body as mine . . . It is incommunicable in the sense that it cannot be exhausted in the logical categories of primary reflection.[38]

Primary reflection fails to explain the relationship between the self as a being among beings, largely because it cannot give an account of the human person as a being, apart from the body's mechanistic function as an existent in the universe. Reflecting on the self as a problem requires the individual to constantly attempt to affirm the self through the individual's own judgment about what the individual can do and how well the individual does: I am a faculty member, a home owner, a parent, a spouse, a daughter, and at times can go beyond the actions I perform in those roles and play a strong game of euchre, hike mountains, drive a manual transmission, or bake a pumpkin bread that would win competitions. On the one hand, this reduction of the self to an object is dangerous because when we treat others as objects, we can discard them as objects as well. Louis Pamplume and Beth Brombert explain that, for Marcel, the objectification of the self is a form of isolation that can lead to my own silencing, "In isolating myself from the world I cut myself off from myself; but by the same token, the world, changed into a ghostly spectacle, thins out, becomes empty, 'finally suppresses itself through the simple fact of ignoring me.'"[39] Yet on the other hand we risk thinking of ourselves in ways that are not suitably self-critical. Marcel thought we should

> resist the temptation of the philosophy of idealism to which so many have yielded who are prone to substitute for the study of man as he actually is elaborations on what he should be, or on the too-flattering self-portrait he is likely to draw when his attention is focused on an essence imprudently dissociated from the existential context.[40]

Existential meaning (as well as moral improvement) seems to require something beyond primary reflection.

The inadequacy of primary reflection does not reside in its mere reduction of objects to functions, especially because of the fact that objects are known through primary reflection for their functions. Rather, the reduction of my existence to that of an object idealizes the self problematically, and so centers Marcel's critique of idealism. In Volume 1 of *The Mystery of Being*, he explains that primary reflection's basic assumption (the translation of sense data into information) cannot provide a positive account of the feeling I have of the body as mine. For primary reflection to adequately explain this feeling, it would have to first have a prior sensation of the self as body ("every kind of message . . . presupposes the existence of sensation"[41]) that could then be translated. A sensation itself cannot be the information or the affirmation of the self. The self-as-body is not given to us in sensation, and so primary reflection is insufficient to account for what Marcel calls the "indissoluble unity" between existence and the self-as-body.[42] If the self is immediately given in experience, without a translational process of sensation to information, then the self-as-body becomes, for Marcel, the existential indubitable.

Primary reflection is also unable to explain the relation of the immediate, unified self as a self among others. Logic cannot join the self to others. In *Existential Background of Human Dignity*, Marcel elaborates,

> It is enough . . . to reflect on a relationship of the kind that the word < with > suggests to recognize how poor and inadequate our logic is. Apart from juxtapositions pure and simple it is in fact incapable of expressing relationships of an increasing intimacy. If I simply *find myself* in a train compartment or in an airplane *next to* someone to whom I do not speak and whose face *tells me nothing*, I cannot really say that I am *with* him. We are not together. I might note in passing that the English noun *togetherness*, which has been unfortunately travestied in popular usage, has no possible equivalent in French. It is as if the French language refused to make a substantive of—that is, to conceptualize—a certain quality of being which is concerned with the "*entrenous*," the "between you and me."[43]

The self's existence is basic and given in experience, and phenomenologically, the presence of the self among other beings resists being reduced to the level of problems.

Whereas most of philosophy (including idealism and empiricism) does not go beyond the level of primary reflection (and it indeed renders science and technology possible), objectifying the self in such a reductive way, Marcel contended, "destroys the participation in Being that is proper to authentic philosophy."[44] The reason that being is not reductive is that the self cannot be reduced to its roles and functions in the world. Relying on primary reflection to think about personal, existential significance can lead to a feeling of meaninglessness, because characterizing human significance as a problem risks "an infinite regress which is bound to appear to a person as an outright dissipation of what he would spontaneously mean in speaking of his substance or his own being."[45] The self is more than its functions and is a situated being among beings. Existentially, to understand the relationship between the self and others in the world (or more basically, the relationship of the self to the self), effective reflection should account for being in the experiences of daily life, and from a moral standpoint, reflection should allow the subject to see how those experiences impinge on the development of future possibilities.

Sam Keen suggests, "In turning aside from a rationalistic, intellectualistic approach to being, Marcel elaborates a new type of reflection—secondary reflection—which searches for being in the concrete realities of experience."[46]

This new type of identified reflection, secondary reflection, looks for the significance of being in the reality of experience. In secondary reflection, the details of the situation are placed into an experiential context at the level of being, so that whereas "primary reflection tends to dissolve the unity of experience which is first put before it, the function of secondary reflection is essentially recuperative; it reconquers this unity."[47] Secondary reflection allows the self to reflect on experiences that are not explicable through a subject-object distinction and contemplate the relation of the self to others within experience. Contemplation and secondary reflection both involve intentional introspection on a level above the problematical. Contemplation is analogous to the physical experience of looking. Throughout the day, we look without any specific purpose, but at times we look for things in a way that serves some practical activity. If I hike across a patch of ground covered in boulders, puddles, or muddy patches, I purposefully direct my vision, careful where I put my feet. My attention is continuously directed toward a wholly definable activity—that of picking my way from one given point to another. The knowledge I seek by looking in this intentional way is specific and focused on a particular end (that of finding my way across the obstacles before me). In looking, I look out, away, and without, to find out what I need to know. In contemplation, I seek inside. Insofar as the word "contemplation" indicates the act by which the self concentrates its attention on its own self or being, we can properly say that contemplation is a turning inward of our awareness of the outer world.[48] This turning inward allows the self to begin to see herself as a being who is able to participate with the needs, desires, and goals of others and not merely as a tool to be used. Although contemplation provides avenues for growth for the self because it involves non-reductive reflection, it still is insufficient to explain the phenomenon the individual has of experiencing *this* body as the self (for Marcel, *moi*). Contemplation can allow the self to concentrate attention on the self apart from its bodily possibilities and limits, but secondary reflection is needed to reflect on the incommunicable experience of the body as mine.[49]

"I am my body" is the point of departure for the individual as a being in the world because it is what is immediately given in experience. To think of the self as a body is to begin to answer the question *Who am I that asks the question 'Who am I?'*. Further reflection on the question reveals the relationship of this situated body with others. For Marcel, the individual as a body cannot help but interact with other bodies. At no time is the individual self-sufficient; rather, the situated self requires that others influence, shape, and justify the view one has of the self. We are more than bodies of objectifiable data analyzed by science, but have a type of relationship with others that can only be described as *mysterious*, a relation that resists the reduction of objectification. Being, for Marcel, is a fundamental and indissoluble bond beneath the level of abstraction and objectification, and is at its root personal, rather than functional.[50] We (as existential persons, selves interacting with selves) are not problems to be solved, but mysteries upon which to reflect.

Secondary reflection, then, takes as its starting point the individual as a being, situated among other beings. The goal of secondary reflection is to explicate existence, which cannot be separated from the individual (as the body), who is in turn situated among others. The introduction of the concept of secondary reflection marks, for Marcel, a further distinction between idealism and his emerging existentialism: The presence of the self in the world is given in the world, does not require the mediation of thought or a rational process, and is fundamentally related to other beings in the world.[51] For Marcel, self-understanding is only possible through secondary reflection, since through it, the self asks itself how and from what starting point the self is able to proceed.[52] Through secondary reflection, the individual realizes the lived body's relation to the self, which is the beginning of the self's ability to turn away from the level of problems and onto being and meaning.

Marcel's rejection of idealism as a system of thought, and his subsequent explication of secondary reflection, aided his shift in focus away from whether objectivity could help explain existence and onto the relationship between existence and being. When Marcel became disillusioned with idealism's emphasis on the impersonal nature of knowledge, he turned toward empiricism (and then, existentialism) to show that the self is always situated in place and time, and knowledge is always personal. Marcel then developed his philosophy to be able to explain the various ways in which the self resists reduction and objectification. Marcel did not believe that the self has rigid designators but is rich in contours. He could not accept an ideal, transcendental ego because it could not itself be experienced, and could not account for the experience the self has as a being in a situation. Yet the self's experiences are concrete and (eventually, for Marcel) personal. Knowledge can be objective, but it must be able to provide an answer to the self's question, "Who am I that asks the question, 'Who am I'?" Objectification leads to an inability to treat the self as a subject, and, worse still, the destruction ("pulverization") of the subject:

It is necessary to see what sort of self-image man fashions when he tends to picture the world in the light of the techniques that it has been given to him to invent. It is true that this image is more and more confused, misshapen, indecipherable, and that this distortion entails incalculable consequences for self-knowledge. The Socratic γνῶθι σεαυτόν [*know thyself*] was, after all, based on the idea of an identity of the knower and the known; and the principle of the identity of the ideal and the real thereby postulated was, in the last analysis, the foundation of the whole of traditional philosophy from Plato to Descartes to Hegel. But is not this postulate annulled, for all practical purposes, by the hyperbolic enlargement of technical skills—that is to say, of "know-how?" Does not the explosion of the objective world whose physiognomy is increasingly strange and threatening, entail in fact a pulverization of the subject? I mean to say that the techniques conceived on the model of those whose efficacy was demonstrated in the realm of nature will now be applied to the subject himself, who will, by the same token, cease to be treated as a subject.[53]

The mature Marcel aimed to show the primacy of the concrete over idealism's Absolute through an authentic subjectivity, wherein the self can relate to itself and others through a discovery of the inner meaning of experience.

The Self as Subject

Marcel's worry over objectifying human existence grew in his later writings to the extent that the term "subject" became a way for Marcel to connote the opposite of an object, thing, or substance.[54] Whereas Fichte and the Romanticists earlier gave Marcel an aesthetic, creative principle of the self, neither the idealism nor empiricism could encapsulate the *moi* Marcel believed confronted the "essential ambiguity" of the self in an absurd world. Marcel sought to protest against idealism because he saw that it was unable to provide an adequate idea of the human subject and the central *personality* of subjectivity. Rather, Marcel sought to adequately, faithfully, and descriptively analyze subjectivity without an ontological system, but within a phenomenological approach to human experience.[55]

After his idealist and empiricist phases, Marcel saw his "continual and central metaphysical preoccupation" as an attempt to "discover how a subject, in his actual capacity as a subject, is related to a reality which cannot in this context be regarded as objective, but which is persistently required and recognized as real."[56] Marcel's development as an existentialist with a focus on the subject's personal experiences shifted the role of thought in the subject to one of mediating and resolving experiences. The mediation of thought involves the subject (who raises questions and reflects on experiences), other subjects (who may also question, who may answer, or who may be present in experience), and objects (which are interpreted by subjects of experience and are indifferent to the interpreters' thoughts and the judgments made by them).[57] Metaphysical cognition binds thought to the incarnation of the self as body, and then brings knowledge of the self and others incarnated. This existential approach to subjects and thought ameliorated Marcel's distrust of idealism's and empiricism's inability to consider the meaning of existence and experience by focusing on the relation of subjects in experience, and fleshing out his view of the ethical self (which leads to freedom), intersubjectivity, and the mystery of being.

Marcel's intersubjective reciprocity is called *communion* and (similar to his conception of incarnation) is a secular invocation to community. Thus Marcel's existentialism is grounded not in a *cogito, sum*, nor *je me sens*, but more closely in *nous sommes* or *coesse*.[58] There is solidarity between subjects when there is knowledge of the self and others as bodies. Intersubjective communion is, for Marcel, existential communion—rooted in the situatedness of incarnate beings. The result is that participation is fundamentally about being with others in a situation. Marcel explained, "It is participation which had priority in my thought . . . and in no way was this a question of participation in an Idea, but of participation in Being."[59] Those who are committed to participating in intersubjective communion engage in the practices of an *ethical life*.

An example of secular communion from Marcel's life can be found in his relationships to other philosophers (and, particularly, atheists). Marcel, a prolific letter writer, was friends with Bertrand Russell, who published one of his exchanges with Marcel in his *Autobiography*:

> I often have imaginary conversations with Leibniz, in which I tell him how fruitful his ideas have proved, and how much more beautiful the result is than he could have foreseen; and in moments of self-confidence, I imagine students hereafter having similar thoughts about me. There is a "communion of philosophers" as well as a "communion of saints" and it is largely that that keeps me from feeling lonely.[60]

In the letter, Marcel suggests that participation with others who have a similar constitution or telos (regardless of the content of their philosophical and theological commitments) creates a community that begins with our situation in the world, and yet transcends the limitations of the body. He identified a secular communion that has actual existential impact (here, on whether Marcel could feel lonely when reading Leibniz and sharing that with Russell).

Communion occurs when the presence of the other (whether the other is physically present is irrelevant) is felt by the subject. Buber and Marcel were similar in calling this felt presence of the other the I-Thou relationship. The intimacy of the I-Thou cannot be considered objectively but is grasped from the interior life of the mind. An attempt to objectify the I-Thou leads to existential despair.[61] Marcel hints at his own view in his letter, that there is not an authentic experience of the self except for an experience of the self with others.

The ethical life is existentially significant on Marcel's account because it is the mark of the subject who is able to have richly meaningful experiences of the interior life that fosters intersubjectivity with others. Existence is the given through which being is reflected, and the life of the mind is part of lived experience. Authentic subjectivity is primary, and the result is that, for Marcel, the subject is not a data point, but reflects a unity of inner and outer experiences that is achieved because she is free.[62] Freedom is not given in experience, but is something that must be developed, honed, and strengthened in intersubjective relationships. Marcel also believed that the freedom of the ethical self would be key in our technological age to overcoming the reduction of humanity to functionality:

> The demand of our times is for an ideology fundamental enough to deal with the problems raised by the human passions of hate, fear and greed, an ideology of freedom, that man's relations with man shall not be governed by how much we can get from one another, but how much we can selflessly give. That is the only guarantee that man's inhumanity to man shall end. Men shall cease to fear each other because their motives will have changed.[63]

The ethical self, then, exists at more than the level of problematicity, takes physical existence as an opportunity to experience participation and presence with others, lives freely, and generates possibilities for existential flourishing (and hope) by being available (*disponible*) to others who share intersubjective reciprocity. The ethical life must be free, since it is only by breaking out of the objectification of the self and the gaze of others that we are able to take responsibility for our choices and growth. The ethical life must be exigent, or committed to reflection and being ontologically present to others, if it is to successfully create relationships and meaning. Finally, the ethical life must foster hope through a creative impulse because hope helps the self see beyond the limits of facticity.

Kenneth Gallagher explains why the ethical self is not an endeavor that can be sought individually: "The acts which found me as a subject-in-communion, as I in the face of a thou, are also those which give me access to being . . . My participation in being is ultimately, then, a creative participation."[64] The ethical life requires an intersubjective participation that creates possibilities for hope for others. But hope is not solely tied to the individual's possibilities—it is not potent at the level of the self without the aid of others. By itself, the "solitary ego, self-hypnotized and concentrating exclusively on individual aims" seeks ambition, which is innocuous, but hope subsists on a different plane.[65] For Marcel, hope creates possibilities only if there is someone for me to share those possibilities. The most significant source of meaning, then, is genuine hope that comes through the individual being available more to others. Rather than being closed up on itself, the participating subject can have community through communion. Marcel ventured as far as to say that there "can be no hope which does not constitute itself through a we and for a we."[66]

Marcel's elucidation of the ethical self as a self-among-selves should not be read as an erasure of the self—far from it. Marcel thinks the ethical self as a being-among-beings is the best, full sense of the free subject. Authentic subjectivity involves incarnation (and the constraints of being a body), but it also requires freedom, which is itself not possible without an awareness of the self. Marcel explained, "If I treat the other as a Thou, I treat him and apprehend him qua freedom. I apprehend him qua freedom because he is also free . . . I help him, in a sense, to be freed, I collaborate with his freedom."[67] Subjectivity facilitates freedom (and so, the fullness of being) in those who experience it.

Marcel suggested that his own early (1914) play *Le Palais de Sable* contained an exchange between characters (the daughter Clarisse and the father Moirans) which, in his later thought, served both as a critique of idealism and demonstrated the need for existential intersubjectivity:

Moirans: Yes, but why did you have to be the victim of this suffering?
Clarisse: The fruitless sacrifice of a life was perhaps necessary to expiate for your having walled yourself in; for you have lived a solitary life among men.
Moirans: In what possible realm does this mysterious notion of yours hold good?
Clarisse: It is a realm that we can affirm simply on the strength of our being able to think of it.
Moirans: And yet if it is not willed by any God?

> *Clarisse*: Father, remember: our thoughts must be capable of sufficing unto themselves; they emanate from no center. They reflect no world apart from them.
> *Moirans*: Ah yes . . . I recognize now what I once thought so wise. Why does it seem so different now?
> *Clarisse*: Because it is something you've lived through.[68]

Marcel was right that the example serves to show some limits of idealism. He contended, "It is obvious that Clarisse has succumbed to the temptation of an idealism that is nothing but a degeneration from an authentic faith which is in itself prereflective" and "Moirans appears as utterly blind; his blindness is that of the idealist whose thought obstructs communication with other people by preventing him from even imagining them in their concrete reality."[69] But the intersubjective bond between characters is not immediately obvious, though it comes through with some analysis. The solitary life (among others) is described as "walled in" and a "fruitless sacrifice." When Moirans replies to Clarisse that her description of the fruitlessness of his solitary life is *mysterious*, Clarisse's reply demonstrates Marcel's retort to idealism: "self-consciousness, far from being an illuminating principle, as traditional philosophy has held, on the contrary shuts the human being in on himself and thus results in opacity rather than enlightenment."[70] *The strength of our ability to think it* means that there is neither a transcendental nor divine ideal that grounds the person, but free human choice in engaging the world through subjectivity should be the source of humanity's search for existential flourishing. Through free action and secondary reflection, the subjective self responds to the other through intersubjectivity in an attempt to navigate the absurdity of the human condition. The result, for Marcel, is an existentialism that responds to the depersonalization of idealism and the reduction of human significance.

Conclusion

The continuum of the Marcelian metaphysics of the subject over the course of his life began with Marcel's flirtation with idealism, and his dependence on an ideal to explain the self, objects in the world, and thought. His personal experiences and philosophical efforts during a changing global political dynamic took Marcel on a search for a view that could explain concrete experiences and human relationships that seemed to transcend the level of the object.

The external world is personal; it begins with individual existence and so, it cannot be separated from the self.

This chapter has shown that shifting philosophy's point of view to the personal allowed Marcel to explore concrete relationships between wholly contingent (yet wholly free) beings. Meaningful existence is, Marcel thought, "a precarious and continually threatened presence, but it is not without the aspiration toward plenitude toward the pleroma. And that plentitude is still being, it is even most truly being, but being insofar as it can in no way be given."[71] The continuing progress of the ethical, authentic self in a world that threatens it is challenging, and is not fundamentally optimistic. Yet creating opportunities for the self and others to flourish is hopeful. And it is this search for hope that truly separates Marcel from the idealists. It allows the subject to be a *homo viator*, the one on a journey, in which the subject's meaning is concretely and inextricably tied to the journey of others. This is, after all, what Marcel thought distinguished his view from those which influenced it. The answer to the question *Who am I that asks the question, 'Who am I'?* cannot be found in a biography, a list of roles, activities, net worth, or (even) relationships. It is an answer whose contours are drawn by *my journey*—never fully answered, but always in progress.

Notes

1. Gabriel Marcel, *The Philosophy of Existentialism*, trans. M. Harari (New York, NY: Citadel Press, 1949), 104.
2. Gabriel Marcel, *The Existential Background of Human Dignity* (Cambridge: Harvard University Press, 1963), 19–20.
3. Gabriel Marcel, *The Metaphysical Journal*, trans. B. Wall (London: Rockliff, 1952), 45.
4. Ibid, 320.
5. Ibid.
6. Marcel, *Philosophy of Existentialism*, 104.
7. Marcel, *Existential Background of Human Dignity*, 97.
8. Johann Gottlieb Fichte, *The Science of Knowledge: With the First and Second Introductions* (Cambridge: Cambridge University Press, 1982), section 7, *Werke* 1, 440.
9. Marcel, *Existential Background of Human Dignity*, 97.
10. Marcel, *Philosophy of Existentialism*, 109.
11. Harold Baldwin Hoyt, "The Concept of the Dehumanization of Man in the Philosophy of Gabriel Marcel" (Ph.D. diss., University of Oklahoma, 1970), 8–9.
12. Marcel, *Philosophy of Existentialism*, 120.

13. Marcel, *Metaphysical Journal*, 329.
14. Marcel, *Existential Background of Human Dignity*, 13–14.
15. Ibid., 29–30.
16. Gabriel Marcel, *Metaphysical Journal* (Chicago, IL: Regnery, 1967), 129.
17. Of course, a reason Marcel later abandoned idealism writ large was because he saw it as a view that deconstructed philosophical systems only to create a new one. See Thomas C. Anderson, *A Commentary on Gabriel Marcel's The Mystery of Being*, (Milwaukee, WI: Marquette University Press, 2006), 148.
18. Gabriel Marcel, *Man against Mass Society*, trans. G. S. Fraser (Chicago, IL: Regnery, 1962), 2.
19. Marcel, *Philosophy of Existentialism*, 109.
20. Anderson, *Commentary on Gabriel Marcel*, 181.
21. Ibid., 148.
22. Kenneth T. Gallagher, *The Philosophy of Gabriel Marcel* (New York, NY: Fordham University Press, 1962), 121.
23. Marcel, *Man against Mass Society*, 155.
24. Thomas Flynn, "Toward the Concrete: Marcel as Existentialist," *American Catholic Philosophical Quarterly* 80, no. 3 (Summer 2006): 357; translation of Jean Wahl, *Vers le concret. Etudes d'histoire de la philosophie contemporaine,* 2nd ed. (Paris: Vrin, 2004), 187.
25. Marcel vacillates between the question "What am I?" and "Who am I?" before landing on the question, "Who am I that asks the question 'Who am I?'" (Gabriel Marcel, *The Mystery of Being, Volume 1: Reflection and Mystery*, trans. G. S. Fraser [Chicago, IL: Regnery, 1950], 125).
26. Marcel, *Existential Background of Human Dignity*, 78.
27. Ibid., 78–79.
28. Ibid., 46.
29. Marcel became keen to repudiate idealism's ability to understand the self as body, because of its need to objectify. Marcel cautioned against the temptation to conceive of the body through a materialist framework, which is understood through primary reflection. "What possible sense could there be," he wrote, "in saying 'I am my body' if my body could be reduced to an extended thing to be exhaustively characterized in terms of objective science? I was even led to introduce the idea of what I called the 'body-subject,' that is, the body insofar as it is inaccessible to the manipulations, real or ideal, to which the scientist can and must submit extended things" (*Existential Background of Human Dignity*, 46).
30. Ibid, 78.
31. Sebestien Mongo-Behon, "The Existential Analysis of Evil and Its Impact on Human Freedom and Hope in the Philosophy of Gabriel Marcel" (Ph.D. diss., Catholic University of America, 1999), 50–61.
32. John R. Crocker, "Realism of Gabriel Marcel" (MA thesis, Loyola University Chicago, 1959), 35.
33. Anderson, *Commentary on Gabriel Marcel*, 53.

34. Marcel, *Existential Background of Human Dignity*, 102.

35. Peter James McNelis, "The 'Social Self' in Social Work Theory and Practice. A Study and Synthesis of the Social Thought of John Dewey and Gabriel Marcel" (Ph.D. diss., Tulane University, 1972), 172.

36. Thomas A. Michaud, "Secondary Reflection and Marcelian Anthropology," *Philosophy Today* 34 (Fall 1990): 223.

37. Gabriel Marcel, *Being and Having*, trans. K. Farrer (New York, NY: Harper and Row, 1965), 117.

38. Rudolf Gerber, "Marcel's Phenomenology of the Human Body," *International Philosophical Quarterly* 4, no. 3 (1964): 453.

39. Louis Pamplume and Beth Brombert, "Gabriel Marcel: Existence, Being, and Faith," *Yale French Studies* 12 (1953): 92.

40. Marcel, *Existential Background of Human Dignity*, 96.

41. Marcel, *Mystery of Being: Volume 1*, 108.

42. Ibid., 90.

43. Marcel, *Existential Background of Human Dignity*, 41.

44. F. C. Copelston, "Existentialism," *Philosophy* 23, no. 84 (Jan. 1948): 37.

45. Marcel, *Existential Background of Human Dignity*, 18.

46. Sam Keen, "The Development of the Idea of Being in Marcel's Thought," in *The Philosophy of Gabriel Marcel: The Library of Living Philosophers*, ed. P. A. Schlipp and L. E. Hahn, vol. 17 (LaSalle, IL: Open Court, 1984), 103.

47. Marcel, *Mystery of Being: Volume 1*, 83.

48. Ibid., 121.

49. I identify the differences between Marcel's primary, secondary, and reflexive reflection in Jill Hernandez, "Gabriel Marcel," *Internet Encyclopedia of Philosophy*, https://www.iep.utm.edu/marcel/.

50. Chad Engelland, "Marcel and Heidegger on the Proper Matter and Manner of Thinking," *Philosophy Today* 48, no. 1 (1995): 96.

51. Gabriel Marcel, *Creative Fidelity* (New York, NY: Noonday Press, 1970), 22.

52. Marcel, *Existential Background of Human Dignity*, 18.

53. Ibid., 165.

54. Thomas C. Anderson, "The Nature of the Human Self according to Gabriel Marcel," *Philosophy Today* 29, no. 4 (Winter 1985): 273.

55. Copleston, "Existentialism," 37.

56. Marcel, *Philosophy of Existentialism*, 127.

57. Marcel, *Metaphysical Journal*, 129.

58. Crocker, "Realism of Gabriel Marcel," 130.

59. Marcel to John R. Crocker, 4 December 1954, in Crocker, "Realism of Gabriel Marcel," 134.

60. Bertrand Russell, *The Autobiography of Bertrand Russell, Vol 1* (New York, NY: Bantam, 1968), 245–46.

61. Donald Stewart, "Man and Fidelity: A Study in Marcel" (Ph.D. diss., University of Hawaii, 1969), 129.

62. Anderson, "Nature of the Human Self according to Gabriel Marcel," 62.

63. Marcel (and contributors) explore this view in the last book he published, an edited anthology entitled *Fresh Hope for the World* (London: Longmans, Green & Co., 1960), 211.

64. Gallagher, *Philosophy of Gabriel Marcel,* xii.

65. Gabriel Marcel, *Homo Viator: Introduction to a Metaphysics of Hope,* trans. Emma Craufurd (Chicago, IL: Harper & Row, 1965), 10.

66. Gabriel Marcel, *Tragic Wisdom and Beyond,* trans. S. Jolin and P. McCormick (Evanston, IL: Northwestern University Press, 1973), 143.

67. Marcel, *Being and Having,* 108–9.

68. Gabriel Marcel, *Le Palais de Sable,* 389–390, in Gabriel Marcel, *Le Seuil Invisible* (Paris: B. Grasset, 1914), 212–398, as quoted and translated by Marcel, *Existential Background of Human Dignity,* 33–4. The first English translation of the full volume was recently published, *The Invisible Threshold,* ed. B. Sweetman, G. Karabin, and M. Traub, trans. G. Karabin and M. Traub (South Bend: St. Augustine's Press, 2019).

69. Marcel, *Existential Background of Human Dignity,* 34.

70. Ibid., 35.

71. Marcel, *Tragic Wisdom and Beyond,* 8.

6

Freedom in Sartre's Phenomenology: The Kantian Limits of a Radical Project

Sorin Baiasu

Sartre's phenomenological existentialism can be safely characterized as a philosophy that places significant emphasis on freedom.[1] The view of freedom Sartre's phenomenological existentialism is standardly taken to promote is radical.[2] As he often presents his views on freedom by contrast with Kant's, his existentialism is regarded as a radicalization of the Kantian account. Given this radical character, Sartre's existentialism is often criticized for its implausible implications. In what follows, I would like to challenge this reading. I focus on one perspective from which freedom is usually discussed and from which existentialism appears as radical. I show that the implausible implications usually attributed to existentialism do not in fact apply. I argue that this reading of Sartre is plausible, since he does object to some aspects of Kant's account. By objecting to Kant in this way, he seems to intend to take his own account in a different, more radical direction. Nevertheless, while Sartre's view of freedom is radicalized by comparison to Kant's, this is the case in a different sense than that standardly attributed to him and without the implausible implications for which he is usually criticized.

S. Baiasu (✉)
Keele University, Keele, UK
e-mail: s.baiasu@keele.ac.uk

107

C. D. Coe (eds.), *The Palgrave Handbook of German Idealism and Phenomenology*,
Palgrave Handbooks in German Idealism,
https://doi.org/10.1007/978-3-030-66857-0_6

In the next section, I distinguish between two claims concerning the radical character of Sartre's account of freedom, I identify their radical implications, and I present some objections formulated to these interpretations or to recent accounts of freedom that are taken to follow in Sartre's footsteps. The third section explains why such a reading is plausible by focusing on a particular objection Sartre formulates to Kant's account of freedom and on the solution he proposes. The fourth section undermines this reading by challenging one of the claims of radicalization. I show that the implausible implication usually criticized does not follow from the account of freedom advanced by phenomenological existentialism. Before I conclude, I show in the fifth section that Sartre avoids the implausible radicalization of Kant's view of freedom considered here, but his view of freedom makes some significant steps away from Kant's account.

The Kantian Background of Sartre's Existentialism

How radical is Sartre's account of freedom? Following a standard reading, quite radical, since it manifests this character both for its conception of what is usually termed "negative" freedom and for its account of autonomy or "positive" freedom. Thus, on the one hand, existentialism is understood as defending a libertarian view of freedom, according to which to be free is to be free from all constraints.[3] This "negative" understanding of freedom—an understanding in terms of what freedom is *not*, namely constraints—suggests Sartre is an incompatibilist, who regards freedom and determinism as incompatible and defends a view of moral agents as free.[4] Call the version of existentialism which asserts this view of negative freedom "libertarian existentialism."

On the other hand, however, Sartrean phenomenological existentialism is also regarded as taking a moral agent's autonomy to the extreme. On this reading, existentialism considers a moral agent as autonomous in the sense of being self-governing. This understanding of freedom is "positive," since it specifies how a moral agent should be in order to be free (to wit, self-governing), rather than presenting it negatively by specifying how the agent should not be (namely, constrained). To govern oneself or others, however, we need a law or set of laws, and existentialism is read as departing from a conception of these laws as merely adopted by the agent in virtue of their validity; instead, on this reading, Sartrean phenomenological existentialism regards a moral agent as autonomous when she authors the standards through which she governs herself.[5] Such standards are not formulated independently from the individual agent, who would then merely adopt them and self-legislate accordingly; instead, they are created by the moral agent, who then governs herself through them. Call this version of existentialism, which asserts this interpretation of positive freedom, "constructivist existentialism."

It is important to note that the negative and positive notions of freedom do not refer to different things—different types of freedom; instead, they are two related ways of presenting the same thing—a free agent. In fact, we can see that the constructivist existentialist view of freedom as autonomy is a particular case of the libertarian existentialist view of freedom presented negatively. If freedom is defined negatively as the absence of constraints, then one particular case of this view of freedom is the case of a free agent who is not constrained in her self-governance by a law or laws formulated independently from her, but who constructs her own standards and governs herself through them. Existentialist autonomy, on this reading, is the result of removing the constraint of a law of self-governance formulated and justified independently from the individual agent.

Interestingly, both these readings of phenomenological existentialism can be seen as historically motivated by the attempt to radicalize a Kantian account of freedom. Moreover, as we will see, in discussing his account of freedom, Sartre often compares his views with Kant's. Although Kant is sometimes read as a libertarian about the metaphysics of freedom, he is by no means a standard libertarian, since he accepts that our actions, while in one sense possibly free from the constraints of the laws of nature, are, in a different sense, determined by these laws.[6] By rejecting this deterministic dimension of the Kantian view of freedom, phenomenological existentialism is read as an extreme version of libertarianism.

Moreover, Kant's account of autonomy defends a view of freedom as self-legislation, but the law through which this process of self-governance is to take place—the Moral Law—is a law which is not authored by the individual agent, but is a structure of practical reason and is justified as normative without reference to aspects of individual agency. By rejecting the status of this law as independent from the individual agent as individual, phenomenological existentialism seems to take to an extreme the Kantian view of autonomy.

Both the libertarian and the constructivist existentialisms, as radical conceptions of freedom, end up with some implausible implications. According to the libertarian account, we are free from all constraints, including the constraints of the laws of nature, and, hence, we can always act freely. Yet this leads to the implausible implication that we are free even in the contexts of very oppressive institutions; moreover, in the context of institutions which generate systemic injustice, the assumption that we are radically free renders any emancipatory discourse superfluous.[7]

According to the constructivist account, we are free whenever we act in accordance with the standards we construct, although it is unclear whether such a process of construction could not be conditioned or even determined by certain internalized norms; furthermore, even assuming that the process of construction is free from such constraints, we end up with the implausible suggestion that acting in accordance with arbitrarily constructed standards would have to be accepted as free agency.[8]

The first charge relies on a reading of Sartre's view of freedom as involved in the traditional metaphysical debate between free will and determinism. Sartre does talk about this debate but frames it in different terms: not as a dispute between a claim to the existence or non-existence of uncaused action, but of an action without motive. The traditional reading might be explained by the choice, in the most popular translation of *Being and Nothingness*, of the French "*motif*" by "cause."[9] For instance, Sartre's claim (at EN 435–36, 480) is not that no factual state can by itself *cause* an act, but that it cannot by itself *motivate* it. Moreover, Sartre does not simply talk about freedom but distinguishes between various aspects of free agency. On Sartre's account actions are always motivated by reasons, and while actions may always be ontologically free, politically they may well be constrained and may need a discourse of emancipation for the individual's liberation.[10]

As already mentioned in the first section, in what follows, I would like to focus on the second charge of implausibility. I will eventually argue that Sartre's account of autonomy is not as radical as standardly interpreted, but accepts the main limitation of the Kantian account that he was taken to remove, although there are aspects of the Kantian account with which he parts company. It follows that Sartre's existentialist phenomenology avoids the implausible position of the constructivist existentialist, although it departs from Kant's position in the attempt to draw more consistently some of the conclusions of the Kantian project. In this way, Sartre's phenomenological existentialism paradoxically turns out to be closer to Kant's account of freedom than he is to the accounts of some contemporary existentialist Kantians.

Now, one question we can begin with is why Sartre has been interpreted as defending a constructivist version of existentialism. Answering this question will be the task of the next section.

Sartre as Constructivist Existentialist

In the second part of *Being and Nothingness*, entitled "Being-for-Itself," Sartre discusses freedom in the context of a section devoted more generally to "Temporality"; there, in part B ("The dynamics of temporality") of the second sub-section ("The Ontology of Temporality"), he contrasts his view of freedom with Kant's account of the spontaneity of a person. Thus, he claims:

> It would be useless to remind us of the passages in the *Critique* where Kant shows that a non-temporal spontaneity is inconceivable, but not contradictory. It seems to us, on the contrary, that a spontaneity which would not escape from itself and which would not escape from that very escape, of which we could say, "It is this," and which would allow itself to be enclosed in an unchangeable denomination — it seems that such a spontaneity would be precisely a contradiction and that it would ultimately be the equivalent of a particular affirmative essence, the eternal subject which is never a predicate. (EN 171, 188)[11]

This is a complex passage, which needs considerable unpacking. For our purposes, however, it will suffice to provide an outline of Sartre's objection in order to see what motivates the interpretation of his account of freedom as a version of constructivist existentialism.[12] We can perhaps already grasp the gist of Sartre's criticism: the general objection is that Kant provides a contradictory account of freedom as non-temporal spontaneity. Without yet mentioning the Kantian context of this objection, we can already outline the argument Sartre advances. For him, change presupposes time. A non-temporal spontaneity, therefore, should be unchanging. As unchanging, spontaneity is viewed as possessing a character that cannot be modified. More precisely, not even a self-generated modification of spontaneity would be viewed as conceivable. Yet the idea of spontaneity is that of self-motivated possible manifestation unrestricted by any pre-set direction as given by a fixed character. Hence, the Kantian idea of a non-temporal spontaneity is contradictory. The free agent understood as non-temporally spontaneous is congealed in an "unchangeable denomination," that of "the eternal subject which is never a predicate."

Although Sartre clearly points here to a contradiction in Kant's idea of freedom as spontaneity, the details of some of the claims are unclear without a brief discussion of Kant's account. The reference seems to be clearly to the discussion of the third antinomy in the *Critique of Pure Reason* (A445–51/B473–79).[13] This is part of Transcendental Dialectic, the second division of Transcendental Logic,[14] where Kant examines the contradictory claims at which we arrive by following logically the claims of reason. On Kant's account, an epistemic agent has the capacity to be affected by the world through her sensibility, the capacity to cognize the world through the understanding (which unifies under concepts what the sensibility senses through being affected by the world), and the capacity to unify this cognition by reason. In the attempt to unify this cognition, reason leads us to make claims about the world as a whole.

We may claim, for instance, that everything in the world, including ourselves, is determined by the laws of nature and there is no freedom. In this case, we are hard determinists. We may equally well claim that not everything in the world is determined by laws of nature and there is freedom. Such a claim is made by libertarians. The two claims are contradictory or antinomical—hence, the name of this contradiction. It is possible for equally rational claims to be contradictory, because these are claims about an object we cannot experience—namely, the world as a whole. Claims about objects which we cannot experience are speculative. Such claims generate controversies between speculative metaphysicians, claims between which we cannot adjudicate. Kant thinks that the existence of such contradiction and controversies is a "scandal" and he is, of course, in a certain sense right (Bxxxiv).[15]

Kant's attempt in the *Critique of Pure Reason* is to deal with this scandal by setting reason on "the secure path of a science" (Bvii). He thinks that his transcendental idealism can show that both antinomical claims concerning freedom are correct, but from different perspectives. In this way, the contradiction in which reason entangles itself is dissolved. His solution to the third antinomy, at least in its very general outline, is well known. From the perspective of what we experience, the perspective of phenomena, everything in the world is determined in accordance with the laws of nature. However, from the perspective of things as they are in themselves, independently from our experience, the world is not determined by the laws of nature and we are free. Hence the thesis ("[t]he causality according to laws of nature is not the only causality, … it is necessary also to assume a causality through freedom") and the antithesis ("[t]here is no freedom, but everything in the world occurs solely according to laws of nature") are no longer contradictory.

This background enables us to understand better Sartre's argument above. Since Kant regards space and time as structures of sensibility, things in themselves, including ourselves regarded as such, are non-temporal. Moreover, since "cause" is a category of the understanding, through which we constitute in our experience the world of phenomena, again, an agent, considered as a being in itself, will be spontaneous, independent from any constraints imposed by natural laws. Sartre is slightly confused when he claims that Kant's freedom is inconceivable [*inconcevable*], but not contradictory. According to Kant, freedom is not cognizable [*erkenntbar*], but it is conceivable or thinkable; in fact to be thinkable is to be free from contradiction for him.[16]

If we understand freedom, with Kant,[17] as the property of a being to which I attribute effects in the world of sense, then there is a way to see freedom as non-contradictory, despite the fact that, with Kant, we view all effects in the world of sense as subject to the laws of nature. More exactly, it is sufficient to accept another kind of causality, that of the spontaneous agent considered in itself, in order to be able to see the effects produced by this alternative causality, even if they are regarded phenomenally, as attributable to the agent, rather than to the laws of nature. The freedom of the agent is, in this way, non-contradictory. It is, however, not cognizable, since, for Kant, cognition requires both concepts and intuitions, and we can have no experience (and hence sensible intuitions) of the agent, regarded as in itself.[18]

The contradiction in the Kantian notion of freedom introduced by the third antinomy is removed by Kant's solution to the antinomy. Yet Sartre continues to regard the Kantian conception of freedom as contradictory. This is because he takes Kant to give a particular determination to freedom, "an unchangeable denomination," a "particular affirmative essence," which makes it impossible even "to escape from itself," let alone "escape from that very escape." We will see shortly how on the dominant interpretation of Sartre's account of freedom, the free agency can be seen as able not only to escape from itself, but also to escape from that very escape. These two conditions are taken by Sartre to be implications of an account of freedom as spontaneity. Yet Kant's account seems unable to meet them: If freedom has such an affirmative essence, as "the eternal subject which is never a predicate," then it cannot escape itself, since to escape itself is equivalent to abandoning this affirmative essence and abandoning this essence is equivalent to becoming something else than freedom (since by definition the essence of something is that without which that thing cannot exist as the thing it is).

To see why Sartre reads in Kant a notion of freedom with an affirmative essence as the eternal subject which is never a predicate, it is sufficient to reflect on the status of the free agent. An agent is regarded as free from the perspective of things as they are in themselves. As such, a free agent is not cognizable and, hence, not predicable—it is similar to an eternal subject, which is never a predicate.

Sartre does not suggest that the Kantian account of freedom should be altogether rejected. He regards Kant's account of freedom as spontaneity as correct, but he thinks Kant's account of spontaneity must be modified. As we have seen, the modification must allow the free agent to be genuinely spontaneous, and Sartre seems to suggest an alternative notion of spontaneity as autonomy: "*This* spontaneity should be allowed to define itself; this means both that it is the foundation not only of its nothingness of being, but also of its being and that simultaneously this being recaptures it to fix it in the given" (EN 171, 188 — translation slightly amended). If the spontaneous being is self-defining, then there is no affirmative essence, which would congeal the supposedly free agent and would undermine its spontaneity. This view of the genuinely free agent as an autonomous spontaneity seems to be the response Sartre provides to the problem he identifies in Kant's solution to the third antinomy.

It is easy to see now why Sartre's existentialism is read as a version of constructivist existentialism. Sartre does suggest that freedom is best conceived of in terms of autonomy, and he clearly sees this autonomy as radical. The agent is self-defining, the "foundation not only of its nothingness of being, but also of its being," a spontaneity which can "escape from itself" and can also "escape from that very escape" (EN 171, 188). The view of the agent as autonomous in the Kantian sense, as governed by a law the individual agent adopts, but which is not formulated or defined by the agent herself, since it is shared necessarily by all rational agents, would be a view of a spontaneity that may escape itself (escapes its individuality and governs itself according to a law, which is her law insofar as she is a rational being), but cannot further escape this very escape (the law cannot be defined by the agent herself, but can only be adopted as valid).

While it may be now understandable why Sartre is sometimes read as a constructivist existentialist, I have claimed that, in fact, this is not an accurate reading. I have claimed that, in fact, Sartre's phenomenological existentialism is closer to Kant's account of freedom than it is to the constructivist version of some of today's existentialist theories. Nevertheless, there is one respect in which Sartre's phenomenological existentialism is more radical than a Kantian account of freedom and specifically than a Kantian account of autonomy. To show these will be the purpose of the next two sections.

Sartre's Account of Freedom and Its Kantian Limitations

The implausible implications of a constructivist existentialist account of freedom follow from the specific view of autonomy held by this account. In particular, this view of autonomy requires that the standard through which the moral agent governs herself be her creation. This requirement must be understood in a specific sense. Imagine a Kantian account of action, according to which human agency is centered on maxims, and maxims are created or devised by agents depending on circumstances and personal features.[19] A Kantian account of autonomy requires that these maxims be objective principles. To determine whether a maxim (which is a subjective principle of action) is an objective principle, we employ the Categorical Imperative.[20] For instance, universalizable maxims are morally permissible and may even be required as categorical imperatives. Hence, acting on such maxims would be autonomous on the Kantian account. Yet it would not be on the constructivist existentialist one, although maxims are created by the agent. This is because the principles of action of the autonomous agent depend normatively on the Categorical Imperative. This, however, is not created by the agent, but it is a structure of practical reason of all moral agents.

To show that the implausible implications of constructivist existentialism do not follow from Sartre's account of freedom, I need to show two claims. Firstly, I will defend the claim that, on Sartre's phenomenological existentialism, not any standard of action devised by the agent is an expression of the agent's autonomy. Secondly, I will argue that the condition which must be met in order for a standard to be an expression of an agent's autonomy is not some arbitrary condition. On the contrary, it is a normative criterion which Sartre takes to be normative for all moral agents. For the first claim, it is sufficient to focus on Sartre's distinction between pure and impure reflection. For the second, we can examine his view of authenticity. On the basis of this value he distinguishes between standards of action which are expressive of freedom as autonomy, and those which are not.

I started the last section with a long quotation from the second part of *Being and Nothingness* entitled "Being-for-Itself." Being-for-itself is a central concept of Sartre's early philosophy, a concept which Sartre still uses in his later philosophy to explain some of the new terminology he introduces there.[21] The notion is part of Sartre's distinction between being-for-itself and being-in-itself, usually simplified to the distinction between the for-itself and the in-itself.[22] These represent two regions of being, corresponding approximately to individual conscious beings and inanimate beings—a person is sometimes referred to by Sartre simply by "for-itself" and an inanimate being by "in-itself." Now, for Sartre, the for-itself's reflective consciousness, whether pure or impure, is one among several forms of consciousness of the for-itself. It is a form of self-consciousness, but relies on a more fundamental form of self-consciousness, called pre-reflective self-consciousness. Moreover, reflective consciousness is a positional type of consciousness. Hence, before introducing the distinction between the for-itself's pure and impure reflective consciousness, we need to examine three other distinctions: between immediate and positional consciousness, between consciousness and self-consciousness, and, finally, between reflective and pre-reflective self-consciousness.

Consider first the distinction between immediate or non-positional consciousness and positional consciousness. When I am perceiving something, I may be conscious of that thing in virtue of an immediate consciousness that I have with regard to it. For instance, most of the time, we are surrounded by countless sounds, which we perceive, but which we do not get to take as the focus of our attention. Immediate consciousness of such sounds is not positional—it will not present its object as coming from a determinate place or as bearing particular properties. Hence, immediate consciousness is not able to make judgments with regard to the world, because it does not posit the object that it perceives. It may, however, subsequently focus on the object and posit it.

Consider now the situation when I am judging something, such as the quality of the paper of the book I am reading. Although, in this instance, I am positing the page and I am involved in the activity of judging the quality of its paper, I may not be reflectively conscious of doing this; on the contrary, I may be absorbed by my activity to the point of forgetting about myself. The focus of my activity is, therefore, the transcendent object of my attention (the page), not my activities, what I am doing.[23]

This leads to the distinction between consciousness and self-consciousness. Self-consciousness, as the name indicates, takes itself as an object. When I am positing my own conscious activities, I am self-conscious and, moreover, I am reflecting on myself. By contrast, when I am positing an object distinct from myself without also positing myself as doing this, I am simply conscious of that object. Finally, consider the distinction between reflective and pre-reflective self-consciousness. Although in the example above, I am trying to establish the quality of the book's paper, I am not reflectively aware of doing this. Yet I cannot say that I am not conscious of myself as doing this. In my mind the thought that it is me who is doing such-and-such a thing does not occur, but I can always explain what I am doing, if someone asks me.

However, I can only explain now what I have just done, if what I have done is inscribed somehow in my memory as having been done by me. But this is not possible, if I have not been somehow aware of myself as having done such-and-such a thing while doing it. Hence, one can be reflectively or pre-reflectively aware of oneself as doing something depending on whether or not one is positionally aware of oneself as doing that. According to Sartre, any form of consciousness is at the same time pre-reflectively conscious of itself. Hence, my positional consciousness of the book in front of me is also pre-reflectively conscious of itself as such a consciousness. This pre-reflective self-consciousness is distinct from reflective consciousness (consciousness of self) and, to mark this difference, Sartre calls it "consciousness (of) self" (EN liv, 20). Reflective self-consciousness presupposes a positional consciousness of oneself, whereby one's self is posited as an object (an "I" or ego). By contrast, pre-reflective self-consciousness or consciousness (of) self, as pre-reflective, cannot be posited, since it would then have to become an object for a positional consciousness and, hence, simply part of a reflective process.

Now, for Sartre, there is a constitutive similarity between self and value (EN 117, 131). The self is for the for-itself what a value is for our actions. We act in pursuit of certain values—some more distant, such as long-term projects and ideals, some more quickly achievable, such as more immediate goals or the satisfaction of certain desires or needs. Pursuing a value implies bringing about states of affairs which realize that value and without which current states of affairs are perceived as lacking in that respect.

Similarly, the for-itself lacks something in relation to the self and constantly attempts to eliminate this lack and achieve the fullness of the self. Through reflection I can determine what I am lacking, what I need to achieve in order to obtain the fullness of self. Self-sufficiency is the stage where the for-itself achieves independence, since it becomes its own foundation: It becomes at the same time an in-itself, which is not lacking, since it simply is, and a for-itself, which alone is able to make sense of things, such as lack, sufficiency and value. This is why Sartre sometimes calls this ideal of a self-sufficient, full self, the "for-itself-in-itself."

We can now examine the distinction between pure and impure reflection. Impure reflection posits the consciousness reflected-on as an object having the ontological structure of an in-itself. This, however, is not a legitimate process, since the consciousness reflected-on, as consciousness, is at the same time a for-itself. Impure reflection attempts to cognize the consciousness reflected-on, that is, to take it as a given in-itself, and not simply to recognize it as already revealed.

The consciousness reflected on by impure reflection is thus transformed into an object of psychic life. For instance, in the attempt to reach self-sufficiency, the for-itself may try to overcome its lack through certain actions. Through these actions the for-itself tries to change the world, which seems to be lacking. In trying to identify the missing part of its self, the for-itself's impure consciousness will reflect on the for-itself and will perceive its lack (and the value of the actions which try to change the world to overcome this lack) as a transcendent unity. Instead of seeing the consciousness reflected-on with its desires, purposes, and hopes as part of consciousness and, hence, the result of freedom, impure reflection turns them into objective entities which transcend consciousness and determine it. The unification performed by impure reflective consciousness posits a particular end of the action as given, rather than as chosen. Every act is the result of a synthesis of different consciousnesses reflected-on. Impure reflective consciousness turns them into transcending unities.

> By acts we must understand all synthetic activity of the person, that is, every disposition of means with a view to ends, not as the for-itself is its own possibilities but as the act represents a transcendent psychic synthesis which the for-itself must live. For example, the boxer's training is an act because it transcends and supports the for-itself, which, moreover, realizes itself in and through this training. (EN 185, 202)

Hence, impure reflection synthesizes and objectifies the result, losing sight of the for-itself, whose possibilities are in this way turned into necessities. Therefore, on the level of the act constituted as an object by impure reflective consciousness, my freedom is simply that of realizing the already given ends.

On the level of impure consciousness the person's sensible desires, emotions, and beliefs are objects that are causally determined by other objects. Hence, one does not see oneself as actually realizing an end or as attempting to realize it, but as determined (causally led) to attempt to realize it. Impure reflection and bad faith are very closely related. Impure reflection is reflection in bad faith, and bad faith is an attitude brought about by impure reflection. In other words, impure reflection and bad faith are mutually constitutive. Sartre explicitly denies the deterministic interpretation of the person on the level of impure reflection. The very idea of transforming a psychological state into an object of reflection presupposes the freedom of the for-itself to make explicit and modify reflectively a consciousness (of) acting into the object of positional consciousness. Hence, by making use of freedom in order to present an account of agency as devoid of freedom, "this reflection is in bad faith" (EN 187, 201).

As against impure reflection, existential psychoanalysis reveals "the ideal meaning of all human attitudes," and the fact that this ideal meaning—as a particular value—is ultimately contingent (EN 646, 690). Sartre claims that existential psychoanalysis is in fact practiced by "many men" even before they have learned "its principles." It is, in other words, a practice which need not have its method explicitly presented in order for a person to engage in it. Since it is a means of escaping bad faith, Sartre also calls it a "moral description" (EN 645, 690).

Existential psychoanalysis aims to realize that catharsis which transforms impure reflection into pure reflective consciousness, since existential psycho-analysis attempts to provide the person with that degree of self-consciousness which, as we will see in the next section, enables her to become aware of her fundamental project. The free choice underlying this fundamental project shows that an action or a psychic state is not determined but is only conditioned by the world.

Hence, a preliminary conclusion we can draw here is that not any projects through which a person defines herself can be considered as ethically good. If such projects are not regarded as grounded in a person's freedom, then their value is not ethically good. Moreover, what drives this criterion for the moral evaluation of a person's project is the value of authenticity, which is seen as valid for all moral agents. These are the two claims I formulated at the beginning of this section as sufficient to demonstrate that Sartre's phenomenological existentialism is not constructivist, in the radical and implausible sense mentioned at the beginning of this chapter. Hence, in this respect, Sartre is closer to Kant than to some contemporary existentialist constructivists.

I have said that another aim of this chapter is to argue that Sartre's phenomenological existentialism does attempt to radicalize Kant's moral theory, but it is not in the sense in which it is usually interpreted to do so. To show this will be the aim of the next section.

Sartre's Moral Theory as a Radicalization of Kantian Ethics

In what follows, my claim will be that Sartre's and Kant's moral theories are structurally similar, but there is a sense in which Sartre introduces into his account some radical aspects. In particular, the second-order standard on the basis of which we can evaluate the moral choices of the agents is in Sartre's case a second-order value, not a law. Moreover, for Sartre, the standards which structure a person's agency are not principles, but values. Whereas in Kant rules of action are guided by the principles the person adopts, in Sartre they are guided by the values they pursue.

On Sartre's account, every action has an end, which can be seen as the instantiation of a more general project. For instance, if I plan to run a marathon, I must also plan to run a few miles every day, and this was the end or purpose of my running this morning. Moreover, for Sartre, even this more general project of running a marathon can be understood on the basis of a more profound project:

> The problem indeed is to disengage the meanings implied by an act—by every act—and to proceed from there to the richer and more profound meanings until we encounter the meaning which does not imply any other meaning and which refers only to itself. This ascending dialectic is practiced spontaneously by most people; it can even be established that in knowledge of oneself or of another there is given a spontaneous comprehension of this hierarchy of interpretations. (EN 457, 535)

To see this more clearly, consider the following example that Sartre discusses in *Being and Nothingness*: I start out on a hike and after several hours my fatigue increases until it becomes painful; I may then either try to resist it and go on walking, or I may give up and let myself fall down beside my knapsack. Here and in general, each of my acts is comprehensible in terms of its end: "I place my knapsack down in order to rest for a moment" (EN 460, 537). The importance of resting at that point is comprehensible from the perspective of a more general end—perhaps that of wanting to have enough energy left to enjoy the evening properly, where enjoyment is one of the more general ends of my actions. Alternatively, I could go on walking in order to overcome this limit, as part of a general project of undertaking physical training, where enjoying an evening, rather than going directly to bed, is no longer part of my end.

The "ascending dialectic" through which Sartre thinks we "disengage the meaning implied by an act—by every act" is part of the cathartic process of existential psychoanalysis presented in the previous section. As we have seen, the aim of this process is to provide a moral description through which the for-itself can escape bad faith. It is this process practiced by many persons even before they have learned its principle or, as he says above, it is "spontaneously practiced by most people."

One important objection Sartre formulates in relation to Kant's ethics concerns the distinction between imperatives and values. More exactly, the key distinguishing feature that Sartre identifies in the comparison between imperatives and values is their normative force. In order for a value to determine my will to act, I have to choose its end as my possibility. This end is normative ("to be realized") insofar as I chose it; otherwise, it does not determine my will and cannot motivate me.

By contrast, in order for an imperative to be a moral imperative, and hence to be normative, an actual choice of its purpose as my possibility is not required. In short, values require actual choice, whereas imperatives do not. What is more, as Sartre acknowledges, even if I tried to choose an imperative, I could still not choose its purpose as my possibility, since its normative force goes beyond my actual choice of a purpose: "[E]ven if all our desires were conformed to our obligation and as a consequence served the pure Will, there would still remain an underlying duality that is the source and ground of all the others" (CM 256, 267). Nevertheless, what Sartre identifies here as a distinction between imperatives and values, and between his account and Kant's account is not so much a difference between two moral theories and type of norms, as a metaethical distinction between a purpose (or a principle), as regarded by a descriptive account of action, and a purpose (or a principle), as presented by a prescriptive account of action. Hence, in order to distinguish between values and imperatives, Sartre makes use of the distinction between a descriptive and a prescriptive account of action.

Thus, when he claims that the end represented by a value is "to be realized," if I actually choose it as my possibility, he formulates the necessary and sufficient condition for a person to act in order to reach, against certain adverse circumstances, an end. This is because, when I choose an end, I regard the end as to be realized and, hence, I act to bring it about. By contrast, when he asserts that the purpose of an imperative is "to be realized" independently of, and even against, my actual choice of it as my possibility, he formulates a condition for how a person ought to act.

For Kant, whether or not a person has adopted a certain principle for the determination of the will and has acted on that principle in a certain situation cannot conclusively help us determine whether the action ought to have been performed. We only learn that the action has been possible, in the sense of being physically possible, but this feasibility is, of course, a necessary condition for both permissible and impermissible principles.

According to Sartre's account, in order to determine whether the end of a value is "to be realized" by a person, we should simply determine whether or not the person has chosen that end; actual choice is in this case both a necessary and a sufficient condition for the normativity of an end. Yet, again on Sartre's account, actual choice is no longer either a necessary or a sufficient condition for the purposes of the normativity of categorical imperatives.

A categorical imperative formulates an obligation and can even claim to obligate a person who chooses to do precisely the opposite of what the categorical imperative commands. The problem with this, however, is that a value or purpose or end will only have normative force if it can still impose an obligation, when they have not actually been chosen as ends of actions. Without such a distinction, whatever value a person happens to adopt, it must be accepted as morally valid. Taken as such, this conclusion encourages again an interpretation of Sartre as a constructivist existentialist about autonomy. It suggests that, on Sartre's account, when a person adopts a standard (a value) and governs herself in accordance with that standard, she is autonomous. Yet, as we have seen, it is not the case that whatever end we adopt, as an end of our action, is also a morally valid end. As Sartre himself acknowledges, values that are chosen in bad faith cannot be morally valid. But since a value which has actually been chosen may not be morally valid, then actual choice cannot be the sufficient condition of moral normativity. And since a value which has not been actually chosen may be morally valid, then actual choice is not even a necessary condition of moral normativity.

This is exactly the situation with Kant's categorical imperatives too: the morally valid imperatives impose an obligation the person ought to follow but cannot determine the person to actually choose it and follow it. For Kant, it is important that this standard be chosen by the person freely because it is the right thing to do. This, however, seems to be also Sartre's requirement— that the standard proposed be followed freely by the person to whom it is proposed, and, hence, be chosen because it is considered to be right.

We end up with two surprising results: an unexpected similarity between Kant's and Sartre's accounts of action and, at the same time, an unexpected difference—the result of Sartre's radicalization of Kant's metaethical views. Thus, for both of them, actions can be described by rules and have ends that represent the projects people have when they act. These projects can also be understood as general policies of action or maxims. Projects and maxims have several rules of action under them and they guide action; hence, they are second-order rules. In turn, these second-order rules seem to be regulated by third-order rules (the categorical imperative, for instance, or the value of authenticity).[24]

Kant's emphasis on rules of action, principles, or maxims and the Categorical Imperative shows that he favors a rule-centered view of action and practical philosophy. By contrast, Sartre's discussion of value, projects, and the higher-order value of authenticity suggests a purpose-centered ethical theory and philosophy of action. There is therefore a radicalization of the Kantian ethical project in Sartre's phenomenological existentialism: the relative rigidity of rules, principles, and imperatives is replaced by the relative flexibility of values, projects, and the ideal of authenticity. Various rules, principles, and imperatives can illustrate the correspondingly same values, projects, and ideal of authenticity. The latter still provide guidance for the agent, and the ideal of authenticity is justified by Sartre as a moral criterion, rather than being formulated by individual agents. It is not here that the radicalization of the Kantian project can be found in Sartre, but in his emphasis on a value- or purpose-centered ethics, as opposed to Kant's rule-centered practical philosophy.

Conclusion

For both Kant and Sartre, freedom is a central value, and the project of an ethical theory or practical philosophy guided by this value is a shared one. This is not surprising: They belong to a tradition of Western modern philosophy, in which human agents adopt as normative standards those standards they freely acknowledge to be valid. Sartre is standardly interpreted as a radical philosopher of freedom, who takes the moral agent to be free from any constraints, including natural laws, relatedly to be the bearer of an absolute responsibility for what happens in the world, and to be autonomous in the constructivist sense of self-legislation by the standards she herself creates. Given that Sartre often formulates his views on freedom by contrast with Kant's account and on the basis of objections to a Kantian account, he is usually regarded as advancing a radicalized version of a Kantian account of freedom.

In this chapter, I have examined some of Sartre's objections to Kant and the way he thinks he can overcome the Kantian problems, in order to explain why he is standardly interpreted as a constructivist existentialist. I have then presented some fundamental aspects of his philosophy of action and ethics, focusing on the central concepts of self, value, possibility, facticity, and reflection. We have seen that impure reflection is a mode of consciousness that presents the world and in particular an agent's values as set-in-stone, already given demands the agent must pursue. By contrast, pure reflection makes evident the freedom of the individual to commit to specific projects in an authentic mode and to pursue these in virtue of their ethical value. This higher-order value of authenticity, which functions as a test of the moral goodness of an agent's projects, shows that the account of autonomy Sartre's phenomenological existentialism advances is not a version of constructivist existentialism. The moral criterion of authenticity is shared by all agents, and it is not a criterion they create and legislate themselves according to it; it is, however, a criterion they adopt due to its validity.

Secondly, we have seen that Sartre's philosophy of action includes some interesting similarities when compared with Kant's account. For Kant, agency is structured by maxims. Agents perform actions whose rules are derived from maxims the agent is committed to. Ethical actions are those actions that are derived from maxims that are at the same time principles, that is, maxims that are valid for all agents who are in the same situation and have the same morally relevant features. Whether or not such maxims are valid is decided in accordance with the Categorical Imperative. Similarly, Sartre takes an agency to be structured by projects, which have purposes that the agent tries to realize through her actions. The more specific purposes of these actions are therefore derived from the projects' purposes. Ethical actions are performed with a view to the realization of ethical projects, and whether or not a project is ethical is decided in accordance with the value of authenticity.

This comparative analysis reinforces the conclusion that Sartre is not a constructivist existentialist à la Korsgaard, but offers an account of freedom and in particular autonomy, which is closer to Kant's account. Yet the same analysis also makes evident a significant difference between Kant's and Sartre's account: the difference between a rule-centered and a purpose-centered practical philosophy. This indicates further that, in fact, Sartre's ethical theory does include an element of radicalization, but perhaps one whose significance has been overlooked by commentators. Sartre still regards an agent's autonomy as made possible by a moral criterion, whose validity is independent from the individual agent, just as Kant does. Yet, unlike Kant, Sartre questions the need for an ethics of rules, principles, and imperatives, and proposes, at least in his early writings, an ethics of purposes, projects, and values, an ethics guided relatively more flexibly by normative standards.

This, however, is only part of the picture of Sartre's existentialist phenomenology. While commentators increasingly discuss the continuity between the early and the later Sartre, they are still to notice the change in Sartre's conception of values and imperatives in the later writings.[25] Although a thorough discussion of this aspect goes beyond the scope of this chapter, research undertaken so far[26] shows both a move closer to Kant, but also a significant way in which Sartre does modify Kant's ethics in the direction of a philosophically more convincing critical ethics.[27]

Notes

1. According to Jonathan Webber, for instance, "as originally defined by Simone de Beauvoir and Jean-Paul Sartre, existentialism is the ethical theory that we ought to treat the freedom at the core of human existence as intrinsically valuable and the foundation of all other values" (Jonathan Webber, *Rethinking Existentialism* [Oxford: Oxford University Press, 2018], 2). Whereas regarding

freedom as central for Sartre's existentialism is not surprising, the interpretation of existentialism as an ethical theory is, I think, more problematic, given Sartre's failed attempts to publish an ethical theory (which is, of course, not to deny the ethically relevant discussions in Sartre's published work, de Beauvoir's *The Ethics of Ambiguity* (trans. Bernard Frechtman [New York: Citadel Press, 1964]) and Sartre's approval of Francis Jeanson's *Sartre and the Problem of Morality* (trans. Robert V. Stone [Bloomington, IN: Indiana University Press, 1980]), as an accurate elaboration of the existentialist ethics implicit in his own works), as well as the significance of the posthumously published or yet unpublished works on or related to ethics (for instance, *Cahiers pour une Morale* [Paris: Gallimard, 1983]; translated as *Notebooks for an Ethics*, trans. David Pellauer [Chicago: University of Chicago Press, 1992]. Hereafter: CM). For conventions concerning the referencing system, see note 11.

2. As we will see in the next section, Sartre's account is read as radical from the two main perspectives freedom is usually discussed.
3. According to Stefanie Grüne, for instance, "for Sartre, in order to maintain that a human being is free it must also be the case that neither his actions nor his choices are causally necessitated by anything" (Stefanie Grüne, "Sartre on Mistaken Sincerity," *European Journal of Philosophy* 11, no. 2 [2003]: 151).
4. Grüne attempts to place Sartre in the contemporary context of the debates between libertarianism, determinism, and compatibilism. This is problematic, since Sartre seems to reject explicitly a libertarian account of freedom and even the debate between libertarianism, determinism, and compatibilism, whereas Grüne contrasts compatibilism with Sartre's account. For a similar interpretation of Sartre, as defending a radical libertarian view of freedom, see also Susan Wolfe (*Freedom Within Reason* [Oxford: Oxford University Press, 1990], 65). Elsewhere I show why this is not the appropriate framework for Sartre's account of freedom and I place his discussion in the appropriate conceptual context (Sorin Baiasu, "Existentialist Freedom, Distorted Normativity, and Emancipation," *Oñati Social-legal Series* 5, no. 3 [2015]: 874–94).
5. This view of autonomy is present also in Christine Korsgaard's account of the sources of normativity and is considered an existentialist aspect of her work. This is well illustrated in the discussions of her position by Gerald Cohen and Thomas Nagel: "In Christine Korsgaard's ethics, the subject of the law is also its author: and that is the ground of the subject's obligation — that *it* is the author of the law that obliges it" (G. A. Cohen, "Reason, Humanity and the Moral Law," in *The Sources of Normativity*, ed. Onora O'Neill [Cambridge: Cambridge University Press, 2000], 170); "[t]hough she accepts the Kantian argument that freedom implies conformity to law, Korsgaard departs from Kant in holding that the content of the law depends on something else, namely our conception of our practical identity. This distinctly unKantian, rather existentialist idea is the heart of her position. It introduces a strong element of contingency and therefore relativism, because depending on how we conceive of ourselves as reflective beings, the law may be egoistic, nationalistic, truly universal, or just

plain wanton" (Thomas Nagel, "Universality and the Reflective Self," in *The Sources of Normativity*, ed. Onora O'Neill [Cambridge: Cambridge University Press, 2000], 203–4). In her reply, Korsgaard acknowledges the existentialist element (Christine Korsgaard, "Reply," in *The Sources of Normativity*, ed. Onora O'Neill [Cambridge: Cambridge University Press, 2000], 237). One implication of this paper is that, against standard readings of existentialism, Sartre turns out in fact to be closer to Kant than to Korsgaard.

6. This leads to what is sometimes taken to be a paradox of Kantian libertarianism. I discuss this paradox and claim to solve it elsewhere (Sorin Baiasu, "Free Will and Determinism: A Solution to the Kantian Paradox," in *The Concept of Will in Classical German Philosophy*, ed. Manja Kisner and Jörg Nöller [Berlin: De Gruyter, 2020], 7–27).

7. For instance, according to Thomas Anderson, "Sartre's views of freedom could lead to a quietistic or Stoical ethics. If human reality is freedom and human freedom is total, absolute, and unlimited, if all situations are equivalent in freedom, then there is no reason to change the concrete conditions in which humans live, even if they appear terribly oppressive" (Thomas C. Anderson, *Sartre's Two Ethics: From Authenticity to Integral Humanity* [Chicago: Open Court, 1993], 25). Associated with this implausible view of negative freedom there seems to be also an implausible notion of responsibility: "What we know as the world is the conglomerate of human projects; there 'is no nonhuman situation.' For example, there are no innocent victims of war. Any war we are in is one we deserve. Human consciousness causes the world to be as it is, and so it is entirely responsible for the world" (Jeanson, *Sartre and the Problem of Morality*, 234–35).

8. Charles Taylor criticizes this aspect of existentialism (Charles Taylor, "What's Wrong with Negative Liberty," in *Philosophy and the Human Sciences*, vol. 2 [Cambridge: Cambridge University Press, 1985]).

9. Sarah Richmond's recent translation renders "*motif*" by "reason," which I think it is much less confusing: Jean-Paul Sartre, *Being and Nothingness: An Essay on Phenomenological Ontology*, trans. Sarah Richmond (London: Routledge, 2018).

10. I have discussed the first charge elsewhere ("Existentialist Freedom, Distorted Normativity, and Emancipation"). I must add that, for the purpose of the comparative discussion of Kant and Sartre, I draw on aspects of a more detailed analysis previously published (Sorin Baiasu, *Kant and Sartre: Re-discovering Critical Ethics* [Basingstoke: Palgrave Macmillan, 2011]).

11. Jean-Paul Sartre, *L'Être et le néant: Essaie d'ontologie phénomènologique* (Paris: Gallimard, 1973); translated as *Being and Nothingness: An Essay on Phenomenological Ontology*, trans. Hazel E. Barnes (New York: Philosophical Library, 1956). Hereafter: EN. For Sartre, abbreviations will be followed by page number of the French edition used. Then, for both Kant and Sartre, the page for the English translations will be given. Emphases are in the original.

12. For a more detailed discussion of this aspect of Sartre's existentialism, see Baiasu, *Kant and Sartre*, esp. ch. 4.

13. Immanuel Kant, *Critique of Pure Reason*, ed. and trans. Werner S. Pluhar (Indianapolis: Hackett, 1996). References to the *Critique of Pure Reason* will follow the A (first edition), B (second edition) convention. In references, abbreviations will be followed by the volume and page number from Kant's *Gesammelte Schriften* (Berlin: vols. 1–22 Preussische Akademie der Wissenschaften; vol. 23 Deutsche Akademie der Wissenschaften zu Belin; vols. 24—Akademie der Wissenschaften zu Göttingen).

14. This represents Part II of the *Critique of Pure Reason* with Part I being devoted to Transcendental Aesthetic.

15. One context for Kant's discussion here is given by scepticism; ancient radical sceptics in the Pyrrhonian tradition used to claim that, for every dogmatic claim, they can defend, with an equally strong argument, the contradictory claim. For them, the result of reflecting on this antinomy was not, as it was for Kant, a scandal; on the contrary, they thought that, in this way, they can suspend judgment [*epoché*] and achieve mental tranquillity or unperturbedness [*ataraxia*], both of which refer to their ideal of the good life (Sextus Empiricus, *Outlines of Pyrrhonism*, trans. Benson Mates [New York: Oxford University Press, 1996], Book 1, §4). It is in this practical sense that Kant's suggestion of a scandal generated by antinomies seems exaggerated and only correct in part.

16. "Now ... from this second standpoint, I cannot ... cognize freedom as the property of a being to which I attribute effects in the world of sense.... Nevertheless, I can still *think* freedom. I.e., at least my presentation of freedom contains no contradiction, if we make our critical distinction between the two ways of presenting (sensible and intellectual)" (Bxxviii).

17. See quotation in the previous note.

18. In the second *Critique*, Kant does see freedom as a practical postulate (4:133). Moreover, he thinks that the postulates of practical reason give objective reality to the ideas of speculative reason, so to freedom too. However, Kant specifies that the postulate is of freedom "considered positively" and that the objective reality of the ideas does not "expand theoretical cognition" (4:133). This explains why in the first *Critique* Kant claims that we cannot have theoretical cognition of freedom considered negatively, but can only show that it is not a contradictory idea. On a more detailed discussion of these aspects, see my "Kant's *Rechtferigung* and the Epistemic Character of Practical Justification," in *Kant on Practical Justification: Interpretive Essays*, ed. Mark Timmons and Sorin Baiasu (New York: Oxford University Press, 2013), esp. Section III.

19. This is a reading that can be found in Otfried Höffe's "Kants kategorischer Imperativ als Kriterium des Sittlichen," in *Zeitschrift für philosophische Forschung* 31, no. 3 (1977): 354–84.

20. I follow here the increasingly common convention of capitalizing this expression, in order to distinguish between the moral criterion on the basis of which maxims are evaluated and the objective moral principles (categorical imperatives, such as "Do not lie!"), which are the results of such an evaluation.

21. For instance, in the *Critique of Dialectical Reason* (Jean-Paul Sartre, *Critique de la raison dialectique* (précédé de *Questions de méthode*). Tome 1: Théorie des ensembles pratiques (Paris: Gallimard, 1960); translated as *Critique of Dialectical Reason*, Vol. 1: Theory of Practical Ensembles, trans. Jonathan Rée, ed. Alan Sheridan-Smith (London: Verso, 2004), 285n1, 227n68.

22. The distinction is in fact fourfold: Apart from the for-itself and the in-itself, significant are also the concepts of the for-others and the for-itself-in-itself. For the purpose of this chapter, I only need to briefly mention the distinction between the first two terms, and between the first two and the last.

23. The object is transcendent, because it is not part of my consciousness. It is an object of my consciousness, beyond it and, hence, transcends it.

24. Moreover, there seems to be an even higher-order rule, which represents the sum of the person's ethical attitudes and which Sartre calls the global project and Kant, the disposition. A discussion of these goes beyond the scope of this chapter, but a comparative analysis can be found in Baiasu, *Kant and Sartre*.

25. This is noticeable particularly in the unpublished notes for the canceled Cornell Lectures. Discussions of these can be found in Juliette Simont, "Autour des conferences de Sartre à Cornell," in *Sur les Écrits Posthumes de Sartre; Annales de l'Institut de Philosophie et de Sciences Morales*, ed. Pierre Verstraeten (Bruxelles: Éditions de l'Université de Bruxelles, 1987); and Pierre Verstraeten, "Imperatifs et Valeurs," *Sur les Écrits Posthume de Sartre: Annales de l'Institut de Philosophie et de Sciences Morales*, ed. Pierre Verstraeten (Bruxelles: Éditions de l'Université de Bruxelles, 1987).

26. See my discussion of this topic in Baiasu, *Kant and Sartre*, esp. §80.

27. I started to work on some of the ideas of this paper when I was a visiting researcher at the University of Vienna, as part of the ERC Advanced Grant "Distortions of Normativity." I would like to thank the project's PI for the opportunity and Keele University for a period of research leave which enabled me to do research abroad.

Part II

Intersubjectivity and the Other

7

Kant and the Scandal of Intersubjectivity: Alfred Schutz's Anthropology of Transcendence

Jan Strassheim

Alfred Schutz, it is often said, used phenomenology to build a philosophical foundation for the social sciences. Although this statement is correct, it can distract from Schutz's contribution to philosophy itself. The following chapter outlines some central ideas of Schutz's philosophy as part of an ongoing dialogue between German Idealism and phenomenology.

As will become clearer, Kant and Husserl differ in how they assess "transcendental" conditions of subjectivity vis-à-vis the anthropological fact that as human beings, we experience the objective world as something that transcends us. Husserl rejects Kant's "anthropological theory" with its idea of "things in themselves." He argues that our world is objective not because it transcends subjectivity, but because the world is *inter*subjective, i.e., based on a relation between subjects. Schutz agrees with this status of intersubjectivity. But he claims that it can only be understood once Husserl's insights are related back to the anthropological level.

A key question of Schutz's anthropology is how we experience the transcendence of the world and the other subjects around us. Tracing this question through three Schutzian concepts ("transcendence," "meaning," and "types"), I will suggest that Schutz's theory allows us to articulate a crucial condition

J. Strassheim (✉)
Institute of Philosophy, University of Hildesheim, Hildesheim, Germany
e-mail: strassheim@uni-hildesheim.de

© The Author(s), under exclusive license to Springer Nature
Switzerland AG 2021
C. D. Coe (eds.), *The Palgrave Handbook of German Idealism and Phenomenology*,
Palgrave Handbooks in German Idealism,
https://doi.org/10.1007/978-3-030-66857-0_7

of intersubjectivity on the anthropological level: human experience is inherently open to an "Other." I will argue that this openness is formulated as an anthropological principle in Kantian philosophy, from which Schutz had started out in the 1920s. Kant's contentious idea of "things in themselves" may help us further develop the account of intersubjectivity which Schutz could not complete before his early death in 1959.

The "Scandal" of Intersubjectivity

Under the title of a "transcendental" philosophy, Kant and Husserl present different ways to cope with the modern turn toward subjectivity and the doubts that came with it. If only the thinking subject's own existence remains certain, then what about the belief, underlying our everyday lives and our sciences, in a world beyond subjective experience?

Kant rejects doubting, let alone denying, the existence of that world, but he also rejects decreeing it by dogma. For him, it is "a scandal of philosophy. ... that the existence of things outside us. ... should have to be assumed merely *on faith*" (CPR Bxxxix). Rather than speculating further about matters that *transcend* experience, philosophers should reflect on characteristics of subjective experience itself. Some of these are "transcendental": they necessarily shape human experience and therefore all the objects it can possibly have. This access to the world is won at the price of accepting strict limits. We can know things as they "appear to us," but we cannot claim knowledge about "the things in themselves," simply because they are beyond human experience. A different kind of subject, God perhaps, might be able to experience things as they are independently of human subjectivity, but we cannot.

Husserl uses "transcendental subjectivity" as "an old term given a new sense" (*Ideas* II, 406). One difference is that he rejects Kant's view as too narrow. The characteristics of experience which Kant calls "transcendental" are restricted to *human* subjectivity. For Husserl, this is only a step toward discovering characteristics of subjectivity *as such*, of *any* kind of conceivable subjectivity, and only these are truly "transcendental." Even God could not, for instance, perceive all sides of a spatial object at once, because this would no longer be a case of *perception* (*Ideas* I, §§42–43). For Husserl, it makes no sense to imagine behind the object a "thing in itself" which could be perceived in some other way, because there is no other way. "Kant's anthropological theory," as he calls it around 1908, is bound up with the concept of "things in themselves," which he deems a "groundless metaphysics."[1] We are right to believe in an objective world, but not because it transcends our subjectivity, but because it is *intersubjective*: the objectivity of "our" world is based on a relation between a plurality of subjects. Understanding intersubjectivity is therefore a vital if difficult task for phenomenology.

Alfred Schutz reaffirms this fundamental status of intersubjectivity—and the difficulty of understanding it. Looking back in 1954, he writes:

> Alluding to a statement Kant made in another context, I suggest that it is a "scandal of philosophy" that so far a satisfactory solution to the problem of our knowledge of other minds and, in connection therewith, of the intersubjectivity of our experience of the natural as well as the socio-cultural world has not been found and that, until rather recent times, this problem has even escaped the attention of philosophers.[2]

Schutz begins to investigate the problem of intersubjectivity several years before he discovers it in phenomenology. In the 1920s, he takes to heart the point made, among others, by the sociologist Max Weber that concepts and methods taken from the natural sciences keep us from understanding the social world. We cannot understand social phenomena through causal laws of behavior as if people were molecules or ants. Instead, we must take into account how actors in a society subjectively experience their situation and that of other actors. For Schutz, this view requires a foundation in a philosophical analysis of subjectivity and of the relation between subjects. He starts looking for an answer in Neo-Kantian thought.[3]

Schutz's earliest extant manuscripts show that after the mid-1920s, he has already moved on.[4] In his view, Kant modeled the relation between subject and world on the mathematical physicist who observes lifeless nature and formulates laws shared within a scientific community. As a result, Schutz claims, Kant's philosophy is built around conceptual logic, which obscures the bulk of our pre-scientific everyday experience. The rich and changing material of our senses, pre-conceptual forms of experience which relate us to ourselves and to the world around us—all of this escapes a formal logic. Moreover, a strict conceptual language shuts out differences in individual experience as well as nonverbal forms of communication between individuals. As long as conceptual experience sets limits of understanding, we cannot analyze these dimensions. However, Schutz thinks, these dimensions cannot be ignored because they are part of the foundation on which conceptual experience and science become possible in the first place.

As an alternative to Kant, Schutz considers Henri Bergson's philosophy of life with its emphasis on the fullness of lived experience beyond conceptual language. But while Bergson's analyses are fruitful, he strictly separates lived experience from conceptual levels, introducing a dualistic split where Schutz wants to show how one level is based on the other. In 1929, when reading Husserl's *Formal and Transcendental Logic*, Schutz realizes that Husserl too plans to clarify intersubjectivity by showing how conceptual logic and science are founded upon pre-logical and pre-scientific structures of experience. He immediately starts reading up on Husserl's published work.

Anthropology on a Phenomenological Basis

According to Husserl, the objective world as assumed in the natural sciences has a basis in our everyday experience. Transcendental phenomenology starts with a critical reflection on the "natural attitude" which governs our daily lives. In the natural attitude, I take it for granted that a world beyond myself exists, and that it corresponds more or less to the way I experience it. The phenomenologist "brackets" the validity of these assumptions and treats the world purely as a "phenomenon" in order to investigate the way it is experienced. As a correlate of this, the experiencing subject is not treated as a human being in their natural attitude, but as a "transcendental ego." This is a pure subject who is not so much living in the world (the existence or non-existence of which has been "bracketed") but, rather the other way around, who experiences the world as a phenomenon within their own consciousness.

With this reflection, Husserl never means to doubt the existence of the world beyond the subject. On the contrary, he seeks to provide it with a foundation in the structures of subjectivity itself. In his *Formal and Transcendental Logic*, he stresses that the "objective" world, as a phenomenon, has the essential meaning of a world which is one and the same "for everyone," it is "our world." As a phenomenon, it points to a subjectivity for whom it is a phenomenon. As "the world," it furthermore implies a *plurality* of subjects who share it. The world is essentially intersubjective.[5]

For Schutz, this argument confirms the significance of intersubjectivity. But within the transcendental framework, it raises what Husserl himself calls an "enigma." If the world is essentially intersubjective, then the way in which it transcends the ego relates back, most fundamentally, to subjects other than the ego. All "transcendencies" that make up the world beyond myself, Husserl writes, point to "others" as the "first affair that is not my Ego's own." However, from the viewpoint of a transcendental ego, other subjects too are phenomena *within* that ego, and their existence or non-existence, as part of the "world of the 'non-Ego,'" is "bracketed." A strictly transcendental phenomenology must then be able to show how the transcendental ego contains within itself the "motivational foundation" for the experience of something as "another Ego."[6] In his 1929 book, Husserl does not yet undertake this task.

But Schutz cannot wait. What he wants is precisely a phenomenology of intersubjectivity. In this situation, he takes a hint from Husserl's 1930 "epilogue" to his earlier *Ideas* volumes (*Ideas* II, 407–30). There, Husserl explains that while the transcendental approach awards insights into the structure of subjectivity as such, these more general insights can be applied to our experience within the "natural attitude" in order to analyze its more specific structure. Schutz chooses this course, termed by Husserl a "constitutive phenomenology of the natural attitude." In 1932, Schutz publishes the results in a book and sends a copy to Husserl, who replies with a letter calling Schutz "one of the very few who have penetrated to the deepest and unfortunately so difficult to penetrate sense of my life work."[7]

At first, it seems odd that Husserl should welcome Schutz's approach. The subject of experience in the natural attitude is not the "transcendental ego" but the "empirical ego," the human being living in the world with others. It is studied by "anthropology," which Husserl opposes to phenomenology. In 1931, Husserl had even toured the *Kant Societies* in three German cities giving a lecture on the superiority of phenomenology over anthropology.[8] Now, in 1932, Schutz presents him with a book which not only skips a transcendental solution to the problem of intersubjectivity, but closes with the suggestion that a full solution would require "an ontology of the human being on a phenomenological basis."[9] Schutz seems to be moving toward an anthropology rather than a transcendental phenomenology, and the word "ontology" (to which I will return toward the end of the chapter) suspiciously sounds like the "groundless metaphysics" that Husserl had found in Kant.

But Schutz's anthropological ambitions are compatible with Husserl's approach because of their "phenomenological basis." The "transcendental ego" embodies the full range of the possible forms which subjectivity in general can take. Therefore, it contains as a subset the more specific possibilities of *human* subjectivity. As Husserl notes in his 1930 "epilogue," transcendental phenomenology contains within it an anthropology. What he rejects as "anthropologism" is the idea that anthropology can replace transcendental phenomenology in its fundamental role (*Ideas* II, 407–8). This will never be Schutz's claim. Nevertheless, Schutz does go on to claim more and more forcefully that the anthropological specification is not an option, but a necessary route to understanding intersubjectivity. Why is this?

The possibilities open to Husserl's transcendental ego include the possibility of experiencing an "other ego" beyond itself. The "enigma" of intersubjectivity then comes down to the question of how and why this possibility is actualized. The transcendental ego consists in a "sphere of ownness" which has been construed by "bracketing" anything "alien" to the ego or "other" than it, including other subjects, who are merely phenomena within the transcendental ego.[10] What would motivate the ego to treat a phenomenon as belonging to something other than itself? In the fifth of his *Cartesian Meditations*, Husserl tries to solve the problem. To put his argument simply: the transcendental ego perceives an object which it realizes is a body similar to its own. It then ascribes to this body a consciousness similar to its own but distinct from it. While the object in question is still a phenomenon within the ego, it now has the meaning "*alter ego*," "another ego." With this step, the ego has entered the intersubjective dimension. Schutz, however, thinks that Husserl's argument begs the question. From the transcendental viewpoint, another subject is "a 'modification' of myself" (CM 115). But what would motivate the ego to "modify" itself in this way? Husserl's argument presupposes that the ego can already experience something as "other" than itself: a body like mine, but *not mine*; a subjectivity, but a *different one*.[11]

Schutz concludes that the insights gained within the transcendental sphere are fundamental, but only their application to the natural attitude in which we experience ourselves from the outset as human beings living in a world with others will allow the phenomenologist to grasp intersubjectivity. The "scandal" of intersubjectivity calls for an anthropology on a phenomenological basis.

Transcendence

For the philosophical anthropologist, the range of possibilities open to a transcendental ego is restricted to those of a human being. Schutz takes into account the facts that make us finite: we can only be in a single place at a time; we have a restricted field of perception; our bodies can only do certain things; we cannot overstay our life span, etc. These are not the same as facts established by sciences such as biology or empirical psychology, since scientific objectivity presupposes the very foundation of human intersubjectivity which the phenomenologist aims to understand. What Schutz looks at is how we *experience* our own finitude.[12]

Husserl's critique of Kant's "anthropological theory" had implied that restricting the possibilities of subjectivity in general to those of human experience produces, as its flip side, the idea of something that transcends this experience, the "thing in itself." In Schutz too, the human subject in the natural attitude assumes from the outset that the world around them as well as the other subjects transcend their experience. But for Schutz, transcendence is a category for various ways in which human finitude appears *within experience*.[13] In this sense, his concept of transcendence is different from Kant's, which refers to what lies beyond all possible human experience. But in what sense do we experience transcendence?

Most obviously, the world around me transcends all that I have experienced up to now and it will transcend whatever I experience in the future. Again, this is not a fact uncovered by a scientific observer, but it is part of my experience: I *know* that I could know more than I presently do. It is "an existential element of all human knowledge" (SCP 5:178): even when I think I have acquired enough information for my purposes, and even when I lack any curiosity in broadening my experience, I am familiar with the fact that there are still things beyond what I know. Schutz uses Husserl's metaphor of "horizons" to express this quality of our experience: although I cannot see *what* lies beyond my horizon here and now, I know that I could go on without coming to an end. Moreover, I know that the world transcends my lifespan; it existed before my birth and will continue to exist when I am gone.

Within the world around us, we experience other subjects, people whose existence transcends ours in several ways. Spatially, the others are "there" as opposed to my "here"; they are at places where I am not right now and where I may never be. Temporally, others have been born before me, and still others will outlive me. And as subjects, others are like myself in that they experience the world around them, but they do so from individual perspectives which may be quite different from mine and which are not immediately accessible to me.

Within the natural attitude, we constantly experience this transcendence of others (SCP 4:238–39). If we look at how experience builds up over time, Schutz claims, the transcendence of others is even among the most primary experiences. Children do not first observe the world around them and then discover that there are people in it. When my mother gave birth to me, I gained access to the world literally through another person. I was then gradually introduced to the world by her and others who taught me most of what I know about the world and the ways in which it transcends me. Even the knowledge that a world existed before I did and will exist after I die is imparted to me by other people whose lifespan or knowledge transcends mine. This line of thought confirms Husserl's idea that the objectivity of the world has its foundation in intersubjectivity.

Furthermore, Schutz thinks that intersubjectivity is fundamental even to the formation of one's own self. A child does not first discover its own standpoint and then experience others as a "modification" of it, but if anything, it is the other way around:

> as long as humans are born of mothers and not produced in test tubes, experience of the *alter ego* will, genetically-constitutionally, precede experience of one's own self. This fact has long been quite familiar to child psychology, which shows how relatively late it is that the child acquires the concept of 'self' [*Ich*], or even that of a body [*Leib*].[14] (SCP 6:261, translation slightly modified)

In this picture, which Schutz paints in the mid-1930s, it makes sense that the *alter ego* cannot be reconstructed from within the transcendental ego but must be presupposed as something that is already there and transcends it. This relation between ego and *alter ego* aptly reflects, on the general level of transcendental phenomenology, the constitution of human experience as it builds up over time (its "genetic" dimension, in the Husserlian terminology which Schutz echoes above).

Meaning

The ways in which we experience transcendence are reflected in the concept of "meaning" (*Sinn*) that Schutz starts to develop in the 1920s. As Schutz tries to capture the structure of experience at a more general level than the conceptual structures Kant focused on, this notion is wider than linguistic meaning. On the most general level, "meaning" refers to the selectivity of experience, to a selective activity on the part of the experiencing subject. This selective activity happens for the most part automatically, without the subject even noticing it. For an embodied human being, any moment holds a potentially infinite richness of sensations, movements, and feelings which overlap and fade into each other as part of a continuous "stream" of experience.[15] Specific phenomena (e.g., a pain in my back, my action of reaching for a glass, the visual perception of an empty bottle, the memory of the night before) are highly *selective* meaning-constructs. That is, a phenomenon is constituted through processes which foreground only certain aspects of the potential richness of the stream of experience and neglect all others. These selective processes carve out the acts, phases, contents, etc., which make up a concrete phenomenon.

The selectivity of meaning implies a specific notion of transcendence within experience. Most aspects of the stream of experience are *not* selected and remain in the background. In this sense, one and the same moment within my stream of experience contains many possibilities of meaning-construction beyond the meaning that is actually constructed. Every moment contains potentially many phenomena that I *could* experience instead of those I actually do.

I am not conscious of the alternatives that are not selected, as they are not actual phenomena for me at the time. I am usually not even aware that my phenomena are selective at all. However, phenomena follow each other within the temporal development of my experience. As different meanings are selected, I can become aware in retrospect that I failed to notice a certain aspect of a past situation, forgot about something, left an item at home, missed an opportunity which I should have recognized, etc. (SCP 4:237–38). In this type of experience, it becomes manifest to me that my own stream of experience transcends the selectivity of what is a phenomenon for me. Correlatively, this type of experience points me to the fact that the situation in which I found myself, with its many aspects, connections, and objects, was far richer than what I took into account there and then. To the extent that I relate my situation to the world around me, the transcendence of the world beyond my experience is reflected *within* such an experience.

As noted earlier, Schutz's initial motivation for researching the structure of experience was to understand the relation between experiencing subjects. His concept of meaning unfolds the complexity of this relation.

On the one hand, the structure of meaning separates subjects. Like my own experience, the experience of another person is carved out of a richer stream. Therefore, their experience transcends mine in a twofold way. First, even in what seems to be the same situation, the other's meaning-selections may be different from mine or from those I attribute to them. For instance, I may describe an accident quite differently from you when asked by the police, or I may be amused about what makes you sad. But even when I "know" what the other is feeling, thinking, or doing, I capture their meaning-selections in form only, while the material provided by the other's stream of experience will be different from mine. I can understand that you are sad about your partner passing away; I may even have had "the same" experience—but only you can feel what my description means in terms of your loss, your memories and regrets, your fears, unanswered questions, etc. No two streams of experience can be precisely the same, for this would require two people to share the same body and biography—to be, in effect, one and the same person. You and I can never have exactly the same experience.

On the other hand, the structure of meaning functions as a bridge between subjects. As much of our experience of ourselves and the world builds on what we learn from others, many of our meaning-selections are based on shared patterns provided by the social groups into which we were born (e.g., a family, a culture, a nation) or by groups we join (e.g., a circle of friends, an adopted country, a profession). Through repeated use, patterns of meaning "sediment" (a Husserlian term) in the individual subject and come to guide them as automatic routines and habitual expectations. To the extent that this happens along similar lines across individuals, the shared patterns allow them to simply "take for granted" that everybody thinks, feels, or acts the same way in a given situation. And even where this is not the case, a mutual interest in coordination often makes it advisable to follow patterns of meaning which, although they fail to do justice to the individual situations, are shared by all parties involved (Schutz's example is the interlinking roles of a mailman and their customer).

This bridge does not erase the transcendence of the other; it anchors that transcendence within our everyday experience. Even when two people "feel the same," each of them knows that nobody can feel *exactly* what another person feels. Where we converse smoothly with people we have never met before, we are usually aware that the shared roles and expectations which enable us to do so are "anonymous" constructs distinct from our individual situations (SCP 1:12).

Again, a variety of occasions manifest the transcendence of the other person in my experience. I may encounter members of other groups who use different patterns of meaning. Members of my own group may have a different standpoint from mine, or a different interpretation of their role. Sometimes I immediately notice such differences: the other does not behave as expected or tells me that I am wrong—or, conversely, I realize that the other is imputing to me a standpoint that is not mine. At other times, I only find out after the fact that such a misjudgment happened. These are constant reminders that shared patterns of meaning at best approximate individual experience, may always prove inadequate, and frequently need to be adapted or changed.

Types

To describe patterns of meaning that are relatively stable yet allow for adaptation or change, Schutz uses the term "types." He is excited when Husserl introduces a similar concept of "types" in his last book, published in 1939, *Experience and Judgment*.[16] Here, Husserl articulates in detail a genetic phenomenology which focuses on the temporal development of experience.

This development is based on motivation. A subject's experiences and expectations are motivated by their past experiences. Some of the connections are motives in the narrower sense of conscious goals we want to reach through voluntary action, but other motives are implicit reasons, leanings, or habits that shape our experience without any reflection on our part.[17]

According to Husserl, any experience "points beyond" itself in anticipation of what might come later. In this way, it "pre-delineates" (*vorzeichnen*) a path for a future experience,[18] which will then relate back to the present anticipation as a confirmation, a modification, or a disappointment. When I see the front side of an object, my perceptual experience already implies an anticipation of what its backside might look like. As Schutz notes, this way in which a present meaning-construct pre-empts a possible future meaning-construct is a core mechanism which makes transcendence immanent to experience: every experience "transcends itself" (SCP 4:235).

Types are part of what gives the "pre-delineated" path its direction. When I see an object, I perceive it from the outset as an object of a type I am already familiar with: I see "a dog" or "a golden retriever." This type connects the present with the future by motivating typical expectations. When I see the head of a golden retriever appearing around a corner, it is part of my experience that I expect to see a typical golden retriever tail at the other end. This expectation will shape the actual experience that follows, whether it conforms to the type or not. What I will see next will be experienced as a confirmation, a modification, or a frustration of what I anticipate now (e.g., as the expected bushy tail; as a different tail or no tail; as a puppeteer controlling what now turns out to be a dog puppet, etc.).

A type does not predetermine the experience that follows, though. Types allow for modifications or disappointments. Typical expectations are *merely* typical; they only concern what happens for the most part. Typical patterns of meaning structure experience, but unlike timeless essences, they do not restrict it. It is true that types often bias and even blind us, becoming stereotypes especially where they work below the radar of our conscious reflection, but this is not always and not necessarily so.[19] Even a well-established type remains open, at least in principle, to exceptions and changes. This openness of types enables us to be surprised, frustrated, and instructed in ways which, as indicated above, help make us acquainted with the transcendence of the world and the others. At the same time, the relative stability of types enables us to cope with this transcendence by coordinating with others in a shared social world. Types, then, would help solve the "scandal" of intersubjectivity.

But the openness of types involves an element we have yet to make clear. To the extent that my experience follows established types, it is a repetition of the same, involving events and objects that fall under familiar concepts. However, Schutz asks, can I not have an experience which is "novel" in that it does not relate to the types I already know (SCP 5:134)? The same question arises even where I simply experience "new" instances of a familiar type. Strictly speaking, every situation to which I apply a type is unique: "although being familiar as to its type, [a new experience] is strange insofar as it is *atypical* in its uniqueness and particularity" (SCP 5:125).

This in turn raises the question: how is an atypical experience motivated? Any experience "transcends itself" into the future along a path of selective anticipation which shapes the following experience. To the extent that the following experience is familiar, we can further assume that this movement is driven by a tendency of experience to conform to established typical patterns. But what would motivate (in the wide sense of "motivation" introduced earlier) the selective meaning which constitutes the novel, atypical portions of my experience, if what they transcend are precisely the types I know?

Schutz offers several possible answers, but his early death in 1959 keeps him from systematically developing them. There is a group of experiences where the unknown forces itself upon us by causing a "problem" (SCP 3:117). My typical expectation is interrupted by an unexpected event; my routine action runs against the "resistance" of the material world[20]; or incompatible types get into each other's way. Such experiences have the quality of a surprise or disturbance that indicates that a type has met an unknown obstacle. But even then the question remains on what basis we experience the atypical "something" once it has indirectly made its presence felt. Furthermore, another large group of experiences attests to a "spontaneous" tendency to leave typical paths that does not need a "problem" to be triggered.

This latter tendency is often found in our interactions with others. For instance, language, as Schutz notes (SCP 1:14), is a chief medium for expressing, transmitting, and applying the types we share among groups. But language is not simply based on the "typical" use of words we might find in a dictionary or grammar book. As more recent research in linguistics has confirmed, we tailor the meaning of words to the concrete situation and apply them in novel ways; we use metaphors, wordplays, and ironical twists which are not prescribed by types. We do all this without hesitation and without even noticing it, and we are understood by others (and understand them) with the same natural ease. In other words, we spontaneously transcend typical patterns.[21] And even where we do conform to shared types, e.g., in straightforward and literal language, or when following "anonymous" professional roles, we apply the types to a "new" situation which, in Schutz's expression cited earlier, is always "*atypical* in its uniqueness and particularity"

(SCP 5:125). Hence, even when a typical script of everyday life is played out by individual interactants, they spontaneously "tune in" to each other in a way Schutz likens to the performance of a classical piece by an ensemble of musicians.[22]

Such observations suggest that there is a tendency, immanent to our experience, to transcend types. This tendency would fill an important place within the argument presented in this chapter. The difficulty that made Schutz seek an anthropology on a phenomenological basis was that Husserl's transcendental ego, while being open to the possibility of recognizing an ego other than itself, lacked an internal motivation to *actualize* this possibility. Only for the human ego in his or her natural attitude, the transcendence of others is part of their experience from the outset, and types, with their combination of stability and openness, play a key role in this. But the openness of types, not unlike that of the transcendental ego, is only an openness in principle to the possibility of experiencing aspects other than typical aspects. Where human beings *actualize* this possibility in the spontaneous ways we observe in people's everyday dealings with each other, once again an internal motivation must be at play. In other words, in order to solve the "scandal" of intersubjectivity, we need to assume a tendency of human experience to transcend types.

Back to the "Things in Themselves"

While Schutz raises questions that point toward a tendency to transcend typical patterns of meaning, he never formulates it as an anthropological principle. However, we can find an analogue in the thinker who was the point of departure for Schutz's philosophical career.

I mentioned at the beginning of this chapter that Schutz criticized Kant for limiting experience to *conceptual* experience. But "concepts" in Kant are similar to "types" in Husserl and Schutz. In Kant, the faculty of understanding (*Verstand*) is a necessary element of human experience. This faculty employs concepts to select certain aspects from the richness of our outer and inner senses, and to unify these aspects in terms of a known kind. This role of the Kantian concept parallels the way types shape our experience in Husserl and Schutz; in fact, both authors refer to Kant and even use the same example: the concept (or type) of a dog.[23] If we are searching for a tendency to transcend types, we should reconsider Kant's notion of "things in themselves" which evade our conceptual experience.

As first sight, this does look like a metaphysical concept, as Husserl had charged. The world we experience is the world as it is given to human subjectivity; it is a world of *phaenomena*, "appearances" or "apparent things." Since "appearances always presuppose a thing in itself" (Pro 4:355) of which they are appearances, we posit *noumena*, "objects of thought," beyond the phenomena. However, in the context of the *Critique of Pure Reason*,[24] Kant traces this distinction to a process *internal* to human experience.

Human understanding selects from material given to it by our senses and organizes it in accordance with established concepts into "things," such as specific objects or events. These are things "as they appear to us," in that their material is given by the human sensorium. When understanding ignores the specific makeup of the human senses but continues its formal work of positing objects, what remains is a thing in itself. But any attempt to further determine this "something," e.g., with the vocabulary of traditional metaphysics, produces "illusions." Even our most abstract concepts would only impose on the thing in itself structures of the world "as it appears to us"; moreover, those concepts would be "empty" as there would be no material for them to select from. *Noumena* then are "beings of understanding" (*Verstandeswesen*): they are objects internal to understanding, which, while exploring its boundaries, never actually leaves the field of human experience (CPR B306–7). Therefore, the word "appearance" (*Erscheinung*) should not be misread as "illusion" (*Schein*; CPR B69). The world of *phaenomena* is the only reality that human beings can ever know and take a reasonable interest in: "what the things may be in themselves I do not know, and also do not need to know, since a thing can never come before me except in appearance" (CPR A276–77/B332–33).[25]

In other words, this level of analysis does not imply any metaphysical commitments about things beyond human experience.[26] What Kant describes is a transcendence *immanent* to experience. "Things in themselves" remain unknown to us because they are constituted through a *negation* of human understanding. By the same token, they remain grounded in human experience: as its negation. To the extent that concepts are equivalent to types, the Kantian "thing in itself" is another word for what is absolutely unknown or unfamiliar with respect to our typified experience. It is a radical expression for what transcends types within our experience.

But what we are looking for in the present chapter is a *tendency* to transcend types. What would motivate us to come up with the strange notion of a "something" that defies our understanding? Kant identifies a driving force which is again immanent to human experience: the faculty of reason

(*Vernunft*), which regulates the use of understanding. By encouraging understanding to posit a thing in itself, pure reason fulfills two functions at once. First, it determines the boundaries of all humanly possible understanding, which cannot go beyond *phaenomena*. Second, it indicates that there might be something beyond these boundaries. The *noumenon* is a "boundary concept" (CPR A256/B310–11): it both connects and separates these two functions.

The first function is crucial to Kant's project in the first *Critique*: to establish the boundaries of any metaphysics "that will be able to come forward as science," as he puts it in the title of his later introduction (the *Prolegomena*) to the *Critique*. The second function represents a tendency to cross these boundaries which, historically, gave us the various metaphysics that the *Critique* aims to rein in. But could this tendency have an anthropological basis which affects not only metaphysicians but people more generally?

In fact, Kant thinks that metaphysics is part of "*the natural predisposition* of human reason.*" He goes on to inquire after the "purposes" of nature behind this predisposition. This question "does not concern the objective validity of metaphysical judgments, but rather the natural predisposition to such judgments, and therefore lies outside the system of metaphysics, in anthropology" (Pro 4:362).

One of Kant's answers[27] to his question is that reason motivates understanding to investigate further and further without ever stopping at the results it has gained so far. As "experience never fully satisfies" it (Pro 4:351), reason seeks out the boundaries of experience to trace a "connection of that with which we are acquainted to that with which we are not acquainted, and never will be," a connection "of the known to a wholly unknown (which will always remain so)" (Pro 4:354). An awareness of boundaries of experience beyond which there might still be "something" sets our understanding into constant motion. Reason reminds us that whatever knowledge we acquire remains a fragment of an unknown whole, the mere "appearance" of an unknown "thing in itself." By relating the known to the unknown, reason opens up "new paths into the infinite (the undetermined) with which the understanding is not acquainted" (CPR A680/B708).

While reason strives to find "peace and satisfaction" (Pro 4:352) in ideas of what would finally be the *whole* of experience and the actual "thing in itself," such "ideas of pure reason" are *noumena*. As such, they must remain empty, because once we try to determine them through concepts taken from our experience, we produce illusions with serious consequences: the false belief that we have found the ultimate answer leads to an unjustified breakoff in our efforts to expand our experience. This mistake results in what Kant calls "lazy reason" (CPR A689/B717), a reason which deceives itself into thinking that its work is done and which thus defeats its "natural" purpose. Where reason avoids this mistake, it keeps driving our understanding beyond whatever experience we have acquired so far. But even so, human reason can "never get beyond the field of possible experience" (CPR A702/B730); this is nothing less than "the result of the entire *Critique*" (Pro 4:361). Paradoxically then, the idea of a "thing in itself" remains devoid of experience and *therefore* works as a force which makes us strive for ever new experiential content, thus making us transcend the concepts we have at any given moment. The Kantian transcendence of what lies beyond all possible human experience can motivate the Schutzian transcendence *within* human experience.

World, Soul, God

To the extent that concepts are equivalent to types, we can conclude that when Kant talks about things in themselves, he describes what Schutz's anthropology needs: a tendency to transcend types which is immanent to experience. This conclusion is strengthened when we compare the areas covered by Kantian *noumena* with the areas of Schutzian transcendence. Among the more specific ideas through which reason motivates understanding, three are linked to classical areas of metaphysics: "world," "soul," and "God."

In the context of this chapter, the Kantian idea of the world would stand for an unattainable whole of experience as opposed to the limited experience that humans can achieve. My own soul too is an unknown thing in itself which underlies the ways I appear to myself. In Schutz's framework, these two ideas would motivate human experience to transcend types which would otherwise restrict our experience. The idea of the world drives us beyond the sum total of our experience so far and into its unexplored horizons. The idea of a soul could be related to the stream of experience. In a first-person perspective, only a fraction of my own stream of experience stands out for me in terms of typified phenomena, but it forms a whole that is unified beyond my grasp. In the intersubjective dimension, the idea of a soul would then drive the assumption that the other person has their own stream of experience which, like my own, transcends all anonymous, socially shared, and individually sedimented types that shape our pictures of ourselves and of others.

What about the third idea? God is the ultimate boundary concept for an anthropology. It marks the sum total of human boundaries *and* situates these boundaries within a larger philosophical space. In Kant's view, it would be an "absurdity" to hope that we can cross the boundaries of human experience. But it would be "an even greater absurdity ... for us to want to pass off our experience for the only possible way of cognizing things" (Pro 4:350–51). God is the idea of a non-human subject who holds together, through their "way of cognizing things," all other things in themselves. And again, while this idea embodies all that transcends our human makeup and our world of *phaenomena*, its function is to push us ever further *within* the limits of our own world.

Like all *noumena*, the idea of God cannot be determined by human concepts. Such anthropomorphism must be avoided—except in the form of analogies which help the idea of God fulfill its function (Pro 4:357). One such analogy is the notion that nature has purposes. When we look at nature as if it were the product of a rational builder, the analogy can serve as a heuristic device for the systematic investigation of nature; in fact, we could replace the name "God" by that of "Nature" (CPR A670–71/B698–99, A699/B727). Since Kant introduced what I interpreted as an immanent tendency to transcend types precisely in terms of a purpose of nature, we have come full circle. Kant's assumption that the natural predisposition of human reason has the purpose to drive our understanding ever further is itself based on a *noumenon*. It should therefore be taken, not as a metaphysical claim, but as a call for further anthropological research.

But can such research be done on a phenomenological basis? In a letter from 1953, Schutz's friend Aron Gurwitsch criticizes what he calls Schutz's "ontologizing inclinations" and insists that phenomenologists should not "accept" what they cannot understand in terms of its intrinsic constitution. Schutz agrees that "the ontological foundation of all understanding and self-understanding is itself in principle not available to understanding." But he adds that it is not up to us to accept or not to accept what is "imposed" upon us: "And what is imposed upon us? Our place as human beings in the cosmos. I mean no more than that this [our place] is simply ontologically there, and that it is only this primal foundation—as life-world—that makes all understanding possible."[28]

The position Schutz states here can be read along the lines of Kantian things in themselves. We see ourselves as placed within a cosmos, a whole of which, as human beings rather than gods, we can only ever experience a part. This anthropological placing, we assume, is "simply there," independently of how, or indeed whether, it appears to us. Furthermore, this relation forms the foundation for our understanding of the world around us and even for our understanding of ourselves as subjects. Since this assumed foundation transcends not only the typifying (conceptual) structure of human understanding, but even the boundaries of human experience as a whole, it cannot be understood in terms of its intrinsic constitution, as Gurwitsch points out. But precisely because these are all purely negative assumptions, they remain within the field of human experience and play a constitutive role in it which phenomenologists can and should account for. When Kant describes the production of such *noumena* by pure reason, he does not make metaphysical claims about what lies beyond human experience.[29] What he analyzes are anthropological conditions of experience which help explain why some people make metaphysical claims. And precisely because the *noumena* thus produced negate all human *phaenomena*, they reflect a motivational force *within* our phenomenal experience: a tendency to transcend types which, together with these types, shapes our everyday subjective and intersubjective experience. Such a tendency is not necessarily characteristic of any conceivable subjectivity, such as that of a god. But it is characteristic of human subjectivity.

Conclusions

In order to understand intersubjectivity, Schutz argues, Husserl's transcendental analysis of the possible forms of subjectivity must be complemented on the more specific, anthropological level. For an anthropology on a phenomenological basis, transcendence becomes a central category.

By transcendence, Schutz refers to ways in which a human being *experiences* the fact that the world and other people transcend his or her experience. Schutz's concept of meaning describes the immanence of transcendence as a basic structure of experience: phenomena are selections from a richer stream of experience. His concept of types captures this relation in terms of a temporal development: meaning-selections follow familiar patterns which are nevertheless open to modifications and changes. Both the typification and the openness of meaning are constitutive for everyday forms of human intersubjectivity, e.g., for the interaction between individual subjects, or our use of language.

However, the openness of types presupposes an immanent motivation of experience to "transcend itself," more precisely, to transcend established *types*. The assumption of a functional equivalence of "types" (Husserl, Schutz) and "concepts" (Kant) leads us to Kant's idea of "things in themselves" which escape all conceptual determinations. This was understood as an anthropological (rather than metaphysical) concept. Human reason, by making us posit the *noumenon* of an "Other" which, despite all efforts, remains forever unknown, drives us to question and transcend whichever degree of understanding of the world or the others around us we achieve. It thus opens our understanding toward ever new aspects of situations and the individual perspectives of others.

I would like to add one final point. If a tendency to transcend types (concepts) is part of human nature, as Kant suggests, and if it is at work in our everyday social interactions, as Schutz suggests, then we might expect to find this fact reflected in ordinary language. This is indeed how Michel Foucault, in his 1961 commentary to Kant's *Anthropology from a Pragmatic Point of View*, interprets the concept of "spirit." In Foucault's reading, part of the *Anthropology*'s method is to clarify the meaning of certain expressions in late eighteenth century everyday German. One of these is "spirit" (*Geist*), which Kant defines as "[t]he principle of the mind that animates by means of *ideas*."[30] Foucault relates this somewhat cryptic definition back to the role of "ideas" in the First *Critique*: ideas "animate" (*beleben*) us by freeing us from the potentially sclerotic effect of established conceptual determinations. Further research into Kant's *Anthropology* might prove fruitful for working toward Schutz's vision of an "anthropology that will be able to come forward as science" (SCP 6:256).[31]

Notes

1. Edmund Husserl, "Gegen Kants anthropologische Theorie" (ca. 1908), in *Husserliana Vol. 7: Erste Philosophie (1923/24). Erster Teil: Kritische Ideengeschichte*, ed. Rudolf Boehm (The Hague: Martinus Nijhoff, 1956), 357–64. On Husserl's stance toward anthropology, see Hans Blumenberg, *Beschreibung des Menschen* (Frankfurt: Suhrkamp, 2006), part I.
2. Alfred Schutz, "Concept and Theory Formation in the Social Sciences," in *Collected Papers* (hereafter: *SCP*) *1: The Problem of Social Reality*, ed. Maurice Natanson (The Hague: Martinus Nijhoff, 1962), 57.
3. For a short account of Schutz's philosophical development by himself, see "Husserl and His Influence on Me," in *SCP 5: Phenomenology and the Social Sciences*, ed. Lester Embree (Dordrecht: Springer, 2011), 1–4.
4. For the following, see Alfred Schutz, "Life Forms and Meaning Structures," in *SCP 6: Literary Reality and Relationships*, ed. Michael Barber (Dordrecht: Springer, 2013), 24–25, 29–30, 39–40. As the English translation is at times faulty, it is best read in parallel with the German original: "Lebensformen und Sinnstruktur," in *Alfred Schütz Werkausgabe 1: Sinn und Zeit. Frühe Wiener Arbeiten und Entwürfe*, ed. Matthias Michailow (Konstanz: UVK, 2006), 45–173.

5. Edmund Husserl, *Formal and Transcendental Logic*, trans. Dorion Cairns (The Hague: Martinus Nijhoff, 1969), §96.
6. Ibid.
7. Alfred Schutz, *The Phenomenology of the Social World*, trans. George Walsh and Fredrick Lehnert (New York: Northwestern University Press, 1967). For Schutz's approach to phenomenology, see 43–44. Schutz kept reaffirming the fundamental role of transcendental phenomenology until his death in 1959 (e.g., "Husserl's Importance for the Social Sciences," in SCP 1:149). Husserl's letter is quoted in SCP 4 (Dordrecht: Kluwer, 1996), 155.
8. Edmund Husserl, "Phenomenology and Anthropology," trans. Richard G. Schmitt, in *Shorter Works*, ed. Peter McCormick and Frederick A. Elliston (Notre Dame: University of Notre Dame Press, 1981), 315–23. The unnamed target of the lecture was Heidegger. Reading *Being and Time* as an anthropology was a misunderstanding which Husserl shared with other readers and which Heidegger rejected (see already BT §10).
9. Alfred Schutz, *Der sinnhafte Aufbau der sozialen Welt. Eine Einleitung in die verstehende Soziologie. Alfred Schütz Werkausgabe 2* (Konstanz: UVK, 2004), 250 (my translation; the 1967 English translation is inaccurate).
10. Husserl, *Formal and Transcendental Logic*, §96.
11. Alfred Schutz, "The Problem of Transcendental Intersubjectivity in Husserl," in *SCP 3: Studies in Phenomenological Philosophy*, ed. Ilse Schutz (The Hague: Martinus Nijhoff, 1966), 51–83. Schutz died in 1959 and never read Husserl's manuscripts on the problem of intersubjectivity published later. Had he known them, he would have found himself in greater agreement with Husserl; see Shinji Hamauzu, "Schutz and Edmund Husserl: For Phenomenology of Intersubjectivity," in *Alfred Schutz and his Intellectual Partners*, ed. Hisashi Nasu, Lester Embree, George Psathas, and Ilja Srubar (Konstanz: UVK, 2009), 49–67.
12. Despite parallels to Heidegger and occasional references to him in Schutz's notes, their basic outlooks were different. Schutz wanted to investigate human experience in order to clarify intersubjectivity. For Heidegger, human experience was only a step, and even an obstacle, on the way toward understanding "being" beyond human existence.
13. "Transcendence" became a central category for Schutz in his 1954 "Symbol, Reality and Society" (SCP 1:287–356; see also "Experience and Transcendence," in SCP 4:234–41), but it was already present in the 1930s (e.g., "The Problem of Personality in the Social World," in SCP 6:272–73).
14. Schutz presumably has Jean Piaget in mind, whose theory of child development he will later invoke together with George Herbert Mead's (see, for example, "The Theory of Social Action: Text and Letters with Talcott Parsons," in SCP 5, 56). While his and Husserl's focus on the temporal dimension of experience already invited a developmental perspective, Schutz's interest in empirical sociology and psychology may have contributed to the fact that he includes

childhood in his thinking more than do many other philosophers. I am grateful to Cindy Coe for raising this point.

15. *The Phenomenology of the Social World*, esp. §§7, 12. Schutz combined Bergson's concept of *durée* with Husserl's metaphor of a "streaming" time consciousness, to which he later added William James's "stream of thought" (see "William James's Concept of the Stream of Thought Phenomenologically Interpreted," in SCP 3:1–14).

16. Since the 1920s, Schutz had employed a concept of "types" inspired by Max Weber's "ideal type." When he met Husserl after sending him his book in 1932, he read some of the manuscripts for *Experience and Judgment* and discussed the concept of types with Husserl.

17. Husserl introduced this concept of "motivation" in *Ideas* I, §47. Again, Schutz used phenomenology to clarify the concept of "motivation" he had originally found in Max Weber (*The Phenomenology of the Social World*, §§4, 17, 18).

18. Edmund Husserl, *Experience and Judgment. Investigations in a Genealogy of Logic*, trans. James S. Churchill and Karl Ameriks (Evanston: Northwestern University Press, 1973), §8.

19. Otherwise, we would be enclosed in a kind of permanent tunnel vision. For an argument to this effect, see Jan Strassheim, "Type and spontaneity: Beyond Alfred Schutz's theory of the social world," *Human Studies* 39, no. 4 (2016): 493–512.

20. Schutz took this idea from Bergson's pragmatism (SCP 6:224) and later concurred with Max Scheler in his critique of philosophies like Kant's and Husserl's which take perception, rather than action, as the core model for our relation to the world (SCP 3:155–56).

21. The significance of this point for a social philosophy is overlooked by "rule" theorists like John Searle or Jürgen Habermas, who believe that such deviations can be idealized away; see Jan Strassheim, "Language and lifeworld: Schutz and Habermas on idealization," *Civitas* 17, no. 3 (2017): 411–34. For a more detailed account of "transcendence" in Schutz, see Jan Strassheim, "The Problem of 'Experiencing Transcendence' in Symbols, Everyday Language and Other Persons," *Schutzian Research* 8 (2016): 75–101.

22. "Making Music Together. A Study in Social Relationship," in *SCP 2: Studies in Social Theory*, ed. Arvid Brodersen (The Hague: Martinus Nijhoff, 1964), 159–78.

23. See CPR A141/B180; Husserl, *Experience and Judgment* §83; SCP 5:125.

24. See esp. CPR A235–60/B294–315; A669–703/B697–731; Pro §§57, 60.

25. Heidegger (BT §7A) captures the complex character of Kant's concept of "phenomena," but then leaves it behind in favor of a different concept of "phenomenon" motivated by his own, ontological interests (§7B, C).

26. It seems to me that this is true irrespective of what Kant wrote elsewhere about "things in themselves." For an interpretation of Kant along these lines, see Kojin Karatani, *Transcritique: On Kant and Marx* (Cambridge; London: MIT Press, 2003), 29–50.

27. I focus on the cognitive function referred to in the *Critique of Pure Reason* (A643–703/B671–731). In the *Prolegomena* (4:362–63) and in his writings on practical philosophy, Kant also refers to morality.

28. Alfred Schutz and Aron Gurwitsch, *Philosophers in Exile: The Correspondence of Alfred Schutz and Aron Gurwitsch, 1939–1959*, ed. Richard Grathoff, trans. J. Claude Evans (Bloomington; Indianapolis: Indiana University Press, 1989), 210–12. "Our place as human beings in the cosmos" is an implicit reference to Max Scheler's 1928 book.

29. Schutz's use of the word "ontology" may therefore be misleading; Kant rejected the title "ontology" in favor of that of an "analytic of the pure understanding" (CPR A247/B303).

30. Immanuel Kant, *Anthropology from a Pragmatic Point of View*, trans. Robert B. Louden (Cambridge: Cambridge University Press, 2006), 7:246. See Michel Foucault, *Introduction to Kant's Anthropology*, trans. Roberto Nigro and Kate Briggs (Los Angeles: Semiotext(e), 2008), 60–65.

31. Funded by the Deutsche Forschungsgemeinschaft (DFG, German Research Foundation)–431058086.

8

Moving Beyond Hegel: The Paradox of Immanent Freedom in Simone de Beauvoir's Philosophy

Shannon M. Mussett

Simone de Beauvoir's philosophy of liberation is largely grounded in the tradition of Hegelian and Marxist theories of revolution and rebellion. Yet she is wary of what she sees as a troubling optimism in the eventual victory of the subordinated over their tyrannizers. Especially regarding Hegel's idealistic confidence expressed at the conclusion of *The Phenomenology of Spirit*, Beauvoir argues that only certain expressions of freedom can lead to concrete change while many others waste away in self-degradation or impotence. In order to institute social structures that will admit the fundamental humanity of the oppressed, it is necessary to destroy the institutions and practices that serve to exclude them from recognition. The dynamic and affirming forces of destruction and creation, so integral to the education of the slave-consciousness in Hegel's narrative, are sometimes denied to those who are not recognized—and therein lies the essential problem to be resolved by Beauvoir's philosophy of freedom. In this paper, I argue that Beauvoir's formulation of empty and abstract dispersions of freedom helps her to avoid the pitfalls of historical optimism, and consequently to give a more robust

S. M. Mussett (✉)
Department of Philosophy and Humanities, Utah Valley University, Orem, UT, USA
e-mail: shannon.mussett@uvu.edu

© The Author(s), under exclusive license to Springer Nature Switzerland AG 2021
C. D. Coe (eds.), *The Palgrave Handbook of German Idealism and Phenomenology*, Palgrave Handbooks in German Idealism, https://doi.org/10.1007/978-3-030-66857-0_8

description of oppression than is found in Hegel's dialectic. Ultimately, Beauvoir's goal is to see actual liberation of oppressed peoples; such work requires discovering and naming the various ways that freedom can be wasted and denied, before showing how freedom can also lead to revolution and creation.

Beauvoir's liberty is partially grounded in the Hegelian idea of freedom as a two-part movement of negativity that is both destructive and productive of the given world. She considers this double movement to be the *transcendent* expression of freedom, which can be linked directly to the master-slave dialectic's focus on productive labor and the fear of death. However, Beauvoir deepens the Hegelian understanding of freedom as negativity in the discussions of certain *immanent* expenditures of freedom, or what she terms *empty* and *abstract* liberty. These latter two expressions, while largely absent in Hegel's master-slave narrative (and thus in the further developments of Spirit) help Beauvoir to show how oppressed existents, while ontologically free, are cut off from transforming their world. Thus, alongside the creative and revolutionary thrusts of freedom as negativity, Beauvoir posits two fundamentally *impotent* expressions in "complaint" (*la plainte*) and "resignation" (*la résignation*). In Beauvoir's philosophy, freedom (understood as negativity) is *both* transcendent and, when trapped in conditions of subjection, paradoxically *immanent*, thereby effectively sublating Hegelian freedom as negativity into her unique analysis of historically concrete situations of oppression.

The chapter begins by tracing Hegel's understanding of freedom as negativity in the *Phenomenology of Spirit*. The essential lesson learned by self-consciousness in the master-slave dialectic is that the essence of freedom is both productive of the self through labor and destructive of limitation in the absolute fear of death. Beauvoir discovers that this conception of freedom as a twofold negativity is open to criticism concerning the inherent optimism of the system; regardless of whether or not the existent is creatively changing the world through work or negating it through revolt, the Hegelian subject *ultimately progresses and advances*. Despite setbacks and dead ends, Spirit will eventually be victorious in the concretization of freedom in the achievement of the We that is I and the I that is We. The paper consequently moves to address Beauvoir's expansion of Hegelian freedom understood as transcendence by supplementing it with her own analysis of freedom in its immanent, i.e., *ineffective* forms. The immanent expressions of freedom found in complaint and resignation show that even though situations of oppression can actually prohibit transcendence in *both* forms, the freedom of the oppressed does not simply disappear. Freedom still finds a way to be expressed in oppressive situations, but only in empty, abstract, and socially ineffective behaviors.

Hegel on the Freedom of the Negative

The centrality of freedom and/as the power of the negative in Hegel's systematic philosophy is unquestionable. Unlike Kant, Hegel claims that reason, rather than falling into antinomies, is in fact capable of *uniting* opposing metaphysical claims into higher and more complete truths. Far from being a mere annihilation of difference, Hegelian synthesis is actually the preservation of difference in a higher unity. This is what Hegel means by the term *sublation* (*Aufhebung*) which he describes in the *Phenomenology* as exhibiting "its true twofold meaning which we have seen in the negative: it is at once a *negating* [*Negieren*] and a *preserving* [*Aufbewahren*]" (PhG 68). Sublation, therefore, involves an alteration and an overcoming of the given that both preserves and destroys what has come before. Sublation is thus the self-alienation of Spirit through negation and the subsequent negation of alienation and preservation in a higher form. The critical idea is that this movement ultimately advances. Whatever does not lead to progression is either outside the concern of Spirit, or made to serve the purposes of advancement by Spirit.

Alienation from negation first results in a kind of subjection to otherness that generates its own surpassing. Ray Brassier describes this as a processual movement of alienation wherein "first, there is subjection to necessity, then an externalization through which Spirit emancipates itself from this subjection, but in a way that is congenitally incomplete, generating another form of subjection."[1] This movement of self-alienation and self-overcoming is precisely the movement of becoming. Furthermore, the movement of self-diremption yields that to which the self is subjected, until the self overcomes the original negation and comes to see what is alien as the self. Progress is therefore enacted through a negative movement that is both productive and destructive of limitation insofar as the subject limits itself by positing itself as what is alien, only to destroy this limitation through experience. Determinate negation works through mediation of self through otherness to advance earlier forms into more complex, later forms.

The dialectic is therefore essentially a movement of generating and overcoming otherness. That which is other produces a kind of bondage to what is not the self. But this otherness also produces the very movement of becoming insofar as it motivates the subject's activity. Negativity is therefore best understood as the driving force in the activity of the subject coming to know itself as such. For Hegel, therefore, negativity overcomes alienation and names the movement of freedom itself—the way in which Spirit prevails over bondage to that which is external to it. The negative is the force operating in all development and change and consequently all progress. This is no more obvious than in the *Phenomenology* where Spirit develops by its own self-negation, or mediation of its immediacy. Spirit's activity is not imposed upon it from the outside; rather, it is itself the basis for its own development. In this light, Hegel's Spirit must not be understood as a thing, but as a freely issuing-forth, *negative process* of positing otherness and overcoming (yet preserving) that otherness in a new shape of truth. He writes:

> The content, in accordance with the *freedom* of its *being*, is the self-alienating Self, or the immediate unity of self-knowledge. The pure movement of this alienation [*Entäußerung*] considered in connection with the content, constitutes the *necessity* of the content. The distinct content, as *determinate*, is in relation, is not 'in itself'; it is its own restless process of superseding itself, or *negativity* [*Negativität*]; therefore, negativity or diversity, like free being, is also the Self. (PhG 490–91)

The content of the absolute subject is thus the free, restless process of negativity: negating the self, negating the original negation by removing the alienation, and the movement into a new stage of development. This negative movement is nothing less than the free movement of the self-relating, or self-conscious subject: "this 'I' = 'I' is the movement which reflects itself into itself ... this identity, being absolute negativity, is absolute difference" (PhG 489). Thus, Spirit as subject *is* the absolute negativity of the setting up and overcoming of otherness and the preservation of this process. In a word, Spirit is the development and memorialization of its own self-surpassing. The negative initiates and maintains the movement of the dialectic.

The Absolute that we find at the conclusion of the *Phenomenology* is the fully mediated concept, or the universal, self-conscious "I" which is "pure negativity or the dividing of itself, it is *consciousness*. This content is, in its difference, itself the 'I', for it is the movement of superseding itself, or the same pure negativity that the 'I' is" (PhG 486). Clearly then, Hegel conceives the essence of freedom to be a process of negation; put in a different way, the *essence of freedom is negativity*. While the journey to the absolute is long and full of frustrations and dead ends, its achievement is teleologically guaranteed. The self-alienation of Spirit will be brought to an end in the attainment of absolute knowing. There is no sense that this actualization is in danger of simply sputtering out in wasted activity or useless effort. The negative driving development will reach its appointed *telos*, and substance and subject will be one. This is because, ultimately, for Hegel, "it is in the nature of humanity to press onward to agreement with others; human nature only really exists in an achieved community of minds" (PhG 43). What doesn't ultimately lead to the fulfillment of a free humanity is left to the "anti-human" or "merely animal."

Hegel's dialectic is profoundly useful for understanding social forms of alienation and objectification (something clearly formative of Marxist thought). As the journey of Spirit is long and difficult, it can be challenging to see the confidence in the final destination at any one stop along the journey. The master-slave dialectic exemplifies this tension. While it is a foundational moment in the education of freedom—moving to the famous dialectical inversion of the master and slave—it is only a moment in the overall development. Spirit will continue to repeat the same patterns as it continues to posit the other (in whatever form it takes) as an alien entity that must be obeyed, subdued, or destroyed. Yet, despite the torturous and violent journey, Hegel's narrative of intersubjectivity remains progressive and therefore necessarily *optimistic* on Beauvoir's critically appropriative reading.

The master-slave dialectic plays such a significant role in Hegel's *Phenomenology* because it is pivotal to what he understands self-consciousness to be in its most essential form. The lessons learned about negativity and its relationship to death and work in this critical moment of the dialectic are carried through up to the emergence of Absolute Knowing. Thus, the magnitude of the fear of death and the role of work cannot be overemphasized in Hegel's account of the passage into and out of the master-slave dialectic. Hegel's notion of freedom as the negative has two distinct and equally necessary moments: a constructive moment, as seen in the formative activity of labor, and a destructive moment, as seen in the experience of absolute fear in the face of death. In existentialist terms, both moments are *transcendent* expressions of freedom, meaning that they succeed in *doing* something. Both production and destruction illuminate the doubled nature of freedom as negativity, and both are necessary in subject formation and expression in Hegelian thought.

Following the initial confrontation and subsequent bondage of the losing party, a relationship based on production and consumption results. The bondsman, who refused to stake a claim on life in the assertion of subjectivity, is reduced to labor for the lord who was initially willing to die in the battle for recognition. While the lord is a purely consumptive subject, the servile consciousness is actually in the essential position of productive self-creation. This is because in laboring for the master, the slave is able to enact the movement of the negative in a way that is more complex than mere consumption and incorporation. Hegel explains that in manipulating the material world, the slave comes into its true nature. In other words, the slave becomes conscious of itself as a force of negativity that forms, shapes, and changes the world. As Hegel says, "work forms and shapes the thing" and in turn, educates the consciousness that is forming and shaping its world (PhG 118). Significantly, Hegel refers to work as a "*negative* middle term" in which the slave's subjective negativity takes on an objective existence (PhG 118). The negative is therefore the central force in creative work. Labor, which is "arrested Desire [*gehemmte Begierde*]," is the expression of sublation that preserves difference even as it overcomes it (PhG 118). Because the slave is involved in the transformation of the environment (and in turn, subjectivity[2]), labor is still fundamentally an expression of freedom as negativity. Labor, as creative, formative activity, fashions both the world *and* the consciousness of the laboring existent. However, Hegel also reminds us that in addition to formative activity having a positive significance in labor, it also has "the negative significance of *fear* [*Furcht*]" (PhG 118). Freedom, in order to be made explicit to itself, must also experience a *purely* negative moment—i.e., a moment of utter dissolution in which all self-identity dissolves in the face of *absolute* negativity, or death.

In the battle for recognition, the slave (in discerning the real possibility of the loss of its life) experiences true terror. Hegel explains, "this consciousness has been anxious, not of this or that particular thing or just at odd moments, but its whole being has been seized with fear [*Angst*]; for it has experienced the fear [*Furcht*] of death, the absolute Master" (PhG 117, translation modified).[3] In its confrontation with the possibility of its own nonexistence, the soon-to-be slave experiences a substantial lesson regarding the nature of self-consciousness. The encounter with this ultimate fear is actually an insight into "the simple, essential nature of self-consciousness, absolute negativity, *pure being-for-self*, which consequently is *in* [*an*] this consciousness" (PhG 117, translation modified). Hegel explains that through the fear of death, the slave experiences the *truth* of self-consciousness in the form of an existential moment of absolute negativity. Instead of objectifying its negativity by transforming the limitations of its world, the fear of death is an experience of the slave's utter loss of the world. As he writes, this is due to the fact that the slave has been totally undone, "has trembled in every fibre of its being, and everything solid and stable has been shaken to its foundation" (PhG 117). The radical possibilities of this moment where all stability melts away lie in that it is the impetus for utterly novel, revolutionary activity because limitation of self, other, and the world as a whole has been momentarily dissolved, leaving pure potentiality in its wake.

Through work and fear, the slave experiences the two sides of freedom—explicitly as the negative movement of forming, shaping, and creating the material world, and implicitly as the dissolution of the self in the absolute fear of the nothingness of death, the melting away of the given, and as a radical break with the status quo. These two moments are integral to freedom and are necessary for the attainment of self-consciousness—both on the level of the individuals living this dynamic and on the level of Spirit coming to know itself through constant alienation and supersession. This is why the master-slave dialectic plays such a crucial role in the *Phenomenology* and consequently, in Beauvoir's Hegelian approach to the different expressions of freedom.

Beauvoir's Critique of Hegelian Freedom: Situation and Oppression

Beauvoir's engagement with Hegel's philosophy is a topic explored by many scholars, partly because it seems to be at odds with her particular formulation of existentialism (one that embraces anti-teleological ambiguity) while clearly informing her general conception of freedom as transcendence.[4] Importantly, Beauvoir's knowledge of Hegel is extensive and offers an original engagement, rather than a simple mapping of the theory.[5] She read Hegel's *Phenomenology* in the early 1940s when Alexandre Kojève's lectures were beginning to appear in publication and when Sartre was detained in Germany as a prisoner of war. One of her first mentions of Hegel is in a letter to Sartre dated July 11, 1940, where she writes, "You know, Hegel's horribly difficult, but also extremely interesting. You must know him—it's akin to your own philosophy of nothingness. I'm enjoying reading him and thinking precisely about expounding him to you."[6] The interest in Hegel in France is largely attributed to Kojève's lectures on the *Phenomenology* and Jean Hyppolite's translation of the *Phenomenology* into French.[7] Significantly, Kojève's reading of Hegel emphasizes the importance of the opening passages of the master-slave dialectic and the role of desire in the construction of the human subject.

In *The Ethics of Ambiguity*, Beauvoir expresses admiration for Hegel's *Phenomenology* because it emphasizes the "inextricable confusion between objectivity and subjectivity," in the constant movement of the dialectic.[8] However, Beauvoir believes that Hegel's emphasis on progress annihilates the role of individual suffering and sacrifice. In addition, she believes that Hegel misconstrues the role of temporality in existence. She writes, "If one denies with Hegel the concrete thickness of the here and now in favor of universal space-time, if one denies the separate consciousness in favor of Mind, one misses with Hegel the truth of the world" (EA 122). While the pitfalls of the absolutism in Hegel's philosophy remain a concern for Beauvoir throughout her philosophical development, there are ways in which freedom, separated from teleological optimism, can provide a useful framework for the development of freedom in situation. For Beauvoir, the situation is one of ambiguity. Human beings are neither fully transcendence (freedom) nor immanence (facticity) but an emergent, fully temporal admixture of both. While transcendence must be encouraged in oneself and others (as opposed to the enforced immanence of oppression) one is never free from the complex webs of social, material, and bodily forces that set the limitations in expressions of transcendence. In order to develop this complex notion of ambiguous freedom, Beauvoir adopts a formulation of Hegelian freedom understood as negativity. Transcendence is expressed in both the creative moment of work and the destructive moment of revolt. However, Beauvoir further develops a conception of immanent, (*negative* or *abstract)* freedom. This latter form accounts for the empty expression of freedoms who are oppressed—those peoples and groups for which Hegel's dialectic cannot adequately account.

Sonia Kruks explores the advances made by Beauvoir over Jean-Paul Sartre on the existence and effects of oppression on human beings.[9] The problem with Sartre's early philosophy lies, as Kruks locates it, in his inability to account for oppression except on a practically irrelevant level. Beauvoir's philosophy, although not specifically constructing a philosophy of freedom in direct confrontation with Sartre's, "quietly challenges" him on the basic assumption that all existents are equally free. Whereas Sartre argues in *Being and Nothingness* that freedoms are always equal regardless of the situation of the existent, Beauvoir explores the impact that given conditions have on the *expression* of freedom and argues that from this perspective, not all freedoms are equal.

In *Pyrrhus and Cineas*, Beauvoir writes, "I am not first a thing, but a spontaneity that desires, that loves, that wants, that acts" and consequently, "what is mine is therefore first what I do."[10] Here Beauvoir makes two central points about freedom. First, she agrees with Hegel concerning the essence of freedom lying in activity rather than a static definition or predicate of a subject. Additionally, she emphasizes that what belongs to me and, in a sense *defines* me, is not what I am but what I *do*. Freedom is thus not a property of a concrete soul or mind, but transcendent activity itself.[11] Later, in *The Ethics of Ambiguity*, Beauvoir explicitly rejects Hegel's conception of the Absolute and the progressive thrust of history; yet she remains committed to his understanding of freedom as self-determination and negativity. In this work, Beauvoir acknowledges that freedom and ethics can be construed within the understanding of the negative operative in the Hegelian dialectic by stating directly that "man is originally a negativity" (EA 118). Just as Hegel's Spirit is not an entity but a negating *process*, Beauvoir insists that we are the free process of what we do—in other words, transcendent activity. Additionally, she consistently maintains that our projection into the future is integral to the movement of transcendence. One of her core criticisms against Hegel is that he betrays his insight into freedom as negativity by constructing a positive future at the end of history: "the Future appears as both the infinite and as Totality, as number and as unity of conciliation; it is the abolition of the negative, it is fullness, happiness" (EA 116). Hegel's optimistic focus on the future as some kind of preordained goal allows for the sacrifice of the present in the name of an abstraction and falsely blankets the essence of subjectivity as negativity (EA 106).[12]

Although Beauvoir agrees with Hegel (and Sartre) that freedom is defined as that which negates the given, she also recognizes that one's situation can sometimes serve not as a limit to be surpassed, but as an unsurpassable, seemingly natural wall imposed around existence.[13] Through her analysis of various marginalized groups in both her ethics and feminism, Beauvoir's conception of situation allows for, echoing what Kruks above calls "gradations of freedom." For example, Beauvoir tells us in *The Prime of Life* that as early as *Pyrrhus et Cineas* she believed that,

> actual concrete possibilities vary from one person to the next. Some can attain to only a small part of those opportunities that are available to mankind at large … Their transcendence is lost in the general mass of humanity, and takes on the appearance of immanence. (POL 661)

In other words, although everyone is ontologically free, not everyone shares the same concrete *possibilities* for expressing this freedom. Some individuals may be in a favorable situation conducive to the expression of their freedom, and others may simply suffer a loss of their transcendence so much so that it takes on the appearance of immanence, i.e., the appearance of givenness. One's situation can in some cases serve not merely as a limitation to be surmounted in an upsurge of freedom, but as an intractable and oftentimes unknown constraint on action.[14]

In oppression, "transcendence is condemned to fall uselessly back upon itself because it is cut off from its goals" (EA 81). Oppression effectively denies existents' unfettered expansion into the future, confining them to a static present or forcing them into a repetition of the past. The facts of the situation therefore appear fixed, immovable, and unchanging: "[r]educed to pure facticity, congealed in his immanence, cut off from his future, deprived of his transcendence and of the world which that transcendence discloses, a man no longer appears as anything more than a thing among things" (EA,100). Yet, in oppression, the ontological freedom of that existent is not simply destroyed (i.e., one is not literally turned into a thing) even if it is prevented from affecting the world: "[n]o social upheaval, no moral conversion can eliminate this lack which is in his heart" (EA 118). By extrapolation, Beauvoir also means to argue that even if one is oppressed, the negativity of freedom cannot be annihilated unless the existent is literally turned into a thing, i.e., a corpse. What then *happens* to the freedom that is employed in transcendent activity, but denied expression in conditions of immanence? If one cannot literally turn a human being into a thing through oppression, where does the transcendent thrust of freedom *go*?

Moving Beyond Hegel: The Paradox of Immanent Freedom

Laura Hengehold writes that Hegel offers Beauvoir "a promise of support, an assurance that immanence might have exits."[15] Immanence is thus not the defining feature even of those people walled up in oppression and mystification. In this light, Beauvoir echoes the Hegelian twofold movement of constructive and destructive negativity, in the closing lines of *The Ethics of Ambiguity*. She writes:

> Man is free; but he finds his law in his very freedom. First, he must assume his freedom and not flee it; *he assumes it by a constructive movement*: one does not exist without doing something; *and also by a negative movement* which rejects oppression for oneself and others. In construction, as in rejection, it is a matter of reconquering freedom on the contingent facticity of existence. (EA 156, italics my own)

Beauvoir here mirrors the lessons learned from the master-slave dialectic in which freedom, understood as negativity, has two distinct manifestations: a productive and a destructive movement. She interprets the constructive moment as *doing* something (i.e., *working*) and the negative moment as *revolt* (against the given).[16] These two movements must be undertaken if freedom is to be transcendent or actual. And both of these activities *change* the face of the world—one through building and modifying, and the other through destroying sedimented structures.

In describing these modes of transcendence, Beauvoir takes over Hegel's distinction between freedom as productive and destructive. However, her adoption is not without criticism. The first criticism can be found succinctly laid out in *The Ethics of Ambiguity* where she writes,

There are thus two ways of surpassing the given…. In these two cases the given is present in its surpassing; but in one case it is present insofar as it is accepted, in the other insofar as rejected, and that makes a radical difference. Hegel has confused these two movements with the ambiguous term "aufheben"; and the whole structure of an optimism which denies failure and death rests on this ambiguity; that is what allows one to regard the future of the world as a continuous and harmonious development. (EA 84)

This first criticism thus centers around Hegel's teleological account of history in which revolution is simply a part of the restlessness of Spirit, and sacrifice is swept up into what she sees as the ideal future of humankind. Beauvoir, however, agrees more with Marx in that true revolt is not integrated into the world, but explodes the static structures of its givenness (EA 84).

There is another criticism of Hegel operative in Beauvoir's philosophy—one that is not so easily determined but upon closer inspection is ubiquitous. What if the givenness of the world is tacitly accepted and thus the surpassing of it practically impossible? What if this kind of prohibition of activity was not simply a dead-end of Spirit's progress but is in fact a recalcitrant set of structures oppressing individuals and communities alike? Certainly, if the oppressed have the means to rebel, theirs is the path of revolution that confronts the awesome negativity of death and tears down social and political institutions that serve to alienate and exclude them. Following revolution, they will then exert the creative expression of transcendence to set up a world of their own invention. Yet, some oppressed existents never attain revolution, and yet cannot be understood as being reduced to the status of "things" and "objects" without freedom. In her inquiry into this dilemma, Beauvoir discovers two *other* expressions of freedom that are absent in Hegel's philosophy and which help to explain the complexity of concrete situations of oppression. Instead of manifesting *transcendent* expressions of liberty, the oppressed expend their freedom in *immanent* agitations and gestures. Since they cannot actively change the situation, they feebly react against or quietly submit to it. Beauvoir's philosophy roots out and describes these expenditures as the initial theoretical move requisite in eventually overcoming them practically.

Both of these attitudes or expressions of freedom—"complaint" and "resignation"—fall under Beauvoir's category of "abstract freedom." It is somewhat confusing because she often addresses these terms under the rubric of "negative liberty" which appears to be a contradiction. If liberty is essentially negativity as argued above, how can negative liberty be a harmful thing? However, it becomes clear in her work that when she employs the term "negative liberty," she means the term "negative" as "empty," "abstract," and/or "impotent," as opposed to a "positive" sense of liberty that implies "concrete," "expressive," and "powerful" freedom in action. Repeatedly throughout her major philosophical works, Beauvoir claims that true freedom is "concrete," that is, like production and revolt, it substantially affects the world of the existent expressing it. However, there is another expression of liberty that Beauvoir labels "abstract." This kind of freedom is often discussed in tandem with immanence, thus drawing a connection between immanence and abstract liberty. To label freedom as immanent (as opposed to transcendent) is a radical claim for Beauvoir to make, given that immanence typically characterizes the existence of things, or of repetitive organic processes.[17] It is therefore tempting to say that those who are condemned to immanence are simply *not* free. But Beauvoir never denies the freedom of the existent, no matter how great the oppression. Instead, as she explains in the *Ethics*, if "his transcendence is cut off from his goal or there is no longer any hold on objects which might give it a valid content, *his spontaneity is dissipated* without founding anything" (EA 30, italics my own). Freedom is thus *dissipated*, not annihilated, disclosing itself in both complaint and resignation.

Complaint is clearly an expression of freedom in that it exhibits a conscious awareness of a situation and a reaction *against* it. But unlike revolt, it does little to nothing to change the situation. Complaint, in the most general sense, is the best example of a revolt that remains empty and as such is "purely negative." This is what Beauvoir means when she writes that "revolt, insofar as it is pure negative movement, remains abstract. It is fulfilled as freedom only by returning to the positive, that is, by giving itself a content through action, escape, political struggle, revolution" (EA 31). In other words, if revolt fails to affect the world through concrete action, it is merely a powerless grievance. The clearest examples of complaint that Beauvoir provides for us can be found in *The Second Sex*, where woman is left to protest without the power to meaningfully change her lot. For example, she writes that woman "does not dare revolt; she submits against her will; her attitude is a constant recrimination ... complaint is the commonest mode of expression" (SS 646). Complaining does not substantially alter the situation, it merely rails against it. This is why further down the page, Beauvoir characterizes woman's situation as one of "impotent anger" (SS 646).[18] Clearly, grumbling about one's situation is an expression of freedom, but unlike creativity and revolt, it is an empty and almost meaningless expression—a mere expenditure that does nothing to improve or undermine the status quo. At best, it is a displacement of the oftentimes unknown structures of oppression limiting action. Instead of complaining about inequitable power distributions, complaint is often about mundane annoyances. It can stir up a reaction, but not one that transforms the given in a positive sense. As shown above, true revolt requires exercising the destructive forces of freedom. *Impotent* revolt is the powerless and sad expression of a transcendence cut off from expression in any consequential sense.[19] Such expressions only serve to make the concerns of the oppressed seem petty and easily ignored, while simultaneously serving to reinforce their resentment. In the case of women's oppression, Beauvoir concludes, "[t]his is why women do not succeed in building a solid 'counter-universe' where they can defy males; they sporadically rant against men in general ... But to truly build this 'world of grievances' that their resentment calls for, they lack conviction" (SS 617). This paralyzed state of women's liberty leads Beauvoir to close her detailed exploration of woman's education from infancy to old age by exclaiming, "in her thoughts as in her acts, the highest form of freedom a woman-parasite can have is stoic defiance or skeptical irony. At no time in her life does she succeed in being both effective and independent" (SS 596). In other words, given her position of enforced immanence, woman's reactions can never attain to concrete action and as such, she remains largely ineffective and dependent.

Yet even complaint shows the *possibility* of enacting some form of change, if only minimally (EA 153). There is a second sense of negative liberty that is defined by acquiescence to the given and renunciation of all hope of changing it. Ironically, this form of negative liberty is more powerful in its powerlessness. Beauvoir writes in the *Ethics* that there is "hardly a sadder virtue than resignation" (EA 28). To resign oneself to the given is not simply to become an object, but to submerge oneself in immanence, to let go of even the desire to set up a project or to change the face of the world. It is, for Beauvoir, the emptiest expenditure of liberty. Through resignation, "one manages only to save an abstract notion of freedom. It is emptied of all content and all truth. The power of man ceases to be limited because it is annulled" (EA 29).

Resignation, like complaint, is not solely a result of the oppression of women. Rather, it can be applied to many groups for whom transcendence has been denied by a situation of enforced immanence. To the existent who is resigned to a situation, the given does not appear as a limitation to be surpassed, or a situation against which to complain, but only as a hopelessly unalterable and static fact. However, as with complaint, some of Beauvoir's strongest descriptions of this attitude of sheer defeatism are found in *The Second Sex*. There she says that on the whole, women "accept what is. One of their typical features is resignation" (SS 642). Returning to her many arguments that enforced immanence (or oppression) is defined by the denial of an open future to an existent, it is clear that if one is forced merely to maintain the present through a repetition of the past, then quite often the only choice left is to resign oneself to such a "destiny." Left no possibility for concrete choice, the existent can, in essence, deny that choice exists and believe that the situation is immutable. This is why Beauvoir writes that, for example, "[a] proud woman can make a lofty virtue" of resignation because in general "women always try to keep, to fix, to arrange rather than to destroy and reconstruct anew; they prefer compromises and exchanges to revolutions" (SS 642). Rather than condemning women for lacking the fortitude to engage in revolution, Beauvoir shifts focus to the awareness that resignation becomes a fallback, even a glorified feminine quality, because of a lack of options to do otherwise. Abandoning even the desire to complain about the situation, the extreme and most triumphant configuration of oppression leads the oppressed to give up the ability to know that their situation is unjust and harmful. The forces of domination are most successful and oppression most complete at this point. True, freedom is expressed in resignation, but its expression is so reduced, so empty, that it can only be called freedom in name only. Uncovering the realities of resignation, bringing what is hidden into the light, provides a kind of kindling to spur the oppressed to change.

The idea of resignation brings up a certain tension in Beauvoir's formulation of subjugation. On the one hand, she maintains that certain extreme forms of oppression essentially rob human beings of their ability to make choices. She confesses that sometimes existents can be so degraded that they are hardly more than beasts. This is the ultimate manifestation of enforced immanence such as the situation of Jews in concentration camps. Reduced to little more than an "animal horde," their revolts "were only the agitations of animals" (EA 101). Can a Jew in a concentration camp or an Algerian in a French torture chamber[20] honestly be said to have even a modicum of choice to resign themselves to their situations? In a very strong sense, no, they cannot, and Beauvoir acknowledges this. However, she refuses to take the position that freedom can ever be completely destroyed in an individual so long as that individual lives. Besides, the freedom to essentially give up is not always done in bad faith, but is often demanded by the brutality of the situation. This is the ultimate goal of all oppression—to reduce existents to such demoralized and dehumanized states that their sphere of choice is reduced to nothing more than obedience and the stark acceptance of their oppression. While this idea may be lurking in the interstices of Hegel's master-slave dialectic, the overall optimism of the dialectical inversion prevents the exploration of how deeply servitude can be externally and violently enforced.

Another component of Beauvoir's analysis that brings her closer to Marx focuses on the mystification of the oppressed to see their situation as natural or given, rather than created and thus transformable. The power of mystification, which forces a fixed identity onto individuals, complicates the "choice" of resignation. Beauvoir is clear that:

> The slave is submissive when one has succeeded in mystifying him in such a way that his situation does not seem to him to be imposed by men, but to be immediately given by nature, by the gods, by the powers against whom revolt has no meaning; thus, he does not accept his condition through a resignation of his freedom since he can not even dream of any other. (EA 85)

Although it seems that resignation is impossible in the aforementioned examples, I argue that Beauvoir's utilization of the category of "resignation" as such includes even the mystified slave in that there is still a tacit acceptance of what is, coupled with a total lack of power to change it. The individuals trapped in concentration camps or taught from birth that they are slaves by nature are still free in the abstract sense, but their freedom is merely a total surrender to the given until the situation changes. Admittedly, this might not seem like freedom in any meaningful sense, but that is precisely Beauvoir's point—freedom merely to accept the situation as unalterable or predetermined is only the exercise of a negative, abstract liberty.

Taking into account the excesses of oppression, Beauvoir forces us to admit that even in resignation there is still freedom. Freedom, in other words, can never be destroyed in human beings, even if it is completely ineffectual in its diffusion. As Kruks observes, freedom "can, in a situation of extreme oppression, be wholly suppressed, *even though it cannot be definitively eliminated*" and therefore, "should oppression start to weaken, freedom can always reerupt."[21] It is thus the *potential* of freedom to overcome oppression to which Beauvoir commands our attention. That said, we can certainly never deceive ourselves that resignation in the face of oppression is an authentic expression of human liberty. Beauvoir reminds us that we must "respect freedom only when it is intended for freedom, not when it strays, flees itself, and resigns itself" (EA 90–91).[22] The freedom to dissipate rather than to alter merely expends energy instead of encouraging the existent's freedom and flourishing. As such, resignation is the lowest and saddest state of affairs resulting from oppression.

Yet, despite the difficulties of extreme oppression, Beauvoir explains in a late interview that it is always necessary to uphold the freedom of the individual *even in the very act of renunciation*: "Well, naturally, the choice itself depends upon a number of things. But after all, there is still some freedom or choice, *even in resignation of course*."[23] For Beauvoir, if we do not hold on to the liberty of even the most degraded and abused human being—the one whose freedom is lost in impotent acts of complaint or resignation—we lose the hope of bringing such oppression to an end and lose sight of the humanity of the oppressed.

Conclusion

Beauvoir's introduction of the categories of complaint and resignation help to reveal the paradoxical manifestation of immanent freedom found in oppression. Although this idea seems contradictory (in that freedom is usually defined as a *transcendent* surpassing of the given toward an indefinite future) Beauvoir's discovery of these immanent dissipations of freedom allows her to move beyond entrenched Hegelian optimism. Hegel did not adequately address the mechanism of this contradictory freedom and thus did not account for concrete oppression in the *Phenomenology*. In contrast, Beauvoir argues that if we fail to understand immanent freedom (or negative liberty) we fail to comprehend how oppression can take on semi-permanent or regressive structures throughout history.

There are many important ramifications on Beauvoir's politics resulting from the above analysis. For one, it shows that we cannot even begin to talk about revolution and creativity—the transcendent expressions of the negativity that is our freedom—before we can understand how freedom can expend itself *without* transforming the world. Certainly, she acknowledges that before real labor can occur, the oppressed must revolt. That is why she writes "the oppressed can fulfill his freedom as a man only in revolt, since the essential characteristic of the situation against which he is rebelling is precisely its prohibiting him from any positive development; it is only in social and political struggle that his transcendence passes beyond to the infinite" (EA 87). Yet, to achieve liberation, the oppressed must first overcome the pitfalls of resignation, complaint, and the mystification that supports their continuance.

Additionally, it is crucial to remember that the Hegelian dialectic of mastery and servitude, which reveals the truth of self-consciousness as negativity, is essentially rooted in a struggle for recognition. When one is, through the machinations of oppression, reduced to the state of simply complaining against or resigning oneself to the givenness of the situation, there has been a total breakdown of recognition. The futile attempts of the existent to expend energy rather than to build or destroy indicate the unqualified isolation of one whose voice, actions, and desires are not even taken up into a dialogue, let alone the public sphere. In construction and dissolution, there is at least an undeclared recognition of the existent's freedom in that it is impossible to deny that the world is transformed through their actions. But in the hollow gestures of complaint and resignation, the powerful can simply ignore the needs of the oppressed by refusing to recognize them.

Clearly then, although Beauvoir admires the Hegelian construction of freedom as a twofold negativity, she goes beyond his analysis by undoing the optimism that freedom is progressively realized, by substituting another, more ambiguous, perhaps cautious optimism of her own. For Beauvoir, there is no historical guarantee that existents will ever move beyond abstract expenditures of freedom—on the individual or universal level—and thus no guarantee that the oppressed will ever be recognized. Nonetheless, her entire philosophical project is oriented toward showing how oppression functions so that it can be countered by those who stand on the side of the oppressed.[24] She thus exhibits a kind of mitigated optimism which refuses to believe that oppression is ever so complete as to annihilate freedom. Because Beauvoir is more attuned to the necessity of understanding and alleviating oppressive structures (structures which only allow certain existents empty and abstract expressions of freedom), she sees something that Hegel's optimism obscures—conditions of stagnation and even regression in human advancement. Beauvoir provides us with an expansion of Hegelian freedom by uncovering sites of powerlessness that must be confronted before social and political emancipation and transformation can become a reality for the oppressed.

Notes

1. Ray Brassier, "Strange Sameness: Hegel, Marx and the Logic of Estrangement," *Angelaki: Journal of the Theoretical Humanities* 24, no. 1 (2019): 101.
2. Hegel concludes that "Through this rediscovery of himself by himself, the bondsman realizes that it is precisely in his work wherein he seemed to have only an alienated existence that he acquires a mind of his own" (PhG 118–19).
3. This experience of fear leads Tadeusz Gadacz to argue perceptively that "the master is not the master of the slave, but the master of death. Likewise, the slave is not the slave of the master, but the slave of death" ("Freedom as Reconciliation: The Essence of the Individual's Freedom in the Philosophy of Hegel," *International Philosophical Quarterly* 27, no. 2 [June 1987]: 177).
4. As Karen Green and Nicholas Roffey observe: "while it is clear that Beauvoir appropriates a great deal from Hegel, she by no means simply accepts his views. Indeed, Beauvoir's use of Hegel is confusing and there is deep disagreement in the literature as to exactly where she agrees with him and where her agreement ends" ("Woman, Hegel, and Recognition in the Second Sex," *Hypatia* 25, no. 2 [Spring 2010]: 382).

5. Meryl Altman's essay, "Beauvoir, Hegel, War," provides an excellent historical framework for teasing out some of the complexities of Beauvoir's utilization of Hegelian philosophy (*Hypatia* 22, no. 3 [Summer 2007]: 66–91).

6. Simone de Beauvoir, *Letters to Sartre*, trans. and ed. Quintin Hoare (New York: Arcade Publishing, 1990), 31. Beauvoir admits that in her eighteenth year, while attending lectures at the Sorbonne, her professors "systematically ignored Hegel and Marx" (*Memoirs of a Dutiful Daughter*, trans. James Kirkup [Middlesex: Penguin Books, 1986], 230). Thus, her interest in these figures was largely self-induced.

7. Kojève's lectures were delivered in Paris between 1933 and 1939, with the official publication of his students' notes in 1947. Beauvoir herself read Hyppolite's French translation of the *Phenomenology*. See Karen Vintges, *Philosophy as Passion: The Thinking of Simone de Beauvoir*, trans. Anne Lavelle (Bloomington: Indiana University Press, 1996), 141. Eva Lundgren-Gothlin artfully discusses the influence of Alexandre Kojève on Beauvoir's Hegelianism in *Sex and Existence: Simone de Beauvoir's "The Second Sex,"* trans. Linda Schenck (Middletown: Wesleyan University Press, 1996), 56–66. See also Nancy Bauer, *Simone de Beauvoir, Philosophy, and Feminism* (New York: Columbia University Press, 2001), 86.

8. Simone de Beauvoir, *The Ethics of Ambiguity*, trans. Bernard Frechtman (New York: Citadel Press, 1996), 153. Hereafter: EA.

9. The freedom espoused by the early Sartre is a freedom devoid of social context in that it pits the lone individual against the given world and the hostile others who want to steal this world away. Regarding the individualism rampant in *Being and Nothingness*, Kruks contends, "Sartre cannot account adequately for the existence of 'collectivities,' of 'general types,' or of such a generality as 'woman's situation.' There is in his work a radical individualism that amounts to a kind of solipsism: each of us construes the meaning of both past and present only from the perspective of our own project" ("Simone de Beauvoir: Teaching Sartre About Freedom," in *Feminist Interpretations of Simone de Beauvoir*, ed. Margaret A. Simons [University Park: The Pennsylvania State University Press, 1995], 86).

10. Simone de Beauvoir, "Pyrrhus and Cineas," in *Simone de Beauvoir: Philosophical Writings*, ed. Margaret A. Simons with Marybeth Timmermann and Mary Beth Mader (Urbana: University of Illinois Press, 2004), 93.

11. Beauvoir never abdicates this position on freedom. Even in *The Second Sex*, which is her monument to the oppression of women and their historically entrenched position as the absolute Other, she maintains that, "An existent *is* nothing other than what he does; the possible does not exceed the real, essence does not precede existence: in his pure subjectivity, the human being *is* nothing. He is measured by his acts" (*The Second Sex*, trans. Constance Borde and Sheila Malovany-Chevallier [New York: Alfred A. Knopf, 2010], 270. Hereafter: SS.) Regardless of situation then, all human subjectivity is the action of pure negativity or transcendence.

12. Beauvoir's critical reading of Hegel at this time leads her away from the more obvious passages of the *Phenomenology* where Hegel does not envision the fulfillment of the Absolute as pure positivity stasis, but as a preservation of past sacrifice and more importantly, as the stage for a new beginning (PhG 492). Nor does she do justice to his deep meditations on the tragic conflict between the individual and the universal running throughout the entirety of *The Phenomenology*. In part, this is because it is not until *The Second Sex* that Beauvoir's reading of Hegel reaches the depth and complexity it deserves. Yet, even there, and with some concessions, Beauvoir maintains a consistent suspicion of Hegelian optimism and absolutism throughout her works.

13. In *The Prime of Life*, Beauvoir writes that she was intrigued by Sartre's discussion of "situation" in *Being and Nothingness*, yet she admits: "I maintained that from the angle of freedom as Sartre defined it—that is, an active transcendence of some given context rather than mere stoic resignation—not every situation was equally valid: what sort of transcendence could a woman shut up in a harem achieve?" Even though she grudgingly conceded the argument victory to Sartre, she still concludes, "Basically I was right" (*The Prime of Life*, trans. Peter Green [New York: Lancer Books, 1966], 523. Hereafter: POL). On Beauvoir's specific formulation of transcendence as "constructive activity," see Andrea Veltman, "The Concept of Transcendence in Beauvoir and Sartre," in *Beauvoir & Sartre: The Riddle of Influence*, ed. Christine Daigle and Jacob Golomb (Bloomington: Indiana University Press, 2009), 222–40.

14. Beauvoir argues that certain people—the aforementioned women in a harem, slaves in the American south, and ultimately many women conditioned as the Other—are "mystified" into believing that they are inferior by nature (not by social conditioning). It is these mystified groups that largely suffer complaint and resignation as their only experience of freedom. I discuss this in greater detail further into the paper.

15. Laura Hengehold, *Simone de Beauvoir's Philosophy of Individuation: The Problem of* The Second Sex (Edinburgh: University of Edinburgh Press, 2019), 37.

16. Karen Vintges calls these two moments, *action* and the *rejection* of oppression (Vintges, *Philosophy as Passion* 82). She argues that Beauvoir eventually produces a "*negative* moral code" which asserts only that, from the perspective of morality, freedom cannot be limited or denied. She continues that Beauvoir abandons the project of constructing a positive ethical system, but rather elucidates a "positive art of living" in addition to the negative moral code (82–83). Vintges is correct in her characterization of the negative element of Beauvoir's ethics, although it is clear from the above discussions that Beauvoir also holds a "creative" component vital to morality, even if she refuses to give it a determinate content.

17. See Shannon M. Mussett, "Nature and Anti-Nature in Simone de Beauvoir's Philosophy," *Philosophy Today* 53, SPEP Supplement (2009): 130–37.

18. Beauvoir goes so far as to say that woman's "life takes place against a background of powerless revolt" (SS 608).

19. For example, even if a woman tries to revolt physically against her situation, often she, "like the child, indulges in symbolic outbursts ... these are only gestures. But above all, through nervous fits in her body she attempts to express the refusals *she cannot carry out concretely*" (SS 609, italics my own).

20. This thematic of extreme oppression essentially robbing the existent of any kind of substantial choice also underlies her analysis of the French atrocities in Algeria as described in her Introduction to *Djamila Boupacha: The Story of the Torture of a Young Algerian Girl which Shocked Liberal French Opinion*, ed. Simone de Beauvoir and Gisele Halimi, trans. Peter Green (New York: Macmillan, 1962). There we are shown cases of torture that force us to ask whether one can be said to choose to resign oneself to the situation in the face of extreme physical and mental violence. And yet, Boupacha was able to emerge from that situation and turn her liberty into a force enacting concrete, political change through it.

21. Sonia Kruks, "Gender and Subjectivity: Simone de Beauvoir and Contemporary Feminism," *Signs: Journal of Women in Culture and Society* 18, no. 1 (Autumn 1992): 100, italics my own.

22. This staunch belief in the hollowness of resignation and the ethical necessity to fight against it leads Beauvoir so far as to posit a figure such as the Marquis de Sade as a "great moralist" because he fiercely rejects the virtue of resignation which "is a stupid submission to the rule of evil, as recreated by society. In submitting, man renounces both his authenticity and his freedom" (Simone de Beauvoir, "Must We Burn Sade?" [London: John Calder, 1962], 66).

23. Margaret Simons, "Two Interviews with Simone de Beauvoir," trans. Jane Marie Todd, *Hypatia* 3, no. 3 (Winter 1989): 16, italics my own.

24. The situation of women brings this belief directly to the surface: "Because of the fact that in woman this freedom remains abstract and empty, it cannot authentically assume itself except in revolt: this is the only way open to those who have no chance to build anything; they must refuse the limits of their situation and seek to open paths to the future; resignation is only a surrender and an evasion; for woman there is no other way out than to work for her liberation" (SS 664).

9

Fanon and Hegel: The Dialectic, the Phenomenology of Race, and Decolonization

Azzedine Haddour

Slavery appears as an ambivalent concept in Georg Wilhelm Friedrich Hegel's work, which at once objectivizes the principles of the rational state and goes against them. His views on slavery and race divide opinion: critics like Stephen Houlgate refer to his ethnocentrism only to ignore it and choose to focus instead on his pronouncements on the rational state and universal freedom[1]; others such as Philip J. Kain find his endorsement of Western racism objectionable, but provide an apology for it. By arguing that it is not "scientific" and does not "cut that deep" and that "essences reside in mind or spirit" and must not be comprehended in natural and biological terms, these critics reproduce Hegel's ethnocentrism which pits *corporeality* against *mind*: the immutability of race against the dialectical progression of spirit in its attainment of "freedom [which] is a potential waiting to be realized in all."[2]

To start with, this chapter adumbrates Hegel's dialectic and teleological narratives of world history before turning to explore Frantz Fanon's critique of Hegel. For Fanon, Hegelianism is not an abstract theory but has very real phenomenological implications. His take on Hegel is historically bound up with the specificities of colonialism and slavery.[3] His critique has two stages:

A. Haddour (✉)
University College London, London, UK
e-mail: a.haddour@ucl.ac.uk

C. D. Coe (eds.), *The Palgrave Handbook of German Idealism and Phenomenology*,
Palgrave Handbooks in German Idealism,
https://doi.org/10.1007/978-3-030-66857-0_9

(i) in *Black Skin, White Masks*, he shows that color is a factor in the dialectic; (ii) in *The Wretched of the Earth*, he discounts the teleological narratives of progress for their complicity in Europe's colonial project. Fanon identifies an otherness which is not situated within the dialectic, a difference which cannot be synthesized and digested by world history and which Hegel uses to justify historical slavery.

Fanon lays bare the ethnocentrism inherent in the dialectic. A close reading of Hegel shows that the racialized subject sits outside the dialectic beyond the processes of sublation as an unchanging being-in-itself and that the narratives of world spirit are structured and ranked according to race and thereby exclude peoples of color from their teleological progress. Hegel's rational state is sustained by an Orientalizing discourse that works to situate historical slavery outside the scope of the dialectic; the crux of Fanon's argument is that, because founded on slavery and servitude, the Hegelian dialectic is useless and inoperative: it is premised on principles which go against the grain of the Hegelian narratives of progress, principles which therefore thwart the actualization of freedom and the development of the rational state.

Hegelian Dialectic: Universal Consciousness, Work, and the Burden of Slavery

The human individual, Hegel argues, separates himself [sic] from nature in order to conquer and exercise power over it.[4] He establishes a "practical relationship" with the world to satisfy his self-seeking appetites—"to turn nature to [his] advantage, to exploit and harness and in short to annihilate it."[5] Through necessity and work, he changes the world and ultimately transforms himself; such transformation is enacted via what Hegel terms the master/slave dialectic and the attendant struggle for recognition. Hegel uses the metaphor of the master/slave to delineate not only human dominance over nature but also intersubjective relations that are inevitably fraught.

In the struggle for recognition, *force* (viz. power and the violence to which it gives rise) is a "necessary and legitimate factor."[6] The master stakes his life and wins the fight. But in doing so, he finds himself at an existential loss, because he is unable to ascertain the truth of his self-consciousness confronting a dependent slave: only a free consciousness affirms the humanity of the master. In this aporetic instance, *mastery* is, in Alexandre Kojève's parlance, an "existential impasse" keeping the master in *servitude* as he becomes dependent on the labor of the slave to maintain his power and prestige. The slave, having failed to stake his life and attain recognition as an independent self-consciousness, turns to the object (i.e., work) and masters it. However, the slave, working for the master, overcomes the inner immediacy of self-seeking appetites and "in this divestment of self ... makes ... the passage to universal self-consciousness."[7] "Through his service," says Hegel, "he rids himself of his attachment to natural existence in every single detail; and gets rid of it by working on it."[8] In Hegel, work humanizes and imparts to the slave "universal self-consciousness [as] the affirmative knowing of one's self in the other self"; work also provides a solution to the existential impasse of the master.[9] While the master does not work and experiences neither objectification nor loss of agency, his self-realization and ultimate freedom are contingent on the freedom of the slave actualized by work. Through work, the slave transcends the particularity of his individual inclinations and achieves truly independent self-consciousness. In Hegel's theorizing, the path to freedom and universal history is paved with the slave's servitude, and genuine reciprocity is borne out of slavery.

Hegel considers the phenomenon of subordination and servitude as an inevitable phase of human history, a necessary condition for the development of universal self-consciousness.[10] Legitimizing the exploitation of those who carry the enormous burden of labor and shoulder the negative weight of the dialectic, he states: "Servitude and tyranny are therefore to *some extent* justified, since they constitute a necessary stage in the history of peoples. No absolute injustice is done to those who remain servants, for whoever lacks the courage to risk his life in order to obtain freedom deserves to remain a slave."[11]

Hegel's dialectic is instituted and maintained by the logic of brute force of slavery and colonialism. Alluding to this logic in *Black Skin, White Masks*, Fanon argues that Hegelian universal self-consciousness substantiates itself as absolute by drawing its worth from its negative side and by sublating itself in the dark night of slavery. Recognition cannot be achieved by a singular and lonely consciousness but through intersubjective mediation; it involves competing desires which seek fulfillment. It is a two-way traffic or, in Hegel's and Fanon's parlance, a "circuit" with a dual interchange: in Hegel's dialectic, two unmediated consciousnesses are implicated in an encounter which is conflictual and self-othering; each consciousness seeks recognition; opposition is overcome and mutual recognition achieved, as each self-consciousness mediates and actualizes the other. As Hegel puts it:

The process then is absolutely the double process of both self-consciousnesses. Each sees the other do the same as itself; each itself does what it demands on the part of the other, and for that reason does what it does, only so far as the other does the same. Action from one side only would be useless, because what is to happen can only be brought about by means of both.

Furthermore:

> Each is the mediating term to the other, through which each mediates and unites itself with itself; and each is to itself and to the other an immediate self-existing reality, which, at the same time, exists thus for itself only through this mediation. They recognize themselves as mutually recognizing one another.[12]

Mutual recognition brings about the spiritual unity of these two separate consciousnesses and the elaboration of the *I* as *We*. Freedom is actualized not in isolation but rather in the coming together of self-recognizing consciousnesses as independent. Individuality is overcome in the union of the one with the other. This universal solidarity comes after a long and unmediated struggle between these consciousnesses which were opposed and unequal.

Hegel, the Racialized State, and World History

In the *Encyclopaedia*, Hegel admirably states that "Man is implicitly rational; herein lies the possibility of equal justice for all men and the futility of a rigid distinction between races which have rights and those which have none." However, he goes on to express his racist bias infantilizing people of color: "Negroes are to be regarded as a race of children."[13] He contends that "[n]o colour has any superiority"; he paradoxically maintains that "one can speak of the objective superiority of the colour of the Caucasian race as against that of the Negro."[14] Hegelian dialectic is predicated on binary opposition (essence/appearance, spirit/nature, self/other, white/black, master/slave), prioritizing one of the terms of the binary and positing "the objective superiority of the whiteness of the skin."[15] Before turning to his views on world spirit and history which are, just as is his dialectic, premised on a Eurocentric and racialized view of the world, it suffices to say that *Black Skin, White Masks* is an acerbic rejoinder to its inherent ethnocentrism.

In Hegel's view, world history is a rational process and spirit is its substance; freedom is one of its fundamental properties.[16] History is the sum total of national spirits as they develop from individual particularity into universal totality. Like individual spirit, national spirit enters the stage of universal history as it overcomes its immediate contexts "to attain knowledge of its own function."[17] The development of universal history is teleological: "Each new individual national spirit represents a new stage in the conquering march of the world spirit as it wins its way to consciousness and freedom."[18] National spirits represent, for Hegel, particular instances through which world spirit ascends, in the course of history, to universality in an "all-embracing totality."[19] World spirit—or what Hegel dubs the "Absolute Idea"—is the embodiment of past and present forms of self-consciousness and all manifestations of spirit which appeared throughout the different stages of its development in history.[20]

Hegel posits patriarchy as a transitional stage in which the family grows gradually into a tribe, nation, and ultimately state.[21] He draws conceptual links between patriarchal authority and theocracy in tribal life, between despotic rule in certain "underdeveloped" nations and "uneducated" cultures before the advent of world spirit and the state. According to Hegel, ethical life starts in the family, but this sort of life is premised on the sentiments of love and interdependence and must be differentiated from world spirit founded on knowledge and freedom.[22]

In nature, argues Hegel, regeneration occurs as a repetitive process within a stasis. Change and development take place not in the natural world but only in the spiritual sphere.[23] Humans differentiate themselves from natural objects and animals by virtue of being natural reality and ideality.[24] Unlike objects and animals in nature, they have "a real capacity for change" and "an impulse of perfectibility."[25] In the natural world, change is a "repetition of identical phases," while in the world of spirit, change is a manifestation of progress.[26] Hegel affirms that progress manifests itself as a sequence of successive stages governed by three main principles which saw the emergence of spirit in the East and its actualization in the West:

> [T]he Far East (i.e. Mongolian, Chinese, or Indian) principle, which is also the first to appear in history; the Mohammedan world, in which the principle of the abstract spirit, of monotheism, is already present, although it is coupled with unrestrained arbitrariness; and the Christian, Western European world, in which the highest principle of all, spirit's recognition of itself and its own profundity, is realised.[27]

To outline the course of world history and the actualization of world spirit, Hegel grounds these principles culturally and geographically, using metaphors pertaining to diurnal rhythm and human biological development: the succession of night and day and the movement of the sun from East to West hypostatizing the birth of spirit and the Enlightenment with the advent of the rational state. Like the human individual, world spirit follows clearly defined stages in its development: infancy, childhood, youth, adulthood, old age, and death. Like human beings, nations come into existence and wither with old age. In Hegel's view, while nations are ephemeral, the existence of the rational state is absolute. The ideal state is one which actualizes "universal happiness" and promotes the "peaceful enjoyment of civic life."[28] In terms which prefigure the Lacanian "mirror stage," Hegel maintains:

> All progress takes the form of following the successive stages in the evolution of consciousness. Man begins life as a child, and is only dimly conscious of the world and of himself; we know that he has to progress through several stages of empirical consciousness before he attains a knowledge of what he is in and for himself. The child starts out with sensory emotions; man next proceeds to the stage of general representations, and then to that of comprehension, until he finally succeeds in recognising the soul of things, i.e. their true nature. In spiritual matters, the child lives at first by relying on its parents and its environment, and is aware of their efforts to guide it in the ways of rectitude, which appear to it to have been laid down arbitrarily. A further stage is that youth; its distinctive feature is that the human being now looks for independence within himself, that he becomes self-sufficient, and that he recognises that what is right and ethically proper, what is essential for him to perform and accomplish, is present in his own consciousness. And the consciousness of the adult contains even more principles regarding what is essential. Since progress consists in a development of the consciousness, it is not just a quantitative progress but a sequence of changing relationships towards the underlying essence.[29]

The development of spirit is gradual, evolving from the stage of nature to that of culture, from arbitrariness to freedom, from particularity to universality. In the first stage of its development, the human individual exists in a state of nature as "unfree particularity." Hegel compares the first stage of spirit's development to "childhood"—a development which is akin to the Lacanian *"infans* stage." For Hegel, this stage characterizes the Oriental world where, immersed in nature, spirit has not yet achieved self-consciousness and still lives in a despotic state. Governed by patriarchal rules "[i]n relation to the will of the One," writes Hegel, "all the others are in the position of children or subordinates."[30] In the second stage, spirit succeeds only partially in liberating itself from the immediacy of nature and its arbitrariness. This second stage consists of the Greco-Roman worlds, which Hegel dubs the "youth of spirit" and its "manhood": a fledgling spirit in Ancient Greece attains maturity with the political and legal status afforded to free citizens by the Roman state. Though "some are free," the majority experience slavery. Hegel calls the third stage "the Christian world"—better still "the old age of spirit"—where "all are free" with the objectivization of the Enlightenment. In this stage, universality and freedom are actualized, and spirit becomes conscious of itself and its nature; it finds itself in the individual.[31]

Driven by progress, world history culminates in the development of spirit's consciousness of its own freedom and the actualization of this freedom, as "the individual comprehends himself as a person."[32] In Hegel's Orientalizing discourse, which infantilizes people of color and excludes them from his teleological narratives of progress, neither India nor China have history because they lack "the essential self-consciousness of the concept of freedom."[33] In his view, the "Old World" comprises three distinct geographical locations extending over three continents: Asia, Africa, and Europe. He considers the Mediterranean as "the heart of the Old World"—better still the "the navel of the earth"—which connects these three continents. Spirit, he contends, was born in Asia and travels West and the Mediterranean is the "the axis of world history."[34] Hegel reconfigures the world map and "twist[s] the pattern of history in order to make it fit his scheme"[35] excluding the "Mohammedan principle" and "Africa proper" from world history. In his description of Africa, he Europeanizes Egypt and North Africa, separating their Mediterranean region from what he dubs "Africa proper," namely sub-Saharan Africa where "man has not progressed beyond a merely sensuous existence, and has found it absolutely impossible to develop any further." Hegel sees the African individual only fit for slavery, physically "exhibit[ing] great muscular strength, which enables him to perform arduous labours."[36]

Africa proper, writes Hegel, "has no historical interest of its own, for we find its inhabitants living in barbarism and savagery in a land which has not furnished them with any integral ingredient of culture."[37] He characterizes Africa as "the land of childhood, removed from the light of self-conscious history and wrapped in the dark mantle of night."[38] In the succession of day and night, Hegel employs a racialized vocabulary to exclude "dark" Africa from Europe's enlightenment: world spirit and history. Africa proper, in his view, "has remained cut off from all contacts with the rest of the world."[39] In this part of Africa, Hegel writes:

> history is in fact out of the question. Life there consists of a succession of contingent happenings and surprises. No aim or state exists whose development could be followed; and there is no subjectivity, but merely a series of subjects who destroy one another.... in the interior of Africa, the consciousness of the inhabitants has not yet reached an awareness of any substantial and objective existence.... The African, in his undifferentiated and concentrated unity, has not yet succeeded in making this distinction between himself as an individual and his essential universality, so that he knows nothing of an absolute being which is other and higher than his own self. Thus, man as we find in Africa has not progressed beyond his immediate existence. As soon as man emerges as a human being, he stands in opposition to nature, and it is this alone which

makes him a human being. But if he has merely made a distinction between himself and nature, he is still at the first stage of his development: he is dominated by passion, and is nothing more than a savage. All our observations of African man show him as living in a state of savagery and barbarism, and he remains in this state to the present day. The negro is an example of animal man in all his savagery and lawlessness, and if we wish to understand him at all, we must put aside all our European attitudes.[40]

Hegel differentiates between "animal humanity" and "animality proper."[41] The former is epitomized by the figure of the child on which the character of humanity is always already inscribed[42]; the latter is incapable of experiencing self-consciousness.[43] Clearly, this distinction serves to dehumanize Africa proper and relegate it outside history. In Africa, Hegel encounters not a "state of innocence" but its "zoological condition"—its "primitive state of nature [which] is in fact a state of animality."[44] In his description, this condition excludes Africa proper from the historical narratives of progress and development; this stasis renders his dialectical schema inoperative.

Hegel attributes cannibalism and African slavery to the Negro's scant regard for human life.[45] In Africa, he argues, Negroes have not attained the consciousness of freedom, and slavery is absolute. "The negroes," he writes, "see nothing improper about it, and the English, although they have done most to abolish slavery and the slave trade, are treated as enemies by the negroes themselves."[46] He is emphatic in his denunciation of slavery in Africa borne out of a state of nature—"a state of absolute and consistent injustice."[47] Paradoxically, he considers the institution of slavery in ancient Greece and Rome as a stage in the development of world spirit and universal history, an important factor in the actualization of freedom and the externalization of reason. In his words: "when it occurs within an organised state, it is itself a stage in the progress away from purely fragmented sensuous existence, a phase in man's education, and an aspect of the progress whereby he gradually attains ethical existence and a corresponding degree of culture."[48] Slavery is, for Hegel, "still necessary"; it represents a "transitional moment" in a dialectical development of world spirit and universal history.

Alluding to the abolitionist movement, Hegel writes: "Slavery is [by definition] unjust in itself and for itself, for the essence of man is freedom; but he must first become mature before he can be free. Thus, it is more fitting and correct that slavery should be eliminated gradually than that it should be done away with all at once."[49] By infantilizing the Negro, Hegel provides an apology for the maintenance of the institution of slavery and an alibi for colonial paternalism which justified Europe's putative "civilizational work" in Africa and Asia and the attendant exploitation of these two continents under the pretext of promoting their enlightenment. He is, however, unapologetic about European slavery and colonialism, commending the French for their colonial endeavor in North Africa.

Hegel considers "intractability" as a defining feature of Negro character: it is symptomatic of a living condition that is "incapable of any development." Assigning to Africa a place outside the development of world history, Hegel presents the whole continent in a stasis ruled by sensuous barbarism and despotism. Africa proper features as a footnote in his discussion of the development of world spirit and universal history: "it is an unhistorical continent, with no movement or development."[50] This Eurocentric account of the beginning of world history is, as Robert Bernasconi observes, "structured by Hegel's understanding of race."[51] Hegel establishes a correlation between history, consciousness, and race—better still, between people of color and the putative obscurity of their history and consciousness.[52] Only those peoples and nations that contributed to "the progress of the Idea"— namely freedom—are, Hegel opines, world historical.[53] In Asia and Africa, "no progress is made: all this restless movement results in an unhistorical history."[54] In other words: "History is still predominantly unhistorical, for it is merely a repetition of the same majestic process of decline."[55] While decrying the arbitrariness of the despotic state and caste system in China and India,[56] Hegel fails to grasp that his discourse articulates ethnocentric and racial biases and "functions in his hands as a caste system, thereby rendering his philosophy of history arbitrary and so devoid of reason."[57]

In summary, Hegel pits the figure of the slave against the master to delineate spirit's upsurge. Significantly, in the *Phenomenology*, this figure works as a mediating agency through which spirit attains mastery over the immediacy of nature and realizes self-knowledge. Hegel opposes spirit and nature, humanity and animality, mastery and slavery, and through this binary opposition, he constructs the slave as a supplement—a negative term in a dialectical schema endowing spirit with the possibility of perfectibility. In *Lectures on the Philosophy of World History*, "Africa proper" is located outside history and its dialectical progression. The crux of Hegel's argument is that the perfectibility of spirit into world spirit is instantiated with the advent of world history and the rational state. Freedom in this state is grounded geographically. Europe is the embodiment of spirit—"the principle of unity in diversity"; Asia is of "unreconciled antithesis between different way of life"; Africa is locked in stasis representing non-identity, physicality, and negativity.

As has been noted, Hegel conceives of the Mediterranean as the crucible where spirit is created—a site where difference is sublated, contained, and overcome and where world history is shaped. Situated outside world history,

Africa proper represents what is kept beyond the processes of sublation which motivate the march of history. Africa proper particularizes racialized difference, namely blackness; such difference cannot be assimilated and, like nature, must be dominated, mastered, and enslaved for the advancement of spirit. I concur with Patricia Purtschert that the trajectory of spirit paved the way to Europe's colonial project.[58] Hegel presents Africa outside the play of history and its dialectical progression. He characterizes Africa proper as unhistorical—as a geographical entity which is destined to remain outside world history. I do not agree with her assertion that Africa "appears both as the beginning and as that which remains outside of world history."[59] Hegel excises blackness from the teleological narratives of progress; he is very clear that history does not begin in Africa proper, which he considers as a supplemental Other to be excluded: a surplus, an excess, an unconscionable difference which always already remains at the margins of world history.[60]

Fanon, Hegel, and the Negro

Although Fanon emulates the struggle for recognition in *Black Skin, White Masks*, he is at variance with Hegel. This discordance is discernible not in Fanon's critique of the Hegelian dialectical schema in Chapter 7, "The Negro and Recognition," but in Chapter 5, "The Fact of Blackness." As Ethan Kleinberg affirms, "Fanon's critique is blunted when he is in the dialectic but it is most powerful in the phenomenological investigation into the conditions prior to the 'Struggle for Recognition.'"[61] The "facticity of blackness" prevents the Negro from taking part in the Hegelian dialectic and its teleological progression. Elaborating on the influence Alexandre Kojève's *Introduction to the Reading of Hegel* had on Fanon, Kleinberg writes:

> There is an incompatibility between the system that Kojève is describing and the system that Fanon is trying to understand, which is not addressed when Fanon steps into the dialectic precisely because the determining moment is prior to the dialectic.
>
> What becomes clear in "The Fact of Blackness" … is that the economy of Hegel's system is such that it does not allow space for a radically Other. Fanon sees that there is no room for the colonized in the historical progression of Hegel as read by Kojève but the Other, the Black, is not denied a place because he is "recognized without struggle" or because "he did not fight for his freedom," which is Fanon's claim. Instead, it is because prior to the moment of confrontation the fact of blackness disqualifies the Negro from participation in the Hegelian teleological progression.[62]

In his critique of Hegel, Fanon inscribes color into the dialectic; it is only by conflating "the teleological Hegelian dialectic with phenomenology that the fundamental incompatibility of the Hegelian system and the colonial system becomes visible."[63] Colonial racism thwarts the possibility of identification and recognition, rendering ontological and intersubjective relations between black and white impossible, and negating any possibility of black self-consciousness. The Negro, sealed into blackness and reduced to thinghood, is denied access to the Hegelian dialectical schema. In Fanon's account, the Hegelian dialectic is thrown of joint, working to exclude people of color from the symbolic exchange "with the result that their desire for recognition is left permanently unrequited."[64]

Three long footnotes in *Black Skin, White Masks*, referencing intersubjective relations in Lacan, Sartre, and Hegel, establish an intertextual framework within which Fanon interprets Hegel through the prism of psychoanalysis and existential phenomenology. It is instructive to provide a cursory review of Lacan and Sartre to help us grasp the infantilizing vocabulary which articulates Hegel's world history and the ethnocentrism which excludes the Negro from the symbolic exchange.

In the Lacanian "mirror stage," i.e., at the age of six months, the child comes to self-recognition and leaves the *infans* stage (a stage prior to the subject's individuation) to enter into the symbolic order. The subject is born with its entry into this order "which essentially distinguishes human society from natural societies."[65] Echoing Hegel, Lacan describes the insertion of the subject into this order as a passage from the world of *nature* to that of *culture*. This passage from the natural to the conceptual is mediated through the rules and taboos that govern society. The function of the mirror stage establishes a relation of reciprocity between the image of the child's body and its reality, or between the *Innenwelt* and the *Umwelt*. In the mirror stage, the child acquires a projection of its body and becomes conscious of itself as an entity.

In *Black Skin, White Masks*, however, the gaze of the Other does not help the Negro acquire a unified representation of the body. Fanon puts Lacanian theory on its head: the Negro's encounter with the white child represents a reversal of the Lacanian mirror stage: it projects a view of the Negro *infantilized*, excluded from the symbolic order, objectified, and degraded to the level of "animality." Fanon's take on Lacan provides two pointers to the ethnocentrism at the core of Hegelian dialectic and world history. Firstly, the dialectic—patterned on a "historico-racial bodily schema"—is rendered dysfunctional and obsolete because racism thwarts its operation and the attendant processes of identification and recognition; intersubjective relations thus become impossible. Secondly, the facticity of blackness excludes the Negro from the symbolic exchange and the Hegelian teleological narrative of progress. In *Black Skin, White Masks*, Fanon dismisses the assertion that the Negro is an exemplar of "animal man" and that, as Hegel says, "if we wish to understand him at all, we must put aside all our European attitudes."

Fanon defines the relation between self and other in Hegelian language, within a dialectical schema which turns purely on biological and racialized terms in a context petrified by colonialism. His interpretation of the Lacanian specular relation reflects and refracts this dialectical schema. His reference to the Lacanian mirror stage must be situated within two contexts. First, it is a long footnote to his argument that "with the Negro the cycle of the *biological* begins."[66] This argument is of central importance to what Fanon calls the "corporeal schema," a notion which he borrows from Jean Lhermitte and Maurice Merleau-Ponty to highlight the shortcomings of ontology and existential phenomenology in dealing with the *Erlebnis* of the black and the consciousness of blackness in a white world. Second, in a footnote in *Black Skin, White Masks* (on p. 138), rebuking Sartre for overlooking historical slavery, Fanon writes: "Though Sartre's speculations on the existence of The Other may be correct (to the extent … to which *Being and Nothingness* describes an alienated consciousness), their application to a black consciousness proves fallacious. That is because the white man is not only The Other but also the master, whether real or imaginary." This footnote announces the reference to Lacan's mirror stage (on p. 161) and the footnote to Hegel's master/slave dialectic (on pp. 220–21):

> When one has grasped the mechanism described by Lacan, one can have no further doubt that the real Other for the white man is and will continue to be the black man. And conversely. Only for the white man The Other is perceived on the level of the body image, absolutely as the not-self—that is, the unidentifiable, the unassimilable. For the black man, as we have shown, historical and economic realities come into the picture.[67]

Unlike Hegel, Sartre assigns a place to the Negro in the teleological narratives of progress in "Black Orpheus." Like Hegel, he conceives of negritude as a negative concept in the progression of the dialectic, which leads to the transcendence of racism and ultimately to the end of class struggle. Fanon excoriates Sartre for abstracting the experience of the black. In dialogue with Sartre and Hegel, he writes:

Help had been sought from a friend of the colored peoples, and that friend had found no better response than to point out the relativity of what they were doing. For once, that born Hegelian had forgotten that consciousness has to lose itself in the night of the absolute, the only condition to attain consciousness of self. In opposition to rationalism, he summoned up the negative side, but forgot that this negativity draws its worth from an almost substantive absoluteness. A consciousness committed to experience is ignorant, has to be ignorant, of the essences and the determinations of its being.[68]

In the above, Fanon echoes Hegel's definition of universality as an abstraction of identity—"the Absolute as the night in which, as we say, all cows are black" and knowledge is "*naively* reduced to vacuity."[69] Hegel's teleology of progress culminating with the advent of the rational state loses itself in the darkness of the night (i.e., the "Absolute") in order to announce the dawning of the Enlightenment, and Fanon bemoans that his blackness is considered as a "minor term" in the dialectic. "Without a Negro past, without a Negro future," Fanon opines, "it was impossible for me to live my Negrohood. Not yet white, no longer wholly black, I was damned. Jean-Paul Sartre had forgotten that the Negro suffers in his body quite differently from the white man. Between the white man and me the connection was irrevocably one of transcendence."[70] Fanon regrets that this "transcendence" is not transcending. Sartre uses the term to describe the subject in its orientation with its objective reality and in its intersubjective relations as transcendence, transcended, and transcending. In Fanon's account, the Negro is objectified and denied any possibilities of establishing intersubjective relations with the white as transcending-transcendence, i.e., as Other whose subjectivity is grasped by another. At the core of the dialectic is the idea of transcendence and surpassing; in Hegel's schema, the Negro is a slave that has "lost the fight"—so to speak—to be recognized as a free self-consciousness. In the Hegelian teleology, the Negro is a sort of "animal man" that cannot develop any further and that is fit only for slavery; the Negro exists outside the redemptive narratives of progress and history and is destined to remain a slave, a beast of burden carrying the negative weight of the dialectic and performing arduous and indentured labor.

In "The Negro and Recognition," Fanon opens the second section entitled "The Negro and Hegel" with the following citation taken from Hegel's *Phenomenology*: "Self-consciousness exists in itself and for itself, in that and by the fact that it exists for another self-consciousness; that is to say, it is only by being acknowledged or recognized."[71] The citation clearly serves as a pointer to the non-dialectical relationship between the white master and the black slave, as Fanon goes on to elaborate:

At the foundation of Hegelian dialectic there is an absolute reciprocity which must be emphasized. It is in the degree to which I go beyond my own immediate being that I apprehend the existence of the other as a natural and more than natural reality. If I close the circuit, if I prevent the accomplishment of movement in two directions, I keep the other within himself. Ultimately, I deprive him even of this being-for-itself.

The only means of breaking this vicious circle that throws me back on myself is to restore to the other, through mediation and recognition, his human reality, which is different from natural reality. The other has to perform the same operation. "Action from one side only would be useless, because what is to happen can only be brought about by means of both…"; "*they recognize themselves as mutually recognizing each other.*"[72]

Kleinberg mistakenly attributes this fundamental incompatibility to Kojève's influence on Fanon. The issue is not, however, that Fanon fails to recognize himself in a Hegelian schema that Kojève distorts; the flaw is intrinsic to the schema itself. In *Black Skin, White Masks*, the circuit is closed—the dialectic is inoperative—the other is stymied and kept shut within itself. In *The Wretched of the Earth*, vying for self-recognition, Fanon battles to re-enact the dialectic by breaking the vicious circle that thwarts the other.

Historically, the colonial master never sought recognition from the black slave to ascertain the truth of his self-consciousness. Taking issue with Hegel, Fanon argues that the dialectical operation is "useless," because there is no reciprocity between the master and the Negro. In the scenario outlined by Fanon, "the master differs basically from the master described by Hegel. For Hegel there is reciprocity; here the master laughs at the consciousness of the slave. What he wants from the slave is not recognition but work."[73] Alluding to Kojève, Fanon rejects the view that work humanizes the slave (and ultimately the master) by attaining "universal consciousness," or as Hegel puts it "the affirmative knowing of one's self in the other." The master expresses contempt for the Negro by usurping his work. The Hegelian dialectic is "useless," for it is premised on slavery and servitude, principles which are not rational and go against the grain of Hegelian teleological development of the state as the objectivization of freedom and rationality. The crux of Fanon's argument is that slavery and colonialism impart to the colonized Negro an inferiority complex and therefore make mutual self-actualization impossible for both slave and master.

In "The Negro and Recognition," Fanon complicates his reading of Hegel by referring to Alfred Adler's *The Neurotic Character* and *Understanding Human Nature*. Fanon's discussion of the Adlerian individual psychology and

of the inferiority complex grounds the master/slave dialectic in the specificities of the Antilles, focussing on two important contexts: slavery and its
abolition. Applying Adlerian individual psychology, Fanon argues that Antil-
lean society ("pre-occupied with self-evaluation and with the ego-ideal") is a
society of comparison; its members are neurotic and "have no inherent values
of their own, they are always contingent on the presence of The Other."[74]
They seek to dominate the Other so as to compensate for their historical
inferiority brought about by slavery. Characteristically un-Hegelian, they do
not realize their freedom at work; they turn not to the object but toward the
master in order to emulate him reinforcing their inferiority: they ascertain the
mastery of the master and replicate the negativity of the dialectic. In Fanon's
conception of the dialectic, the master never acknowledges the slave, and
slavery reproduces a language that does not actualize freedom. Historically,
work kept them under the yoke of dehumanizing slavery and colonialism;
the abolition of slavery in 1848 and the departmentalization of Martinique
in 1946 denied them the possibility to fight for freedom. Fanon's assertion
that the Negro was "recognized without struggle" evokes these two historical
moments.

Explicitly referring to the abolition of slavery in 1848, Fanon ironizes that
the white master decided to be nice to black slaves by declaring that "slavery
shall no longer exist on French soil." This gesture smacks of colonial paternalism; this gift of freedom is emblematized by "the impressive number of
statues erected all over France and the colonies to show white France stroking
the kinky hair of this nice Negro whose chains has just been broken."[75] "Historically," Fanon affirms, "the Negro steeped in the inessentiality of servitude
was set free by his master. He did not fight for his freedom." "Out of slavery,"
Fanon goes on to add, "the Negro burst into the lists where his masters
stood."[76] "The Negro is a slave who has been allowed to assume the attitude of a master"[77] and Fanon bemoans that "the Negro knows nothing of
the cost of freedom, for he has not fought for it."[78]

Echoing Hegel's *Phenomenology*, Fanon contends that the upsurge of
universal consciousness depends on the concept of recognition. The Hegelian
being-for-another, albeit fraught with danger, hypostatizes for Fanon the
meaning of life: recognition is crucial for the actualization of self-
consciousness, and "human worth and reality depend on it."[79] The encounter
with the other, while endangering its physical being, engenders desire which
is essential to the affirmation of human dignity.[80] In dialogue with Hegel,
Fanon writes:

As soon as I *desire* I am asking to be considered. I am not merely here-and-now, sealed into thingness. I am for somewhere else and for something else. I demand that notice be taken of my negating activity insofar as I pursue something other than life; insofar as I do battle for the creation of a human world—that is, of a world of reciprocal recognitions.[81]

Fanon, as a Negro and a descendent of a registered slave, risked his life and battled for the creation of a human world. In World War II, he fought to uphold the master's freedom and justice, albeit "white" freedom and justice. In the Algerian War, he fought until his dying breath to bring about decolonization. The armed struggle in Algeria—which came to symbolize for Fanon the revolution of Africa as a whole—strengthened his belief in the Hegelian axiom that freedom was something that could not be given but must be fought for. Alluding to Nkrumah's inaugural speech at the Accra Conference, and discounting colonial ethnocentrism that excluded Africa from world history, Fanon writes: "We have nothing to lose but our chains and we have an immense continent to win."[82]

I concur with Kleinberg that Fanon's Chapter 5 "The Fact of Blackness" and Chapter 7 "The Negro and Recognition" must be read in tandem to elicit Fanon's interpretation of Hegel. The ramifications of this reading become explicit in the opening chapter of *The Wretched of the Earth*, "Concerning Violence," as Fanon becomes the indefatigable champion of those who were consigned to exist outside Hegel's dialectic, world spirit, and history. Simply put, "The Negro and Recognition" announces the theme of anti-colonial struggle and violence in *The Wretched of the Earth*, as Fanon refuses to surrender his claim for recognition, discounting the Hegelian view that the slave, before acquiring self-consciousness and freedom, must first exhaust his self-seeking appetites in the service of the master. Fanon is adamant that the institutions of slavery and colonialism do not humanize the slave: they worked only to turn indentured labor into surplus capital which Europe exploited to build its wealth.

Teshale Tibebu adroitly captures the problematic at the center of Fanon's critique: the Hegelian dialectic never envisages "[t]he *resistance of the servant against the master*."[83] In Hegel's dialectic, the slave overcomes nature. Ultimately, the slave's victory is not a victory against the master but against his own immediate nature.[84] In *Black Skin, White Masks*, Fanon problematizes Hegel's master/slave dialectic by overturning its terms. It is not by serving his master but by staking his life that the slave will restore his subjecthood and bring about "the transformation of subjective certainty into objective truth." "In a savage struggle," he avers, "I am willing to accept convulsions of death, invincible dissolution, but also the possibility of the impossible."[85] In *The Wretched of the Earth*, Fanon battles to make possible that which was considered "impossible"—that is staking his life to actualize the freedom of those who were colonized and enslaved.

Fanon: The Inoperative Dialectic and the Struggle for Recognition

The implications of Fanon's reading of Hegel are clearly outlined in *The Wretched of the Earth*: "Concerning Violence" and the concluding pages continue the critique of Hegelian dialectic and world history which Fanon initiates in *Black Skin, White Masks*. The colonial world is, in his words, "characterized by the dichotomy it imposes upon the whole people"; this "motionless" and "Manichaeistic world" marked by division is governed by the rules of an "apartheid."[86] Fanon describes the cartography of the colonial space as constituted of two opposed zones which are mutually *exclusive*.

> The zone where the natives live is not complementary to the zone inhabited by the settlers. The two zones are opposed, but not in the service of a higher unity. Obedient to the rules of pure Aristotelian logic, they both follow the principle of reciprocal exclusivity. No conciliation is possible, for of the two terms, one is superfluous.[87]

The logic demarcating this compartmentalized world—a world which is "cut in two" and "inhabited by two different species"—is racialized.[88] Fanon is cognizant of the fact of belonging to a given race determines the terms of the dialectic. Couching these terms in a Hegelian phraseology, he announces: "The serf is in essence different from the knight, but a reference to divine right is necessary to legitimize this statutory difference."[89] Ostensibly, "the ordering of the colonial world" is governed not by a speculative agenda objectivizing the rational state but by pure force. Decolonization is neither "a rational confrontation of points of view"; nor is it "a treatise on the universal, but the untidy affirmation of an original idea propounded as an absolute."[90] Colonial Manichaeism imposes on this world terms which are dehumanizing and pertain to zoology. Invoking the diurnal rhythm which motivates the development of Hegelian world spirit and leaves people of color without agency and history, Fanon writes:

Those hordes of vital statistics, those hysterical masses, those faces bereft of all humanity, those distended bodies which are like nothing on earth, that mob without beginning or end, those children who seem to belong to nobody, that laziness stretched out in the sun, that vegetative rhythm of life—all this forms part of the colonial vocabulary. General de Gaulle speaks of "the yellow multitudes" and François Mauriac of the black, brown and yellow masses which soon will be unleashed. The native knows all this, and laughs to himself every time he spots an allusion to the animal in the other's words. For he knows that he is not an animal; and it is precisely at that moment he realizes his humanity that he begins to sharpen the weapons with which he will secure its victory.

Fanon's point of criticism targets Hegel; de Gaulle and Mauriac's "colonial vocabulary," clearly, draws its significance from the author of *Phenomenology* and *Lectures on the Philosophy of World History*. Critiquing Hegel and his view on Western Enlightenment, Fanon writes: "it so happens that when the native hears a speech about Western culture he pulls out his knife."[91] In *The Wretched of the Earth*, decolonization re-enacts the Hegelian dialectic bringing two protagonists face to face in a decisive encounter, and Fanon conceives of this encounter as "a real struggle for freedom," overthrowing the superstructures of bourgeois and colonial thought which alienate and shut the individual within the solipsism of subjectivity.[92]

Fanon calls into question the "immobility" to which the colonized people are condemned[93] and challenges the Hegelian teleological narratives of progress that the colonial master makes history. Citing Engels' *Anti-Dühring*, he argues that the dialectical operation[94] depends for its success on "the implements of violence; and the more highly-developed of these implements will carry the day against primitive ones." Simply put, the "triumph of violence" is determined by production—by the economy of the state and "the material means which that violence commands."[95]

The project of decolonization, Fanon contends, inaugurates a new diplomacy: "a diplomacy which never stops moving, a diplomacy which leaps ahead, in strange contrast to the motionless, petrified world of colonization"—a diplomacy which guarantees "the progress of the masses towards a state of well-being and the right of all peoples to bread and liberty."[96] In *The Wretched of the Earth*, decolonization "takes the form of an armed and open struggle," overturning the discourse of the master and replicating the terms of the Hegelian dialectic without following its teleological pretensions. As Fanon elaborates:

He of whom *they* have never stopped saying that the only language he understands is that of force, decides to give utterance by force. In fact, as always, the settler has shown him the way he should take if he is to become free. The argument the native chooses has been furnished by the settler, and by an ironic turning of the tables it is the native who now affirms that the colonialist understands nothing but force. The colonial regime owes its legitimacy to force and at no time tries to hide this aspect of things.[97]

It is worth reiterating that Hegel considers force as a "necessary and legitimate factor" motivating the dialectic. Fanon turns the tables on Hegel by inscribing decolonization within a dialectical schema and characterizing it as a "duel," a "murderous and decisive struggle between the two protagonists," an encounter marked by violence.[98] "To work," Fanon explains, "means to work for the death of the settler," that is, the destruction of colonialism.[99] In Hegelian dialectic, work transforms the world as well as the relationship between the master and the slave, as the latter in his service to the former achieves universal consciousness and freedom. For Fanon, it is not work but the fight which "secures victory" and helps both ultimately attain this universality. In his own words: "Violence is thus seen as comparable to a royal pardon. The colonized man finds his freedom in and through violence. This rule of conduct enlightens the agent because it indicates to him the means and end."[100] Fanon maintains that the Manichaeism of the colonizer engenders that of the colonized: their violence and counter-violence "balance" and "respond to each other in an extraordinary reciprocal homogeneity."[101] In the period of decolonization, argues Fanon, violence "constitutes their [the colonized's] only work, invests their characters with positive and creative quality."[102]

In terms that invoke Hegel, Fanon describes decolonization as an encounter which brings about the upsurge of being of those who are enslaved and colonized:

> it influences individuals and modifies them fundamentally. It transforms spectators crushed with their inessentiality into privileged actors, with the grandiose glare of history's floodlights upon them. It brings a natural rhythm into existence, introduced by new men, and with it a new language and a new humanity. Decolonization is the veritable creation of new men. But this creation owes nothing of its legitimacy to any supernatural power; the "thing" which has been colonized becomes man during the same process by which it frees itself.[103]

Fanon re-enacts the master/slave dialectic and the processes of sublation, as the "thing" becomes "man" in a battle for self-recognition, but now inscribing self-actualization in the violent confrontation of colonizer and colonized. Decolonization represents "the moment of the boomerang"[104]: a returning violence that comes back to assail its perpetrators. The violence of decolonization is the sum total of colonial oppression: it is nothing but the exteriorization of a single violence, that of the colonial masters. Fanon conceives of decolonization as a struggle for self-recognition; it is "no less than man reconstructing himself."[105]

In the Hegelian teleology, violence was the midwife of world history. World spirit was engendered and maintained by such violence; it was, by Hegel's own admission, genocidal. Hegel condones Europe's colonial project and legitimizes the supremacy of white European spirit. He admits that the indigenous inhabitants were "subjected to far greater violence, and employed in gruelling labours"; however, their degradation seemed warranted for Hegel because of their "inferiority" and "submissive" predisposition.[106] The laws of dialectical progression of spirit and history sanctioned colonial genocide; the annihilation of indigenous cultures in North America and elsewhere instantiated and provided justification for Hegel that "[c]ulturally inferior nations such as these are gradually eroded through contact with more advanced nations which have gone through a more intensive cultural development."[107] As Bernasconi observes, "Hegel's blanket proposal, directed even at China, was colonization. Hegel seems to have regarded colonialism not only as a fact of history but as a law of history."[108]

In stark contrast to Hegel's teleological narratives of progress and world history, Fanon outlines what he calls "the geography of hunger":

> It is an under-developed world, a world inhuman in its poverty…. Confronting this world the European nations sprawl, ostentatiously opulent. This European opulence is literally scandalous, for it has been founded on slavery, it has been nourished with the blood of slaves and it comes directly from the soil and from the subsoil of that under-developed world. The well-being and progress of Europe have been built up with the sweat and the dead bodies of Negroes, Arabs, Indians and the yellow races.[109]

This geography is at the antipodes of Hegel's map of world spirit that excluded peoples of color and legitimized their exploitation. Europe's historical progress, its Enlightenment, and its material wealth were founded on slavery and colonialism—"built up with the sweat and the dead bodies of Negroes, Arabs, Indians and the yellow races." Hegelianism embodies the logic of capitalism and bourgeois thinking. M.A.R. Habib dubs Hegel "the archetypal philosopher of capitalism" and describes the global impetus of his dialectic as one of the logical outcomes of the structural workings of global-ization and its totalizing processes.[110] As Habib observes, "imperialism is not accidental or peripheral in Hegel's system; it is sanctioned by the authority of the Absolute Idea itself, by its absolute imperative to conquer all otherness in realizing itself. For Hegel, the overcoming of otherness glides seamlessly from epistemology to economics, from self-realization to imperial domina-tion, from freedom to Empire."[111] Hegel's dialectic is determined by "the reality of capitalism as the specific outgrowth of European history."[112]

Alluding to Hegel's Eurocentric views on the obscure consciousness of people of color and the putative obscurity of their history, Fanon is explicit in his critique of Hegel's world spirit and history:

> Let us waste no time in sterile litanies and nauseating mimicry. Leave this Europe where they are never done talking of Man, yet murder men every-where they find them, at the corner of every one of their own streets, in all the corners of the globe. For centuries they have stifled almost the whole of humanity in the name of a so-called spiritual experience.... Europe undertook the leadership of the world with ardour, cynicism and violence.... That same Europe ... where they never stopped proclaiming that they were only anxious for the welfare of Man: today we know with what sufferings humanity has paid for every one of their triumphs of the mind.[113]

The reference to Hegel's *Phenomenology of Spirit* is obvious. Fanon denounces the so-called "spiritual adventure" of the West: "It is in the name of the spirit, in the name of the spirit of Europe, that Europe has made her encroachments, that she has justified her crimes and legitimized the slavery in which she holds four-fifths of humanity."[114] Fanon debunks Hegel's dialectical progression of world spirit and history. "When I search for Man in the technique and style of Europe," writes Fanon, "I see only a succession of negations of man, and an avalanche of murders."[115]

Fanon deconstructs the Hegelian teleology, affirming that the Enlight-enment failed to objectivize universal freedom and break the vicious circle of the master and slave dialectics that kept Europe shut within an inter-minable solipsism. He is adamant that Hegel and his narratives of progress held Europe in a stasis, and that this "motionless movement" is gradually changing the dialectic into the "logic of equilibrium" so as to maintain its hegemony. He also discounts the dialectic and its workings as colonial, excoriating Europe for its "increasingly obscene narcissism."[116]

Nevertheless, the theme of violence does not constitute the centrality of Fanon's project. Violence, for Fanon, is a negative moment in the process of decolonization, which must pass through two phases: the breaking-up of the colonial state and the emergence of the postcolonial nation. He affirms that this process seeks "to change our ways" of being in the world and "shake off the heavy darkness in which we were plunged, and leave it behind."[117] In the concluding pages of *The Wretched of the Earth*, Fanon celebrates a new humanism announcing the advent of post-Hegelian world history. "It is a question of the Third world starting a new history of Man, a history which will have regard to the sometimes prodigious theses which Europe has put forward, but which will also not forget Europe's crimes, of which the most horrible was committed in the heart of man, and consisted of the pathological tearing apart of his functions and the crumbling away of his unity."[118]

Conclusion

Two lines of argument run in Fanon's work providing a sustained critical engagement with Hegelian dialectic and teleological narratives of world history. In *Black Skin, White Masks*, Fanon seeks to restore human relations corrupted by racism and to amend "the pathological tearing apart of [human] functions" brought about by historical slavery and colonial oppression. In *Lectures on the Philosophy of World History*, Hegel opines, "*slavery* is the basic legal relationship in Africa. The only significant relationship between the negroes and the Europeans has been—and still is that of slavery."[119] Hegel's denigrating remark—"When the negro slaves have laboured all day, they are perfectly contented and will dance with the most violent convulsions throughout the night"[120]— instantiates Fanon's claim that the Hegelian master derides the consciousness of Negro slaves recognizing them only as subjects of indentured labor. Fanon discounts the dialectic for being a "useless" and dysfunctional operation—an exclusive operation which works to marginalize people of color and legitimize their exploitation. In the *Encyclopaedia*, Hegel affirms that the Absolute Idea is essentially European shaped by the laws of the dialectic and its successive transformations. "The European mind," he argues, "opposes the world to itself, makes itself free of it, but in turn annuls this opposition, takes its Other, the manifold, back into itself, into its unitary nature. In Europe, therefore, there prevails this infinite thirst for knowledge which is alien to other races.... the European mind strives to make manifest the unity between itself and the outer world. It subdues the outer world to its ends with an energy which has ensured for it the mastery of the world."[121] The Hegelian subject reconciles itself with its outer world only to conquer it. This unity does not externalize the universality of the individual but brings about its disintegration and neurosis. In the dialectic, Hegel infantilizes people of color, denying them any possibilities of development and progress. Founded on slavery, the dialectic thwarts the externalization of freedom. In *The Wretched of the Earth*, Fanon rejects European knowledge for instituting the colonial state. He shows that Hegel's phenomenology of mind is counterintuitive: world spirit is not governed by rationality and freedom is not one of its properties, as Hegel postulates that it is European and white.

Notes

1. Stephen Houlgate, *An Introduction to Hegel: Freedom, Truth and History* (Oxford: Blackwell, 2005).
2. Philip J. Kain, *Hegel and the Other* (Albany: State University of New York Press, 2005), 254–56.
3. Fanon was the grandson of a registered slave and that this lineage was determined by the history of a society which had been "enslaved, freed, re-enslaved, colonized, assimilated and 'departmentalized.'" *Black Skin, White Masks*, written as a critique of the republican tradition that failed to deliver on the promise of universal fraternity, is a complaint against racism. In its concluding section, Fanon reminds his readers that he risked his life in World War II to uphold this tradition and that he fought for the ideals of universal brotherhood. Yet he felt amputated by white racism.
4. Georg Wilhelm Friedrich Hegel, *Hegel's Aesthetics: Lectures on Fine Art*, trans. T. M. Knox (Oxford: Clarendon, 1975), 465–66. Taking a cue from Ethan Kleinberg, it is important to underscore the gendering of the subject: "From its ontological inception in Hegel's system, the 'I' that first speaks, that has animal Desires and overcomes those Desires, that struggles for recognition and progresses toward Self-consciousness is a European 'I,' a white 'I,' and by all indications a male 'I'" (Ethan Kleinberg, "Kojève and Fanon," in *French Civilization and its Discontents*, ed. Tyler Stovall and Georges Van Den Abbeele [Oxford: Lexington Books, 2003], 122).
5. Georg Wilhelm Friedrich Hegel, *Hegel's Philosophy of Nature*, vol. 1, trans. and ed. Michael J. Petry (London: Routledge, 2002), 195.
6. Georg Wilhelm Friedrich Hegel, *Hegel's Philosophy of Mind*, trans. William Wallace (Oxford: Clarendon Press, 1971), 173.
7. Hegel, *Hegel's Philosophy of Mind*, 175.
8. Georg Wilhelm Friedrich Hegel, *Phenomenology of Spirit*, trans. A. V. Miller (Oxford: Oxford University Press, 1977), 117.
9. As Hegel puts it: "Universal self-consciousness is the affirmative awareness of self in an other self: each self as a free individuality has his own "absolute" independence, yet in virtue of the negation of its immediacy or appetite without distinguishing itself from that other. Each has "real" universality in the shape of reciprocity, so far as each knows itself recognized in the other

freeman, and is aware of this in so far as it recognizes the other and knows him to be free." Hegel, *Hegel's Philosophy of Mind*, 176. See also Georg Wilhelm Friedrich Hegel, *Hegel's Philosophy of Subjective Spirit*, vol. 3, trans. Michael J. Petry (Dordrecht: Reidel, 1979), 73.

10. Translator's comment in Georg Wilhelm Friedrich Hegel, *Phenomenology of Mind*, trans. J. B. Baillie (London: Allen & Unwin Ltd., 1971), 228.
11. Hegel, *Hegel's Philosophy of Subjective Spirit*, vol. 3, 69.
12. Hegel, *Phenomenology of Mind*, 230–31.
13. Hegel, *Hegel's Philosophy of Mind*, 41–42.
14. Hegel, *Hegel's Philosophy of Subjective Spirit*, vol. 2, 47.
15. Ibid.
16. Georg Wilhelm Friedrich Hegel, *Lectures on the Philosophy of World History*, trans. H. B. Nisbet (Cambridge: Cambridge University Press, 1975), 47.
17. Ibid., 61.
18. Ibid., 63.
19. Ibid., 65.
20. Ibid., 150–51.
21. Ibid., 99.
22. Ibid., 100.
23. Ibid., 124–25.
24. Ibid., 49–50.
25. Ibid., 125.
26. Ibid., 128.
27. Ibid., 128–29.
28. Ibid., 117.
29. Ibid., 129.
30. Ibid., 130.
31. Ibid., 130–31.
32. Ibid., 144.
33. Ibid., 145. As he explains: "A nation is only world-historical in so far as its fundamental element and basic aim have embodied a universal principle; only then is its spirit capable of producing an ethical and political organisation" (145). Governed by principles predicated on natural determinations, namely the caste system India has no history (136). "Given this state of bondage in an order based firmly and permanently on nature," he opines, "all social relations are wild and arbitrary, an ephemeral activity—or rather madness—with no ultimate end in the shape of progress and development" (137).
34. Ibid., 171.
35. Joshua Foa Dienstag, "Building the Temple of Memory: Hegel's Aesthetic Narrative of History," *The Review of Politics* 54, no. 4 (1994): 716n. Cited in Robert Bernasconi, "With what must the philosophy of world history begin? On the racial basis of Hegel's eurocentrism," *Nineteenth-Century Contexts* 22 (2000): 185.
36. Hegel, *Lectures on the Philosophy of World History*, 172.

37. Ibid., 174.
38. Ibid.
39. Ibid.
40. Ibid., 176–77.
41. Ibid., 133.
42. Hegel contends that "[the child] remains a purely natural being which has only a latent capacity for existing in and for itself as a free human being" (154).
43. Ibid., 133.
44. Ibid., 178.
45. Ibid., 182–85.
46. Ibid., 183.
47. Ibid., 184.
48. Ibid.
49. Ibid.
50. Ibid., 190.
51. Bernasconi, "With what must the philosophy of world history begin? On the racial basis of Hegel's eurocentrism," 171.
52. "Nations whose consciousness is obscure, or the obscure history of such nations, are at any rate not the object of the philosophical history of the world, whose end is to attain knowledge of the Idea in history—the spirits of those nations which [have] become conscious of their inherent principle, and have become aware of what they are and of what their actions signify, are its object" (Hegel, *Lectures on the Philosophy of World History*, 12).
53. Hegel, *Lectures on the Philosophy of World History*, 209.
54. Ibid., 199.
55. Ibid.
56. Ibid., 80.
57. Bernasconi, "With What Must the Philosophy of World History Begin? On the Racial Basis of Hegel's Eurocentrism," 191.
58. Patricia Purtschert, "On the Limit of Spirit: Hegel's Racism Revisited," *Philosophy and Social Criticism* 36, no. 9 (2010): 1045.
59. Ibid., 1041.
60. The figure of the Black is excluded from the dialectic and "function[s] as a criterion of otherness" (Sander L. Gilman, "The Figure of the Black in the Thought of Hegel and Nietzsche," *The German Quarterly* 53, no. 2 [March 1980]: 147).
61. Kleinberg, "Kojève and Fanon," 120.
62. Ibid., 120–21.
63. Ibid., 116.
64. Ibid., 123.
65. Jacques Lacan, *Ecrits: A Selection* (London: Tavistock, 1977), 148.
66. Fanon, *Black Skin, White Masks* (London: Pluto Press, 1993), 161.
67. Ibid.

68. Ibid., 133–34.
69. Hegel, *Phenomenology of Mind*, 79. See also Hegel, *Phenomenology of Spirit*, 9. My italics.
70. Fanon, *Black Skin, White Masks*, 138.
71. Ibid., 216.
72. Ibid., 217.
73. Ibid., 220.
74. Ibid., 211.
75. Ibid., 220.
76. Ibid., 219.
77. Ibid.
78. Ibid., 221.
79. Ibid., 217.
80. Ibid., 218.
81. Ibid.
82. Frantz Fanon, "Accra: Africa Affirms Its Unity and Defines Its Strategy," in *Toward the African Revolution* (Harmondsworth: Penguin, 1970), 167.
83. Teshale Tibebu, *Hegel and the Third World* (Syracuse, NY: Syracuse University Press, 2011), 62.
84. Ibid.
85. Fanon, *Black Skin, White Masks*, 218.
86. Fanon, *The Wretched of the Earth* (Harmondsworth: Penguin, 1990), 35, 40 and 29.
87. Ibid., 30.
88. Ibid., 29 and 31.
89. Ibid., 31.
90. Ibid.
91. Ibid., 33.
92. Ibid., 36.
93. Ibid., 39–40.
94. "In the same way that Robinson [Crusoe] was able to obtain a sword, we can just as well suppose that [Man] Friday might appear one fine morning with a loaded revolver in his hand, and from then on the whole relationship of violence is reversed: Man Friday gives the orders and Crusoe is obliged to work" (Fanon, *The Wretched of the Earth*, 50).
95. Ibid.
96. Ibid., 61.
97. Ibid., 66.
98. Ibid., 28 and 67.
99. Ibid., 67.
100. Ibid., 67–68.
101. Ibid., 69.
102. Ibid., 73.
103. Ibid., 28.

104. Jean-Paul Sartre, *Colonialism and Neocolonialism* (London: Routledge, 2001), 147.
105. Ibid., 148.
106. Hegel, *Lectures on the Philosophy of World History*, 164.
107. Ibid., 163.
108. Bernasconi, "With What Must the Philosophy of World History Begin? On the Racial Basis of Hegel's Eurocentrism," 190.
109. Fanon, *The Wretched of the Earth*, 76.
110. M. A. R. Habib, *Hegel and Empire* (Cham: Springer Nature, 2017), 2–4.
111. Ibid., 7.
112. Ibid., 59.
113. Fanon, *The Wretched of the Earth*, 251.
114. Ibid., 252.
115. Ibid.
116. Ibid., 253.
117. Ibid., 251.
118. Ibid., 254.
119. Hegel, *Lectures on the Philosophy of World History*, 183.
120. Ibid., 219.
121. Hegel, *Hegel's Philosophy of Mind*, 45.

Part III

Ethics and Aesthetics

10

Guidance for Mortals: Heidegger on Norms

David Batho

There is, plausibly, a distinction between merely conforming to a standard and genuinely following a rule. Intuitively, a child at a chessboard who makes the moves she is told to perform is doing something different to an adult who is trying to figure out what move to make. Granting that such a distinction is there to be drawn, how are we to do so? It is natural to account for this difference in terms of our "distance" from norms. Indeed, Robert Pippin puts the question to both Hegel and Heidegger in just these terms:

> what is it about the *"way* we go on," the way we *follow* social norms … that could explain my "distance," as it were, *from* the norm, my not merely responding and initiating appropriately, but in the *light of*, and so with some possible alteration or rejection of, such presumed shared sense of appropriateness?[1]

According to Pippin, Hegel's discussion of self-legislation provides a sophisticated answer to this question. We have distance from norms to the extent that we are able to give norms to ourselves: "for something to function as a norm, it must be *self-imposed*."[2] We act in the light of norms to the extent that we recognize the norms we have given ourselves "as in some sense justifiable,"[3] that is, as having universally valid authority that outstrips, with the power

D. Batho (✉)
University of California, Santa Barbara, Santa Barbara, CA, USA

© The Author(s), under exclusive license to Springer Nature
Switzerland AG 2021
C. D. Coe (eds.), *The Palgrave Handbook of German Idealism and Phenomenology*,
Palgrave Handbooks in German Idealism,
https://doi.org/10.1007/978-3-030-66857-0_10

to overrule, our merely subjective preferences. The distinctively Hegelian twist on this recognizably Kantian thesis is that our ability to give norms to ourselves for reasons we recognize as universally valid is fully realizable only in a social order that has an appropriate structure, where this structure has "something to do with real mutuality of recognition among free, rational beings."[4]

As well as providing an interpretation of Hegel's view of what it means to act in the light of norms, however, Pippin also argues that despite promising overtures, Heidegger fails to deliver. For despite having a detailed account of the *failure* to act in the light of norms—he has in mind Heidegger's analysis of "average everydayness" and the mindless, absorptive conformism of *Das Man*—when it comes to articulating a positive alternative, Heidegger has nothing coherent to say:

> what positive answer there is in Heidegger to the question of the possibility of a non-individualist, non-mentalist account of our sensible, norm-governed dealings with the world is undermined by his own analysis, and … we are only left with rejected alternatives.[5]

If this challenge were left unanswered, it could seem to pose a serious problem for Heidegger. If he cannot account for the possibility of acting in the light of norms, Heidegger has no viable account of normativity, since he has no way of distinguishing between adult mastery, on the one hand, and mere "appropriate responsiveness," on the other.

Steven Crowell has attempted to meet Pippin's challenge. Across a series of essays, he argues that Heideggerian authenticity bears a necessary connection to an obligation to assess the validity of the norms we live by, in light of which assessments our norms can be accepted, modified, or abandoned.[6] In this way, Crowell hopes to emphasize and exploit Heidegger's inheritance of German Idealist thought around the topic of self-legislation to provide a Heideggerian answer to Pippin's question that bears a striking resemblance to the answer Pippin finds in Hegel. For, if Crowell is right, Heidegger would account for our "distance" from norms by reference to our capacity to give norms to ourselves. And he would analyze our ability to act in the light of norms as an ability to follow norms which we have given to ourselves for reasons we stake and defend as universally valid.

In this chapter, I have two principal aims. Firstly, I shall argue that Crowell's reading fails as a defense of Heidegger. Secondly, I shall lay out an alternative reading of Heidegger's position as providing a partial answer to Pippin's question. I take each task in turn.

Crowell on Heidegger on Norms

Crowell's reconstruction of Heidegger begins with the claim that it is only in virtue of self-understanding that we are able to inhabit specific contexts of relevance in terms of which entities are meaningfully disclosed. It is only because I understand myself to be a carpenter, for example, that a hammer can show up to me as for hammering within a workshop.[7] To understand yourself as a carpenter, Crowell argues, is to be able to be a carpenter. He takes this to mean that self-understanding consists in trying to be a particular sort of person. So, on his account, it is a condition on the possibility of anything showing up to you as something or other that you are trying to be a particular sort of person in whose projects the entity can matter in some particular way.[8] In trying to be a particular sort of person, he argues, you have to take up the everyday, socially accepted way of being that sort of person as a preliminary guide. But the norms that describe the everyday way of being, for example, a father do not settle the question of what it is to be a father, so in trying to be a father you are not bound to act as all fathers do:

> the norms that measure what *Dasein* is trying to be are themselves *at issue* in that trying. In acting for the sake of being a father, I measure myself by what I *take* being a father to mean. And if, in doing so, I must start from the norms typical of my time and place, this does not mean that the normative force of these norms (their first-personal way of binding me as actual measures, "internal" reasons) is independent of my uptake—including critical uptake—of them. My comportment … discloses what I take a "good" father to be, and such comportment can bend the rules, even quite radically. To be a father is to exemplify a certain way of going on in the matter of fatherhood, to embody an interpretation of what it means to be a father. As Heidegger will begin to say around 1928, in acting for the sake of being a father I stand as an exemplar of what a father *should* be.[9]

Existing in a meaningful world necessarily involves understanding yourself through some number of commitments, such as a commitment to being a father. But to be a father is to try to be a father. And to try to be a father is to have a take on what it means to be a good father and to strive to live up to that standard, thus embodying your take on fatherhood as the measure of your striving. Further, to have a take on what it means to be a good father is to stand as an exemplar of what fathers should be. So standing as an exemplar is part of the existential structure that makes possible the meaningful disclosure of entities.

By this point in his argument, Crowell's Heideggerian conception of self-legislation has begun to take shape. The norms by which you measure yourself are not impositions of nature, culture, parents, or God: They are what you *take* it to mean to do well by your commitments, your interpretative transpositions of socially accepted standards. Consequently, if he has succeeded, then he has shown that Heidegger does have an account of our "distance" from norms. We are distant from norms, on Crowell's reading, because we live by standards we have given ourselves, our "takes" on what counts as success with respect to some commitment. It is central, however, to the thought of both Kant and Hegel (and Pippin's reconstruction of the latter), that for something to be genuinely binding, and thus to serve as a norm, it cannot be a reflection of mere subjective preference. Something that shifted with changes in what it was supposed to measure could have no more authority than a yardstick that shrank or grew to match whatever was held against it. Thus, to explain the possibility of acting in the light of *norms*—standards with genuine force over conduct—we need to show more than that we have given them to ourselves, and in that sense have distance from them; we need also to account for the independence of their authority from merely subjective preference. What *constrains* my "takes," on Crowell's account, such that they amount to something other than a reflection of my mere idiosyncrasies?

Through standing as an exemplar, Crowell argues, your comportment embodies a public judgment, such that your way of going about things "is always also an address to others, a kind of petition to consider [my commitment] as I do."[10] So not only must you exemplify a particular take on your commitments, you cannot but embody a publicly addressed judgment that this is how anyone similarly committed should go about things. But since your comportment embodies a demand that others should understand their commitments as you do, you are in effect making a claim on their behalf. And this means, Crowell continues, that you are answerable to those on behalf of whom you are making this claim:

> This demand on others entails a corresponding obligation to engage with them, to account for myself.... Because accountability belongs to the phenomenological character of authentically measuring myself against a norm, then, exemplary necessity entails an obligation to enter into the game of giving and asking for reasons.[11]

Although Crowell holds that we cannot but embody a claim as to the validity of some take on the commitments we live by, he does not believe that we always acknowledge this. On his view, the life of inauthenticity involves a failure to take responsibility for the validity judgments that we must embody:

The first-person character of mindless coping is such that this exemplarity is mostly occluded, (inauthenticity), but it can become "transparent" to itself in that mode of self-awareness in which the stakes of being a father include both my responsibility for the normative force of the norms in light of which I act and my answerability to others for acting on them in this way (authenticity).[12]

Thus, on pain of living a lie we are required to take responsibility for our existential situation, to own up to our claim to exemplarity, and to be prepared to engage in the assessment and adjustment of our guiding norms in the give and take of reasons. In so doing, Crowell hopes to demonstrate that Heidegger secures a connection between authenticity and the practice of giving justificatory reasons through which our takes are genuinely constrained, rather than reflective of mere personal idiosyncrasies. As I shall now argue, however, there are problems with Crowell's argument.[13]

Critical Remarks

As we have seen, central to Crowell's account is the claim that the norms that structure the commitments you live by are your own interpretative transposition of prevailing cultural standards. On this account, a moment of self-legislation is built into all self-understanding: to understand yourself as a father just is to live by norms you have taken for yourself. Crowell's appeal to the notion of "exemplary necessity," as it putatively figures in Heidegger's thought, is supposed to explain how such self-imposed norms could aspire to the universal validity required for them to be genuinely binding. For if it is true, as Crowell claims, that to have a take on what it means to be a good father just is to stake oneself as an exemplary father, and thereby to claim universal validity for the norms embodied in your comportment, then the mere possession of an interpretative take on fatherhood entails entry into the practice of giving reasons, in which one's take is held as in need of justification by reasons that are also authoritative for those others to whom the claim of exemplarity—and the defense of this claim—are addressed.

But why should we accept that any comportment whatsoever, simply by being structured by a commitment, involves a claim to exemplarity that entails an obligation to justify yourself?[14] The claim is certainly surprising, not least because it seems to invert the role of the exemplar as it is understood at key moments in the post-Kantian tradition. In Romantic thought, for example, exemplars are often taken to play a central role in ethical development through being taken as examples to emulate.[15] Two features of this conception are worth emphasizing here. Firstly, the exemplarity of the exemplar is not necessarily claimed by the exemplar herself. Rather, the exemplar is exemplary in relation to some individual who finds her worthy of emulation. Secondly, the exemplar's example sets the standard that others may follow and, therefore, is not fully justifiable in terms of norms antecedently available to those who regard her as exemplary.[16] On the Romantic conception, then, the exemplar need not make a claim to her own exemplarity in order for her example to be taken as such. And even if she were to make a claim to exemplarity, her claim could only be justified ostensively by her example, which would speak for itself, rather than by discursive argument in the practice of giving reasons.

As well as inverting classic discussions, however, Crowell's portrayal of exemplary necessity is also highly counter-intuitive in its own right. To be sure, it is quite possible to assert oneself as exemplary with respect to some commitment. But it also seems quite possible to take oneself as a novice with respect to some commitment and for that reason to find oneself a far cry from exemplarity. I might, for example, find myself having to figure out what it means to be a father as I go along, never taking myself to be in possession of the sort of wisdom that might ground a claim to my own exemplarity. It seems quite possible, in other words, to go about your commitments with modest reservation.[17]

Even granting that it is possible to take a more unassuming posture with respect to your own commitments, however, would not such a mode of comportment itself involve an assertion of exemplarity, albeit at a higher order? I might, for example, take myself to be a novice in the context of my commitment, while taking such an attitude toward my current understanding of my commitment to be exemplary, exhorting others to follow my lead in just this respect. But even granting the substance of this reply, which we might wish to question, it would not solve the problem.

Suppose that I do not take myself to be an exemplar with respect to my commitment to being a father, relative to the norms that guide my decision to "go drinking with my buddies and skip my son's Little League game,"[18] but only relative to my higher-order relation to such norms as tentative stages on the way of my continual apprenticeship in fatherhood. In that case, I would not be petitioning others to consider the validity of the norms that guide my decision, since I do not assert them as valid, but petitioning others to consider the validity of my orientation toward any such norms, namely, my withdrawal of any claim to be an exemplar of my commitments. Any exemplary necessity claimed at this higher order, however, would not entail that my interpretation of what it means to be a good father—encoded in the norms I embody in making my concrete decision—itself issues a claim for which I am obliged to give reasons. Consequently, the assertion of this higher-order exemplarity would not secure the connection between the takes on my commitments that guide my concrete decisions, on the one hand, and the external constraint supposedly provided by the practice of giving reasons, on the other, to which Crowell appeals to explain the bindingness of norms.

So either Crowell's claim regarding exemplary necessity is restricted to our relation to the norms that we follow in living up to our commitments—in which case it inverts classic discussions of exemplarity and, more seriously, implausibly denies the possibility of sustaining a commitment in a modest way—or it refers to a higher-order form of exemplarity—in which case any claim of exemplarity attaches to our relation to the norms we follow, rather than the norms themselves. In either case, the appeal to exemplary necessity does not explain the possibility of external constraint on the formation of our interpretative takes on the norms that constitute our commitments. Consequently, Crowell's defense of Heidegger from Pippin fails: Lacking a plausible explanation of the possibility of external constraint on the formation of our takes, it offers no explanation of the possibility of the genuine bindingness of norms. We remain left with nothing but "rejected alternatives."

Beyond Self-Legislation

What, then, can be said on Heidegger's behalf? To begin we can note that the problems with Crowell's account stem from his acceptance of a premise that he shares with Pippin, namely, that our distance from norms is to be explained in terms of self-legislation. It is because he accounts for our distance from norms in this way that it is incumbent on him to explain how the norms we "take" for ourselves have any authority over us. And it is the dependence of his answer to this question on his problematic discussion of exemplary necessity that undermines his defense as a whole. But must Heidegger accept this problematic premise?

To be sure, the claim that our distance from norms must be explained in terms of self-legislation is contestable. John McDowell, for example, has contested it.[19] The tree in the garden is normative with respect to my thought and judgment about it. I might feel the urgency of a demand to scrutinize the credentials of my experience, perhaps if I am in some doubt over exactly what is in my tea. But if everything is in order and the tree itself is given, there is no obvious logical space to ask whether the perceived tree should hold sway over what I think and say about it. The tree is authoritative, and

I can acknowledge it as authoritative, in light of which authority I can freely think and judge. But I do not establish its authority, indeed, there is no clear sense of what this could mean.[20]

My aim here is not to vindicate McDowell's position, although I am sympathetic. At this stage, I wish only to point out that there are philosophical reasons to challenge the assumption that acting in the light of a norm entails the ability to self-legislate.[21] Consequently, we need not accept as obvious the demand that any account of the former must account for the general possibility of the latter. We are at liberty to return to Heidegger's texts with the aim of exploring how he might explain the possibility of acting in the light of norms, unburdened by the requirement of explaining this possibility in terms of self-legislation. This is the task that I take up in what follows.

I shall argue that on Heidegger's account, acting in the light of norms requires acknowledging your mortality, and that acknowledging your mortality entails acknowledging the questionability of yourself and the matters that concern you through which you understand yourself, which acknowledgment does not reduce to a process of questioning the validity of the norms that you follow. I reconstruct Heidegger's reasoning as follows. You cannot act in the light of a norm unless you acknowledge that norm *as* a norm. A norm just is a piece of guidance providing orientation with respect to some interest or concern over which its authority ranges. But, on Heidegger's account, any such interest or concern is ultimately for the sake of the cessation of your own existence. So the failure to acknowledge mortality is a failure to act in the light of norms, since it is a failure to act in the light of what a norm *is*, namely, a guide for a mortal life. To acknowledge your death in the manner in which you follow norms, I shall argue, involves letting the norms you follow be in question with respect to your existence as a whole, and— what amounts to the same thing—to let yourself be in question in terms of concerns that you acknowledge as questionable, in a sense I shall elaborate.

To be clear at the outset, I shall not be claiming that acknowledging your mortality is sufficient for acting in the light of norms. All I intend to show is that if Heidegger is right (as I read him), then any account of acting in the light of norms that left acknowledged mortality out of the picture would for that reason be lacking. So although the reading I develop below will not give a complete answer to Pippin's question, it offers a substantial portion and, moreover, identifies a desideratum of any satisfactory answer, one that is overlooked when exclusive focus is given to the recognition of the rational authority of norms.

Heidegger on Norms for Mortals

Heidegger's discussion of death is one of the most contentious areas in Heidegger scholarship, so nothing I say here will be uncontroversial. That said, it is not my aim to defend the superiority of the reading I present over all others. If my reading is tenable and helps with the problem at hand, that will be good enough for me.[22] I shall limit myself to arguing that the following claims are tenable attributions to Heidegger. The first claim is that death is a way of existing for the sake of something. The second is that that for the sake of which we exist in death is the cessation of Dasein's existence. (As I shall explain in detail later on, I do not mean that Dasein aims for the cessation of its existence as its *goal*.) The third is that Dasein necessarily exists in this way. The fourth is that Dasein always relates to its death in some way, either transparently or opaquely. With these claims established, I will argue that, on Heidegger's view, every norm we follow just is a piece of guidance with authority over a way of living out a mortal life, such that to come to act in the light the norms you follow—to follow norms *as* norms—has to involve acknowledging your death in the manner in which you act.

Death, Heidegger claims, is a possibility of Dasein's being.[23] "Possibility" is a Heideggerian term of art: A possibility is a way of existing for the sake of something.[24] To return to a by now familiar example, fatherhood is a possibility, in Heidegger's terminology, since it is a way of existing for the sake of something, namely, your children. Heidegger distinguishes existing for the sake of something from acting in order to achieve a goal.[25] In acting in order to achieve a goal, I have a more or less determinate aim in view that I strive to realize and attain. I might, for example, set as my goal the end of attaining the legal status of being a father. In this way, I have a determinate end in sight that I can work to realize once and for all. In contrast to acting in order to achieve a goal, to exist for the sake of something is to harbor a form of concern in terms of which the goals I might seek to attain, and the entities I encounter along the way, matter to me.[26] To exist for the sake of my children, for example, is not to have my children as my goal, but for the possible goals that are open to me, and the entities I encounter as I pursue them, to be conditioned in their salience by my concern for my children.[27] So, for example, to act in order to secure the legal status of being a father would be to act for the sake of my children, if the possibility of attaining that status was lent salience by my concern for my children. But seeking to attain the legal status of a father need not be for the sake of your children; you might be seeking to attain that goal for the sake of some other concern. Before same-sex marriage was legalized in the USA, for example, some couples chose to adopt one another in order to secure legal status for their relationship.[28]

As a way of further elaborating the notion of a possibility as a way of existing for the sake of something, it may be helpful to introduce the idea of a horizon by way of comparison. A horizon is not an objective feature of the world but the constitutive limit of a perspective. Consequently, a horizon persists only so long as the perspective of which it is the limit is sustained. In addition, a horizon is a vanishing point at the end of any orientation within a perspective. Since a horizon is not a place in the world, but a limit of a perspective within the world, it is not a place one can occupy, so it is not a place one can seek to occupy either. A horizon is, thus, the constitutive, non-occupiable, limit of a perspective toward which a perspective is directed, without being a place within a perspective or a goal one can seek to attain. Similarly, an end for the sake of which Dasein exists is a constitutive, non-attainable limit of a form of concern toward which any particular activity is directed. My children are an end of my action, in this sense, not because they are a goal I am trying to attain, but because my concern for them conditions the salience of the available goals that I can aim for. Since my children persist as an end in this way only so long as the form of concern is alive in me, they are a constitutive aspect of a way of existing.

In claiming that death is a possibility, then, Heidegger is claiming that death is a way of existing, a form of concern for the sake of something that conditions the salience of what Dasein encounters. This is a point worth emphasizing. Heidegger is not claiming that death is the cessation of existence, the terminus of all ways of life. He is making the counter-intuitive claim that death is a way of existing, in some respects similar to other ways of life, such as being a father.[29] In other respects, however, death is unlike other possibilities. For one thing, other ways of existing are contingent to Dasein's particular circumstances. Death, in contrast, is a way of existing upon which Dasein has already embarked whatever else it does. Death, Heidegger claims, is a possibility of Dasein's *being*. He means that Dasein cannot exist without existing in this way; Dasein *is* this way of existing. He also means that death conditions the salience of everything Dasein encounters and every one of its possible undertakings. Where my concern for being a father and my other everyday commitments project local horizons within my life which may collapse or expand in time, my death projects the global horizon of my life as a whole that ranges over my life. So when Heidegger claims that death is the "not to be bypassed possibility of Dasein,"[30] on my reading he does not mean that death is an eventuality we cannot avoid.[31] He means that it is a way of existing for the sake of something in which Dasein is already underway, that it cannot abandon, and which projects the all-encompassing horizon of its existence as such: "*I myself am this constant and utmost possibility of myself*, namely, to be no more.... Dasein is essentially its death."[32]

As we have seen, Heidegger distinguishes death, which is a way of existing for the sake of something, from the cessation of Dasein's existence. Death is not unrelated to the cessation of Dasein's existence, however, since the cessation of Dasein's existence is that for the sake of which Dasein exists in death, the horizon that conditions the salience of everything Dasein encounters. This is, I take it, what Heidegger means when he claims that death is not the *end* of Dasein, but *being-toward-the-end* of Dasein,[33] "the possibility of the absolute impossibility of any existence in general,"[34] and the possibility of "being no more."[35] If a "possibility" is a way Dasein exists for the sake of something, then an "impossibility" is the absence of a way for Dasein to exist for the sake of something and the "the absolute impossibility of any existence at all" is the absence of any way for Dasein to exist for the sake of anything. The cessation of existence is the absolute impossibility of any existence at all, on this reading, since it marks the collapse of Dasein's existence in *every* way, and thereby constitutes its annihilation. So death, as a possibility of Dasein's being, is an unavoidable way of existing for the sake of something. That for the sake of which Dasein unavoidably and inextricably exists, however, is its end: the impossibility of any existence at all, the cessation of its existence: the "moment at which ... possibility becomes impossibility."[36] As Heidegger elaborates it, then, death is not an event whereby Dasein ceases to exist, but the way of existing toward the horizon of the cessation of its existence.[37]

As well as claiming that Dasein is its death, Heidegger also claims that Dasein relates, essentially, to its death. The relation that we take toward our own death is what Heidegger calls "dying": "let 'dying' stand for that *way of Being* in which Dasein *is towards* its death."[38] He differentiates between two ways of dying: We can acknowledge death or we can cover over death. He calls the first form of dying "authentic being-towards-death."[39] You might comport yourself, for example, as though you were free to let your mortality be relevant to what matters to you some time from now. If so, you would be relating to yourself as though the cessation of your existence did not always already condition the salience of every moment of your life. You might, in contrast, acknowledge that the cessation of your existence is always already the horizon within which anything you care about matters, and let yourself see the matters that concern you in the light it already casts. So by distinguishing death from dying, Heidegger is distinguishing a way of existing that we cannot avoid and cannot abandon, on the one hand, from two ways of relating to that way of existing, on the other: acting in acknowledgment of the light cast by the cessation of your own existence, the form of concern that you always already are, and acting absent such acknowledgment.

Taking these tendentious points of interpretation as established, let me draw a number of corollaries. Dasein *is* its death: It is constituted by the projection of the cessation of its own existence as the horizon of its existence as a whole, such that the cessation of Dasein's existence conditions the salience of everything Dasein encounters, rather as my children condition the salience of what I encounter, so long as my concern for them is alive in me. Consequently, everything Dasein does just is a way of existing for the sake of the cessation of its existence, even if it is not acknowledged as such. A transparent understanding of Dasein's activity, then, must involve seeing what it is doing in the context of is existence as a whole, that is, the form of concern for the cessation of its existence.

This claim is presented in the course of Heidegger's elaboration of the connections between entities, goals, and that for the sake of which the goals are pursued:

> [The] thing at hand which we call a hammer has to do with hammering, the hammering has to do with fastening something, fastening something has to do with protection against bad weather. This protection "is" for the sake of providing shelter for Dasein, that is, for the sake of a possibility of its being.[40]

The phrase translated as "providing shelter for Dasein" is "*des Unterkommens des Daseins.*" A very literal translation of *unterkommens* would be "coming under." It can mean "seeking accommodation"; you can *unterkommen* at a friend's place when visiting another city. But it can also be used as an expression of being exposed to something new, even shocking: If someone has been especially aggressive to you in the Hauptbahnhof, you might say "*Das ist mir noch nie untergekommen!*"; it means "I've never come across *that* before!" Thus, the term is ambiguous between going under something you are sheltered by and undergoing something you are exposed to. So while "providing shelter for Dasein" is an appropriate translation, the connotations of the original German are lost. The importance of this point can be seen in connection with another issue with the translation. Heidegger claims that hammers are used for tasks such as fastening things in order to protect against bad weather. The word rendered as "bad weather" (*Unwetter*) is more suggestive of a severe storm than sub-optimal conditions for a picnic. Thus, to protect against bad weather is plausibly both to seek to provide shelter and to be exposed, indeed: to seek to provide shelter in the face of exposure. So Heidegger is indicating a connection between productive activity in the form of seeking to provide shelter, on the one hand, and passivity in the form of exposure before nature, on the other.

In this passage, I suggest, Heidegger is drawing connections between everyday forms of productive activity and death. He is suggesting that if we take a wide-angled view on the humble act of driving a nail, we can see this act in connection with the practice of construction, we can see the practice of construction in connection with our concern for building, we can see our concern for building in connection with our concern to provide shelter, and we can see our concern to provide shelter in connection with our vulnerability before nature as mortal beings.[41] He is not claiming, absurdly, that all hammering is subsumed under the "highest-order project" of seeking to provide shelter, as though the provision of shelter were the distal goal of all our use of hammers. I can, after all, use my hammer to dismantle your shelter. His view is that since Dasein *is* its death, the cessation of Dasein's existence is, essentially, the horizon within which all of Dasein's possibilities are conditioned in their salience. This has the implication that all of our practices are, as ways of existing, ways of living in the shadow of death, whether we acknowledge them as such or not. Heidegger is, further, suggesting that certain experiences, such as anxious vulnerability before a storm, confront us with the place of our practices within the ultimate horizon of the cessation of our existence. In seeing our possibilities transparently in light of the cessation of our existence, we come to see those practices within the horizon of our life as a whole and, thereby, for what they are: ways of leading a mortal life. To see the point more clearly, we can consider a second example.

At a young age, a child might begin to imitate the map-reading behavior she sees in the adults around her. We can imagine this imitative behavior growing more refined until, as a teenager, she has attained a mastery of the practice, such that she is able to engage in orienteering exercises without adult guidance. There may come a point, however, at which she finds that she is lost, and feels anxious before an approaching storm. Now this vignette is very sketchy. But it has enough detail for us to highlight a few salient features. Firstly, the example should be familiar enough to draw into view the sort of experience I believe that Heidegger had in mind when indicating the connection between hammering and seeking shelter: In both cases, an everyday practice is received in a new light through an experience of vulnerability.[42] This example also helps us to see why such an experience could give an opportunity to deepen your understanding of norms you might already take as justified. The teenager had mastered the practice of map reading as part of her broad schooling. Her prospective vision, we might say, was limited to that context: She projected her practice, and the norms that constitute it, toward a future horizon she took as established and secured by her parents, teachers, and adults in general. Through the experience of vulnerability, however, she newly found herself to be relevantly like her parents and teachers: without a horizon established and secured by "Others," the adults. In this way, we can imagine that she finds her prior vision of the world to be a fantasy that has now dropped away, leaving her with her capacities, practices, and concerns exposed as situated in the context of her *own* life, her *ownmost* possibility. We might describe this transition, occasioned by an anxious sense of her own vulnerability, as one in which her practices (and the norms that structure them) are seen as having a place in the world as such, as opposed to the "world" of the "Others," that is, the childish fantasy of existing in a horizon sustained and secured by adults.

This way of taking Heidegger's remarks on death and anxiety has the benefit of giving us traction on some seemingly occult passages in which he appears to refer to a vanishingly rare, if at all plausible, experience of "hovering" above the world, somehow able to see and grasp things for what they are despite having become radically disconnected from the practical contexts in which their salience could be disclosed.[43] We can bring Heidegger's remarks down to earth, however, if we read them as analyzing the sort of experience I have been trying to elaborate. Through experiences of anxiety—such as vulnerability before storms and the feeling of being lost—the fantasy of your educative environment as encompassing the world drops away as a whole and can offer nothing to you, except a chance to recoil from your newly lucid vision. On this reading, it is not the *world itself* that drops away beneath you; on the contrary, the world comes rearing up at you, newly liberated by the removal of a stand-in. This is why, I take it, Heidegger describes the world revealed in terms of mortality as *unheimlich*—uncanny or unhomely. For in seeing what matters to me in light of my mortality, through anxious experiences of vulnerability, I find that my home is not the world and that the world is not my home.[44]

Let me now bring these considerations to bear on the problematic we are pursuing here, namely, the question of what explanation Heidegger can provide for acting in the light of norms. A norm just is a piece of guidance providing orientation with respect to some interest or concern over which its authority ranges. But, by Heidegger's reckoning, any interest or concern is, ultimately, for the sake of the cessation of your existence. To understand a norm *as* a norm, then, and to follow it as such, is to understand not only how it guides, but what it is for it to guide at all: to direct a mortal being. To put the point in contemporary terms: You are only responding to reasons *as* reasons if you understand them for what they are, namely, considerations that speak in favor of something in the context of an interest undertaken over which they have authority, ultimately, for the sake of the cessation of your existence. In this way, I submit, Heidegger's account entails that acting in the light of norms must involve acknowledging your mortality in the manner in which the norms are followed, as part of the acknowledgment of what it is for a norm to be a norm. So acknowledgment of your mortality is a necessary condition on acting in the light of norms.

Although the acknowledgment of your mortality in the manner in which you follow norms is part of following norms in light of what they are, it is not a matter of attaining a new critical vantage point from which your norms might be assessed. Consider, again, the case of the teenager whose mastery at orienteering is newly received in light of her mortality. There may be, for her, no live question as to the suitability of the guidance of the map for the task at hand; that matter may be settled. In coming to see the norms that structure the practice of map reading in light of her death, the teenager comes to understand what it is to follow norms, to need guidance in view of her death. This is not reducible to a development in her sense of the justification of the norms of the practice in which she is participating.[45]

I have argued that, on Heidegger's reckoning, transparently projecting the norms you follow in participating in practices against the horizon of the cessation of your own existence, is necessary for acknowledging those norms for what they are; that this involves becoming disabused of the fantasy of having horizons secured by others (principally, "the adults" of one's educative environment); and that certain experiences of anxious vulnerability make this possibility salient. I have also denied that taking up this possibility is reducible to a refinement of your competence in seeing or assessing the validity of norms. In this way, I have argued that acting in the light of norms requires acting in the light of your death, where this goes beyond acknowledging the justified authority of the norms that you follow. I have, however, said next to nothing about what it is to follow norms in light of your mortality. In the next section, I begin to elaborate a positive account. I do so by attributing to Heidegger two further claims. The first is that Dasein's death is indefinite. The second is that the indefiniteness of Dasein's death entails the questionability of the significance of the matters that concern it.

Indefiniteness and Questionability

Death is indefinite because it is a possibility and possibilities are, in general, indefinite: "indefiniteness ... characterizes every factually projected potentiality-of-being of Dasein."[46] Heidegger discusses the indefiniteness of possibilities in a number of places, through which he delineates two aspects of the phenomenon. The first aspect of indefiniteness is temporal: that for the sake of which Dasein exists in death—the cessation of its existence—is not a prospectively datable event. Heidegger is not making the narrowly epistemic point that we do not know when we will die; he is claiming that the continual imminence of death casts a uniform light over life as a whole, regardless of whether we let ourselves see by this light, such that our lives are always and everywhere in the shadow of death, regardless of whether this is acknowledged.[47] Death is temporally indefinite, in other words, because it matters equally all the time, not just particularly for some particular time: "This indefiniteness as to when death comes positively refers to the possibility that it can come at any moment. It in no way weakens the certainty of its coming, but rather gives it its sting and the character of an utmost and constant possibility which Dasein is."[48]

The second aspect of indefiniteness of possibilities to which Heidegger draws attention concerns the role of possibilities as a source of developing self-understanding:

> "He studies history" … With history something definite is factually meant—in factual life experience cogiven with it in its life-context—however, *in the character of indefiniteness*. What is meant by this indefiniteness? I know of someone that he studies history in the first semester. I can explicate this opinion by bringing to mind that he always goes to the seminars of Finke and Below, sits in the library and carries large codices home with him, works on medieval papal documents; one never sees him working in the natural sciences institutes. That is a rough explication in the style of factical life experience. One can pursue it further. Studying history is after all not simply reading, collecting, excerpting, acquiring knowledge; it is a wanting to grow into a method, into a goal-directed acquisition of knowledge that occurs in going through certain provisions of the individual steps of knowledge. The study of the science of history is accompanied by the study of the historical past. Studying history therefore means to make the historical world accessible to oneself, but in the form of growing into historical research as science.[49]

Heidegger is linking the indefiniteness of the discipline of history to the way in which it can serve as a source of development of self-understanding, that is, as something into which the historian can continually grow and thereby develop her understanding of herself as a historian and the world as historical. Why should we think that the availability of the discipline of history as a source of self-understanding should have anything to do with "indefiniteness"?

To see what Heidegger is getting at, we can consider again the way in which your children matter for you when you exist for their sake. Your children definitely mean a lot to you. What they mean to you is manifest in the way they make a difference, that is, the way your concern for them conditions the salience of possibilities for action you undertake and entities you encounter along the way. But although your children definitely mean a lot and definitely make a difference, what they mean to you, the difference they definitely make, is indefinite, that is, not already given except as yours to work out. Through working out the difference your children definitely make with respect to some matter, you come to develop your understanding of what they mean to you and, thus, how you understand yourself in relation to them, that is, how you understand yourself as a father. A father, for example, might wonder whether he is reinforcing problematic stereotypes by letting his son have the toy he has had his eye on, or whether he is moralistically imposing ideals that will only serve to expose his son to bullying, and so on. In this way, the father is looking to get a grip on what he would be doing if he were to let his son have the toy. The father's concern for his child exerts a definite pressure on him in the form of a definite problem: It is up to him to figure out the significance of his actions in connection with his concern for his child. But his concern does not give a definite answer to his problem, it just gives that problem to him as one to work through. So his child definitely matters with respect to the significance of his possible action, but in an indefinite way. Equally, how his son matters to him is indefinite: there to be worked out through working out the significance of the action.[50] Similarly, the discipline of history is indefinite, in the sense of raising ever-new problems and questions through which the historian can grow into the practice, develop her self-understanding, and thereby open up stretches of the historical world.[51]

With that in mind, we are now in a position to see what Heidegger means when he claims that death is indefinite. Since death projects the ultimate horizon of all existence, death matters continually over existence, thereby continually allowing for the question of the significance of the matters that concern Dasein in terms of its existence as a whole. Just as my children are indefinite in the sense that they pose a question over the significance of my actions with respect to my concern for them, the form of my existence as a whole is indefinite in the sense that it leaves a question over the significance of any particular concern with respect to my life as such.

Now, to be in this condition of indeterminacy—such that the significance of your actions is indefinite in terms of your concerns, and the significance of your concerns is indefinite in terms of your life as a whole—is to be at stake both in what you do and what concerns you. This is, I take it, the central idea behind Heidegger's claim that Dasein is essentially at issue. I am at stake in what I do, since whether I am realized as a father in "going drinking with my buddies and skipping my son's Little League game," depends on whether this action is or can be found to be intelligible as a way of being a father. Suppose I let on to my friends what I have given up in choosing to be with them. They might conceivably respond by proclaiming: "that's no way to look after your children!" The challenge presented in these terms does not simply target the justifiability of the action; the challenge targets the intelligibility of the action as an expression of myself as a father. Doing that is not caring for my child; in acting in this way I was not being—was not realized as—a father. Just as my concerns are at stake in my actions, I am at stake in the concerns that I harbor, since whether or not I myself am realized depends on whether I am or could be found to be intelligible as myself in a concern realized in my actions. To extend our example, should I come to the realization that my decision to go drinking with my buddies was not, despite my initial protestations, intelligible as a way of being a father, I might pause to reflect on whether this possibility—the form of concern for my children—is really intelligible as a way of being myself. On finding that I can indeed find myself intelligible in these terms, or even that I cannot avoid thinking of myself in these terms, I might then come to reflect that when I left my child to whistle, *I was not myself*.[52]

In sum, the question of the significance of an action that is opened by the indefiniteness of a possibility is situated within the broader question of the significance of the possibility that is opened by the indefiniteness of the ultimate horizon of one's existence as a whole: the cessation of one's existence. In so doing, death opens the question of whether you can make sense of your concern in terms of your action, and vice versa, and whether you can make sense of yourself in terms of your concern, and vice versa. Taking these points as established, we can now close our discussion by turning to the question of what it would mean to acknowledge the indefiniteness of death in your mode of comportment, and thus to act in light of norms as offering guidance for a mortal life.

Acting in Light of Mortal Norms

The first thing to note is that to acknowledge that one is at stake in the ways I have outlined does not require one to stake an interpretation as valid. I might regard my understanding of what it means to be a father as insufficient for determining whether I was realized as a father in my actions. I might also regard my understanding of my life as a whole as insufficient for determining the significance of my concern for my children and, therefore, whether I myself would be realized through realizing that concern in my actions. In either case, I would regard myself as at stake in both what I do and what I care about. But in neither case must I suppose myself to be in possession of the sort of understanding that would support an assertion of my actions as really intelligible as expressions of my concerns or an assertion of my concerns as really intelligible expressions of myself.[53] In either case, if I am to acknowledge the way that my mortality puts me at stake, I do not need to take myself to be in possession of an interpretation of what it means to be a good father, embodied in my comportment and the validity of which I stake. What matters is whether I acknowledge that the realization of a concern in my actions and the realization of myself in my concern is at stake in what I do and what I care about, and I need not stake myself to do so.

From these reflections we can finally identify a minimal condition of what acknowledging mortality in the way you follow norms must involve that points in precisely the opposite direction to staking oneself as an exemplar. Since my life as a whole is nothing I can get within my power, nothing I can come to grasp in such a way that it could serve as a definite point of reference in terms of which the question of the significance of a concern could be closed once and for all, my understanding of my life as a whole must be insufficient for determining whether any particular form of concern, itself at stake in my actions, would genuinely count as a realization of myself. To acknowledge *that* in one's mode of comportment—and thus to be transparent in one's comportment to death, the form of one's existence as a whole—would, I submit, require one to withdraw any premature claim to being in a position to assert one's own example as valid for all fathers, friends, and so on. It would, instead, require an altogether different mode of comportment that we might wish to call "reticence."[54]

Conclusion

Let me conclude by briefly recollecting the argument I have pursued across the course of this essay and highlight one ambiguity that remains. We began with a problem. Any account of normativity will have to explain the difference between mere appropriate responsiveness, on the one hand, and acting in the light of norms, on the other. Robert Pippin has argued that while Hegel's discussion of self-legislation provides a sophisticated explanation of this distinction, Heidegger has no corresponding positive account.

We saw how Steven Crowell attempted to meet Pippin's challenge head on, by arguing that Heidegger has his own account of self-legislation that fits the bill. I argued, however, that Crowell's defense relies on a problematic account of exemplary necessity and, for that reason, does not provide a satisfactory answer to Pippin's challenge. In response, I argued that Heidegger is under no obligation to account for acting in the light of norms in terms of self-legislation. On my view, Heidegger's discussion of death entails that the acknowledgment of mortality is a necessary condition for acting in the light of norms. In this way, I argued that Heidegger's discussion of death provides a partial, albeit substantial, answer to Pippin's challenge, by highlighting a desideratum of any account of our distance from norms that is overlooked by any theory that seeks to account for the phenomenon exclusively in terms of the acknowledgment of the rational authority of norms. But what does it mean to acknowledge your mortality? I argued that this involves acknowledging the questionability of the matters that concern you in light of the indeterminateness of death, where this is not reducible to assessing the validity of the norms you follow, and minimally involves withdrawing any claim to already understand the significance of the matters that concern you.

Be that as it may, one final ambiguity should be acknowledged. Toward the close of my argument, I spoke as though the question of significance opened by the indeterminacy of death is just like any question of significance opened by the indeterminacy of a form of concern, albeit at a higher order. But there is reason to suppose that there is a significant discontinuity here. We can represent the indefiniteness of possibilities by way of a representative question: "how does x matter with respect to f?" The x variable denotes some matter that may concern me (e.g. buying a toy) and the f variable denotes something for the sake of which the value of the x variable matters (e.g. my children). Death, however, is the possibility of Dasein's being; the cessation of Dasein's existence is the global horizon of its existence as a whole. Consequently, death opens up the question of the significance of a matter with respect to Dasein's existence as a whole, as opposed to with respect to this or that local concern. As the horizon of Dasein's existence as a whole, however, the cessation of Dasein's existence is not something determinate within the world, just as a horizon is not something determinate within the perspective it describes. But if the cessation of existence is not anything determinate, then it is not something in terms of which a determinate question of significance can be asked. When it comes to death, the value of the f variable remains an open question to the person for whom it matters. If that is right, however, then question of significance raised by the indeterminateness of death is discontinuous with any question of significance raised by this or that possibility in at least one striking way: the question of significance raised by the indeterminateness of death raises the question of its own intelligibility as a question, since it is a question of which a key term remains a riddle for the subject of the inquiry.[55]

Notes

1. Robert Pippin, *Idealism as Modernism* (Cambridge: Cambridge University Press, 1997), 387.
2. Ibid., 428.
3. Ibid.
4. Robert Pippin, *The Persistence of Subjectivity* (Cambridge: Cambridge University Press, 2005), 216.
5. Ibid., 387.
6. I focus on what I take to be the clearest statement of Crowell's position: Steven Crowell, "Exemplary Necessity: Heidegger, Pragmatism, and Reason," in *Pragmatic Perspectives in Phenomenology*, ed. Ondrej Švec and Jakub Čapek (London: Routledge, 2017), 242–56. This article develops and clarifies the position articulated in Steven Crowell, *Normativity and Phenomenology in Husserl and Heidegger* (Cambridge: Cambridge University Press, 2013), esp. Part III.
7. On some of Crowell's formulations of this point, the claim made is patently false. He claims, for instance, that "It is my ability to make a birdhouse, for example, that allows entities to show up for me as hammers, nails, and lumber" ("Competence Over Being as Existing" in *Giving a Damn: Essays in Dialogue with John Haugeland*, ed. Zed Adams and Jacob Browning [London: MIT Press, 2017], 81). This claim is patently false because one can recognize a hammer without being able to build a birdhouse. I take it that Crowell means, however, that I must be trying to be *someone or other* (and able to do *something*) in view of which I have some way of letting hammers matter as such practically, rather than that I must be able to build a birdhouse in order to be able to see a hammer as such. We might still demur, however, since it is far from obvious that in order to *be* a friend I have always to try (are not the closest friendships those in which companionship is "effortless"?), just as it is far from obvious (if not obviously false) to suppose that in order to *do* something I have always to try.
8. Crowell, "Exemplary Necessity," 248.
9. Ibid., 259. Crowell provides no reference for the claim that Heidegger holds that acting for the sake of something entails staking yourself as an exemplar ("around 1928"). I have found no evidence to support it.
10. Ibid., 259.
11. Ibid., 251.
12. Ibid., 249–50.

13. Even accepting Crowell's argument up to this stage, more work remains to be done. For if the practice of giving and taking reasons were itself guided by norms that were merely contingent to a cultural milieu, then the deliverances of that practice with respect to the validity of any particular "take" would be no less contingent and no more binding than the norms that permit the judgments. Crowell recognizes this problem and attempts to solve it by appeal to Jürgen Habermas's account of communicative rationality. The second leg of his argument depends on his first, though, so we need not reconstruct the argument in its entirety to assess its strength as a whole.

14. Suppose that Søren Kierkegaard is right to describe Johanne Luise Heiberg's performance as manifestation of the ideal of Juliette by way of the recovery of the role as a *source* of possible interpretations. Could she coherently take herself to be an exemplar to an understudy? Her exemplification to her understudy would be curiously paradoxical, in the sense that she would have to exemplify non-reliance on exemplars: She would have to somehow teach her student, by way of example, to refuse her own example as exemplary. For discussion, see Daniel Watts, "Kierkegaard, Repetition and Ethical Constancy," *Philosophical Investigations* 40, no. 4 (2017): 414–39.

15. See James Conant, "Nietzsche's Perfectionism: A Reading of *Schopenhauer as Educator*," in *Nietzsche's Postmoralism: Essays on Nietzsche's Prelude to the Philosophy of the Future* ed. Richard Schacht (Cambridge: Cambridge University Press, 2001), 191–96.

16. For a more recent discussion of the role of exemplars in defining ethical standards, see Linda Zagzebski, *Exemplarist Moral Theory* (Cambridge: Cambridge University Press, 2017).

17. Crowell's reading of Heidegger is markedly close to a number of points that Jean-Paul Sartre makes in *Existentialism is a Humanism* (I am grateful to Simon Thornton to alerting me to this connection): "When we say that man chooses himself, not only do we mean that each of us must choose himself, but also that in choosing himself, he is choosing for all men. In fact, in creating the man each of us wills ourselves to be, there is not a single one of our actions that does not at the same time create an image of man as we think he ought to be.… Choosing to be this or that is to affirm at the same time the value of what we choose, because we can never choose evil. We always choose the good, and nothing can be good for any unless it is good for all. … I am therefore responsible for myself and for everyone else, and I am fashioning a certain image of man as I choose him to be. In choosing myself, I choose man" (Jean-Paul Sartre, *Existentialism Is a Humanism* [London: Yale University Press, 2007], 24–25). And further: "In this sense, we can claim that human universality exists, but it is not a given; it is in perpetual construction. In choosing myself, I construct universality; in construct it by understanding every other man's project, regardless of the era in which he lives.… The fundamental aim of existentialism is to reveal the link between the absolute character of the free commitment, by

which every man realizes himself in realizing a type of humanity—a commitment is always understanding, by anyone in any era—and the relativity of the cultural ensemble that may result from such a choice" (ibid., 43). My view (which I work out in detail below) is that the Crowell/Sartre position differs from Heidegger's in roughly the following way. Where Crowell and Sartre hold that we *stake ourselves* merely through acting, by implicitly or explicitly asserting the norms or values that we follow as valid for all, Heidegger holds that we are *at stake* in acting, in the sense that whether or not we (and those who act like us) are realized *as* the sort of person we (and relevantly similarly others) understand ourselves to be (e.g., good fathers) is dependent on whether our actions are or can be found to be intelligible as those of that sort of person. Heidegger's position is, in this respect, markedly Aristotelian. For a discussion of Aristotelian reflections on this point, see David McNeill, "The Virtue of Error: Solved Games and Deliberation," *European Journal of Philosophy*, forthcoming.

18. Crowell, *Normativity and Phenomenology*, 226.

19. See John McDowell, *Having the World in View: Essays on Kant, Hegel, and Sellars* (London: Harvard University Press, 2009), 185–207.

20. In more recent work, Pippin has sought to rebut this response, claiming that all the thesis of self-legislation amounts to is the claim that a standard is authoritative only so long as it is accepted as such: "norms governing what we think and do can be said to govern thought and action only insofar as subjects, however implicitly or habitually or unreflectively (or as a matter of 'second-nature') accept such constraints and sustain allegiance" (Robert Pippin, *Hegel on Self-Consciousness* [Princeton: Princeton University Press, 2010], 22). Pippin seems to be taking the substance of McDowell's criticism as follows: The thesis of self-legislation entails that norms are normative only because they have been inaugurated as such in some moment of decision by an individual, a community, or whomever, which is implausible. Against this, Pippin is claiming that there need be no such moment for a norm to be genuinely self-legislated: a norm need only be sustained as authoritative by its continued acceptance, which can be implicit, unreflective, habitual, and so on. But this reply misses the nerve of McDowell's objection. McDowell targets the claim that the authoritativeness of norms is established by subjective activity, not the claim that the authoritativeness of norms is established by a particular sort of subjective activity, namely, an explicit act of inauguration. His point is that if we claim that the authority of a norm is actively established by us, then however we describe this activity we cannot account for the externality required for the possibility of empirical knowledge, since the authoritativeness of the norm could be traced back to factors entirely within the pale of our subjectivity. This is why McDowell claims that the tree must be *acknowledgeable* (rather than *acknowledged*) if it is to be normative. This formulation does not entail that the normativity of the tree depends upon its actively being established as such, whatever this establishment consists in. His example of perception is supposed to demonstrate the point, by highlighting the absurdity of supposing there to be a real possibility

of rejecting the authority over thought and judgment of what we veridically perceive. That seeming absurdity stands even if we accept Pippin's more modest reading of the thesis of self-legislation. For what could it mean for a subject (or community) to implicitly, or habitually, or unreflectively refuse to accept and thereby undermine the authority of the deliverances of veridical experience over our thought and judgment? But if we cannot make sense what it might mean to reject or refuse, and thereby undermine, the perceived tree as authoritative, regardless of how we characterize the rejection, then no sense has been given to the claim that we accept it in an authority-bestowing way.

21. McDowell is not denying that some form of subjective activity is required to present something over which the deliverances of perception are normative, just that this activity does not establish the authority of what perception discloses as authoritative over thought and judgment. The tree exerts no authority if there are no subjects actively pursuing interests over which its authoritativeness can range. But that does not entail that subjects have power over whether the tree is an authority over the interests they sustain.

22. Stephen Mulhall's interpretation of Heidegger on death is probably closest to the position I sketch below. See Stephen Mulhall, "Human Mortality: Heidegger on How to Portray the Impossible Possibility of Dasein," in *A Companion to Heidegger*, ed. Hubert Dreyfus and Mark Wrathall (London: Blackwell, 2005), 297–310. For a helpful discussion of the main positions in this debate, and for his own contribution, see Iain Thomson, "Death and Demise in *Being and Time*," in *The Cambridge Companion to* Being and Time, ed. Mark Wrathall (Cambridge: Cambridge University Press, 2013), 260–90.

23. The phrase "possibility of being" (*Möglichkeit seines Seins*) appears only three other times in *Being and Time*, each in connection with Heidegger's discussion of death: "We are asking about the ontological meaning of the dying of the person who dies, as a possibility-of-being of *his* being, and not about the way of being-with and the still-being-there of the deceased with those left behind" (Martin Heidegger, *Being and Time*, trans. Joan Stambaugh [Albany: State University of New York Press, 1996], 239, translation modified. Hereafter, H. All 'H' numbers refer to the marginal pagination in all editions of *Being and Time*.); "For the most part, everyday Dasein covers over its ownmost, nonrelational, and insuperable possibility of being" (H 257); "The calling back in which conscience calls forth gives Dasein to understand that Dasein itself—as the null ground of its null project, standing in the possibility of its being—must bring itself back to itself from its lostness in the they, and this means that it is guilty" (H 287).

24. See H 86–88; H 143–44.

25. For a sustained discussion of the "for-the-sake-of-which" in which Heidegger vociferously rebuts the claim that the "for-the-sake-of-which" is a sort of higher-order goal, in the context of refuting a charge of metaphysical egoism, see Martin Heidegger, *The Metaphysical Foundations of Logic* (Bloomington: Indiana University Press, 1984), 186.

26. In formulating Heidegger's position in this way, I am attempting to avoid the implication that we have the ability to begin or abandon a form of concern by elective choice alone. It is a Heideggerian thesis that we find ourselves thrown into ways of caring that we cannot collapse by fiat. To be sure, this raises some interesting and difficult questions regarding the plausibility of describing a thrown form of concern as something Dasein *does*. For a discussion of "medio-passive" modes of agency, see Béatrice Han-Pile, "Nietzsche and Amor Fati," *European Journal of Philosophy* 19, no. 2 (2011): 224–61; "Hope, Powerlessness, and Agency," *Midwest Studies in Philosophy* 41, no. 1 (2017): 175–201; and "'The Doing is Everything': A Middle-Voiced Reading of Agency in Nietzsche," *Inquiry* 63, no. 1 (2020): 42–64.

27. I therefore deny that the "for-the-sake-of-which" is a higher order project. Here is a typical paragraph from the secondary literature in which this claim is made: "Projects have a nested structure, where the pursuit of larger projects consists of a series of smaller projects. Typing on a laptop might serve the immediate project of sending an e-mail, while sending the e-mail might serve the further project of arranging a meeting, which might in turn serve the further project of planning a budget for the coming fiscal year, and so on. If we follow this chain of projects up far enough, we come to what Heidegger calls a 'for-the-sake-of-which' … these projects contribute to realizing a distinct possibility of Dasein's being" (David Egan, "Rule, Following, Anxiety, and Authenticity," *Mind*, forthcoming).

28. Koa Beck, "How Marriage Inequality Prompts Gay Partners to Adopt One Another," *The Atlantic*, November 2013. https://www.theatlantic.com/national/archive/2013/11/how-marriage-inequality-prompts-gay-partners-to-adopt-one-another/281546/.

29. For a discussion of this point, see William Blattner, "The Concept of Death in *Being and Time*," *Man and World* 27 (1994): 49–70. Blattner holds that death is the possibility of a local collapse of self-understanding, and thus an event that one can pass through. As will become evident below, I disagree with him on this point. On my account, localized collapses of forms of self-understanding *foreshadow* death. But death, as projecting the *ultimate* horizon within which any such local collapse could occur, must transcend all such local events.

30. H 258–59.

31. Piotr Hoffman reads Heidegger in this way. He claims that, according to Heidegger, death is certain for Dasein insofar as Dasein has an unavoidable "rendezvous" with death. See Piotr Hoffman, "Death, time, history: Division II of *Being and Time*," in *The Cambridge Companion to Heidegger*, ed. Charles Guignon (Cambridge: Cambridge University Press, 1993), 199.

32. Martin Heidegger, *The History of the Concept of Time: Prolegomena* (Bloomington: Indiana University Press, 1985), 313.

33. H 249.

34. H 262.

35. Heidegger, *History of the Concept of Time*, 313.

36. H 308.

37. Death, then, is Dasein's way of existing for the sake of the cessation of its existence. But the cessation of Dasein's existence is an event that will be realized. It is also an event that Dasein can set as a goal and actually bring about. This might seem to stand in some tension with my claim that, for Heidegger, the cessation of Dasein's existence is that for the sake of which it exists. This appearance is mistaken. Heidegger distinguishes between the *concept* of a goal we act towards and the *concept* of the end for the sake of which we exist. One and the same thing can instantiate each concept simultaneously, and thus fulfill two different logical roles.

38. H 247.

39. Since death is *being-toward-the-end of Dasein* (H 249), being-toward-death (H 251) must mean *being-toward-being-toward-the-end* of Dasein. "Being-toward-death" is thus synonymous with "dying": Dasein's way of relating to being-toward-the-end. Demise is the "intermediate phenomenon" in which Dasein dies without authentically dying (H 247). In other words, in demise Dasein relates to itself as other than being-toward-the-end and thereby covers over itself. In authentic being-toward-death, in contrast, "Being-toward-death is the anticipation of a potentiality-of-being of that being whose kind of being is anticipation itself. In the anticipatory revealing of this potentiality-of-being, Da-sein discloses itself to itself with regard to its most extreme possibility" (H 262). I read Heidegger as meaning that in authentic being-towards-death, Dasein relates to itself (i.e., comports itself towards itself) transparently *as* being-toward-its-end.

40. H 84.

41. We might want to describe this development as one in which we come to grasp the *point* of our practices. I think this would be a mistake. By the "point" of the practice, I mean the set of needs, interests, and values that informs and is betrayed in the pursuit of the practice. (Here I draw liberally from Matthieu Queloz, "The points of concepts: their types, tensions, and connections," *Canadian Journal of Philosophy* 49, no. 8 [2019]: 1122–45.) Contemporary discussion of the point of something, in this sense, has typically focused on the point of concepts. The application of the *concept* "millennial," for example, might be thought to be informed by particular valuations and interests of a speaker, such as a negative valuation of perceived character traits of a younger generation and an interest in endorsing the perceived authority of an older generation, both of which are betrayed in the (disquotational) application of the concept. But the idea extends naturally enough to discussion of practices, since the pursuit of a practice might be thought to be informed by evaluative aspects of the viewpoint of the agent that is betrayed in her non-ironic participation. Straightforward participation in the practice of taking holy communion, for example, might be thought to betray a set of affective and evaluative orientations of the participant that come with having been brought up into the Christian faith. If so, then to grasp the point of a practice in this sense

would mean either to come to share, or at least to come to be able to imaginatively occupy, the evaluative perspective that guides it. This need not amount to coming to a refined propositional articulation of the matters that inform the practice; it might simply be expressed in an aversion to taking part. In coming to see a practice in light of her vulnerability and, hence, her mortality, does the teenager come to grasp the point of the practice in this sense? Appeals to the points to concepts or practices are supposed to help us explain why we have and apply some concepts or practices rather than others. If we come to see what interests, needs, and values inform and motivate the application of the concept of "the millennial," for example, the hope is that we will come to see the specific place of the concept in the lives of the people who have mastered it, and will thereby better understand why that concept, as opposed to any other, might have emerged in the first place. It is, however, implausible to suppose that an appeal to mortality could contribute to an explanation of the emergence of any *specific* concept. If we accept the Heideggerian claim that death relates equally to every context, then it follows that our mortality indiscriminately conditions *every* context in which we might form or apply concepts or practices. But if there is no particular explanation that mortality can provide to the formation or application of any particular concept, then it is not clear what use—indeed, what point—there would be to saying that mortality is the point of any particular practice: no particular point is no point at all.

42. Heidegger claims that any mood at all has three structural moments: that in the face of which we have the mood, the mood itself, and that about which we have the mood. In the case of fear: that in the face of which we have the mood is a range of fearsome possibilities; the mood itself is fear; that about which we have the mood is our own well-being and, therefore, ultimately ourselves (H 141–42). In the case of anxiety, in contrast: that about which we have the mood is being-in-the-world as such; the mood itself is anxiety; and that about which we have the mood is being-in-the-world as such as well (H 188). The examples I have presented might seem to be better analyzed as *fear*, rather than anxiety, since it seems that that in the face of which the agent has her mood is not being-in-the-world as such but, rather, the possibilities laid bare by the approaching storm. As I understand the examples, however, while the agent's anxiety is *occasioned by* "innerworldly" events, she is not merely fearful before these events. Being-in-the-world as such is made salient through the experience of vulnerability, which is distinct from an experience of fear, in which the salient object of concern is not being-in-the-world as such but, rather the object that occasions the experience of anxious vulnerability. In this connection it is worth nothing that Heidegger describes fear as inauthentic anxiety (H 189). I take it that he has in mind the analysis I have just proposed: events that can give rise to fear primordially occasion anxiety through disclosing being-in-the-world as such; such experiences of anxiety can be "covered over," however, by focusing on the range of possibilities that occasions the anxiety, rather than that which the occasioned anxiety discloses (e.g., the fearsome possibilities held out by the

storm, rather than being-in-the-world as such). This founded mood is fear, and since it covers over the anxiety on which it is founded, it is inauthentic.

43. The following sets of claims are representative: "In anxiety what is environmentally ready-to-hand sinks away, and so, in general, do entities within-the-world. The 'world' can offer nothing more, and neither can the Dasein-with of Others" (H 232); "In anxiety, we say, 'one feels uncanny.' What is 'it' that makes 'one' feel uncanny? We cannot say what it is before which one feels uncanny. As a whole it is so for one. All things and we ourselves sink into indifference. This, however, not in the sense of a mere disappearance. Rather, in their very receding, things turn toward us. The receding of beings as a whole, closing in on us in anxiety, oppresses us. We can get no hold on things. In the slipping away of beings only this 'no hold on things' comes over us and remains" (Martin Heidegger, *Pathmarks* [Cambridge: Cambridge University Press, 1998], 88).

44. In this connection, I read Heidegger's remarks on anxiety in the direction of post-Kantian reflection on the experience of the sublime. For a discussion of the sublime in Kant, Schopenhauer, and Heidegger, see Julian Young, "Death and Transfiguration: Kant, Schopenhauer, and Heidegger on the Sublime," *Inquiry* 48, no. 2 (2006): 131–44.

45. If acting in the light of norms is internally related to the acknowledgment of our mortality, and if the acknowledgment of our mortality is internally related to an acknowledgment of our vulnerability before nature, then the desire to "leave nature behind" (see Pippin, *Persistence of Subjectivity*, 186), and thus for nature to drop out of the system, looks more like a refusal to act in the light of norms than an aspiration to achieve it.

46. H 298.

47. Heidegger's discussion of St. Paul's first letter to the Thessalonians draws out the point at issue (see Martin Heidegger, *The Phenomenology of Religious Life*, trans. Matthias Fritsch and Jennifer Anna Gosetti-Ferencei [Bloomington: Indiana University Press, 2004], 67). The Thessalonians cared about when, exactly, Christ would return. In this respect, Heidegger's Paul believes, the Thessalonians were not relating to the Parousia in the right way. Because the Parousia could happen at *any* moment, *every* moment is affected equally. In urging the Thessalonians to give up worrying about when exactly the Parousia will occur, Paul is not trying to correct a simple mistake about the limits of what they could know of the future. His worry is that they have yet to accept the Parousia as the horizon of their worldly lives and, therefore, as something that is already and equally conditioning every moment of their existence.

48. Heidegger, *History of the Concept of Time*, 317.

49. Martin Heidegger, *Phenomenology of Intuition and Expression*, trans. Tracy Colony (London: Continuum, 2010), 34.

50. Stanley Cavell seems to have a similar point in mind when he writes: "What you do and fail to do are permanent facts of history, and the root of responsibility. But the trunk and branch of responsibility are what you are *answerable* for. And where your conduct raises a question, your answers will again be elaborative. I

have described moral arguments as ones whose direct point it is to determine the positions we are assuming or are able or willing to assume responsibility for; and discussion is *necessary* because our responsibilities, the extensions of our cares and commitments, and the implications of our conduct, are not obvious; because the self is not obvious to the self" (Stanley Cavell, *The Claim of Reason* [Cambridge: Cambridge University Press, 1999], 312).

51. A second way in which your children might definitely matter "in the mode of indefiniteness" can be seen through consideration of a form of self-alienation, in which you find that none of your possibilities are readily intelligible as ways of acting for the sake of what you care about. In such cases, you sustain a form of concern, on account of which you feel the weight of the problem. But the problem is that you cannot see what you are able to do *as* any way of realizing your concern. A parent might, for example, think that the right thing to do is to let her child be taken from her and placed into quarantine while he receives treatment. Having made this decision, she might feel that she has lost any way of continuing to care for her child, at least for the time being. Now that her child is in the care of others, it is far from obvious how whatever she does has to do with what she cares about (see M. Kars et al., "Parental experience at the end-of-life in children with cancer: 'preservation' and 'letting go' in relation to loss" in *Supportive Care Cancer* 19 [2011]: 27–35); for discussion see David Batho, "Experiences of Powerlessness in End-of-Life Care," https://powerlessness.essex.ac.uk/experiences-of-powerless ness-in-end-of-life-care-green-paper). In this case, her child definitely matters to her, and the way the child definitely matters is indefinite. But the way that her child definitely matters in "the mode of indefiniteness" is different from the first case. In the first case, the parent had the definite problem of having to work out the salience of a matter with respect to her child and, concomitantly, the meaning of her child with respect to this matter. In the second case, the parent has the definite problem of not having any obvious problems through which she could work out the meaning of her child for her; her problem is to work out a way of letting her child raise the sort of problem that the first parent faces.

52. For a connected discussion and an interpretation of Heidegger on this point that diverges from my own, see Mark Wrathall, "Who is the Self of Everyday Existence?" in *From Conventionalism to Social Authenticity: Heidegger's Anyone and Contemporary Social Theory*, ed. Hans Bernhard Schmid and Gerhard Thornhauser (London: Springer, 2017), 9–28.

53. See Kierkegaard: "Now, inasmuch as death is the object of earnestness, here again earnestness is: that we should not be overhasty in acquiring an opinion with regard to death. In all earnestness the uncertainty of death continually takes the liberty of making an inspection to see whether the opinion-holder actually does have this opinion—that is, makes an inspection to see whether his life expresses it. With regard to something else, one can express an opinion and then if one is required to act by virtue of this opinion, that is, show that

one has it, innumerable escapes are possible. But the uncertainty of death is the pupil's rigorous oral examiner, and when the pupil recites the explanation, uncertainty says to him, 'Well, now I will make an inquiry as to whether this is your opinion, because now, right now at this moment, all is over, for you all is over; no escape is thinkable, not a letter to be added; so I will find out whether you actually meant what you said about me.' Alas, all empty explaining and all verbiage and all embellishing and all concatenating of earlier explanations in order to find an even more clever one, and all the admiration for this and the trouble with it—all this is merely diversion and absentmindedness in intellectual abstraction—what does the uncertainty of death think about that?" (Søren Kierkegaard, *Three Discourses on Imagined Occasions* [Princeton: Princeton University Press, 1999], 100).

54. For an extended discussion, see David Batho, "Reticence," *European Journal of Philosophy* 26, no. 3 (2018): 1012–25.

55. See Stephen Mulhall, *The Great Riddle: Wittgenstein and Nonsense, Theology and Philosophy* (Oxford: Oxford University Press, 2015).

I am grateful to Matteo Falomi, Béatrice Han-Pile, David McNeill, Joseph Schear, Simon Thornton, Dan Watts, and the audience of the Post-Kantian Seminar at the University of Oxford, for helpful discussion and feedback. Thanks are also owed to Kathrin Bachleitner, Anika Knüppel, and Timo Jütten for help with points of translation. Finally, I wish to thank Margherita Belgioioso, without whose support this paper could not have been written.

11

Husserl's Idealism in the *Kaizo* Articles and Its Relation to Contemporary Moral Perfectionism

Takashi Yoshikawa

Edmund Husserl is the most prominent "idealist" of the twentieth century and his philosophy is defined as transcendental idealism. Initially he refrains from asserting his metaphysical position, and in *Logical Investigations* [LI] (1900–01), the thesis of "metaphysical neutrality" is stated. However, starting around 1908, he starts to seriously consider transcendental idealism in some manuscripts.[1] *Ideas Pertaining to a Pure Phenomenology and to a Phenomenological Philosophy: First Book* (1913) is a systematic philosophy of phenomenological idealism. In *Cartesian Meditations* (1931), he more clearly declares that his phenomenology is transcendental idealism.

> Carried out with this systematic concreteness, phenomenology is *eo ipso* "*transcendental idealism*," though in a fundamentally and essentially new sense.... We have here a transcendental idealism that *is* nothing more than a consequentially executed self-explication in the form of a systematic egological science ... (Hua I, 118–19 [86])[2]

This passage emphasizes the character of self-explication in phenomenological idealism, and here we may discover the remains of subjectivism as a legacy of modern philosophy. As the title of the book suggests, its roots can be

T. Yoshikawa (✉)
University of Kochi, Kochi, Japan
e-mail: yosikawa@cc.u-kochi.ac.jp

C. D. Coe (eds.), *The Palgrave Handbook of German Idealism and Phenomenology*,
Palgrave Handbooks in German Idealism,
https://doi.org/10.1007/978-3-030-66857-0_11

sought in Descartes.[3] Phenomenological philosophy appears to start with the *cogito* and understand the existence of the world as a result of construction by transcendental subjectivity.

However, despite Husserl's terminology, his transcendental idealism is not subjectivism in the sense of reducing all beings to the ego or deducing them from it. He acknowledges the existence of the world independent of our consciousness, and his idealism is compatible with a kind of realism. In order to understand his idealism accurately, we must trace its stages of development. Husserl began to consider transcendental idealism as a thesis around 1908 (XXXVI, 3–72) and asserted the idealistic thesis that the real world depends on consciousness in *Ideas I* (Hua III/1, 103–107 [109–12]).[4] But in the publications of the 1920s and 30s, he came to insist repeatedly that his idealism is not a "product of sportive argumentations" (Hua I, 119 [86]), a "thesis" or "theory" (Hua V, 152 [419]).[5] Furthermore, Husserl's transcendental idealism from a certain period is developed as a moral philosophy, which regards the self as a finite being and asserts that living with modesty is a virtue. Although Husserl's idealism is often discussed in relation to epistemology rather than ethics, his ethical idealism is important in the context of contemporary ethics because of its affinity with "moral perfectionism." This moral philosophy is systematically formed and articulated in his articles published in the Japanese magazine *Kaizo* in 1923–24.

The purpose of this chapter is to examine several versions of Husserlian transcendental idealism and to make clear the significance of the moral-philosophical version in the *Kaizo* articles. It will show that Husserl's phenomenology starts with epistemology and becomes transcendental idealism by dealing with the problem of reality; the phenomenological analysis of the perception of real things reveals the finiteness of our cognition and puts into question the practical meaning of scientific investigations that fail to reach their goals; by examining this question, transcendental idealism inevitably turns into ethical idealism and finally leads to philosophy as a way of life.

Epistemological Idealism

The term idealism is used in LI, which is the starting point of Husserl's phenomenology, although it does not mean the transcendental idealism of the later period. There Husserl emphasizes that the exploration of the "possibility" of cognition is concerned with the ideal as species, and that idealism represents "the possibility of a self-consistent theory of knowledge": "To talk of 'idealism' is of course not to talk a metaphysical doctrine, but of a theory of knowledge which recognizes the 'ideal' [das Ideale] as a condition for the possibility of objective knowledge in general, and does not 'interpret it away' in psychologistic fashion" (Hua XIX/1, 112 [LI/1 238]).[6] To clarify the terms "knowledge" and "the ideal," the framework of *LI* should be briefly explained. Husserl's epistemology tries to avoid "psychologism," which dissolves logical truth into empirical subjectivity.[7] While the subjective experience of judging is generated or dissolved in time, objective truths continue to be valid as the propositional contents of judgments. We begin to judge and stop judging or we become incapable of judging through death or loss of cognitive ability. But as it is said that "truth ... is 'eternal,' or, better put, it is an Idea [Idee], and so beyond time," the truth in itself is established independently of our experience (Hua XVIII, 134 [LI/1, 85]). Since the Pythagorean theorem was discovered in Greece around 2500 years ago, it has been reflected on by different people and languages. Even so, the proposition, as truth itself, remains the same in every place and period.

In authentic cognition, truth is related to subjective experience. Husserl states that "inner evidence is rather nothing but the 'experience' of truth" (Hua XVIII, 193 [LI/1, 121]) and notes that the experience connected with truth has a special character of evidence. In cognition, truth as an Idea and experience as an individual are linked together. Husserl says, "*truth is an Idea, whose particular case is an actual experience in the inwardly evident judgment*" (Hua XVIII, 193 [LI/1, 121]) and, accordingly, he maintains that the relationship between truth and evident experience is that of exemplification. Moreover, it is worth noting here that individual psychological experiences have no value in epistemology. Rather, truth is correlated with the ideal possibility of evident experience, and the Pythagorean theorem has been established as something that can be experienced evidently even if not actually experienced: "There evidently is a general equivalence between proposition *A is true* and *It is possible for anyone to judge A to be true in an inwardly evident manner*" (Hua XVIII, 187 [LI/1, 117]). LI's epistemology looks at the ideality of truth and the ideal possibility of evident experience in order to explore the conditions of the possibility of objective cognition.[8] Idealism here considers the realm of the "ideal" contrasted with the factual and individual as the condition of possibility of the cognition and, accordingly, it is not subjectivism in any sense, but rather objectivism. The basic framework of LI is supported by the theory of meaning as species. The propositions as contents of judgments exist as species independently of the factual experience of them.

Although LI prepares the fundamental concepts of Husserl's idealistic phenomenology, it is in a later period that Husserl characterizes his philosophical position as "transcendental idealism."[9] In his analysis of the relationship between the real world and consciousness from around 1908, he begins to examine the thesis of transcendental idealism that "real things are dependent on consciousness." Although the term "transcendental idealism" is not used in *Ideas I* (1913), this systematic book shows the results of the examination of transcendental idealism. What makes *Ideas I* different from LI is that it reports the results of Husserl's studies of the perceptional cognition of real things. Although perceptions and accidental expressions are considered in LI, they are not the central issue for epistemology, which is rooted in the ideality of species. However, in the lecture on "Thing and Space" (1907) the phenomenology of perception is developed, and in the lecture on "Theory of Meaning" (1908)—where empirical judgments about perceived things are considered in earnest—the concept of meaning as species is modified and the prototype of meaning as noema in *Ideas I* arises. Based on the results of these lectures, *Ideas I* treats in full scale the problems of perception or empirical judgment of objects in the real world. It is through consideration of the correlation between the real world and consciousness that Husserl characterizes his phenomenology as transcendental idealism.

Starting around 1908 Husserl repeatedly points out that real things are related to "actual consciousness." Real things exist in space and time and are given as existing for actual consciousness, which means the experience of ego in the "here and now" and "I see" in the broadest sense of the word (includes hearing, touch, etc.). When we actually experience things by perception, they are experienced through "appearing in person [*Leibhaft-Erscheinen*]." Their bodily presence is characterized as "originary givenness" (Hua III/1, 316 [328]): "*The world of transcendent "res" is entirely referred to consciousness and, more particularly, not to some logically conceived consciousness but to actual consciousness*" (Hua III/1, 104 [110]).

In *Ideas I*, although Husserl offers no further explanation of the actuality of consciousness, it has a deep connection with time consciousness and the body. On the one hand, actual consciousness is a stream of consciousness called "living presence," which is continuous changes in the form of "now." On the other hand, it has an original location of "here" in the perceiving body and is also linked to the sense of movement of the body, known as "kinesthesis." Hence, real things are experienced by consciousness in the here and now rather than by possible cognitive subjectivity: "We recognize that something necessarily must be experienceable not merely by an Ego conceived as an empty logical possibility but by any *actual* Ego as a demonstrable unity relative to its concatenations of experience" (Hua III/1, 102 [108]). It can be thought that there could be a diamond as big as the sun and a subject who experiences it with evidence. However, thinking about the possibility of such a thing and subject has nothing to do with the truth about the real world. When we think about them, we are not considering the situation of this world (the realm of the real) at all.[10] This type of possibility through thinking is called "empty possibility," "unfounded possibility," and "mere logical possibility" (Hua XVI, 291; Hua XXXVI, 37, 61).[11] To confirm that real things truly exist in the real world, something more than logical possibility is required. Husserl believed that for real things to be given as truly existent, they require a relationship with actual consciousness. This does not mean, however, that only what is actually perceived really exists. If so, that would mean that when we close our eyes, or when we fall asleep, things do not exist. In order to avoid such subjectivism, here again Husserl appeals to a certain kind of possibility, that is, to "real possibility."[12] Even when things in the real world are not given in the actual consciousness of the here and now, they potentially exist as things I can experience actually.[13] This potentiality is the "real possibility" or the "possibility grounded in motivation" (Hua XVI, 291; Hua XXXVI, 37, 61). Husserl writes that *"experienceableness never means a mere logical possibility, but rather a possibility motivated in the concatenations of experience"* (Hua III/1,101 [106–7]) and elaborates on the concept of real possibility by addressing problems about the perception and perceptual judgments of real objects.

What is more important here is that things are always and only given in a one-sided way. Realities comprised in the name "nature" cannot be given in complete determinateness. In this regard there is always room for new perceptions to more precisely determine the indeterminate parts. That the real thing appears only "inadequately" in a closed appearance means that it is "transcendence" while consciousness is immanence because it is given adequately. Its transcendence is expressed in the limitlessness of the progression of its experiences.

Such a phenomenological analysis of the perception of things yields surprising results in the context of epistemology. According to Husserl's basic concept, *"to every 'truly existing' object* there corresponds *the idea [Idee] of a possible consciousness* in which the object itself is seized upon *originarily* and therefore in a *perfectly adequate* way" (Hua III/1, 329 [341]) and accordingly the truly existing thing demands seeing it in a perfectly adequate way. It follows that since our perception cannot define things completely, it cannot reach the truth of things. However, it is crucial that *"perfect givenness is nevertheless predesignated as 'Idea'* [Idee] (in the Kantian sense)" (Hua III/1, 331

[342]) and that the true existence of a thing is possible as "Idea," which is not reached by our perception. According to Husserl, while the real thing can only be given inadequately and remains transcendent for us, this transcendence is equivalent to the "Idea" of completeness, which can be approximated in the real possibility of "I can," although in the limitlessness of the progress of experience. His phenomenology regards the existence of real things as an "Idea" and deserves to be called idealism in the very matter of the real thing.[14]

The Primacy of Practical Reason: A Kantian-Fichtean Heritage in Husserl

Epistemological transcendental idealism reveals to us the one-sidedness of perception, the incompleteness of cognition, and the unattainability of the truth of the real world. According to Husserl, this brings us to the question of the practical meaning of theoretical cognition. In the lecture on "Thing and Space" (1907), "great problems" are revealed: "Does not this turn cognition into an aimless enterprise? Or should we make peace with an infinite task? Who would reasonably set him or herself a task the solution of which can only be achieved through an infinite process or, better said, cannot be achieved at all by its very nature?" (Hua XVI, 138; see also XXVIII, 183).[15] Our theoretical cognition of the real world is incomplete, and not only the structure of our perception but also our deaths and natural disasters prevent us from achieving its goal. If this is true, then what is the meaning of scientific activity? What is the point of pursuing an unattainable goal? Why do we live in pursuit of truth in spite of the necessity of its failure?[16] The question of the meaning of pursuing truth in the irrational world is also a question of the meaning of life as a scientist or philosopher.

It should be noted that *Ideas I* does not address this issue. The central problem for epistemological idealism is that of the truth of the real world and it is finally considered as Idea in the Kantian sense. But this Idea means only possibility envisioned by our philosophical thinking.[17] Here it is not questioned whether it can be realized by our practical activity, including scientific investigation. However, the problem that Husserl faces is related to the practical dimension of the Idea and also includes the ethical problems of how we should live, what is the right aim for our life, and what is the meaning of our life.

We should examine the extent to which the moral philosophy in *Ideas I* can answer those questions. Phenomenological philosophy analyzes intentional consciousness relating to objects through meaning and considers the possibility of objective judgments, in setting up the semantic problem of the correspondence between meaning and the object.[18] In *Ideas I*, every act is considered to be an objectifying one and has a relationship with its own object: "Any act whatever—even emotional and volitional acts—are 'objectivating [objectifying],' 'constituting' objects originaliter" (Hua III/1, 272 [282]). Since here the objective validity of the various kinds of judgments (including moral judgment) can be elucidated, Husserl's philosophy can be seen as a phenomenology of reason, including not only theoretical but also practical and evaluative reason.[19] *Ideas I* is a systematic philosophy under the primacy of theoretical reason in a broad sense because all the contents of consciousness are transformed into judgments with a logical form (Hua III/1, 272 [282]).

However, Husserl realizes that ethical questions about how to live cannot be asked within this framework, because the truths of objective moral judgments and of personal life are different.[20] Husserl does not believe that this moral philosophy is the final achievement and seeks to find clues to the solution to these questions in the concept of the primacy of practical reason of Kant and Fichte.[21] From the lectures "Fichte's Ideal of Humanity" given in 1917–18, we can read the relationship between Husserl and German Idealism.[22] In this text, the moral philosophy of Kant and the religious philosophy of Fichte are favorably introduced.

Husserl focuses on the unique character of practical reason in Kant, the "postulates of practical reason."[23] The "transcendent essential beings" like "God, immortality and freedom" cannot be known or shown in theory, but they must be assumed to truly exist if moral laws are not to lose their practical meaning (Hua XXV, 273 [116]).[24] Here practical reason can approve, in the form of postulates, the reality of an "ideal" [Ideal] that cannot be proved or refuted by theoretical reason; this is called the "primacy of practical reason." What he learns from Kant is the logic to affirm the rationality of the practical ideal—namely, to understand the significance of the goal we pursue. While, in an epistemological context, the Idea is said to be thinkable and its rationality as a goal is not mentioned, in an ethical context, the significance of pursuing the ideal as a goal is affirmed in terms of practical reason. Though there is not complete consistency in Husserl's terminology, the unattainable but meaningful goal of practical action is called the "ideal." The postulate of practical reason interpreted in a manuscript of 1923 does not insist on the existence of transcendence in an objective dimension, but instead the significance of transcendent aims for an agent in a personal dimension. We are required to act as if we are immortal or as if our actions are not hampered by disaster. This "practical as if" makes our goal meaningful for us (Hua VIII, 349–54).[25]

Furthermore, Husserl learns of another dimension of practical reason from Fichte, who establishes a teleological philosophy of action toward the ideal of practical reason: "Prior to the acting, ... there lies nothing. The beginning, when we think ... of the history of the subject, is not a fact (*Tatsache*) but an 'action' (*Tathandlung*)" (Hua XXV, 275 [117]). Husserl focuses on Fichte's insistence that all acts of ego are a kind of striving: "All life is striving, is drive for satisfaction. This drive pervades all our still incomplete satisfaction. The ideal goal is therefore always pure and full satisfaction. In a word, it is blessedness" (Hua XXV, 285 [125]). In Husserl's understanding, any kind of intentionality can be considered a practical act. Scientific cognition is also a practice and is deeply connected to the meaning of our lives. We are finite and are asked to strive for the unattainable goal. In this striving, we finite beings can live meaningfully. The primacy of practical reason, when combined with the concept of striving, is understood by the phenomenological analysis of experience.

Even more noteworthy, Fichte's practical philosophy focuses on a personal way of life: "This voice of my conscience commands me in every special situation of my life, what I am determined to do in this situation, what I have to avoid in it" (Fichte, GW/II, 258).[26] This insight in *The Vocation of Man* (1799) is adopted in Husserl's phenomenology. In a manuscript around 1920, Husserl says: "The *Daimon* which leads to the true vocation, speaks through love. Therefore, it is not mere objective goods or the objectively highest good that matters, but everyone has her sphere of love and her 'duties of love'" (Hua Mat IX, 146n1).[27] In the lecture "Introduction to Philosophy" (1923), Husserl states, by use of the term of Fichte's *The Way to the Blessed Life* (1806), "every scientifically insightful action [*Jedes wissenschaftlich einsichtige Tun*] ... is in itself a blessed life" (Hua XXXV, 44).[28] It indicates that we can attain personal blessedness through scientific activity if we live as a scientist or philosopher who loves the truth.[29]

Based on the primacy of practical reason, Husserl's moral philosophical idealism in the 1920s establishes the phenomenology of practical reason from which the practical meaning of theoretical activity can be studied. The results of these investigations are published in the *Kaizo* articles.[30]

Ethical Idealism

At the heart of the new style of practical reason is "self-consideration (*inspectio sui*)," in which the experiences of self-knowledge, self-evaluation, and self-creation are at work (Hua XXVII, 23). Self-knowledge is directed toward the self rather than an object in the world, and in this sense, it is not an objectifying act. Self-evaluation is consciousness of one's self-worth and reveals a better self. Moreover, self-creation is the intentionality of will, which creates the future of the self. Here, our self-consideration reveals what we are and brings us into what we should be.

The concept of "practical possibility" in section three, "The Constitution of the Spiritual World," of *Ideas II*, which is established in the period between *Idea I* and the *Kaizo* articles, is important here. The real possibility used in epistemology has the meaning of "practical possibility" when it is interpreted in the context of the theory of action, which takes into account the bodily action of "I do." It is the possibility of "I can" and my possibility because of originating in my bodily ability and my surrounding world: "It is only between practical possibilities that I can decide, and only practical possibilities ... can be a theme of my will" (Hua IV, 258 [270]).[31] I cannot run a hundred meters in ten seconds or less. I cannot kill someone. Although these are all logically possible, I cannot do them because of my restricted ability or factual environment and my motivation (resistance).[32] My practical possibility is constrained by the facticity of my life in this world or the habitually effective norms and sometimes I have a consciousness of "I cannot."

In practical self-consideration, the possible future lives of the self are examined as practical possibilities. A person observes her life and "consciously strives ... to shape her life into a satisfying, a blessed one" (Hua XXVII, 25). The value of the self is examined here, and though not an objectively valid value, it is valid for the self and tied to its satisfaction. It is called "absolute value," "value of love," "value of life," or "my value"[33]:

> In reviewing and evaluating her future life, someone may be certain that values of a certain kind, which she can choose at any time as goals for action, has the character of being *unconditionally desired* for her, without whose continuous realization she could not find satisfaction. Therefore, she now decides to dedicate herself and her future life to the realization of such values. (Hua XXVII, 27)

For some, art is of value; for others, learning is of value; and for others, family is of value. If I am a genuine artist, I "love it from the innermost center of the personality 'with all my soul'" because it is "something which inseparably belongs to me who I am" and it is the object of my personal love (Hua XXVII, 28).

It is important that the absolute value brings the highest satisfaction to the subject and thereby unifies her life. A person converges her own future potential to an absolutely worthwhile life and orientates the self toward its value. Husserl characterizes this identification of the individual personality through absolute value by the concept of "vocation [*Beruf*]"[34]:

> So art is a vocation for the genuine artist, and science is a vocation for the genuine scientist (the philosopher); it is a field of spiritual activities and accomplishments, for which she knows she has a calling, so that only the pursuit of these goods can give her the most "inner" and most "pure" satisfaction, and each succeeding can give her the consciousness of "blessedness." (Hua XXVII, 28)

Clearly, this style of personal self-consideration, the concepts of "blessedness" and "love" and the metaphors for voice like "vocation" are inherited from Fichte. Moreover, Fichte's moral and religious philosophy relies on the conception of the development of the ego, so Husserl's consideration here has this in mind. The life of vocation is positioned as a prelude to an even higher life, an "ethical life." The life of vocation can either be a life of blind acceptance of irrational habits or an unjust one. Our consideration of a vocation does not ask whether the value is true and genuine. In contrast, ethical life consists of "the desire and the will to form a personal whole life in the sense of reason with respect to *all* its personal activities": "The person who lives in the consciousness of her capacity of reason, knows that she is responsible for right and wrong in all her activities" (Hua XXVII, 32; see also 76–82). However, it is impossible, due to our finiteness, to examine all activities to see whether they are right or not and to take responsibility for them. The more a human being reflects on the possibilities of future lives and influences, the more the potential for disillusionment and disappointment becomes apparent. The life of genuine humanity as a completely pure and blessed life is an unattainable ideal and remains "the absolute limit" as "the pole beyond all finiteness" or "the conducting pole from [the] unreachable far away" (Hua XXVII, 33, 36). While for epistemological idealism in *Ideas I* the complete determinateness of the world is considered to be the "Idea" as the limit of the real possibility of our cognition, for ethical idealism in the *Kaizo* articles the full authenticity of the person is considered to be the "ideal" as the limit of the practical possibility of our action: "Every ethical human being carries it in her own mind, yearning for it infinitely, loving it, and believing that she knows she is always infinitely far from it" (Hua XXVII, 33–34). We are motivated by our ideal because we love and aspire to it.

It is important to note here that Husserl understands ethical life not as the realization of an ideal of humanity, but as a process of moving toward that ideal, just as Fichte emphasizes "striving."[35] We are only living in time, and our lives are in the midst of becoming. Thus, the ethical demand means "to do the best possible thing at the present time and thus to become better and better after the present possibility" (Hua XXVII, 36). Husserl understands the ideal of perfect humanity in relation to "the human ideal of becoming in the form of human development" (Hua XXVII, 36). As Husserl says, "Ethical life is really by its nature a life from renewal" (Hua XXVII, 42), and ethical life is a never-ending journey of progress. An ethical person in this world would be one who lives with the virtue of "modesty," in knowing the finiteness of her life and the contingency of the world.[36] This shows the style of rationality of our living within the facticity or irrationality of the real world.

Husserl's ethics presupposes an imperfect agent, who is bound to a particular situation and does not make decisions in a fully autonomous way because of her finitude.[37] Since she cannot know something from all sides, she anticipates the consequences of her actions only with probability, not certainty. Hence, its success or failure must depend on luck and chance. Nevertheless, she lives her life believing in the reachability of the goal and thinking of probability as a certainty (XXXXII, 317 fn.1).[38] Her life is meant to be a kind of "try" (Hua VIII, 352). Moreover, this agent can be torn by a conflict of incommensurable values because she is not free to alter or ignore the inconvenient situation. Here the tragedy of sacrifice can occur. For example, we can face the dilemma as to whether we should stay with our mother or participate in resistance for our country. This means that our two "vocations" contradict one another and two loves divide our identity.[39] If we choose one, we "sacrifice" the other (Hua XXVII, 28). Our decision is tragic because we must lose something important.

Being a Philosopher in a Situation

The European and international situation in the 1910–20s should not be overlooked as the backdrop to the lectures on "Fichte's Ideal of Humanity" and the *Kaizo* articles. Husserl lived as a father, as a German, and as a philosopher in World War I and post-war situation, and through this period his transcendental idealism acquired special meaning and expression.

World War I had a great influence on Husserl's private life in that his sons and disciples went to the battlefield.[40] In 1916, his son Wolfgang was killed in battle, and his son Gerhard was injured. In 1917, his pupil Adolf Reinach, a leader in the Munich-Gottingen School, was killed in the war. Husserl had feelings of patriotic exaltation about the war and deep despair over the subsequent results, because he was aware of his German identity and lived as a father of sons fighting on the battlefields. In other words, he was torn by love for his country and love for his sons. While many philosophers and novelists were driven by patriotism, some of those who had a relationship with Husserl, such as Rudolf Eucken, Paul Natorp, and Max Scheler, had made nationalistic statements since the beginning of the war.[41] Husserl was officially silent about his nationalistic enthusiasm, although, in his private letters, he made various remarks about his hopes for German victory. Husserl heard the warning voice by his "daimonion" and took on his "mission" of being an academic philosopher rather than a practitioner.[42] Although he were torn between the loves for his sons, his country, and the truth, he publicly lived as a philosopher and "didn't write about war" due to his vocation.[43]

Moreover, the economic and cultural context after World War I cannot be ignored. Germany was hit by an economic crisis caused by inflation, and Husserl was in dire financial straits; he wrote the articles for Japanese readers in order to "make money."[44] What is noteworthy here is the situation of Japanese society at that time and the policy of the Japanese publishing company Kaizo-sha. Japan achieved economic development by modernization after the Meiji Restoration (1868), extended its hegemony through First Sino-Japanese war (1894–95) and Russo-Japanese war (1904–05), and did not suffer any serious damage from World War I. In the 1920s, Japanese society was economically and culturally rich and was introducing the latest Western science, philosophy, and art. International academic exchange was also highly active, and many Japanese students attended German universities, including the University of Freiberg, where Husserl taught phenomenology. It is said that one of these students, Hazime Tanabe, who came to be a famous philosopher of the Kyoto School, acted as an intermediary between Husserl and Kaizo-sha.[45]

The president of Kaizo-sha was Sanehiko Yamamoto, who was also a journalist, and Tadayoshi Akita was its editor.[46] Yamamoto's company developed various projects that are significant in the history of Japanese publishing: It not only published general magazines such as *Kaizo* but also pioneered "media mix," by publishing novels and showing associated films.[47] Internationally famous researchers and writers such as Bertrand Russell, Albert Einstein, Margaret Sanger, and George Bernard Shaw were invited to Japan by Kaizo-sha. For example, Russell was invited to Japan by Akita in 1921, while he was staying in China. Einstein stayed in Japan for forty-two days in 1922 and received a telegram informing him that he had won the Nobel Prize on his way to Japan. In addition to Husserl, Heinrich Rickert, Romain Rolland, Leon Trotsky, Rabindranath Tagore, Paul Claudel, and Lu Xun contributed articles to *Kaizo* magazine. Kaizo-sha published the complete works of Marx and Engels in 1928–35 and conveyed the labor movement and socialist ideology of China to Japanese readers. When Husserl wrote the five papers for *Kaizo* magazine, Japan was experiencing a time of freedom of speech before World War II, which is called the "Taisho democracy," and Yamamoto was on a mission to introduce Western and Chinese culture to Japan.[48]

However, soon after Husserl's first paper was published both in Japanese and German in the magazine, the Great Kanto Earthquake struck Tokyo in 1923. In the aftermath of the disaster, two papers were published only in Japanese because most of the printing houses with Latin printing types had been destroyed.[49] The last two of Husserl's five articles were left unpublished, and he did not receive the full payment.[50] In 1925, the Maintenance of Public Order Law was enacted, which provided legal precedent for the forthcoming suppression of Marxism (in 1933 Takiji Kobayashi, a prominent Marxist novelist, died under torture). In 1931, the Manchurian Incident occurred, and relations between Japan and China became tense. Starting in the late 1930s, Kaizo-sha's magazines and books began to have a nationalistic or fascist tendency, and the complete works of Benito Mussolini were published in 1944. But in the same year the publication of *Kaizo* ceased, and the company was dissolved by order of the government. The publication of Husserl's papers in Japan was possible due to the personality of Yamamoto, who lived in his own vocation, and the international circumstances of that time.

This situation at the time is closely related to Husserl's philosophy, especially the style of his philosophical expression. The lectures held in 1917 and 1918 on "Fichte's Ideal of Humanity" are an exception in which Husserl talks about the war publicly. He basically introduces the thought of Fichte, with occasional critical comments. But he addressed his audiences (those connected with the war effort) bearing in mind Fichte's lecture "Speech to the German Nation" (1808) during the Napoleonic Wars. Husserl emphasized the need to understand the significance of German Idealism and insisted that the meaning of "Ideas and Ideals [*Ideen und Ideale*]" should be regained (Hua XXV, 270 [112]).[51] Attention should be paid to the tone of the lecture. Husserl evaluates "the philosopher of the war of liberation" as "educator," "foreseer," and "prophet" (Hua XXV, 269–70 [212–13]) and reproduces the voice of Fichte a hundred years previously by superimposing the times of Fichte and Husserl. Philosophy here is neither a mere logical demonstration nor purely phenomenological description, but an appeal through voice, which asserts optimistic idealism. Philosophical messages spoken in the war situation with Fichte's voice are now spoken again with Husserl's voice. When the two philosophers speak of the ideal, they try to lead their audiences to it through their lectures.

In one of the *Kaizo* articles, Husserl makes readers aware of the situation in his time: "Renewal is the universal call in our recent, sorrowful age" (Hua XXVII, 3). And he appeals to his readers by using the first person plural: "Something new must arise. It must arise in us and by ourselves" (Hua XXVII, 4). He speaks of "renewal" as a task for him and his readers, and asks them to re-examine their way of life with him.[52] According to Husserl, philosophical truth in itself can be found in eternity over time, but it is in certain times or circumstances that we, as philosophizing human beings, are actually involved in philosophy. Husserl's ethical idealism sheds light on the life of the philosophers as lovers of the ideal, and appeals to readers for the restoration of the ideal of humanity.

Moral Perfectionism

Husserl's ethical idealism is not an anachronistic relic of the past but is worth considering in the contemporary context. It has an affinity with the position called "moral perfectionism," which Iris Murdoch and Stanley Cavell espouse. It is especially remarkable that Husserl and Murdoch have many ideas in common, though it has not yet been thoroughly studied. Husserl's ethics not only aims to justify objectively valid judgments but also to consider one's way of living, including one's beliefs, feelings, habits, and so on. One is motivated in one's own environment and has one's task to be realized for the future. This conception can be regarded as perfectionism in that it is essential for morality that each person lives in their surrounding world and pursues their own way of life. Moral perfectionism is not a moral theory, such as utilitarianism or deontology, but a dimension of moral thinking on a different level than theory and can be related to it in various ways.[53] When a theory makes a rational judgment on a problem, it can leave the question of how one should live. Elizabeth Costello, a character in *The Lives of Animals* by J. M. Coetzee, is hurt and troubled despite acknowledging the theoretical correctness of a kind of animal ethics.[54] When we are involved in issues that are not taken into account by the dominant theories in our society, we have to decide our lives without relying on those theories. When, in Ibsen's *Dollhouse,* Nora learns that her husband and his friends cannot understand her situation despite of being rational, she gives up speaking with them and leaves her home.[55] For moral perfectionism, the person is not only the central theme of moral thinking but also the clue for revision of our thoughts by critical consideration. Namely, moral perfectionist thinking considers the person as an "exemplar"[56] and can question theories or judgments by showing the concrete person, who has her own voice.[57]

Murdoch criticizes modern ethics, which she claims that focuses only on actions and judgments, and she tries to treat moral agents as substantive selves who have inner lives. The question of morality concerns moral agents, not momentary acts or judgments, and therefore moral thinking must analyze the chain of experiences of the agent as "a continuous fabric of being" (SG 21)[58]: "I want to talk about consciousness and self-being as the basic mode or form of moral being" (MGM 171).[59] This insight overlaps with Husserl's moral philosophy, which analyzes personal motivations. In her first philosophical work, *Sartre: Romantic Rationalist,* Murdoch notes that phenomenology, which describes a variety of experiences, has great significance as a moral philosophy, although she later expresses her dissatisfaction that Husserl's description is made in technical terms.[60] According to Murdoch, when the web of consciousness is morally good, it is directed by "seeing" or "attention," and thus the moral problem is "what we attend to, how we attend, whether we attend" (MGM 167). Murdoch's ethics are the ethics of "vision" as "moral seeing."[61] To see something is to sink deeply into what we love, and we can see people in detail through love. The object of love as moral activity is the real, and the encounter with reality through this love releases our souls from our dreams. The reality as an idea of the good exists as "an ideal limit of love or knowledge," which is always distancing itself from us (SG 27).

Moreover, there is no end to our moral inquiry, and our efforts must remain incomplete.[62] Thus, "we are changed by love and pursuit of what we only partly see and understand" (MGM 222), and when we love something, our inner beliefs and concepts may change radically. The "inevitable imperfection" of moral activity originates in our finite being, and our moral life follows the moral imperative of "Act lovingly," "Act perfectly" (SG 99): "Life is a spiritual pilgrimage inspired by the disturbing magnetism of *truth,* involving *ipso facto* a purification of energy and desire in the light of a vision of what is *good*" (MGM 14). The point of Murdoch's perfectionism is that life is a journey, which is not completed. Morality means that we are aware of our finitude and make a journey toward a further state. Murdoch points out that "the good man is humble" and adds, "the humble man, because he sees himself as nothing, can see other things as they are" (SG 100–1). The similarity between Husserl and Murdoch is evident.[63]

What is interesting when considering Husserl's transcendental idealism is that Murdoch characterizes her position as realism. Like Husserl, Murdoch's perfectionism emphasizes that a moral life leads to an idea of the "good" in a Platonic meaning. As a realist, Murdoch acknowledges the existence of someone beyond us. The more we realize that others exist independently of and are different from us, and the more we understand that they have pressing needs and desires like us, the harder it is for us to treat them as objects. Here, the Platonic realism of the idea of the good comes into play as our moral stance. "The vision of a reality separate from ourselves" or "unsentimental, detached, unselfish, objective attention" (SG 46, 64) means overcoming egoism by recognizing an existence beyond us. This "realism" is considered as a "moral achievement" and understood "in a normative sense" (SG 62, 64). As long as Husserl sees intentionality as the site of the solution of philosophical problems and he makes sense of all objects in the intentional correlation, he does not call himself a realist. But his transcendental idealism also regards reality as a kind of norm (an aim to be reached or conducting principle) and insists that we should live toward something beyond us.

Conclusion

Having revealed the possibility of several versions of Husserlian transcendental idealism, I close this chapter by considering its features in relation with German Idealism.

The development of Husserl's transcendental idealism is similar to a historical change in German Idealism, which—according to Frederick Beiser—means a struggle with subjectivism to recover reality.[64] Husserl never hesitates to acknowledge the objective reality of the world and does not fall into a subjectivism that denies it. His epistemological idealism in *Ideas I* connects the existence of the real world with actual consciousness, but does not dissolve it into subjective ability. The existence of the world is understood as Idea in the Kantian sense. Furthermore, ethical idealism in the *Kaizo* articles examines how humans as finite beings live within their own circumstances. An agent of moral deliberation is dependent on her situation and has no complete control over the world. Here, to live ethically implies a never-ending renewal toward a further self. Under the influence of Fichte, Husserl interprets transcendence as the goal to be reached—namely, the ideal in normative sense. He constantly takes the real world to be transcendent for finite being.

In Husserl, as in Kant and Fichte, transcendental idealism is not incompatible with empirical realism. In our ordinary view, the world exists in its own right, independently of us. In contrast, from a philosophical perspective, how we experience the objective world is elucidated and it becomes clear that it is difficult to fully understand the world.[65] Here, Husserl uses the term "change of attitude" from a natural attitude to a transcendental attitude by "phenomenological reduction." Although nothing changes the existence of the world before or after philosophy, our attitude or vision dramatically turns out to be another. In the transcendental attitude, we are aware of the structural incompleteness of our perception and the situational dependency of our action. This philosophical endeavor means our living with the virtue of "modesty," by which we avoid the firm assumptions that the world objectively exists or that this good should be realized over other things.[66] To "carry out" transcendental idealism as "self-explication" means to live as a transcendental idealist, i.e., to live modestly with a vision of the infinite world. We can accept Husserl's cryptic assertion that transcendental idealism is not theory, thesis, or argument, in the terms of the philosopher's way of life.[67]

Notes

1. Robin Rollinger and Rochus Sowa, Introduction to Hua XXXVI, *Transzendental Idealism. Texte aus dem Nachlass (1908–1922)*, ed. Robin Rollinger and Rochus Sowa (Dordrecht: Kluwer, 2003), iv–xxxvii.
2. Hua I, *Cartesianische Meditationen und Pariser Vorträge*, ed. Stephan Strasser (The Hague: Martinus Nijhoff, 1950); translated as *Cartesian Meditations*, trans. Dorion Cairns (The Hague: Martinus Nijhoff, 1973).
3. Husserl characterizes his transcendental phenomenology as "neo-Cartesianism" (Hua I, 3[1]).
4.   Hua III/1, *Ideen zu einer reinen Phänomenologie und phänomenologischen Philosophie. Erstes Buch: Allgemeine Einführung in die reine Phänomenologie*, ed. Karl Schuhmann (The Hague: Martinus Nijhoff, 1977); translated as *Ideas Pertaining to a Pure Phenomenology and to a Phenomenological Philosophy, First Book: General Introduction to a Pure Phenomenology*, trans. Fred Kersten, *Collected Works: Volume 2* (The Hague: Martinus Nijhoff, 1982).
5. "Nachwort," in Hua V, *Ideen zu einer reinen Phänomenologie und phänomenologischen Philosophie. Drittes Buch, Die Phänomenologie und Die Fundamente der Wissenschaften*, ed. Marly Biemel (The Hague: Martinus Nijhoff, 1977), 138–62; translated as "Epilogue," in *Ideas Pertaining to a Pure Phenomenology*

and to a Phenomenological Philosophy, Second Book, Studies in the Phenomenology of Constitution, trans. Richard Rojecewicz and Andre Schuwer (Dordrecht: Kluwer, 1989), 405–30. The non-theoretical trend is pointed out by Naberhaus (Thane M. Naberhaus, "Husserl's Transcendental Idealism," *Husserl Studies* 23 [2007]: 255).

6. Hua XVIII, *Logische Untersuchungen. Erster Band: Prolegomena zur reinen Logik*, ed. Elmer Holenstein (The Hague: Martinus Nijhoff, 1975). Hua XIX/1–2, *Logische Untersuchungen. Zweiter Band: Untersuchungen zur Phänomenologie und Theorie der Erkenntnis*, ed. Ursula Panzer (The Hague: Martinus Nijhoff, 1984); translated as *Logical Investigations, Volumes 1 and 2*, trans. J. N. Findlay with a new Preface by Michael Dummett, ed. Dermot Moran (London: Routledge, 2001).

7. Husserl's critique of psychologism is a critique of his past self because his *Philosophy of Arithmetic* (1891) insisted that the experience of counting produces numbers.

8. I borrow the concept of LI conceived as a system of "objective epistemology" to Genki Uemura, *Shinri, Sonzai, Ishiki: Husserl no Rongrigaku Kenkyu wo Yomu* [*Truth, Being, and Consciousness: Reading Husserl's Logische Untersuchungen*] (Tokyo: Chisen Shokan, 2017).

9. Husserl uses the term transcendental idealism in 1918, but he had been considering this thesis since 1908 (Rollinger and Sowa, 2003, iv).

10. He examines this issue in 1913 in a draft for a rewrite of LI (Hua XX/1, 255–71). Hua XX/1, *Logische Untersuchungen. Ergänzungsband. Zweiter Teil: Texte für die Neufassung der VI. Untersuchung. Zur Phänomenologie des Ausdrucks und der Erkenntnis*, ed. Urlich Melle (Dordrecht: Springer, 2002).

11. Hua XVI, *Ding und Raum: Vorlesungen 1907*, ed. Claesges Ulrich (The Hague: Martinus Nijhoff, 1973).

12. Rudolf Bernet, "Husserl's Transcendental Idealism Revisited," *New Yearbook for Phenomenology and Phenomenological Philosophy* (2004): 1–20.

13. I am now looking at the desk actually from the front while I am potentially aware of the back of it.

14. In his lecture "Kant and the Idea of Transcendental Philosophy" (1924), Husserl states: "In purely transcendental consideration *the world* ... is ultimately *only an Idea lying in infinity*, which draws its sense of purpose from the *actuality* of consciousness" (Hua VII, 274). Hua VII, *Erste Philosophie (1923/24). Erster Teil: Kritische Ideengeschichte*, ed. Rudolf Boehm (The Hague: Martinus Nijhoff, 1956).

15. Hua XXVIII, *Vorlesungen über Ethik und Wertlehre 1908–1914*, ed. Ullrich Melle (Dordrecht: Kluwer, 1988).

16. See Sebastian Luft, "From Being to Givenness and Back: Some Remarks on the Meaning of Transcendental Idealism in Kant and Husserl," *International Journal of Philosophical Studies* 15, no. 3 (2007): 367–94.

17. It is a real possibility, but not yet practical possibility.

18. The philosophy of language on "expression and meaning" in LI is centered on the function of meaning in relation to the object: "To use an expression significantly, and to refer expressively to an object (to form a presentation of it) are one and the same" (Hua XIX/1, 59–60 [LI/1, 201]).

19. In personal documents from 1906, Husserl seriously considers the implications of Kant's system of critical philosophy: "In the first place, I mention the general task I have to solve for myself if I am able to call myself a philosopher. I mean: a critique of reason. A critique of logical and practical reason, of evaluative reason in general" (Hua XXIV, 445). Hua. XXIV, *Einleitung in die Logik und Erkenntnistheorie:Vorlesungen 1906/07*, ed. Ullrich Melle (The Hague: Martinus Nijhoff, 1984). Husserl understands Kant's critical philosophy as an exploration of the conditions of possibility for objectively valid judgments, and *Ideas I* is considered to be the successor of Kant's critique of reason.

20. Ullrich Melle distinguishes rationalistic ethics from an ethics of love. "Husserl: From Reason to Love," *Phenomenological Approaches to Moral Philosophy* (Dordrecht: Springer, 2002), 229–48. He finds the ethics of love in the later manuscripts in 1920–30s, but I think that Husserl's ethics of love and sacrifice is established in the *Kaizo* articles, and the later manuscripts are significant as the clue of a deeper understanding of them.

21. See also, Iso Kern, *Husserl und Kant: eine Untersuchung über Husserls Verhältnis zu Kant und zum Neukantianismus* (The Hague: Martinus Nijhoff, 1964), 34–39, 293–303.

22. James G. Hart, "Husserl and Fichte—With Special Regard to Husserl's Lectures on Fichte's Ideal of Humanity," *Husserl Studies* 12, no. 2 (1995): 135–63.

23. Husserl appreciates the method of postulates as "the greatest of Kant's discoveries" in a letter to Ernst Cassirer, 3 June 1925 (BW/V, 6). Hua: *Dokumente, Band 3: Edmund Husserl Briefwechsel-V*, ed. Karl Schuhmann (Dordrecht: Springer, 1994). Hereafter: BW.

24. Edmund Husserl, "Fichtes Menschheits ideal," Hua XXV, *Aufsätze und Vorträge: (1911–1921)*, ed. Hans Rainer Sepp and Thomas Nenon (Dordrecht: Martinus Nijhoff, 1987), 267–92; translated as "Fichte's Ideal of Humanity [Three Lectures]," trans. James G. Hart, *Husserl Studies* 12 (1995): 111–33.

25. Hua VIII, *Erste Philosophie (1923/24). Zweiter Teil: Theorie der phänomenologischen Reduktion*, ed. Rudolf Boehm (The Hague: Martinus Nijhoff, 1959). In this period, Husserl seems to understand the practical ideal as regulative (not constitutive) in that he emphasizes its significance as a goal. According to him, a "regulative Idea" is defined from our infinite progress (Hua VIII, 349). When, in the lecture of 1910–11, Husserl refers to the same problem and talks about the concept of "Idea" or "the ideal" (XXVIII, 185–90, see also BW/VI, 48), there is a clear distinction between the ideal and the real, the former is considered a "constitutive principle" for the latter (XXVIII, 190). Here the ideal seems to be understood within the framework of LI.

26. Johann Gottlieb Fichte, *Fichtes Werke, Band II*, ed. Immanuel Hermann Fichte (Berlin: Walter de Gruyter, 1971).

27. Hua, Materialienband IX, *Einleitung in die Philosophie. Vorlesungen 1916–1919*, ed. Hanne Jacobs (Dordrecht: Springer, 2012).

28. Hua XXXV, *Einleitung in die Philosophie: Vorlesungen 1922/23*, ed. Berndt Goosens (Dordrecht: Kluwer, 2002).

29. Husserl answers the question of the significance of pursuing the unattainable Idea in terms of a personal way of life. Personal belief in an infinite Idea has a kind of religious significance, but it is Husserl's factual experience, it is a phenomenological fact for him. This answer is a very interesting result of thinking by practical reason, but it does not have universal validity.

30. Edmund Husserl, "Fünf Aufsätze über Erneuerung," Hua XXVII, *Aufsätze und Vorträge. 1922–1937*, ed. Thomas Nenon and Hans Rainer Sepp (The Hague, Kluwer, 1988), 3–124.

31. Hua IV, *Ideen zur einer reinen Phänomenologie und phänomenologischen Philosophie. Zweites Buch: Phänomenologische Untersuchungen zur Konstitution.* ed. Marly Biemel (The Hague: Martinus Nijhoff, 1952); translated as *Ideas Pertaining to a Pure Phenomenology and to a Phenomenological Philosophy, Second Book: Studies in the Phenomenology of Constitution, Collected Works: Volume 3*, trans. Richard Rojcewicz and André Schuwer (The Hague: Kluwer, 1989). We can find the term of "practical possibility" in the manuscript from 1914, which deals with transcendental idealism (Hua XXXVI, 139).

32. Husserl faces the problem of "imaginative resistance."

33. See Melle, "Husserl: From Reason to Love."

34. For more on the historical implications of vocation, see J. Hart, *Who One Is: Book 2: Existenz and Transcendental Phenomenology* (Dordrecht: Springer, 2009). In Husserl, this concept is related to Bernard Williams' "Grand Project" in the context of contemporary philosophy. See Bernard Williams, "Persons, Character and Morality," in *Moral Luck: Philosophical Papers 1973–1980* (Cambridge: Cambridge University Press, 1981), 1–19.

35. The concept of striving in Fichte connects the finite ego and the infinite ego. See Frederick C. Beiser, *Enlightenment, Revolution, and Romanticism: The Genesis of Modern German Political Thought, 1790–1800* (Cambridge: Harvard University Press, 1992), 69–74.

36. Hanne Jacobs, "Phenomenology as a Way of Life? Husserl on Phenomenological Reflection and Self-Transformation," in *Continental Philosophy Review* 46, no. 3 (2013): 349–69.

37. What phenomenological thinking has in mind is not a self-regulating agent, but an akratic or "weak-willed" agent. See Takashi Yoshikawa, "Akrasia and Practical Rationality: A Phenomenological Approach," in *New Phenomenological Studies in Japan*, ed. Shigeru Taguchi and Nicolas de Warren (Dordrecht: Springer, 2019), 1–15.

38. Hua XXXXII, *Grenzprobleme der Phänomenologie: Analysen des Unbewusstseins und der Instinkte. Metaphysik. Späte Ethik. Texte aus dem Nachlass 1908–1937*, ed. Rochus Sowa and Thomas Vongehr (Dordrecht: Springer, 2014).

39. See Jean-Paul Sartre, *L'existentialisme est un humanism* (Paris: Edition Nagel, 1946). According to Sartre, this should be resolved by his free decision without depending on any emotion. In contrast, Husserl would insist that the young man already loves both his mother and his country.

40. I owe my understanding of Husserl and the War to Nicolas de Warren's presentation. "Die Tragik der Person—Husserl at War," presentation at Okayama University, 11 August 2017.

41. Nicolas de Warren and Thomas Vongehr (ed.), *Philosophers at the Front: Phenomenology and the First World War* (Leuven: Leuven University Press, 2017).

42. BW/IV, 409.

43. Ibid.

44. BW/III, 45. As a result, the articles are the highest achievement in Husserlian ethics and he seemed to have wanted them to be published in Germany. See Martin Heidegger and Karl Löwith, *Briefwechsel 1919–1973*, ed. Alfred Denker (München: Karl Alber, 2017), 75. However, his publications did not resonate among Japanese readers (we cannot find any response in Japan at that time).

45. Thomas Nenon and Hans Rainer Sepp, Introduction to Hua XXVII, 1988, xi. Here it is pointed out that Tanabe may be the translator of Husserl's papers. Heidegger's letter to Löwith from 1922 suggests that H. Rickert introduced Husserl to Kaizo-sha (ibid., 75).

46. Kazue Matsubara, *Kaizo-sha to Yamamoto Sanehiko* [*Kaizo Campany and SanehikoYamamoto*] (Kagoshima: Namposhinsha, 2000).

47. See Tatsuya Shoji, Wataru Nakazawa, Ikuko Yamagishi (eds.), *Kaizo-sha no Media Senryaku* [*The Media Policy of Kaizosha*] (Tokyo: Sobunsha-Publisher, 2014).

48. Christopher T. Keaveney, *The Cultural Evolution of Postwar Japan: The Intellectual Contributions of Kaizō's Yamamoto Sanehiko* (New York: Palgrave Macmillan, 2013), 2.

49. See H. Tanabe's letter to Husserl. BW/IV, 512.

50. Nenon and Sepp 1988, xi.

51. In a letter to Mahnke in 1921, Husserl wrote that the lecture was "the synthesis of Fichte and Plato's theory of eros" (BW/III, 429).

52. "Kaizo" is better translated as "reconstruction" or "reform" than "renewal." Russell's *Principles of Social Reconstruction* was translated as *Shakai-Kaizo no Genri* in 1919. Husserl understands that "Kaizo" is translated to "reconstruction" (BW/III, 45).

53. According to Cavell, perfectionism is not "a competing moral theory" or "a competing theory of moral life" but a "dimension of any moral thinking" or "a dimension or tradition of moral life" (Stanley Cavell, *Conditions Handsome and Unhandsome: The Constitution of Emersonian Perfectionism: The Carus Lectures, 1988* [Chicago: University of Chicago Press, 1990], 2, 62).

54. J. M. Coetzee, *The Lives of Animals*, ed. Amy Gutmann (Princeton: Princeton University Press, 1999), 15–71. See also Cora Diamond, "The Difficulty of

Reality and the Difficulty of Philosophy," in Stanley Cavell, Cora Diamond, John McDowell, Ian Hacking, and Cary Wolfe, *Philosophy and Animal Life* (New York: Columbia University Press, 2008), 43–90.

55. See Cavell, *Conditions Handsome and Unhandsome*, 101–26.

56. Cavell's concept of "exemplars" comes from Kant (Eli Friedlander, "On example, representative, measures, and standards, and the ideal," in *Reading Cavell*, ed. Alice Crary and Sanford Shieh [London: Routledge, 2006], 204–17). Husserl also envisions an ethics that takes person as an exemplar (BW/VI, 49). "Socrates-Buddha" seems to be a manuscript on this issue (Edmund Husserl, "Socrates-Buddha," trans. Arum Iyer, *The New Yearbook for Phenomenology and Phenomenological Philosophy* 15 [2017]: 398–415).

57. For Cavell "voice" is a central topic and one element of his method. See Timothy Gould, *Hearing Things: Voice and Method in the Writing of Stanley Cavell* (Chicago: University of Chicago Press, 1998).

58. Iris Murdoch, *The Sovereignty of Good* (London: Routledge, 1970). Hereafter: SG.

59. Iris Murdoch, *Metaphysics as a Guide to Morals* (Vintage Classics, Penguin Books, 1992). Hereafter: MGM.

60. Iris Murdoch, *Sartre: Romantic Rationalist* (Cambridge: Bowes & Bowes, 1953): Introduction. See MGM 171–72.

61. Murdoch criticizes an ethics that devalues "seeing" (SG 34–35). Husserl understands the central message of his *Ideas I* as "See!" "Learn to see" (BW/IV, 413) and finds ethical implications of "cognitive-ethical" or "responsibility" therein in the *Kaizo* articles (Hua XXVII, 40: 81–85). Seeing and paying attention plays an important role in practices of expert nurses: Patricia Benner, Christine Tanner, and Catherine Chesla, *Expertise in Nursing Practice: Caring, Clinical Judgment & Ethics*, 2nd ed. (Dordrecht: Springer, 2009), 137–60.

62. Cavell understands "perfection" in the sense that each of the self is final: Each state constitutes a world, not in the sense of the perfectibility or the last state of the self (Cavell, *Conditions Handsome and Unhandsome*, 3). Husserl's ethics can also be considered perfectionist insofar as it affirms that each person lives his or her own life.

63. There are also significant differences between the two philosophers: Husserl links morality to self-understanding more than Murdoch. Morality as a form of self-understanding can be read in Murdoch, but it is not clearly expressed (see Cavell, *Conditions Handsome and Unhandsome*, xviii–xix). Murdoch noted that the depth of seeing is linked to changes in the use of language (SG 28–29; 32–34). This aspect is inherited by Cora Diamond: "Eating Meat and Eating People," *Philosophy* 53, no. 206 (1978): 465–79. Husserl lacks the argument that the use of language is morally important.

64. Frederick C. Beiser, *German Idealism: The Struggle against Subjectivism 1781–1801* (Cambridge, MA: Harvard University Press, 2002), 1–14.

65. For a more detailed analysis of Fichte's two perspectives, see Matthew C. Altman, "Fichte's Transcendental Idealism: An Interpretation and Defense," in

The Palgrave Handbook of German Idealism, ed. Matthew C. Altman (New York: Palgrave Macmillan, 2014), 320–43.

66. Husserl's ethics questions various beliefs or sensibilities within oneself and is deeply connected to the discussion of "epistemic injustice" in contemporary contexts. See Miranda Fricker, *Epistemic Injustice: Power and the Ethics of Knowing* (Oxford: Oxford University Press, 2007) and José Medina, *The Epistemology of Resistance: Gender and Racial Oppression, Epistemic Injustice, and Resistant Imaginations* (Oxford: Oxford University Press, 2013).

67. Pierre Hadot interprets phenomenological philosophy from the perspective of "philosophy as way of life" since ancient Greece (*Philosophy as a Way of Life: Spiritual Exercises from Socrates to Foucault*, ed. Arnold Davidson, trans. Michael Chase [Malden, MA: Blackwell, 1995]). I can agree with this claim in that in his ethical idealism Husserl understands the philosopher as a person living in the love of truth as vocation. See also Jacobs, "Phenomenology as a Way of Life."

12

The Blindness of Kantian Idealism Regarding Non-human Animals and Its Overcoming by Husserlian Phenomenology

María-Luz Pintos-Peñaranda

The great figures of our Western philosophical tradition have not only grown up immersed in the circumstances of their present time, but have also evolved intellectually from them. Afterward, they have put down in writing their position on such circumstances and, by doing so, each philosopher's resulting style is the expression of the commitment to "his" time, as could not be otherwise. Hence, Kant and Husserl show significant differences in their respective philosophical ideas, due to their belonging to quite different periods and circumstances. They could not have therefore agreed on numerous topics, as is the case with their clear opposition on the matter of the "transcendental subject" and, accordingly, non-human animals.

In our attempt to understand the differences between Kantian idealism and Husserlian phenomenology as regards the matter of non-human animals, it is important to bear in mind various circumstances surrounding both philosophers, which were the main breeding ground for both the singularity and major divergences of each one's thought concerning the issue being discussed here. Two questions must be then raised now: what does Kant focus on, what is his main concern and why; and what does Husserl focus on, what is his main concern and why?

M.-L. Pintos-Peñaranda (✉)
University of Santiago de Compostela, Santiago de Compostela, Spain
e-mail: mariluz.pintos@usc.es

© The Author(s), under exclusive license to Springer Nature Switzerland AG 2021
C. D. Coe (eds.), *The Palgrave Handbook of German Idealism and Phenomenology*, Palgrave Handbooks in German Idealism,
https://doi.org/10.1007/978-3-030-66857-0_12

(a) Kant belonged to an age which was becoming increasingly convinced that the main purpose of humanity was to achieve happiness and, at the same time, was enthusiastic about the recent discovery of how powerful human reason can be when we are allowed to use it, as investigation and rational creativity are instrumental to meeting all the individual purposes leading to the basic aim of universal happiness.

During the last two-thirds of the eighteenth century, Kant had witnessed firsthand all the continuous developments that were taking place thanks to the Galilean *New Science*, whose innovative feature was to join observation and experimentation with a quantitative measurement of nature by means of an "exact" mathematical calculation. Kant was pleasantly impressed by everything that could be achieved through proper scientific research based both on "exactness" and, therefore, overall *certainty* of its verifiable conclusions.

At that time, the natural sciences were not only able to provide a rational explanation for nature across all its dimensions, but scientists also aimed at putting this explanation into practice through a series of "laws." These laws of nature were an attempt to scientifically express the process that drives nature, with all its changes and diversity. In the end, the practical implementation of knowledge of these laws would serve to exploit natural resources. It is hard to imagine that an eighteenth-century person, like Kant himself, would not be enthused by modern science, namely the new techniques and new machines which were sprouting in a breathtaking and uninterrupted succession. However, perhaps what most mattered to Kant was that science had managed to find a procedure to accomplish two significant achievements: firstly, a *non-speculative explanation* of how nature works, and secondly, the extraction of the *internal causes* that govern it. This procedure deriving from physical-mathematical reason has been the foundation for modern sciences, which made possible great advances and—at least as seen at that time—improved the lifestyle of humanity.

Encouraged by this productive route of science, Kant attempted a similar task, although—and this was his own contribution—not in the domain of nature but in the field of knowledge: it was an attempt to theoretically explain the process of knowledge that allows us to know reality because science is what it is only thanks to this process. Moreover, he considered this to be the task of philosophy and, correspondingly, his own at that particular time in which he happened to live. The modern commitment to using reason had brought along certain questions that he believed were imperative to answer: What are the conditions that allow objective experience and, therefore, scientific knowledge of nature to be possible? and, what are the limits within which that knowledge is possible? Because it is one thing to have perceptive knowledge of your surroundings and another to make assumptions about what cannot be experienced in a perceptible way. The objects of knowledge of metaphysics are beyond what can be experienced, and thus metaphysics does not meet the conditions to be considered science. Were Kant to find answers to those questions, on the one hand, he could make the philosophical contribution of clarifying the very foundation of science, the pride and focal point of that time; on the other hand, philosophy itself would greatly benefit from it. Science had emerged as a model of knowledge by having solely relied on the objective knowledge of nature, which allowed establishing the laws governing it. Kant therefore wished to remedy the general disrepute that philosophy had fallen into due to having used speculative reason devoid of any justification (CPR A845–46/B873–74, A849–50/B877–78).

Modern physics is based on what is perceived and draws its conclusions in a mathematical way according to what can be confirmed or refuted experimentally. This approach has resulted in reliable knowledge, which has turned physics into a model to be followed by metaphysics. In order for there to be perception, it is absolutely essential for there to be a subject who establishes the conditions for that perception. The knowledge of the human subject already entails the conditions that allow sensorial experience to have sense— an objective sense. It is the subject himself (the *transcendental subject*) who sets out such conditions. All sensible acts take us back, then, to the *transcendental subject*. We will be only able to discover those conditions by mimicking the method of sciences: if sciences formulate laws of nature, philosophy will formulate the laws of our knowledge by finding the conditions of perception, and thus of knowledge. Put briefly, science's method was enthusiastically praised in Kant's own time, and, accordingly, philosophy intended to emulate the same modus operandi in its effort to be "scientific" and to keep up with the times as well.

(b) Husserl was born in 1859, fifty-four years after Kant's death. He was reared in the idealist and neo-Kantian philosophical atmosphere of the nineteenth century, surrounded by a strongly positivist society that worshipped both science and the extraordinary ability of human reason, since the latter was seen as the protagonist and creative force behind the technological-industrial-scientific progress. However, while this progress seemed to follow an unstoppable and successful course throughout the century, one of the keys to the genesis of Husserlian phenomenology was that, around 1900, the existing *cultural* situation in Europe evinced that the blind faith in mathematical-physical reason was entering a period of deep crisis. Husserl witnessed this crisis in person, having lived during the last four decades of the nineteenth century and the first four of the twentieth century. In the nineteenth century, he became fully aware of the lack of clarity of science with itself as well as of the "naturalization of consciousness" by psychology—the new science that intended to reduce everything human to psychophysical aspects.[1] In the twentieth century, he experienced the horror of the First World War, which made use of scientific technology for destruction on a scale never seen before. The seriousness of these issues stemmed from the fact that whether physical reason—i.e., the great "modern" novelty of the culture of the West—is questionable, then so is Western culture itself due to its increasing identification with science, to the point that the two had become an inseparable unit.

Husserl's critical positioning regarding science meant a significant contrast when compared to Kantian enthusiasm for it, so much in vogue during the eighteenth century. Husserlian criticism was not focused on science itself but on the orientation it had been taking over the years, an evolution with obvious negative repercussions in the course of Western society and, ultimately, on humanity. While what Kant most valued and appreciated about science was that it appeared as the realization of reason and therefore of human nature itself too, Husserl underscored the abandonment of rational and ethical aspirations from which modern science emerged. Reason had become to be understood as merely "instrumental."[2] The ideal of a better world for all was abandoned, and with it the purpose of having our rational capacity always at the service of the aforesaid ideal. The objectivistic paradigm consigned to oblivion the life-world—the one of concrete subjects—and all the issues (subjectively) of concern for them (how they feel, what matters them, what motivates them, etc.). The original aim of science was gradually abandoned in favor of devoting all efforts to a practical result-oriented approach, and there came the crisis (see FTL 5; Krisis §§1–7 and 342).[3]

This process became so evident for Husserl that he increasingly turned his attention toward the causes of what he defined as twisting of the purpose with which the new science had emerged in the Renaissance. Finding—unmasking and denouncing—those causes became Husserl's core task as a philosopher. Only by establishing clarity on the causes of the diversion from reason and science, will we be able to overcome the collapse of faith in reason and retrieve the lost ideal, that is, "the capacity and possibility of man to confer a rational sense to his individual and collective human existence" (Krisis §5: 11).

Now the question is as follows: what role do the "naïve" perspective regarding science—according to Kant's idealist approach—and the "critical" perspective—according to Husserl's phenomenology—play when it comes to addressing the issue of non-human animals? In this matter, is it decisive that

Husserl, unlike Kant, focuses his attention on the problems generated within science and on the mentioned negative repercussions in culture and society? Undoubtedly it is so, as we will see later. But before that, a brief reference should be made to various diametrically different aspects that are collateral to the two philosophers' different stances with regard to science.

The Traditional Image of the "Subject"

The current debate on the issue of non-human animals poses a major paradox: we humans cannot find a strong moral link with non-humans if we start from what differentiates us. Why? Because the "meeting" point that we may reach will never be as originary, essential, or unquestionable as the "essential difference" from which we make our start. However, this approach has become chronic in the present debate and entails the following three big errors.

First, when starting to compare non-human and human animals, we always privilege certain characteristics that we humans consider deeply "ours," as very "human" and that define us very well: the neocortex, bipedalism, hand configuration, the soul, freedom, self-consciousness, reasoning and symbolic language, ideation, the making and usage of tools, etc.

Second, once these features have been selected among all the others we have, what follows is searching for their presence in non-human animals, with a twofold aim: (1) verifying if they have them and to what extent, or if, on the contrary, they lack them; (2) then, comparing those animals with us humans on the basis of whether we share those characteristics. This is the customary procedure, never the opposite. We do not select characteristics of the other animals in order to compare ourselves with them and see whether we have them or not. For instance, we dare not compare ourselves with them in terms of the ability to "fly," which would mean that while birds do fly, we "do not"; nor do we select the ability to perceive ultrasound, which would be followed by the recognition that, while bats are capable of this perception, we are "not." Third, if we detect characteristics regarded as properly human in the other animals, in a third moment they are considered slightly human, to the extent possible, which is tantamount to recognizing the similarity.

As may be seen, this is therefore a matter of comparing non-human animals with us, of taking ourselves—anthropocentrically—as a model and doing this in line with those certain features that have been previously decided to stand out from the many others we have.

In my view, the major recurring problems and errors when dealing with the issue of non-human animals spin around an ever-present and singular focus of attention, which is whether or not to acknowledge that non-human animals are subjects, after having taken this characteristic as defining of our human identity.

Humans' self-image always runs parallel to the image of other animals. If we humans look at ourselves as subjects and, even further, if we believe that we are the only animals under that category, then, correspondingly, we will have the idea that the rest of them are simply objects. *Those who are not subjects can only be "objects."* We are traditionally bound by this twofold belief that we often cast no doubt upon, and we confine ourselves solely to acting without question in this regard.

Conceptualizing non-human animals as non-subjects is never a neutral categorization, nor is it limited in scope at a purely theoretical level. Regrettably, a conceptual categorization (a notion, an interpretation, an idea, a concept, or a belief) always has a very tangible and real impact in practice. In this case, it is that the beings who are not subjects but only objects receive a valuation inferior to the one corresponding to those who are subjects (the superior ones). As a result, the *notion* of being merely objects, in conjunction with the *valuation* of inferiority, will encourage an irretrievably asymmetrical and speciesist *course of action* against them. Actually, this approach has always been the foundation for perpetrating intolerable atrocities against non-human animals: once categorized as objects and mere "nature," they are considered to be so different and foreign to us (i.e., so "other") that, theoretically, we find no moral objection to damaging their habitats to the point of causing them unsustainable living conditions, to exploiting them for our convenience while harming their own interest, to mercilessly ill-treating them by inflicting unnecessary suffering, etc.

The idea that rational cognition is the essence of human being comes from Greek antiquity and has grown strongly through the centuries in our Western tradition until today. There is no such thing as reason in the animal kingdom. This idea is linked to the judicial notion of humans: we are a subject or a person with rights and duties by virtue of our essential characteristic as *rational and free beings* in relation to the pressures of biological nature. The "subject of rights" is only the rational and free being who is, as such, able to understand his duties and claim his rights—rights that, in turn, his peers must uphold. In short, rights and duties have a judicial origin and require a being endowed with autonomy and reason: someone who is able both to give himself moral laws and to comply with them, i.e., able to rationally create moral and judicial *sense*. Such is a "subject" or "person."

It is obvious that, under this interpretation, non-human animals are neither rational nor free beings and, accordingly, they *cannot* be considered as subjects, and far less as "subjects of rights." They have the judicial condition of "things" and, as such, they can only be an "object" of judicial relationship, in terms of being useful and interchangeable. Non-human living beings are, then, opposed to how a human being is defined, since they are legally an "object" or instrumentalizable things, as seen from the superior level of humans as a "subject," and they are *interchangeable* since they are not "persons," i.e., not unique.

It must be pointed out that the judicial field, in which Kant had a substantial influence, privileges the rational aspect over other components of the human being: firstly, in the definition, in a negative way, of the other animals as not being a "subject"; and secondly, in that only those beings who are a "subject" or "person" are able to fulfill duties can be rights holders.[4]

However, what really matters to us now is that Kant's philosophy truly illustrates the traditional prejudices against non-human animals by (1) linking the quality of subjecthood to rational understanding; (2) exploiting this link to say that such animals are not a "subject"; (3) establishing such an abysmal difference between human species and other animal species that all the similarities they could have will prove less important than the insurmountable differences outlined earlier.[5] Thereby, Kant's thought results in breaking the bond with nature and with the non-human living beings dwelling therein.

By contrast, the phenomenological ontology of animal life not only does not share those prejudices but diverges from the traditional mainstream in a very innovative way, which can serve as an inspiration for current ecological and non-human animal rights movements. From a phenomenological outlook, non-human animals are indeed fully a subject, despite not being human.[6] Non-human animals need not be human or rational in order to be a subject, and we are referring to "subject" here both as a "subject of rights" in the judicial sense of the term and as a "transcendental subject" according to its philosophical meaning.

The Blindness of Kantian Idealism as Seen from the Phenomenological Perspective

Naturalism is our problem, says Husserl, and here lies the origin of the crisis of culture (see Krisis 318, 327). Naturalism is an attitude that consists either in ignoring everything related to subjectivity, or despising it as the objectivist

264 M.-L. Pintos-Peñaranda

method of science does not apply to it, or considering subjects as "objects" or things. Kant lacked the appropriate method to penetrate constituent subjectivity. As a son of his time, he thinks that the subject's interior already comes with "its capacities as forces attached to it in a naturalistic mode," as Husserl says (Krisis 117). The Kantian transcendental subject brings along a set of *a priori* logical laws, structures, or logical relationships; it is a pure thinking I who is indifferent to everyday experience and, consequently, to existence.[7] Naturalism is therefore at the heart of Kantian philosophy as the source of its misinterpretations, one of whose side effects is the narrow view on non-human animals (see Krisis §30).

In response to this Kantian naturalistic logic, Husserl emphasizes that the purely psychical is the primordial-life-world experience (see Krisis 224), which is essentially a subjective-relative and bodily-perceptive experience, where "another logic" rules: not any principle of formal logic (the logic of objective knowledge and science) but what he calls "transcendental logic," which is the logic operating in the life-world (see Krisis 144; FTL §86 and *passim*), i.e., in the world of daily living. His obsession with pure thinking together with his naturalistic approach blinded Kant from seeing that there is something which is *evident* by itself for every subject (in the shape of self-evidence), and which is not obtained through any formal logic at the level of thought (see Krisis 137). For every subject, whether human or non-human, the world, as their first perceptive evidence, is the soil which "is already there." This is a self-evidence that is not connected in any way with scientific evidence because the former "is given in inner experience," says Husserl. Therefore, this self-evidence is prior to the evidence obtained via formal logic and underlies it at all times. It is a pre-reflective one that operates as *a priori* life-world: the world already is and it counts for me in the simple experience of living at every moment (see FTL 141, Krisis §§28–29). This experience of living, interacting in a bodily-perceptive way with what one comes across, is a sort of "primitive belief" (*Urdoxa*) merely lived by the subject. Other equally pre-reflective and pre-scientific self-evidences are given on the grounds of this self-evidence lived as *Urdoxa* or primordial faith (*Glaube*). For instance, for me as a human as for the other animals living on the ground, this is the motionless soil on which one can move around, and this is not something "thought" but lived and, hence, taken for granted.[8]

Thus, Husserl confronts Kant by claiming that, on the one hand, we humans, before acting as theoreticians or scientists, raising questions and seeking answers, are subjects in the life-world, acting in accordance with this soil of self-evidence. This is why Husserl, unlike Kant, is interested in bringing to light the constitution of sense such as is implemented by the living subject in the immediate experience of the "life-world," since this is the primordial experience that is the soil for any theoretical or scientific intention (see Krisis §30:118; §34:135; §65:229).[9] On the other hand, the self-evidence, due to being constituted in the simple acting-perceptive-bodily experience and by means of a sort of pre-reflective transcendental logic, is not unique to humans but *shared* by all the other non-human animals. It is therefore a basic feature of animality.

As a result, it can now be understood that, whereas for Kant the science of his time is a model for philosophy, and he himself attempted to imitate its method, for Husserl that science, and even the contemporary version, could never be a model for philosophy because the former leaves out precisely what is the *prius* of all, the first and most primordial experience (both in time and in importance), that is, the subjective immediate experience of the lifeworld (see Krisis 149).

As the Spanish phenomenologist José Ortega y Gasset rightly said,

> It was a terrible error of the modern age ... to be in the belief that the primordial being of man lies in thinking, that his primordial relationship with things is an intellectual one. This error is called "idealism." The crisis we are experiencing is but the fine we pay for that error. Thinking is not, then, the being of man; man does not consist of thinking; this is only an instrument, a faculty he owns....[10]

The new phenomenological perspective seems then to place us in a starting point very different from the traditional approach whenever it comes to understanding what the essence of a—human or non-human—animal is, and whether or not there is any *ontological* relationship between human and non-human animals. Having considered that the privilege of the "intellective" relationship with the world on which we have traditionally built our notion of both human being and subject lacks foundation, we are now obliged to be consistent by redefining and modifying the image of the other animals with which that traditional notion was coupled.

According to phenomenology, every animal is, fully, *a subject* in this practical-perceptive-corporeal interaction. Every animal specimen is, in performing his[11] practical-perceptive-corporeal relationship with his surroundings and without intervention of reflective cognition, a subject by himself—as will be shown below. Thus, it can be clearly seen how Husserl portrays a novel image of the (animal) *transcendental subject*, and how phenomenology claims for a new attitude "towards men and animals ... as men (or animals) that own their bodies as their somas" (Krisis 310): "Scientists of spirit should not be satisfied with considering spirit as spirit, but should go back to corporeal foundations…. As animal spirituality, that of animal and human 'souls' … is coincidentally founded, on all and every one of the individual cases, in the corporeality, it goes back to it" (Krisis 316).

Husserl's Novel Image of the (Animal) Transcendental Subject, and His New Attitude Regarding Non-human Animals

When compared to Kantian idealism, phenomenology has brought forward major developments, which resulted in a new concept of "transcendental consciousness" and, consequently, in a new approach to non-human animals.

Firstly, the pre-reflective understanding of the world and the corresponding constitution of sense is a capacity we have not as humans, but merely as animals. This is why Husserl speaks about the "transcendental I" referring to the psyche both linked to human and animal corporeality, i.e., the "transcendental consciousness" is tied up to *corporeality*, be it a human or non-human animal.[12]

Secondly, this means that, as for phenomenology, the perceptive-corporeal activity of the subject—of *every* animal subject—is by itself a constituting power that is prior to any rational thinking, and this power is what defines the transcendental subject.

Thirdly, while Kantianism focuses its attention on the *a priori* form of consciousness that makes possible the experience of what is given as object of theoretical knowledge, phenomenology addresses *worldly experience* because sense is only produced in the very moment of the (intentional) encounter between subject and object, being in this encounter where subjectivity *constitutes* that sense, which is, then, a subjective (*Erlebnis*) *lived* sense.[13]

Fourthly, whereas for Kant the capacity of transcendental constitution is uniquely human as it depends on the rational element, for Husserl it is an animal capacity because the primordial generation of sense (the transcendental constitution) is carried out regardless of reason via somatic body and its perceptive-corporeal activity. It is important to understand that if we humans are endowed with this capacity, it is precisely because this is a legacy received from the animals that preceded us in the evolutionary ladder. Such capacity is inherent to animal biology, to *animality*. In humans, the "plus" that rational cognition adds up is the possibility of "taking consciousness" of this capacity and analyze it, but without intervening in its production.[14]

In other words, the Kantian and Husserlian "transcendental subjects" differ more than they share.

As to phenomenology, the perceptive-corporeal activity of the subject, which is by itself constituent production, not only conveys a new image of the human subject, but also that of the non-human animal subject. Our interaction with the world *as the animals that we are* is not—primordially—organized by the rational understanding of the individual, but by the practical-perceptive corporeality, which is exactly the case with the other animals.

Now, some steps will be taken to further develop the above issue in the following three sections: (1) animal selfhood; (2) lived space and the corresponding capacity to spatialize; and (3) inner temporality and the corresponding capacity to temporalize. This analysis will prove to be useful to delve into ideas and key concepts of phenomenology, and to assess how different this philosophy is from Kantian idealism.

Animal Selfhood (*Ichlichkeit*), Bodily Ruling, and Being a Subject of Will

Husserl's own terminology of a "biologic a priori" (Krisis 482n) shared by all species indicates that this *a priori* is in no way related to an intellective cognition, and let alone to a conscious reflection, but to previous capabilities that, as adaptative strategies, *every* living corporeality already brings with them and through which any animal specimen, human or non-human, procures the most elemental, important, and basic thing they need: getting-along-with-the-world and, correspondingly, acting-with-sense with regard to it. Otherwise, they would fail to preserve their most precious asset: life.

Every animal individual brings along in their corporeality a certain number of capabilities that can be described and analyzed separately, yet in fact are manifestations of what is one and the same capability found in all species: the one the animal individual has of feeling affected by the surrounding world, the one to decipher and interpret from within himself—in a pre-reflective way—the sense of what the individual is perceiving, and the capability to act in consonance with the sense that the individual gives to the situation surrounding him. There is a reason for this emphasis on "from within himself."

We all animals live "constantly in I-related acts," states Husserl (Krisis 230; see CM §44). The animal lives in acts of an I as he moves his body by himself and rules it as an I, as the I of his movements and the I interacting with his world in an active way. As simple as we may believe an animal to be, his being subject of his acts will be never absent, that is, an "I-subject." For instance, when he makes his way towards that thing, it is "he"—and not another one—who makes his way toward that thing, and if the animal lifts his head, it is he as an I who is in that moment the I-subject lifting his head. The body is moved freely by an I, and the I is the very subject of both its perception and free movement. The subject is an "I can," i.e., as an I can-move-freely (within my abilities and opportunities offered by the situation where I am) (see Ideen II §22 and Ideen III 134–37). An insect that is walking comes across a stone and it is he—he as an I-subject acting from his own subjective perception of himself and of what surrounds him—who resolves to find a way around it, over it, or to turn back. It is the animal who has the will to carry out his decision by choosing among the various alternatives available. The example of the insect has been given here to show that, despite being an animal with strong instinct, he will never behave completely as an automaton.

Therefore, a "subject of will" is not merely the animal that is able to take a rational decision and act according to a rationally premeditated project in view of a given purpose. Bodily ruling bears no relation whatsoever to consciousness, reflection, and rational premeditation, but rather to the fact that *every animal, spontaneously and pre-reflectively, can*—thus he is an "I can," to the extent possible, simpler or more complex—*control his perceptive-motor movements providing them, from within himself, with target-oriented guidance, without the need of having awareness of himself and of his acts at any time.*

This orientation from within himself as I-subject is feasible because the animal experiences, inasmuch as he is a lived body (*Leibkörper*), his own somatic body, which he feels as his own albeit without thematizing it. For instance, if a cat happens to lose one of his front legs, he will try to walk focusing on keeping his balance because it is he, the I-subject of his body, who is—pre-reflectively—realizing that he misses the foothold he once had and, as a result, will rearrange his position and movements.

The fact that every animal rules their corporeality and behavior as an I is an indispensable basis to navigate the world at any time. Every animal is corporeal in two ways: (1) as *Körper*, in terms of *res material* and *res extensa*, and (2) as *Leib* or *soma*, since, in terms of living corporeality, his life evolves in an environment with which he establishes, from his selfhood, passive and active interaction, by always perceiving, interpreting and acting *with a purpose.*

Indeed, an animal does not live in chaos. On the contrary, he moves in an organized, orderly, and structured way with purpose and sense—i.e., the one he himself bestows on things at any given time. After all, this is what is meant and required to be alive and survive.[15] In this respect, again we have to say that every animal is always the *subject* of his life, and even in his interaction with environment he does not have just movements but behavior, i.e., *oriented* movements towards something. In short, each animal already brings in his biology the capacity to organize his own life and, therefore, endow it with sense (which he gives to any situation that may come up).[16]

Lived Space and the Capacity to Spatialize

We will now focus on the capacity to carry out spatialization, which is one of the capacities for organization that every animal subject has implemented in their corporeal-perceptual interaction with their surrounding world and situation at all times. Such capacity is considered as "transcendental" in phenomenology, in reference to the animal subject's capability to give spatial sense by organizing, from his corporeality, his surroundings, i.e., "spatializing"—or, in other words, acting as the *constituent* subject of that spatialization. This power is both biological and transcendental—in equal measure. On this matter, Husserl provides a different approach, far from the beaten track. Biological animal corporeality already entails this power without any need for rational knowledge to intervene. It is a fact that every animal manages to direct their movements, regardless of whether or not their brain allows them a rational cognition similar to the human one.

Let us explore this, but bearing in mind a change in attitude is called for. Space for physics is the external, objective space—an idealized space. Physics does not deal with nature in the same way as (every single) human being apprehends and lives it in their own experience, in the subjective experience. However, when phenomenology looks at the transcendental capacity to constitute space, it attends both to (a) the capacity to spatialize, carried out by every subject, (b) and the lived space, which is lived by every subject in a unique way—subjectively. Hence the needed shift in attitude. First, all these theories of science are to be disregarded and "not resorted" to—doing an *epoché* (see CM §8)—in our descriptive analysis. This, of course, does not mean denying the achievements made by science in the field of investigation, new techniques, and instrumental technology, but rather only setting those established theories aside. Secondly, we are able to address the issue of the subject's experience. When doing so, at the level of both humans and the other animals, we notice this is not about the experience of a supposed space, which is objective, homogeneous, neutral, pure extension. The "idea" of space in physics is one thing, but space for living beings is quite another.

All of us subjects are only in a *lived space*, and we solely experience the *lived space*, i.e., the space in which we live, in which we move. The inhabited space—which is qualitative and not quantitative—is the only one every subject has experience of, and is where the animal subject navigates his everyday life to ensure his survival.

We animal subjects already are in a *lived space* where our innate biological strategy is at work, as follows: the subject's animal corporeality embodies a system of spatial coordinates that allow the individual concerned to accomplish at least these three extremely important things: (1) placing (situating) himself in space; (2) placing perceived things surrounding him; and (3) orienting all his movements spatially (behaving in relation to his environment). Living animal corporeality is thus situated (never de-situated), and it is from his situation where the animal subject manages to place everything around him in context so as to orient his movements as he perceives or behaves this way or that. The animal's own body is the foundation for the subject to place himself in space, to organize his surroundings spatially and, accordingly, arrange his movements with (spatial) sense. His body is, indeed, for him the core of all spatial orientation, i.e., his "zero point" in—and from—which he is simply situated due to the natural fact of being a perceptive living corporeality (Ideen 65 and §41). Thus, every animal subject's body is, for him, the original place of spatializing perception.

In light of the foregoing, perception is qualifying, since an animal never perceives in indifference, nor "everything the same." Quite the contrary, perceiving is distinguishing, differentiating. Otherwise, he would not be able to interpret and decipher what he perceives, let alone orient his movements. It is therefore obvious that every animal is the *subject* of his qualifying differentiation.

According to that differentiation and to the fact of putting distance between himself and things or other animals, which he perceives by one or several senses of his organism, the animal creates or establishes *routes* (for instance, to go from his "here" to that "there," to make that "there" become his "here"), routes or paths which forge *severance* or *de-severance* (separation or non-separation); he organizes his surroundings in a spatial way establishing *places,* i.e., spaces he differentiates as such (though this differentiation is not already there in a natural and physical way); he organizes what he perceives differentiating between figure and background in such a way that the animal subject perceptively highlights, for himself, something which has perceptive *presence* as center or figure of his perception; what his perception raises as the central figure stands out as such a figure above the perceptive field or background; this field or background is made up of everything the subject is not paying perceptive attention to at that time, but which is there occurring as co-presence, and the truth is that without this co-presence as background nothing could stand up as a central figure. The field or background is what is indeed there as materially present in the situation but without being heeded to at this point (see Ideen I §27, Krisis §28).

Therefore, it seems that animal spatialization is part of everyday life since establishing places and, in addition, tracing and following paths or routes is a strategy inherent to every animal subject as it is indispensable in surviving and successfully interacting with what surrounds them, both nature and other animals, whether members of the same species or not.

It is living corporeality itself, as the "zero point," which makes it possible to organize the surroundings in a spatial way pre-reflectively, instantaneously, and spontaneously differentiating between here-there-over there, near-far, up-down, something reachable-unreachable with the body (depending on what the animal can or cannot reach by means of his bodily features and movements), in front-behind, on this side-on the other side, and inside-outside.

We therefore say, from phenomenology, that the only space that the animal subject really experiences in his daily life is the qualitative *space*, that is, the *qualified space*, as inhabited by him from his central position or "zero point." This space is qualified by him, as a subject and in every particular case, in perceptive dimensions that are absolutely subjective and non-transferable: his here, his there, his over there, his in front, his behind, his on this side, his on the other side, his up and his down, his near, his far, his farther, so far away he cannot reach at all.

The assertion that there is no world for any individual animal (of whatever species)—i.e., perceived by him—before his own, subjective, and non-transferable perception thereof has its foundation on the fact that each living individual inhabits the perceptive world from his own corporeality (with his own physical characteristics such as height, his reach of sight, ear, smell, his way of moving and how long it takes him, etc.) and thus from his standpoint, with the motivation or immediate aim driving him at all times. The animal individual is a full-fledged subject in this regard, and it could not be any other way—save some disabling physical condition. There is no single animal who does not live in an organized territory (i.e., in "his" territory, perceived as such from himself; or, rather, organized in this way from himself). No animal could live surrounded by spatial disorganization, chaos, or spatial perceptive indifference. This is why every animal, from himself as the center or zero point of the world—the world for him—differentiates in a perceptive way. Take, for example, places. Differentiating places is a way of saying that any animal—as the subject he is—organizes or structures what he perceives in a spatial way. By being able to differentiate places, and by this means alone, is why *he can act in an oriented way*, i.e., bestowing a good spatial sense on his movements, always based on his motivation at that given moment. For example, if there is a place which is "far" for the subject to reach (far from the situation in which he is corporeally, and from the possibilities of his body in general and at that moment), he will plan a route, a path, a way to go from his "here" to the "there" where he wishes to situate himself. If scared due to being stalked from his right, he may decide to remain still in his "here" to avoid detection, or may even decide to run away and escape. However, in the latter case, he will not take the route to his right, but will endow his escape response with the sense of "stepping away" from the "there" where, on his right, an animal is lying in wait for his prey. Certainly, every animal, whether human or non-human, needs—and manages—to devise paths laden with sense for his survival, in other words, well oriented spatially according to his body possibilities and right motivation. Otherwise, he neither would be able how to organize his movements so as to get food, shelter, a mate, etc. nor how to escape from danger.

What is more, the non-human animal, as well as the human one, perceives what he perceives by placing it within the framework of an outer horizon, which implicitly accompanies every perceptive object and involves other animals, things, activities, emotive valuations (if the animal species is endowed with that ability), and expectations (what "he can" do and/or expect from that animal or thing that he perceives; or even, from that animal or thing that he remembers or imagines, in case of having the appropriate cognitive capacity) of the "family of sense" to which he belongs.

Everything involved in his current perception is neither given in presence nor in physical co-presence in such perceptive situation, but is somehow implied in the current perception of what he is perceiving, as meaning that he is *operating, i.e.,* taking action—*in a passive way*—in his givenness of current sense.

At the same time, that "family of sense" is linked to another "family of sense" and to other ones within the framework of that "outer" horizon in which perception of something takes place. Without the need for the animal subject to do it in a premeditated and conscious way, he manages to perceive what he is perceiving as he in some way understands it as belonging to a certain network of sense which is already at work internally, and from that network he fits together everything perceived in each new perception.[17]

Lived Time and the Capacity to Temporalize

Temporalization (*Zeitigung*) and the inner time flow of lived experiences are part of the capacities that each animal subject has, irrespective of how simple or complex the organism of the species in question is, be it a vertebrate or invertebrate animal.

What follows from the previous section is that spatialization is inseparable from temporalization. This could have already been glimpsed when we said that the subjective spatialization of the animal, carried out in every moment of perception, goes hand in hand with a field of co-presence and an outer horizon, which, as we mentioned, are involved—i.e., passively involved, with their elements operating, but not in current presence. The foregoing has also been approached when dealing with selfhood: that the subject of acts is like an I ruling each one of the lived experiences and acts, that it is he himself in his starting point and that he remains undivided in all of his acts, being, as for the latter, identical with himself.

We animals spatialize and, likewise, *we temporalize as well, i.e., we give temporal sense*. In other words, we temporalize in a qualitative way, creating temporal sense such as it is lived by the animal in question. Due to this temporalizing dimension of the animal corporeality (and not to an alleged rational cognition, which not all species even have), the perceptive subject organizes, structures, or gives temporal sense to his surrounding world at all times.[18]

The experience of temporalizing is to transcendentally constitute temporal sense, always lived (i.e., not thought). If, as stated earlier, things in perception are never presented spatially to the animal subject as being the same but are rather perceived by him from a process of differentiation, now something similar should be said about the experience of temporalizing. The time which goes by is lived by every animal as a short or a long time, so he will act according to his way of qualifying *in a qualitative way* (not in a quantitative way as objective physics does). For instance, if I leave my dog tied up at the entrance of a supermarket when I go inside to do some shopping, the waiting time for my dog will usually seem long, though only five minutes have elapsed according to my watch. My dog is the subject of his own temporalizations, which are subjective and non-transferable.[19]

Every animal always carries out temporal constitution from his inner temporality, which is subjective and non-transferable. It is not obvious that the Husserlian terminology for this inner temporality (such as inner flow of lived experiences, inner temporal horizon, lived duration, or inner time flow) may also be applied to non-human animals.[20] However, this difficulty may diminish when using another wording: all vertebrate animals have temporal memory, whether big or small depending on the needs of the species.[21] Animal memory is a biological one, i.e., part of the abilities or strategies needed for survival. We animals have memory, in principle, to protect ourselves in the present and in the future. We carry past experiences so that they can operate in a present that always comes after what we have experienced directly or indirectly in the past. Such experiences are kept in us to be eventually used in situations which are yet to come. If we animals did not have this capacity, facing a completely new situation from scratch and without experience gathered would be exceedingly costly for our lives. Every animal must learn (self-learn), even despite having instinctive behavior. The process of learning always acts in the present and in the future contingent on the past experience, either to avoid dangerous situations to life or to successfully take advantage of opportunities. This inner temporal carrying-forward has absolutely nothing to do with reflective cognition, but with pre-reflective cognition. For example, it is well known now that a bee that until now has never left her hive is unable to return home when released at a certain distance, even if it is short. "In order to return"—states Karl von Frisch—"she has to know the surroundings. This learning starts when, by the tenth day of her life, she first goes out. The flight hardly lasts six minutes and is aimed at getting to know the situation of the hive and surroundings."[22] Thus there is no instinct here but self-learning, which will be carried by the animal for life. If this inner carrying-forward of that first experience takes place in the life of insects, it goes without saying with regard to life of vertebrate animals. Vertebrate species add the strategy of associative memory. So, when perceiving something, those relationships and interconnections established at the time of perception between an object, action, animal, etc. and other objects, actions, and animals are the result of *habits* the individual already has within himself. Such habits result from the different perceptive experiences that he lived at earlier stages and that now, in his current perceptive situation, are acting from within himself. All this is what allows the individual to give sense the way he does to what he perceives, always with the intervention of the (not conscious) consciousness of unity. Things are constituted for the animal in the continuously unitary multiplicity of sense perceptions. What is perceived already contains a reference to previous past experiences, which are related to what is being perceived. Every animal, since he is permanently perceiving, can never abandon his subjective point of view.

Now therefore it seems that we need to substantially bring up to date our knowledge about non-human animals and accept the fact that they live their life as subjects due to having the *transcendental* capacity to interpret and organize their way of living from within themselves. Similarly, we deem it necessary to stay current on the unexpected findings provided by science when observing animals.

Conclusions

Thanks to his insight and intellectual courage, Husserl achieved major advances, about which we still feel conceptually uneasy today: recovering corporeality as the basic component of the transcendental subject; bringing humans back to the life-world and ceasing to privilege in them the area of Kantian "pure thinking"; showing that being a transcendental subject is not unique to human animals; and thus his contribution to eliminating the glaring and unbridgeable difference between non-human and human animals.

Descartes was therefore flawed in his interpretation of the body by reducing it to a sort of automaton. Similarly, Kant did not understand that the purely psychical is the living-worldly experience of the subject and that we—like all other animals—are perceptive beings in the world (in the *Umwelt*, in the *Lebenswelt*), and we originally experience this world in a pre-reflective way that is valid by itself. There is both a (human) reflective cognition and a prior and more basic one: a pre-reflective cognition tied up to our animal corporeality. This perceptive corporeality is the common background that ontologically links us to all animals,[23] since it is what enables and forces us all alike to act as transcendental subjects.

Thus, if at the beginning of the chapter, specific emphasis was placed on the fact that a philosopher is heir to his own time, now it should also be highlighted that his grandeur lies in having been able to build a sound foundation aimed at addressing the greatest issues and concerns of his time. In this sense, Husserl has outstandingly contributed, in an indirect and inadvertent way, to the current urgent need to overcome anthropocentrism and speciesism, which rely on an asymmetry between animal species that is at present as conceptually unsustainable in Kantian terms as it is conceptually inconvenient due to its legal-political implications.

Notes

1. The psychology practiced in Europe at the end of the nineteenth and beginning of the twentieth century was a laboratorial, naturalistic, or experimental one; in short, "psychologism" (G. T. Fechner or W. Wundt). It was a science in the spirit of what was known as "science" at that time, deriving its theoretical results from an application of the methodology of physical and chemical sciences. As for these sciences, there only exists what has physical or material existence; therefore, the psychic phenomenon is understood exclusively as a psycho-physical one. Husserl's objections raise questions of this kind: based on

the knowledge of facts and on the physiological functioning of the brain and the whole human organism, can the human being be understood as a subject who makes decisions about acting with ethical responsibility?

2. "In the century of science … the world has not become more understandable at all, only has become more useful for us" (Ideen III 95).

3. The following major works by Husserl are referenced in the text parenthetically, using the abbreviations listed below:

CM   *Cartesianische Meditationen.* Hamburg: Meiner, 1987.

Krisis   *Die Krisis der europäischen Wissenschaften und die transzendentale Phänomenologie.* Den Haag: Nijhoff, 1962.

FTL   *Formale und transzendentale Logik.* Hamburg: Meiner, 1992.

Ideen I   *Ideen zu einer reinen Phänomenologie und phänomenologischen Philosophie.* 1 Buch. The Hague: Nijhoff, 1950.

Ideen II   *Ideen zu einer reinen Phänomenologie und phänomenologischen Philosophie.* 2 Buch. The Hague: Nijhoff, 1950.

Ideen III   *Ideen zu einer reinen Phänomenologie und phänomenologischen Philosophie.* 3 Buch. The Hague: Nijhoff, 1952.

4. For Kant, "*Respect* [i.e., *rights* and *duties* required when respecting someone] is always directed only to persons, never to things" (CPrR 5:76). And when the latter are, he says, animals, we do not feel respect, but emotions such as affection, fear, etc.

5. Heidegger is also a good case in point of the previous position despite the close relationship with his disciple. *Da-sein* on one side, living beings on the other, and in between an abyss (*Abgrund*). See Martin Heidegger, "Brief über den Humanismus," in *Gesamtausgabe.* Band 9 (Frankfurt am Main: Klostermann, 1976), 323–26.

6. See below Note 14.

7. "Descartes and, above all, Kant *untied* subject or consciousness showing that I would not be able to apprehend anything as existent if, first, I did not feel as existent in the act of apprehending it" (Maurice Merleau-Ponty, *Phénoménologie de la perception* [Paris: Gallimard, 1945], III).

8. As regards humans, above this layer of self-evidences new ones emerge, but as beliefs of reason, as "cultural beliefs," in which reasoning comes into play— for instance, believing that democracy is the best political option or that the objectivistic paradigm is better than others. Besides, there are "personal beliefs," which belong to each individual as a person; for example, believing that traveling by train is better than by bus.

9. See Ludwig Landgrebe, "La signification de la phénoménologie de Husserl pour la réflexion de notre époque," in *Husserl et la pensée moderne*, ed. H. L. van Breda (Den Haag: Nijhoff, 1969), 226.

10. José Ortega y Gasset, "En torno a Galileo," in *Obras Completas.* Tomo VI (Madrid: Taurus and Fundación José Ortega y Gasset, 2006), 470.

11. When referring to a non-human animal hereinafter, "he," "him," "his," "himself" will be used instead of "it," "its," and "itself."

12. The Husserlian idea that non-human animals have their transcendental side as well—i.e., *constituent*—has been explored by Javier San Martín, "La subjetividad trascendental animal," *Alter*, no. 3 (1995): 383–406, and by Javier San Martín and María-Luz Pintos-Peñaranda, "Animal Life and Phenomenology," in *The Reach of Reflection: Issues for Phenomenology's Second Century. Volume 2*, ed. Steven Crowell, Lester Embree, and Samuel J. Julian (Boca Raton, FL: Center for Advanced Research in Phenomenology, 2001), 342–63. This issue has been dealt with by the author of this chapter in several other publications.

13. The method of "phenomenological reduction" is conducive to clarifying this "intentional" constitution. Any philosophy (and the Kantian one is a good example) which does not carry out this reduction is, for Husserl, a worldly, dogmatic, and "naive" philosophy because it holds the concept of the world as a set of things that are there by themselves, thus remaining in the "natural attitude." See Eugen Fink, "Die phänomenologische Philosophie Edmund Husserls in der gegenwärtigen Kritik" (in *Studien zur Phänomenologie 1930–1939* [Den Haag: Nijhoff, 1966], §§22–23).

14. This analysis is achieved by means of a re(con)duction going backward—the "phenomenological reduction"—as well as by bracketing the various theories established so far, doing an *epoché* of them.

15. See "The Cambridge Declaration on Consciousness": On this day of July 7, 2012, a prominent international group of cognitive neuroscientists, neuropharmacologists, neurophysiologists, neuroanatomists, and computational neuroscientists gathered at The University of Cambridge to reassess the neurobiological substrates of conscious experience and related behaviors in human and non-human animals.

16. To be a person is a different thing. For Husserlian phenomenology, the concept of person entails *something else*, a *plus*: i.e., the possibility and capacity to take thematic consciousness about oneself and one's surroundings, about what happens, has happened or could happen; theorization and taking of consciousness of what pertains to the pre-reflective and naïve sphere; consciousness and analysis of one's and other people's emotive valuations; all kinds of aspirations and wishes of wishes. Among all these, the aspiration to act well in an ethical and political way is at the core, i.e., abiding by the rules of society and/or by what one considers to be right. Freedom is essential to carry out all of the above. Besides, for Husserl, a person is a member of a community which has, he says, "its moral and legal systems, its modes of operation with other communities and persons," etc. A person is a member of the community, family, social class, municipality, state, church, etc., who knows himself to be a member of these institutions and dependent on them. However, non-human animals do not need to be humans and, thus, to be persons as described here to be subjects (see Krisis §73).

17. An example: let us consider foxes' "nets of meaning": "lair-quietness-warmth-protection from rain-licking the body for cleaning-litter-feeding the litter-etc."; "feeding-outside-seeking-walking-hunting-killing-prey."

18. Unlike temporality in Kant, for phenomenology it is not necessary to postulate an I that synthesizes temporal multiplicity from outside through an act of voluntary rational thinking (see *Cartesianische Meditationen* §9; Ideen II §10 and §§32–33; *Phenomenology of Internal Time Consciousness, passim*).

19. Someone might wonder how we can be sure what this waiting feels like to the dog. I would like to recall that basic emotions, such as surprise, fear, anger, sadness (being down!) or joy (being up!), are not originally human but a legacy from our ancestors, the most primitive mammals; emotions originated with the cerebral limbic system. Then, I can be sure, for example, that the dog will be afraid that his owner will not return to get him. We both, the dog (mammal animal) and I (mammal animal), share this pre-reflective cognitive characteristic of emotions. When I conclude the dog is scared, I am not projecting from myself but simply empathizing. Empathy is the adaptive strategy that enables us to understand what the other feels. For empathy to work, and for emotions to be transferred from one subject to another, they must evidently share this characteristic. And, in this example, they certainly do.

20. Husserl speaks of "the flow of states of mind of every *animal* subject" (Ideen III 48; see Ideen II 309).

21. We animals have (temporal) memory as a strategy that mainly serves to protect us from the future. What we experienced earlier remains within ourselves in order to provide help for later experiences. This is, primarily, a biological memory.

22. Karl von Frisch, *Aus dem Leben der Bienen* (Berlin: Springer, 1927), 106.

23. "Biology hides an ontology within itself" (Krisis 483).

13

Morality and Animality: Kant, Levinas, and Ethics as Transcendence

Cynthia D. Coe

In his phenomenology of responsibility, Emmanuel Levinas consistently notes the proximity of his work to Kant's practical philosophy.[1] A core element of that convergence is a refusal to ground morality in nature, which both Kant and Levinas understand in quasi-Darwinian terms—the self-interested instinct that seems to govern the primitive motivations of all beings. Such an account leaves no room for a sense of duty or obligation, and morality must then be understood as a form of transcendence of the animal parts of ourselves. However, the forms of that transcendence differ significantly: whereas Kant describes a moral law that binds us without being reducible to a natural cause, Levinas uses the language of anarchy to analyze responsibility.

In this chapter, I read Levinas's references to the anarchical quality of ethics as a radicalization of Kant's anti-naturalistic moral thought. For Levinas, the ethical is anarchical in two related dimensions: responsibility to and for the other exceeds any principle or law that I might comprehend, and responsibility arises prior to any origin that I can represent. Both of these dimensions resist the reduction of responsibility to one event among others, experienced by a self-governing, intentional subject. Instead, I encounter a

C. D. Coe (✉)
Philosophy and Religious Studies, Central Washington University,
Ellensburg, WA, USA
e-mail: cynthia.coe@cwu.edu

C. D. Coe (eds.), *The Palgrave Handbook of German Idealism and Phenomenology*,
Palgrave Handbooks in German Idealism,
https://doi.org/10.1007/978-3-030-66857-0_13

singular other whose demand remains unjustified by any shared characteristic or prior commitment on my part. Although Levinas praises Kant for the "primacy of practical reason"—how the ethical exceeds the domain of theoretical knowledge—the language of "anarchy" should be heard as a critique of the Kantian moral agent, whose self-possession is not fundamentally displaced by responsibility.[2] Writing from a post-Darwin and post-Shoah historical context, Levinas argues that reason is continuous with egoistic instinct rather than functioning as a way to transcend it. In Levinas's account, responsibility interrupts the self-interest behind animal instinct *and* human reason.

Kant: The Moral Law as Transcendence of Animality

For Kant, moral experience points back to the possibility of autonomy, where autonomy means the capacity to set one's own ends, or to govern oneself, according to the demands of practical reason. This self-governance is not merely the ability to choose (negative freedom), but the ability to choose rationally, without being determined by desires or external influences—which Kant sometimes calls "*bruta necessitas*," animal necessity.[3] In both the *Groundwork* and the *Critique of Practical Reason*, Kant contrasts the moral law with natural law, as a way of drawing out the nature of normative constraint: "Everything in nature works in accordance with laws. Only a rational being has the capacity to act *in accordance with the representation* of laws, that is, in accordance with principles, or has a *will*. Since *reason* is required for the derivation of actions from laws, the will is nothing other than practical reason" (G 4:412). Reason is the only ground of moral law.

What commands respect is the lawfulness of the law itself. Kant treads carefully here in describing a form of constraint that would leave intact the possibility of autonomy: the bindingness of the moral law does not function as a form of determination, as if actions were effects resulting from causes. Moral obligation works on the basis of authority rather than force—a distinction that Levinas also makes. Respect is "a feeling *self-wrought* by means of a rational concept"—in contrast to feelings "*received* by means of influence" (G 4:401n). Although respect is an affect, then, it is an affect proper to autonomous subjects, one that reflects their ability to give the law to themselves rather than merely be determined by natural forces. Accordingly, the ground of moral obligation cannot be found in either knowledge or psychological impulses. The peculiarity of moral obligations—which exceed what can be theoretically justified—is a form of constraint that reflects not only the negative freedom of choice but the positive freedom of autonomy: decisions based on recognition of one's duty.[4] This is not subjective caprice, in the sense of following my whims and impulses, and it is not external constraint, but something we are called to impose upon ourselves.[5] This constraint approximates the binding force of natural law, but none of its content—a "sense of law or necessity that consciousness possesses always already."[6] Because moral commands have no causal force, they may be ignored, but so long as we are (imperfectly) rational creatures, we are bound to follow them. In this sense, the moral law does not originate in us, in the sense of contingent choice or fabrication, and nor is it imposed upon us by an external force: it is "issued from the rational part of oneself."[7] As rational beings, we can escape the tyranny of self-interested instinct and inclination.

The lawful quality of moral obligation guarantees that I am not acting selfishly or out of arbitrary sympathy (for instance), from hypothetical imperatives that are only contingently binding. Instead, I am governed, or govern myself, according to the formal condition for the possibility of all obligation: the categorical imperative, which places upon me the duty to treat myself and all rational beings as moral agents with inherent, incomparable value. It is the formal capacity for lawfulness that matters here, since Kant defines autonomy as the "property of the will by which it is a law to itself (independently of any property of the objects of volition)" (G 4:440). That is, autonomy is a formal commitment to law-governed activity, where heteronomy "seek[s] the law" in a particular object of the will, and so allows itself to be governed by natural law (G 4:441).

The fact of reason, our experience of moral obligation, shows us that we are law-governed and law-governing: we can act contrary to our desires, rather than our behavior being the mere product of natural laws, in the form of instincts or impulses. We become aware of this law as a fact "because one cannot reason it out from antecedent data of reason, for example, from consciousness of freedom … and because it instead forces itself upon us" (CPrR 5:31). Moral obligation "announces itself as originally lawgiving," in contrast with a natural fact, which would have some condition behind it (CPrR 5:31). What it announces, what it testifies to, is the autonomy of the subject. Respect is both what autonomous subjects feel with regard to the law and what we owe to other lawgivers. The binding quality of the law rests on the rationality of the subject and its formality: the fact that it applies universally, regardless of particular needs, desires, and interests. Its authority derives from its blindness—or its refusal to attend morally—to the singular *qua* singular. The individual instantiates a rational person, and that is what is morally significant about them. Moral experience is thus fundamentally a recognition of autonomy, both in myself and in others. Responsibility functions as an affirmation of my freedom and rationality, and as an affirmation of my status as a subject worthy of respect (G 4:428). Accordingly, the moral law impartially binds every subject, thereby avoiding the capriciousness that Kant associates with heteronomy.

Morality should be understood as a rational transcendence of the motivations that govern the natural world, including the instincts or inclinations that humans share with animals. Hence Kant draws a sharp distinction between beings who are morally considerable in their own right and those that are not, on the basis of reason:

> Beings the existence of which rests not on our will but on nature, if they are beings without reason, still have only a relative worth, as means, and are therefore called *things* [*Sachen*], whereas rational beings are called *persons* [*Personen*] because their nature already marks them out as an end in itself, that is, as something that may not be used merely as a means … (and is an object of respect). (G 4:428)

Nonhuman animals are mere things, although how we behave toward them may psychologically predispose us to behave in similar ways toward human animals.[8] But what it means to respect humanity in ourselves and in the person of others is to offer respect to rational, purpose-giving beings, rather than treating such beings as tools for external ends. That quality of moral constraint that outweighs self-interest is fundamentally alien to the natural world as Kant understands it.

What Levinas most admires about Kant is his refusal to contain ethics within the theoretical—his acknowledgment of the inability of reason to ground its obligations in the knowledge that we are free persons. This excess is precisely what allows morality to resist reduction to the natural world of causes and effects, as the last sentence of the *Groundwork* emphasizes: "we do not indeed comprehend the practical unconditional necessity of the moral imperative, but we nevertheless comprehend its *incomprehensibility*; and this is all that can fairly be required of a philosophy that strives in its principles to the very boundary of human reason" (G 4:463). But to conceptualize moral obligation as law-governed is to establish a set of obligations that can be justified through reason, and to which all rational beings are obligated. Levinas echoes Kant's attempt to carve out a space for morality that cannot be explained by or grounded in a Darwinian struggle for existence, but he suspects that reason is fundamentally continuous with self-interest rather than a way to constrain self-interest; he thus looks for a different register to describe how the ethical transcends the natural or the animal.

Levinas: The Ethical as Transcendence of the *Conatus*

Levinas's project is a phenomenology of the ethical subject: What is the lived experience of responsibility, and what is the significance of that lived experience? What does it mean to be a subject in relation to the other, and how does the ethical relation to the other disrupt (and precede) other ways we have of relating to others—as fellow citizens in a social contract, as objects of knowledge, as rivals for resources?[9] In this approach, Levinas consistently questions the privileging of consciousness that is prevalent in both German Idealism and phenomenology, by asking whether consciousness exhausts subjectivity. His criticisms of modern European philosophy, and Kant and Hegel in particular, center on their emphasis on the rational subject, as a figure who attempts to comprehend the surrounding world, including others within that world, and thus disavows the possibility of responsibility as Levinas understands it. I argue in this section and the one that follows that Levinas takes this account of subjectivity to be profoundly complicit in the moral catastrophes of the twentieth century.

In "The Name of a Dog, or Natural Rights," Levinas suggests that the demarcation between the human being and the nonhuman animal can be blurred, just as the distinction between domesticated dogs and ravening wolves may become unclear. The French colloquialism "*entre chien et loup*" literally means "between the dog and the wolf," but generally means twilight, or any place of ambiguity or uncertainty. Levinas describes an uncertainty about whether "under his dogged faithfulness" the dog still "thirsts for blood" just before discussing his memories of being interned, as a Jewish soldier serving in the French Army, in a German prisoner of war camp.[10] That historical setting implies that human beings, despite their social training, all too easily shed the binding quality of morality: he writes in "the twilight [*entre chien et loup*] (and what light in the world is not already this dusk?)," in which we cannot differentiate the dog from the wolf. Levinas is preoccupied in this essay with the ease with which the line between human and nonhuman animals is traversed: the tendency of human beings to slip out of the moral bounds of responsibility to become savage toward one another, and the corresponding tendency to dehumanize others by refusing to see them as morally considerable beings. In his experience in the internment camp, guards and bystanders do not address the prisoners as persons: those encounters "stripped us of our human skin. We were subhuman, a gang of apes.... How can we deliver a message about our humanity which, from behind the bars of quotation marks, will come across as anything other than monkey talk?"[11] How does one convince another person to respect one's humanity, unless that respect is already established, in the willingness to be addressed? The refusal to hear is not a matter of lack of understanding, but a disavowal of the very condition of understanding, a refusal to respond to the other. Levinas doubts that reason will adequately protect that moral attention to the other and thus prevent a move into moral savagery.

The singular dog mentioned in the title of the essay is Bobby, a stray dog who spends a "few short weeks" at the prison camp, who would "appear at morning assembly and was waiting for us as we returned, jumping up and down and barking in delight. For him, there was no doubt that we were men."[12] For those greetings and the recognition it implies, Levinas describes Bobby as the "last Kantian in Nazi Germany," based on an "animal faith" rather any intellectual acknowledgment of one's obligations to persons.[13] It is difficult to know how to read this praise for a dog: certainly it expresses horror at Nazism as a possibility within modern German history—the way in which recognizing every other person as morally significant became corrupted by anti-Semitism and other forms of hatred. But it is also peculiar because Levinas mostly describes animals as amoral, in being governed by self-interested instincts for survival: what would "animal faith" in the personhood of others mean?

For Levinas, ethics is an interruption of the struggle for existence in which selfish motivations rule: fundamentally, the desire to protect one's life and one's way of life. Levinas's version of that association between nature and violence takes self-preservation to be instinctive, in both human and nonhuman animals. His repeated references to the *conatus essendi* gesture to Spinoza, who uses the term to claim that all finite beings strive to "persevere in [their] being."[14] Following its connotations among the Stoics and Descartes, the *conatus* is a way of explaining motivation: what moves us to act in certain ways. That striving sets up a basically self-interested set of desires, in which others are primarily positioned as competitors and enemies. Levinas explicitly links this attitude of the *conatus* with Darwin, but we should recognize that this is Darwinian theory as it has been popularly interpreted. Darwin's account of what motivates behavior in the natural world (including both human and nonhuman animals) is considerably more nuanced, with attention to how species that live in societies display a wide variety of self-risking and self-sacrificing actions, and how human morality may have developed out of such origins. I will discuss this complication in more detail towards the end of the chapter.

Levinas wonders how ethics is possible, if we accept that the struggle for existence defines our lives—how it is that anyone could ever experience responsibility, be brought up short by someone else's suffering, or perform acts of self-sacrifice? What would challenge the disavowal of our responsibility for the other? In describing the *conatus*, Levinas contrasts the possibility of ethics with the biological:

> The widespread thesis that the ethical is biological amounts to saying that, ultimately, the human is only the last stage of the evolution of the animal. I would say, on the contrary, that in relation to the animal, the human is a new phenomenon.... I do not know at what moment the human appears, but what I want to emphasize is that the human breaks with pure being, which is always a persistence in being. That is my principal thesis. A being is something that is attached to being, to its own being. That is Darwin's idea. The being of animals is a struggle for life. A struggle for life without ethics.[15]

The above passage begins with the idea that the ethical has biological underpinnings (which is a fair reading of Darwin's position) and ends with the claim that animal life, essentially characterized by the struggle for existence, is devoid of all ethics. We get a chain of associations here, from Spinoza to Darwin, and then to the Nazi philosopher Kurt Schilling and Heidegger. As Robert Bernasconi reminds us, Schilling was a German political philosopher and proponent of social Darwinism, who explicitly discusses race in terms of a "struggle for existence."[16] Social Darwinism promoted a picture of violent, self-interested rivalry—"a gladiatorial struggle in which each animal ... seeks to perpetuate its existence at the expense of its neighbor," in Peter Atterton's phrase.[17] We might also recognize the legacy of Hobbes in Levinas's description of animal and animalistic life: "Being's interest takes dramatic form in egoisms struggling with one another, each against all, in the multiplicity of allergic egoisms which are at war with one another and are thus together."[18] The term "allergy" here refers to a reaction to the other person that frames them as a threat, which needs to be violently expelled or controlled. If the *conatus* dominates our lives, there indeed is a great deal of reason to fear that the boundary between domesticated dogs and ferocious wolves, or humans in their animal and moral dimensions, is shadowy and permeable.

The kind of animality that Levinas is most interested in is the animality within human beings, the possibility that we might all be wolf-like in our approach to others[19]: "To be: already an insistence on being as if a 'survival instinct' that coincided with its development, preserving it, and maintaining it in its adventure of being, were its meaning."[20] Levinas calls this "the origin of all violence.... The life of the living in the struggle for life; the natural history of human beings in the blood and tears of wars between individuals, nations, and classes ..."[21] In such a struggle for existence, there is no room to question one's *right* to existence, or to exist in the way that one does. Concern for the welfare of others will appear to be a distraction or delusion; this account worries that we "are duped by morality" in a reality dominated by the war of all against all.[22]

For Levinas, ethics represents a break with such a state of nature: it is the "shattering of indifference—even if indifference is statistically dominant" as an ethical event.[23] He also describes ethics as breaking up "the materiality of matter," "the solidity of the solid," "the obstinacy of being."[24] Responsibility is "not a natural benevolence…. It is against nature."[25] That is, ethics is absolutely discontinuous with the natural motivations of self-interest, even expanded self-interest, by interrupting the complacency with which we preserve our own being and even the complacency that legitimizes the anxiety we might feel about preserving our own being.

Levinas: The Anarchy of the Ethical

Thus far, Levinas shares Kant's characterization of the natural world as amoral, devoid of ethics. Like Kant, Levinas tries to capture the quality of how we are bound, ethically, without an appeal to natural causes, including instincts, desires, or emotions. In our ethical vocation, we are called by an "authority," which he distinguishes from "a force" or a cause—hence the fragility of the ethical demand, its capacity to be ignored or reduced to an intentional object.[26] In a very Kantian note in *Otherwise than Being*, Levinas writes that responsibility "weighs" on the one who is responsible, "but otherwise than the way a cause weighs on an effect."[27] To represent this normative power, Levinas experiments with a range of rhetorical convolutions that are very much *not* judicial in their imagery: transcendence, height, the face, proximity, the trace, and trauma, among others. The ethical is an *inversion* of the *conatus*, in the sense that one finds oneself responsible, or morally implicated in the life of the other, without having made a promise or acting to contract such an obligation: "Being persisting in being, that is nature. And that there can be a rupture with nature, yes; but one must not attribute to it the same force as nature has."[28] This rupture destabilizes the subject's sense of self-possession and ability to understand the quality of the obligation—hence Levinas's references to the traumatic impact of responsibility. Responsibility obligates us prior to our ability to comprehend the source of that obligation, and in a way that calls into question the assumption at the root of the *conatus*, the inherent and self-evident justification of one's existence.

Despite his praise for Kant's emphasis on the primacy of practical reason, Levinas critiques the Kantian moral framework of a law-governed set of obligations, because a law still represents too "archical" a source of moral authority. That is, the moral law establishes obligations that can be comprehended, and its obligatoriness should be understood as applying universally, to all rational subjects. The *arkhe*, the "place of commencement and commandment" (in Derrida's terms), positions the moral subject as autonomous: capable of understanding and imposing its obligations upon itself.[29] The language of the law and duty, while avoiding the tyranny of natural causes, lends itself to rational adoption of principles. We find ourselves under an obligation, but through an authority that we recognize and participate in: "reason is an archeology" that seeks to understand the origins of obligation.[30]

In speaking of responsibility as a trauma, Levinas reaches beyond that model of moral obligation to focus on the ethical significance of incomprehensibility. The subject is *affected by* and *provoked to* responsibility for the other, beyond any principle or law that could be rationally adopted by the subject. Comparing Kantian and Levinasian ethics, Catherine Chalier asks: "Does the source of moral behavior toward the other lie in a subject's principles, independent of any encounter the subject might have with the sensible and concrete exteriority of individuals, or is it in fact produced by that encounter, independent of preexistent principles?"[31] A principle will not function traumatically. It may call upon a subject to justify their actions but not challenge their very right to be or displace the right of the rational subject to establish the limits of their obligations.[32] Being provoked to responsibility is not fundamentally an affirmation of my own status as a moral being, who is worthy of respect.[33] It is as if I am accused before I have deliberated and committed myself to an action. This radical displacement of the self-possessed subject entails an intractable uncertainty about my obligations to the other, and a basic inability to rest in the knowledge that I have fulfilled those obligations. I find myself obligated, in an "anarchic being affected"[34] that Levinas names heteronomy, in a "rehabilitation" of that word.[35] In opposition to Kant's privileging of autonomy, he suggests a "reconciliation" between autonomy and heteronomy, in the sense that in responsibility I am responding to a demand that cannot be declined: "The inscription of the order in the for-the-other of obedience is an anarchic being affected, which slips into me 'like a thief' through the outstretched nets of consciousness."[36] The ethical destabilizes the dynamic of intentional possession of and compliance with a delineated set of duties.

Levinas's refusal to ground ethical transcendence in a juridical model also generates the asymmetry of responsibility. The subject responding to the other is not one rational being among others, fulfilling universally distributed and reciprocal duties. Instead of a legalistic moral framework, one whose authority explicitly rests on its formality and universal constraint of rational beings, Levinas uses the rhetoric of singularity:

> Proximity appears as the relationship with the other, who cannot be resolved into "images" or be exposed in a theme. It is the relationship with what is not disproportionate to the *arkhe* in thematization, but incommensurable with it, with what does not derive its identity from the kerygmatic logos, and blocks all schematism.[37]

For Kant, the schematism is what allows concepts to be related to sensation, or what brings sensations under a rule or concept, so that we can meaningfully represent the objective world. Levinas uses this term to describe how responsibility resists such comprehension by the subject. Proximity is "already an assignation … an obligation, anachronously prior to any commitment. This anteriority is 'older' than the a priori."[38] Although I confront the authority of the moral law in the Kantian fact of reason (as a practical rather than a theoretical stance), I recognize it as a principle grounded in reason and to which I am bound as one rational being among others.

Levinas radicalizes this authority by describing responsibility as arising out of an immemorial past, an obligation that bears upon me without any recognition on my part of its foundation or justification. Time here has a moral significance, rather than marking the domain of determinism foreign to autonomy. In that sense, responsibility is a traumatic force that strikes me without warning, without the possibility of amortization or "deadening," a force that imposes meaning without being able to be comprehended, even retrospectively. Given his emphasis on how responsibility exceeds comprehension, Levinas describes the face of the other as a "trace" rather than a phenomenon: "I wonder if one can speak of a look turned toward the face, for the look is knowledge, perception. I think rather that access to the face is straightaway ethical."[39] The "straightaway [*d'emblée*]" imposes a different temporality than a moral law that allows us to establish obligations that are transparent to reason: "*d'emblée*" means immediately, from the start, but has the connotation of being taken by surprise. More precisely in contrast to Kant, "ethics arises in the relation to the other and not straightaway by a reference to the universality of a law."[40] One way to get at this distinction is that for Levinas, the ethical begins in the encounter with a singular other, whereas for Kant universality, or treating oneself or another as a generic rational person, guarantees the non-capricious, duty-bound nature of one's motivation: the universalizability of one's maxims ensures that one is treating oneself and all others as rational beings, equally obligated by the moral law.[41]

Levinas juxtaposes the ethical to a different form of tyranny than Kant does: where Kant worries about how we are dehumanized or dehumanize ourselves by being governed by forces external to reason, Levinas associates tyranny with totalization—the refusal to respond to the singular other that allows the subject to detach itself from the immediacy of the ethical demand. That detachment may then normalize and justify violence of various kinds, as in Levinas's experience in the Nazi prison camp. In Chalier's words, "If tyranny, as Levinas says, is characterized by the impossibility of looking the other in the face, then the impersonal law of rationality, because it does not find the face of the other, does not suffice to abolish tyranny.... A law that disregards faces remains violent."[42] Reason cannot guard against that self-protective lapse and may indeed facilitate it. Levinas explicitly claims that the categorical imperative is thus "defenseless against tyranny."[43] The problem with appealing to law as the foundation of morality is that it acknowledges the call to normativity, but it also limits the radicality of that call by providing a structure for determining our obligations. Levinas's interest is in the moment of being-called or provoked to responsibility, which is a moment that decenters or "denucleates" our status as rational, autonomous subjects, rather than reaffirming the reciprocity of duties among morally considerable beings.

Although the formality of the categorical imperative calls us beyond our self-centered impulses and desires, it also reinforces a narrative in which the moral subject can map out its duties and understand the source of its obligations. The moral law is beyond our theoretical knowledge, but reason establishes the nature of our obligations in accordance with that law. In this sense, the Kantian emphasis on autonomy does not leave room for a consideration of how moral principles may be used to deflect the traumatic quality of the ethical demand and thus serve to rationalize acts of violence. An emphasis on reason can be complicit with the forms of moral failure that most concern Levinas because of its tendency to abstract away from the singularity of the other, and to treat the other as a token of a type, even if we are enjoined to see the other as an alter ego, as sharing our status as autonomous beings:

The interhuman perspective [responsibility for the other] can subsist, but can also be lost, in the political order of the City where the Law establishes mutual obligations between citizens. The interhuman, properly speaking, lies in a non-indifference of one to another, in a responsibility of one for another, but before the reciprocity of this responsibility, which will be inscribed in impersonal laws, comes to be superimposed on the pure altruism of this responsibility inscribed in the ethical position of the *I qua I*.[44]

Where Kant emphasizes the moral insignificance of differences between rational subjects in order to guard against the selfish motivations of our animal selves, for Levinas this turn to an abstract law that is universally binding on all subjects misses what is binding about responsibility—that it strikes me as a singular subject responding to the need of another singular subject, and that I can conceptualize neither the source nor the scope of my obligations to the other.[45]

To think of responsibility in reciprocal terms is to reduce the other to an alter ego, another subject sharing my status, and this intellectualized understanding of responsibility removes the traumatic significance of my exposure to the other. In the move away from singularity toward conceptual abstraction, the anarchic temporality of responsibility is transmuted into an obligation that can be represented and justified:

> The order concerns me without it being possible for me to go back to the thematic presence of a being that would be the cause or the willing of this commandment.... it is not even a question here of receiving an order by first perceiving it and then subjecting oneself to it in a decision taken after having deliberated about it. In the proximity of the face, the subjection precedes the reasoned decision to assume the order that it bears.[46]

Like Kant, Levinas worries about self-interest, in describing the *conatus* as a form of deafness to the ethical demand, in the ego's preoccupation with its own preservation. But he connects the *conatus* to the intentional subject, who dispassionately observes and makes judgments about a world of objects. In that sense, he is concerned about a dimension of the *conatus* that converts the ethical demand into a principle or a proposition that can be comprehended by rationality, and in that conversion loses its traumatic or anarchic quality. Reason thus functions to uphold the self-protective, amoral motivations of the *conatus* rather than challenging them.

Levinas's historical position makes a difference in his interpretation of rationality. He is reacting not only to the Shoah itself, but the various ways in which Darwin's ideas were (mis)used to justify genocide and other forms of racial violence: if all of life should be understood as a struggle for existence, then the moral obligation to respect all other persons will be restructured by a racialized understanding of who actually counts as a person, of whose life matters. Moral theories that treat the normative concept of a "person" as self-evident ignore the reality of racial hierarchies, among others, that distinguish persons from subpersons, those who belong to the same biological species but are socially and politically positioned in an inferior status. Comparing the idealized reciprocity between rational persons of Kantian moral theory to the actual workings of *Herrenvolk* morality that rationalized white supremacy in the United States, Charles Mills argues that while those seen as rational persons owe each other respect, subpersons owe persons deference and in return are owed contempt by persons.[47] Subpersons are seen as capable of reasoning and moral responsibility within certain limits, but also are not recognized as full persons, morally or legally. This dehumanization is how human beings may not be able to address others and demand respect from them, how they may be socially disqualified from moral considerability. The principle that all rational persons must be respected as ends in themselves does not settle the question of who will be considered a person. For Levinas, the social customs or rationalizations that *do* settle those questions, often in ways that normalize injustice, can only be interrupted by a more anarchical moral force, my immediate sense of responsibility when I confront another singular being's vulnerability and suffering.

By calling the dog Bobby "the last Kantian in Nazi Germany, without the brain needed to universalize maxims and drives," Levinas points to the paradox of how easy it is for human societies to rationalize dehumanizing others.[48] Llewellyn and other critics of Levinas's anthropocentrism take this passage to be consigning Bobby to moral inconsiderability as a "stupid beast," a being without reason or speech.[49] But my reading is much closer to Diane Perpich's: "The dog, even without reason, managed to do more and do better ethically speaking."[50] In moral twilight, which does not allow us to distinguish easily between the dog and the wolf—the one who will respond and the one who will refuse that responsibility, Levinas warns us about the fragility of the ethical. From his perspective, moral failure arises less from inclinations overcoming the demands of practical reason than from a basic continuity between reason and inclination that attempts to deflect responsibility.

The egocentric quality of the *conatus* is insufficiently interrupted by the moral law, which affirms the moral considerability of the rational subject first and foremost, as a condition of having obligations to others, and a subject whose obligations can be predictably established through a principle. In various writings Levinas distances the commandment of responsibility from a rational constraint, and also from an egocentric struggle to preserve one's life:

> That's Darwin's idea: the living being struggles for life. The aim of being is being itself. However, with the appearance of the human—and this is my entire

philosophy—there is something more important than my life, and that is the life of the other. That is unreasonable. Man is an unreasonable animal.[51]

That is, there is no justification for *why* the other's life should come before my own. If there were such a justification, which could be grasped by even practical reason, the ethical would not have a traumatic impact upon us. In the same interview, Levinas restates the claim that it is not a rational limit that interrupts the self-interest of *conatus*:

> In the *conatus essendi*, which is the effort to exist, existence is the supreme law. However, with the appearance of the face on the inter-personal level, the commandment "Thou shalt not kill" emerges as a limitation of the *conatus essendi*. It is not a rational limit. Consequently, interpreting it necessitates thinking it in moral terms, in ethical terms. It must be thought of outside the idea of force.[52]

The distinction between a natural cause (a force) and a rational law has blurred here, in the sense that neither of these forms of constraint decenter and expose the subject to responsibility.

I read this skepticism about the moral force of reason in a historical context. For Levinas, the Shoah demonstrates the fragility of the ethical response, and how easy it is to rationalize indifference to the suffering of the other. If Auschwitz is emblematic of a "failure of morality," then what is the morality that remains after that failure?[53] For Levinas, it will be anarchical, unsystematic, and promising no "happy end."[54] The ethical means responding to a singular other, in a particular situation, not a generic set of obligations which I apply to a particular rational person or people affected by my current action. Levinas acknowledges that we always have obligations to more than one other, and that an awareness of "the third" demands that we must deliberate about how to distribute our resources. This is the realm of justice, in Levinas's terminology: "in justice the dissymmetry that holds me at odds with regard to the other will find again law, autonomy, equality."[55] In this register, the other is treated as a member of a genus, one among many to whom I have obligations. But even here, Levinas argues that more universalistic, formal considerations of justice cannot be isolated from the anarchic quality of responsibility. I am called upon to respond to the suffering and vulnerability of all others, but that response begins in responsibility to a singular other. Whatever system of justice is established, the subject's responsibility to a singular other will continue to trouble that settled list of obligations and how they are fulfilled, such that I can never lapse into moral complacency.

That emphasis on an unceasing, unfulfillable moral obligation is for Levinas consistent with resisting the amorality of the *conatus* and the satisfactions of a "happy end" that might be held out as a promise for dutiful action. As animals, we are one self-interested species among others, but as humans, we transcend that nature:

> The interest of pure practical reason is beyond the interests of sensible nature and hence a break with a theology (and also with a politics) which assures satisfaction to natural man.... The God of disinterested interest survives the death of the great Pan, who was simply one supreme force among the forces traversing nature and governing like him (or under his orders) the interests of men, those "rational animals" who have lost their exceptional significance in the present crisis of western humanism.[56]

A focus on fulfilling the selfish interests of human beings produces a God who gives us a "happy end" and a Hobbesian politics, and a view of human beings as governed by the *conatus*. Seeing ourselves as "rational animals" is continuous with this picture. But the ethical (or "disinterested interest") has no place in that account, and its possibility arises elsewhere than in the brutality of the *conatus* or even the affirmation of oneself as an autonomous person.

Writing in the wake of the Shoah, Levinas claims that the vision of a Kantian kingdom of ends, in which rational persons mutually respect the humanity of others, does not capture the immediacy of responsibility in the face of others, or interrupt the moral complacency of the *conatus*, in which others are first and foremost enemies. Instead, it may foster a "primal disrespect" for the other *as* other.[57] In a short preface (written in 1990) for an essay (written in 1934) called "Some Thoughts on the Philosophy of Hitlerism," Levinas raises the question of whether a liberal attention to rights or respect for one's fellow man all that is needed for morality:

> the source of the bloody barbarism of National Socialism lies not in some contingent anomaly within human reasoning, nor in some accidental ideological misunderstanding. This article expresses the conviction that this source stems from the essential possibility of *elemental Evil* into which we can be led by logic and against which Western philosophy had not sufficiently insured itself. This possibility is inscribed within the ontology of a being concerned with being ..., that famous subject of transcendental idealism that before all else wishes to be free and thinks itself free. We must ask ourselves if liberalism is all we need to achieve an authentic dignity for the human subject.[58]

Reason does not disturb the moral complacency of the *conatus* but may instead be used to justify the drive to self-preservation. Recognizing oneself as

a rational, self-determining subject does not on its own awaken us to responsibility, because that move establishes the centrality of one's own subjectivity,
as the ground of moral duties to others.

A Darwinian Complication

To this point in the chapter, I have argued that Levinas radicalizes Kant's
attempt to separate morality from the instincts and inclinations that rule
behavior in the natural world, but both of them are attempting to carve
out a moral realm in opposition to a Darwinian struggle for existence. We
should note that Levinas's account of the *conatus* and Kant's account of
natural self-interest are a particular interpretation of the state of nature, one
accepted by social Darwinists: an interpretation that associates self-interested
violence primarily with nonhuman animals and reserves for the human the
capacity to interrupt that violence.[59] However, Darwin devotes a significant
portion of *The Descent of Man* to discussing altruism and social bonds among
nonhuman animals, including the behaviors of cooperative hunting, warning
others in one's group of danger, and feeding the disabled, the elderly, and the
young. He claims that "the moral sense" is one of the most significant ways in
which humans differ from nonhuman animals, but he sees that as a difference
in degree rather than kind:

> The following proposition seems to me in a high degree probable—namely,
> that any animal whatever, endowed with well-marked social instincts, the
> parental and filial affections being here included, would inevitably acquire a
> moral sense or conscience, as soon as its intellectual powers had become as
> well, or nearly as well developed, as in man.[60]

Darwin resists reducing these social acts to a self-interested motivation and
takes the motivation to act for the good of the group to be a "primary impulse
and guide."[61] He acknowledges, however, that such sympathetic social bonds
function only within limited communities: relatively non-social animals like
tigers may exhibit it only toward their own offspring, whereas baboons will
identify with the members of their troop. Not even all members of the same
species will be seen as morally considerable. Darwin speculates that human
beings, as they "advance in civilization," will "extend his social instincts and
sympathies to all the members of the same nation" and from there "to the
men of all nations and races," and from there "to all sentient beings."[62] Our
instincts for preserving ourselves and members of our own family underwrite
our capacity for broader, more principled forms of moral attention.

For Kant and Levinas, this account of morality is an insufficient ground for the binding quality of our moral obligations, insofar as it grounds morality in the contingency of our biological natures. But it offers a more complicated representation of the connection between animal behavior and morality than we get from conventional philosophical accounts of the state of nature. For Darwin, we need to contest the anthropocentric dynamic of projecting onto nonhuman animals an amoral savagery and then disavowing our bonds to nonhuman animals. By contrast, the understanding of nature in Kantian and Levinasian thought has a definite function: it acts as the foil against which the possibility of duty, respect, and responsibility emerge. Neither philosopher thus fundamentally disrupts the anthropocentric glorification of traits that they take to be the exclusive possession of human beings, which open up the possibility of ethics.

Conclusion

In their accounts of morality, Kant and Levinas affirm a quasi-Darwinian account of the natural world, or more specifically the animality within humanity: the self-interested struggle for existence is what is transcended in morality. But Kant and Levinas express two different worries about how we may be tyrannized by that self-interest, in their thinking about moral failure. Kant worries about how we may treat ourselves as mere pieces of the natural world, so that we justify behavior that results from feelings or inclinations. Following those impulses leads to self-centered capriciousness, and thus autonomy, the ability to recognize the authority of the moral law, becomes the core of moral conduct. Levinas worries instead about the violence latent within intentionality itself, or the continuity between our selfish impulses and the activity of reason. Appealing to a moral law does not interrupt that activity radically enough or destabilize the position of the subject at the center of the moral world. Responsibility thus must become anarchic rather than law-governed: anarchic both as an infinite, incomprehensible obligation to the other and as an obligation without an origin, one that precedes any deliberate commitment on my part. If I cannot categorize the other as a person (like myself) who deserves moral consideration, and if I cannot subsume my responsibility under an abstract principle, the singular other functions as the interruption of egoism, its deflections of responsibility of and to the other, and the metaphorical and literal violence that such deflections normalize.

In our own historical context, we need to challenge Levinas and Kant's shared characterization of the natural world as self-interested and amoral.

We may look back on the legacy of the Industrial Revolution, racism, and colonialism as establishing naturalized boundaries between the morally considerable and the morally inconsiderable—boundaries that have often been drawn within the human species, depending on who is seen as fully rational or civilized. Depictions of people of color and other marginalized groups as animals have invoked the worst elements of Darwinian theory as it has been popularly interpreted: the natural world is a place of violence, competition, and self-interest. Those invocations have then been used to justify forms of violence and exploitation suffered by whatever and whomever is perceived as belonging to the natural world. We might think here of how frequently in the last hundred years immigrants or those perceived as foreigners have been systematically dehumanized through animal metaphors, and the forms of oppression that those characterizations have rationalized. Those others are cast out not only from a particular community but from the circle of morally considerable beings—that is, their suffering and death go unremarked and un-mourned, as if they belonged within a natural world in which mortality is inevitable and unworthy of moral attention. In this way, migrants drowning at sea or dying of exposure in deserts or being held indefinitely in cages may not provoke moral outrage but instead be normalized.

Kant's insistence on respect for persons and Levinas's account of anarchic responsibility intend to hold open the possibility of expanding our habitual sense of obligation—of expanding whose suffering and deaths are framed as mattering and whose can be comfortably ignored. But perhaps the most effective way of resisting that political tactic is not to reaffirm the humanity of human beings and the animality (the brutality, the bestiality) of animals. The separation between those who deserve our sympathy and protection, and those who are morally inconsiderable, is one more attempt on the part of the *conatus* to limit the scope of our ethical obligations, and the opposition between an amoral natural world and a moral human one feeds into that dynamic. Kant's description of an obligation that cannot be reduced to a causal force demands that we critically reflect on our inclinations and socially mediated judgments. By discussing responsibility as a form of traumatic exposure to the other, Levinas reminds us that we cannot understand ourselves as wholly immersed in a struggle for existence. We need not reinforce the distinction between animality and humanity in order to make those claims. Moral obligation and self-interested violence are both possibilities within the human.

For Levinas, who was on intimate terms with the dehumanization of persons, transcending our self-interestedness requires more than respect for the moral law—it requires a traumatic disruption of the autonomous subject.

By radicalizing Kant's rejection of instinct and inclination as the ground of morality, Levinas also echoes Kant's refusal to subordinate practical reason to theoretical reason: responsibility leaves us fundamentally uncertain as to the origin, scope, and nature of our obligations to others, and thus whether we have ever fulfilled those obligations. This is an anarchy and a heteronomy that works against moral complacency, a complacency that we can better resist if we recognize it as a human tendency rather than projecting it upon nonhuman animals and animalized humans.

Notes

1. See, for instance, Emmanuel Levinas, *God, Death, and Time*, trans. Bettina Bergo (Stanford: Stanford University Press, 2000), 64–65.
2. Emmanuel Levinas, "The Primacy of Pure Practical Reason," trans. Blake Billings, *Man and World* 27 (1994): 445–53.
3. Immanuel Kant, *Lectures on Ethics*, ed. Peter Heath and J. B. Schneewind, trans. Peter Heath (Cambridge: Cambridge University Press, 1997), 27, 344.
4. See Allen Wood, *Kant's Ethical Thought* (Cambridge: Cambridge University Press, 1999), 46.
5. See Darin Crawford Gates, "The Fact of Reason and the Face of the Other: Autonomy, Constraint, and Rational Agency in Kant and Levinas," *The Southern Journal of Philosophy* 60 (2002): 501–2.
6. Richard S. Findler, "Kant's Phenomenological Ethics," *Research in Phenomenology* 27 (1997): 177.
7. Catherine Chalier, *What Ought I to Do? Morality in Kant and Levinas*, trans. Jane Marie Todd (Ithaca: Cornell University Press, 2002), 64–65.
8. Kant, *Lectures on Ethics*, 27: 459.
9. For a more thorough discussion of Levinas's relation to phenomenology, see John Drabinski, *Sensibility and Singularity: The Problem of Phenomenology in Levinas* (Albany: State University of New York Press, 2001); Richard Cohen, *Elevations* (Chicago: University of Chicago Press, 1995); and Bettina Bergo, "What Is Levinas Doing? Phenomenology and the Rhetoric of an Ethical Un-Conscious," *Philosophy and Rhetoric* 38, no. 2 (2005): 122–44.
10. Emmanuel Levinas, "The Name of a Dog, or Natural Rights," in *Difficult Freedom*, trans. Seán Hand (Baltimore: The Johns Hopkins University Press, 199), 152.
11. Ibid., 153.
12. Ibid.
13. Ibid. For more discussion of Levinas's views on nonhuman animals, see Matthew Calarco, *Zoographies: The Question of the Animal from Heidegger to Derrida* (New York: Columbia University Press, 2008), 55–78; Bob Plant, "Welcoming Dogs: Levinas and the 'Animal' Question," *Philosophy and Social Criticism* 37, no. 1 (Jan. 2011): 49–71; Peter Atterton, "Levinas and Our Moral

Responsibility Toward Other Animals," *Inquiry* 54, no. 6 (Dec. 2011): 633–49; Peter Atterton and Tamra Wright, eds., *Face-to-Face with Animals: Levinas and the Animal Question* (Albany: State University of New York Press, 2019); and Diane Perpich, *The Ethics of Emmanuel Levinas* (Stanford: Stanford University Press, 2008), 150–76.

14. Benedict de Spinoza, *Ethics*, trans. Samuel Shirley (Indianapolis: Hackett, 1992): IIIp9.

15. Emmanuel Levinas, "The Paradox of Morality," in *The Provocation of Levinas: Rethinking the Other*, ed. Robert Bernasconi and David Wood (New York: Routledge, 1988), 172.

16. Robert Bernasconi, "Levinas and the Struggle for Existence," in *Addressing Levinas*, ed. Eric Sean Nelson, Antje Kapust, and Kent Still (Evanston: Northwestern University Press, 2005), 170–71.

17. Peter Atterton, "Nourishing the Hunger of the Other: A Rapprochement between Levinas and Darwin," *Symploke* 19, nos. 1–2 (2011): 31.

18. Emmanuel Levinas, *Otherwise Than Being, or Beyond Essence*, trans. Alphonso Lingis (Pittsburgh: Duquesne University Press, 1998), 4.

19. John Llewellyn, *Middle Voice of Ecological Conscience: A Chiasmic Reading of Responsibility in the Neighborhood of Levinas, Heidegger, and Others* (New York: St. Martin's Press, 1991), 50.

20. Emmanuel Levinas, Preface to *Entre Nous: Thinking-of-the-Other*, trans. Michael B. Smith and Barbara Harshav (New York: Columbia University Press, 1998), xii.

21. Ibid.

22. Emmanuel Levinas, *Totality and Infinity: An Essay on Exteriority*, trans. Alphonso Lingis (Dordrecht: Kluwer, 1991), 21.

23. Levinas, Preface to *Entre Nous*, xii.

24. Emmanuel Levinas, "Dialogue on Thinking-of-the-Other," in *Entre Nous: Thinking-of-the-Other*, trans. Michael B. Smith and Barbara Harshav (New York: Columbia University Press, 1998), 202.

25. Levinas, *Otherwise than Being*, 197n27.

26. Levinas, "Provocation of Morality," 169.

27. Levinas, *Otherwise than Being*, 198n28.

28. Levinas, "Provocation of Morality," 176.

29. Jacques Derrida, *Archive Fever: A Freudian Impression*, trans. Eric Prenowitz (Chicago: University of Chicago Press, 1995), 1.

30. Emmanuel Levinas, "Humanism and An-archy," in *Humanism of the Other*, trans. Nidra Poller (Urbana: University of Illinois Press, 2006), 49.

31. Chalier, *What Ought I to Do*, 18. For further discussion of the dialogue between Levinas and Kant, see Michael L. Morgan, *Discovering Levinas* (New York: Cambridge University Press, 2007), 236–59, 415–17; Adriaan Theodoor Peperzak, *Beyond: The Philosophy of Emmanuel Levinas* (Evanston: Northwestern University Press, 1997), 198–203; and Inga Römer, "Levinas and

Early Modern Philosophy," in *The Oxford Handbook of Levinas*, ed. Michael L. Morgan (New York: Oxford University Press, 2019), 184–87.

32. Chalier, *What Ought I to Do*, 47.
33. Emmanuel Levinas, *Of God Who Comes to Mind*, trans. Bettina Bergo (Stanford: Stanford University Press, 1998), 17.
34. Levinas, "Humanism and An-archy," 148.
35. Emmanuel Levinas, *Is It Righteous to Be? Interviews with Emmanuel Levinas*, ed. Jill Robbins (Stanford: Stanford University Press, 2001), 273.
36. Levinas, *Otherwise than Being*, 148.
37. Ibid., 100.
38. Ibid., 101.
39. Emmanuel Levinas, *Ethics and Infinity: Conversations with Philippe Nemo*, trans. Richard A. Cohen (Pittsburgh: Duquesne University Press, 1985), 85.
40. Levinas, *Is It Righteous to Be*, 114.
41. See Kevin Houser, "Facing the Space of Reasons," *Levinas Studies* 11 (2016): 132–46.
42. Chalier, *What Ought I to Do*, 74.
43. Levinas, "Freedom and Command," in *Collected Philosophical Papers*, trans. Alphonso Lingis (Pittsburgh: Duquesne University Press, 1987), 17.
44. Emmanuel Levinas, "Useless Suffering," in *Entre Nous: Thinking-of-the-Other*, trans. Michael B. Smith and Barbara Harshav (New York: Columbia University Press, 1998), 100.
45. See Houser, "Facing the Space of Reasons."
46. Emmanuel Levinas, "Diachrony and Representation," in *Entre Nous: Thinking-of-the-Other*, trans. Michael B. Smith and Barbara Harshav (New York: Columbia University Press, 1998), 171.
47. Charles W. Mills, *Blackness Visible: Essays on Philosophy and Race* (Ithaca: Cornell University Press, 1998), 6–7, 71.
48. Levinas, "The Name of a Dog," 153.
49. John Llewellyn, "Am I Obsessed by Bobby? (Humanism of the Other Animal)," in *Re-reading Levinas*, ed. Robert Bernasconi and Simon Critchley (Bloomington: Indiana University Press, 1991), 236.
50. Diane Perpich, *Ethics of Emmanuel Levinas*, 154.
51. Levinas, "Provocation of Morality," 172.
52. Ibid., 175.
53. Ibid., 176.
54. Ibid.
55. Levinas, *Otherwise Than Being*, 127.
56. Levinas, "Primacy of Pure Practical Reason," 451.
57. Emmanuel Levinas, *Totality and Infinity*, 298.
58. Emmanuel Levinas, prefatory note to "Reflections on the Philosophy of Hitlerism," trans. Seán Hand, *Critical Inquiry* 17 (Autumn 1990): 63.
59. See Barbara Jane Davy, "An Other Face of Ethics in Levinas," *Ethics and the Environment* 21, no. 1 (2007): 43.

60. Charles Darwin, *The Descent of Man, and Selection in Relation to Sex*, ed. Carl Zimmer (New York: Penguin, 2007), 157. See also *Descent of Man,* 193.
61. Ibid., 187.
62. Ibid., 189.

14

Aesthetic Disinterestedness and the Critique of Sentimentalism

Íngrid Vendrell Ferran

The notion of "aesthetic disinterestedness" has played a prominent role in aesthetics since its development as an autonomous discipline 200 years ago. The expression is used not only to describe the aesthetic experience, but also to prescribe how we should engage with aesthetically valuable objects. According to this normative use, appropriate responses to art must be free of practical concerns. This chapter examines how the notion "aesthetic disinterestedness" has been the underlying force behind attacks on the emotions in the arts. In particular, it focuses on the critiques of sentimentalism—a form of engagement with art aimed at experiencing emotions—developed by Moritz Geiger and José Ortega y Gasset within the field of phenomenological aesthetics.[1] The idea of "aesthetic disinterestedness" is a relatively recent philosophical notion whose origins are somewhat unclear. In a prominent article, Jerome Stolnitz argued that the notion was forged amid eighteenth-century British Empiricism. First employed in ethics, the term became progressively more significant for philosophical aesthetics. In the context of a differentiation between fine arts (related to beauty) and crafts (activities realized with a purpose), "disinterestedness" was used to refer to a specific form of engagement with aesthetic objects, becoming a common trait of experiences

Í. Vendrell Ferran (✉)
Goethe University Frankfurt, Frankfurt, Germany
e-mail: vendrell@em.uni-frankfurt.de

© The Author(s), under exclusive license to Springer Nature
Switzerland AG 2021
C. D. Coe (eds.), *The Palgrave Handbook of German Idealism and Phenomenology*,
Palgrave Handbooks in German Idealism,
https://doi.org/10.1007/978-3-030-66857-0_14

called aesthetic.[2] However, this view has since been challenged from various angles. It is not clear that the authors belonging to the empiricist tradition actually employed the concept to refer to a specific mode of perception that was purely aesthetic; nor is it clear that they were the first to use the term in this sense (Cassirer, who later seems to have changed his mind on this point, and Spaemann trace the origins of the concept to Leibniz).[3]

Though the connection between "disinterestedness" and the domain of the "aesthetic" existed long before Kant, it only became a *topos* in aesthetics after Kant used it in his seminal work *Critique of the Power of Judgment* (1790) to characterize *ex negativo* a quality of the judgment of taste. To be precise, Kant himself does not speak of disinterestedness, but rather of the absence of interest (CJ 90). As he puts it: "taste is the faculty for judging an object or a kind of representation through a satisfaction or dissatisfaction without any interest. The object of such a satisfaction is called beautiful" (CJ 96). The judgment of taste is based on a satisfaction without any interest, and as Guyer has shown: "The fact that a particular pleasure is felt apart from any interest, further, may be referred to as the disinterestedness of that pleasure."[4] According to Kant, not only does the pleasure in the beautiful originate apart from any interest, it is also not connected to the existence of its object and does not create any interest in the object: it is merely contemplative.

Unlike logical judgments, which are based on a concept, judgments of taste are based on a feeling of pleasure. Kant utilizes the absence of interest to justify the judgments of taste: it implies the exclusion of personal concerns, leading us to judge that the object contains a ground of satisfaction for everyone. In this context, the judgment of taste is defined as a universally valid judgment, which is based on a feeling of satisfaction.

Kant's view of aesthetics as independent of practical concerns, and his focus on the constitution of the object independently of its existence, resonated in the development of the discipline. It led to the view that we have to engage with art by adopting an aesthetic attitude akin to contemplation (aesthetic attitude), that we have to attend to the features and values of the work rather than the emotions elicited by it (intellectualized view of appreciation), and that artistic form is more important than content (predominance of form over content). By contrast, sentimentalism, as an attitude that leads us to focus on the emotions, is regarded as an aesthetic defect. Our emotional responses to art might be fueled by egoistic and selfish interests; they might be disproportionate, leading to an incorrect interpretation of the work, interfering with its appreciation; and they might distract us from important elements in the work. Sentimentalism, then, is seen as the opposite of disinterestedness and the antipole of enjoying art for art's sake.

It is precisely in this context, dominated as it is by the idea of "aesthetic disinterestedness," that we have to understand the various critiques of the emotions in the arts that have been formulated since Kant's time. For instance, Hanslick's influential diatribe against the role of emotion in music in *On the Musically Beautiful* (1854) was articulated in this context. Thus, though the idea does not originate in Kant's work, his aesthetics provided a substantive framework that facilitated the development of such critiques.[5] It is also against this background that we need to survey Geiger's and Ortega's respective critiques of sentimentalism, since both authors endorse the view that pleasure in art must be "disinterested."

It is particularly intriguing to note how the Kantian idea of aesthetic disinterestedness continues to motivate phenomenological aesthetics, despite the fact that in the field of ethics, phenomenology presents itself as breaking with Kant. For instance, in light of his value ethics, Scheler claimed that Kant was blind to values. Yet despite this dismissive posture in ethics, in aesthetics the analyses of Geiger and Ortega offer a different picture, insofar as they both share the Kantian view that pleasure in the arts must be free of practical concerns. However, as will become clear, their views of (what can be called in contemporary terms) "appreciation" differ from the view endorsed by Kant.

The chapter proceeds through three main sections. In the next two sections I present the critique of sentimentalism as a thread that runs through Geiger's aesthetics (section "Inner and Outer Concentration and the Dilettantism of the Aesthetic Experience") and explore its main argumentative axes (section "Aesthetic Value, Aesthetic Experience, and Aesthetic Attitude"). I then discuss Ortega's elaboration of Geiger's views (section "Artistic Sensibility, Blind and Seeing Pleasures, and Two Types of Interest"), before closing with some remarks on the plausibility of their critique in light of current philosophy of emotion.

Inner and Outer Concentration and the Dilettantism of the Aesthetic Experience

Moritz Geiger (1880–1937) was first trained in Wundt's experimental psychology, but soon moved to Munich to study with Lipps and became familiar with the phenomenology of Husserl, Pfänder, and Scheler. Geiger became one of the main representatives of the Munich Circle. In aesthetics, his main concern was to reconcile the objectivity of aesthetic values with the subjectivity of the aesthetic experience.

Geiger's aesthetics appears in "fragmentary" form.[6] Besides a few papers published during his lifetime, his aesthetics was developed in a series of manuscripts that were part of a book that he was planning already in the 1920s, but that remained unfinished due to his emigration and premature death. The posthumously published book *Die Bedeutung der Kunst* (1976) contains many of his published aesthetic papers and unpublished manuscripts. This book was partially published in English as *The Significance of Art* (1986), but unfortunately the main essays entailing his critique of sentimentalism have not been translated. In what follows, I will present Geiger's critique as one of the threads that run through his aesthetics.

Already in "Zum Problem der Stimmungseinfühlung" ("On the Problem of Mood Empathy") (1911), we can find a critique of the sentimental attitude in art that contains *in nuce* many of the aspects developed in later works. Here Geiger is concerned with how we experience inanimate objects—such as the painting of a landscape—as being melancholic, cheerful, tranquil, festive, or joyful. Employing a term coined by Lipps, he refers to this phenomenon as "empathy of mood."[7] For Geiger, being melancholic, cheerful, tranquil, festive, joyful, etc. are objective properties that can be "grasped" thanks to a non-propositional form of "knowing."

The subject who grasps such properties can adopt a "contemplative attitude" in which she contemplates the cheerfulness of the color and experiences it as something objective, or an "immersive attitude" in which not only does she perceive that the object has a property, but she is also touched by it.[8] Four main types of immersion are distinguished: (1) objective immersion: though being passive toward the perceived property, we experience it as "spreading" within us; (2) position-taking immersion: we adopt a stance toward the property and this stance in turn affects the way in which we perceive the aesthetic object; (3) sentimentalist immersion: we are not interested in the object, but only in how the property affects us; and (4) empathic immersion: we are completely absorbed by the property and become one with it.

Geiger's rejection of sentimentalism is presented in his discussion of the third form: "sentimentalist immersion." Unlike the first two, the sentimentalist is not interested in the properties of the object, but only in how these properties affect her. She focuses on the affective states elicited by the aesthetic object, and not on the object itself. While in the case of empathic immersion, we are aware of experiencing an emotion as a response to a property of the aesthetic object, in sentimentalist immersion, the object matters only insofar as it elicits emotions we can enjoy.

In *Beiträge zu einer Phänomenologie des ästhetischen Genusses* (*Contributions to a Phenomenology of Aesthetic Enjoyment*) (1913), Geiger develops these objections in more detail. The analysis is devoted to the phenomenon of aesthetic enjoyment which, according to him, has been neglected in research. He analyzes the main moments that are characteristic of enjoyment and applies them to the case of aesthetic enjoyment. These moments are the feeling of "depth" (a concept that he takes from Lipps and that later will play an important role in determining our engagement with art), the attitude of contemplation characterized by a distance toward the object, the mode in which it is experienced, the character of the object (appearances), and the constitution of the object as having a content of human significance.[9] Aesthetic enjoyment presupposes an aesthetic attitude of contemplation, i.e., a distance with respect to the object.

Geiger introduces here a distinction between two possible orientations while engaging with art: "inner concentration" (*Innenkonzentration*) and "outer concentration" (*Außenkonzentration*).[10] This distinction becomes a cornerstone of his aesthetics and helps to articulate his critique of sentimentalism. The terms refer to two possible directions in which our attention can move. With "inner concentration," the subject addresses herself inwardly, focusing on the affective states elicited by the aesthetic object and enjoying them. Geiger distinguishes two forms of "inner concentration": inner concentration *in* the emotion (*Innenkonzentration in Stimmungen*) and inner concentration *towards* the emotion (*Innenkonzentration auf Stimmungen*). Though the differences between the types are not easy to trace clearly, I propose to understand them as follows: the first consists in attending to the *experience* of the emotion (wherein the boundaries between ourselves and the emotion blur), while the second consists in attending to *the emotion* experienced (here the boundaries between self and emotion are preserved, and I am directed toward my emotion enjoying it).[11] With "outer concentration," the subject addresses herself to the aesthetic object and its values.

Though usually our engagement with works of art involves both kinds of attention, for Geiger only the enjoyment experienced in the "outer concentration" is genuinely aesthetic since it is only focused on the work itself and its values. Only this form is "disinterested" because it is free of the subject's concern for her own emotions. Regarding "inner concentration," he makes two observations. The enjoyment elicited by inner concentration *in* the emotion is pseudo-aesthetic: the work is used as a pretext to feel emotions and to enjoy feeling them (he mentions here Hanslick and his condemnatory view of emotions in the appreciation of music). The enjoyment elicited by inner concentration *towards* the experienced emotion, where the boundaries between self and emotion are preserved, can be aesthetic. However, this enjoyment does not focus on the aesthetic object, but on the emotions elicited by it, and as such it is not limited to aesthetics: it is not that we enjoy our aesthetic emotions, but that we aesthetically enjoy our emotions (aesthetic or not). We enjoy aesthetically our own feeling of vitality, emotions of success, and even negative emotions of sadness.

What Geiger had previously criticized in "Zum Problem" as "sentimental immersion" is now described in terms of "inner concentration." His conclusion is that genuine aesthetic enjoyment requires the containment of the self in order to focus on the object: this is only possible through "outer concentration."

The critique of sentimentalism is mainly developed in a collection of essays entitled *Zugänge zur Ästhetik* (*Approaches to Aesthetics*) (1928). In the Preface, Geiger warns of two aesthetic aberrations: sentimentalism as a remnant of Romanticism and, related to this, the conflation of surface and depth effects in the arts.[12] In contrast to its common use to describe the attitude of the artist, in the essay "Vom Dilettantismus im künstlerischen Erleben" ("On Dilettantism in Artistic Experience") the term "dilettantism," as used in the expression "dilettantism of the artistic experience,"[13] refers to the attitude of the subject who engages with art.

For dilettantism, two conditions are necessary: (1) that a work of art elicits in us an experience that has nothing to do with the values of the work, i.e., an experience that is inadequate to the values of the work; and (2) that the dilettante is unaware that this inadequate experience is not an authentic artistic experience. A person who focuses only on the superficial effects of an artwork is not a dilettante as long as she does not take such effects to be genuine artistic experiences (in this case, the first condition is given but not the second). In a similar vein, when a person engages with art for the sake of putting herself in a certain mood, she is not a dilettante (here too the second condition is missing).

All forms of dilettantism infringe Geiger's "basic principle of the aesthetic experience" according to which only those experiences that owe their origins to the value of the aesthetic object can be considered to be aesthetic experiences. Geiger discusses three forms:

1. The first consists in *focusing on the wrong aspects of the aesthetic object*— i.e., instead of focusing on the aesthetic values of the work, the dilettante focuses on its subject matter, on the induced emotions, or on the emotions elicited by empathy.[14]

   (a) In the *dilettantism of the subject matter of the work*, attention is paid to the content of the work rather than its artistic form. The patriot is enthusiastic about novels and dramas about his country, the religious man about images and novels dealing with religious topics, the worker with those depictions of problems pertaining to his social class, etc.

(b) In the *dilettantism of the induced emotions*, the focus lies on the emotions elicited by the work of art. The subject takes the content of the work as if it were real, instead of taking it as material of artistic creation; he experiences emotions and focuses on them.

(c) A complex case is constituted by the *dilettantism of empathic emotions*. Here, the subject puts herself in the shoes of the protagonists and experiences their emotions through a process of identification, allowing herself to experience emotions often repressed in real life. She focuses on such empathic emotions and takes them for authentic artistic experiences.

2. A specific case of dilettantism consists in *misjudging the aesthetic object*. Here we focus not on the value of the artwork, but on associations, images, or fantasies that are not essential to the work but that arise in connection with it.

3. The most problematic form of dilettantism is the *dilettantism of inner concentration*. According to Geiger, it is possible to take a stance toward the emotion as it occurs and relate to it without altering it. This view expands some of his previous work on the consciousness of feelings in *Das Bewußtsein von Gefühlen* (1911). In experiencing sadness, we can abandon ourselves to this emotion or we can distance ourselves from it. This stance is not a reflection about the emotion, but a mode in which we are affectively involved with our emotions in the moment they occur.

As in the previous texts, experiences that arise in inner concentration are described here as typical of "sentimentalism." What is new in *Zugänge* is that Geiger employs these terms not only to refer to two *modes of attention*, but to what can be interpreted as *habits* in our engagement with art.

For Geiger, some lovers of art consider art only as an instrument to induce and enjoy emotions of all kinds. For such people, art is hardly any different from alcohol or any other drug; the only difference being that engaging with art is considered to be a "noble" activity. Following Hanslick, Geiger seems to complain about music lovers who just want to be transported by it and to experience a certain mood.[15]

In the text, he also discusses the *historical origins* of dilettantism by analyzing how emotions became progressively central for art.[16] Geiger notes three moments of particular significance. First, Romantic arguments advocating for the unity of art, religion, and philosophy, as well as for the unity of all arts, are built on the idea that what unifies all these different spheres is a feeling. Second, Romanticism understands the world as a creation of the subject and, at a smaller level, the work of art is understood as being dependent upon the experiencer and her feelings. Finally, Romanticism brought with it an emphasis on emotion in the arts (especially in music), which meant that artworks were only seen to be of value when they induced emotions. Romanticism put the emotions—the most subjective of all our mental states—at the center of aesthetic experience. After Romanticism, the next generations contributed to the development of inner concentration, fostering dilettantism.

Geiger's analysis proceeds by identifying the main *psychological sources* of dilettantism. The first is that of "comfortableness," the attitude of abandonment to the emotions. When art is thought to relax and entertain, there is no place for outer concentration, which requires intellectual effort. The second source is an "excess of self-concern" that is typical of some people who are preoccupied with themselves and who lack the ability to focus on the aesthetic object. A third source is what Geiger calls "auto-aestheticism" (analogous to auto-eroticism). "Soft" and "feminine" natures are, in his view, receptive of emotion and take pleasure in having emotions of all kinds: they enjoy the joy of a success or of being in love, and they also enjoy the sadness over the loss of a loved one.

Next, Geiger identifies the *conceptual frames* that have paved the way to the "effect view of art."[17] The latter view (which Geiger sees as dominant at the time) fosters inner concentration because it focuses on the effects of art on us (such as emotions). According to Geiger, during the Enlightenment, the aesthetic experience was described as a form of judgment and knowledge. Even for the proponents of the idea that it is a "sentiment," this sentiment was associated with knowledge (a vague and indistinct form of knowledge). A change began to take place with Rousseau, and later with Tetens, Mendelssohn, and Kant, since, for these authors, the emotions took on the status of a faculty of the mind. Nevertheless, even in Kant the word "emotion" preserves the double meaning of the word "sentiment," having both an intellectual and an affective meaning: pleasure is, for Kant, not just a sensation, since it is directed toward an object (pleasure in the harmony of the faculties). This primitive cognitive function of the emotions is still tangible in the metaphysical aesthetics of the nineteenth century. For these authors (even in Schopenhauer), in the artistic experience there is a knowledge of something metaphysical. All this changed with the advent of psychological aesthetics, a theoretical frame which, in Geiger's view, gave dilettantism its ultimate conceptual support. A process in which the emotions become free of intellect, and in which the aesthetic experience is simply one of passive pleasure elicited by an object, finds its culmination in psychological aesthetics (though he does not mention specifically the representatives of this view, we can suppose that he has in mind the likes of Fechner and Wundt). This "effect view of art" interprets the aesthetic experience as pure emotion, free of any intellectual content, and the value of a work of art is reduced to the value of its effects on us.

Against the backdrop of a divide between an "emotion-free intellectualism" and an "intellect-free sentimentalism," Geiger proposes a third way: the "emotional grasping of artistic values." I will examine this notion in more detail below, but for now let me note that the description of the grasping of value—a key term of Geiger's aesthetics—in terms of a "feeling" or "emotional grasping" (which is cognitive because it makes values accessible) makes clear that his critique of sentimentalism is not a critique of the emotions per se, but rather a critique of an exclusive focus on the emotional responses to the work as mere feelings that are devoid or independent of cognitive elements.

In his posthumously published "Pleasure and Enjoyment" and "The Aesthetic Attitude," Geiger again describes sentimentalism as a "false inner attitude to the work of art" and characterizes it as "irresponsible."[18] We have to focus on the work and its values, and not on the emotions elicited by it.

Aesthetic Value, Aesthetic Experience, and Aesthetic Attitude

Why did this critique come to occupy such a central place in his thinking? This section argues that sentimentalism goes against Geiger's understanding of aesthetic appreciation. Rather than grasping the values of the work and allowing them to move us existentially, sentimentalism focuses exclusively on the surface effects of the work and on our enjoyment. To develop my argument, I examine how sentimentalism undermines the three main pillars of his aesthetics built on the notions of value, experience, and attitude. I also show that underlying his critique is the concept of aesthetic disinterestedness. However, the version of this notion endorsed by Geiger differs from that of Kant in some significant respects, and Geiger was cautious in making the differences visible to his reader.

(a) Aesthetic value

For Geiger, aesthetics is "the science of the forms and laws of aesthetic value."[19] At that time, it was not uncommon to understand aesthetics as a value science (similar views can be found in Lipps and the authors of the Graz School), but Geiger was the first to put the concept of value at the core of phenomenological aesthetics (a path followed by Ingarden, Hartmann, and Hildebrand).

Against absolutism, which considers values to be independent of the subjects who experience them, and against relativism, which reduces aesthetic value to subjective experience (mainly emotions), Geiger defends an objectivist view, according to which values are experienced as being objectively there for the subject who grasps them. Objectivism was widely endorsed by other phenomenologists, particularly in the field of ethics. For Geiger, as well as for Reinach and Scheler, values are given to us in the "grasping of values."[20] This is a *sui generis* capacity that is irreducible to perception, emotion, or belief. The landscape is not cheerful because we perceive this cheerfulness as we perceive its color (none of our senses presents the cheerfulness), nor do we grasp this cheerfulness by way of an emotion (we can "see" the cheerfulness of the landscape despite being depressed), nor do we judge the landscape to be such (we do not apply general categories to a specific case in order to evaluate it). The capacity to grasp values is an immediate disclosure of the evaluative properties of objects.

This view does not imply that values are "absolute," but only that they have "phenomenological objectivity," i.e., we experience them as being objectively there for us.[21] Geiger distinguishes this phenomenological objectivity from actual or concrete objectivity. Thus, being given objectively, values might be the object of disagreement between subjects according to their subjective preferences.

In "Pleasure and Enjoyment," Geiger applies the thesis of the "grasping of values" to aesthetics and refers to it as a "pleasure" or "liking" (*Gefallen*). This kind of "pleasure" has to be distinguished from "enjoyment" (*Genuss*). Pleasure is the act through which we come to grasp aesthetic values, while enjoyment is pure feeling, excitement, but does not grasp the value. The statement "I like this picture" or "this picture pleases me" involves adopting an inner attitude—a "yes"—to the picture: "The picture is there before me and raises in me the question of what attitude to adopt toward it. And the answer may turn out to be positive or negative: I may like or dislike the picture. This is not an intellectual yea-saying or nay-saying; it is a pre-intellectual attitude conforming to feeling."[22] On the contrary, enjoyment is not an answer to a question that the work of art poses, but an emotional reaction to the work.

The differences between pleasure and enjoyment can be summarized as follows: (1) liking has an opposite, namely disliking (pleasure/displeasure), but enjoying has no direct opposite; (2) pleasure is an active attitude toward the object, while enjoyment is passive; (3) in pleasure, we are open to the value qualities of the object. It is a "yes" to the values of the object or a "no" to its disvalues. It is a pleasure *in* the values of the object. Enjoyment is enjoyment of the effects upon oneself. In short: "pleasure has sight; enjoyment is blind."[23] An additional argument can be seen in the fact that pleasure and enjoyment might come into conflict: it is possible to see the defects of a melody and be displeased by them, and yet psychologically enjoy the experience of being transported by it. We hear something like the voice of aesthetic conscience, but our emotions proceed regardless and enjoy the melody though being displeased by it. Against this backdrop, we can understand how in Geiger's view, sentimentalism is the attitude that focuses exclusively on our enjoyment rather than on liking and disliking the values of the work; that is to say, it ignores the fact that the main task of engaging with art is not to enjoy its effects on us, but to grasp its values.

In the manuscript "Aesthetischer Absolutismus" ("Aesthetic Absolutism"), Geiger describes a movement from absolutism to relativism in aesthetics in which Kant is seen as acting as a juncture between both positions. For Geiger, Kant's aesthetic judgment is a judgment about our pleasure, but not a judgment about a property of the object.[24] Though the judgment "this table is round" seems similar to the judgment "this painting is beautiful," the first is a judgment about a property of the table, while the second is essentially different: it means that the painting is an object of my pleasure. Thus, Kant's aesthetic judgment is a "judgment of reflection," a judgment about an emotional response, and as such it is subjective and individual. However, as Geiger indicates, Kant formulates it as if it were a universal judgment and, as a result, his view entails a paradox: a judgment based on the most subjective of our experiences, on an emotion, is at the same time universal. In contrast, for Geiger, an aesthetic judgment cannot be based on an emotional response (in terms of enjoyment or satisfaction), since what counts for him is the grasping of the values of the work and, as we have already seen, this grasping of values (or pleasure in the work) is clearly different from the enjoyment elicited by the work.

Despite this critique, Geiger's view of Kant is quite ambivalent. On the one hand, in distinguishing between aesthetic judgment, logical judgment, and the judgment of the agreeable, Geiger views Kant as having paved the way for aesthetics to become an autonomous discipline. On the other hand, the

paradox presented by Kant led to two different but, for Geiger, equally problematic solutions: it led to the claim that aesthetic judgment is not grounded
on subjective emotion, but is universal (Geiger attributes this view to German
Idealism); and it led to the claim that aesthetic judgment can be explained in
terms of the judgment of the agreeable, leaving the door open to aesthetic
relativism (the view endorsed by the "aesthetics of effect"). Against both,
Geiger proposes the objectivism of aesthetic value.

(b) Aesthetic experience

Geiger's view of the aesthetic experience, as noted above, is condensed in
the basic principle of aesthetics: only those experiences that originate from
the values of the work are aesthetic. This idea is at work in "Surface and
Depth Effects of Art" where he discusses the conflation of superficial and deep
effects of the arts. Geiger's main line of attack is against those theories that do
not distinguish between the aesthetic and our everyday experiences, thereby
leading to a "leveling" of the aesthetic experience.[25] The distinction between
surface and depth effects is not a distinction between inferior and superior
levels, but rather one between artistic and non-artistic (or extra-artistic) levels
of engagement. It refers to the capacity of art to affect us in the vital and
personal spheres. This distinction is based on the phenomenological idea of
different levels or strata of the person—an idea that was chiefly developed by
Scheler.[26]

Depth effects "appeal to the depths of the self and lay hold of its deeper
nature."[27] The notion of depth, which already appeared in Geiger's *Beiträge*,
is used here to indicate that a work of art can attract and mobilize central
aspects of our person. Depth effects affect the personal sphere: they touch the
core of the self and elicit "happiness" (Glück) which is "the core of aesthetic
experience."[28] Depth effects require that we consciously grasp the artistic
values, and that we allow them to affect us. This happens only in "outer
concentration."[29] In contrast, surface effects are not uniform in their nature:
"amusement" or "pleasure effects" (we are amused by a farce or a joke), but
also having feelings evoked by sentimental songs, the delight in the excitement of a melodrama, or the tension felt while engaging with an adventure
story would count as such surface effects. Surface effects are related to non-
aesthetic effects, to the vital sphere, and can be found outside the arts. This
distinction makes his critique of sentimentalism intelligible: sentimentalism
remains focused on the work's surface effects.

This description complements Geiger's description of the aesthetic experience set out in "Pleasure and Enjoyment" where he describes it as a mixture

of effects and the grasping of values of the work, as a combination of pleasure and enjoyment. All aesthetics based only on enjoyment (basically all
aesthetics of effect) is incomplete, because it reduces the value of the artwork
to the value of its effects on us. Kant, despite being presented as defending a
hybrid position between the aesthetic of value and the aesthetic of effects, is
described here as the "first to recognize that aesthetic judgment is concerned
with the effect upon ourselves."[30] Kant and empiricism are presented as
fostering the development of an aesthetics of effect. After Kant, the progressive focus on the effects of art prompted the development of an aesthetics
based on enjoyment rather than on pleasure and value. Other factors that
influenced this development include the conviction that value has no place
in science; the rise of relativism; the new conception of emotion as a faculty of
the mind; the idea that values must be psychological (leading to the reduction
of values to feelings); and a "leveling" tendency in aesthetics.

(iii) Aesthetic attitude

For Geiger, happiness—the central aspect of the aesthetic experience—
can only be achieved in the aesthetic attitude in which the existential self is
exposed to grasp the values of the work. This claim is based on a distinction
between the "active self" of our everyday life and the "existential self" that is
involved on the vital and personal levels. As he puts it in the "The Aesthetic
Attitude": "The aesthetic attitude is the one in which aesthetic values are
grasped and it is the prerequisite needed for these values to find their way
into the existential self."[31]
By using the label "aesthetic attitude," Geiger is arguing for a view in which
the notion of "outer concentration" is central. However, outer concentration alone cannot explain the aesthetic attitude. The person of action and
the scientist are also in an attitude of outer concentration. Thus, "aesthetic
outer concentration" involves two further elements: "aesthetic intuition" and
"contemplation." Intuition is not conceptual knowledge, but an immediate
grasping of the values and value patterns of the work. Aesthetic intuition
differs from the active attitude of our everyday life: while in active life, objects
are considered in their "use value," in the aesthetic attitude, we consider them
in their "sensuous appearance." To grasp the sensuous character in intuition,
the work of art must be contemplated. While we are usually absorbed in
different activities, in "contemplation" we isolate and grasp the sensuous character of the work, separating the self from the object. This view enables us to
understand why sentimentalism is wrong: it focuses on surface effects that
affect the vital sphere, rather than on those effects on the personal level that

move the existential self. It arises from an attitude of inner concentration and not of the attitude of aesthetic outer concentration.

Geiger's account of the aesthetic attitude motivates a twofold discussion of Kant.[32] According to Geiger, Kant distinguishes between "free" and "dependent" beauty, with only pure beauty being genuinely aesthetic (though Geiger does not mention it, Kant develops the distinction in §16 of the third *Critique*). The beauty of a human being is beauty mixed with values with other origins. For human appearance must be conceived in terms of man, and this entails placing it under the concept of "man." However, since beautiful is only that which pleases "without a concept," for Kant man is not an object of pure aesthetic satisfaction. The problem with this classification, according to Geiger, is that Kant does not distinguish between conceptual classification and the sensuous, immediate grasping of values. Geiger's understanding of the grasping of values as immediate acquaintance with values without the necessity of a concept makes it applicable to objects of different kinds (objects that may or may not involve a concept).

Geiger connects these reflections to a discussion of Kant's notion of "disinterested pleasure." The "profound truth" of this phrase—as Geiger puts it—is that "[o]ne must not take any personal interest in the work of art, any interest that arises from one's empirical ego."[33] Here, Geiger observes that the word "interest" has two meanings, which neither Kant nor his critics keep clearly distinguished. Interest is essential in relating to objects of significance for us, but the term can also be employed to refer to specific practical interests of the empirical ego. In Geiger's view, Kant includes both meanings in his idea of "disinterested pleasure." For Kant, "disinterestedness" means the exclusion of the empirical ego and the absence of the will, and he introduces the concept in order to distinguish the aesthetic judgment from other forms of judgment and to explain how it is universal. However, Kant does not see that while personal practical interests are excluded from our engagement with art, our main motivation for engaging with art is that we are interested in extracting its value. For Geiger, Kant ignores the fact that the exclusion of personal interests is necessary above all to allow the values of the artwork to affect the existential self.

Geiger's ideas about value, experience, and attitude converge in a specific view of what can be called "aesthetic appreciation" (though Geiger does not use this term), according to which phenomenologically objective aesthetic values are grasped in acts of pleasure (in the sense of liking or disliking). These values might affect us at the vital and personal levels and serve as a source of enjoyment and happiness. As a prerequisite for aesthetic experience, we must adopt an aesthetic attitude of contemplative distance between the self and the work, so that the values of the work can be intuitively grasped and can affect the existential self.

As Geiger notes, this view of appreciation differs substantially from the one put forward by Kant. Geiger does not ground the aesthetic judgment on an emotion of pleasure, but on grasping the objective aesthetic values of the work. Thus, his main interest is in values, not effects. He distinguishes between pleasure *in* the work as a form to extract its values and enjoyment *as a response to* the work, and between empirical practical interests that must be excluded and existential ones that guide our engagement with the work.

Nevertheless, these differences aside, underlying Geiger's aesthetics and motivating his critique of sentimentalism is the idea of "aesthetic disinterestedness," the "profound truth" laid out by Kant. Thus, while endorsing a different view of appreciation, he shares with Kant the idea that aesthetic pleasure must be free of practical concerns. It is not without reason that he feels compelled to present his view by having frequent recourse to Kant as a critical foil.

The motive of "aesthetic disinterestedness" is present in his intellectualized view of appreciation and his notion of aesthetic attitude. Regarding the first, Geiger is embedded in a long tradition for which any focus on the emotions interferes with rather than enables and enhances appreciation, thereby defending an "intellectualized view of appreciation."[34] Attending to the emotions while engaging with art draws attention away from the important aspects of the work: its formal features and values. Though the intellectualized model is typical for authors who defend formalism, Geiger advocates a version of it. However, he did not endorse formalism because he considered the content of the work to be significant, though to a lesser extent. Against the dilettante of inner concentration, he argues that we should attend to the values of the work, rather than its subject matter or its effects on us (the elicited emotions). Attending to the content or the emotions is motivated by the practical concerns of our everyday life (interest in the destinies of others, in emotions and feelings, etc.).

Moreover, the notion of "aesthetic disinterestedness" underlies his description of the aesthetic attitude in terms of the contemplation and distance between the subject and the object of appreciation, which excludes only practical, empirical, selfish concerns (the experience of certain contents, imaginings, associations, and emotions regardless of the aesthetic values of the work), but not the deep interest in extracting the values of the work and in being moved by it. This view is extremely appealing in the context of contemporary attacks on the notion of the aesthetic attitude. Dickie—one of the most prominent detractors of the idea of an aesthetic attitude—argues that this notion is a "myth" because it assumes the possibility of a "disinterested attention" and a "disinterested pleasure."[35] However, the notion of aesthetic attitude defended by Geiger does not employ any of these assumptions. First, his model does not employ the notion of disinterested attention. He distinguishes two forms of attention—the inner and the outer—involved in appreciation and claims that only the second is genuinely aesthetic. Outer concentration is not "disinterested": it is a form of attention "interested in" grasping the aesthetic values of the work, which as such must exclude practical concerns. Second, when Geiger speaks of a disinterested pleasure, this concerns only the pleasure that arises out of our engagement with the work as effect, but not the pleasure "in" the values of the work (the liking and disliking) which moves us to extract its value.

Artistic Sensibility, Blind and Seeing Pleasures, and Two Types of Interest

Geiger's work remained unknown to the wider public, but his ideas on inner and outer concentration found a fervent reader in José Ortega y Gasset (1883–1955), the ambassador of phenomenology in the Spanish-speaking world. Ortega was deeply influenced by Kant and the neo-Kantianism of Hermann Cohen and Paul Natorp. However, his interest in examining the concept of experience led him to phenomenology. As a reader of the *Jahrbuch*, he knew well Geiger's *Beiträge* and took up the distinction between the inner and outer concentration to develop his own critique of sentimentalism, which was widely discussed.[36]

Ortega's objections against sentimentalism can be traced back to "Musicalia I" and "Musicalia II" where he (probably under the influence of Hanslick) argues that the new music lacks popularity because the public cannot recognize their own emotions in it.[37] This idea is expanded to other arts (painting, poetry, and theater) in *The Dehumanization of Art* (1925). In his view, modern art is essentially unpopular, even "antipopular," and it will always have the masses against it. This is not a question of personal taste, but one of the capacity to understand it: "It is not that the majority does not *like* the art of the young and the minority likes it, but that the majority, the masses, do not *understand* it."[38] Using terminology that echoes Scheler's vocabulary on the feeling of values, Ortega claims that some persons possess "an organ of comprehension" denied to others and that the average person realizes that he is blind to understand modern art.

The pleasure that arises from participating in the joys and sorrows of the figures is, for Ortega, indistinguishable from pleasure in ordinary life. We are in the same practical attitude and remain oriented to the "human aspects" (human affairs, fates, and emotions) of the work. This kind of pleasure is not genuinely aesthetic because it considers the artistic form only as an instrument through which to participate emotionally in the work. For Ortega: "Not only is grieving and rejoicing at such human destinies as a work of art presents or narrates a very different thing from true artistic pleasure, but preoccupation with the human content of the work is in principle incompatible with aesthetic enjoyment proper."[39] Genuine aesthetic pleasure is incompatible with the enjoyment of the content of the work and of the elicited emotions. The incompatibility is described in terms of an "optical problem," or to put it otherwise, in terms of modes of attention. If we are seeking to be moved by the content of the work, then we have to take the destinies of the protagonists as if they were real, but in order to enjoy a work of art, we have to see it as a work of art and not as something real. Moving from literary examples to paintings, Ortega claims that in order to see a portrait, we have to see the portrait and not the person presented in it. In short, the perception of human reality in art (or, as he calls it, of "lived reality") and perception of artistic form are incompatible because they call for different forms of attention.

This critique of sentimentalism has two different sources. First, the claim that we can only appreciate the work of art if we attend to its constitution and not to the emotions is a clear restatement of Geiger's idea that only outer concentration is genuinely aesthetic. However, unlike Geiger, Ortega advocates for formalism and, again unlike Geiger, argues for the incompatibility of both modes of attention. The incompatibility thesis is developed by taking Husserl's phenomenology of image consciousness, i.e., of how it comes to be that we see represented objects in paintings, as a source. In changing his examples from literature to portraits, Ortega reflects this influence and seeks to make clear that when we engage with art, we have to see the work of art as art and not as merely representing a specific theme. To see a portrait, we have to see the portrait as an artistic representation, and not the real person represented in it. Both modes of consciousness (being conscious of a portrait as portrait and being conscious of the subject represented in it) are incompatible, since they refer to different levels of the artwork.

According to Ortega, the sensibility of the new art is the power to focus on images and not on the content of the work. Given that the majority can focus only on the content of the work and on the elicited emotions, the new art is unpopular among the masses. One of the features of the new style and the new sensibility is that they tend to "dehumanize" art. What does this mean? By means of an example, Ortega illustrates how the same reality can be lived from different points of view, each being authentic. Imagine a dying man with his wife, his doctor, a reporter, and a painter at his bedside. The situation remains the same, but the way in which each of these individuals lives the situation is radically different. The degree of "emotional distance" in each person differs. While the dying man, the wife, and the doctor *live in* the situation (though each from a different perspective: the man is dying, the wife is suffering for him, and the doctor is trying to alleviate his pain), the reporter *pretends to live* it while the painter is in a "*purely perceptive attitude*" observing reality.[40] The human point of view is one in which we "live" in situations; it is not one in which we pretend to live them or are merely an observer. According to Ortega, the art of the middle of the nineteenth century aims at giving the depicted objects the same appearance that they have as part of the lived and human experience, while in modern painting the opposite is the case: namely it goes *against* reality, shattering the human aspects, "dehumanizing" it. In this new sensibility, emotions are only of secondary importance.

At this point, Ortega introduces a distinction between blind and seeing pleasures. "Blind pleasures" are those (and he uses an analogy with a drunken man) in which our happiness is blind: blind pleasures are caused by the work, but do not grasp its values. "Seeing pleasures" are of a different kind: we are happy about something, conscious of what motivates the happiness. In his view, "aesthetic pleasure must be a seeing pleasure,"[41] insofar as it must grasp the values of the work. This distinction is close to Geiger's distinction between enjoyment and pleasure developed three years later in *Zugänge* (though the idea was already present in an elemental form in the *Beiträge*). Like Geiger and the other early phenomenologists, Ortega is endorsing the claim that values are grasped in a feeling. In his essay "Qué son los valores?" he refers to this as the capacity to "estimate" (*estimar*), and on the basis of this capacity he sketches an "estimative" (*estimativa*) as the science that explains how we grasp values.[42]

The critique of sentimentalism appears in "Note on the Novel" (1925) and is linked to a distinction between "action and contemplation."[43] What happens in the plot of a novel might be necessary to enjoy it, but in itself it does not have aesthetic value (here again, only outer concentration is aesthetically valuable). Contemplation and interest (as practical interest, action) are presented as "polar forms of consciousness which in principle exclude one another."[44] Underlying this view is the idea that aesthetic appreciation must be disinterested. Yet, for Ortega, pure contemplation does not exist. The optimum condition for contemplation is when we have been moved first by an interest in the work of art. With this, he distinguishes between practical interests derived from our everyday life and the deeper interests of contemplation that move us to engage with the dimension of the aesthetic values of the work.

Unlike Geiger, Ortega's critique of sentimentalism is linked to a defense of formalism. Some have seen in this defense the direct influence of Kant.[45] It is likely that he was also influenced by Hanslick. In addition, their methodological approaches are quite distinct: Geiger analyzes the self and self-consciousness, while Ortega focuses on a specific cultural manifestation of the new art and its lack of popularity. However, as in Geiger's work, we find in Ortega an intellectualized view of appreciation and a description of the aesthetic attitude defined in terms of contemplation. Given his view that the arts strive to realize, in their respective media, the aesthetic values, it is not surprising that he regards sentimentalism as an aesthetic defect. Thus, despite endorsing a view of appreciation that differs from that of Kant, Ortega leaves the central idea of the Kantian aesthetics untouched, namely that our engagement with art must be free of practical concerns.

Concluding Remarks

This chapter has examined Geiger's and Ortega's phenomenological critiques of sentimentalism. These critiques are articulated around three main argumentative axes: the existence of an aesthetic attitude in which we are not moved by practical interests; an intellectualized view of appreciation, according to which emotions might distract us from attending to the aesthetic values of the work; and the predominance of form over content. Underlying these claims is the idea of "aesthetic disinterestedness," an idea that became a major theme in aesthetics after Kant placed it at the center of his system, though the phenomenologists examined here defend substantially different views of appreciation than the one endorsed by Kant.

The phenomenological attacks on sentimentalism are not directed at sentimentality per se or at being emotionally moved by art; rather, they are aimed at the tendency to focus on the emotions instead of the values of the artwork. However, against the background of contemporary emotion theory and the new views of appreciation that attribute a cognitive function to the emotions, we might ask whether the phenomenological critique is legitimate and whether a focus on the emotions might indeed contribute to appreciation, for instance, by drawing our attention to significant elements of the work, by fostering our imaginings, and by making the grasping of aesthetic values more complete.[46]

Notes

1. The phenomenological aesthetics developed by Geiger, Ortega y Gasset, Ingarden, Hartmann, or von Hildebrand has been largely neglected. This chapter aims to fill this lacuna by discussing two representatives of the first generation.

2. Jerome Stolnitz, "On the Origins of 'Aesthetic Disinterestedness,'" *The Journal of Aesthetics and Art Criticism* 20, no. 2 (1961): 131–43.

3. For objections against Stolnitz, see Miles Rind, "The Concept of Disinterestedness in Eighteenth-Century British Aesthetics," *Journal of the History of Philosophy* 40, no. 1 (2002): 67–87; for an overview of the concept of "disinterestedness," see Werner Strube, "Interesselosigkeit: Zur Geschichte eines Grundbegriffs der Ästhetik," *Archiv für Begriffsgeschichte* 23, no. 2 (1979): 148–74.

4. Paul Guyer, *Kant and the Claims of Taste* (Cambridge, MA: Harvard University Press, 1979), 167.

5. In the Anglo-American tradition, the idea that Hanslick's work is rooted in Kantian aesthetics is widely accepted. However, this thesis is controversial, since there is a lack of convergence regarding the foundations of Hanslick's thought. See Christopher Landerer and Alexander Wilfing, "Eduard Hanslick's *Vom Musikalisch-Schönen*: Text, Contexts, and their Developmental Dimensions; Towards a Dynamic View of Hanslick's Aesthetics," *Musicologica Austriaca* (2018).

6. For introductions to Geiger's aesthetics, see Klaus Berger, "Die Bedeutung der Kunst," in Moritz Geiger, *Die Bedeutung der Kunst. Zugänge zu einer materialen Wertästhetik*, ed. Klaus Berger and Wolfhart Henckmann (München: Fink, 1976), 14; Wolfhart Henckmann, "Moritz Geigers Konzeption einer phänomenologischen Ästhetik," in *Die Bedeutung der Kunst. Zugänge zu einer materialen Wertästhetik*, ed. Klaus Berger and Wolfhart Henckmann (München: Fink, 1976), 550; and Klaus Berger, "Editor's Introduction," in Moritz Geiger, *The Significance of Art*, ed. Klaus Berger (Lanham, MD: University Press of America, 1986), ix–xx.

7. Theodor Lipps, *Ästhetik: Psychologie des Schönen und der Kunst* (Hamburg/Leipzig: Leopold Voss, 1903), 93–223.

8. Moritz Geiger, "Zum Problem der Stimmungseinfühlung" (1911), in *Die Bedeutung der Kunst: Zugänge zu einer materialen Wertästhetik*, ed. Klaus Berger and Wolfhart Henckmann (München: Fink, 1976), 41.

9. Moritz Geiger, *Beiträge zur Phänomenologie des ästhetischen Genusses* (1913) (Tübingen: Niemeyer, 1974), 582.

10. Ibid., 636.

11. Ibid., 639.

12. Moritz Geiger, "Zugänge zur Ästhetik," in *Die Bedeutung der Kunst. Zugänge zu einer materialen Wertästhetik*, ed. Klaus Berger and Wolfhart Henckmann (Wilhelm Fink Verlag: München, 1976), 133.

13. Ibid., 137.

14. Ibid., 140.

15. Ibid., 153.

16. Ibid., 156 and 169.

17. Ibid., 166.

18. Geiger, *The Significance of Art*, 77–78.

19. Ibid., 61.

20. Adolf Reinach, "Die Überlegung; ihre ethische und rechtliche Bedeutung" (1912/1913), in *Sämtliche Werke. Textkritische Ausgabe* 1 + 2, ed. Karl Schuhmann and Barry Smith (München: Philosophia, 1989), 295; and Max Scheler, *Formalism in Ethics and Non-formal Ethics of Values* (Evanston, IL: Northwestern University Press, 1973), 259, where Scheler clearly describes the value-feeling as an "organ" for the apprehension of values.

21. Geiger, *The Significance of Art*, 65.

22. Ibid., 62.

23. Ibid., 63.

24. Geiger, "Zugänge zur Ästhetik," 368–69.

25. Geiger, *The Significance of Art*, 46.

26. Scheler, *Formalism in Ethics*, 295.

27. Geiger, *The Significance of Art*, 47.

28. Ibid., 181.

29. Ibid., 52.

30. Ibid., 69.

31. Ibid., 186.

32. Ibid., 190.

33. Ibid., 202.

34. This expression was coined by Susan Feagin, "Affects in Appreciation," in *The Oxford Handbook of Philosophy of Emotion*, ed. Peter Goldie (Oxford: Oxford University Press, 2013), 636.

35. George Dickie, "The Myth of the Aesthetic Attitude," in *Introductory Readings in Aesthetics*, ed. John Hospers (New York: The Free Press, 1969), 37. Dickie is reacting in particular to Stolnitz's "The Aesthetic Attitude," in *Introductory Readings in Aesthetics*, 17–27.

36. For an analysis of Geiger as the main source of Ortega's aesthetic views, see Nelson R. Orringer, "Esthetic Enjoyment in Ortega y Gasset and in Geiger, a Newly Discovered Source," *Revue de Littératur comparée* 89 (1974): 36.

37. Published in the journal *El Sol*, Madrid, March 8, 1921, and March 24, 1921, respectively.

38. José Ortega y Gasset, "The Dehumanization of Art," in *The Dehumanization of Art and Other Essays on Art, Culture, and Literature* (Princeton: Princeton University Press, 2019), 5.

39. Ibid., 10.
40. Ibid., 17.
41. Ibid., 27.
42. José Ortega y Gasset, *Introducción a una estimativa: Qué son los valores?* (Encuentro: Madrid, 2004).
43. José Ortega y Gasset, "Notes on the Novel," in *The Dehumanization of Art and Other Essays on Art, Culture, and Literature* (Princeton: Princeton University Press, 2019): 80–87.
44. Ibid., 83.
45. Francisco Abad Nebot, "La estética de Kant en España (Notas en el segundo centenario de la Crítica del Juicio)," *Anuario de la Sociedad Española de Literatura General y Comparada* VIII (1990): 28.
46. For a defense of sentimentality in the arts, see Robert C. Solomon, "In Defense of Sentimentality," in *Emotion and the Arts*, ed. Mette Hjort and Sue Laver (Oxford: Oxford University Press, 1997), 225–45. For theories of appreciation focused on the role of feeling, see Jenefer Robinson, "Emotional Responses to Music. What Are They? How Do They Work? And Are They Relevant to Aesthetic Appreciation?" in *The Oxford Handbook of Philosophy of Emotion*, ed. Peter Goldie (Oxford: Oxford University Press, 2013), 651–80, and the chapter by Susan Feagin mentioned above. For the view that emotions enhance appreciation, see Íngrid Vendrell Ferran, "Emotion in the Appreciation of Fiction," *Journal of Literary Theory* 12, no. 2 (2018): 204–23.

Part IV

Time, Memory, and History

15

Redeeming German Idealism: Schelling and Rosenzweig

Jason M. Wirth

On April 15, 1918, Franz Rosenzweig (1886–1929) wrote to his mother of the preeminence of Schelling in his own thought, calling him his "patron saint."[1] Rosenzweig had discovered the famous 1797 *System* fragment in the Prussian State Library in Berlin,[2] which, despite being in Hegel's hand, was the collaboration of Hegel, Hölderlin, and Schelling. When Rosenzweig published his "handwritten find," he argued that it must have been Hegel's transcription of Schelling's thought. Although disputes over such claims seem endless,[3] it spoke to Rosenzweig of a way out of the profanely closed system, a system without absolute exteriority, that he identified with Hegel. As is well known, Rosenzweig had a dramatic break with Hegel in particular and German Idealism more broadly, as strikingly evidenced in his magnum opus, *The Star of Redemption* (*Der Stern der Erlösung*). In the third or 1815 draft of *Die Weltalter* (*The Ages of the World*), Schelling writes that while "all knowledge must pass through the dialectic," striving to break free from the formal structures of thought into the singularities of history, becoming "so vital that knowledge, which, according to its matter and the meaning of the word, is history, could also be history according to its external form" (I/8,

J. M. Wirth (✉)
Department of Philosophy, Seattle University, Seattle, WA, USA
e-mail: wirthj@seattleu.edu

© The Author(s), under exclusive license to Springer Nature
Switzerland AG 2021
C. D. Coe (eds.), *The Palgrave Handbook of German Idealism and Phenomenology*,
Palgrave Handbooks in German Idealism,
https://doi.org/10.1007/978-3-030-66857-0_15

205).[4] Schelling continued his turn toward what he called "positive philosophy," philosophy attuned to the revelation of singularities. This emerges "*toto caelo*" differently than from the "universality" and "indeterminacy" of what Schelling called "negative" thought, which remains formal and structural, and transpires within reason, as does the dialectic. The positive does not occur as a generality within reason but rather *beyond* and *before* being and thought. Negative philosophy "clears the way" for positive philosophy by opening reason up to its outside, making it "ecstatic." It does not allow reason to reconcile itself to the forms of its own activity, but is rather the "incessant overturning of reason [*der fortwährende Umsturz der Vernunft*]," demonstrating to "reason, in so far as it takes itself as the principle," that it "is capable of no actual knowledge."[5] The latter requires the exposure of reason to what is beyond reason.

In fact, Schelling's *Weltalter* was not only decisive to Rosenzweig's break from Idealism, but it was at the burning heart of *The Star of Redemption*. His admiration for this text was great. Robert Gibbs reports that "Rosenzweig had a copy of the 1913 Reclam edition with him at the front during World War I and refers to it in correspondence of that time. In a later letter, Rosenzweig declares: 'It is a great book to the last. Had it been completed, nobody except for Jews would give two hoots for the *Star*.'"[6]

In what follows, I would like to consider the relationship to Schelling's *Weltalter* that emerges in Rosenzweig's *Star of Redemption* as the latter, in a manner of speaking, completes the *Weltalter* project, thereby casting new light on Schelling's thought as well as clarifying and developing it in strikingly original and provocative ways. In so doing, I would like to reflect on the sense of philosophy that emerges after the reign of German Idealism. I concur with Benjamin Pollock who contends in *Franz Rosenzweig and the Systematic Task of Philosophy*[7] that *The Star of Redemption* should not be relegated to a "Jewish book," nor is it the collapse of all systematic thinking in favor of becoming willy-nilly "attentive to existential concerns." It is indeed attentive to the latter, although it endeavors, as did the "system of freedom" in the *Weltalter*, to do so in a systematic fashion, albeit one that is not limited to the formal negative thought that characterizes German Idealism. It emerges from the latter in a "system of freedom" that tracks the historic life of "existential concerns." And although *The Star of Redemption* is no more a "Jewish book" than the *Weltalter* is a "Christian book," their systematic, historical, and existential purview—their *life*—cannot be separated from the emerging life of "existential concerns" traditionally labeled religious. A new "image of thought" (to use Deleuze's felicitous phrase), a new sense of philosophy, emerges from the liminal space between these two works, one that is vital, existential, and, as such, *redemptive*.

I

Speaking of the importance of Schelling's thought for both Kierkegaard and Rosenzweig, Saitya Brata Das rightly remarks that "for both of them Schelling revealed the outside of philosophy by almost violently introducing an irreducible caesura at the heart of philosophy."[8] This caesura at the heart of philosophy features decisively in Schelling's seminal mid-period works, especially the 1809 so-called *Freedom* essay and the drafts of *The Ages of the World* (*Die Weltalter*, 1811–15). This caesura is Schelling's barbarian principle, a nomadic force, which always comes to being unexpectedly ("unprethinkably, *unvordenklich*") from within being, yet which resists our settled modes of thinking as it nomadically dwells outside of philosophy. It consequently reveals the double bind within philosophical thinking: that thinking can neither comprehend nor ignore its groundless ground. Schelling in the *Freedom* essay[9] calls this caesura *erste Natur*, that which is an "incomprehensible ground" and *ein nie aufgehender Rest*, "an irreducible remainder that cannot be resolved by reason even with the greatest exertion" (I/7, 360).

Rejecting the Enlightenment's reduction of nature and being to what can be thought as the death of nature, that is, the exclusion of its incomprehensible but active ground and the demotion of nature and natural science to positivism, Schelling charged that "the whole of modern European philosophy since its inception (through Descartes) has this common deficiency—that Nature does not exist for it and that it lacks a living ground" (I/7, 356). Nature does not exist for modern philosophy because nature is only nature insofar as it is, at least in principle, thinkable nature. Nature is simply, as Schelling adapted a distinction first found in Spinoza, *natura naturata*, nature insofar as it has appeared as nature. Repressed and consequently unthought is *natura naturans*, nature in the act of becoming nature, nature in its generativity. The Enlightenment and the restriction of nature into thinkable, observable, manifest nature cannot think the barbarian principle of nature. As Schelling articulates this in the *Weltalter*, the work that was so decisive for Rosenzweig:

> This is a people that, in the good-natured endeavor towards so-called Enlightenment, really arrived at the dissolution of everything in itself into thoughts. But, along with the darkness, they lost all might and that … barbarian

principle that, when overcome but not annihilated, is the foundation of all greatness and beauty. (I/8, 342–43)

In the first part of Rosenzweig's three-part *Star of Redemption*, a structure that presumably imitates Schelling's proposed three divisions of *Die Weltalter* (the past, the present, and the future, or for Rosenzweig, creation, revelation, and redemption), the barbarian principle immediately undoes philosophy's pretense to self-possession and internal cohesion by confronting its inability to assimilate death. Although the putative identity of thought and being wages that it can succeed, death resists all assimilation. Since death cannot be known in itself positively—for otherwise the knower would be dead—it is neutralized as unknowable and, here comes the trick, as such, it is of no real concern. What matters to philosophy is being insofar as it can be known. If it cannot be known, if reason knows that it cannot know death, death in itself ceases to matter to philosophy. In the dialectic, the negativity of death matters only insofar as it is the promise of a new *Aufhebung*. For Rosenzweig as well as for Schelling, its unknowability is a critical matter, for its unknowability does not mean that it is therefore nothing. It opens up an absolute exteriority before which one is not simply nothing, an exteriority that is also at work as the living ground of nature. This is the exteriority of the past and the future that modern philosophy constitutively denies, an exteriority that simultaneously reveals nature as natality (Schelling) and creation (Rosenzweig) as well as fatality (an absolute future).

The resonance of the barbarian principle with death also featured prominently in Schelling's thought. Schelling, for example, memorably alluded to Plato's claim in the *Phaedo* (64a) that "I am afraid that other people do not realize that the one aim of those who practice philosophy in the proper manner is to practice for dying and death."[10] This practice for dying and death for Schelling is the price of admission for philosophical thinking. In order to philosophize, one has to abandon claims to know its ground. One "who wants to place themselves at the beginning point of a truly free philosophy, must abandon even God."[11] It commences only for those who "had once left everything and who were themselves left by everything" and who, like Socrates contemplating his demise in the *Phaedo*, "saw themselves alone with the infinite: a great step which Plato compared to death" (IPU, 18–19). One empties oneself of oneself, and empties the world of itself, jettisoning all attachments and expectations.

What Dante had written on the gate of the Inferno could also in another sense be the entrance into Philosophy: "Abandon hope all you who enter here." The one who wants truly to philosophize must let go of all hope, all desire, all

Sehnsucht. They must want nothing, know nothing, feel themselves bare and poor. They must give up everything in order to gain everything. (IPU, 19)

For Schelling, one does not just enter philosophy by reading books about it or engaging in conversation about whatever tickles one's fancy or arouses one's curiosity. The first step of what will be three steps (for both Schelling and Rosenzweig) is to empty oneself of oneself, to release oneself to the ground-less ground of both oneself and nature. In the later Berlin lectures on the *Philosophical Introduction to the Philosophy of Mythology*, Schelling articulates this initial step by adapting a distinction found in the Catholic archbishop François Fénelon (1651–1715) in which the self seeks to empty itself. "The ego seeks to consummate the act of self-forgetting or abnegation of itself. This presents itself in mystical piety … which consists in the person seeking as much as possible to void [*vernichtigen*]—but not to annihilate [*vernichten*]—themselves and all the merely accidental being pertaining to themselves" (II/1, 557). *Vernichtigen* is to make oneself nothing, void and invalid, "to count one's self as nought," but in the sense here of emptying oneself of oneself, undergoing the Pauline κένωσις at the heart of nature and oneself.

This, it should be emphasized, is not an end in itself, but rather merely an opening to a movement that takes one toward a redemption of the world. Were it to be left to itself, one is stranded on the periphery of being, detached from the center, a fate that Schelling powerfully characterized as evil in the *Freedom* essay. In breaking the bonds of nature, I risk detaching myself, however empty, from nature and becoming the new ground. This is a way of understanding the pith of Schelling's criticism of Fichte, whom he accused of falling from nature into the ground of the transcendental subject as the new starting point. However free and unknowable to itself the subject may be, nature consequently appears as what contests and obstructs its freedom, much as nature appeared in Sartre's *Being and Nothingness* (*L'Être et le néant*, 1943) as a "coefficient of resistance" to the free subject's "fundamental project."

This danger was present to Schelling early on. For example, in the 1797 edition of his *Ideas for a Philosophy of Nature* he argued that philosophy as such would be impossible if it were part of the causal chain of nature. We would merely think whatever we were determined to think. Philosophy begins when the prisoner in the cave of nature realizes her freedom and steps back from an absorption in the present and "strives to wrench herself away from the shackles of nature and her provisions" (I/2, 12). In discovering a ground within the philosophizing subject that is separable from the ground of nature, philosophy, as well as art, are born of what the poet John Keats in 1817 memorably dubbed "negative capability."[12] Severing the bond with nature, which is the condition for the possibility of philosophically considering nature or creating art, is the disobedient rebellion at the heart of both reflection and creation. Wonder, doubt, angst, confusion, and speculation all assume an initial break with the vice grip of nature. Who am I? Is the world what I am told it is? Why is my experience of myself and my world different than what others experience?

Such radical questioning interrupts the experience of nature as an experience of unrelenting necessity and delivers oneself to oneself in one's freedom, although one also risks becoming marooned in this break. Reflection as an end in itself is what we might now call a *déformation professionnelle*, and what Schelling strikingly diagnoses as *eine Geisteskrankheit des Menschen* (I/2, 13), a psychopathology or, taken literally, a sickness of the spirit. One pulls away from the center of nature and its stubborn hold and retreats to the periphery of reflection. However, if one remains on the periphery, isolated in the delusion of one's ipseity, assuming that one is grounded in oneself, this is the experience of sickness and radical evil. In the language of the introduction to the *Ideas*, when reflection reaches "dominion over the whole person," it "kills" her "spiritual life at its root" (I/2, 13). Reflection only as has a "negative value," enabling the divorce from nature, but it should endeavor to reunite with that which it first knew only as necessity. Reflection, as well as *vernichtigen* or even the realization of Fichte's transcendental ego (in Schelling's account), is consequently "merely a necessary evil [*ein notwendiges Übel*]" (I/2, 13).

Rosenzweig similarly begins his great work by decisively exposing both the self and philosophy to its proximity to absolute exteriority. Having initially been taken with the Hegelian dialectic, which resurrects after every encounter with the negative and hence never really dies, but rather finds a way to ameliorate the threat of death by keeping its relevance internal to the system, Rosenzweig came to reject this pretense in no uncertain terms.[13] In a manner that would critically influence Levinas, Rosenzweig begins his tripartite project (past, present, and future, or creation, revelation, and redemption) by charging that the totalizing philosophical hubris that would know (*erkennen*) the "All" is born of "the fear of death" and the angst that drives one to "toss away" earthly things in order to avoid the "poisonous sting of death and the miasma of hell."[14] The Idealist (Hegelian) system swallows up death, rendering it nugatory—"an All would not die and in the All nothing would die" (SE I, 8).

Although the sting of death is contained by finally being reduced to nothing, its sting neutralized on grounds of relevance, this is doomed to fail. "In truth, this is no final conclusion, but rather a first beginning, and death is truthfully not what it appears, not nothing, but an inexorable some-thing that cannot be disposed of" (SE I, 9). Although death is beyond being, it is not ultimately nugatory. It is rather an opening to an implacable first beginning, an indispensable something, which can be read as Rosenzweig's version of Schelling's *ein nie aufgehender Rest*, "an irreducible remainder that cannot be resolved by reason even with the greatest exertion" (I/7, 360). This barbarian principle is external to the All, yet inseparable from it. As such, it is metaphysical, beyond being, metaethical, for ethics and the law are constricted within the All (SE I, 21), and metalogical in that the logic of the "All from Parmenides to Hegel" has no "protection" from the something "external" to its truths (SE I, 22). As Peter Gordon articulates it, death "names a 'something' in being that exceeds reason's grasp" that "becomes Rosenzweig's heuristic for seizing upon this naked existence."[15] The exteriority revealed by death, as well as birth, cannot be thought positively. This does not mean that it therefore has no relevance. To consign it to nothing is to put all of the stress, as does positivism, on what has been presented, ignoring presentation itself. The domain of freedom that opens up in Kant, and which threatens to explode in the *Critique of Judgment*, cannot be known in itself, but for Rosenzweig, following Schelling, it does not therefore cease to matter. It is an irreducible and barbarian remainder. This is the force of Rosenzweig at first calling this exteriority, demoted by modern philosophy to nothing on grounds of relevance, "something [*Etwas*]." There is not some thing that it is. The *Etwas* simply marks it as not nothing. Because it is not yet a thing, it is not therefore nothing. It is, in the Kantian idiom, to realize an intimacy with the life of the "to us unknown root." Its life is not found by conceiving the *Etwas* as some kind of thing, but by tracing the history of its genesis and the promise of its futurity.

This external "something," this movement, to put it more precisely, "from the nothing to what is not nothing [*nicht nichts*]" (SE I, 34), is not a rejection of systemic thinking, but rather the elevation of metaphysical, metaeth-ical, metalogical systemic thinking over totalizing thinking. Like Schelling's "system of freedom," Rosenzweig endeavored, as Karin Nisenbaum felici-tously articulates it, "to unveil the *ontological ground* of the nonidentity of being and thinking."[16] In *Die Weltalter*, Schelling locates this initial contradiction at the heart of being:

We grasp that the first existence is the contradiction itself and, inversely, that the first actuality can only persist in contradiction. All life must pass through the fire of contradiction. Contradiction is the power mechanism and what is innermost of life. From this it follows that, as an old book says, all deeds under the sun are full of trouble and everything languishes in toil, yet does not become tired, and all forces incessantly struggle against each other. (I/8, 321)

In Rosenzweig, this contradiction is first revealed in the *Verwesung* of the ego before death itself. *Verwesung*, which Rosenzweig links to the "mystical term" *Entwesung*, is a decomposition, a coming apart, a disintegration of the putative self-contained totality of the ego. But it does not just dissolve into the "formless night of the nothing," the refuge of Mephistopheles (SE I, 35). It is a negation of the self, and I note here that Rosenzweig uses *Vernichtung* (annihilation) to describe what Schelling in the discussion above called *Vernichtigen* (becoming nothing, self-emptying) that opens up to the positive. Standing before my death, before its decomposition of my body and dissolution of my mind, I am before what is external to myself and my world. Yet this external "not nothing"—the infinity of God—is not just my future and the future of the world (a future denied by the totalitarian version of the Idealist system), but it is simultaneously the most ancient past. This past is not an actual past, that is, it is not a past that has taken place. It is a ground that does not take place in whatever actually takes place. It is older than the oldest happening. This past becomes the most ancient past by suspending itself in presenting itself, by happening as something. It is the most ancient past sublimated by *any* actual past or present. In suspending the actuality of myself and my world, as they shatter before the absolute externality of death and reveal the sublimated infinity of birth, externality is not nothing. For the idealist, if it cannot be brought into the system then it is nothing to the system. For Rosenzweig, however, the "not nothing" exposed by human mortality is the once and future absolute positivity. It is simultaneously, as Schelling put it in the *Freedom* essay, what is "most ancient in nature," more ancient than nature itself, and the absolute something that is always still to come.

Rosenzweig does not deign, as did Schelling, to borrow from Jakob Böhme (1575–1624), to express this, however poetically and nominally, with phrases like the "dark ground." Rosenzweig's "primordial word [*Urwort*]" is simply "the Yes," pure positivity: "*Im Anfang ist das Ja*, In the beginning is the Yes" (SE I, 37). The Yes is the not nothing, an infinity and boundless positivity beyond being. Nothing can precede the Yes because it is the infinity before the, so to speak, big bang of actuality. Negation births actuality by repressing the Yes, much in the way that the Lurianic Kabbalah speaks of divine contraction (*tzimtzum*, צמצום), or the Japanese philosopher Nishida Kitarō (1870–1945)[17] spoke of absolute nothingness as "self-predication through self-negation" and the "self-identity of an absolute contradiction." This contraction is how Rosenzweig understands the "wandering" of the

Shekhina (הניכש), a term that denotes the "domiciliation [*Niederlassung*]" or dwelling of the divine. It was "represented as a cision [*Scheidung*]"—a critical term also in Schelling's *Weltalter*—"that transpires within God. God severs [*scheidet*] Himself from Himself and gives Himself away to His people; He suffers with their suffering and goes with them in the misery of their exile and wanders with their wanderings" (SE III, 192). (The Lurianic Kabbalah also speaks of the Shekhina, as does the *Zohar*.)

In order to be, including to domicile with the Jews, God says No to His Yes. Temporally, therefore, the No is "younger" than the Yes (SE I, 40). While God's essence is the infinite Yes, God's freedom is the No, the contraction of pure positivity into actuality. For God to be, God must be something, and that is the contradiction of revelation and κένωσις.

II

Schelling had envisioned *Die Weltalter* in its tripartite temporal structure, and Rosenzweig consummates it. This tripartite structure, however, is not the formal or negative structure of the dialectic in which death is annihilated and infinite positivity is contained. For Rosenzweig, the trinity is rather the infinite Yes older than any actuality (the past), miraculously revealed as the present, yet always still to come. God as the furthest star, infinitely beyond yet at the heart of the intimacy of being, redeems both humanity and God. God, the world, and the human come together redemptively in the fullness of time. Although Schelling's lectures on *Mythology and Revelation* resonate deeply with Rosenzweig's work, the present and the future are only hinted at in the unfinished *Weltalter*. (A small fragment of the second volume, The Present, appeared a few years after Rosenzweig's death.) The third or 1815 draft of Schelling's first volume, the only one available to Rosenzweig at the time, takes up the past as the barbarian principle older than nature, which Rosenzweig in his reworking calls the "elements" or "everlasting fore-world [*immerwährende Vorwelt*]."

Rosenzweig also systemically develops this tripartite temporality in its tripartite spatiality (God, the world, humanity). Hence, in the first volume, dedicated to the elemental, absolutely external, ever-enduring fore-world of the Yes, Rosenzweig expounds it systemically in these three spatial dimensions. Each of these ways marks a *beyond* or a "meta."

God is *metaphysical*, or beyond being (before being, ahead of being, and presently contracted within being). Rosenzweig engages in his own philosophy of mythology and revelation, arguing that even mythological manifestations of God, in which God does not yet love and redeem the world, nonetheless display God's metaphysical detachment and externality (SE I, 54).

The world is *metalogical*, and its sense (*Sinn*) is not the immanent logic of the world. The logic of the world is immanent to the world, but the ground of that logic is absolutely external to that world. Beyond the world and beyond its present meaning is its meta-logical pre-world. The being of the world does not exhaust its potential meaning merely by being what it is. To some extent, Rosenzweig anticipates Alain Badiou's adaptation of Cantor's set theory in *Being and Event* (*L'Être et l'événement*, 1988) in which the event of worlds is "forced" like Cantor's sets. The pre-world (or pre-event) is neither one nor nothing, but marked by Badiou by a proper name, the "empty set." For Rosenzweig, "because this affirmation [*Bejahung*, yes saying] must affirm [*bejahen*, say yes to] an infinity, the affirmed not-nothing here cannot mean being, as is also the case with God. For the being of the world is no infinitely resting essence" (SE I, 57). The world is not just what it is, but rather there is "something other in it, something always new, thrusting forth, overwhelming. Its womb is insatiable in its conceiving and inexhaustible in its giving birth" (SE I, 60). Unlike "philosophy from Parmenides to Hegel" where there can be nothing absolutely surprising, or, in Schelling's felicitous term, wholly "unprethinkable [*unvordenklich*]," this is "the appearance of the always-new—the miracle of the spiritual world" (SE I, 62). In totalitarian or closed Idealism, absolute spontaneity—a non-dialectical surprise, for example—is unthinkable because that would "deny the omnipotence of the logos" (SE I, 62). Rosenzweig's metalogical world, in contrast to closed Idealism's "completely full world," is plastic, being fulfilled and shaped (SE I, 69). The metalogical structure of the Whole also exposes the singularity of each part of the world, almost as if they were singular monads, each of which reflected the Whole in its unique way.

> The Whole [*das Ganze*] is precisely not the All, it is actually simply Whole. For this reason, many ways lead from the part to the Whole. Or put more precisely, each part, insofar as it is actually a part, is actually "individual," has its own way to the Whole, its own trajectory. (SE I, 69)

Again, just as with God as metaphysical but not as loving and involved, the world as metalogical is itself only a first step. The world has its infinite externality, but merely to leave it there abandons the world, allowing it to continue to "sleep." Even if one can no longer deny "this externality [*dieses Außen*]," one does not require it. There may be a God, but only so long as God remains outside and is not part of the world, only so long as God's existence is invisible to the macrocosm" (SE I, 80). God, the world, and humanity are redeemed when one requires this externality and affirms it as the lifeblood of the Whole.

Completing the spatial extension of the past, humanity is *metaethical*. Here we recognize the immense influence that Rosenzweig had on Levinas. The good is not intrinsic to the logic of the world any more than it is found within an appeal to human nature or immanent to human character. In the latter, "the only humanity that it knew were its own four walls … reaping all ethical order for its own ethos" (SE I, 108). Just as God shatters the egoism of thought and tears open the self-contained dialectical seal in Idealism between being and thought, revealing the externality and infinite creativity in the birthing of the world, the self-infatuation of humanity begins to shake before the metaethical.

Conclusion: Redeeming Idealism

Although he frequently announced its imminent appearance, Schelling never finished *Die Weltalter*, despite copious drafts. A whole chest full of drafts was destroyed during the Allied Bombing of Munich, although other pieces have been found in Berlin, where Schelling had worked from 1841 until his death in 1854. Moreover, it is not much of a stretch to hypothesize that the immense number of pages and copious lectures on the philosophy of mythology and revelation, inaugurated with Schelling's 1815 address, *On the Deities of Samothrace*,[18] which Schelling explicitly called a "supplement" to *Die Weltalter*, are themselves implicit parts of this overall project. They even hint at the present (the miracle of being at work) and the future, what Schelling called the event of the Johannine Church, which expresses the fullness of time, the holding together of the past, present, and future. The Church to come is the Church not merely *in* the future but *of* the future, that is, a church that liberates time and activates the creativity of the future, a church *of the whole of time*. Schelling's John is the "apostle of the future" (PO, 317). He was "actually not the apostle for his time." Peter expanded the form of the Church all over the world, but it took the Pauline radicality of Luther to reveal the mystery of God's externality and sever the totalizing subsumption of God into the world and into human comprehension. But this metaphysical, metalogical, and metaethical alterity—God's inscrutable solitude and mystery—is not yet an externality that interrupts, manifests in, and redeems the world. This is what is to come: a God who loves the world, an externality that can neither be assimilated nor discarded by the world. Schelling recalls that the "Lord loved" John, "that is, in him he knew himself."[19] The Johannine Church, the church for everyone and everything—for all things human and for the mysterious creativity of the earth itself—is the "being everything in everything of God" (U, 708–709), a "theism that contains within itself the entire economy of God" (U, 709).

Rosenzweig similarly recognized the Church as torn between its body (the Petrine) and its soul (the Pauline) (SE III, 25–28) and the task for "the Christianity of the future" is to realize their "inner nexus," the same nexus that holds together human life as a Whole with the Whole of worldly life" (SE III, 30). Rosenzweig calls this the "Johannine consummation" (SE III, 32), the formless Church of Alyosha Karamazov, who, we here recall, fell to the earth and watered it with his tears of gratitude as the earth below and the heavens above were no longer simply two. This was also for Rosenzweig the hope at the heart of Judaism, that not only must the Christian now "immediately convert the pagan within themselves," but the Jew, in "the beginning of the fulfillment of the Ages, must convert the pagan in the Christian" (SE III, 33). This is not the triumph of a new institution that supplants the former ones, because the Johannine Church, "formless and necessarily unfounded," is "not built; it can only grow" (SE III, 33). The Petrine Church "only grew in space" (SE III, 35). Time merely measured its growth "unto all the world." The Pauline Church is invisible as it plunges back into the mystery of time, but in forgoing space, time stood still. This is the time of the invisible and eternal mystery. It is therefore the task of the Johannine Church to create "an actually living time," the fullness of time (creation, revelation, and redemption), that becomes a stream that carries each moment out to space, not to lose it, but to let it irrigate and bring life to space (SE III, 36).[20] But how to bring this about? How to introduce "an accelerating force"?

For Rosenzweig, this first begins with the transition from mystery to miracle, "the everlasting mystery of creation is the always new for all time miracle of revelation" (SE I, 118), and it remains the profundity of Rosenzweig's project to follow Schelling's sometimes halting efforts to change the very image of thought. Thinking is no longer wholly rational. As Nisenbaum articulates it, "Both for Schelling and Rosenzweig, the ultimate meaning of the conflict of reason is our tendency to deny our human finitude and shun our vocation."[21] This is interrupted by the absolute externality of the repressed infinity of appearance. Thinking is fundamentally mysterious. Yet that is also to say too little, because if thinking cannot account for itself, it can nonetheless just soldier on. Gödel's incompleteness theorems, or the important and equally radical arguments in its wake like Tarski's "undefinability theorem" (1933), which argues in essence that arithmetical truth cannot be proven within arithmetic, did nothing to halt the activity of mathematics or logic. The metalogical, left merely beyond the immanent logic of the world, renders logic incomplete, unable to account for itself within itself, but it remains logical nonetheless and the "omnipotence of the logos," while injured, limps on. Given that the world is caught in the net of reason, it does not ask, as Schelling often insisted, how it got there.

The key is to transition from the *mystery* of thought and appearance to the *miracle* of thought and appearance, the present as the miraculous revelation of the mystery of the Yes. This is part of what Schelling would call positive philosophy, the cataphatic yet incomplete presence of the mystery. Yet, this too, is not enough, this too is but a threshold (*Schwelle*) to illumination or enlightenment (*Erleuchtung*).

How does one bring the grace of being into proximity? How does one participate in revelation? How does one—or philosophy for that matter—become intimate with revelation and thereby redeemed by it? In a way, *this is the prayer of philosophy*. Prayer [*das Gebet*] "is an appeal for enlightenment: Enlighten my eyes—they are blind so long as the hands create" (SE III, 10). So long as love is directed to whatever happens to be at hand, to whatever and whomever is next or neighbor to it, it is blind. Prayer unbinds love insofar as it "appeals for enlightenment" and "without overlooking the neighbor, but "seeing through and beyond the neighbor [*über das Nächste hinweg*], sees, insofar as it is enlightened, the whole world" (SE III, 10). Rosenzweig does not restrict the "neighbor" to the person next to one, which would typically be *der Nächste*; *das Nächste* is whomever and whatever is near at hand. Enlightenment sees, and more importantly loves, the near as an enlightenment of the infinitely far and absolutely external, the neighbor as both at hand and barbarian, "proximate and farthest away." For when "prayer enlightens, it shows the eyes the farthest goal" (SE III, 14).

If for both Schelling and Rosenzweig, the first book is the past (the metaphysical, metalogical, and metaethical older than nature, before the big bang of being), and the second book is the present (the present as the miraculous revelation of the mystery), and the third book, scarcely hinted at by Schelling, but confronted directly by Rosenzweig, is the future, the prayer of philosophy and the redemption of idealism appear in a fundamentally new way. Prayer casts light "into the darkness of the future" that reaches its furthest extreme while illuminating the present as love keeps pace with it (SE III, 17). This is not something that one does just because one is a Jew, or a Christian, or a Muslim, because prayer belongs to the believer and the unbeliever. It is a prayer to redeem philosophy from its resistance to that which absolutely contests reason at the very heart of reason. This is the task of giving the future a genuine future, of bringing about the always still to come *today*. "Eternity must be accelerated; it must always already be able to come today" (SE, III, 37). Moreover, this is not merely the perpetual advent of the new. The natality and mortality of beings confirm that we already have this. Beings are always coming and going, and the Janus-face of death is not simply the ending of the old, but the promise of the new. It is rather that the *externality of coming and going must itself keep coming back as the fullness of time*, as what Schelling, with reference to the Johannine Church, called the "entire economy of God" (U, 709). This is what Rosenzweig calls the moment as *nunc stans*, or the "hour," the circle of time circling back upon itself, the hour containing the fullness of moments (SE III, 39). These in turn are cultivated by the weekly rituals of turning fleeting moments into the fullness of the hour (SE III, 40–41).

Idealism is redeemed when truth is grabbed with both hands, not just the single hand of philosophy, which renders the Yes nugatory, or the other hand of theological dogma, which renders it comprehensible. For Rosenzweig, "God is truth" and truth is the "seal by which God can be known" (SE III, 155). It is the hour of the constant revelation in which "our Verily, our Yes and Amen, with which we answer God's revelation … also exposes the beating heart of the eternal truth," the "burning of the farthest star" (SE III, 170). This is the new image of thought that emerges in and between Schelling and Rosenzweig: reaching out to the farthest star, *die ewige Über-welt*, what is eternally beyond or external to the world, in its always coming near to hand within the fullness of time.

Notes

1. Franz Rosenzweig, *Briefe*, ed. Edith Rosenzweig (Berlin: Schocken Verlag, 1935), 299. See also Werner J. Cahnman, "Schelling and the New Thinking of Judaism," *Proceedings of the American Academy for Jewish Research* 48 (1981): 50.
2. See Diana I. Behler's translation, *Philosophy of German Idealism*, ed. Ernst Behler (New York: Continuum, 1987), 162–63. "Das sogenannte 'Älteste Systemprogramm," *Materialien zu Schellings philosophischen Anfängen*, ed. Manfred Frank and Gerhard Kurz (Frankfurt am Main: Suhrkamp, 1975), 110–12. This text first appeared in 1917 as "Das älteste Systemprogramm des deutschen Idealismus: Ein Handschriftlicher Fund," *Sitzungberichte der Heidelberger Akademie der Wissenschaften* 5 (1917).
3. See *Das älteste Systemprogramm: Studien zur Frühgeschichte des deutschen Idealismus*, ed. Rüdiger Bubner, Hegel Studien, Beiheft 9 (Bonn: Bouvier Verlag, 1973).
4. Schelling citations, unless otherwise noted, follow the standard pagination, which adheres to the original edition established after Schelling's death by

his son Karl. It lists the division, followed by the volume, followed by the page number. Hence (I/1, 1) would read: division one, volume one, page one. This pagination is preserved in Manfred Schröter's critical reorganization of this material. *Schellings Sämtliche Werke*, ed. K. F. A. Schelling (Stuttgart-Augsburg: J. G. Cotta 1856–1861); *Schellings Werke: Nach der Originalausgabe in neuer Anordnung*, ed. Manfred Schröter (Munich: C. H. Beck, 1927). Translations are my own.

5. F. W. J. Schelling, *Philosophie der Offenbarung* (1841–42), ed. Manfred Frank (Frankfurt am Main, 1977), 152. Henceforth PO.

6. Robert Gibbs, "The Limits of Thought: Rosenzweig, Schelling, and Cohen," *Zeitschrift für philosophische Forschung*, Band 43, Heft 4 (Oct.–Dec. 1989), 625. Gibbs also reports that "Rosenzweig did not, however likely know the late Schelling, the lectures which were published as *Philosophy of Mythology and Philosophy of Revelation*. He writes to Rudolph Stahl (#1156, 2 June 1927) 'At that time [1911] I still knew nothing of the late Schelling.' But on 18 March 1921, he writes to Hans Ehrenberg 'I'm reading the *Philosophical Empiricism* of 1827. It is surely worse than the *Weltalter*'" (625n6).

7. Benjamin Pollock, *Franz Rosenzweig and the Systematic Task of Philosophy* (Cambridge: Cambridge University Press, 2009), see esp. 1–13.

8. Saitya Brata Das, *The Political Theology of Schelling* (Edinburgh: Edinburgh University Press, 2016), 27.

9. The *Freedom* essay or *Freiheitsschrift* is Schelling's 1809 masterpiece, *Philosophische Untersuchungen über das Wesen der menschlichen Freiheit und die damit zusammenhängenden Gegenstände*.

10. Plato, *Phaedo*, trans. G. M. A. Grube, rev. John M. Cooper, in *Five Dialogues* (Indianapolis: Hackett, 2002), 101.

11. F. W. J. Schelling, *Initia Philosophiæ Universæ* (1820–21), ed. Horst Fuhrmans (Bonn: H. Bouvier, 1969), 18. Henceforth IPU. This is an early critical edition of the *Erlanger Vorlesungen*. These lectures formed the basis of Schelling's essay, *On the Nature of Philosophy as Science* (1821).

12. In a letter to his brothers, Thomas and George, dated 22 December 1817, Keats defined negative capability as "when a man is capable of being in uncertainties, mysteries, doubts, without any irritable reaching after fact and reason" (John Keats, *The Complete Poetical Works and Letters of John Keats, Cambridge Edition* [Boston: Houghton, Mifflin and Company, 1899], 277).

13. See Gibbs: "Thus whenever we place a limit on thought, and assert that beyond that limit lies the infinite, Hegel challenges us, claiming that in doing that thinking, we already re-appropriated that infinite and transcended the limit. Hegel's true infinity is one which is present in the finite. This dialectical move is the main point of Rosenzweig's interpretation of Philosophy in general, and of Hegel in particular: the willful desire to know it all cannot tolerate anything

beyond the limits of thought. Rosenzweig denies this re-appropriation emphatically, claiming that he has to shatter Hegel's genuine infinity in order to make the 'bad' infinity visible" (Gibbs, 621).

14. Franz Rosenzweig, *Der Stern der Erlösung*, three volumes (Berlin: Schocken Verlag, 1930), vol. I, 7. Henceforth SE, followed by volume number and page number. Translations are my own. I have used the old three-volume edition, which literally preserves the tripartite conception announced in Schelling's *Die Weltalter* but achieved in Rosenzweig's magnum opus.

15. Peter Eli Gordon, *Rosenzweig and Heidegger: Between Judaism and German Philosophy* (Berkeley: University of California Press, 2005), 168.

16. Karin Nisenbaum, *For the Love of Metaphysics: Nihilism and the Conflict of Reason from Kant to Rosenzweig* (Oxford: University of Oxford Press, 2018), 226. A clear strength of this monograph is Nisenbaum's spot-on grasp of the centrality of Schelling to Rosenzweig's project.

17. I have an additional reason for inserting Nishida here, namely, to offset Rosenzweig's vexingly ignorant reading of all Asian philosophical traditions. Dao, for example, is "only effective without acting [*tatlos Wirkende*]" and hence "keeps as quiet as a little mouse" (SE I, 50). Or the scandalously misconceived account of the Asian world as "unplastic" (SE I, 76–79).

18. A new, and for the first time complete, translation and critical edition of this seminal and dramatic lecture is forthcoming from Indiana University Press, edited and translated by Alexander Bilda, Jason M. Wirth, and David F. Krell.

19. *Urfassung Philosophie der Offenbarung*, two volumes, ed. Walter E. Ehrhardt (Hamburg: Felix Meiner Verlag, 1992), 703. Henceforth U. This is a much completer and more exciting version of the *Philosophy of Revelation* than the one that appeared in the edition prepared by Karl Schelling. It is derived from the 1831–1832 original version of the course and preserved in a carefully dictated handwritten manuscript, which the editor found in the university library of the Catholic University Eichstätt.

20. Kevin Hart also draws our attention to this parallel. "Again, Rosenzweig draws from Schelling (though surely with a bow to Joachim of Fiore as well), this time to give himself the three ages of Christendom: the Petrine (or Catholic) age, beginning with the Edict of Milan in 313; the Pauline (or Protestant) age, beginning with Luther's posting of the ninety-five theses to the door at the Wittenberg Castle Church in 1517; and the Johannine age, which has been developing since 1800, the symbolic year that for Rosenzweig marks the fulfillment of German Idealism and the beginning of *Weltanschauungsphilosophie*" (Kevin Hart, "From the Star to the Disaster," *Paragraph* 30, no. 3 [2007]: 90–91). It should be noted here that Schelling also explicitly draws on the legacy of the Medieval thinker, Joachim of Fiore (Gioacchino da Fiore, c. 1135–1202) as do more recent thinkers like Gianni Vattimo, for whom the advent of the Johannine Age does not name the revelation of a particular event or teaching

because it "stresses not the letter but the spirit of revelation" (Gianni Vattimo, *After Christianity*, trans. Luca D'Isanto [New York: Columbia University Press, 2002], 31).

21. Nisenbaum, 252.

16

Heidegger on Hegel on Time

Markus Gabriel

In the concluding paragraphs of *Being and Time* Heidegger gives an account of the origin of what he calls the "vulgar concept of time [*vulgärer Zeitbegriff*]," the critical examination of which culminates in the aporetic question with which the book ends: "Does *time* itself reveal itself as the horizon of *being*?" (BT 415). In this context, he argues that the vulgar conception of time is paradigmatically articulated by Aristotle (BT §81) and inherited by Hegel (BT §82), who merely radicalizes it.

The thrust of Heidegger's claims is familiar from other parts of the book. A vulgar conception of something is a conception that arises out of everydayness. Yet our everyday interaction with objects in our agential environment is not as such transparent to us. It is possible and, according to Heidegger, quite natural for the kinds of beings we are to think of a fundamental aspect of human sense-making as latching onto an independent, external reality.

In Heidegger's account, the vulgar conception of time is a mistake of the following form: beings like us (*Dasein*) tend to mistake our meaning-laden experience of reality for a feature of a mind-independent external world. In the case of time, this means that we think of time as a sequence of present moments. Heidegger speaks of "*now-time*" (BT 401). What was is no longer,

M. Gabriel (✉)
University of Bonn, Bonn, Germany
e-mail: gabrielm@uni-bonn.de

C. D. Coe (eds.), *The Palgrave Handbook of German Idealism and Phenomenology*,
Palgrave Handbooks in German Idealism,
https://doi.org/10.1007/978-3-030-66857-0_16

and what will be is not yet, as if time passed through the bottleneck of a metaphysically privileged present moment.

In this chapter, I will explore Heidegger's reading of Hegel on time. I will argue that Heidegger seriously misrepresents Hegel on time. Correcting some of the elements of Heidegger's mistaken interpretation leads to an insight into a central shortcoming of *Being and Time*: its incapacity to think of ourselves as historically situated, embodied, free agents who are capable of accounting for their own position and conceptual framework. Heidegger sets our everyday understanding of fundamental concepts—such as time—and the philosophical-phenomenological account in an opposition which makes it hard, impossible even, for him to retain some of the core aspects of the manifest image of the human being.

I will first reconstruct the outlines of his reading of Hegel in *Being and Time*, §82. Then I will contrast this with a closer and more complete reading of the paragraphs on space and time in Hegel's *Encyclopedia* (§§254–59), which is also Heidegger's own reference text. In the final part I will sketch a reconstruction of Hegel's method in order to demonstrate that Hegel's account of historical time is precisely not that of an automated, ontotheological process of absolute spirit's self-revelation, but rather a conception of the human being as free agent. Heidegger has no room for such a self-conception of the human being, as he erroneously tries to replace the notion of the human being with a formal counterpart (*Dasein*), a project which fails due to the misguided attempt to sever temporality from our experience of time and its physical representation.

Heidegger on Hegel (BT §82)

In BT §82 Heidegger offers a cursory reading of selected passages from EPN §§254–59. His goal is to defend the view that Hegel's account of the relationship between space and time remains thoroughly within the confines of what he calls the "the vulgar understanding of time" (BT 407). In this part of my chapter, I would like to reconstruct Heidegger's interpretation before I compare it to a different reading that arguably does more justice to Hegel than Heidegger's problematically superficial take.

Heidegger rightly emphasizes that Hegel offers a dialectic transition from space to time. The starting point of this endeavor is the concept of space as "the abstract multiplicity of the points distinguishable in it" (BT 407). In a word, the concept of space is that of a pure "multiplicity of points" (BT 407). Space is a boundless, infinite manifold of points. According to this concept, no point is privileged in any way. They are all equally valid, which is the notion of "indifference [*Gleichgültigkeit*]" (EPN §254). This contrasts with the idea that a given point stands out either in virtue of being occupied by a distinguished entity or, say, in virtue of being represented as distinguished (e.g., as a consequence of someone's literal perspective and therefore spatial location). Pure space is not occupied by any entity, nor is it as such related to a subject's point of view.

At this juncture, Heidegger claims that points are themselves something spatial. "The differentiations themselves have the nature of what they differentiate" (BT 408). At the same time, no given point is identical to pure space as such. In this regard, then, a point is a negation: It is spatial without being space itself. Space is thereby differentiated into infinitely many points or rather a pure manifold of points.

Heidegger maintains that this is the meaning of Hegel's claim that space is "punctuality" (BT 408). Space is its own negation in that the points that can be found everywhere in space without any particular conceptual or ontological privilige are constitutive of pure space. The purity of space is the fact that all space points are equal. Space then depends for its being what it is on a manifold of points that can be described as negations.

The next step in the argument that Heidegger ascribes to Hegel is rather obscure. He rightly mentions that a negation of negation takes place that leads to the concept of time, but he does not offer a plausible reconstruction of that transition. Heidegger himself clearly struggles with the dialectical transition he offers and therefore grants himself the right to offer an interpretation to which there is supposedly no intelligible alternative: "If this discussion [*Erörterung*] has any demonstrable meaning at all, it can mean nothing other than that the positing of itself for itself of each point is a now-here, now-here, and so on" (BT 408). Let us take a closer look at Heidegger's own "discussion [*Erörterung*]" (BT 408) which leads to his bewilderment and motivates his own alternative route. Beforehand, let me make the wordplay explicit here. Heidegger's term for "discussion" in this context is "*Erörterung*" which contains the word "*Ort*," i.e., place. On this level, Heidegger ironically points out that in his view Hegel's discussion of time is an "*Erörterung*" and, therefore, a spatialization of time, which is part of his worry about Hegel.

However, instead of specifying this worry in a careful manner, Heidegger simply assumes that dialectic somehow moves from thesis and antithesis to synthesis. Yet this does not correspond to Hegelian dialectics and plays no recognizable role in the paragraphs from the *Encyclopedia* that Heidegger is interpreting. Actually, there is not a single passage in the *Encyclopedia* where dialectics is couched in these simplified terms. As a matter of fact, the opposition of thesis and antithesis only shows up in the addition to §48 in the context of a critical discussion of Kant's dialectic. Hegel nowhere provides us with the schema thesis-antithesis-synthesis as a model of dialectics, which is further evidence that Heidegger does not really bother to articulate the Hegelian method in its own right, as his agenda is to maintain that Hegel inauthentically follows in the footsteps of "the *traditional* concept of time" (BT 410n30). In light of these considerations, Heidegger offers the following reading of the transition from a negation to a negation of negation: "In the negation of negation (that is, punctuality) the point posits itself *for itself* and thus emerges from the indifference of subsistence. Posited for itself, it distinguishes itself from this or that point; it is *no longer* this one and *not yet* that one" (BT 408). A possible way of beginning to make sense of this goes like this: (The concept of) pure space is (the concept of) a manifold of points. Each point is itself something spatial. Each point thereby differs in space both from space itself and from all other points. Yet there is no actual reason to distinguish any given point from any other given point; they are all equal. Hence, any given point both is and is not different from all other points, which is the starting point of a dialectical contradiction.

Heidegger assumes that the dialectical contradiction inherent in the notion of a point already contains some kind of quasi-temporal flow so that every point is a part of a proto-temporal series. However, this is not Hegel's line of argument. Rather, his idea is that points are not by themselves distinguishable from each other so that we need different spatial units (beginning with the line) in order for the various points in space to become spatial.

Hegel here introduces a nice wordplay which Heidegger does not fully account for. He claims that each point "'rebels' against all the other points" (BT 408), as Heidegger puts it. The verb "*sich aufspreizen*," translated as "rebels" here, takes on at least two meanings. On the one hand, it is idiomatic and means puffing oneself up. Any given point in that sense lays an unjustified claim to being distinguished in virtue of just being this point. However, this gesture is pretty idle if the concept of a given point is merely the concept of one point in a manifold. No point is as special as it would deserve to be, were it actually individuated by something that transcends its purely spatial nature.

The second meaning at play here is that of spreading out. Given that the concept of a pure point in pure space is the concept of something that precisely cannot distinguish any point in contradistinction to any or all others, we realize that all points are on equal footing, which gives us access to the concept of a densely populated space, an absolute continuum ("absolutely *continuous*"), as Hegel himself introduces the concept (one of the many aspects of Hegel's own treatment Heidegger ignores) in EPN §254.

In order to fill in the many steps of the actual argument in Hegel (which we shall discuss in the next section), Heidegger jumps to the next concept in the dialectic, that of time, in order to help himself to a better understanding of space. Without much further ado, Heidegger introduces his main objection against Hegel on time, namely: "We do not need any complicated discussion [*Erörterung*] to make it clear that in his interpretation of time, Hegel is wholly moving in the direction of the vulgar understanding of time" (BT 409). His evidence for this strong interpretative claim is a comparison of some words in the *Encyclopedia* with an earlier Jena discussion of space and time, which certainly borrows vocabulary and some central concepts from Aristotle.

In order to understand how Hegel—according to Heidegger—remains within a vulgar framework while radicalizing it, it is important to look at the relevant contrast between the vulgar and the phenomenological account of time, a distinction which lies at the very heart of the enterprise of *Being and Time*.[1]

A conception of something (time [BT 17 and passim], conscience [BT 258], Dasein [BT 24], phenomena [BT 29 and *passim*], guilt [BT 282], etc.) is vulgar if it originates in our ordinary, inauthentic mode of being-in-the-world. This is in contrast with the authentic, phenomenological understanding of a phenomenon that does not merely articulate how reality strikes us from the standpoint of everydayness, but transcends that very limitation. The vulgar conception of time corresponds to the pre-phenomenological experience of the passing of time through the bottleneck of the specious present. Simply put, the vulgar conception of time is a kneejerk, unsophisticated account of presentism. The present seems to be absolutely privileged in comparison with past and future in virtue of being the only real point in time: the past is not (anymore) and the future is not (yet).

Famously, Heidegger develops a very different account of temporality according to which the vulgar experience of time is embedded in a space of possibilities. According to him, it is possible to experience time as primarily driven by our orientation toward the future. As Dasein, we fundamentally transcend the given moment and can only conceive of ourselves as historically situated agents if we give up the notion that to be is to be here, as it were (which is one of the reasons why Heidegger uses the term *Da-Sein*, Being-There in order to characterizes the being of those who understand).

In Heidegger's reading, Hegel is a radical presentist who denies the reality of past and future and therefore thinks of the present as eternity. Time, then, is a movement from one point to another point whereby each point gains the questionable advantage of standing out simply in virtue of being designated as salient. Heidegger calls this notion of time the "succession of nows" (BT 410).

Borrowing a famous distinction alien to both Hegel and Heidegger, we might say that Heidegger reads Hegel as reducing time to the C-series, i.e., to a pure order of conceptually orderly, atemporal points so that the A-series (past, present, future) turns out to be in some sense unreal, a line of thought notoriously defended by the Hegel-inspired British idealist John M. E. McTaggart.[2]

The central aspect of Heidegger's worry is that Hegel interprets time through the lenses of an indifference of time-points. Points in time are nothing over and above points in space. Time, then, is just, as it were, the illusion of a movement in space. Nevertheless, for Heidegger, Hegel achieves some distance from the vulgar notion of time as a consequence of his theoretical sophistication. Hegel avoids the trap of the metaphor of the river of time by introducing the pure concept of becoming. The pure concept of becoming is simply the notion of a *movement* of pure space points. Time thereby turns into a pure form, the form of the negation of negation of space.

> So even when he characterizes time as becoming, Hegel understands this becoming in an "abstract" sense that goes beyond the representation of the "flux" of time. The most appropriate expression for Hegel's conception of time thus lies in the determination of time as the *negation of negation* (that is, of punctuality). There the succession of nows is formalized in the most extreme sense and leveled down to an unprecedented degree. (BT 410)

Hegel on Space and Time (EPN §§254–259)

In this section, I would like to offer a more detailed reading of the argumentative, dialectical transition from space to time in Hegel's actual philosophy of nature, as laid out in his most mature presentation in the *Encyclopedia*. Hegel dedicates EPN §254–256 to space, i.e., to the concept of space.

The first of those dense paragraphs, §254, introduces the first determination of nature: "the abstract *universality of Nature's self-externality*." Nature is externality. The idea behind this vocabulary can be illustrated with recourse to the widespread notion that nature is "out there" and that it antedates and differs in category from mindedness. Roughly, nature is the domain of entities and processes such that *prima facie* there is no relevant metaphysical sense in which that domain depends on our conceptualization of and presence in it. Nature is mind- and language-independent. As I put this elsewhere, nature corresponds to the idea of a "world without spectators."[3] Nature's self-externality on my proposed reading is its being external to a self where this aspect is implicit in its concept and made explicit by a dialectical analysis.

If you abstract from the details of nature, as we find it, we are therefore left with the abstraction of sheer "out-thereness." This abstraction is what Hegel calls "space." Space is nature's most minimal determination, its being simply there, ready to be discovered by thinkers as soon as they enter the stage. Given that we have not introduced any further concept that would allow us to distinguish actual occupants of positions in space as long as we just think of it as the form of being out there, space is "absolutely *continuous*." On this level, there are no actual points in space.[4] An actual point is a negation of space in that space itself—i.e., the pure concept of space—does precisely not contain points. Contrary to Heidegger's reading, space is not constituted by actual points, but by their very absence.

The second paragraph on space, §255, introduces the notion of "three *dimensions*" of space. The reason why space has three dimensions is that space is a concept, which is an immensely puzzling claim grounded in Hegel's logic. Hegel here relies on results from the logic that precedes the philosophy of nature. Here is one way of making sense of the relationship between concept and space.[5]

Let *logical space* be the totality of concepts linked together by inferential patterns.[6] What is thinkable can be brought under a concept and if we bring concepts under concepts, we recognize higher-order patterns (functions of functions) that constitute a tree of genera and species. Regardless of Hegel's specific account of the architecture of logical space, we are entitled to assume that there are patterns of intelligibility that we capture by way of articulating them as logical forms.

Firstly, logical space encompasses the totality of the thinkable; it is a concept introduced in logical theory to make sense of concepts and what it is for something to fall under them. In this respect, logical space is *universal*: All other concepts fall under the concept of logical concept.

Secondly, in order for there to be many concepts, we need to add the notion that logical space is internally differentiated. We therefore require a concept of concept specification. Hegel calls this concept "the particular." The particular is a set of rules of specification we rely on when thinking of a given concept (such as the concept of concepts) as subsuming more specific concepts.

Thirdly, logical space is itself a concept. It is the unique concept under which all concepts fall in such a way that they are bound together by logical forms. Hegel labels the singularity of logical space, the fact that there cannot be more than one domain of thinkables logically hanging together, "the individual." The fact that the concept of concepts falls under itself without thereby being one of the special concepts, means that the concept of concepts, logical space, is a paradigmatic example of an individual. It is both fully determinate (an *ens omnimodo determinatum*) in virtue of it encompassing all more specific (logical concepts) and falls under a concept (namely under its own concept).

Universality, particularity, and singularity are the three dimensions of the concept of space. The three-dimensionality of space is not geometrical, and Hegel adds in the *Remark* that it is not to be confused with the distinction between *height, length,* and *breadth.*[7] Hence, §255 does not introduce the idea that pure space is Euclidean in some special, *a priori* sense, as Kant is typically read.[8] Rather, as the next paragraph (EPN §256) explicates, the three dimensions of space are point, line, and plane. Contrary to Heidegger, for Hegel the point is precisely not yet spatial. A point has no extension; it does not occupy any position in space. In that exact sense, the concept of a point is that of "the *negation* of space itself" (EPN §256). The next step involves the kind of dialectical operation Heidegger locates one step too early. Here, Hegel writes: "(β) But the negation is the negation *of space*, i.e. is itself spatial. The point, as essentially this relation, i.e. as sublating itself, is the *line* [and not time, as Heidegger claims], the first other-being, i.e. spatial being, of the point" (EPN §256).

A line is a relation between a point and space. Remember that Hegel is thinking of space in terms of a domain of thinkables "out there." A straight line is "the shortest distance between two points" (EPN §256 R). A line is a spatial (because continuous) connection between two endpoints. It thus establishes a spatial relationship between points. Points are not spatialized, but the relationship between points is spatialized so that the negation of space provides us with the second conceptual dimension of space. The third dimension, the plane, is the "negation of the negation." Space is now itself something spatial and can be thought of as constituting "an *enclosing surface* which separates off a *single* whole space."

The order of dimensions is structured by negation. In general, "negativity" in Hegel concerns abstraction. The most abstract concept, being, is therefore pure negativity or nothing, as he famously puts it (SL 59). Space is an abstraction performed on the ground of the concept of a reality "out there." It is impossible to determine actual points in space. The attempt to think of space as both continuous and consisting of actual points according in Hegel's analysis leads to space as a plane. Determining a point by drawing a distinction between universal, particular, and individual aspects of space, is what Hegel calls "time." Time is negativity "posited for itself" (EPN §257).

Time arises in virtue of the fact that no actual point in space can be determined without separating space into smaller units (planes and lines) so that we can think of a point as an endpoint of a spatial figure. Time is the invisibility of actual points, their inexistence in continuous space. It is "that being which, inasmuch as it *is*, is *not*, and inasmuch as it is *not*, *is*: it is Becoming directly *intuited*; this means that differences, which admittedly are purely *momentary*, i.e. directly self-sublating, are determined as *external*, i.e. as external to *themselves*" (EPN §258).

This is very far from the vulgar conception of time, as Heidegger portrays it. Rather, Hegel here draws on his logic: Becoming is a transition from being to nothing and vice versa, i.e., represented as coming-into-being and destruction. Time is tied to intuition in Hegel's sense, i.e., to a conscious direct experience of how things strike as sentient, embodied agents. In pure becoming, there is no stability.

Actually, what Hegel discusses under the heading of "time" in his mechanics is a purely conceptual operation that establishes a relationship between spatial points. A point both is and is not in space. It is an ideal limit of space designed to draw distinctions in an absolute continuum. These distinctions immediately vanish in the medium itself which *qua* absolute continuum does not allow for a real separation.

In §259, Hegel introduces the "dimensions of time, *present*, *future*, and *past*." Analogously to his treatment of the point (and contrary to Heidegger's interpretation), the now does not really or actually exist. It is pure vanishing, the objectless transition from nothing to being and from being to nothing. Time is precisely not a succession of nows, but rather pure becoming realized in nature *qua* a domain of processes "out there."

> The immediate vanishing of these differences [between coming into being and ceasing to be] into *singularity* is the present as *Now* which, as singularity, is *exclusive* of the other moments, and at the same time completely *continuous* in them, and is only this vanishing of this its being into nothing and of nothing into its being. (EPN §259)

In this context, Hegel explicitly rejects the position that Heidegger ascribes to him, namely the idea of time as succession of nows, and actually provides an account of temporality related to what Heidegger discusses under his master-rubric of *Dasein*. In the Remark to §259 he even writes:

> Furthermore, in Nature where time is a *Now*, being does not reach the *existence* of the difference of these [i.e., temporal] dimensions; they are, of necessity, only in subjective imagination, in *remembrance* and *fear* or *hope*. But the past and future of time as *being* in Nature, are space, for space is negated time; just as sublated space is immediately the point, which developed for itself is time. (EPN §259 R)

Hegel does not reduce space and time to forms of nature, as Heidegger mistakenly assumes. On the contrary, the dimensions of temporality only *exist* outside of nature, in the realm of spirit. Heidegger entirely misconstrues this in BT §82 b. by confusing topics from the *Phenomenology of Spirit* and Hegel's philosophy of history with the discussion of time in the context of mechanics. Remarkably, he leaves out Hegel's explicit claim that the three dimensions of time as well as the now are essentially related to modes of *Dasein*: remembrance, fear, or hope, which, among other things, sets Hegel's account of the subjectivity of time apart from Kant's famous notion that they are pure forms of intuition.

The Keyword Is the Method

One crucial methodological result of Hegel's *Science of Logic* is the insight that metaphysics does not contain *basic object-level claims*.[9] In the context of thinking about nature, a basic object-level claim is a claim about the mind-independent furniture of physical reality. Hegel's discussion of space, time, movement, etc., takes place in the context of mechanics, as a section of the philosophical discipline called "philosophy of nature." What sets philosophy of nature and philosophy of spirit apart as two parts of the *Encyclopedia* are different kinds of concepts. The concepts of philosophy of nature are designed to refer to entities and processes in a mind-independent reality "out there" by largely abstracting from the embodied presence of thinkers who deploy those concepts in explanatory contexts. By contrast, the concepts of philosophy of spirit deal with human mindedness, our subjective mental faculties grounded in human animality (subjective spirit), their historical and institutional embedding (objective spirit), and the highest-level representations of human mindedness in art, religion, and philosophy (absolute spirit) as so many ways of thinking of oneself as minded.

When discussing spirit in Hegel, Heidegger mostly refers to the Jena *Phenomenology of Spirit* rather than discussing the sections on it in the *Encyclopedia*. This is a problematic maneuver, as Hegel changed his views about the architecture of the system and, therefore, about the conceptual structure of mind and nature themselves, between the Jena *Phenomenology* and the mature system.[10] Yet, even if we look at the textual basis of Heidegger's reading, he misses some of the crucial aspects of Hegelian dialectics.

In this section of the chapter, I want to focus on Hegel's notion of "conceptually grasped history [*begriffene Geschichte*]" (PhS 467),[11] which corresponds to the stance of "absolute knowing" at the very end of the *Phenomenology*. The crucial passage in which Hegel transforms the temporalized series of shapes of consciousness into a single, multi-layered, a-temporal account reads as follows:

> *The aim*, absolute knowing, or spirit knowing itself as spirit, has its path in the recollection of spirits as they are in themselves and are as they achieve the organization of their realm. Their preservation according to their free-standing existence appearing in the form of contingency is history, but according to their conceptually grasped organization, it is the *science of phenomenal knowing*. Both together are conceptually grasped history, they form the recollection and the Golgotha of absolute spirit, the actuality, the truth, the certainty of its throne, without which it would be lifeless and alone. (PhS 467)

Hegel's use of the German word "*Geschichte*" contains a wordplay which Heidegger (of all people!) misses. "*Schicht*" means layer and "*Ge-schicht-e*" represents the idea that the shapes of consciousness presented in the *Phenomenology* are so many layers of the kind of mindedness of which Hegel is reflexively giving an account.[12] This corresponds to the philosophical method Hegel deployed throughout his works. The master term for the method in the *Phenomenology* is "*determinate* negation" (PhS 53). The basic function of this concept can be characterized as follows.

A shape of consciousness is an enacted account of intentionality, i.e., of our capacity to think about a mind-independent reality. Intentionality is a paradox-ridden notion. For it seems to be mysterious how the mind can be directed at entirely mind-independent objects and facts. If mind-independent objects and facts are absolutely independent from our grasp of them, how can we ever determine that any of our representations get them right? How can we avoid postulating a "limit which completely separates [*schlechthin scheidende Grenze*]" (PhS 49) mind and world to such an extent that we wind up with a devastating form of skepticism?[13] But if mind-independent objects are essentially knowable or graspable by us, in what exact sense are they mind-independent after all? How could we possibly separate the mind-dependent from the mind-independent parts of the allegedly mind-independent world?

Each of the shapes of consciousness discussed in the *Phenomenology* is an attempt to solve this problem by specifying a ratio of mind-dependence and mind-independence for a given paradigm case of intentionality (such as sensory intuition, perception, abductive inference). Some of the higher, more complex shapes of consciousness (beginning with self-consciousness) involve ordered layers of intentionality such as second-order other-intentionality (i.e., thought of someone's thought of mind-independent objects, etc.).

In order to redeem the claim to necessity and completeness (see PhS 53) so as to overcome both a dogmatic claim to absolute knowing and its associated skeptical threat, Hegel moves in the smallest possible steps. The next shape of consciousness in each case replaces the most minimal assumption of the preceding one so that the theorist is able to construct an ordered succession of attempts to think about ourselves as intentional agents.

A simple example of this method of determinate negation might suffice to illustrate my point. The first shape of consciousness is "sensuous-certainty [*sinnliche Gewißheit*]." The basic idea of sense certainty has it that we immediately grasp parts of the mind-independent world simply by directing our overall gaze at it. The mind-independent world reveals itself to us without further conceptual ado. However, how is it possible to distinguish particular items (objects) as patterns if we are bombarded by mind-independent reality? In particular, how can we account for the fact that we sometimes get things wrong if we are immediately in touch with how things really are, if how things really are is revealed to us? Sense certainty is deficient, as it leaves us with no account of our own fallibility.

The second shape of consciousness, perception, tries to fill in this lacuna by adding mental activity on our side to the picture: in perception we bundle aspects of the mind-independent world together into objects that are not immediately given to us. Yet how can we establish that we ever bundle the right aspects together if this kind of synthesis merely reflects the activity of our minds? This creates a whole series of problems (well-known from discussions in philosophy of perception in the wake of British empiricism), which all follow from the assumption that properties of objects only hang together in the object itself if we establish their relationship to the object.

Hegel operates on two levels. On one level, he ontologically commits to there being sense certainty, perception, etc. They really are layers of the human mind. Yet, the theoretical investigation into their systematic unity articulates paradoxes and shortcomings that are not transparent to the mind itself on the level of its basic encounter with reality. The function of philosophy is to make explicit the assumptions built into mental reality itself. Mental reality, then, is not merely a mentalistic vocabulary designed from the intentional stance and to be explained away by a full-fledged theory (of whatever sort), but a reality which historically unfolds until it reaches the point where the mind is capable of reconstructing its layers in a systematic self-conception.[14]

Heidegger misses Hegel's method, as he always portrays him as mired in ontotheology. In Heidegger's reading, Hegel basically does not have a method, but actually looks at historical reality from a fundamentally Christian perspective for which all of historical reality moves toward an endpoint of revelation which is achieved in the Hegelian system.[15]

To be sure, in *Being and Time* Heidegger is trying to formulate the following more specific point as a critique of Hegel: Temporality ontologically precedes the mind's capacity to rationally reconstruct its layers. For Heidegger, there is no such thing as the human mind potentially struggling to get hold of a mind-independent reality in the first place. What there is, is fundamentally temporal, the groundless manifestation of reality as the facticity of our own being-in-the-world. However, formulating such a picture of the human being, despite Heidegger's insistence on radicality, resoluteness, and authenticity, does not even begin to address the problem of how the existential modes by which being manifests itself to us fit into nature, a topic Heidegger barely addresses in *Being and Time* and which is a crucial element in his own insight into its ultimately subjectivist shortcomings. Heidegger is not able to avoid the skeptical conundrum that results from the rejection of the very possibility of achieving an insight into the systematic unity of human activity.

This is why Heidegger after *Being and Time* resolutely sticks to his guns and thinks of history as a history of being rather than of mindedness. Being transforms itself into various shapes of *Dasein* (a plurality of worlds of meaning) without revealing any kind of underlying unity, purpose, or directedness. History turns into a chaotic series of transformations, variations without a recognizable invariant.

Yet this raises the decisive question of why anyone would be entitled to accept Heidegger's ominous claims about the history of being, all written in a code that over the decades becomes increasingly opaque and is heavily intertwined with stereotypical and paranoid (including anti-Semitic) ruminations associated with Heidegger's autobiography.[16] Heidegger after (and already to some extent within) *Being and Time* loses control of his phenomenological method, as he desperately tries to replace the conception of the human being as rational animal by the idea of a mysterious temporality engaged in unsystematic self-revelation.

In this context, it is possible to formulate a Hegel-inspired criterion for theory success, which I have elsewhere described as the "principle of intelligibility"[17] and the "indispensability thesis"[18] respectively. The upshot of these can be summarized as follows: *No philosophical theory should make it* a priori *that we are incapable of addressing the ontological relationship between knowledge (claims) and what they are about. For this reason, we need to be able to accommodate the fact that human beings are both parts of reality and in the epistemically distinguished position of knowing it in our conception of what there is. Our conception of what there is needs to account for the central epistemic position we occupy, lest we wind up with epistemological disaster.*

Hegel has developed his own complex version of how to respect this principle. It would take a reconstruction of the entire system laid out in the *Encyclopedia* to give an account of this. What matters most in a discussion of Heidegger's interpretation of Hegel is the fact that the Hegelian system is actually incompatible with the idea that history is an unfolding of an originally transcendent ontotheological absolute spirit who manifests itself to finite thinkers at privileged points in historical time. Hegel himself rejects any such view as religious "picture thinking," which, to be sure, has a place in the structure of the human mind's capacity to think of itself. For Hegel, a religious account of historical time as the revelation of the divine does indeed contain a grain of truth in that it indirectly directs our attention to ourselves as rational, free agents who transcend the domain of that which can be explained from a purely observational point of view.

Conclusion

In this chapter, I have argued that Heidegger in BT §82 (as elsewhere) misinterprets Hegel on various levels. He imputes a vulgar conception of time to Hegel by suggesting that Hegel merely voices Aristotelian prejudices in an inauthentic manner, prejudices inherited from generation to generation of philosophers lapsing into the world. Remarkably, he himself is subject to that criticism, as he precisely does not offer a detailed and critical reconstruction of Hegel's actual conceptual maneuvers dealing with the transition from space to time. Hegel's dialectical method comes to bear at the joints of conceptual transition, a method entirely absent from Aristotle's account of time in the context of his *Physics*.

Heidegger misses the important methodological architecture of Hegel's systematic approach to philosophical theorizing because he assumes that

Hegel's system is a historicized form of ontotheology, i.e., a somewhat sophisticated version of a Christian history of salvation, which Heidegger, beginning with his intention to break with the "*system* of Catholicism," tries to supersede throughout his entire philosophical work.[19] However, closer inspection shows that an ontotheological reading of Hegel is incompatible with his account of the dialectical method, not to mention with the explicit anti-Platonic arguments in the *Science of Logic* which show that temporal reality cannot be conceived of as the manifestation of an eternal transcendent realm of pure structure.[20]

Hegel himself already realizes that time cannot in general be an abstract flow or ordered series of points, as this undercuts our experience of time as embodied, historical agents. Our situation as embodied, historical agents is only made explicit in the philosophy of spirit, which is based on the full development of the concepts of the philosophy of nature. Time is thus in no way in general reduced to mechanical time, which does not mean, in turn, that there is no mechanical time.

The discussion of space and time in the mechanics is restricted to a rational reconstruction of fundamental concepts of the philosophy of nature and therefore needs to be relegated to an analysis of the vocabulary of physics *qua* discipline dealing with anonymous processes in the mind-less universe. This analysis does not entail that time in general could or should be reduced to physical time. On the contrary, part of the transition from the philosophy of nature to the philosophy of spirit within the Hegelian system consists in understanding that the concepts deployed in explaining natural processes are not nearly sufficient to give an account of the modes of self-conception constitutive of historically situated, free agents.

In this chapter, I suggested that Heidegger's project fails vis-à-vis both nature and history. Actually, Heidegger never really addresses the relationship between physical time and existential temporality and is consequently in no position to give an account of how our understanding of being is related to the fact that we are embodied thinkers, rational animals. Instead, he notoriously tries to transcend the human standpoint, which makes him a forerunner of more recent post- and transhumanist trends in contemporary philosophy. But thereby hangs a tale.

Notes

1. See the crucial passage at Martin Heidegger, *Being and Time*, trans. John Stambaugh (Albany, NY: State University of New York Press, 1996), 17: "We intimated that a pre-ontological being [*Sein*] belongs to Dasein as its ontic

constitution. Dasein *is* in such a way that, by being [*seiend*], it understands something like being. Remembering this connection, we must show that *time* is that from which Dasein tacitly understands and interprets something like being at all. Time must be brought to light and genuinely grasped as the horizon of every understanding and interpretation of being. For this to become clear we need an *original explication of time as the horizon of the understanding of being, in terms of temporality as the being of Dasein which understands being.* This task as a whole requires that the concept of time thus gained can be distinguished from the common [in the German Heidegger says: "vulgar"] understanding of it."

2. John M. E. McTaggart, "The Unreality of Time," *Mind* 17, no. 68 (1908): 457–74.

3. Markus Gabriel, *Why the World Does Not Exist* (Cambridge: Polity Press, 2015).

4. See G. W. F. Hegel, *Philosophy of Nature: being part two of the "Encyclopaedia of Philosophical Sciences,"* ed. and trans. A. V. Miller (Oxford: Clarendon Press, 2004), §254 R: "It is not permissible to speak of *points of space*, as if they constituted the positive element of space, since space, on account of its lack of difference, is only the possibility and not the actual *positedness* of being-outside-of-one-another and of the negative, and is therefore absolutely continuous; the point, the being-for-self, is consequently rather the *negation* of space, a negation which is posited in space."

5. This account draws on Anton Friedrich Koch, *Die Evolution des logischen Raums: Aufsätze zu Hegels Nichtstandard-Metaphysik* (Tübingen: Mohr Siebeck, 2014) and Markus Gabriel, *Transcendental Ontology: Essays in German Idealism* (New York: Continuum, 2011).

6. Markus Gabriel, "Hegels Kategorienkritik," in *Kategoriendeduktion im Deutschen Idealismus*, ed. Rainer Schäfer et al. (Berlin: Duncker & Humblot, forthcoming). For a philosophically lucid account of the function of Hegelian categories see the *opus magnum* Robert B. Brandom, *A Spirit of Trust: A Reading of Hegel's Phenomenology* (Cambridge, MA: The Belknap Press of Harvard University Press, 2019).

7. EPN, §255 R: "The reason, therefore, why it cannot be said how *height, length,* and *breadth* differ from each other is that these three dimensions only *ought* to be different, but that they *are* not yet differences."

8. See the excellent discussion in Michael Forster, "Kants transzendentaler Idealismus: Das Argument hinsichtlich des Raumes und der Geometrie," in *Raum erfahren: Epistemologische, ethische und ästhetische Zugänge*, ed. David Espinet, Tobias Keiling, and Nikola Mirković (Tübingen: Mohr Siebeck, 2017), 63–82.

9. Markus Gabriel, "What Kind of an Idealist (if any) Is Hegel?" *Hegel-Bulletin* 27, no. 2 (2016): 181–208; Gabriel, *Transcendental Ontology*. For an excellent overview of the different accounts of Hegel's metametaphysics and a strong defence of a reading based on the doctrine of essence, see Andrés Felipe Parra Ayala, *Das spekulative Geschehen: Über die Bedeutung der Metaphysik in Hegels Wissenschaft der Logik* (Bonn Dissertation, 2019).

10. On this topic, see Hans F. Fulda, *Das Problem einer Einleitung in Hegels Wissenschaft der Logik* (Frankfurt am Main: Vittorio Klostermann, 1965); Michael N. Forster, *Hegel's Idea of a Phenomenology of Spirit* (Chicago: University of Chicago Press, 1998).

11. Quotations from the *Phenomenology* are from Georg Wilhelm Friedrich Hegel, *Phenomenology of Spirit*, trans. Terry Pinkard (Cambridge: Cambridge University Press, 2018). Hereafter: PhS.

12. Thanks to Michael Forster for making me aware of this wordplay. For more on this see Markus Gabriel, *Propos réalistes* (Paris: Vrin, 2018), 205–207.

13. See Michael N. Forster, *Hegel and Skepticism* (Cambridge, MA: Harvard University Press 1989); Gabriel, *Transcendental Ontology*, 2–34; Brandom, *A Spirit of Trust*, 35–62.

14. For more on Hegel's method in philosophy of mind see Markus Gabriel, "Hegel's Account of Perceptual Experience in His Philosophy of Subjective Spirit," in *Hegel's Philosophy of Spirit: A Critical Guide*, ed. Marina F. Bykova (Cambridge: Cambridge University Press, 2019), 104–24; Markus Gabriel, "Intuition, Representation, and Thinking: Hegel's Psychology and the Placement Problem," in *The Palgrave Hegel Handbook*, ed. Marina F. Bykova and Kenneth R. Westphal (London: Palgrave Macmillan, forthcoming).

15. See Martin Heidegger, *Hegel's Concept of Experience: With a Section from Hegel's* Phenomenology of Spirit *in the Kenley Royce Dove Translation* (San Francisco: Harper & Row, 1989).

16. See Markus Gabriel, "Was heißt ‚denken'? Heidegger und das Problem der Philosophie in den Überlegungen II-XI," in *Heideggers »Schwarze Hefte« im Kontext: Geschichte, Politik, Ideologie*, ed. David Espinet, Günther Figal, Tobias Keiling, and Nikola Mirković (Tübingen: Mohr Siebeck, 2018), 173–94.

17. Gabriel, "What Kind of an Idealist (if any) Is Hegel?"

18. Markus Gabriel, *I Am Not Brain: Philosophy of Mind for the 21st Century* (Cambridge: Polity Press, 2017); Markus Gabriel, *Neo-Existentialism: How to Conceive of the Human Mind after Naturalism's Failure*, with contributions by Jocelyn Maclure, Jocelyn Benoist, Andrea Kern, and Charles Taylor (Cambridge: Polity Press, 2018).

19. Martin Heidegger, "Letter to Father Engelbert Krebs (1919)," in *Supplements: From the Earliest Essays to* Being and Time *and Beyond*, ed. and trans. John van Buren (Albany: State University of New York Press, 2002), 69: "Epistemological insights extending to a theory of historical knowledge have made the *system* of Catholicism problematic and unacceptable to me, but not Christianity and metaphysics—these, though, in a new sense."

20. For a detailed excellent reconstruction of Hegel's account of the nature of metaphysics in that regard, see again Parra Ayala, *Das spekulative Geschehen: Über die Bedeutung der Metaphysik in Hegels Wissenschaft der Logik*.

17

Sedimentation, Memory, and Self in Hegel and Merleau-Ponty

Elisa Magrì

Often, we think of institutions as the embodiment of some type of authority that establishes normative rules. Religious, social, and educational organizations, for example, are usually characterized as instituting practices, principles, and norms that contribute to public discourse and collective customs. However, this notion of institution in the robust sense of social normativity does not do justice to the historical dimension that informs and constitutes it. An institution is not created *ex nihilo* but is generated in the course of time, building on the assent of individuals to certain beliefs and collective practices, as well as on the transformation of the social and collective landscape that is informed by those customs. In this respect, the concept of institution refers to the enactment of the social, cultural, and affective ties that are sedimented across history at both individual and collective levels. On this view, institution is closely related to the concept of tradition but is not restricted to it, for the former primarily appeals to the *processes* of signification that generate and establish traditions of thought and normative frameworks while remaining open-ended.

Merleau-Ponty's 1954–55 lectures on passivity and institution at the Collège de France examine the notion of institution in this specific sense as a process of donation of sense (*Sinngebung*) that is pivotal in the constitution

E. Magrì (✉)
Philosophy Department, Boston College, Chestnut Hill, MA, USA

C. D. Coe (eds.), *The Palgrave Handbook of German Idealism and Phenomenology*, Palgrave Handbooks in German Idealism,
https://doi.org/10.1007/978-3-030-66857-0_17

of meaning across different dimensions, including the aesthetic, the affective, and the historical domain.[1] Merleau-Ponty was interested in exploring how meaning is deposited in human experience, producing traditions of feeling and thought that allow for change and transformation. In this respect, institution, for Merleau-Ponty, is inseparable from sedimentation, which bestows meaning indirectly or laterally, namely via symbols, art, and the unconscious. The most significant characteristic of sedimentation is that, even though it typically begins with a particular person, action, or place, its main tendency is toward a generalization that is not directly governed by the mind.[2]

Consider, as an illustration of this, Merleau-Ponty's favorite example of institution in the artistic domain, such as the use of planimetric perspective in the Renaissance. As Merleau-Ponty puts it, the relation between space and body was not conceived in its generality by Renaissance artists, who "saw only a mode of reporting, not the principle of the report."[3] Merleau-Ponty's argument is that planimetric perspective allowed artists to establish constant relations between height, breadth, and depth with respect to the distance from the eye. In turn, this choice produced "stability, consistency, compossibility, and rationality."[4] Yet planimetric perspective was not any truer than previous strategies of artistic expression. The use of perspective in painting was an "aesthetic-social choice," not "a law of nature or even the acquisition of a pictorial, critical consciousness which would be ultimate."[5] By making space a dimension that precedes the positions of objects, Renaissance artists found a way to juxtapose different elements on the same plane without suppressing their gradation in depth. Yet they did not *conceive* of space as an *a priori* dimension. This new form of pictorial practice was an attempt to make sense of space from within the practice of visual representation, but the artist did not make any choice involving space as an object of perception. If anything, the artists' choice consisted in their diverging from a given norm; the same divergence that would later allow the Baroque to entirely re-interpret the meaning of perspective.

On this view, the sedimentation of a given practice, while being contingent to particular events and places, institutes lasting nexuses between form and content, theory and praxis, norms and uses, which are never definitive. With regard to this, it is noteworthy that Merleau-Ponty's reflections on institutions are intended to also offer a revision of Hegelianism. For Merleau-Ponty, Hegel's philosophy represents "the discovery of the living, real and original relation between the elements of the world. But Hegelianism situates this relation in the past in order to subordinate it to the systematic vision of the philosopher."[6] In his notes, Merleau-Ponty praises the Hegelian aspiration to understand the nexuses that hold together history, nature, and thought. This was the aspiration to understand experience through logic, to paraphrase Hyppolite,[7] whose existentialist reading of Hegel's *Phenomenology of Spirit* deeply influenced Merleau-Ponty.[8] At the same time, however, Merleau-Ponty also manifests his distance from Hegelianism, which he finds committed to "the systematic vision of the philosopher." The worry here is that systematic philosophy fails to do justice to the contingency of the real as well as to the ephemeral character of the present. This is a constant *leitmotif* of Merleau-Ponty's constant dialogue with Hegelian philosophy.[9]

Already in his 1946 paper on "Hegel's Existentialism," for example, Merleau-Ponty argues that Hegel's philosophy could enrich and revive contemporary existentialist theories, but such a task could only be achieved by the *Phenomenology of Spirit* and not by Hegel's late philosophy. In the former, Merleau-Ponty envisaged the possibility of vindicating the role of reason over the anxiety and the contradictions of the human condition.[10] In contrast to this, for Merleau-Ponty, the Hegel of 1827 fell victim to the fallacy of interpreting history through the lenses of logical reasoning. Hegel failed to contextualize and interpret his own position in history as a philosopher. The historical process described by Hegel's late lectures could only lead—for Merleau-Ponty—to the establishment of a hierarchical social order governed by reason and inhabited by none other than the philosopher himself. Instead, the Hegel of 1807 was concerned with revealing the logic at work at the levels of society, culture, religion, and philosophy. Unlike the late Hegel, the young Hegel would not replace human experience with universal thought but rather retrieve the latent logic sedimented in collective life. Only in this way does absolute knowledge, the culminating moment of the *Phenomenology of Spirit*, become "perhaps not a philosophy but a way of life."[11]

Ten years after the publication of "Hegel's Existentialism," Merleau-Ponty's skepticism toward Hegel's mature philosophy reflects the same worry. His greatest preoccupation concerns the contemplative attitude that resurfaces in the very notion of an absolute knowledge independent from space and time. Pointing out the co-implication of Hegel's philosophy of history and the cunning of reason, Merleau-Ponty claims that "the one who observes the opacity [of history] sets himself up outside of history, becomes a universal spectator."[12] If reason underlies the course of history and if the philosopher is the only one who can grasp the sense of such an unfolding, it turns out—Merleau-Ponty argues—that the cunning of reason is nothing but philosophical knowledge. And in order to obtain such a knowledge, which abstracts from accidental events and particularities, philosophers are compelled to be indifferent to contingency, thereby becoming spectators of the universal.

Merleau-Ponty's critical remarks are still fruitful today, despite being partly outdated. To be sure, the opposition that Merleau-Ponty draws between the young and the late Hegel does not seem to acknowledge Hegel's generative view of social norms or the relevance of historical transformations within philosophy of history.[13] Furthermore, Merleau-Ponty tends to overlap absolute knowledge, absolute spirit, and the spirit of world history, without distinguishing between the account of absolute knowledge outlined by the *Phenomenology of Spirit* and the notion of absolute spirit that appears in the third part of Hegel's system in his *Encyclopedia of the Philosophical Sciences*. Such a distinction is typically based on the different systematic transitions that link together objective spirit and history across the two works.[14]

Nonetheless, Merleau-Ponty's worry concerning the contemplative attitude engendered by Hegel's philosophy still deserves further examination today, not simply as an isolated issue in the Hegelian scholarship but rather as a fundamental philosophical question. If absolute knowledge was indeed meant to represent "a way of life," what sort of life would that be like? The ending of the *Phenomenology*, in particular, posits relevant issues because of the emphasis it places on spirit's self-recollection and inwardization (PhG §808).[15] Is absolute knowledge meant to initiate a new historical beginning, or does it sublimate the course of history into the ecstatic dimension of speculative thought?

Given the limited scope of this chapter, my analysis will be restricted to Hegel's account of absolute knowledge in the *Phenomenology of Spirit*. Deepening Merleau-Ponty's appraisal of this work, I argue that Hegel's view of absolute knowledge in the *Phenomenology* consists in a process of sedimentation that is very much in line with Merleau-Ponty's in that it revolves around a phenomenological-inspired view of institution. Contrary to Merleau-Ponty's skepticism, however, I suggest that absolute knowledge is compatible with an account of ethical memory that reactivates potential new beginnings in history and society as a form of critical awareness. For Hegel, memory is not simply the *locus* of transmission of sense but rather the activity through which concepts are instituted in order to be communicated, shared, and taken up in history. On this view, subjectivity is not a mere shell that is left aside once a more mature and solid knowledge is established, for it corresponds to the source of reference of ethical memory.

Accordingly, this chapter primarily shows that both Hegel and Merleau-Ponty employ a theory of institution that is fundamentally linked to sedimentation, memory, and self. By exploring the connection between these concepts in both philosophers, my aim is to provide a ground to critically reconsider contemporary discussions of ethical memory, such as the account put forward by Avishai Margalit.

The Interiority with Escape: Merleau-Ponty's Dialectic of Sense

Merleau-Ponty's course notes on passivity and institution are heavily indebted to Husserl's late manuscripts, particularly *The Crisis of European Sciences,* including the appendix on *The Origin of Geometry* (C: Appendix VI). In these manuscripts, Husserl explores the original meaning of mathematics and geometry, discussing the relation between science and culture, and issues of universal history in general. Husserl's key insight is that Galileo Galilei introduced a whole new paradigm in the history of Western thought by conceiving of geometry as the language of nature. As Husserl remarks, this was less a product of deliberate choice than a natural development of geometry as a science, namely as a lively forward movement of acquisition and transmission of knowledge. The hallmark of Galilei's pioneering demonstrations, however, lies—for Husserl—in the use of geometry as idealization of the experiences that characterize the natural attitude. In the translation operated by geometry, bodies become limit-shapes, namely ideal entities whose relations can be converted into numbers in order to verify the consistency of the physical laws underlying their movements. As Husserl writes:

> In place of real praxis—that of action or that of considering empirical possibilities having to do with actual and really [i.e., physically] possible empirical bodies—we now have an ideal praxis of "pure thinking" which remains exclusively within the realm of pure *limit-shapes*.... Through a method of idealization and construction which historically has long since been worked out and can be practiced intersubjectively in a community, these limit-shapes have become acquired tools that can be used habitually and can always be applied to something new—an infinite and yet self-enclosed world of ideal objects as a field for study. Like all cultural acquisitions which arise out of human accomplishment, they remain objectively knowable and available without requiring that the formulation of their meaning be repeatedly and explicitly renewed. (C §9, 26)

The mathematization of nature corresponds to the translation of ordinary experience into the ideal language of forms and symbols. In this respect, sedimentation is operative in two main senses. In one way, meaning is sedimented in mathematical symbols without the necessity of a concomitant intuition. This means that mathematical formulas are abstractions of regular movements and interactions that occur between physical objects. The original intuition underlying the apprehension of those relations is not required in the application of the formula. In this sense, Galilei's law of gravitation provides a shortcut for dealing with physics problems without having to go through the steps of Galilei's experiment. In a similar way, Husserl argues that cultural objects, such as pincers or scissors, are habitually seen and employed as tools for cutting and gripping things and not as aesthetical or material objects. We perceive cultural objects as embedded with the practical significance that we habitually bestow upon them. Thus, in another and deeper sense, the root of sedimentation is habituality, conceived as the temporal stratification of acts of apprehension. Sedimentation represents a form of "living retention" without which there could not be any science, for retention provides the transmission of sense originally grasped by evidence.[16]

From this point of view, the problem of the mathematization of nature can be explained in terms of the failure to reactivate the living retention that underlies acts of meaning apprehension. According to Husserl, geometry was originally meant to pass on its goal of deductive reasoning, enabling the formation of logical nexuses between propositions without necessarily abstracting from, but rather preserving, their reference to concrete reality. Unfortunately, such a *desideratum* was not fulfilled, as geometry was employed by natural sciences as a formal discipline, severed from the concrete experience of nature. This means not only that the ties with concrete experience are cut off in favor of a formalistic approach to truth. The subject of experience is also replaced by an impersonal reference point that is devoid of self-relation. As Husserl points out, to be a person means to have a position in space through the constant and peculiar reference to one's own body, in and through which the surrounding world becomes available.[17] Thus, spatiotemporal localization is an inadequate characterization of personal individuation, for the latter depends on the temporal succession of lived experiences that inform the psychic sphere. Husserl's view, which is also elaborated in *Ideas* II,[18] is that the sedimentation of the lived experiences through which the ego takes a stance and develops a personal attitude, is a *habitus* that projects the self into the world, motivating their choices and actions.

Merleau-Ponty's course notes draw further attention to the dimension of emptying out of meaning (*Sinnenentleerung*) that is distinctive of natural sciences. And yet, for Merleau-Ponty, the emptying out of meaning is not exclusive of geometry but intrinsic to the institution of a domain of knowledge. Merleau-Ponty argues that signification is "not timeless," "it does not descend from the principles to the consequences." On the contrary, and in a quite Hegelian fashion, true "idealization raises itself up above itself by means of recurrence, does not surpass it without preserving it."[19] If a domain of knowledge is to have meaning at all, its transmission and universalization can only be obtained in virtue of the donation of sense (*Sinngebung*) that is actualized in every instance of knowledge acquisition. However, like Husserl, Merleau-Ponty was aware that traditions can be passed on even when the ability to reactivate their originary source of sense is lost. What guarantees, then, the persistence of sense across history? Merleau-Ponty's concern can be summarized as follows: If science and culture are understood in terms of sedimentation of knowledge, and if the reactivation of knowledge is necessary for the transformation of the latter into a tradition, how can there be tradition in the face of forgetfulness and mechanization?

Merleau-Ponty's approach to this problem is eminently dialectical. The core idea of his reflections is that every institution involves a dialectic between meaning constitution and forgetfulness. Once meaning is generated and established, its genesis is forgotten and yet the sign that carries the meaning remains. *Prima facie*, Merleau-Ponty's approach seems to resonate with Horkheimer and Adorno's famous claim that "all reification is forgetting."[20] However, the process of sedimentation that underlies the notion of institution cannot be reduced to reification, for it is not the end result of a productive activity. For Merleau-Ponty, the sign is not the residual of the process of signification. For the sign, along with the consciousness that interprets it, produces a field of sense that is capable of being reactivated at any new emergence of the sign in other contexts of experience.

This is what sedimentation is: the persistence of the trace of the forgotten, "and thereby a call to thought which depends on itself and goes further."[21] Without a community of selves who take up the solicitation to thinking that is preserved in the sign and who, thereby, think through it, there would not be any truth or knowledge. In this sense, Merleau-Ponty speaks of a "double horizon"[22] that is not restricted to the holder of the experience in the now but that also includes, as a virtuality, the possibility of an extended generalization. In order to illustrate Merleau-Ponty's argument, it is helpful to consider the example that he provides in both his 1949–52 lectures[23] as well as in his 1954–55 notes on institution and passivity.[24]

Drawing on Wertheimer's *Gestalt* psychology, Merleau-Ponty recalls how learning competencies are acquired in geometry, specifically when calculating the surface of the parallelogram. This requires that one understands the underlying *Gestalt* or organizing principle of the figure. In Wertheimer's example, a five-year old who has already learnt how to calculate the surface of the rectangle and has fully grasped the sense of the geometrical demonstration seeks "to straighten out" the parallelogram. She proceeds by cutting off a triangle from one end, moving it around to the other side, thereby turning the parallelogram into a simple rectangle. Whether the parallelogram is presented in the classic, horizontal way or turned around (Fig. 17.1), the child is not taken aback, because she has developed "structural understanding."[25] This means that the child does not proceed by blind recollection of the teacher's demonstration. On the contrary, the child's learning is activated by the application of part-function relations.

To acquire a genuine understanding of the equivalence between the parallelogram and the rectangle one needs to activate productive thinking, i.e., synthetic, interpretative insights that bestow sense on symbolic forms. Gestalt psychologists like Wertheimer understood apprehension in terms of grasping and intuiting the inner structure or organization of the object. Such an approach challenges associationism in that it maintains that knowledge is produced by trials and errors, producing changes in the way items are grouped and constructed in order to satisfy the structural requirements of the situation.

Interestingly, Merleau-Ponty does not use this example to emphasize the productivity of thinking activated by the *Gestalt*. On the contrary, he insists on the retention that is necessary to laterally extend the proof of the demonstration to variations of its examples. For Merleau-Ponty, Wertheimer's investigations show that the generalization of sense underpinning geometrical transformations and constructions *retains* signification.[26] Generalization does not proceed from empirical facts to ideas but rather from the transformation of a field of knowledge into another. On this view, the truth of geometry

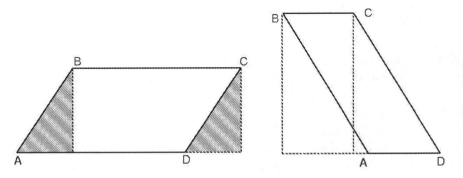

Fig. 17.1 Wertheimer's parallelograms. Credits: Aaron Sloman (https://www.cs.bham.ac.uk/research/projects/cogaff/misc/orthogonal-competences/), Creative Commons License

(as of any domain of true knowledge) is based on the idealization that transforms the field of experience into a symbolic order that yields the possibility of a repetition. Therefore, Merleau-Ponty repeats that signification cannot be obtained without a "return to the concrete" or without "recurrence."

Recurrence is not sheer repetition, which would lead to the mechanization of the formula as well as to the blind acceptance of the demonstration. On the contrary, recurrence refers to the way in which meaning is taken up and renewed in an actual field of experience.[27] To put it in other words, the institution of a domain of knowledge is not established once its formal truth has been demonstrated, for it requires a living and continuous dimension of apprehension and recreation of the original truth, which in turn extends, modifies, and enriches the very field in which that truth was originally grasped. This is the reason why Merleau-Ponty conceives of institution as the enactment (not the result) of the sedimentation of sense.

While the model that Merleau-Ponty presents is dialectical, it also differs from Hegel's approach. For Merleau-Ponty, universalization "is thought in perceptual terms (*soil* of knowledge, *horizon*)"[28]; it does not evolve by becoming other than itself, but rather by returning to the empirical origin as an "interior." What Merleau-Ponty hints at here is the possibility of a critical engagement with the past within a field of knowledge that allows always new ways of thinking through the original model, whether this is a scientific intuition, an artistic innovation, or an emotional breakthrough. The interior is the domain of experience that is enlarged and progressively transformed by the active relation to a concrete object of experience. On this view, knowledge is generated by engaging traditions of thought, thereby reactivating in a lateral way the principles and intuitions that are sedimented in the past.

Such a task is not accomplished by a plurality of subjects working in a parallel way, each having his or her underlying intentional grasping of the object. Crucial to the transmission of geometry as a field of knowledge is the co-participation in the "soil" of pre-geometric experiences. After all, geometry demonstrations are not elaborated *in a vacuum* but developed within a context that is later integrated in the epistemic principle. Accordingly, the transmission and sedimentation of a given tradition of thought is not realized by a plurality of minds working independently from one another, but rather accomplished by a community of consciousnesses, each embodying a position within a common field that guarantees continuity of knowledge. Only in this way does the resumption of the past in the present leave the former "in its originality, does not truly 'surpass' it, does not falter itself to contain it all [in its entirety] plus something else."[29] At this level, Merleau-Ponty distances himself from Hegel's "logic of history":

In its interiority with escape, this passage from decentering to decentering, without absolute decentering, in this exteriority which does not forbid encroachment, there is truly union of exteriority and interiority, at each moment, while Hegel unifies them only by pushing them to the absolute: absolute real or fact, absolute rational or concept, being unified as absolutes.[30]

For Merleau-Ponty, Hegel's philosophy precludes the opening of new possibilities, closing up the dialectic of sign and meaning into an absolute, speculative unity. Before discussing, in the next section, the alleged lack of "escape" of Hegel's approach, it is worth noting that Merleau-Ponty's appeal to the resurrection of the past in the present is essentially a form of collective memory. As put by Vallier, memory for Merleau-Ponty is neither restricted to personal memory nor based on phenomenological analyses of egoic retention: "It is not about recalling what I did last Friday night; it is about reanimating a past, even a past that was not my own, in order to understand it and to alter the landscape of my present."[31]

This type of non-personal memory, as it were, is characterized by a non-egoic modality of retention, which manifests itself as consciousness of a field of knowledge. This is the form of retention that animates the work of the intellectual historian, who seeks to further explore the nexuses between past and present by inquiring the conceptual framework in which determinate traditions of thought originated. Certainly, historians do not have to be personally involved in their research in order to generate knowledge. And yet their commitment to explicate the moral and political significance of past events informs their quest for accuracy and understanding.

Thus, on a deeper level, non-egoic retention represents the modality in and through which intersubjectivity becomes an instituting power in that it motivates consciousness to further appropriate its sense and history. That there is intersubjectivity and not just a plurality of views means, for Merleau-Ponty, that the fitting together of many different subjective viewpoints is brought about by history, tradition, and culture as a foundation that does not have any ultimate foundation. Once the concept of institution is understood as a form of sedimentation, the former does no longer operate as archaeological anteriority or as normative authority. On the contrary, an institution constitutes a horizon of sense that informs the present, and whose persistence calls to the exercise of thought in the now.

Absolute Knowledge as Sedimentation in Hegel's *Phenomenology of Spirit*

Hegel's *Phenomenology of Spirit* is best described as a journey of formation. Like Goethe's *Wilhelm Meister's Apprenticeship* or *Faust*, the *Phenomenology of Spirit* describes the journey of human spirit through different phases of development that culminate in absolute knowledge. The systematic development that Hegel describes has generally been taken to characterize the substance of Hegel's dialectical method. To be sure, the evolution of the *Phenomenology of Spirit* is the development of a subjective mind that experiences the dialectical contradictions arising within its own experience of the world. On the one hand, truth is presented as an organized whole; while, on the other hand, knowledge unfolds and sediments as the result of spirit's journey. And yet, both sides are cognate dimensions of a single comprehensive experience that is supposed to lay the ground for a holistic theory of truth.

However, it is worth noting that, strictly speaking, at the beginning of the *Phenomenology of Spirit*, consciousness does not yet qualify as a *subject* of experience. As pointed out by Russon,

> the *Phenomenology of Spirit* demonstrates that the sense of ourselves that we typically live with—a coherent sense of ourselves as independent agents, coherently integrated with the human and natural world—is an achievement (indeed, a complex negotiation with the conflicting infinities of reality, desire, and others) and not our "given" state.[32]

Subjectivity is not given from the outset, but it is achieved in the process of actualization of spirit as a self that relates to an external world. Such fundamental directedness to the world, which is perceived as being independent but no longer alien to the self, represents the most significant outcome of the fourth chapter of the *Phenomenology*, which has for very good reasons been at the center of a number of divergent interpretations. Here, Hegel shows that the relation between self and world requires the activity of consciousness as a subject of desire that is capable of transforming reality, thereby actualizing thinking and abstract thought.[33] By defending a developmental view of the self, which is always enacted as a pole of desire, action, and thought in the world, Hegel allows the distinction between a minimal and a more robust view of self. While the former is the prerequisite for any theory of truth, the latter refers to the constitution of reality that the self brings about through practical agency and theoretical understanding. If the minimal view of the self is the logical condition for having knowledge, the robust view refers to the self-determination of subjectivity and its constitutive role in shaping the very reality of which knowledge is about.

On this view, absolute knowledge is science in that it coincides with the conceptual organization of what spirit has learnt throughout the phenomenology. Absolute knowledge encompasses both subjective and objective processes of spiritual self-determination. This notably includes the actualization of the personal self but it also covers struggles, pain, and conflicts. For spirit's development[34] is bound to other selves and evolves by going through self-fragmentation, conflicts, and social and cultural crises. In this sense, the development of spirit is tied to temporality, and yet absolute knowledge does away with time consciousness. What is appropriated by absolute knowledge is neither an event nor the transcendence of an absolute value. At the level of science, all the experiences that characterize the journey of spirit precipitate onto spirit itself, making it absolute, namely stripped out of temporality. More specifically, absolute knowledge is linked to the concept (*Begriff*), which is defined as the content that is developed and brought about by spirit and that is finally apprehended and appropriated as the self's own doing.[35] The insistence on the sphere of the self (*Selbst*) at the end of the *Phenomenology of Spirit* is worthy of attention because the self of absolute spirit does not amount to the self of subjective spirit or to any subjective stance. This is precisely the reason why a reader like Merleau-Ponty would be put off by the concluding chapter of the *Phenomenology of Spirit*. What kind of subjectivity is involved at the level of absolute knowledge? Since the self of absolute knowledge is not an individual, how can it possibly inform the substance of absolute knowledge? In relation to this issue, it is possible to identify three main readings: a meta-philosophical approach, a genetic reading, and a cultural-historical inspired interpretation.

The first position is best represented by Winfield. According to Winfield, absolute knowing posits the necessity of removing the form of representation that is tied to spirit's temporal evolution in order to achieve the pure element of knowing. This reading aims to explicate the link between the *Phenomenology* and the *Science of Logic*. By culminating in absolute knowledge, the *Phenomenology* paves the way for the "minimal initial characterization of science...: the thinking of thinking or logic."[36] In this sense, the self of absolute knowledge would correspond to a meta-philosophical position that is meant to introduce to an entirely new realm of philosophical thinking, namely the logic.[37]

The second position is that of Ferrarin,[38] according to whom the self or "I" in Hegel takes up different senses depending on whether it appears to us in the form of spirit or in that of the concept. Ferrarin emphasizes that the "I" in Hegel is said in many ways. In the case of absolute spirit, Ferrarin stresses the dialectic of alienation that is distinctive of self-consciousness and that Hegel radicalizes at the level of absolute knowledge in order to show the transformation of metaphysical substance into metaphysical subjectivity.

The third position is represented by Nuzzo, according to whom absolute knowledge differs across the *Phenomenology* and the *Encyclopaedia,* respectively. While she recognizes that absolute knowledge in the *Phenomenology* institutes a new speculative beginning, she argues that the account of absolute knowledge provided by the *Encyclopaedia* puts forward a theory of absolute memory that does justice to a renewed and ethical sense of collective subjectivity.

In a way, each reading testifies to the systematic value of Hegel's account of absolute knowledge. Yet Ferrarin's and Nuzzo's positions take very seriously the possibility that absolute knowledge represents more than a transitional step in Hegel's system. Focusing more closely on Nuzzo's approach, I intend to further discuss the connection she establishes between absolute knowledge and memory.

Nuzzo proceeds by distinguishing two distinct and yet interconnected levels of memory in Hegel's *Phenomenology of Spirit.* On the one hand, she identifies memory as the inner force and reactivating power of the *Phenomenology of Spirit.* On such a reading, memory operates as the texture of the *Phenomenology* in that it channels the shapes of consciousness into a unitary process, propelling the advancement of spirit forward. The distinctive character of such a process is that every moment of spirit's development dialectically institutes the possibility of a new beginning. As Nuzzo argues, "memory seems to be, for Hegel, more of the future or of the present, than of the past."[39] Memory serves the goal of opening up the future, while dialectically positing the reality of spirit. On the other hand, Nuzzo argues that memory is present in the *Phenomenology of Spirit* as a distinct figure or *Gestaltung,* namely as ethical memory. By ethical memory, Nuzzo refers to the process of social recollection that is distinctive of the *Phenomenology of Spirit* once spirit becomes reason, establishing itself as a historical dimension.

For Nuzzo, the emergence of memory as ethical memory in the *Phenomenology of Spirit* is tied to the constitution of ethical life, in which individuality and universality are mediated with each other. This means that memory must abandon "its merely psychological, individual, and accidental character, and reach its 'higher determination' or 'common sense' (*Gemeinswesen*)."[40] Memory becomes ethical insofar as the negativity of forgetfulness is preserved but also overcome through collective acts of social and historical significance. Antigone, Christianity, and the Terror become figures of acts of memorialization that cement the unity of the community. At the level of absolute spirit, however, history "is translated and overcome in the atemporal and aspatial dimension of the pure 'concept.'"[41]

Interestingly, Nuzzo identifies a second, more compelling dimension of ethical memory, which she calls "absolute memory," in the account of absolute knowledge that Hegel provides in the *Encyclopaedia* §§552–53. On her view, unlike the *Phenomenology*, which inscribes the work of memory into history only to let this vanish in the shadowy dimension of pure thought, the concluding paragraphs of the *Encyclopaedia* are systematically related to and dependent on world history. In this case, Nuzzo argues that absolute spirit enacts a form of memorialization that inscribes the works of spirit in a trans-historical or eternal dimension. As Nuzzo writes, "The works of absolute spirit are the 'sites' of a meaningful recollection of history in the dimension of a present that is no longer national or political but cultural in a universal sense, that is, at once, individual and truly global, historical (and, systematically, 'post-historical') and eternal."[42] The significance of this form of dialectical memory is that it does not bring back to the past, but "posits the past as spirit's eternal present."[43] As an example of this, Nuzzo refers to specific intersections of personal and collective memories that can be found in the works of Toni Morrison as well as in Primo Levi's memoir of surviving Auschwitz in *Se questo è un uomo* (*If This is a Man*).

As Nuzzo argues, Morrison's writings represent a form of literary archaeology, which—unlike any historical or autobiographical accounts—uses fiction in order to institute the truth. For Morrison, the writer who seeks to find and expose the truth about the interior life of people who did not write their own story (e.g., slave narratives) draws on the "recollection that moves from the image to the text. Not from the text to the image."[44] A photograph, the corner of a room, the memory of a voice, even when dimly recalled, track a journey along which the writer reconstitutes the interior life, the world-horizon of a forgotten event, person, narrative. The writer (or the philosopher, for Hegel) does not try to conjure up a fictional reality, but rather aims to inscribe in the realm of language the truth, namely the personal and intrinsic world-relatedness and stance of the subject. In this sense, truth consists in positing a new present, a new work, wherein what is missing (because it was forgotten) is re-posited, and what has never been there (because it belongs to the aftermath) can live in images that generate new awareness.

Images and not facts, for "facts can exist without human intelligence, but truth cannot."[45] This is why Nuzzo argues that "it is only from the standpoint of a memory that is truly absolute because it is not made of facts (psychological or historical) but of images, that the world—subjective and objective, internal and external—can be (re-)created and lived anew."[46] Similarly, Levi's narrative of the lager camp serves the.

> function of absolute memory—that is, of a memory animated by imagination, feeling, and empathy, but also by reason; a memory that conjoins the personal and the collective in the dimension of a concrete and shared humanity, a memory unequivocally bound to time and history and yet also permanent and eternal.[47]

For Nuzzo, absolute knowledge in the *Encyclopaedia* represents the space that reason inhabits when it enacts itself as absolute memory, namely as a rational reconstruction of the meaning that informs history, including testimony of horrors and abuses such as Levi's. Drawing on Nuzzo's account of ethical memory, it is however possible to re-read Hegel's account of absolute knowledge in the *Phenomenology* as a form of absolute memory that does justice to the sedimentation of self across time.

Written between 1945 and 1947, *Se questo è un uomo* is the lucid account of Levi's imprisonment in the concentration camp of Auschwitz, following his capture by the Fascist militia in 1943 due to Levi's affiliation with the Resistenza movement. Shortly after his arrival in a detention camp for prisoners of war, Levi was selected by a German SS squad to be transferred to the Auschwitz camp along with other Jewish people. A worldwide classic in the literature on genocide, *Se questo è un uomo* is also—at the same time—a powerful illustration of testimony and trauma that exposes the absolute annihilation of human corporeality and individuality.

As has been noted,[48] Levi's narrative strikes us not only because it reveals the daily dehumanization inflicted to the Auschwitz prisoners. Levi's writing transfixes the reader also because it begins with a reconstruction of how Levi was imprisoned (an account given in the past tense) that suddenly shifts to the present tense when Levi recalls his arrival and subsequent time spent in Auschwitz. "This is hell. Today, in our times, hell must be like this."[49] In re-enacting the experience of the concentration camp, Levi cannot help but relive the trauma of Auschwitz in diachronic continuity in the effort to situate and understand it. In this way, a traumatic experience becomes an eternal present that informs the existence of the survivor. As aptly put by Caruth:

> The insistent reenactments of the past do not simply serve as testimony to an event, but may also, paradoxically enough, bear witness to a past that was never fully experienced as it occurred. Trauma, that is, does not simply serve as

record of the past but precisely registers the force of an experience that is not yet fully owned.[50]

The difficulty of owning one's experience, especially traumatic experience, lies at the core of memory as an exercise in self-appropriation. From this point of view, it appears that the function of ethical memory is not restricted to historical time but to a process of self-owning. While Levi's memoir epitomizes a collective experience, its intersubjective character and the very possibility of its communicability rest on the persistence and transformation of the self across the different transitions of one's narrative. Levi's memoir, just like Morrison's writing, are paradigms of absolute knowledge in that their "absolute" character rests on the appropriation of the self as the author of one's actions and thinking. In this sense, the self represents the only condition that guarantees continuity of acting and thinking. Hence, it is not surprising that Hegel elevates it to the form of absolute knowledge in the *Phenomenology*.

In emphasizing the presence of the self, Hegel argues that absolute spirit *owns* the content of its experience, and such ownership represents a universal principle that admits lateral universalization, namely it provides the basis for philosophical reflection and appropriation. The recollection of the different shapes of spirit at the end of the *Phenomenology* indicates the continuity and necessity of the self, i.e., the fact that spirit is a concrete form of self-reference that is constantly modified and enriched by experience. By owning its own doing, spirit posits self-reference as the condition of its own truth, namely it establishes the possibility of philosophical or scientific understanding. In apprehending itself as a universal principle, absolute spirit institutes science as the space of conceptual thinking, where all the past experiences of spirit can be narrated and thematized as its own doing. In this sense, absolute spirit does not achieve self-knowledge by contemplating its past development, but rather by appropriating and recognizing itself.

Here lies the possibility of the repetition, the productive and fertile "recurrence" of which Merleau-Ponty speaks with regard to personal and cultural institution. Once again, repetition is not the mechanical transmission of a given content but the actualization of a possibility that is deeply and firmly rooted in the appropriation of one's development. While the self is always the result of a specific process, its permanence and evolution across different experiential, practical, and theoretical domains require a continuous act of re-appropriation. In order to own itself, spirit needs memory not as the subjective faculty of remembering but rather as the institutionalizing power that lets thought and experience sediment, thereby creating spaces for inquiry, reflection, and ethical interrogation. In this sense, memory is, like habit, a second nature that spirit gives itself in order to crystallize its own spontaneity, thereby laying the foundations for its critical reappropriation.

The importance of owning one's experience can be further appreciated if one considers the political uses of memory where individual narratives are deprived of their sources of agency and reduced to narratives that either hypostatize or victimize the role of the agents. This is, for instance, the case of Giulio Regeni, the Cambridge graduate abducted and tortured to death while researching Egypt's independent trade unions. Depicted by the press either as unconscious spy or as a martyr of the Egyptian Revolution, his story is still waiting to be narrated transnationally, avoiding the reduction to either political polemic or sheer rhetoric.[51] The value of absolute memory consists precisely in the fact that memory cannot be separated from the self who has enacted its own story. And yet, since memory is by definition tied to the negative and the forgotten, its intrinsic connection to ownership is a call to interrogate the author of any shared narrative.

Thus, the "living retention" that is necessary to activate productive thinking is, for both Hegel and Merleau-Ponty, tied to the appreciation of trans-historical and trans-cultural subjectivity. Ethical memory works by instituting nexuses and relations between self and other that are sedimented across time in shared fields of knowledge, and whose reactivation requires dialectical thinking, which is not bound by time or space. This is why, memory is, for Hegel, one of the most complex and sophisticated abilities of the mind, which is closely related to both habit and thinking.[52]

Rethinking Ethical Memory with Hegel and Merleau-Ponty

What kind of memory is at stake when we speak of ethical memory as a form of intersubjective institution? Certainly, ethical memory is not a variation of our episodic memory, whereby we recollect events and facts of the past by representing them to us. Ethical memory is not semantic memory either, for it does not imply that a subject S remembers the events of its past as these occur at $t1$, $t2$, etc. Semantic memory does away with the self, whereas ethical memory requires personality. Ethical memory works as a form of sedimentation once the essential moments that constellate history are preserved *as* relational nexuses between self and alterity. This is why absolute spirit in Hegel, just like the concept of institution in Merleau-Ponty, does not depend on the conscious remembering of the mind, for it consists in the reactivation of a principle and not in representational thinking. In this sense, ethical memory is connected or indexed to a self without this self being the subject of an act of remembering.

It follows that the actualization of ethical memory is not the mere flow or gallery of past images. It is rather a communication of meaning and sense that circulates back and forth in the realm of culture, thereby instituting new beginnings. Indeed, the culmination of absolute spirit in the *Phenomenology* is the impulse to become something other, namely to evolve and to enact itself once more in time and history. In this respect, Hegel's view of ethical memory complements and integrates Merleau-Ponty's insights on institution and sedimentation. For Merleau-Ponty, memory institutes the possibility of a new beginning as a power of decentering, that comprehends in itself a plurality of perspectives. Likewise, for Hegel, ethical memory is enacted on an absolute level when knowledge and being no longer stand opposed to each other, but rather reactivate each other in an open-ended activity.

This is, for Nuzzo, the most significant feature of absolute memory, namely the ability to express and name what is otherwise inexpressible. This does not mean that absolute memory provides history with *ad hoc* and *a posteriori* justifications. The main achievement of absolute memory actually consists in naming and addressing what is otherwise doomed to be anonymous, empty, or forgotten. The possibility of instituting freedom as a space for conceptual communication is rooted in the presence of the self, which is the condition of identity and unity, but also of difference and fragmentation. Hegel links the presence of the self to the ethical responsibility of dialectical thinking, which is autonomous in the practice of looking for the truth but always bound to the systematic and co-evolving development of reality.

At this stage, it is legitimate to wonder whether there is a *space* where ethical memory can be enacted. To be sure, ethical memory is not a space for contemplation, but a space for knowing and acting. The difference between ethical life and absolute knowledge is that the latter is not a historical and material transmission of knowledge and norms. And yet, as ethical life facilitates common criteria of making sense of the world, likewise absolute knowledge enables conceptual communication. Ethical memory can be enacted only as form of "recurrence" in Merleau-Ponty's words, namely as a task of re-actualization of former traditions and narratives in the present. In this sense, ethical memory is not tied to historical spaces or times but represents the critical power that interrogates the past to better understand the matrix of the present and to project such awareness in the future as a form of responsibility. This is particularly relevant in order to appreciate a specific value of memory, namely its power of resistance.

With regard to this, I would like to draw a few conclusions concerning the ethical value of memory in contemporary discourse. In his well-known discussion on the ethics of memory, Margalit distinguishes between common and shared memory. While the former aggregates the memories of all the people who remember a certain episode that each of them experienced individually, the latter requires communication:

> A shared memory integrates and calibrates the different perspectives of those who remember the episode—for example, the memory of the people who were in the square [during 9/11], each experiencing only a fragment of what happened from their unique angle on events—into one version. Other people in the community who were not there at the time may then be plugged into the experience of those who were in the square, through channels of description rather that by direct experience. Shared memory is built on a division of mnemonic labor.[53]

As Margalit points out, we cannot be held responsible for the accuracy of what we remember. We cannot be morally or ethically praised for remembering or for failing to remember. Yet Margalit defends the paradigmatic value that memory has when it creates a legacy or a heritage that guarantees the continuity of the remembrance of those events that are laden with ethical value, whether they inspire respect, gratitude, or horror. Such a commitment institutes, for Margalit, communities of memory.

In a way, Margalit's account of shared memory reminds us of Merleau-Ponty's reflections on cultural and historical institutions, which depend on dynamics of intersubjective responsiveness. Drawing on Hegel, however, it is possible to integrate this view of shared memory with a critical stance. In this revised sense, ethical memory allows reason to distance itself from the past, never accepting any event as absolute or definitive, but actually warning against the possibility of stagnation and hypostatization. This is possible in that memory does not neutralize the self, but rather institutes its permanence. The self stands for the immanent principle that allows the institution of logical, affective, social, or historical nexuses between form and content, theory and praxis, norms and social institutions. By uncovering the dimension of the self that is in place in absolute memory a critical distance between thought and history is obtained. For philosophy is essentially the exercise of critical thought, independent from external authority.

Indeed, by instituting nexuses of identity and difference, memory helps us to not repeat past mistakes. It is in light of such a capacity that I would then like to re-read the conclusion of the *Phenomenology of Spirit*, when Hegel writes that comprehended history represents the Golgotha of absolute spirit, without which the life of spirit would be "lifeless and alone" (PhG §808, 493). Here, the emphasis lies on the solitude of absolute spirit once it is deprived of its capacity of reactivating a new beginning. Hence, at the end of the *Phenomenology of Spirit*, Hegel reminds us that the life of absolute spirit cannot do without others. This capacity is, I believe, inseparable from the sedimentation of the self in absolute memory, and only in the cultivation of the latter as critical thinking does memory open up a new dimension for thinking and acting, namely a new form of life and collective engagement.[54]

Notes

1. Maurice Merleau-Ponty, *Institution and Passivity. Course Notes from the Collège de France (1954–1955)*, trans. L. Lawlor and H. Massey (Evanston: Northwestern University Press, 2010).
2. For a thorough discussion of this crucial aspect in relation to Merleau-Ponty's philosophical project, see Enrica Lisciani-Petrini, "Merleau-Ponty: Potenza dell'istituzione," *Discipline Filosofiche* XXIX, 2 (2019): 71–88.
3. Merleau-Ponty, *Institution and Passivity*, 43.
4. Ibid., 45.
5. Ibid., 46.
6. Ibid., 79.
7. Jean Hyppolite, *Logic and Existence*, trans. L. Lawlor and A. Sen (Albany: State University of New York Press, 1997).
8. For a discussion of Hegel's readings in twentieth-century France, see Michael S. Roth, *Knowing and History: Appropriations of Hegel in Twentieth-Century France* (Ithaca: Cornell University Press, 1988); and Alison Stone, "Hegel and Twentieth-Century French Philosophy," in *The Oxford Handbook of Hegel*, ed. D. Moyar (Oxford: Oxford University Press, 2017).
9. See also Enrica Lisciani Petrini, *La passione del mondo. Saggio su Merleau-Ponty* (Naples-Rome: Edizioni Scientifiche Italiane, 2002), 156–68; and Luca Vanzago, *The Voice of No One. Merleau-Ponty on Nature and Time* (Milan: Mimesis, 2017), 35–44.
10. Maurice Merleau-Ponty, "Hegel's Existentialism," in *Sense and Non-Sense*, trans. Hubert L. Dreyfus and Patricia Allen Dreyfus (Evanston: Northwestern University Press, 1964), 65.
11. Merleau-Ponty, "Hegel's Existentialism," 64.
12. Merleau-Ponty, *Institution and Passivity*, 63.
13. For a critical re-assessment of Hegel's argument in his *Lectures on the Philosophy of History* see Simon Lumsden, "Second Nature and Historical Change in Hegel's Philosophy of History," *International Journal of Philosophical Studies* (2016): 74–94.

14. See Angelica Nuzzo, *Memory, History, Justice in Hegel* (New York: Palgrave, 2012). Nuzzo's argument will be discussed more in detail in the next sections.

15. Ernst Bloch famously drew attention to this aspect of Hegel's philosophy in his Hegelian meditations, where he suggested that Hegel's philosophy was inhibited by the phantom of *anamnesis*: Ernst Bloch, *Subjekt-Objekt. Erläuterungen zu Hegel* (Frankfurt am Main: Suhrkamp, 1951). For an appraisal and contextualization of the role of temporality in the *Phenomenology of Spirit*, see Joseph C. Flay, "Time in Hegel's *Phenomenology of Spirit*," *International Philosophical Quarterly* 33, no. 3 (1991): 259–73; Remo Bodei, *La civetta e la talpa. Sistema ed epoca in Hegel* (Bologna: Il Mulino, 2014); and Valentina Ricci, "The Role of *Erinnerung* in Absolute Knowing: History and Absoluteness," in *Hegel on Recollection*, ed. Valentina Ricci and Federico Sanguinetti (Newcastle: Cambridge Scholars, 2013), 1–20. For a normative approach that does away with the problem of temporalization, see Robert Pippin, "The 'logic of experience' as 'absolute knowledge' in Hegel's *Phenomenology of Spirit*," in *Hegel's* Phenomenology of Spirit: *A Critical Guide*, ed. Dean Moyar and Michael Quante (New York: Cambridge University Press, 2008), 210–26.

16. Edmund Husserl, *Formal and Transcendental Logic*, trans. Dorion Cairns (The Hague: Martinus Nijhoff, 1969), Appendix II, §7, 328.

17. C, *Beilage* I, which is unfortunately not translated in Carr's English edition of the *Crisis*.

18. Edmund Husserl, *Ideas Pertaining to a Pure Phenomenology and to a Phenomenological Philosophy. Second Book. Studies in the Phenomenology of Constitution*, trans. Richard Rojecewicz and André Schuwer (Dordrecht: Kluwer Academic Publishers, 1989), §§50–55.

19. Merleau-Ponty, *Institution and Passivity*, 54.

20. Max Horkheimer and Theodor Adorno, *Dialectic of Enlightenment*, trans. Edmund Jephcott (Stanford: Stanford University Press, 2002), 191.

21. Merleau-Ponty, *Institution and Passivity*, 59. Interestingly, Adorno develops a similar line of interpretation in his aesthetic theory, where he argues that "aesthetic success is essentially measured by whether the formed object is able to awaken the content [*Inhalt*] sedimented in the form." See Theodor Adorno, *Aesthetic Theory*, trans. Robert Hullot-Kentor (London: Continuum), 139. I am very grateful to Gareth Polmeer for the pointer.

22. Ibid., 61.

23. Merleau-Ponty, *Child Psychology and Pedagogy: The Sorbonne Lectures 1949–1952*, trans. Talia Welsh (Evanston: Northwestern University Press, 2010).

24. Merleau-Ponty, *Institution and Passivity*, 55.

25. Max Wertheimer, *Productive Thinking*, ed. Michael Wertheimer (New York: Harper & Row, 1959), 35.

26. Merleau-Ponty, *Institution and Passivity*, 55.

27. On this aspect, see also Derrida's commentary of Husserl's *Origin of Geometry*. See Jacques Derrida, *Edmund Husserl's 'Origin of Geometry'. An Introduction*, trans. John P. Leavey (Lincoln: University of Nebraska Press, 1962).

28. Merleau-Ponty, *Institution and Passivity*, 59.

29. Ibid.

30. Ibid.

31. Robert Vallier, "Memory—Of the Future: Institution and Memory in the Late Merleau-Ponty," in *Time, Memory, Institution: Merleau-Ponty's New Ontology of Self*, ed. David Morris and Kym McLaren (Athens: Ohio University Press, 2015), 119.

32. John Russon, "The Project of Hegel's *Phenomenology of Spirit*," in *A Companion to Hegel*, ed. Stephen Houlgate and Michael Baur (Oxford: Oxford University Press, 2011), 57.

33. See Judith Butler, "Desire, Rhetoric, and Recognition in Hegel's *Phenomenology of Spirit*," in *Subjects of Desire: Hegelian Reflections in Twentieth-Century France* (New York: Columbia University Press, 1987), 17–59.

34. Naturally, spirit translates *Geist*, which in Hegel's philosophy captures the complex reality of subjectivity, understood both as a psychophysical reality (characterized by consciousness and practical agency) as well as objective reality (in terms of practical achievements that involve sociality, law, and culture). While it is customary to capitalize "spirit" in the English-speaking literature, in the following I prefer using it in lowercase to avoid any hypostatization of the self that emerges in the course of the development of *Geist*.

35. "The concept requires the content to be the self's own act. For this concept is, as we see, the knowledge of the self's act within itself as all essentiality and all existence, the knowledge of this subject as substance and of the substance as this knowledge of its act" (PhG §797, 485). As is well-known, Miller translates *Begriff* with the "Notion," which I have here replaced with "concept" (in lowercase) to preserve the meaning of "comprehension" that is implicit in the German *begreifen*.

36. Richard Winfield, *Hegel's* Phenomenology of Spirit: *A Critical Rethinking in Seventeen Lectures* (Lanham: Rowman & Littlefield, 2013), 379.

37. The *vexata quaestio* concerning the exact role of the PhG with respect to the system is an object of open debate. See, for instance, Hans-Friedrich Fulda, "'Science of the Phenomenology of Spirit': Hegel's Program and Its Implementation," in *Hegel's* Phenomenology of Spirit: *A Critical Guide*, 21–42.

38. Alfredo Ferrarin, *Thinking and the I: Hegel and the Critique of Kant* (Evanston: Northwestern University Press, 2018). My response to Ferrarin's reading can be found in "Review of Alfredo Ferrarin, Il pensare e l'io. Hegel e la critica di Kant (Rome 2016)," *Critique*, February 2018: https://virtualcritique.wordpr ess.com/2018/02/18/elisa-magri-on-alfredo-ferrarins-il-pensare-e-lio-hegel-e-la-critica-di-kant/.

39. Nuzzo, *Memory, History, Justice*, 23.

40. Ibid., 29.

41. Ibid., 48.
42. Ibid., 154.
43. Ibid.
44. Toni Morrison, "The Sites of Memory," in *The Source of Self-Regard: Selected Essays, Speeches, and Meditations* (New York: Alfred A. Knopf, 2019), 239.
45. Ibid.
46. Nuzzo, *Memory, History, Justice,* 161.
47. Ibid., 163.
48. Katharina Kraske, "Il corpo come testimone. La corporeità come esperienza centrale del lager nelle tesimonianze di Primo Levi e Liana Millu," *DEP: Deportate, esuli, profughe: Rivista telematica di studi sulla memoria femminile* no. 29 (2016): 43–55.
49. Primo Levi, *If This Is a Man,* trans. Stuart Woolf (New York: Orion Press, 1959), 15.
50. Cathy Caruth, Introduction to *Trauma: Explorations in Memory,* ed. Cathy Caruth (Baltimore: The Johns Hopkins University Press, 1995), 151.
51. Franco Palazzi and Michela Pusteria, "Remembering against the Tide: Giulio Regeni and the Transnational Horizons of Memory," *Open Democracy,* 25 January 2018: https://www.opendemocracy.net/en/north-africa-west-asia/giulio-regeni-murder-transnational-memory-egypt-italy.
52. Hegel, *Philosophy of Mind,* trans. Michael Inwood (Cambridge: Cambridge University Press, 2007), 131, 198.
53. Avishai Margalit, *The Ethics of Memory* (Cambridge, MA: Harvard University Press, 2002), 51–52.
54. I presented earlier versions of this paper at the University of Oxford, the University of Padua, and Boston College between 2018 and 2019. I am grateful to all participants in those talks for their helpful questions and comments, especially to Susanne Hermann-Sinai, Gareth Polmeer, Francesca Menegoni, Luca Illetterati, and Vanessa Rumble.

18

Max Scheler's Idea of History: A Juxtaposition of Phenomenology and Idealism

Zachary Davis

From the very earliest of his writings to the end of his life, Scheler attempted to chart a middle course between Hegel's idealism and Marx's historical materialism. Upon the early discovery of Husserl's *Logical Investigations*, Scheler understood phenomenology to be the proper approach and attitude to guide him through this precarious course. In this value theory, phenomenology provided him the access through which to demonstrate the possibility of a material *a priori*, navigating between the formalism of Kant's ethics and the materialism of Aristotle's virtue ethics. As his thought matures, his attention shifts increasingly to the growth and development of culture, or more generally conceived, to the idea of history. It is in working through the meaning and structure of history where Scheler embarks upon a systematic account of the middle course between Hegel and Marx, or as he expresses it in his later works, a course between idealism and realism. A middle course would rescue the important insights from both idealism and realism but would expunge the errors of both. In this paper, I examine the development of Scheler's middle course in respect to his idea of history and the stark influence that idealism has had on this development. My interest is not necessarily the veracity of Scheler's account or critique of Hegel and idealism. Rather I seek to show

Z. Davis (✉)
Department of Philosophy, St. John's University, New York City, NY, USA
e-mail: davisz@stjohns.edu

C. D. Coe (eds.), *The Palgrave Handbook of German Idealism and Phenomenology*,
Palgrave Handbooks in German Idealism,
https://doi.org/10.1007/978-3-030-66857-0_18

how Scheler's idea of history becomes more deeply influenced by idealism in this later work.

Immediate evidence of this influence is found in the title of his final published work on history, "The Human Being in the World Age of Balance" ("Der Mensch im Weltalter des Ausgleichs"). Although Scheler does not make the reference explicit, the title is a clear reference to Schelling's famous work, *The Ages of the World* (*Die Weltalter*). In his essay, Scheler—like Schelling and Hegel—sought to think history at its end, at the conclusion of the development of human cultures. While Scheler rejects Hegel's notion of absolute knowing or the Idea of universal history, he does introduce the possibility of a new form of knowing, a knowing embodied by a new human type, the *Allmensch*. This new human type, as I argue, is a form of knowing that emerges out of a "new" cosmopolitanism, or what he calls a cosmopolitanism of spirit. He describes this cosmopolitanism as the result of a "great discussion" among the leading thinkers of diverse and irreducible cultures in the world, a concept he explicitly borrows from Schopenhauer. The present "World Age of Balance" offers the opportunity for different cultures to relax the tensions among them and balance out the necessary one-sidedness found in each. In fragments posthumously published, Scheler further refers to this age of human history as the noetic stage, a stage where humanity as such becomes for the first time fully emancipated from the real and material conditions of existence to gain a self-conscious and cosmopolitan view of its history, of its own meaning. It is precisely in Scheler's descriptions of this final stage where we find the growing influence of idealism on Scheler's thought, an influence that allows Scheler to use phenomenology as a means to articulate the meaning of the end of history.

The Time of History: Scheler's Early Approach to History

The earliest writings that we have from Scheler regarding his idea of history stem from lectures he gave in 1909 at the University of Munich, lectures titled "Grundlagen der Geschichtswissenschaft" ("Foundations of the Science of History"). Scheler's relatively brief time in Munich (1906–10) was a remarkably influential period for the development of his approach and understanding of phenomenology. In 1902, Scheler was introduced to Husserl's *Logical Investigations*, which enabled Scheler to overcome the dead end he had reached in his habilitation, *Die transzendentale und die psychologische Methode* (1900). Yet perhaps the greatest influence on Scheler was his participation in the discussions with the famous Munich Circle consisting of some of the most promising early phenomenologists such as Alexander Pfänder, Moritz Geiger, and Theodor Conrad. Evidence of this rather experimental period in early phenomenology is found throughout Scheler's lectures on history. Two problems in particular that were very much in discussions among the Munich Circle members figure prominently in his lecture on history: (1) the distinction between the natural scientific attitude and the historical attitude; and (2) the experience and account of time. Working through these two problems, Scheler provides an initial glimpse into the type of access phenomenology gains into the meaning of history.

Curiously, despite the intensity of his participation in the phenomenological approach at this time, Scheler does not make any explicit reference to phenomenology in these early lectures. This is not wholly unusual for Scheler. In many of his writings, he does not describe his analysis as phenomenological. The distinction that Scheler makes between natural science and historical science does in many respects mirror the distinction he makes in his later work between the natural worldview and the phenomenological attitude. While it is important that Scheler's understanding of historical science and phenomenology are not conflated, there are distinct similarities that suggest his account of history and phenomenology bear an intimate relation.

According to Scheler, there is an essential difference between how natural science and historical science regard both the meaning of the past and the meaning of a historical development.[1] Natural science views the past events in respect to their general character and laws of development. This is what makes it possible to describe the development or evolution of a species over time. By contrast, historical science is idiographic and concerned with the concrete individual.[2] For the natural scientist, past events are used to make sense of the present in the respect that this sense-making clarifies the natural laws governing the development. The purpose of describing these laws is to have a better understanding of why things happen the way that they do in order to then better control future events. For the natural scientist, there is no history, only laws of natural development. "The primary aim of historical science," writes Scheler, "is to bring to intuition and understanding the particular sense-content of past events."[3]

This is not to say that the past has no relation to the present. What is crucial for Scheler is that "historical phenomena" are taken as a particular type of phenomenon and not treated as first brought about by a thought process that is not historical.[4] Because natural science treats all phenomena as the same, it remains naïve to the experience of history and to what it means for an event to be historical. Historical science recognizes the integrity of the historical event and seeks to clarify what it means for the event to be historical. "The *essence* of all history exists in not merely that some B follows some A like one movement follows a different movement, but that B is *experienced* as following A."[5] Hence, historical science is concerned about the way in which an event is given as historical. In this respect, the historian examines the sense of a phenomenon that presently gives itself, but yet gives itself as having been. It is thus not a matter of going back to the past, as if historical science was a form of time travel, but a matter of the present sense of the historical event. There is no anachronism here. The past is not being made sense of in light of the present. It lies rather in the meaning of historical science to make sense of how an event has come to be historical, has come to be given as historical.

By placing the emphasis on the way in which the past is given, Scheler aims to address the problem raised by skeptics regarding the historian's access to the past. Although Scheler does not make this assumption explicit, he draws a parallel between a person's access to her own memories and the access the historian has to her cultural events. For this reason, Scheler dedicates his attention to the problem of history to an analysis of memory. As the historical scientist attempts to bring to intuition and thereby make evident the sense of a past event, memory, for Scheler, is a piece of one's past that is brought to intuition.[6] Similar problems arise as in the case of historical investigation regarding access to the meaning of this event in one's past. An individual is not the same person in the present as one was in the past. Is not the meaning of memory of the past event different for the person at present than in the past? Is not the original meaning of this past event lost?

Both the natural scientist and the skeptic assume a much different concept of time than the historian.[7] "The time of the natural scientist is a continuum of now-points or now-phenomena whose content we ignore."[8] Anticipating the publication of Husserl's time-consciousness lectures, which were very much a part of the discussion in the Munich phenomenology circle, Scheler makes a distinction between the objective time of the natural scientist and the phenomenological account of time. Although Scheler does not refer to his account as phenomenological, the account he frames in terms of the historical sense of time assumes the structure both he and Husserl describe phenomenologically as the living present.[9] The immediate present is not a point on a time line, but a unity of the past, present, and future. Regardless of whether the person is consciously aware of the past, the past persists and thus still lives in the present.[10] Not only do past events inform the meaning of present events, but also inform how future events are anticipated. Every event has its past and future horizons, horizons that help to make sense of the present and show how the present event is distinct from the past. In this respect, the "past" for the historian has an "existential dimension" entirely unknown to the natural scientist.[11]

For the individual person, the collective past "exists" in the past, a past that remains bound to the present: "Nothing is lost."[12] In his analysis of memory, Scheler makes a distinction between an immediate past and a sedimented past. The events of the immediate past are still retained in the present, retained in present awareness. A sedimented past remains inscribed in the life of the individual, but one is not immediately aware of it. This past is brought back in the act of remembering. Yet, because the past, whether consciously or not, still lives in the present life of the person, the meaning of this event is still with the person and thus accessible. Over the life of the individual, it is the "weight" of the past that changes.[13] The meaning of this past event remains unfinished as it still lives in the present as past. Hence, the question is not whether we are able to access the past, but rather a matter of how this past is brought to present consciousness.

In a parallel fashion, the past of a people or culture continues to live in the present. This past informs the present in the form of a tradition:

> Through tradition, the generational epochs are connected into a living continuity, which is entirely independent of the conscious memory of it. Hence, in us lives Greek thinking and feeling, Christian living, entirely independent of what we know of this history and judge about it. At no time could we say: what would we be, if this or that piece was cut out of the past. Thus, never is a part of the past exhausted of its effectiveness.[14]

The skeptic fails to realize that the past remains accessible through the present. Or as Scheler writes further, "from the outset the entire history of a people continues to live in its current present: this history is not past like a natural event, but is in the depths as effective present."[15] None of these notions such as tradition introduced in this early lecture on history are worked out in detail. Certainly, many questions remain. Yet, what is clear is that Scheler understands history to be a unified whole, a unity wherein the beginning remains to the end.

The influence of idealism, or more specifically the idealism of Hegel in his Introduction to *The Philosophy of History*, leaves its mark through Scheler's lectures. For Hegel as well, "nothing in the past is lost."[16] Hence, historical thinking is not a retreat from the present in a return to the past. Rather the past is thought historically through the present, through its continued effectiveness and meaning for the past and present. The sense or idea of history is in a process of development and has a meaning that changes as new future horizons emerge through ever emerging new meanings in the present. Scheler shares with Hegel the conviction that there is an "idea" in history that develops over the life of a culture or people.

In Scheler's early lectures, there are the first signs of Scheler's decisive break from Hegel and what he understands idealism to be. We find in these early lectures the seeds of Scheler's rejection of the Hegelian approach of thinking history merely in terms of the accomplishments of spirit, of an idea working itself out dialectically. There are two factors responsible for the unfolding of history, the spiritual values and ideas on the one hand and the material or life forces on the other. The course of history is not propelled by spirit alone, by an Idea there from the beginning. For Scheler, individual persons do indeed introduce into history new ideas through spiritual accomplishments such as works of art and philosophy. Yet these ideas alone have no effectiveness if they are not adopted into the "masses," into the interest of the people. The suggestion for Scheler that history is moved by ideas is the equivalent of saying Rafael could paint without hands or that the genius is possible without means of education.[17] There are, in short, material conditions necessary for ideas to take root and for history to develop. Historical thought must then not only account for the ideas of history, but also for the conditions that allowed certain ideas to be "chosen," to attract the interest of the people. This distinction that Scheler draws between himself and the idealists leads him to think the idea of historical progress differently as well. Progress is not spirit coming to consciousness fully of itself, of finally reaching the possibility of absolute knowing. The goal of history is rather to "complete socialization of the material conditions and a simultaneous complete individualization of spiritual values."[18] There is no end of history, only the task of history. The ideas that move history spring from the purely spiritual acts of individual persons and the greater material freedom persons have to create and think, the more open history will be to new and original ideas.

The Age of History: Scheler on the Structure of History

Scheler's early criticism of idealism focused primarily on the impersonal nature of its conception of spirit. While Scheler shares with idealism that the growth of a culture and thus of history is brought about by the spontaneity of spirit and the manner by which spirit inspires the new, he rejects the idea that spirit is a type of "logos" working itself out through persons and the gestalts of history. Spirit is for Scheler fundamentally personal and thus history develops according to the genius of particular individuals in history. In his later thought, Scheler strengthens his critique and places idealism in a Western philosophical tradition that has harbored a "dangerous" misconception of spirit. According to Scheler, since Plato the dominant view in the Western tradition is that "ideas have their own power, their original power and activity, and their own effectiveness."[19] Idealists such as Hegel and Fichte assume this classical theory of spirit as well. In his later work, Scheler commits himself to the position that spirit bears no trace of power or effectiveness.[20] At stake here is whether ideas and values on their own accord can effect change in the movement of history. The great danger in the Western tradition in holding that spirit can alone determine the course of history is that ideas and values remain abstract and fail to address the vital concerns of a people. By insisting upon a personal account of both spirit and history, Scheler is committed to an account of history wherein the ideas that move history are the ones that directly attend to vital needs and desires.

There are significant questions and deep-seated problems that immediately arise regarding Scheler's later work when he commits himself to a powerless spirit. I do not wish to address them here.[21] My interest in this section is how this sharp distinction that Scheler maintains between him and the idealist tradition leads him to think of history in biological terms and as a consequence the necessary role that "real factors" play in the movement of history. This is not to suggest that Scheler commits himself to a form of historical materialism. Both the real and ideal factors have an essential role wholly independent of one another: "Everything that happens takes place in the historical interplay of ideas and the power drives simultaneously."[22]

The real factors are rooted in the basic life drives of the human being and are the ways in which these drives are expressed collectively by a people relative to a particular geographical and historical period. There are three human life drives: the appetitive or accumulation drive, the power drive, and the reproductive drive.[23] Each of these life drives correspond to three social institutions: the economic, political, and familial, respectively.[24] These three life drives of the human being are the particular human manifestation of life or urge (*Drang*).[25] Life is wholly independent from spirit and has its own structure and end. The distinction Scheler draws between life and spirit is not, as he remarks, a distinction based on a substance dualism of the type introduced by Descartes. They are distinct "movements," and the human being is the *Treffpunkt*, the meeting place wherein these two movements must contend with one another.[26] While spirit is directed toward ever-deeper personal values, life is structured according to the aim of the maximization of reality (*Realen*) and a minimization of strenuous energy output.[27] This striving for every greater expression of life is infinite in scope. There is never a time when there is not the urge to be: "Urge, the urge toward existence is nothing more than existence."[28]

The introduction of these two independent movements, spirit and life, does further introduce a "new dualism" in Scheler's late work.[29] That there are different, if not competing, aspects of the human being are not in itself a concern. The difficulty with Scheler's new dualism is how these two independent movements directed at two distinct ends are able to create, at the very least, a functional unity. Scheler refers to the process by which spirit and life form a unity is the process of spiritualization, the process by which the life drives come to be directed by the deeper spiritual values. Social institutions such as economics, politics, and family are all the expression of some form of spiritualization. There are two factors complicating the process of spiritualization. Because Scheler rejects the "traditional" notion of spirit, spirit has no "power" on its own to control the movement of life. The only power that spirit has to direct and channel the life drives is through inspiration, a form of attraction. Yet spirit's "power" of attraction is by virtue of the depth of value. According to Scheler, the life drives are value blind[30]: "The urge is, however, even without spirit always goal-oriented, but also a logical, value free, and purposeless."[31] If all that spirit has at its disposal are the deeper personal values, how can it direct and channel that which is blind to value itself?

Scheler offers no immediate or direct solution to this perplexing problem in his late work. However, working toward a solution with the clues we are given does make clearer the "danger" Scheler warned of regarding the idealist assumption that spirit has its own power. Scheler's experience during and immediately after the Great War had taught him a hard lesson. He had counted on the power of the deeper spiritual values to guide Germany and Europe out of their cultural crisis and depression on their own accord without having to directly contend with the present real factors. In Scheler's own thought, this faith in the power of spirit led to a dangerous abstraction from the horrors of war. He further warned of a growing divide between the spiritual and real factors as the Weimar Republic began to crumble[32] and as fascism began to grow in its public appeal.[33] The great danger in the belief that spirit has its own power is that the life drives such as the power drive go unchecked and are allowed to express themselves without any moral guidance whatsoever.

For this reason, Scheler turns his attention ever more directly to an analysis of the life drives and indirectly to the question of how a powerless spirit can guide and channel the movement of the value-blind life drives. The real factors may indeed be value blind, but they are not mechanistic. They are rather "biological."[34] For Scheler, this means that the end to which life is directed, the maximation of reality with the least amount of resistance, cannot be measured in merely quantitative terms. Life rather is directed through the power of attraction, an attraction to the production of the beautiful life.[35] In this respect, the maximization of reality must be rendered in qualitative terms, in terms such as health and the robustness of life. Spirit therefore can only direct and channel life if it appeals to this drive to be beautiful, if spirit can meaningfully contribute to the future and growth of the organism.[36] The spiritual values do not guide the real factors because they are good, but because they are beautiful, because the life drives experience a greater vitality through the course indicated by the spiritual values.

In this all-too-brief excursion into Scheler's late metaphysics, it may appear that we have come a long way away from the idea of history. Yet, for Scheler, history is nothing other than the spiritualization of life.[37] While empowerment of spirit and the ideation of power is a metaphysical belief,[38] it does clarify the specific roles of spirit and life in the movement of history. Spirit is the determining factor in history, determining the expression of life in terms of values and ideas, a *liberté modifiable*. By contrast, the real factors are the *fatalité modifiable*, allowing as sluice gates certain values and ideas to be realized.[39] The realization particular to spiritual values and ideas, in other words, does not take place according to the power of these ideals, but how they have become attractive to the social institutions such as economics, politics, and the family. What mediates the relation between the ideal and the real is the will of persons.[40] Given Scheler's metaphysical descriptions of the interaction between spirit and life, it is tempting to think of these movements as overarching courses working themselves out through the lives of persons. Not only is spirit always personal, but the life drives are also communal, expressed through the collective lives of a people. The elite may inspire the people; however, it is the will of the people, the actions and decisions by those co-living and co-experiencing the life drives of each individual that ultimately direct and channel the course of the real factors. Spiritualization, and thus the course of history, is determined by the implicit and explicit choices of the people who share a culture. Idealism with its mistaken view of spirit underestimates the power of the will of the people to realize the deeper values and ideals of the person.

The biological underpinnings of history also determine the "essential order of the phases of time."[41] Scheler rejects the modern conception of time as a series of now points, progressing linearly and without end. Both time and space are for Scheler "forms of activity" and thus understood as vital experiences.[42] Understood in biological terms, the order of time proceeds according to the life of the organism. In the case of history, the order is relative to the being of a culture. There is then a parallel between the temporal order of an individual person and that of a culture or collective person. As the individual finite person moves through distinct stages in life, so too does a culture. According to Scheler, there are three main phases of a culture: a youthful stage, a blossoming stage, and a maturing phase.[43] A culture ages in the same course as the body.

In respect to the aging of a culture, these distinct phases are determined by the predominance of a particular life drive. The early or adolescent stage of a culture is marked by the rise of the reproductive drive over the other two. For Scheler, this is why the early phase of a culture is predominantly concerned with the family structure. The second stage is marked by the rise of the power drive and hence the introduction of the state and politically regulated institutions and rights. The third stage is the rise of the accumulation drive as the primary drive and with it the rise of late capitalism. In the final section of this chapter, I examine what it means to be at the end of these phases. Regardless of whether Scheler's descriptions of the life of a culture are accurate, it is clear that part of his criticism of idealism is the meaning of time. The time of history for Scheler is biological in nature and thus moves according to the rhythm of life. Every culture is wholly unique but shares in this basic structure of the life of a culture or rather the aging of a culture.[44]

The three different phases in the aging of a culture are not a mere happenstance of one life drive moving to prominence over the other two. This movement of a culture's history follows a lawful direction according to the spiritualization of power. In fact, Scheler understands each phase of history as a particular expression of power. The rise of the reproductive drive assumes the "power of human beings." In the progression of a culture, power continues to be spiritualized. In the second stage, the political and "blossoming" stage of a culture, power is expressed as the power over both humans and things. The later stage of a culture, the economic phase, power is expressed only in terms of the power over things.[45] According to Scheler, every culture has its own particular development curve that follows the trajectory of the spiritualization of power. It is the general tendency of the transformation of violence to political power, of the right of power into the power of right, and of physical power to spiritual power.[46] Scheler is well aware that this developmental curve of history that follows the arc of the spiritualization of power is not a linear progression of decreasing physical violence. He repeatedly warns of the possibility of World War II and unimaginable violence in the near future.[47] Despite his commitment to a curve tending toward spiritual power, he declares total ignorance as to where humanity in 1926 stands on this curve.[48] As we are all too aware almost a hundred years later, humanity was nowhere near the end of this curve. The ubiquity of violence in history does not deter Scheler from holding the "eternal idea of peace" as a real possibility and the ideal bringing ultimate shape to the developmental curve of history.[49] Such a conviction does not commit Scheler to a teleological idea of history, an idea he finds in Hegel, but, rather, to an idea of history wherein power is confronted and thereby transformed by the will of the people inspired by the deeper spiritual ideals and values. The process of spiritualization and the historical tendency to a decrease in violence in no way entails that there is a moral trajectory to history. Power can be spiritualized in accord with negative values and ideals, promoting forms of injustice such as institutionalized racism or misogyny. Peace is indeed a positive value, but not one guaranteed through a decrease in violence and the process of spiritualization.

The End (or Beginning) of History: Scheler on the Meaning of Human History

The distinctive stages of a history of a culture, stages that unfold in accord with the biological course of aging, leave at least one obvious question unanswered: What is to come at the end of the third stage? Scheler writes often of the death or end of a culture. Because each culture has access to a unique view of the world, the death of a culture is the loss of such access and thus the loss of that world. His defense of German aggression at the outset of World War I was motivated in part by the fear of losing the German and European culture. War was a means to defend Germany against the hegemony of the "English," the bearers of the onslaught of late capitalism and the mechanization of nature.[50] Hence, cultures can die through usurpation and annihilation, the imposition of one ethos on another. Scheler is also well aware that cultures have disappeared for a myriad of reasons other than war and cultural conflict. Yet if we take Scheler's biological analysis of history seriously, it would seem that cultures have a natural death, an end of their time. And if the West is in the twilight of its history, having entered into its third stage, then the West would appear to be at the end of its history and awaiting its cultural death.

In contrast to thinkers, such as Oswald Spengler, who had foretold of the "decline of the west," Scheler writes of a new cultural beginning. This new beginning at the end of history breaks from the process of spiritualization that

Scheler had developed up to this point. It is no longer a matter of guiding and directing the life drives, but solely a matter of knowing and the introduction of a new worldview. Despite his criticisms of the idealist tradition, Scheler articulates the end of history in terms of spirit alone. Hence, the grounds for a new beginning are not found in a transformation of the real or material conditions, but in a synthesis of different existing worldviews, a process Scheler calls *Ausgleich* or balancing.

Though the notion of *Ausgleich* is scattered throughout Scheler's late work, his only attempt to clarify what he means by this notion is in one of his final essays, "The Human Being in the World Age of Balance." The use of the term, world age, in the title is an explicit reference to the idealist tradition and in particular to Schelling's famous final work, *Die Weltalter* (*The Ages of the World*). Curiously, Scheler does not provide any further explanation as to why he uses this term of Schelling's. As was the case with his early work on history, Scheler finds it necessary to distance himself from the idealist tradition as he develops his own account of spirit while at the same time appropriating much of the tradition as well. This is certainly the case with this term, world age.

On the one hand, Scheler's use of the term assumes the inner conflict that Schelling describes in his *Ages of the World*. As Schelling writes,

> The existence of such an eternal antithesis could not elude the first deeply feeling and sensitive people. Already finding this duality in the primordial beginnings of nature but finding its source nowhere among that which is visible, early on one had to say to oneself that the ground of the antithesis is as old as, nay, is even older than, the world; that, just as in everything living, so already in that which is primordially living, there is a doubling that has come down, through many stages, to that which has determined itself as what appears to us as light and darkness, masculine and feminine, spiritual and corporeal.[51]

In a quite similar fashion, Scheler writes of the coming balancing of opposing forces that not only includes the masculine and feminine, but also the East and West, the conflict of the classes, and of national and economic tensions. A world age is that moment in history when it becomes possible to grasp the necessity of both forces, which is a grasping of the whole, of the world.

Yet, on the other hand, Schelling and Scheler have quite different understandings of how history has come to the point when the whole, the world as such, can be grasped in totality. For Schelling, it is a process by which history is "internalized," when human beings become the "living witnesses of the truth."[52] By contrast, the world age of balance is made possible, for Scheler, by virtue of the Great War, the first collective experience of humanity in its entirety.[53] As a consequence of the war, an ever growing part of humanity has been placed in the same fate.[54] In this respect, Scheler maintains that there is a material condition for the current world age. It is not a question of the transformation of the material conditions, but rather of what has made it possible for humanity to share in the same history. The shared fate once again rests on the drive of power. The Great War has shown that the world must now contend with the ever-present possibility of tremendous violence and even the annihilation of humanity as such. Both Schelling and Scheler understand the world age as the time when humanity must contend with the opposition and tensions brought into sharp focus at the end of history. The difference is that for Scheler these tensions are not only spiritual in nature. They bear the trace of a war to end all wars.

Because the world age of adjustment is characterized by the political task of avoiding unprecedented violence, it is not possible for Scheler to resolve these tensions of oppositions dialectically by understanding the necessity of opposing forces. What is necessary is the relaxation of the tensions, the task of the coming *Ausgleich*, a balancing.[55] The source of these tensions is the diversity of cultures, a diversity inherent to the meaning of culture itself. World War I was also, for Scheler, the result of cultural differences. The present world age presents a new possibility for resolving these tensions. Every culture assumes its own particular access to the meaning of the world, its worldview. This access is only "partial."[56] Consequently, every culture harbors its own limitations or one-sidedness, as Scheler describes it. The peculiar and partial access a culture has remains hidden for most of its history. Only through the introduction of the alien cultures is this prejudice of one's own culture disclosed to itself. This is precisely the opportunity the world age of balancing affords, the opportunity to recognize critically the partial nature of one's cultural worldview.

While Scheler mentions many different tensions in this world age, the tension that garners most of his attention and one that serves as the balancing possible is the tension between the so-called East and West. According to Scheler, who is painting in very broad strokes in his characterization of incredibly diverse cultural traditions, the East and West have developed two distinctive psychic techniques in respect to suffering, techniques informing the way in which these two traditions have spiritualized power. The East has spiritualized power through a turn inward, through an art of toleration.[57] By contrast, the West has predominantly attempted to end suffering by turning outward. In the modern era, this turn outward by the West has been expressed through the domination of nature. My interest is not in the accuracy of

Scheler's description of these two traditions, but by how the *Ausgleich* of them takes place.

Scheler is insistent that the aim of the balancing that takes place during this world age is not to realize some "world best" as the singular form of culture.[58] He understands such a project as the project of the dominant forms of "internationalism," a project wherein all cultures are reduced to one under the ruse of modernization and capitalism. The end of history does not rid history of cultural diversity. Rather it signals the opportunity for self-criticism, the opportunity to call attention to the one-sidedness of one's own culture. In respect to the *Ausgleich* of the East and West, Scheler is only speaking to the balancing of the West, taking the genius of the East and its unique historical development as a means to address its failure to resolve tensions through means other than the domination of what is other. The world age of balance thus offers a means of cultural growth through self-conscious critical reflection. This critical self-reflection would not be possible without the introduction of the spiritual development of an alien culture.

As a means to cultivate such a form of self-criticism, Scheler seeks to develop what he calls a cosmopolitan worldview or philosophy. Prior to the world age of balance, the emergence of a worldview took place by means of the insights by the genius of one's culture. These insights introduced something novel, but consistent within the tradition. A cosmopolitan worldview emerges as a result of a "sublime and great discussion," a notion Scheler takes from Schopenhauer.[59] Modeled in part by the type of international discussion that the leading scientists were having at this time, Scheler had hoped for a similar type of discussion between the cultural "elite." Yet, rather than an international form of cooperation, wherein the goal is a singular point of agreement, the great discussion would seek a cosmopolitan cooperation. Through such a cooperation, a fuller sense of the meaning of the world would emerge, but one that maintained the irreducibility of each and every culture.

Scheler found in Hegel a similar type of cultural synthesis. Yet he was critical of Hegel for only understanding this historical synthesis through a European lens.[60] A cosmopolitan cultural synthesis retains the unique and irreplaceable history of a culture and does not seek to discover the logos to history.[61] There is not a singular history of humanity. The world age of balance is the convergence of the history that takes place in the form of a cooperative discussion. Scheler insists that this form of synthesis is organic in nature, unpredictable in advance and is not a matter of merely selecting the "roses" of different cultures.[62] There is no accumulation in the course of history, only disclosure.[63] Through the cosmopolitan discussion, the meaning of the world becomes ever richer and ever deeper. The insights elicited from other cultures demonstrate that the meaning of the world can in principle never be fully disclosed, that there is no singular idea. There is only a growing multitude of insights that cooperate collectively that the meaning of the world is inexhaustible.

It is in this context of the emergence of a cosmopolitan world philosophy that Scheler describes the becoming of a new type of human being, the *Allmensch*.[64] In his philosophical anthropology, Scheler had described the different human types that had arisen in the history of the West, types such as the human being as rational animal. The world age of balance signals the end of this history. However, it also provides the resources for a new type, a type that personifies the diversity of cultures. In this respect, the *Allmensch* is not an *Übermensch*, an overcoming of what has come before. It is rather a manner of being open to that which is other, of deepening one's understanding of the world by listening to different worldviews. The *Allmensch* has not achieved any absolute knowing, but rather the self-awareness that the world is other for other persons and that access to this world is only gained through the insights only others can grant by virtue of their own worldview. As Scheler had attempted to do in his earlier approach to history, he is seeking this in later work to personalize the idea of history. The understanding possible in the world age of balance only happens with other persons, an understanding that assumes cooperation from the outset.

In working notes only published later in the collected works, Scheler describes the present world age of balance as the beginning of a fourth epoch or stage in history. He refers to this new stage as the noetic stage.[65] The unfinished nature of these manuscripts leaves open the question of whether Scheler was fully committed to this idea of a new stage in history. What is clear is that this new stage is not simply one further stage in the aging of a culture, as was the case with the earlier stages. At the very least, this new stage of history does not follow the same form of spiritualization that had taken place in three previous epochs. The world age of adjustment has given rise to a new self-consciousness in respect to history itself, a self-consciousness that understands itself at the end of its own history as well as the diversity of other cultures and histories. "The highest aim of history," as Scheler writes, "is that the human being brings forth meaningfully the human being as the creator of history."[66] In his all too brief descriptions of this fourth stage, Scheler comes quite close to what both Hegel and Schelling understood as the "completeness of spirit," namely, freedom.[67] The world age of adjustment is the transition from the end of history to the beginning of history, of a new history. History up to this point had been the "most concentrated participation in the life of the becoming of the spiritual world."[68] Through the great discussion, the cosmopolitan world philosophy becomes possible and as a consequence "spirit has moved in history from the selected to the selecting."[69] For Scheler, this freedom is the freedom of the human being to decide for itself what it is. The world age of balance affords the human being the opportunity to see itself critically in the history of humanity and no longer to live naively in the narrowness of its own worldview, not knowing that it does not know of its own limitations. Though Scheler insists on referring to the knowing at the end of history as cosmopolitan and not absolute, he remains very much a part of the idealist tradition as he thinks history at its end and what this would mean for the time to come.

Notes

1. Max Scheler, *Schriften aus dem Nachlaß. IV. Philosophie und Geschichte, Gesammelte Werke XIII*, ed. Manfred S. Frings (Bonn: Bouvier Verlag, 1990), 173. Hereafter: GW XIII. All translation from the original German texts are my own.
2. Ibid., 170.
3. Ibid., 172.
4. Ibid., 187.
5. Ibid., 180.
6. Ibid.
7. Ibid., 189.
8. Ibid., 191.
9. For a comprehensive account of Husserl's notion of time-consciousness, see Klaus Held, *Lebendige Gegenwart: die Frage nach der Seinsweise des tranzendentalen Ich bei Edmund Husserl, entwickelt am Leitfaden der Zeitprobleme* (The Hague: Martinus Nijhoff, 1966).
10. GW XIII, 188.
11. Ibid., 191.
12. Ibid., 197.
13. Ibid., 193.
14. Ibid., 193–94.
15. Ibid., 194.
16. Georg W. F. Hegel, *The Philosophy of History*, trans. J. Sibree (Buffalo: Prometheus Books, 1991), 79.
17. GW XIII, 229.
18. Ibid., 230.
19. Max Scheler, *Späte Schriften, Gesammelte Werke* IX, ed. Manfred S. Frings (Bern: Francke Verlag, 1976), 50. Hereafter: GW IX.

20. Max Scheler, *Die Wissenformen und die Gesellschaft*, *Gesammelte Werke* VIII, ed. Maria Scheler, 1st and 2nd ed., ed. Manfred S. Frings, 3rd ed. (Bern: Francke Verlag, 1976), 21. Hereafter: GW VIII.

21. For an analysis of this problem, see Zachary Davis, "Scheler and the Task of Human Loving," in *Phenomenology 2010, Volume 5: Selected Essays from North America—Part 1: Phenomenology within Philosophy*, ed. Michael Barber, Lester Embree, and Thomas Nenon (Bucharest: Zeta Books, 2010), 123–54.

22. GW XIII, 80.

23. GW VIII, 101.

24. Ibid., 19.

25. The notion of life and urge are introduced in Scheler's later work. For the sake of simplicity, I will use the term life to refer to the basic impulse of life. For a fuller and rich discussion of this notion, see Angelina Sander, "Askese und Welbejahung: Zum Problem des Dualismus in der Anthropologie und Metaphysik Max Scheler," in *Vom Umsturz der Werte in der modernen Gesellschaft, II. Kolloquium der Max-Scheler-Gesellschaft*, ed. Gerhard Pfafferott (Bonn: Bouvier Verlag, 1997), 34–52.

26. Max Scheler, *Schriften as dem Nachlaß, III. Philosophische Anthropologie*, *Gesammelte Werke XII*, ed. Manfred S. Frings (Bern: Francke Verlag, 1987), 226. Herafter: GW XII.

27. Max Scheler, *Schriften aus dem Nachlaß, II. Erkenntnislehre und Metaphysik*, *Gesammelte Werke XI*, ed. Manfred S. Frings (Bern: Francke Verlag, 1979), 186. Hereafter: GW XI.

28. GW XI, 161.

29. Scheler himself refers to his later metaphysics and philosophical anthropology as supporting a "new dualism" (GW XII, 412). There are a number of other passages throughout his work where he claims that the relation between spirit and life is a dualism (Max Scheler, *Vom Ewigen in Meschen, Gesammelte Werke V*, ed. Maria Scheler [Bern: Francke Verlag, 1954], 360; and Max Scheler, *Schriften aus dem Nachlaß, I., Zur Ethik und Erkenntnislehre, Gesammelte Werke X*, ed. Maria Scheler [Bern: Francke Verlag, 1957], 146; GW XI, 193). In his earlier work, *Formalism in Ethics and Non-Formal Ethics of Value*, Scheler rejects the traditional dualism of two substances such as Descartes' dualism of mind and body. Scheler maintains to the end of his life that traditional dualism is merely two different regards of the lived-body, a manner of inner perception (psyche) and outer perception (body) (Max Scheler, *Der Formalismus in der Ethik und die materiale Wertethik. Neuer Versuch der Grundlegung eines ethischen Personalismus, Gesammelte Werke II*, 5th ed., ed. Maria Scheler [Bern: Francke Verlag, 1966], 397–402). Scheler's contention is that this type of traditional dualism found in fails to grasp the unique character of spirit. Needless to say, there are significant questions and problems that arise with Scheler's own dualism. Here is not the place to resolve these issues and problems.

30. GW XIII, 144. For a discussion of the Scheler's notion of the value blind life drives, see Eugene Kelly, "Vom Ursprung des Menschen bei Max Scheler," in *Person und Wert: Schelers "Formalismus"—Perspektiven und Wirkungen*, ed. Christian Bermes, Wolfhart Henckmann, and Heinz Leonardy (Bonn: Alber, 2000), 252–71.
31. GW XII, 262.
32. GW XIII, 72.
33. GW IX, 86.
34. GW XIII, 144.
35. Max Scheler, *Schriften aus dem Nachlaß, V. Varia I, Gesammelte Werke XV*, ed. Manfred S. Frings (Bonn: Bouvier Verlag, 1993), 161.
36. GW XII, 131.
37. GW XIII, 144.
38. Ibid., 94.
39. GW VIII, 23.
40. Ibid., 40; GW XIII 142–43.
41. GW XIII, 138.
42. GW VIII, 270.
43. Ibid., 41.
44. Aging is a notion that Scheler develops quite early in his phenomenological development. See Manfred S. Frings, *LifeTime: Max Scheler's Philosophy of Time* (Dordrecht: Kluwer, 2003) and also my work on Scheler's notion of aging. The parallel between the individual person and culture is an idea Scheler maintains in *Formalism is Ethics and Non-Formal Ethics of Value*. So it is quite consistent with his thought that he would apply his phenomenological account of aging to the aging of a culture, a collective person. Nonetheless, it is also very likely that Scheler was influenced by Oswald Spengler's *The Decline of the West*. Scheler speaks sparingly of Spengler, both in critical and complimentary terms. Yet, in regard to the understanding of culture in respect to the rhythm of life, the influence of Spengler is unmistakable. For instance, Spengler writes, "We know it to be true of every organism that the rhythm, form, and duration of its life, and all the expression-details of that life as well, are determined by the properties of its species. 'Mankind,' however, has no aim, no idea, no plan, any more than the family of butterflies or orchids. 'Mankind' is a biological expression, or an empty world. But conjure away the phantom, break the magic circle, and at once there emerges an astonishing wealth of actual forms—the living with all its immense fullness, depth and movement—hitherto veiled by a catchword, a dry as dust scheme, and a set of person 'ideals.' I see, in place of that empty figment of one linear history which can only be kept up by shutting one's eyes to the overwhelming multitude of facts, the drama of a number of mighty cultures, each springing with primitive strength from the soil of a mother-region to which it remains firmly bound throughout its whole life-cycle; each stamping its material, its mankind, in it own image; each having its own idea, its own passions, its own life, will and feeling, its own death"

(Oswald Spengler, *The Decline of the West, Volume One, Form and Actuality*, trans. Charles Francis Atkinson [New York: Alfred A. Knopf, 1926], 21). As we will see in the next section, Scheler does not share Spengler's pessimism regarding the "decline of the west." He sees rather a new beginning brought about by the cosmopolitan balancing of cultures.

45. For a further description of this lawful direction of power, see the editor's afterword in GW XIII, 246.
46. GW XIII, 93–94.
47. GW IX, 153.
48. GW XIII, 94.
49. Ibid., 91.
50. Max Scheler, *Der Genius des Krieges und der deutsche Krieg, Politische-pädogogische Schriften, Gesammelte Werke IV*, ed. Manfred S. Frings (Bern: Francke Verlag, 1982).
51. F. W. J. Schelling, *The Ages of the World, Third Version*, trans. Jason M. Wirth (Albany: State University of New York Press, 2000), 6.
52. Schelling, *Ages of the World*, xxxvii.
53. GW VIII, 91.
54. GW XIII, 93–94.
55. GW IX, 153.
56. GW V, 199.
57. GW IX, 160.
58. GW XIII, 60.
59. GW VIII, 162.
60. Ibid., 36.
61. Ibid., 27.
62. GW XIII, 161.
63. Ibid., 145.
64. GW VIII, 146.
65. GW XIII, 138.
66. Ibid., 139.
67. Hegel, *Philosophy of History*, 35.
68. GW XIII, 161.
69. Ibid., 145.

Part V

Ontology and Epistemology

19

The Presence of Kant in Stein

Mette Lebech

Stein's understanding of phenomenology was from the outset marked in equal measure by Husserl's and Reinach's. This is to say that she, like both of them, understood phenomenology to be a discipline of which different practitioners could hold different views, but which as such was and is what it is, defined by the adequate investigation of the phenomena. Her realist tendency makes her distance herself from Husserl's idealism and instead turns her attention towards preserving Reinach's heritage by finalizing and publishing his *Gesammelte Werke* after his death. Nevertheless, she accepts Husserl's transcendental turn in consequence of both his and Reinach's emphasis on the *a priori*, but rejects its egocentrism and in its place allows for faith in God, as creator and redeemer.

Both Reinach and Husserl held Kant to have "discovered" the *a priori*, which phenomenology was to explore methodically, but also to have unduly limited it and even held a psychologisticp view of it. Kant did of course not "discover" it, since the idea and expression was present since Euclid and played an important role in the Leibnizian/Wolffian school. Emilie du Châtelet, to whom Kant referred in his first publication "Thoughts on the True Estimation of Living Forces" (1747), linked it with essence, like the

M. Lebech (✉)
Department of Philosophy, Maynooth University, Maynooth, Ireland
e-mail: mette.lebech@mu.ie

C. D. Coe (eds.), *The Palgrave Handbook of German Idealism and Phenomenology*, Palgrave Handbooks in German Idealism, https://doi.org/10.1007/978-3-030-66857-0_19

phenomenologists.[1] As Kant abandoned the idea of essence in his later critical writings,[2] Stein's (and Husserl's and Reinach's) understanding of the *a priori* remains closer to du Châtelet's than Kant's, undoing, as they all do, this abandonment.

Despite the agreement between Reinach and Husserl in their critical assessment of Kant, it nevertheless on a closer view takes them in opposite directions, frequently referred to, respectively, as a realist and an idealist direction. Stein, always keen to recognize in each what is right, accepts both, and would probably have sidestepped the confrontation to side with du Châtelet's synthesis of empiricism and rationalism inspiring Kant, had she been aware of it. Although the *Edith Stein Lexikon* therefore is right in its assessment that "Kant was not an independent teacher for her ... on the road to knowledge of essence,"[3] it is nevertheless in her engagement with Kant that she discusses most extensively and interestingly the nature of idealism and realism as epistemological and metaphysical positions, both of which she declines to take. It is particularly in her early years that she sharpens her methodological phenomenology in this engagement with Kant, but she brought the *Critique of Pure Reason* with her when she entered the convent, and must thus have expected to use it or to have to engage with it again. In her later work, however, the role of catalyst for the discussion of idealism and realism is taken over by Heidegger, as she engages in *Finite and Eternal Being* in a *Seinslehre*, which she characteristically does not refer to as metaphysics.[4]

In what follows, I shall trace her engagement with Kant (or "Kant" in so far as it is an engagement mediated by Reinach's and Husserl's engagement with "Kant," which in turn has the ulterior purpose of clarifying the phenomenological method) in three steps. First, I shall look at the period between Stein assisting at Husserl's lectures on Kant in the winter semester 1913/14 and the winter semester 1918/19, respectively. The writing and publication of her own dissertation on empathy falls in this period, and her work for Husserl, in particular her editing of his *Introduction to Phenomenology*, planned as a response to the neo-Kantian criticism of phenomenology in *Kant-Studien*, does as well. I shall entitle this section "Phenomenology as extending and purifying Kant's understanding of the *a priori*: unknowingly recovering du Châtelet," since I shall also recover the du Châteletian underlay connecting essence and the *a priori* as an illustration of a position coming very close to Stein's.[5] Next, I shall look at Stein's more personally involved discussions of Kant in *Philosophy of Psychology and the Humanities* (written 1919–20, published 1922) and *Introduction to Philosophy* (1916–20), both marked by a position taking and a clarification of her own understanding of phenomenology, now in contradistinction from Husserl's, which she understands as marked by a metaphysical idealism. I shall entitle this "Causality and idealism as a metaphysical choice," since we shall discuss both as pulling in opposite directions for Stein's phenomenology. Finally, I shall discuss Stein's "What is Phenomenology?" (1924), "What is Philosophy?" (1929) and "The Significance of Phenomenology for a Worldview one might have" (1930/31), where the critical position taking in relation to Husserl's unfolding idealism continues, and continues to be cast in a discussion of Kant. Here, however, confirmed by her other writings, a new motif occurs, namely that Kant marks the beginning of a philosophy thinking it possible to dispense with faith. I shall entitle this section "Distance to Kant's criticism of religion."

Phenomenology as Extending and Purifying Kant's Understanding of the *a Priori*: Unknowingly Recovering Du Châtelet

Stein recalls from her early years of study at the University of Breslau that among the activities of "the four-leaved-clover," consisting of herself, two friends and her sister Erna, was an attempt at reading *Critique of Pure Reason*.[6] As she moved to Göttingen to study under Husserl, she attended his lectures "Kant and Modern Philosophy" (winter semester 1913/14), while at the same time attending Reinach's "Introduction to Philosophy" and his exercises for advanced students. It was during this time that Reinach gave his well-known lecture "Concerning Phenomenology" to the neo-Kantians in Marburg. The editors of Reinach's *Sämtliche Werke* summarize Reinach's intent in this very substantial paper in the following way: "Reinach is here first and foremost concerned to show that *a priori* knowledge is subjectivized in Kant and those who follow him, especially through its being impoverished and limited to the formal."[7] For Reinach, as for all the phenomenologists, there is a material *a priori*, which determines the regions with which each science concerns itself, and of which eidetic analysis is not only possible, but also necessary for the satisfactory development of the ensuing sciences:

> Up to now[,] I have been dealing with the subjectification of the *a priori*. No less an evil is what I have previously called the "impoverishment" of the *a priori*. There are few philosophers who have not in some way acknowledged the fact of the *a priori*; but there are none [who have not[8]] in some way reduced it to a small province of its actual kingdom. Hume enumerates a few relations of ideas. They are, surely, *a priori* connections. But why he restricted such connections to relations and then only to some few of them, is not clear.

And, finally, the restrictiveness with which Kant conceived of the *a priori* could not but become disastrous for subsequent philosophy. In truth, the realm of the *a priori* is incalculably large. All objects known have their "what," their "essence"; and of all essences there hold essence-laws. All restriction, and all reason for restriction, of the *a priori* to the, in some sense, "formal" is lacking. *A priori* laws also hold true of the material—in fact, of the sensible, of tones and colours. With that there opens up for investigation an area so incalculably large and rich that yet today we cannot see its boundaries.[9]

Husserl also was critical of Kant. In a planned formal answer to the Kantian criticism of phenomenology entitled *Introduction to Phenomenology* (1917/19), which Stein as his assistant elaborated in the first half of 1917, §10 treats of "the transcendent presuppositions in Kant's formulation of the problem,"[10] and §11 of "the necessity of abandoning the naturalistic foundation and Kantian limitation of the problem." We can thus see a very different emphasis compared to Reinach's:

For what concerns Kant, it certainly sounds harsh to count even him among the psychologists. But, one needs only to read the original formulation of the problem of his critique of reason … and compare it with the elaboration of the problem in the second edition of the completed work … to convince oneself that he remained far from the radical formulation of the problem of knowledge. Repeatedly, he operates with transcendent presuppositions stemming from the natural conception of the world…. It is transcendencies under the title "affecting thing in itself" derived from the natural thesis of the world outside the subject, partly from the naturally given material external world, partly, under the title "transcendental capacities and functional laws," from the natural reality of the subject as an in actual conscious living announcing capability subject, a human person…. We can take it to be certain that Kant himself never took the step from the presupposition-based to a radical [formulation of the] problem, and that all reinterpretation attempts in this regard are hopeless.[11]

In Stein, we find both Reinach's and Husserl's points accepted. She accepts Reinach's point to be that there is in Kant a restriction of the *a priori* and therefore of the field investigated by phenomenology, and she accepts Husserl's point that there is an inconsistency in Kant. This inconsistency, however, she interprets as a sign that Kant unawares adopts a metaphysical standpoint, much like Husserl himself does. Husserl, in contrast, seems to reproach Kant for not being radical enough in his idealism.

There can be such opposite criticisms of Kant (on the one hand, he denies the extent of the *a priori,* and on the other, he affirms it for what Stein would refer to as the "empty form" of the thing[12]) because it is not clear what role Kant accords to information stemming from the senses for *identifying* a thing. Maybe Husserl's criticism reflects that it remains equally unclear whether Husserl accepts both a causal input in the constitution of a thing and a being to its essence. At any rate, neither accepts the simple position found in du Châtelet: "That which is impossible cannot exist, for one calls impossible that which implies contradiction. Now if what implies contradiction could exist, one thing could both be, and not be at the same time: which is demonstrated as false for all men."[13] That the essence, which is the possibility of something, is *a priori* in the sense that it must by necessity (i.e. in itself and therefore for the mind) be what it is and not what it is not, is a principle not relying on anything, and thus primary.[14] However, it does not exclude a causal input through the senses out of which the things are identified, whose essence is *a priori*. The self-consistency of the essence is precisely what we mean by it being *a priori* and by the principle of non-contradiction being a fundamental principle. Insofar as Kant "situates" or attributes the logical principle, and with it its consequences for space, time, and categories *in or to the mind* his position is vulnerable to the criticism of psychologism that the phenomenologists were so keen to expose. The "thing in itself" *a priori* for both du Châtelet and Stein, and supposedly for all the phenomenologists insofar as intentionality is the law of all fully constituted consciousness, seems to be a problem for Husserl in the quotation above because he understands it as transcendent, and sees transcendencies as affecting or effecting something transcendental. Causality, however, for du Châtelet, obtains for all contingent being because of the principle of sufficient reason, which "is neither less fundamental nor less universal than that of contradiction."[15] It is equally *a priori*, since its negation leads to contradictions and the loss of meaning:

> For as soon as one accepts that something may happen without sufficient reason, one cannot be sure of anything, for example, that a thing is the same as it was a moment before, since this thing could change at any moment into another of a different kind; thus truths, for us, would only exist for an instant.[16]

If everything in the universe is understood to have a sufficient reason when it is understood, there is no need for the thing in itself to be transcendent in Husserl's sense. For du Châtelet the principle of sufficient reason has the same status as the principle of non-contradiction: it obtains for being (in this case for contingent being) in itself and therefore for thought.

It could be in prolongation of du Châtelet, that Kant, in his early, "pre-critical" work, defines essence as "the inner possibility," "that of which the cancellation eliminates all that can be thought."[17] To du Châtelet, all possibility is *a priori* as first principles are for Kepler,[18] and as geometry is in relation to the physical world according to Euclid's *Elements*. She is, however, making the point that experimentation cannot be dispensed with in natural science, and that to make sense of it, hypotheses are necessary. They should not, as they often are, be mistaken for *a priori* truth, but we can test them precisely because we have the *a priori* principles of non-contradiction and sufficient reason. Nevertheless, the idea of experimental testing relies on there being contingent truth and contingent being of which we can come to know something. In contrast with Kant, du Châtelet would not consider what we can come to know as attributable to the mind (only). If she did, she would not have been a natural scientist or indeed a natural philosopher, since her (ultimate) object in that case would have been the mind.

For Stein as for Husserl (and Reinach), the *a priori* is likewise the (whole of what is) ideally possible, the *mathesis universalis*,[19] the investigation and clarification of which gives rise to the *philosophia perennis*, the most convincing attempt at which is phenomenology. Kant clearly represents a branching out from the development towards its realization, a branching out compared to du Châtelet and the experimental scientists who knew they were applying necessary principles to experience in order for it to yield "laws," i.e. further (hypothetical) regularities characteristic of the physical world.

Although essences are be constituted, for Stein as well as for Husserl, and that genesis and habit therefore indeed play roles worth investigating, Stein will insist with Hering, that *essentialities* explain our recognition of something as something which in turn allows us to constitute essence.[20] Essences may thus, to stay in the vocabulary of du Châtelet, function as *hypotheses* in relation to contingent being, but what is *a priori* in them and in relation to them (the principles of non-contradiction and sufficient reason) allows us to investigate whether they are truly possible (in eidetic variation) and therefore might be. These principles are assisted, for the purpose of constituting essences, by the essentialities for Stein.

Accordingly, Stein in her *The Criticism of Theodor Elsenhans and August Messer*, authored as an appendix to the abovementioned *Introduction to Phenomenology*, and planned as Husserl's response to Kantian critics of phenomenology for the *Kant-Studien*, attributes to categorial objects a being parallel to but different from that of real being.[21] These objects are "seen into" as "ideal (or essential) possibilities,"[22] in the same way as mathematical objects are, on the background of freely forming imagination varying the object in all its possible variations. What cannot be imagined to be one cannot be a possible shape in space, for example,[23] although such *a priori* insights do not make reasoning error proof.[24] That which Stein later will refer to as "essential" being, is not all being, however. She confides to Ingarden from Breslau, where she is on holiday, in a much-quoted passage that:

> quite suddenly a breakthrough has occurred to me, according to which I imagine more or less to know what constitution is—but while breaking with idealism! An absolutely existing physical nature on the one hand, a subjectivity of a specific nature on the other seems to me presupposed for a vivid [anschauliche] nature to constitute itself. I have not yet arrived at confessing my heresy to the Master.[25]

It seems that Stein comes to this insight by elaborating the *Introduction* and adding the *Appendix* just referred to, in which we in fact see the position referred to. However, the fact that she knows it will be regarded by Husserl as unorthodox means that she is putting forward as his an opinion that she knows to be hers and to possibly differ from his. Husserl concentrates on transcendental idealism resulting from understanding the *a priori* as ideal,[26] but nevertheless affirms a distinction between *a priori* and *a posteriori* being: dubitability characterizes the real as distinct from the *a priori*.[27] It may thus be better to say that Stein recognized in Husserl a tendency towards idealism, which she could not quite reconcile with his overall thought. Insofar as transcendental idealism means that that which is known is known in and through its *a priori* essence (and not the metaphysical position that *nothing exists* beyond this), she also was sympathetic to it, much like du Châtelet was sympathetic to Descartes, while still insisting on empirical, experimental observation. Stein could not convince Husserl and was convinced of his sincerity.[28] As it took quite a while to bring these "Kant" texts towards publication,[29] she had time to measure her own newfound insight against the sincerity of Husserl. This doctrinal divergence—Stein refusing to take any position towards idealism and realism regarding both as metaphysical positions versus Husserl embracing idealism as part of phenomenology—no doubt contributed to Stein eventually resigning from her position.

Causality and Idealism as a Metaphysical Choice

In prolongation, perhaps, of Reinach'scritique of Kant, Stein criticizes Kant for making of causality a category, which does admittedly explain what natural science is concerned with, but does not correspond to a phenomenon explained. Stein relies for her own investigations (*Philosophy of Psychology and the Humanities* and *Introduction to Philosophy*) on material from *Ideas*

II (which she has left behind unpublished with Husserl) and a work by Erika Gothe entitled *Cause and Condition*,[30] which unfortunately seems lost apart from an excerpt kept by Husserl.[31] Erika Gothe was with Stein as she tried to persuade Husserl to finalize *Ideas II* instead of being side-tracked by the *Kant Beiheft*.[32] It seems they both had an interest in seeing the phenomenon of causality further clarified by Husserl, but their persuasion attempt did not succeed.

Stein's idea is that *psychic* causality is the paradigmatic case of causality, the description of which is the phenomenon of causality sought for.[33] This makes of death and all its precursors the paradigmatic instance of a caused, experienced event.[34]

> Without a doubt, we have the right to claim this phenomenon of causality in the experiential sphere as analogous to causality in the realm of physical nature, and indeed to the paradigmatic case of causality (to which physics attempts to reduce all other causal relations): mechanical efficacy. As a rolling ball induces movement to another on which it impacts; as the induced movement in direction and speed depends on the "power" of the impact—so the "push" coming from the life-sphere determines the kind of proceeding of further experience, not only its quality but also the "strength" of the effect depends on the cause, only is the strength here not measurable as in the realm of physical nature.[35]

The phenomenon of causality is of course not found by making it, as Kant does, a synthetic *a priori* concept of reason, through which "alone something of the manifold of perception" is understood and an object thought.[36] Kant

> deduces causality as one of the conditions of possibility of the exact natural sciences, he shows that nature in the sense of natural science without causality is unthinkable. That is an indisputable fact, but it is no solution to the problem of causality and not a satisfactory answer to Hume's question.... To this question, which undoubtedly represents a genuine problem for knowledge, a consideration like the Kantian one where only a "*natura formaliter spectata*" is involved, provides no answer. It is not interested in the phenomena, and the causality it deduces is a form, which allows for many fillings; it designates only a necessary relation in time; of what kind this relation is, can the "transcendental deduction" in Kant's sense not teach us. To accomplish this, we need a method of analysis and description of phenomena, i.e. objects in the concrete fullness in which they present themselves to us, and of the consciousness corresponding to these.[37]

Stein attempted to describe the phenomenon as occurring in conjunction with motivation in the first part of *Philosophy of Psychology and the Humanities*, entitled *Psychic Causality*. The analysis of this phenomenon and the discussion of how it can be seen to be the paradigmatic case of causality are not our task here. The fact is that Stein believed she had shown it, and this may explain her confession to Ingarden of a (re-)conversion to idealism,[38] as she is now envisaging the phenomenon of causality to show up as an aspect of the stream of experiences itself. Although she remains critical of *Ideas II–III*, it is thus not at the time by disagreeing with their idealism; it is rather because she considers them insufficiently thought through.[39]

Stein accepts the Kantian idea, adopted by Husserl, that natural causality "belongs to the categories which makes a natural science 'possible in the first place' as an exact mathematical science."[40] Nevertheless, this is not sufficient to determine the object of a science: the object must be concretely (empirically) experienced as well, for the science to obtain and be able to choose between the different types of formalization available to it.[41]

> The natural scientists generally have the standpoint that different theories to explain reality are possible and that all are equally justified, which provide such an explanation. But, on the one hand "reality" provides certain limits to freedom in its choice of a useful explanation, and on the other only one of these can be the true, the one namely, which corresponds to something in reality—that lies in the concept of truth, from which the entire observation proceeds. Only through engagement with the object itself, not through random "thought elaborations," can I press on to its real elements and elemental laws. That goes for the investigation of its factual nature as for that of its constitution.[42]

This insistence, whether or not understood as idealism, nevertheless expresses a realist tendency, which probably prompts Ingarden, knowing her well, to claim her to "love reality." Stein's response is characteristic:

> Yes, I do love reality, but not simply, a very specific [part of it]: the human soul, that of the individual and that of the peoples.... And yes, I also love ideals, for their own sake; for I am strongly theoretically inclined—and moreover as the only reliable guiding star of our lives, without which we unredeemably lose our way.... In this sense I am an unrepentant "idealist."[43]

Two weeks later Stein reports reviewing Gertrud Kutznitzki's *Experience of Nature and Consciousness of Reality*,[44] in which "the problem of reality and knowledge of reality is central."[45] The program she recognizes in this work is in many ways taken over by herself and many concepts occur in it, which Stein will use in her later work. Kutznitzki understands the experience of nature to be experienced "through the essence of reality."[46] Thus, reality "divides itself" "according to fundamental *a priori* structures."[47] "Reality is unity of experiential matter and form, fullness and meaning content. But the form is not from the outside—through consciousness—drawn into fullness, but grounds in it and is given as one with it."[48] Stein criticizes what she sees as an inconsistency left over from the neo-Kantian background, namely that the formal categories (in distinction from the material ones) are understood to be functions of consciousness. The material categories Kutznitzki nevertheless recognizes as "essentialities independent of the forming activity of the subject."[49] Stein asks: "Should it not equally be grounded in the structure of the sensual material, *that* objective entities, individual objects, constitute themselves, as it according to the author depends on the 'fullness' of what kind the constituted objects are?"[50] This question deserves, according to Stein, sustained investigation: it would involve discussion of the constitution not only of reality but also of the formal and material categories.[51]

> Only through it can finally also the choice between "idealism" and "realism" be made. (NB. I want to stress, that a choice for one or the other side is not implied, when one does not recognize categories to be subjective forms and acknowledges to them the same independence of consciousness as reality. The meaning of this independence remains to be investigated for all objectivities.)[52]

This leads us to Stein's most substantial discussion of Kant (and of idealism versus realism) in her *Introduction to Philosophy*. Marièle Wulf helpfully introduces this work as follows[53]:

> "Introduction to Philosophy" intervenes in the struggle between eidetic and idealistic phenomenology. While eidetic phenomenology only methodically brackets the positing of existence, but regards as possible a knowing access to the empirical thing, transcendental phenomenology takes another route: it considers relevant for phenomenological research only the in consciousness given object. Stein takes her methodical point of departure here *and does not take it to be absolute*. To her not only consciousness is indubitably given, but also the thing intended.[54]

Stein refuses in the introduction to characterize what she calls the "objective attitude," i.e. "with completely open eyes in self-less dedication conceiving the things themselves" as either allowing or disallowing for a Kantian thing-in-itself.[55] She attributes the discipline of "critique of reason" to him and describes it as a better name for epistemology, which in turn investigates:

how it is possible that consciousness directs itself to objects outside itself, which have their own, independent being, a transcendent being, as is often said[.] The phenomenon of the self-transcending consciousness, of the comprehension of the object, forms the centre of the discipline we have designated as critique of reason.[56]

A dialectic between epistemology and ontology thus serves as an avenue to introduce beginners to phenomenology:

Although the critique of reason seems referred back to ontology, it is neverthe- less possible to say in another sense that the critique of reason in its turn still is "presupposition" for ontology. For it must be shown, for the *a priori* structures of being just as for all objectivities, how a knowledge of them is possible. Thus arises the reciprocity and inseparability of the two fundamental philosophical disciplines.[57]

She formulates the insight with which *Psychic Causality* ends in language suited for her audience of beginners:

That all that happens in nature has a cause is an axiom upon which natural science as a systematic investigation of causal connections is based.[58] This axiom states something which already is implicit in natural experience (already the naive human being understands everything as happening for a reason, whether known or unknown), which however in no way can be justified by [this] experience. A philosophy based on mere experience is thus just as absurd as one based on experiential science.[59]

Du Châtelet calls this *a priori* axiom the principle of sufficient reason. Her understanding of space as *a priori*[60] also foreshadows Stein's, who does not follow Kant in its subjectivization as a "form" of perception. Thus, "it remains possible that there might be an experience of spatiality. All experience of nature includes an experience of space, on the basis of which (as an exem- plary substrate) knowledge of essence is possible.... Spatiality [belongs] to the essence of the natural object."[61]

Although Stein identifies Kant as a critical idealist, whose goal is to demonstrate the impossibility of metaphysics, she nevertheless claims, in prolongation of Husserl's criticism, that in his *Critique*

metaphysical perspectives play a role in a twofold way: 1. he works with specific metaphysical presuppositions. 2. The problem of the reality of the outer world has whether one likes it or not two sides—an epistemological and a metaphys- ical—, and thus it is not easy to say something about one of these without (implicitly at least) taking a standpoint in relation to the other. The metaphysical presuppositions of the Critique—that there are things in themselves and that the subject is "affected" by them—constitutes a transgression of the idealistic (and the criticist) standpoint and is therefore of no use if we want to characterise it. What is of relevance here is thus only those metaphysical views of Kant, which so to speak form the reverse of his epistemology: the things of our experience are not things in themselves, but appearances and as such dependent on the forms of perception and reason, i.e. on the consciousness to which they appear. They hold their structure and being from the forming activity of the subject, which conceives its sensations in forms, pertaining to every consciousness. The lowest synthesis is the sensual, which organises the sensual material according to the forms of perception space and time. On this builds the formation of the perception through the pure concepts of reason or categories, e.g. substance and causality.[62]

Stein's own position, which she understands to be the phenomenological position, is similar in many respects as she herself says.[63] She admits of a "schema," according to which sensual impressions are synthesized, and which can be analyzed in what she calls "ontological observation," investigating the essence of the experienced object.[64] She allows also for categories as the root concepts (*Stambegriffe*) out of which a schema-like "thing" forms (i.e. is constituted).

But here we must already stop. The Kantian understanding of the categories and the forms of perception as functions of subjectivity go beyond the results of our analysis. Our schemata seemed to us as fundamental structures of objectivity and at the same time as the laws regulating the constitution of objects.... Then we have in the schemata an *absolute being* before us, in no way to be seen as a being at the mercy of subjectivity. One could say that they only apply, and function, where an experiencing consciousness obtains—but their being is not dependent on it. This being fits the predicates with which Plato characterises his ideas: uncreated, indestructible, unchanging. The schemata are furthermore like the Platonic ideas in that they are "archetypes" of the real objects. However, with the absoluteness of the schemata or categories nothing has yet been said of the independence of being of what we call the real outer world. The thing's schema is not itself a real thing; it is what makes every real thing a thing, that in which it participates (to use the Platonic image of the relationship between the idea and its realisation), but it displays everywhere a different filling in, and the thing's subsistence is never exhausted by its correspondence with the schema. Thus the question remains open of whether of the two domains of being—consciousness and reality (in our case: nature)—one has the priority of absoluteness of existence over the other, while the other only has meaning as its correlate.[65]

With the affirmation of the independent *a priori* being of the categories, she distances herself from the Kantian position, and by leaving open the question of whether either consciousness or being has any kind of priority, she also leaves behind Husserl's idealism. That the *a priori* is necessarily possible does not make it a feature of subjectivity. It rather contributes to account for the difference between nature (real being) and spirit (consciousness *and* ideal being): our experience of the world is both *a priori* and factual, a position expressed by du Châtelet's position that the will of God is the source of actual existence, but not of the possibility of things.[66]

Stein also remarks, that even the idealist philosopher, whether Kant or Husserl, does not want to relativize "other co-experiencing subjects."[67] The solipsist, as soon as he presents his point of view and by this very fact, in practice refutes it or acts inconsistently with it, in that he takes others as others who might be convinced: "were he to be consistent, he would have to remain silent."[68] Of the pure I of the other one cannot say that it in its structures or for its constitution depends on the functions of the perceiving subject, whether the "cannot" here is a moral ought or not:

> Naturally a conceiving consciousness also corresponds to him [the other], and one may also of him, as of things, say, that it means a regularity determining a specific proceeding of this consciousness. That he would only be that, that his existence would have no other meaning than as the regularity of a certain proceeding of consciousness; that is not either accepted by the forms of idealism dominant today. To them, every consciousness counts as [an] equally valuable being. We emphasise this fact, which seemingly has nothing to do with natural philosophy, so much, because with it the possibility of a being, which is independent from the corresponding knowing consciousness, is recognised.... Of this "external" experience now obtains that that which is experienced in it, in its being is completely independent of it.... Here we thus have an experience, which transcends itself.[69]

In order for idealism to show itself to be credible, it would thus have to *show* (to others) that nature or reality according to its essence (i.e. *a priori*, necessarily) cannot exist without a consciousness perceiving it. "This task appears to me in advance to be not sufficiently treated by the idealist philosophy to whom it falls [to investigate it]."[70] Whether sufficiently accounted for or not, Kant did see the categories as functions of subjectivity or reason.

> If one does that, one must say: The functions can function and the subject can experience by means of them without itself conceiving of them. Such blind ruling functions could not be characterised as *concepts* of reason, and one could not say that the object-"thought" and the categories determining

it more closely, could be conceived in thought and brought to bear on the material available in knowledge.[71]

The automaticity of the function thus seems to rule out that there is an experience of the object at all:

> Is not with the fact that one takes the categories to be functional laws and only that the thought of objectivity sacrificed? The result of epistemology would then be that the object, such as intended by all knowledge: as something founded in itself; and knowledge as what it claims to be: a universally valid grasping of obtaining matters of fact, both would be deceptive appearances. [They would] dissipate when one reveals the functional laws out of which it results that consciousness must, according to its essence, run such a course that the belief in objects independent of it grow in it. At one point this theory must break through itself: the being of consciousness and moreover the subsisting of the functional laws which rule the process of consciousness must be recognised as independent of the consciousness that posits their being. For would one further say that the functional laws do not in truth obtain, but that belief in them is due to the fact that consciousness runs through certain regulated processes, then one obviously ends in an infinite regress. With "truth" and "validity" generally would thus also the truth and validity of the proposed theories expire.[72]

Stein concludes:

> We have had to decline interpreting [the material categories] as functions of subjectivity because it would mean the suspension of knowledge. We attribute to them just as to the formal categories a being independent of all subjectivity; no real existence, but an ideal being, *a priori* to all existence and experience, making these possible "in the first place." In viewing the categories as conditions of possibility of knowledge and its objects, we are in agreement with Kant.[73]

Because of Stein's insistence on the irreducibly *a priori* nature of the essentialities (of or from which essences are constituted), her Reinachian criticism of Kant ends by excluding the possibility of the Husserlian criticism (given that the empty form "object" also is *a priori* for what is intended). It is thus by insisting on ideal being that she expresses her "realism," while probably still understanding it as idealism, at least in the sense, maybe teasingly, introduced by Ingarden, of having high ideals. She stays true to the phenomenological principle that experience is experience of something.

Distance to Kant's Criticism of Religion

In "What is Phenomenology?" (1924) Stein claims that Kant represents modern philosophy as Aquinas represents Scholastic philosophy: two traditions she sees dividing the philosophical scene of her time.[74] Husserl is portrayed as finding his independent way between these two directions, coming into contact with the first through Brentano and the second through the neo-Kantian environment. In Husserl's increasingly affirmed idealism "lies in fact a moving closer to Kant and a radical difference with Catholic philosophy, for which the independent being of the world is clear."[75] That Catholic philosophy would affirm the thesis of the natural attitude is no doubt motivated by the intersubjective availability of the world as much as by the dogma of the creation of the world by God. Leo XIII's *Aeterni Patris*, responding to the modernist crisis, indeed came close to a dogmatic recommendation of it. Husserl's idealism was however criticized by his students irrespective of such dogmatic recommendation, and regarded by Stein as "a personal metaphysical basic conviction, not an indubitable result of phenomenological research."[76]

"What is philosophy?" (1928) is an imagined dialogue between Husserl and Aquinas discussing their most important differences, in the course of which they also come to discuss Kant. The mention Aquinas makes of him is significant, especially in the light of Stein's own development:

> Kant also has said that the limits of reason must be established before it can embark on its real business. But to him, as to all modern philosophy, it was obvious that it would be the task of "autonomous" natural reason itself to establish these. I could here throw in the question of whether it would not need, in order to solve this question an Archimedean point outside itself, and of how it would be possible for it to reach to this point.[77]

Here Stein suggests, through her character of Aquinas, that reason might need a kind of support from an Archimedean point outside itself, a kind of 'circumcision,' a definite limit up against which it can support itself in its growth, and without which its efforts remains fruitless because they are without a hold on ... well, reality. For Stein's Aquinas there is no doubt that that Archimedean point is God, God of the philosophers, and that that Archimedean point has made itself available to us through the Christian revelation. That Aquinas would think so is hardly controversial. That he would suggest in dialogue with Husserl, that Husserl also would need this Archimedean point because thought as such needs it, is the point that Stein conveys: philosophy is in need of religion broadly speaking, of God more precisely, in order to make sense. This in fact is a very radical claim, and it is not one Stein is making lightly. Could it really be that our belief in the reality of an external world is in need of dogmatic support from the side of religion? Is the world real for the sake of the human being, as part of its "wherefrom?" and "whereto?" In that case, it is a concern legitimately falling under the authority of the Church, and discussed at length in Stein's anthropology *The Structure of the human Person/What is the human being?*

This thread is taken up in "Die Weltanschauliche Bedeutung der Phänomenologie" (1930/31). Here it is claimed that (self-) critical philosophy is one that is aware of its own limits, in order to concentrate on its task. Since Kant, this self-critical philosophy concentrated not on collating the results of science to complete a "scientific worldview," "but [on] testing the presuppositions of the individual sciences, in order to place them on secure ground and thereby first make them truly into sciences."[78] Stein thus also attributes the return to the Aristotelian enterprise of founding the sciences to Kant. This is of importance in *Finite and Eternal Being*, in that this project, which also remains Stein's, is seen, not only to be shared between ancient and moderns, but also to be accomplishable (only?) by a (Christian?) philosophy, supporting itself on the revealed knowledge of the wherefore and the whereto of the human being.

Conclusion

Stein's engagement with Kant, like perhaps no other theme, reflects her own development in relation to the questions of idealism and faith. Throughout Stein's development as a philosopher Kant thus plays an important role in representing modern idealism alongside Husserl. Stein deploys Reinach's criticism of Kant in relation to both, which means Kant comes to play a decisive role in her discussion of her own phenomenological position, particularly as regards the metaphysical and epistemological positions of idealism and realism, which she continuously insists remain separate from methodological phenomenology. Kant finally becomes the catalyst for her adopting an explicitly Christian position, where the independent being of the essentialities is light for the constitution of the world. As far as reality is affirmed for reason of charity, Stein's engagement with Kant reveals how she can equally be called a pragmatic realist and a Christian transcendental phenomenologist.

Notes

1. See section 'Phenomenology as Extending and Purifying Kant's Understanding of the *a Priori*: Unknowingly Recovering Du Châtelet' of this chapter.
2. For an analysis of the development of Kant's understanding of essence, see Mette Lebech, *On the Problem of Human Dignity: A Hermeneutical and Phenomenological Investigation* (Würzburg: Königshausen und Neumann, 2009), 205–12.
3. Harald Seubert, "Kant," in *Edith Stein Lexikon*, ed. Marcus Knaup and Harald Seubert (Freiburg: Herder, 2017), 211. Unless otherwise stated, all translations are my own.
4. Edith Stein, *Endliches und ewiges Sein*, in *Edith Stein Gesamtausgabe*, 11/12, 5. Hereafter: ESGA. Stein uses this term, and not *"Ontologie,"* which she could have done. What is meant by it must no doubt be seen in the light of Hedwig Conrad-Martius' *Realontologie*, which constitutes a phenomenological attempt at describing (the phenomenon of) reality, which Husserl, apparently, could not own. Given that Stein could, and indeed was highly appreciative of it, her own *Seinslehre*, honing in on the being of both ideal and real being, from within the Cartesian experience of the being of the I and acknowledging the decisive nature of faith in Christ, is more of a response to Heidegger's "fundamental ontology" than expressing a metaphysical position taking.
5. Many discussions with Ruth Hagengruber, Centre for the History of Women Philosophers and Scientists, over the period of a sabbatical semester September 2019–February 2020 on du Châtelet and Stein, as well as on the role of women philosophers in the history of philosophy, must be recognized here. Although I am deeply indebted to these, they do not hold her, of course, to agree with me on particulars of this interpretation.
6. Stein, *Leben in einer jüdischen Familie*, in ESGA 1, 88.
7. Adolf Reinach, *Sämtliche Werke. Textkritische Ausgabe 1–2*, ed. Karl Schumann and Barry Smith (München: Philosophia Verlag, 1989), 769. This edition subsumes and replaces Stein's Adolf Reinach, *Gesammelte Werke* (Halle: Max Niemeyer, 1921).
8. The translation is corrected to accord with the German of the *Sämtliche Werke*. The passage shows that Reinach was very likely not familiar with du Châtelet.
9. Adolf Reinach, "Concerning Phenomenology," trans. by Dallas Willard, quoted from the *Phenomenology Reader*, ed. Dermot Moran and Timothy Mooney (London: Routledge, 2002), 192–93.
10. §10 of "Phenomenology and Epistemology," *Husserliana* XXV, 140–41, corresponding to §6 of the same treatise in *"Freiheit und Gnade" und weitere Beiträge zu Phänomenologie und Ontologie*, ESGA 9.
11. §7 in ESGA 9, 246; Husserliana XXV, 140–41. The publication was to have appeared under Husserl's name, and Stein elaborated it with that in mind.
12. E.g., *Endliches und ewiges Sein*, ESGA 11/12, IV, §3, 18.

13. §33 (Chapter 3) of *Foundations of Physics*, trans. by Katherine Brading et al. made available at https://www.kbrading.org/translations [consulted 8/4/20]. *Institutions de Physiques*, Paris, 1742, available at https://reader.digitale-sammlu ngen.de/de/fs1/object/display/bsb10130894_00011.html [consulted 8/4/20].

14. §38 (Chapter 3) op. cit.: "For one wants to know here how the Being is possible, and what makes it possible. One must therefore assemble determinations of this Being that do not conflict with one another, and that do not follow necessarily from other antecedent determinations (as, for example, two of the sides and the subtended angle in a triangle; for the third side and the two other angles are only possible once the two sides and the angle made from them are posited, so one must posit the two sides and this angle prior to the third side and the two other angles). Thus, the primordial determinations are those which constitute the essence of a Being." A being is thus possible by or in its essence.

15. §8, *Institutions*. Also available in Emilie du Châtelet, *Selected Philosophical and Scientific Writings*, trans. Isabelle Bour and Judith Zinsser, ed. Judith Zinsser (Chicago: University of Chicago Press, 2009).

16. Ibid., 129.

17. *The Only Possible Argument in Support of a Demonstration of the Existence of God* (1763) in Immanuel Kant, *Theoretical Philosophy*, trans. D. Walford and R. Meerbote (Cambridge: Cambridge University Press, 1992), 172.

18. Emilie du Châtelet, *Commentary on Newton's* Principia, X, note (g); quoted in Emilie du Châtelet, *Selected Philosophical and Scientific Writings*, 269.

19. For Stein, *Zur Kritik an Theodor Elsenhans und August Messer*, appendix to *Introduction to Phenomenology*, ESGA 9, 310–11. For Husserl, *Introduction to Phenomenology* §3, ESGA 9, 236; Husserliana XXV, 130.

20. Stein, *Endliches und ewiges Sein*, ESGA 11/12, Chapter 3, §3. Jean Hering, "Bemerkungen über das Wesen, die Wesenheit und die Idee," *Jahrbuch für Philosophie und phänomenologische Forschung* IV, 495. Stein read Hering's work already in January 1917, well before its publication in 1920 (see Letter to Roman Ingarden, 28 January 1917, ESGA 4, 35).

21. This is a characteristic doctrine as we shall see, even when she as here speaks "as Husserl," ESGA 9, 315.

22. ESGA 9, 316.

23. See du Châtelet *Institutions* §34: "All that is possible can exist, for given that a thing contains nothing that is contradictory, one can imagine nothing that opposes the possibility of its existence. The possibility of things depends, therefore, on the non-contradiction of their determinations; and when a thing contains nothing that is contradictory, this alone suffices for its possibility." See also §§38, 39, 45 and 46.

24. ESGA 9, 318. See du Châtelet, *Institutions* §5 for a similar insight.

25. Letter to Ingarden 3 February 1917, ESGA 4, 40. I have not been able to consult *Self-Portrait in Letters: Letters to Roman Ingarden*, trans. Hugh Candler Hunt, Collected Works of Edith Stein XII (henceforth CWES) (Washington, DC: ICS Publications, 2014) due to COVID 19 restrictions. Translations are thus my own.

26. E.g. ESGA 9, "Phänomenologie und Erkenntnistheorie," 251; Husserliana 147. The *Einleitung*, noted down in one go February to April 1917 (Sepp and Nenon, xix), and probably in some kind of reaction to Stein requesting revisions of *Ideas II* on the elaboration of which she had embarked, was one of those texts Husserl left unpublished.

27. ESGA 9, 266.

28. Letter to Ingarden, 20 February 1917, ESGA 4, 46.

29. Stein's *Bearbeitung* of Husserl's notes took from after Pentecost until the summer holidays (Letter to Ingarden, 6 July 1917, ESGA 4, 62). It consisted in transcription from stenography, stylistic elaboration and "ventriloquism." Cfr. Marianne Sawicki: *Body, Text and Science. The Literacy of Investigative Practices and the Phenomenology of Edith Stein* (Dordrecht: Springer, 1997), 153. We might compare with Reinach's manuscript of his *Introduction to Philosophy*, now printed in his *Sämtliche Werke I*, 369–513, of which she writes to Ingarden on 10 April 1918 that it should "in better times be elaborated as a book" (ESGA 4, 76). If she has worked as much on the *Kant Beiheft* as she here envisages in relation to Reinach's notes, it is considerable.

30. *Ursache und Bedingung*.

31. Karl Schumann: *Husserl-Chronik. Denk- und Lebensweg Edmund Husserls* (Den Haag: Martinus Nijhof, 1977), 198.

32. Letter to Ingarden 9 April 1917, ESGA 4, 52.

33. *Beiträge zur Philosophischen Begründung der Psychologie und der Geisteswissenschaften*, ESGA 6, First treatise: *Psychic Causality*. The treatise is describing the phenomenon in great detail and claims it to be the phenomenon that allows us to identify the psyche (as distinct from soul, consciousness and spirit), the proper object studied by psychology. As she is not addressing the phenomenon of causality in its entirety, she is only suggesting that this phenomenon is more "original" in the sense of us having a more immediate experience of it, and then leaving it to one side for further investigations. It remains an extraordinarily interesting idea, which as far as I am aware has not been followed through as yet.

34. Ibid., 16. Due to COVID 19 restrictions, I have not been able to consult *Philosophy of Psychology and the Humanities*, trans. Marianne Sawicki and Mary Catherine Baseheart, CWES vol. VII (Washington, DC: ICS Publications, 2000). Translations are thus my own.

35. ESGA 6, 16. See also Marianne Sawicki, "Edith Stein's Critique of Hume's Association Theory" in *Yearbook of the Irish Philosophical Society 2004*, ed. Mette Lebech (Maynooth: The Irish Philosophical Society, 2004), 141–50.

36. *Critique of Pure Reason* A80.

37. *Beiträge*, ESGA 6, 7. Beate Beckmann helpfully comments in a note: "Die 'natura formaliter spectata' (lat. 'Natur unter formaler Hinsicht') ist das Produkt der Verständestätigkeit des menschlichen Subjekts, von dem her sie konstituiert wird. Husserl übernam diesen Ausdruck von Kant und bezeichnete damit die ontologische Gesetzlichkeit der Natur, auch mit dem Ausdruck ‚Form der Natur ', z.B. *Ideen III*, s. 36." She also refers to Kant's *Critique of pure Reason*, B164-5: "Nun ist das, was das mannigfaltige der sinnlichen Anschauung verknüpft, Einbildungskraft, die vom Verstande der Einheit ihrer intellektuellen Synthesis, und von der Sinnlichkeit der Mannigfaltigkeit der Apprehension nach abhängt. Da nun von der Synthesis der Apprehension alle mögliche Wahrnehmung, sie selbst aber, diese empirische Synthesis, von der transzendentalen, mithin den Kategorien abhängt, so müssen alle möglichen Wahrnehmungen, mithin auch alles, was zum empirischen Bewusstsein immer gelangen kann, d.i. alle Erscheinungen der Natur, ihrer Verbindung nach, unter den Kategorien stehen, von welchen die Natur (bloß als Natur überhaupt betrachtet), als dem ursprünglichen Grunde ihrer notwendigen Gesetzmäßigkeit (als natura formaliter spectata), abhängt."

38. Letter to Ingarden 24 June 1918: "Husserl hat kürzlich die Abhandlung vom vorigen Jahr über Phänomenologie und Erkenntnistheorie vorgenommen und dabei an einer Stelle meine Forderung vermerkt gefunden, dass er seine Argumentation noch einmal durchdenken und dort in puncto Idealismus unumwunden Farbe bekennen sollte. Das möchte er nun gern tun. Er sucht alles zusammen, was er über die Frage hat, und sprach in den letzten Tagen mit mir darüber. Ich habe alle andere Arbeit vertagt, lese die Ideen und kreide mir an, was mir bedenklich scheint. N.B. ich selbst habe mich zum Idealismus bekehrt und glaube, er lässt sich so verstehen, dass er auch metaphysisch befriedigt."

39. Ibid: "Aber es scheint mir, dass vieles, was in den Ideen steht, anders gefasst werden muss, und zwar in Husserls Sinn, wenn er nur alles zusammennimmt, was er hat, und nicht im entscheidenden Moment etwas von außer Betracht lässt, was notwendig zur Sache gehört."

40. *Beiträge*, ESGA 6, 100–1. This would correspond to accepting that the principle of sufficient reason *a priori* applies to all contingent being—as indeed du Châtelet claimed it did.

41. Ibid., 102.

42. Ibid., 103.

43. Letter to Ingarden 10 December 1918, ESGA 4.

44. Letter to Ingarden 27 December 1918, ESGA 4. Since the work is dated "Breslau, 1919," she must have been sent an early copy by *Kant-Studien*, for which she reviewed the work.

45. "(Besprechung von:) Gertrud Kuznitzky, *Naturerlebnis und Wirklichkeitsbewusstsein* (1920)" in ESGA, 3, 9.

46. Ibid.
47. Ibid., 4.
48. Ibid.
49. Ibid., 5.
50. Ibid.
51. Ibid.
52. Ibid., 5–6.
53. Letter to Ingarden 30 April 1920, ESGA 4, 128.
54. *Einführung*, ESGA 8, xii. Emphasis mine.
55. Ibid., 7–8.
56. Ibid., 11.
57. Ibid., 12.
58. According to du Châtelet the principle of sufficient reason is self-evident like the principle of non-contradiction, despite the fact that it was not known to the ancients (*Institutions* §7): "all men naturally follow it; for no one decides to do one thing rather than another without a sufficient reason that shows that this thing is preferable to the other."
59. *Einführung*, ESGA 8, 16.
60. *Institutions* §79: "we form the idea of Space, which is nothing other than the idea of extension joined with the possibility of restoring to the coexistent and unified Beings, from which the idea was formed, the determinations that we had already stripped from them by abstraction. Thus, we are right to define Space, the order of Coexisting things."
61. *Einführung*, ESGA 8, 31–32.
62. Ibid., 70–71.
63. Ibid., 71.
64. Ibid., 69.
65. Ibid., 71–72.
66. *Institutions*, §121. Du Châtelet understands, like Leibniz, monads to account for extension: simple beings must account for all there is, otherwise it would not be. Husserl's understanding of monads as subjects makes of intersubjectivity all there is: a position Stein could not accept, given her understanding of the absoluteness of the being of the schemata. Indeed, the other subject could not be identified were it not for this absolute being of ideal being.
67. *Einführung*, ESGA 8, 77.
68. Ibid.
69. Ibid., 78–79.
70. Ibid., 79.
71. Ibid., 87.
72. Ibid., 88.
73. Ibid., 97.
74. "*Freiheit und Gnade*," ESGA 9, 85.

75. Ibid., 89.
76. Ibid.
77. Ibid., 98 (123 in non-dialogical version: "Husserls Phänomenologie und die Philosophie des hl. Thomas v. Aquin. Versuch einer Gegenüberstellung").
78. Ibid., 144.

20

Heidegger on Fichte's Three Principles

M. Jorge de Carvalho

Should one ask why the path of Heidegger's thought led him to an examination of Fichte's three principles in his philosophy, the *Wissenschaftslehre*, an essential part of the answer lies in the fact that Fichte regards the "absolutely certain knowledge" his *Wissenschaftslehre* is all about as something that can only be found in "what *underlies* all knowledge or knowing as such [*was allem Wissen als solchem zugrunde liegt*]" or in "what renders knowing as such possible [*was es als ein solches ermöglicht*]."[1] Accordingly, the purpose of the *Wissenschaftslehre* is to expose *what is already contained in all knowing*, or to "start from the fact of knowing and exclude everything except what cannot be thought away [*was sich nicht wegdenken lässt*], what thus reveals itself as that which in all thinking is already necessarily thought [*als das, das notwendig in allem Denken schon gedacht ist*]."[2] In short, the task of the *Wissenschaftslehre* is to discover *what "we never do not think"* or "what we never fail to think [*was wir nie nicht denken*]."[3] This *constant thought*, or rather the *thinking of this constant thought*, is what renders all knowledge

M. J. de Carvalho (✉)
Departamento de Filosofia, Faculdade de Ciências Sociais e Humanas da Universidade Nova de Lisboa, Lisboa, Portugal
e-mail: mj.carv@fcsh.unl.pt

Departamento de Filosofia, Instituto de Estudos Filosóficos da Universidade de Coimbra, Coimbra, Portugal

C. D. Coe (eds.), *The Palgrave Handbook of German Idealism and Phenomenology*, Palgrave Handbooks in German Idealism, https://doi.org/10.1007/978-3-030-66857-0_20

(viz. all knowing) as such possible. But, on the other hand, none of this prevents what is "never not thought" from remaining *hidden*, and indeed *hidden* in such a way that it takes the *Wissenschaftslehre* to uncover it (so that Fichte's *Wissenschaftslehre* is but a discovery of what is latently present in all our thoughts, representations, etc., without exception).

One need only recall Heidegger's definition of the *phenomenon in a phenomenological sense* to recognize the essential connection.[4] For the *phenomenon in a phenomenological sense*, which his *Daseinsanalytik* is meant to uncover, is nothing other than that "which already shows itself in appearances, prior to the commonly understood phenomenon and accompanying it in every case, albeit unthematically."[5] Or, as he also puts it: it is that

> which initially and in most cases does *not* show itself at all; that which, in contrast to what initially and in most cases does show itself, lies hidden, but which at the same time essentially belongs to what initially and in most cases shows itself; and it belongs to it in such a way as to constitute its meaning and ground.[6]

In Heidegger's view, "phenomenology" stands for ἀποφαίνεσθαι τὰ φαινόμενα: "to let that which shows itself be seen from itself in the very way in which it shows itself from itself [*das, was sich zeigt, so wie es sich von ihm selbst her zeigt, von ihm selbst her sehen lassen*]."[7] The point is that, paradoxically enough, the very *core* of appearing *hides* in—and from—*appearing itself*: appearing somehow *eludes itself* and must *be uncovered to itself*. And "phenomenology" stands for a somewhat more radical version of Goethe's "What is hardest of all? That which seems to you the easiest, / to see with your eyes what is lying before them."[8]

The "phenomenon in a phenomenological sense," which Heidegger's *Daseinsanalytik* strives to uncover, also corresponds to what Kant calls the "*bathos of experience*,"[9] the *a priori*, or the "transcendental form of appearances."[10] And the expression that Heidegger takes over from Kant, according to which the philosopher's business consists in "analyzing the secret judgements of common reason [*die geheimen Urtheile der gemeinen Vernunft*],"[11] also applies to his phenomenology.

In short, Fichte and Heidegger follow in Kant's footsteps. They walk in the same basic direction, and to such extent that in both cases the return to the constant latent φαίνεσθαι—or appearing—underlying all that appears represents the very opposite of a discussion about a harmless detail. On the contrary, the investigation of the *a priori* is conducted in such a way as to call into question, from top to bottom, the entire horizon of what appears to us.

But what kind of discussion of the *a priori* can we find in the principles of Fichte's *Wissenschaftslehre*? And which direction does Heidegger's interpretation of these principles take? Heidegger's reading of Fichte's three principles enhances certain aspects and connects the dots in a certain way. Our task here is to reconstruct its baselines.

Heidegger on the First Principle

A closer consideration of the first principle can help clarify the specificity of the *Wissenschaftslehre*'s principles and the way in which Heidegger interprets them.

The first principle refers to the fact that the positing of anything whatsoever presupposes the positing of a fundamental rule, namely $A = A$, or *if A, then A*. This fundamental rule refers not merely to a particular A (namely the A in question in each different case). Rather, it is *universally* valid. The fundamental rule in question indicates the existence of a necessary connection between any given A and A itself—absolutely, without justification. For what is at stake is the necessary condition of any positing whatsoever—in such a way that without this fundamental condition every positing is annulled or disintegrates. Yet neither is the fundamental rule in question to be understood as though it would only apply in retrospect, presupposing the existence of particular positings and relating to them as a mere consequence, or lagging behind them, as it were. The exact opposite is true. This fundamental rule is posited *in advance*. It constitutes a kind of *Ursetzung* or *proto-positing*, without which no other *Setzung* or positing is possible: by positing an A, I have posited in advance an *if-then connection (if A, then A)*—a "*Wenn-so-Zusammenhang (wenn A, so A)*," and in such a way that I subject myself to that *if-then connection*—that is, to its "*absolute bindingness [absolute Verbindlichkeit]*."[12]

Fichte's discussion of the first principle therefore amounts to the exposition of what *any* positing (or any *being posited*), by its very nature, *already* presupposes, so that it is *always there*. Hence, any positing is of such a nature that it "stands and falls," so to speak, with the identity principle (with the "$A = A$; if A, then A"). And the identity principle is the limit, as it were, between positing and complete non-positing.

The identity principle therefore represents a constitutive condition (in the truest sense of the word, a *sine qua non*) of *anything* as such, or of *something as something*. But Fichte does not simply highlight this. He also points out that any particular positing presupposes the positing of this fundamental condition (not the positing of A—that a particular A exists—but the positing of the *being-A of any given A*). That is to say, every positing is primarily the *positing of the fundamental rule of being-posited as such*—and only by being the positing of this fundamental rule can it also be the positing of a particular content. But the discussion of the first principle also makes this much clear: the positing of the *fundamental rule* of identity simultaneously entails the positing of *everything that can come under a rule*, or rather the positing of the *entire domain of every possible positing*. To use Heidegger's language, it corresponds to the opening of the *horizon* of every possible positing, which can only take place *in this horizon*, as an *inner* development or a *moment* thereof.[13]

In short, the discussion of the *Wissenschaftslehre*'s first principle ultimately comes down to the fact that any positing is, by its very nature, *complex*. For one thing, the proto-positing (*Ursetzung*), i.e., the positing of the fundamental rule, does *not* give rise to a *self-enclosed* sphere. As mentioned above, it also constitutes, by its very nature, the positing of *everything that can come under the fundamental rule* in question. And secondly, the particular positing of any given A is constitutively something *regulated* and presupposes as its condition the *proto-positing* of the identity principle as such.

It is thus no wonder that Heidegger should find in Fichte a forerunner of his fundamental claim about the *vorgängige Hinblicknahme auf die Seinsverfassung* (the *previous view-taking of the ontological constitution*)—viz. the *vorgängige Erschlossenheit der Seinsart*: the previous openness *of the form of being* of any entity (*Seiendes*) as a necessary condition for relating to it. And this is the first main feature of his reading of Fichte's three principles: he sees them in the light of his claim that what he terms *Seinsverständnis* (*understanding of being*), or *ontologische Erkenntnis* (*ontological* knowledge), must precede and underlie what he calls *ontic* knowledge (*ontische Erkenntnis*).

But this is not all. For the essential point lies in the way in which the aforementioned *proto-positing of the identity principle* relates to the *I*.[14]

At first glance, the I is also something particular that is subordinated to this rule. "A is A" is apparently more general. "I am I" seems to represent a further instance, a particular application of the fundamental rule that underlies every positing as its condition of possibility.[15] But this impression is illusory. Far from a mere application or instantiation of the principle of identity, the I constitutes, on the contrary, the *origin* of the fundamental rule in question, and therefore the real *Ursetzung* (the real *proto-positing*). The I "is the very possibility of something like a condition in general."[16] And "everything that is [*alles, was ist*]" is so only "insofar as it is posited *in* the I, *through* the I and *for* the I."[17] In other words, the "I am I" (*Ich bin ich*)—the identity of the I with itself—is so far from being a further instantiation of the universally valid proto-rule that it constitutes, on the contrary, the actual and only "content" of this proto-rule, i.e., the proto-rule or *Ursetzung* (the proto-positing) itself.

This is not easy to understand, not least because what Fichte terms "I" is not what one usually takes this word to mean. For the I is commonly perceived as a fact among others (or as something *posited* among other posited things). But Fichte points out that the I has in fact an entirely different nature—a nature that remains concealed as long as it is perceived as a fact. For the I is a *fact-act* (*Tathandlung*), the product of its own deed— and hence a fact (*Tatsache*) *that is actually none*, for it is only possible, by its very nature, as *action* (*Handlung*).

The big question, then, is how the I is to be understood, or how the understanding of the I that is here in question can shed light on the role ascribed to it.

Heidegger tries to settle this question by: (1) highlighting the specific nature of Fichte's claims about the I; (2) identifying the specific nature of the fundamental phenomenon the term "I" stands for; (3) showing the specific nature of the *identity* (i.e., the *sameness*) of the I with itself, viz. the absolute uniqueness of the *I am I*; and (4) highlighting the specific role played by the I—namely the way in which the I (viz. its identity) constitutes the essential prerequisite or *sine qua non* of *any positing whatsoever* (and hence the *Ursetzung* or *proto-positing*).

According to Heidegger, the claims found in Fichte's discussion of the I must be understood as *ontological*—i.e., as *essential propositions* about the being of the I, viz. about *I-hood* (*Ichheit*) as such, and not about this or that *vorhandenes* I (an I which is allegedly present-at-hand before us).[18] The difference lies mainly in the fact that Fichte's approach is not guided by an average understanding (*durchschnittliches Verständnis*) of what the word "I" stands for; it does not presuppose this understanding and does not limit itself to ascribing this or that characteristic to the I (or rather to an I) or to pointing out that this or that feature is contained in the determination "I," etc., but without ever focusing on the I as such. Fichte's approach is characterized by the fact that it concentrates on *I-hood* (*Ichheit*) *itself* and tries to determine *what it amounts to*: *what constitutes the I as such*. His discussion of the first principle thus adopts a specific point of view, which questions what the terms "first person" or "I" ultimately mean. It tries to work out what this peculiar determination—namely the "I"—stands for, what it is made of, etc.

In other words, more often than not discourse about the I (the focus on the I) takes the form "I am: X" and thereby *skips* or *misses* the I itself (the determination that constitutes the "I" in the first place: the determination that posits and defines the I itself, as such). The point being that all determinations of the form "I am: X" already presuppose this fundamental positing—or, as Heidegger puts it, die *Vorgabe des Ich*, that is to say at the same time (a) the I as the fundamental *pre-givenness* (*Vor-gabe*) and (b) the I as a "*prefixation*" (viz. the fundamental "prefix" of everything else) and the fundamental *blueprint* for everything else.[19] In Heidegger's view, it is very much to Fichte's credit that he counters this tendency and concentrates on the "*Vorgabe des Ich*."

However, the decisive aspect lies in the fact that the I is a very particular "what"—i.e., its mode of being is fundamentally different from that of all other entities and does not constitute a "what" in the same way that the others do.[20] The I is characterized by its "total otherness with regard to all other entities," an otherness reflected in the fact that the I, strictly speaking, *is* not, and can only occur in the specific mode of being of the "*am* [*bin/sum*]."[21]

One tends to understand this difference as if it corresponded merely to a kind of *specific* difference—i.e., a not very significant variation of the genus *Vorhandenheit* (*presentness* or *present-at-handness*), so that the "am" constitutes nothing more than a variation of the "is": a "*Vorhandenes*" (something *present-at-hand*) that is rendered more specific through the addition of further predicates. As a result, *present-at-handness* (the mode of being of *Vorhandenheit* as such) seems to be essential for the determination of the "am," or the I. This, however, is fundamentally wrong and shows that one remains blind to the specificity of the phenomena in question. For the *Vorhandensein* (the being-*present-at-hand*) of a *Vorhandenes* (of whatever is present-at-hand) has absolutely nothing to do with I-*hood*, viz. with the "am" (the "sum"). And, conversely, the being-I of an I, namely the "am" or "sum" as such, has nothing to do with the *Vorhandensein* (the being-*present-at-hand*) of a *Vorhandenes*. The two forms of being are, by their very nature, *completely heterogeneous*. To borrow Kant's words, the "am" comes "*aus besonderer fabrike*" (from a special factory), and indeed so much so that (a) the being-*present-at-hand* of a *Vorhandenes* represents *a zero-degree* of I-hood (and of "am"/"sum"), and (b) I-hood (and "am"/"sum") as such represents a *zero-degree of present-at-handness*.[22]

First, this is due to the fact that the *Vorhandensein* of *Vorhandene* (the being-present-at-hand of entities that are present-at-hand) is not there *for them*, whereas the being of the I must be there *for it*.[23] Otherwise there is no I, no "am" or "sum." But this is not all. For the point lies precisely in the fact that the I (or the "am") is characterized by the particular way of being of the "for": it is essentially that *for which* this or that can be there. The I constitutes a condition of the sphere of the "*for*" as such, and in such a manner that it (1) corresponds to the center of this sphere, so to speak—to that *for which* something is there, and (2) is not some *Vorhandenes* (a present-at-hand entity) contained in this sphere; rather, it is entirely constituted by the mode of being of the "for."

It should be noted, moreover, that this peculiar mode of being of the I, i.e., the "am" or "sum," also relates to the way in which the I *identifies* with itself. *Self-identity* is a key feature of being-I.

The I is not only of such a nature that its being must exist *for itself*; its very specific constitution also implies that the I "*belongs to itself* [*sich zu eigen ist*]."[24] Regarding the *Vorhandensein* (the present-at-handness) of a *Vorhandenes* (a present-at-hand entity), "it cannot be said either that it belongs to itself or that it does not belong to itself."[25] For it does not relate to itself. The I, on the contrary, can only be by *relating* to itself, and indeed in such a way that it *belongs to itself*. This means, for one thing, that the "for" (that for which this or that is there) is there *for itself* as well. Positing, in this case, is not the positing of something other that is there for the I, but rather the positing *of one's own self* (i.e., the positing of that *for* which this or that is—or can be—posited). Put another way, the positing we are referring to (a) *posits itself positing*, and (b) posits itself positing *for itself* (and thereby posits the "for" as such), so that this very positing of the positing as such and of the "for" as such is what the I and the "am" are really all about.

This means that, in this case, the I does not posit *an other*, nor is it posited by *an other*. The I *posits its own self* and is (or, more precisely, *I am*) only in this self-positing. Its *Setzen* is a *Sich-Setzen*: its *positing* can only take place as a *self*-positing. And no I can be without this *self*-positing. Heidegger writes:

> I = being-I, I-hood; I = I posit. It is because I am I, i.e. I am 'I posit', that I am simply and absolutely *with* and *in* being posited—Being [*Ich = Ich-Sein, Ichheit; Ich = Ich setze. Weil ich Ich bin, d. h. ,Ich setze' bin, bin ich schlechthin, mit und im Gesetztsein—das Sein*].[26]

Fichte tries to convey this essential point by writing: "I am simply and absolutely because I am [*Ich bin schlechthin, weil ich bin*]," a sentence that fits with the phenomena in that the I exists, as we have seen, *through its own positing* (i.e., through its own *Tathandlung* or fact-act).[27] And he adds: "I am simply and absolutely what I am [*Ich bin schlechthin, was ich bin*]."[28] That is to say, "the I is its own essence [*das Ich ist sein Wesen*]." Or, as Heidegger also puts it, "the I *brings to pass* its essence [*das Ich west sein Wesen*]"[29]; even more accurately, *I bring to pass my essence* (*Ich wese mein Wesen*), namely the I-hood that consists, in fact, in its own (or rather in *my own*) selfhood.[30] I am primarily nothing other than I. And only by being such ('only' such: namely, the pure *self-coincidence* or *sameness* with myself) can I be, if at all, something else.[31] This, in turn, implies that the I, as Fichte puts it, can only be *for itself* (*nur für sich sein kann*).[32] Not necessarily because the I is absolutely "alone" or "on its own"—or, according to the so-called metaphysical egoism, because it is the only thing that exists. Rather, because the I "as such is only ever for itself [*als solches je nur für sich*]": its form of being is such that it can only be *in* its self-coincidence or sameness with itself, *through* this self-coincidence or sameness with itself (and only in it and through it can it manifest itself and be what it is for others—namely, I).[33]

The I is therefore a very particular "what," consisting entirely *in its relating to itself* (so that, in a way, it is not a "what" at all). For Heidegger, the most decisive aspect of Fichte's discussion of the first principle is his working out this essential feature of the I, namely the particular nature of its sameness with itself. Heidegger highlights the fact that Fichte thereby draws attention to the basic phenomenon of *selfhood*, the singular form of being of the "*am*," the "sum," the "I am it [*Ich bin es*]"—i.e., the "fundamental experience of the 'I am' [*Grunderfahrung des 'ich bin'*]," in which "it is all radically and purely about myself [*in der es radikal und rein um mich selbst geht*]," so that *I am at stake*.[34] In short, the point is the basic phenomenon of "*mea res agitur*": by positing itself, *the I becomes its own concern*: the "*I am I*" at the heart of the I, viz. of the "am"/"sum" makes *me* my concern.

The "I am I," around which the discussion of the first principle ultimately revolves—the "fundamental rule of identity [*Grundregel der Identität*]" that determines the positing of the I—is thus anything but an *empty*, purely *formal* identity. On the contrary, what is at stake is the unique *identity* or *sameness* of the I—and indeed so much so that, as Heidegger underlines, an entity that is not an I can never be identical with itself in the way in which the I *is itself*.[35] And this unique identity is of such a nature that the middle point of the I's relating to itself (a relating, as we have seen, that constitutes the I as such) is occupied precisely by the unique form of *self-belonging* (*Sich-zu-eigen-Sein*) that Heidegger describes in the following terms: the I is an entity "whose being is for it anything but random or casual [*dessen Sein für dieses Seiende nicht etwas Beliebiges ist*],"[36] or:

> The I is an entity that takes over its being as such [*sein Sein als ein solches übernimmt*], it is a taking over of the being of the entity that it is, i.e., by taking [it] over is it this entity as a self [*ein Übernehmen des Seins des Seienden, das es ist, ist, d. h. als Übernehmendes ist es dieses Seiende als ein Selbst*].[37]

Here, Heidegger's interpretation brings out an essential point: *selfhood*, the identity of the I with itself (*my sameness with myself*) is constituted in such a way that it *burdens me with my being*. In other words, my sameness *with myself* imposes a *non-indifference* on me. It radically prevents any *indifference* or *neutrality* with regard to my own self and forces me to *refer* to myself, to be *affected* by myself, to *deal* and *engage* with myself, and to *dedicate* myself to my own being, as it were. To put it in a nutshell: "The essence of the I is for the latter never merely an object of a consideration of essence, but the task of being."[38]

This aspect emerges very clearly from Heidegger's discussion of Fichte's view on *thetical* judgments, and particularly on the original and highest thetical judgment: "I am."[39] The "am" is anything but a present-at-hand entity (*ein Vorhandenes*). The "am" is constituted in such a way that it is "detached from all present-at-hand."[40] And the "I am I" is such that it ultimately comes down to being *concerned with oneself* or *assigned to oneself* —to being *entrusted with oneself* or *left to oneself*. Heidegger speaks of "being saddled with oneself [*Sich-selbst-anheim-gegeben-sein*]"[41] and "having the task of oneself [*Sich-selbst-aufgegebensein*]."[42] Accordingly, "I am I" means nothing other than: I am in such a way that *my being is of utmost interest to me*. Or, to use Heidegger's famous formulation: I am a being "which is concerned in its being about this being [*dem es in seinem Sein um dieses selbst geht*]"[43]:

> My being is never something present-at-hand, but the task I am saddled [charged] with. The being of the I is an *ought-to-be,* this way or that—which is at stake, this way or that [*Mein Sein ist nie ein Vorhandensein, sondern was mir selbst zur Aufgabe anheimgegeben ist. Das Sein des Ich ist ein Soll-Sein, so oder so,—worum es geht, so oder so*].[44]

Here, however, a further point must be emphasized, for without it this brief outline of Heidegger's interpretation of the first principle runs the risk of missing the main point.

What has been said thus far can give the impression that Heidegger is only interested in the unique form of being of the self (I-hood, the "am" or the "sum" as such), so that his discussion of the first principle would simply disregard the fact that for Fichte it plays the role of the absolute *sine qua non* or prerequisite of *any* positing as such (and has to do with the question of the *Ursetzung* or *proto*-positing). Yet this impression is illusory, for the existential *Daseinsanalytik* shows that Heidegger does not regard the unique mode of being of the self as a mode of being among others, with a merely *regional* significance, but rather as the *original positing* (*Ursetzung*), which must underlie all others.

What interests Heidegger in Fichte is precisely the fact that the latter not only focused on the particular form of being of the "I am I," but also understood *this* form of being as the basic *prerequisite* or *ur-condition* of *any* positing as such. Put another way, in Heidegger's view Fichte was absolutely right in pointing out that the I must be involved in the proto-positing—and in such a way that the proto-positing can be nothing else than the positing of the I, that is to say of its singular *sameness* or *identity*. For, whether one notices it or not, any positing as such presupposes that *for which* what is posited is posited. Consequently, the positing of any present-at-hand (*Vorhandenes*)—i.e., the fundamental rule of identity, A = A, understood as the positing of the basic rule of *present-at-handness* or *Vorhandenheit*—simply cannot be the proto-positing. The ur-condition or basic prerequisite—the proto-positing—is what was previously termed the "sphere of the 'for.'" And this sphere has, by nature, the form of being of the "am" (the "sum": *I-hood*), that is, the identification or sameness of the I with itself.[45] To put it in Heidegger's language: the ontological understanding (the previous view-taking or *vorgängige Hinblicknahme*) of the form of being of the *self*—i.e., the *existential* understanding of being—is the proto-form of the understanding of being (the previous view-taking or *vorgängige Hinblicknahme*) *überhaupt* and the origin of the sphere of the "for" *in general* (even when what is posited is something other than the self).[46]

But it should be borne in mind that the self-identity or sameness that is here in question—namely the identity of the "I am I"—is the one corresponding to the aforementioned basic relation of *taking over* one's own self (i.e., of being *assigned to oneself*, left *to oneself*, *saddled* with oneself and *entrusted with the task of oneself*). In Heidegger's view, everything revolves around the "existential" A = A or this "existential" self. This basic form of relating to itself is a major feature of the self (of I-hood, the "sum") as such. And it is this kind of self that is responsible for the proto-positing and thereby marks the limit between *positing* as such and a *complete non-positing*.

This also emerges very clearly from Heidegger's interpretation of the second principle.

Heidegger on the Second Principle

The second principle, which has to do with contradiction and is expressed by the *principle of contradiction*, is characterized by the fact that it is *conditioned* (*bedingt*) with regard to its *content* (*dem Gehalt nach*)—and, more specifically, conditioned *by the first principle*.[47] The second principle *presupposes* the first and is *bound* to it. For "I-hood is absolutely conditioning for every positing."[48] However, the second principle also presupposes the first insofar as it refers to what is *counter-posited* (*entgegengesetzt*). According to its own nature, the latter requires the previous positing of *that against which* I posit something when I *counterposit*.

This does not mean, though, that the second principle can be *derived* from the first. The second principle corresponds to the following rule: *~A is not equal to A*. One can also say that *~A is not A*. But this formulation is misleading, for the second principle has nothing to do with the fact that ~A is equal to ~A (in which case ~A would simply be a further case of A, and the second principle would have the form of the first).[49]

This puts us on the right track: what is decisive about the second principle is the *is-not* (*istnicht*) as such: *~A is not A*—that is, *the opposite of A is not equal to A*.[50] And this is precisely what cannot be traced back to the first principle: what is absolutely *underivable*, and in this sense also *original*. In other words: "what constitutes ~A as such [*was ~A zu einem solchen macht*]"[51]—"the mode of positing that is a counter-positing [*die Weise des Setzens, die ein Entgegensetzen ist*]"[52] (i.e., the specific positing "*is not*" and the posited "*~A*")—or "the counter-posited as such ..., the opposite in general, the counter-posited insofar as it is something *counter*-posited [*das Entgegengesetzte als solches ..., das Gegenteil überhaupt, das Entgegengesetzte, sofern es ein Entgegen-Gesetztes ist*]"[53]—this is completely *underivable*. This means, however, that

> the counter-positing as such, *the positing* in the *specific mode of the counter*, is absolutely posited. It does not arise from the positing; rather, it is equally original [equiprimordial] with the latter [*das Entgegensetzen als ein solches, das Setzen im Wie des Entgegen, wird schlechthin gesetzt. Es entspringt nicht aus dem Setzen, sondern ist mit dem gleichursprünglich*].[54]

It is also itself an "absolute act [*eine absolute Handlung*]"[55]—or, as Heidegger says, an "absolute counter-positing [*ein schlechthinniges Entgegensetzen*]."[56]

This is why, as far as its *form* is concerned (*seiner Form nach*), the second principle is *absolutely unconditioned* (*schlechthin unbedingt*).[57] What is characteristic about it is precisely the fact that, on the one hand, on the basis of its *content*, it is *conditioned*, but on the other hand, on the basis of its *form*, it is absolutely *unconditioned*. The second principle thus corresponds to a kind of "*conditioned a priori* [*bedingtes Apriori*]"[58]—something that is simultaneously *conditioned* and *absolute*—so that there is "condition and conditioned" "within the absolute (Apriori)."[59]

To be sure, the discussion of the second principle is no longer about highlighting what *any* positing, by nature, always presupposes. But it does amount to highlighting what any positing *that differs from the proto-positing*, by nature, always presupposes: what any positing that is not aimed at the I "never does not think [*nie nicht denkt*]."[60] The second principle corresponds, therefore, to an *ur-counterpositing*—to the absolute act of the proto-counter-positing Fichte expresses in the following terms: "by virtue of the sheer counter-positing, the opposite of all that belongs to the I must belong to the Not-I."[61] The second principle therefore opens up the sphere of the not-I. It is the *Ursetzung* or proto-positing of the Not-I and hence the *proto-not-I* (the *ur-not-I*) as such.

But this is still not all. For it should also be borne in mind that, while the second principle refers to the not-I, it has to do with an *act* of the I and is mentioned in the context of what Heidegger terms an "outline [or projection] of the I-hood of the I [*ein Entwurf der Ichheit des Ich*],"[62] so that it actually says "something about I-hood"—i.e., about the self.[63] In other words, the second principle refers to the not-I, "but not to this Not-I as an entity that would be another entity as opposed to the I as an entity; rather, [it refers] to the Not-I as an essential feature of I-hood."[64]

This, in turn, means two different things.

Firstly, it means that the positing of the not-I the second principle refers to is by no means the positing of *some particular entity* devoid of I-hood. As a matter of fact, it is the positing of a *sine qua non*—the *prerequisite* or the fundamental rule—of *any* positing of an entity devoid of I-hood, i.e., the positing of what any positing of an entity devoid of I-hood, by its very nature, *always presupposes and already implies*. It is thus the positing of a *fundamental rule*, or rather the positing of a *horizon*; or, to be even more precise, the second principle is the *proto-positing of the understanding* of any entity devoid of I-hood—and, in this sense, the proto-positing of the "objectiveness of the object [*Gegenständlichkeit des Gegenstandes*]" in general.[65]

However, a second point is equally important, namely the fact that the horizon in question is indeed the horizon of every entity devoid of I-hood, *but not as though the latter had nothing to do with the I*. Contrary to what might be assumed, the not-I is not to be conceived as something *absolute, totally independent from the I*. The not-I—the *entire* horizon of entities devoid of I-hood, and hence *any* entity devoid of I-hood—is rather something that exists *for* the *I*, or *for* the *self*.[66] Fichte's—and, for that matter, Heidegger's—point lies precisely in the fact that the not-I (the "objectiveness of the object") is, by its very nature, something *counter-posited* (*Entgegengesetztes*); or, more precisely, it is posited *by* the I *in counterposition to the I* (or *by* the self *in counterposition to the self*).[67]

Both aspects are emphatically highlighted by Heidegger:

> To the essence of the I there belongs something counter-posited as such [*Entge-gengesetztes als solches*]; the I as I relates to a *counter-*or-*against-which* [*zu einem Wogegen*]. This counter-or-*against-which* is not yet the entity devoid of I-hood itself, but the *horizon* into which the I as I extends itself [*der Horizont, in den das Ich als Ich sich hineinhält*].[68]

He then adds:

> "The I posits absolutely the not-I" does not mean: The I creates the entity that it is not in the manner of a creation … but rather: If the self-positing forms the being of the I as such, then counter-positing-to-the-self [*das Sichentgegensetzen*] indicates a feature of being-I [*einen Charakter des Ich-Seins*].[69]

And he insists on this idea: "Not-I: by no means this or that which comes our way [*dieses oder jenes Entgegenkommende*], but the *field* of what comes our way made available in the I as such [*der im Ich als solchem vorgehaltene Spielraum des Entgegenkömmlichen*]."[70] He then makes the following remark: "This positing of the Not-I is thus not the ontic positing of this entity. It means, rather: counter-positing-to-oneself something in general [*Dieses Setzen des Nicht-Ich ist also nicht das ontische Setzen dieses Seienden, sondern es heißt: das Sich Entgegenhalten von etwas überhaupt*]."[71] And he summarizes his claim as follows:

> Or: The I does not posit this or that object; it rather relates to a field of objec-tiveness [*zu einem Spielraum von Gegenständlichkeit*] within which an object can come to meet the positing I. If it did not put itself in counterposition to something [*würde es sich nicht entgegenhalten zu …*], in the first place, there might well be various entities, and they might well intrude upon the I, but none of them could ever show itself and manifest itself as the entity that it is independently from the I. For an entity in itself to be able to reveal itself to an I as something completely on its own, this I must put itself in counterposition to such an entity [*muss dieses Ich sich für ein solches Seiendes entgegenhalten*].[72]

The bottom line is as follows: the *not-I* is that "which, while belonging to I-hood, forms the counter-element in it [*was zur Ichheit gehörig das Entgegenhafte an ihr ausmacht*]."[73] Or, to borrow the language of the *Dasein-sanalytik*, the second principle refers to the overarching prerequisite of all that Heidegger calls *categorial*, as opposed to *existential*.[74] For Heidegger, Fichte's discussion of the second principle shows, quite rightly, that the essence of the *categorial* is in fact the *existential*, and that the former presupposes the latter.

In Heidegger's eyes, Fichte must therefore be credited with (1) having pointed out the essential role of the previous understanding (the *previous view-taking* or *vorgängige Hinblicknahme*) of the form of being of an entity as a condition for any relation to it; (2) having worked out the unique mode of being that Heidegger terms *Existenz*—i.e., the unique form of being of the "am" (of the self) and its complete otherness with regard to all other entities; (3) having thus contributed to rectify the commonly accepted primacy of *present-at-handness* (*Vorhandenheit*)—i.e., of an *average conception* of being that throws everything in the same pot (namely the pot of an *indifferent present-at-handness*); and (4) pointing out the singular role played by the primordial mode of being of the self, and paving the way for the insight into how the *existential* understanding of oneself constitutes a condition for any form of *categorial* understanding of being.

Heidegger on the Third Principle

An in-depth discussion of Fichte's third *Grundsatz* (viz. of Heidegger's interpretation thereof) would go far beyond the scope of this chapter. But we must highlight some key aspects that (a) can help us better understand how Heidegger interprets Fichte's *third* principle (and indeed the whole set of three principles), and (b) provide a first insight into the particular way in which the aforementioned affinity of approach or philosophical "closeness" entails a certain "distance"—and indeed *considerable distance*—between Heidegger and Fichte.

Fichte's third principle is bound up with the fact that the first and the second principle (viz. *I-hood* and *Not-I-hood*) *cancel* each other out.[75] To be sure, the I is the essential condition (or a *sine qua non*) both for the Not-I and for the *counterposition* (*Entgegensetzung*) between them; for without the I there can be no counterpositing—viz. no counterposition—and hence there is simply no place for the Not-I as such. But it nevertheless remains true that the positing of the I and the positing of the Not-I are, by their very nature, *mutually exclusive*. On the one hand, the positing (or rather self-positing) of the I posits the I and nothing but the I itself (and hence corresponds to the *non-positing of the Not-I* [*Nichtsetzung des Nich-Ich*]). On the other hand, the positing of the Not-I posits the Not- I and nothing but the Not-I itself (and hence corresponds to the *non-positing of the I* [*Nichtsetzung des Ich*]). In short, there is, as it were, a missing link between the I and the Not-I, without which they cannot be bound together.

And this is what the *third* principle is all about. It has to do with the fact that the whole framework of the two first principles—that is, (a) the essential structure of all positing as such (the very core of the two said original ways of positing or *Ursetzungen* that are inherently entailed in each and every other positing as such) and (b) the whole horizon of all possible positing-acts (*Setzungen*) and of whatever can be posited by them—is at variance with itself, or, as Heidegger puts it, is "intrinsically and thoroughly contradictory, incongruous and essentially inconsistent [*in sich durch und durch widersprechend, nicht einstimmig, wesenhaft unstimmig*]."[76]

Fichte's third principle stems from a specific action (*Handlung*)—viz. from a further intrinsic component of the original fact-act (*Tathandlung*), namely one that "unifies I and Not-I as absolutely posited [*Ich und Nicht-Ich als schlechthin gesetzte einigt*]."[77]

The key is therefore something like the *unification* or *combination* (*Vereinigung*) of the two said original *Setzungen*, I and Not-I. The point being, (a) that the unification or combination we are talking about is *not analytically entailed in them*, so that (b) it requires its very own specific positing, i.e., a further original action (*Handlung*): nothing less than a *third proto-positing* or *Ursetzung*. In Fichte's view, this new *Handlung* (this new proto-positing, *or Ursetzung*) must be of such a nature that the two said absolute acts of positing (*schlechthinnige Setzungen*)—I and Not-I—do not cancel or eliminate each other completely, but *only in part*.[78] That is, the third principle stems from the positing of what Fichte terms *limitation* or *restriction, divisibility* and *capacity for quantity* (*Einschränkung, Teilbarkeit* viz. *Quantitätsfähigkeit*).[79] Its special feature is what Fichte terms *Teilbar-Setzen* (*positing as divisible*).[80] And the third *principle* is expressed in the following terms: "In the I, I counterposit a divisible Not-I to the divisible I [*Ich setze im Ich dem theilbaren Ich ein theilbares Nicht-Ich entgegen*]."[81]

By means of this third proto-action "both the I and the Not-I are absolutely posited as divisible [*wird … schlechthin das Ich sowohl als das Nicht-Ich theilbar gesetzt*]."[82] Heidegger comments as follows:

> I-hood: divided, restricted or limited being-posited. Positing as divisible is positing in the mode of "both/and." I-hood is by nature a "both/and," it is both essentially such and essentially not such, both I and Not-I [*Ichheit: teilbare, geteilte, eingeschränkte Gesetztheit. Teilbar-Setzen ist Setzen im Charakter des Sowohl-als-auch. Ichheit ist ihrem Wesen nach ein Sowohl-als-auch, ist sowohl solche als auch wesenhaft nicht solche, sowohl Ich als auch Nich-Ich*].[83]

Heidegger puts the emphasis not so much on divisibility and the particular nature of the *Teilbar-Setzen* (of the *divided positing* or the *positing that posits divisibility*) as on the connection between the positing of the I (i.e., the *first* principle), on the one hand, and the *Teilbar-Setzen* (i.e., the *third* principle), on the other. In other words, he stresses the fact that the I itself entails divisibility in the sense that it is "both essentially such and essentially not such," "both I and Not-I"—i.e., is *intrinsically affected by an internal tension or conflict*.

On balance, the conclusion is that the third principle brings into the equation what Heidegger describes as a "*preserving* (or *retaining*) counterposition [*bewahrendes Entgegenhalten*]":

> The I is not only equal to itself, but at the same time, as I, it is constantly opposed to itself [*sich selbst entgegengesetzt*]. In so far as being-an-I is posited in self-positing, [self-]identity is posited. And this [self-] identical [element] *überhaupt* is that in relation to which there is counterpositing [*Und diesem Identischen überhaupt ist entgegengesetzt*]; i.e., in [the framework of] this [self-]identical element none other than the limited [restricted] I, which counterposits to itself a Not-I, maintains itself and proves itself [*d. h. in diesem Identischen erhält und bewährt sich gerade das eingeschränkte Ich, das sich ein Nicht-Ich entgegensetzt*]. While counterpositing, it does not cancel [suppress, revoke or repeal] itself, but rather it proves itself[84] [*Im Entgegensetzen hebt es sich nicht auf, sondern bewahrt sich gerade*].[85]

Heidegger insists on this point:

> What is posited by counterpositing is not destroyed [annihilated, wiped out] by it, it is rather also preserved by it [*das zernichtet es nicht, sondern erhält es gerade auch*]; counterpositing is, of course, counterpositing, but, as such, it is also a retaining counterposition [*ein bewahrendes Entgegenhalten*]. To "posit-as-not" [*Nichten*] cannot be the same as to annihilate (a Not-positing)[86] [*Das Nichten darf kein Vernichten sein (ein Nicht-Setzen)*].[87]

Hence, the third principle also corresponds to the basic phenomenon Heidegger describes as the previous view-taking of the ontological constitution. But what is at stake here is a *specific* kind of previous view-taking or *vorgängige Hinblicknahme*, namely "das *Seinsverständnis des Sowohl-als-auch*" (the ontological understanding of the "*both/and*," viz. the ontological understanding of the "*both-I-and-Not-I*" as such). In other words, what is at stake here is the basic underlying ontological understanding of the union (the *unification, combination* or *composition*) *between I and Not-I*. It could also be said that the third principle highlights and expresses the ontological understanding of the "*face-to-face*" *between I and not-I*: the fundamental inner articulation that splits the whole sphere of the "for" into two domains: the *existential* (the realm of what is intrinsically *I-related* or rather *self-related*) and the *categorial* (the realm of what is intrinsically *thing-related*).

But there is something else we should bear in mind: Heidegger emphasizes that at the end of the day the third principle does not constitute a *third* moment. It must rather be *presupposed*—and has in fact *already* been *presupposed—from the very beginning*, and indeed so much so that it is simply impossible to think of the proto-positing (*Ursetzung*) without the *third* principle—i.e., without positing it.[88]

The above provides some insight into what Heidegger's criticism of Fichte's three principles is all about.

Heidegger writes: "Hence, in his discussion of the first and second principle Fichte makes an attempt to think purely what basically cannot be purely thought [*das rein zu denken, was sich im Grunde genommen so nicht denken lässt*]; and the impossibility of this attempt becomes apparent in the third principle."[89] And he remarks:

> The I is something limited/restricted by the Not-I. And the I cannot be thought of otherwise than so that its positing means: to limit/restrict [*darf nicht anders gedacht werden als so, dass das Setzen heißt: Einschränken*]. And the exposition of the first and second principles is therefore only an abstraction that does not capture the essential nature of the I. And yet this exposition has its justification, in so far as what is posited in the first principle is that the I is the condition of possibility for Identity in general.[90]

But what does this mean?

First of all, it means that for Heidegger the connection between the three principles is such that they are *equiprimordial*, and indeed so much so that the interaction and cooperation of all three principles is a condition without which the horizon in which we find ourselves—viz. the sphere the first principle is already all about, namely the sphere of "something" (*etwas*) in general—cannot be opened. "Only when positing takes the form of *Einschränken* is [there] something posited [*Erst wenn Setzen Einschränken ist, wird etwas gesetzt*]."[91] In Heidegger's view, this is a key point: "Only through *Einschränkung* something (ens) [*Durch Einschränkung erst etwas (ens)*]."[92] And this key point can never be overemphasized: "Only now are the posited I and the posited Not-I something—, i.e., determined as such [*Erst jetzt sind das gesetzte Ich und das gesetzte Nicht-Ich etwas, d. h. als solche bestimmt*]."[93]

For Heidegger, this is the real significance of the third principle, which reads: "In the I I counterposit a divisible Not-I to the divisible I [*Ich setze im Ich dem theilbaren Ich ein theilbares Nicht-Ich entgegen.*]"[94] As he puts it:

> That is, I am I as something essentially limiting and this means as something limited by itself. To the very essence of the I, i.e. of I-hood, belongs this: finitization into itself [*Verendlichung in sich selbst*]. Only in this positing is there uni-ty, not only as self-sameness, but as wholeness, to wit, the specific wholeness of the finite I [*Erst in diesem Setzen ist Ein-heit, nicht nur als Selbigkeit, sondern Ganzheit, und zwar die spezifische des endlichen Ich*].[95]

In other words, the I is *itself Verendlichung* (finitization or limitation). It is intrinsically *finite*. It is as much *limitation* and *tension* as *proto-self-sameness*. It is as much *confined* as *all-embracing*. It is as much a *part* as it is the *whole*. It is as much something *lost* in the middle of the maze as the *maze itself*.

And here what is particular to Heidegger's interpretation of Fichte's three principles begins to emerge: "The essence of positing—and hence of the I—is finitude [*Das Wesen des Setzens—damit der Ichheit—ist die Endlichkeit*]."[96]

The fact that the *third* principle is taken by Heidegger to be *primordial* and *uncircumventable* (as primordial and uncircumventable as the *first* and the *second*) also has a further important meaning. For it means not least that in Heidegger's view the insight into the internal structure of the proto-positing or *Ursetzung* is *itself limited or restricted*. Heidegger points out that the very core of the *a priori*, although not totally opaque, is not—and cannot become—entirely transparent either.

The difference between Heidegger and Fichte (N.B. the difference between Heidegger and Fichte as perceived by *Heidegger*) can be made clear in the following terms: Fichte tries to carry out a complete analysis of the *a priori*: one that traces back the intricate structure of the proto-positing (*Ursetzung*) to its basic components (to what Aristotle termed "τὰ πρῶτα") and penetrates these basic elements, so that it reaches a pure and unrestricted knowledge of these elements (and therefore pure and unrestricted knowledge of the *a priori*). By contrast, Heidegger tries to show (a) that, at the end of the day, Fichte's analysis fails to fulfill its task, and indeed (b) that such a complete analysis of the *a priori* is simply *not possible*.[97]

In other words, Heidegger's discussion of Fichte's three principles does not limit itself to highlighting finitization (*Verendlichung*) as a key feature of the *a priori*. His views on finitude are notable for another reason: they try to evince that we are marked by finitude in yet another sense, namely because we must consider the proto-positing (the *Ursetzung*) from a *restricted* point of view. The *a priori* Fichte's *Wissenschaftslehre* tries to uncover is marked by finitude to such an extent that finitude is at the very heart of the proto-positing or the

Ursetzung—and indeed so much so that all our relation to the *a priori* and to the finitude lying at its core is itself very strongly and irretrievably marked by *restriction/limitation* (*Einschänkung*) and *finitude*.

This is closely connected with a further key point. Heidegger emphasizes that Fichte's analysis of the third principle sees itself forced to invoke a decree of reason (*Machtspruch der Vernunft*).[98] In Heidegger's view, this recourse to a decree (*Machtspruch*) shows that Fichte's attempted *deduction* of the *a priori*—the attempted "construction [*Konstruktion*]" of the *a priori* in the Fichtean sense—is not successful.[99] In other words, Fichte's recourse to a *Machtspruch* speaks volumes: it is by no means just a residual point of resistance Fichte's deduction or *Konstruktion* does not manage to master. It is rather the *neuralgic point* or the *crux* of the whole endeavor.[100]

Heidegger writes:

> The content presented by the third principle is not deduced or obtained, it is rather always already presupposed [*ständig schon vorausgesetzt*]. The key point, namely how positing in general is to be understood as limitation [*Einschränkung*] rests on a decree of reason [*Machtspruch der Vernunft*]. There is nothing we can do about this power, we must submit ourselves to it, and, what is more: we must invoke it and recognize we are consigned to it [*müssen uns ihr unterstellen, ja uns auf sie berufen, als ihr überantwortet anerkennen*].[101]

Fichte's exposition of the three principles and, above all, his approach to finitization and finitude "is by no means a derivation of viz. a gaining [of insight into] the finitude of the I *ex nihilo*, but rather just becoming aware of what there is already [*keineswegs eine Herleitung, eine Gewinnung der Endlickeit des Ich aus dem Nichts, sondern bringt nur zum Bewusstsein, was schon ist*]."[102]

To be sure, Fichte does not overlook the basic phenomenon of finitude. It is even no exaggeration to say that finitude lies at the heart of his discussion of the three principles. But Heidegger's point is that Fichte tries to capture and understand finitude *from a higher standpoint*—namely one which masters finitude and rises above finitude. As a result, his approach is marked by a tendency to "bring to the horizon of foundation even that which cannot be founded [*selbst das Unbegründbare in den Horizont der Begründung zu bringen*]."[103] Hence, he fails to investigate "what cannot be founded [*das Unbegründbare*]."[104] In short, Fichte tries "to bring finitude under control, [and] to make it disappear, instead of the reverse: trying to work it out [*der Endlichkeit Herr werden, sie zum Verschwinden bringen, statt umgekehrt sie auszuarbeiten*]."[105]

In other words, Fichte's insight into the finite I (and the whole framework of the three *Ursetzungen* it is all about) does not break the "spell" of finitude. It is itself *caught in finitude*. It is but an intrinsically *finite* view on the intrinsically *finite I*. And, according to Heidegger, Fichte overlooks the full extent of this and its implications.

It thus becomes apparent that the question of finitude plays a major role in the parting of ways between Heidegger's and Fichte's views on the first principles. And it also becomes clear that what we are dealing with here is by no means a minor detail. It is rather the point at which their paths diverge— and indeed in such a manner that they lead to very different destinations, far apart from each other. In Heidegger's view, Fichte's examination of the three principles, viz. of the *a priori*,[106] suffers from the fact that, even though it uncovers very important phenomena and major essential features of what is at stake, it nevertheless lets the phenomena and essential features in question slip out of its hands. According to Heidegger, the main reason for this is Fichte's desire for *compelling proof* or *absolute certainty*, viz. what Heidegger in his winter semester 1923/24 lectures terms "*die Sorge um die erkannte Erkenntnis*" (the "concern for known knowledge").[107]

Heidegger writes:

> However—and here starts the debate—Fichte places all emphasis on the path and on justification [*auf den Weg und die Begründung*] and not on what already is, as such [*und nicht auf das, was schon ist, als solches*], i.e. on the basic question that is implied in all this, (namely:) what is it—the finite I which is already there—and how is it already [there] [*was das ist—das endliche Ich, das schon ist—und wie es denn schon ist*]? Fichte—and this is the basic feature of metaphysics as a Doctrine of Science—gives precedence to certainty over truth. Not what truth is and how it is truth, but rather whether it is sufficiently sure or certain (i.e.) absolutely certain [*Nicht was und wie das Wahre sei, sondern ob es hinreichend, schlechthin gewiss sei*].[108]

The point is that in Heidegger's view, as far as philosophical insight into the nature of our existence is concerned, the idea of absolute truth (particularly in the sense of absolute certainty) is a "soporific opiate [*ein einschläferndes Opiat*]."[109]

And this is closely connected to another aspect: according to Heidegger, Fichte gives into the temptation to deal with the constellation of phenomena and essential features that he uncovers (and at least to some extent also highlights) by following the guidelines of traditional logical and metaphysical concepts (notably "subject" viz. "absolute subject")[110] and by applying a dialectical procedure.[111] And, what is more, he regards the basic phenomena in question as something absolutely certain and as the basis for (or the *foundation* of) nothing less than a philosophical *system*, in the strictest sense of the word.[112] In doing so Fichte overlooks the fact that precisely the phenomena in question (i.e., what Heidegger tries to highlight in his reading of Fichte's three principles) get in the way of the recourse to such categories (or, for that matter, to the said dialectical procedure), and indeed get in the way of the whole project of a philosophical *system* in the strictest sense of the word.

The bottom line is: in Heidegger's view, Fichte overlooks some of the key results of his own investigation of the first principles. And this is the main reason why the *question about finitude*—according to Heidegger the question about the basic phenomenon in which we find ourselves and which we are ourselves—falls by the wayside in Fichte's hands. In short, Heidegger's appraisal of Fichte is *double-edged*. On the one hand, he stresses the possibility of interpreting Fichte's *Grundlage* as an outline of fundamental insights of his own *Daseinsanalytik*. On the other hand, he points out that Fichte's concern for certainty and his attempt to build a system of knowledge distract him from examining key problems and prevent him from exploring the paths that lead to Heidegger's "existential temporal analysis of *Dasein*."[113]

Whether this diagnosis is true, what Heidegger's question about finitude really looks like, and where it ultimately leads to—this is another problem. The above outline raises these issues, but they must be left for another occasion.

Notes

1. Martin Heidegger, *Gesamtausgabe* (Frankfurt a. M.: Klostermann, 1976), V28, 53.
2. Ibid., V28, 54.
3. Ibid.
4. Martin Heidegger, *Sein und Zeit* (Tübingen: Niemeyer, 1927), §7. See also Heidegger, *Gesamtausgabe*, V20, §9.
5. Heidegger, *Sein und Zeit*, 31. Translations borrowed from Martin Heidegger, *Being and Time*, trans. J. Stambaugh (Albany: State University of New York Press, 1996), with slight changes.
6. Heidegger, *Sein und Zeit*, 35. See Heidegger, *Gesamtausgabe*, V18, 377.
7. Heidegger, *Sein und Zeit*, 34.
8. "Xenien aus dem Nachlaß," 155, in J. W. Goethe, *Werke Hamburger Ausgabe*, I Gedichte und Epen I (München: DTV, 1998), 230.
9. Immanuel Kant, *Prolegomena*, in *Kant's gesammelte Schriften*. hrsg. v. der Königlich Preußischen Akademie der Wissenschaften (Berlin: Reimer/de Gruyter, 1900–), IV, 380.
10. See Heidegger, *Sein und Zeit*, 31.

11. Kant, *Kant's gesammelte Schriften*, XV, 180. See Heidegger, *Sein und Zeit*, 4, 23; Heidegger, *Gesamtausgabe*, V63, 74–77, V20, 266, and V21, 197, 201 (see also V25, 22).

12. See Heidegger, *Gesamtausgabe*, V28, 60.

13. Ibid., V28, 61: "Now when/if I posit X—by positing the rule—[by the same token] I co-posit whatever is subject to being ruled by it. If …, i.e. if *something* is at all, then it *is* something." By positing the rule as such I posit something as something. "X is possible only in relation to an A" (I, 194). See J. G. Fichte, *Sämmtliche/nachgelassene Werke*. hrsg. v. I. H. Fichte. repr. (Berlin: de Gruyter, 1971), I, 94. Translations borrowed from J. G. Fichte, *The Science of Knowledge* with the First and Second Introductions, trans. Peter Heath and John Lachs (Cambridge: Cambridge University Press, 1982).

14. Fichte's discussion of the three principles of the *Wissenschaftslehre* might be construed as a radicalized version of Aristotle's discussion of the ἀνυπόθετον and ἐσχάτη δόξα *in Metaphysics* IV. Fichte's approach to these matters is notable precisely because it gives a *leading role* to the I, so that the I turns out to be the ἀνυπόθετον and its positing the ἐσχάτη δόξα. And this holds true, first and foremost, for the first principle.

15. Heidegger, *Gesamtausgabe*, V28, 62, 64.

16. Ibid. V28, 62n.

17. Ibid., V28, 173.

18. Ibid., V28, 115.

19. Ibid., V28, 106. The *Ursetzung* (the *proto*-positing or *ur*-positing) of the I is distinguished precisely by the fact that it constitutes a *thetical* (i.e., neither a *synthetic* nor an *analytic*) judgement. See Fichte, *Sämmtliche/nachgelassene Werke*, I, 116: "Ein thetisches Urteil … würde ein solches seyn, in welchem etwas keinem anderen gleich- und keinem anderen entgegengesetzt, sondern bloss sich selbst gleich gesetzt würde … Das ursprüngliche höchste Urteil dieser Art [der thetischen] ist das: Ich bin, in welchem vom Ich gar nichts ausgesagt wird, sondern die Stelle des Prädikats für die mögliche Bestimmung des Ich ins Unendliche leer gelassen wird." ("A thetical judgment … would be one in which something is asserted, not to be like anything else, but simply to be Identical with itself … The first and foremost judgment of this type is 'I am,' in which nothing whatsoever is affirmed of the self, the place of the predicate being left indefinitely empty for its possible characterization").

20. See notably Heidegger, *Gesamtausgabe*, V28, 103, 115, 122.

21. Heidegger, *Gesamtausgabe*, V28, 106–7, 109.

22. Kant, *Kant's gesammelte Schriften*, XV, 395.

23. See Heidegger, *Gesamtausgabe*, V28, 286.

24. Ibid., V28, 66.

25. Ibid.

26. Ibid., V28, 68.

27. Ibid., V28, 67, 286.

28. Ibid., V28, 67: "The I is its own I-hood, it brings the latter to pass. The I is not this or that, but rather *its own essence*. "*I am absolutely what I am*" (I, 98). But what I am, [namely] I, is such that I am *what* I am because *I* am it [*Das Ich ist seine Ichheit, es west sie selbst. Das Ich ist nicht das und das, sondern sein Wesen. "Ich bin schlechthin, was ich bin" (I, 98). Aber was ich bin, Ich, ist so, dass ich das bin, was ich bin, weil ich es bin*]." See also V28, 286.

29. Heidegger provides guidance as to how the above quote should be read. He writes: "*Um Ich sein zu können, muß es in Ichheit, d. h. dieses Wesens und dieses Wesen sein. ('Wesen' (Infinitiv): das Wesen selbst sein, nicht nur ein Wesen 'haben.'—gehört [?] "Wesen" überhaupt für "Sein." Es west, ist das, was es ist.)* (To be able to be an I, it must be *in* [the mode of] *I-hood*, i.e. [it must] be [both] of this essence (*dieses Wesens*) and this essence (*dieses Wesen*). ('Wesen' infinitive: to be itself the essence (*Wesen*), not just to 'have' an essence (*ein Wesen*). —[it] takes [?] 'Wesen' in the first place for 'Being.' It *brings to pass* (*west*), [and] is [itself] what it is)" (Heidegger, *Gesamtausgabe*, V28, 67) Heidegger points out that (a) *Wesen* should be understood verbally *as an infinitive*, (b) strictly speaking, the I viz. the "am" does not *have* a *Wesen*: it *is* itself its own *Wesen*—that is, both (c) it *brings itself to pass*, and (d) it *brings to pass what it is* (*its own I-hood*).

30. See Heidegger, *Gesamtausgabe*, V28, 111: "The human being is an absolute subject, i.e., it is what it is purely in relation to itself. In its essence as [an] I it is related to itself in its I-hood.) [*Der Mensch ist absolutes Subjekt, d. h. er ist, was er ist, rein im Hinblick auf sich selbst. Er ist in seinem Wesen als Ich auf sich selbst in seiner Ichheit bezogen*]."

31. Only by being an I (and bearing the imprint of an "am" or "sum") can I be tall or short, the son of A, the holder of the passport number X, etc. None of these features is what it takes to make an I. And, for themselves, they would have nothing whatsoever to do with *me*.

32. Heidegger, *Gesamtausgabe*, V28, 66, 286.

33. Ibid., V28, 286.

34. Ibid., V64, 43.

35. Ibid., V28, 67n., and 287.

36. So that it makes no difference whether it is this way or that.

37. Heidegger, *Gesamtausgabe*, V28, 66, 286.

38. Ibid., V28, 67, 107.

39. Ibid., V28, 102, 104, 108–115, 123. See note 23 above.

40. Ibid., V28, 111.

41. Ibid., V28, 107.

42. See ibid., V28, 112: "But this 'being-a-task for myself' is precisely my specific being as [an] I, i.e. as 'I act'. (But the task is not an 'ought' or a value hovering over me; this 'being-the-task' is rather the very character of my own being as existence. I am, myself, the task [before me] [*Dieses mir Aufgegebensein aber ist gerade mein spezifisches Sein als Ich, d. h. als 'Ich handle.' (Die Aufgabe ist aber*

nicht ein Sollen und ein Wert, der über mir schwebt, sondern diese Aufgegeben-heit ist der Charakter meines Seins als Existenz. Was da aufgegeben ist, bin 'ich' selbst]."

43. Heidegger, *Sein und Zeit*, 42, 141, 179, 191, 231, 235, 406.

44. Heidegger, *Gesamtausgabe*, V28, 107. The semantic charge of *Soll-Sein* is difficult to render. For it stands both (a) for something along the lines of "*ought-to-be*" and (b) for a *be/ought-to-be* (i.e., a "*being-that-is-an-ought*").

45. In other words: The basic rule of identity (A = A) preceding and under-lying all other rules and the entire horizon of whatever is regulated by them concerns the "for" as such—i.e., the "am" (the "sum") as such. Positing any present-at-hand entity (and this also means: positing the fundamental rule for present-at-handness viz. *Vorhandenheit*—positing the *Vorhandenheit-related* A = A) requires the previous positing of the "for" as such and its fundamental rule (i.e., the original A = A: the intrinsically *I-related*—"*am*"—or "*sum*"-*related*—A = A), i.e., the *sameness* of the "for" viz. of the I (the "am" or the "sum") with itself.

46. See Heidegger, *Gesamtausgabe*, V28, 108, 242.

47. Ibid., V28, 69, 73, 75, 76, 290. See Fichte, *Sämmtliche/nachgelassene Werke*, I, 48, 101.

48. Heidegger, *Gesamtausgabe*, V28, 69.

49. Ibid., V28, 71, 288.

50. Ibid., V28, 70.

51. Ibid., V28, 72.

52. Ibid.

53. Ibid., V28, 73.

54. Ibid., V28, 72.

55. Ibid., V28, 73.

56. Ibid., V28, 75.

57. Or, as Heidegger also puts it: "dem Wie nach" (what is at stake is the *Wie des Handelns*)—see Heidegger, *Gesamtausgabe*, V28, 69, 73, 76, 290. See Fichte, *Sämmtliche/nachgelassene Werke*, I, 101.

58. Heidegger, *Gesamtausgabe*, V28, 70.

59. Ibid., V28, 75; see also V28, 290.

60. See note 3 above.

61. Fichte, *Sämmtliche/nachgelassene Werke*, I, 104.

62. Heidegger, *Gesamtausgabe*, V28, 76.

63. Ibid.

64. Ibid.

65. Ibid., V28, 78.

66. Ibid., V28, 77: "As something absolutely posited it is something posited in the I (i.e., for!) [*Als schlechthin Gesetztes ist es im Ich Gesetztes (d. h. für!)*]."

67. Contrary to what may seem to be the case, the not-I is by no means an *original* and *independent* determination. It is, rather, *intrinsically apophatical*.

68. Heidegger, *Gesamtausgabe*, V28, 77.

69. Ibid.
70. Ibid.
71. Ibid., V28, 291.
72. Ibid.
73. Ibid., V28, 77.
74. See ibid., V28, 108, 113, 242. "Existential" stands for whatever pertains to the sphere of the self (and its non-indifferent relation to itself). "Categorial" stands for whatever pertains to the sphere of the *non*-self: beings *von nicht daseinmäßigem Seinscharakter* (beings whose mode of being is *unlike Dasein*). "Existenzialien" ("existentials") stands for the basic components of the former, shaping everything else (and upon which everything else depends) in the *existential* sphere; they are, as it were, the specific 'categories' of the "existential" sphere. *Kategorien*—categories proper—are the basic components of the "categorial" (of the *non-self*, of whatever is *unlike Dasein*), shaping everything else (and upon which everything else depends) in the *categorial* field.
75. See Heidegger, *Gesamtausgabe*, V28, 84.
76. Ibid., V28, 85.
77. Ibid., V28, 86.
78. Ibid., V28, 87; see Fichte, *Sämmtliche/nachgelassene Werke*, I, 108.
79. Ibid., V28, 87; see V28, 88, 90, 94, 99, and 124. See Fichte, *Sämmtliche/nachgelassene Werke*, I, 108.
80. Ibid., V28, 87. See V28 87, 94, 131, 142, 153, 293, and 305. See Fichte, *Sämmtliche/nachgelassene Werke*, I, 109.
81. Fichte, *Sämmtliche/nachgelassene Werke*, I, 110. See Heidegger, *Gesamtausgabe*, V28, 90.
82. Fichte, *Sämmtliche/nachgelassene Werke*, I, 109. See Heidegger, *Gesamtausgabe*, V28, 87.
83. Heidegger, *Gesamtausgabe*, V28, 87.
84. Or proves its worth.
85. Heidegger, *Gesamtausgabe*, V28, 89.
86. In the *corpus heideggerianum*, there are several instances of the verb "nichten," as opposed to "vernichten." In a number of these cases, it seems to be clear that Heidegger uses "nichten" to express an essentially *Nichts*-related (i.e., *nothing*-related) action that is not the same as "annihilate" or the like. This use of "nichten" has been variously rendered into English (to "nihilate," to "nullify," to "noth"). See, for example G. Stern (Anders), "On the Pseudo-Concreteness of Heidegger's Philosophy," *Philosophy and Phenomenological Research* 8 (1948): 337–71, in particular 344; S. Rosen, "Thinking about Nothing" in *Heidegger and Modern Philosophy*, ed. M. Murray (New Haven: Yale University Press, 1978): 116–37; A. C. Danto, *Connections to the World: The Basic Concepts of Philosophy* (London: University of California Press, 1997), 60; E. Waibl and P. Herdina, *Dictionary of Philosophical Terms/Wörterbuch philosophischer Fachbegriffe*, 2: English-German/Englisch-Deutsch (London: Routledge, 1997), 20; M. Inwood, "Does the Nothing

Noth?", in *German Philosophy Since Kant*, ed. A. O'Hear (Cambridge: Cambridge University Press, 1999), 271–91, in particular 275; and M. Groth, *Translating Heidegger* (Toronto: University of Toronto Press, 2017), 64, 90. But if we are not mistaken, what we are dealing with here is something altogether different. For in this case Heidegger's "nichten" is not intrinsically "*Nichts*"-related. It is rather "*nicht*"-related: it has to do with the "not" (the "~") as such. "To not," although perhaps the best translation, might be syntactically confusing. And this is why we have chosen to translate the way we did: "positing-as-not."

87. Heidegger, *Gesamtausgabe*, V28, 88.

88. And this notwithstanding the fact that the third principle is, as Fichte puts it, doubly conditioned: both in its *content* and in its *form*.

89. Heidegger, *Gesamtausgabe*, V28, 91; see also 294.

90. Ibid., V28, 293. For Heidegger's examination of this key component of Fichte's view, see notably Heidegger, *Gesamtausgabe*, V28, 87, 141, 160, 245, 293, 313, and 317.

91. Heidegger, *Gesamtausgabe*, V28, 293.

92. Ibid., V28, 89.

93. Ibid., V28, 88.

94. Fichte, *Sämmtliche/nachgelassene Werke*, I, 110.

95. Heidegger, *Gesamtausgabe*, V28, 90; cf. 124.

96. Ibid., V28, 91; see V28, 294.

97. That is, for Fichte the interconnection between the three principles (i.e., Heidegger's "equiprimordiality") shows *Wechselwirkung* or interdependency: it has to do with an *organic unity* between them. Fichte is well aware that there are contradiction and tension—namely those the theoretical part of his *Wissenschaftslehre* proves unable to resolve and only the "Gordian solution" provided by the practical part (see Fichte, *Sämmtliche/nachgelassene Werke*, I, 144 and 156) manages to "master." But in his eyes, none of this affects the clarity of the three principles or the quality of the insight into them. For Heidegger, the said equiprimordiality means that there is a *punctum coecum* or blind spot, as it were, at the very core of Fichte's *Ursetzungen*. Or, if I may be allowed to express it this way, there is something of a Möbius loop about them. In Heidegger's view, Fichte comes across a transcendental imbroglio. And this is what Heidegger's emphasis on finitude is all about.

98. Fichte, *Sämmtliche/nachgelassene Werke*, I, 105, 144. '*Machtspruch*' stands for an *authority-based*—that is, a *power*-based—decision. It cannot be over-emphasized that it has to do with *Macht* (*power*), i.e., with a decision resting on a *power claim*.

99. For Heidegger's interpretation and discussion of Fichte's *Machtspruch,* see notably Heidegger, *Gesamtausgabe*, V28, 80, 86, 91, 100, 143, 152, 157, 160, 246, 248, 292, 298, 313, and 318.

100. Heidegger, *Gesamtausgabe*, V28, 82.

101. Ibid., V28, 91. Heidegger is, of course, referring to the connection between *decree* (*Machtspruch*) and *power* (*Macht*). See note 115 above.
102. Ibid., V28, 91. See Fichte, *Sämmtliche/nachgelassene Werke*, I, 114: "Wir haben im dritten Grundsatze eine Synthesis zwischen dem entgegengesetzten Ich und Nicht-Ich, vermittelst der gesetzten Theilbarkeit beider, vorgenommen, über deren Möglichkeit sich nicht weiter fragen, noch ein Grund derselben sich anführen lässt; sie ist schlechthin möglich, man ist zu ihr ohne allen weiteren Grund befugt." ("In the third principle we have established a synthesis between the two opposites, I and Not-I, by positing them each to be divisible; there can be no further question as to the possibility of this, nor can any ground for it be given; it is absolutely possible, and we are entitled to it without further grounds of any kind.")
103. Heidegger, *Gesamtausgabe*, V28, 294; see also V28, 296.
104. Ibid., V28, 296.
105. Heidegger, *Gesamtausgabe*, V28, 47. N.B.: '*Ausarbeiten*' not in the sense of 'solving it,' but in the sense of *facing it* and *dealing with* it.
106. I.e., Fichte's examination of what Heidegger terms the "phenomenon in phenomenological sense."
107. Heidegger, *Gesamtausgabe*, V17, 60, 71, 81, 87, 89, 93, 100, 106, 114, 119, 126, 195, 221, 224, 229, 266, 270, 280, 302.
108. Ibid., V28, 91. Cf. 50, 74, 91, 119, 121, 130, 138, 144, 170, 183, 243, 247, 295, 307.
109. As he puts it in his 1921/22 lectures (Ibid., V61, 164).
110. Ibid., V60, 17: "Especially in Fichte's treatment of this material problem, the "subject" is a new form of objecthood (*Gegenständlichkeit*) vis-à-vis other "objects." Nonetheless, we find here too, in Fichte's departure from Kant's practical philosophy and his utilization of Kantian anticipations (*Vorgriffe*), a basically attitudinal tendency *(einstellungshafte Tendenz)*." For the English translation, see Martin Heidegger, *The Phenomenology of Religious Life*, trans. M. Fritsch and J. Gosetti-Ferencei (Bloomington: Indiana University Press, 2010), 12. For Heidegger's phenomenology of what he terms "theoretical attitude" (*theoretische Einstellung*) viz. "attitudinal tendency" (*einstellungshafte Tendenz*), see M. J. de Carvalho, "Fichte, Heidegger and the Concept of Facticity," in *Fichte and the Phenomenological Tradition*, ed. V. L. Waibel, D. Breazeale, and T. Rockmore (Berlin: De Gruyter, 2010), 223–60, in particular 258.
111. Heidegger, *Gesamtausgabe*, V28, 47, 102, 122, 150, 155, 164, 169, 246, 250, 279, 292, 294, 299, 302, 305, 330.
112. Ibid., V28, 46, 74, 101, 121, 129, 144, 150, 165, 170, 243, 247, 258, 301, 307.
113. See notably Heidegger, *Gesamtausgabe*, V28, 30, 46, 50, 57, 74, 80, 91, 97, 101, 104, 119, 121, 125, 139, 145, 166, 170, 175, 183, 243, 247, 262, 295, 302, 307, 329, 334.

21

Hegel's Phenomenological Method and the Later Movement of Phenomenology

Jon Stewart

Although the term "phenomenology" had been used before, Hegel is known for coining the word as a description of a methodological approach that concerns the study of appearances.[1] It has long been an open question the degree to which the later philosophical school of phenomenology in fact follows the actual method developed by Hegel or if it merely co-opted the name and used the term in a different way. Is Hegel's use of phenomenology really the same as that developed by Husserl and then later by Heidegger, Sartre, Merleau-Ponty, and others? Or are the later phenomenologists using a method that is significantly different from what goes by the name "phenomenology" in Hegel's writings?

There are a number of works that treat the question of the relation of Hegel's phenomenological method to that of the phenomenological movement in the twentieth and twenty-first centuries.[2] This includes both general comparisons and works that explore Hegel's relation to specific phenomenologists such as Husserl. Moreover, there is a broad range of opinions on this question in both the primary and the secondary literature. It should be said here at the outset that it is misconceived to think of this relation as a strict dichotomy, claiming either that Hegel's phenomenology is the very

J. Stewart (✉)
Institute of Philosophy, Slovak Academy of Sciences, Bratislava, Slovakia
e-mail: js@jonstewart.dk

457

C. D. Coe (eds.), *The Palgrave Handbook of German Idealism and Phenomenology*, Palgrave Handbooks in German Idealism, https://doi.org/10.1007/978-3-030-66857-0_21

same as the later school of phenomenology or that it is radically different and has nothing whatsoever to do with it. The difficulty involves teasing out the points of similarity and difference between the two.

Initially, there was great skepticism that Hegel had anything at all in common with the later tradition of phenomenology. This skepticism came from the fact that, somewhat oddly, Husserl seemed never to have made a close study of Hegel or to have regarded him as an important forerunner. On the contrary, in his few mentions of him, he criticizes Hegel rather sharply. Given Husserl's critical assessment, it might appear that the connection between Hegel and later phenomenology is simply a linguistic deception. While Hegel and Husserl both use the term "phenomenology," it was thought, they take it to refer to quite different things.

However, the picture changed somewhat with the French phenomenologists, who, in contrast to Husserl, seem to embrace and acknowledge Hegel.[3] Sartre and Merleau-Ponty both made a careful study of Hegel and openly adopted specific elements of his thought.[4] In a famous essay, Merleau-Ponty identified what he regarded as existentialist elements in Hegel's philosophy, which are arguably connected to the phenomenological method.[5] This would seem to suggest a more positive basis for a comparative analysis. At the very least, it is an indication of the fact that what is understood by "phenomenology" today is something both complex and heterogeneous.

In this chapter, I will argue that there are in fact some important points of continuity and that it is quite legitimate to regard Hegel as a forerunner of the phenomenological movement. While there are, to be sure, some important differences, some of the basic philosophical intuitions that inform phenomenology can be found in both Hegel and the later phenomenologists. In both cases, there is at work a rejection of a commonsense correspondence theory. I will begin by discussing how Hegel conceives of the subject matter or scope of phenomenology. This suggests an important point of continuity with the diverse applications of the method in modern phenomenological research. Then in the second section, I will analyze Hegel's clearest methodological statement about phenomenology from the Introduction to the *Phenomenology of Spirit*. In the third section, an analysis of Hegel's use of the term "phenomenology" in the *Encyclopedia of the Philosophical Sciences* will be presented. In the fourth section, I examine Husserl's criticisms of Hegel in order to determine how these are relevant for the conception of phenomenology. In the fifth section, I will explore the more positive reception of Hegel in the works of the French phenomenologists Sartre and Merleau-Ponty. In the final section, I will use these accounts of Hegel as the basis for comparison with the later school of phenomenology. I will try to enumerate significant points of comparison and contrast. I wish to show that Hegel has two conceptions of phenomenology, one broad and one narrow. The latter fits best with Husserl's original conception, whereas the former fits best with the later developments in phenomenology where the method is applied to any number of different spheres of human experience. In other words, the basic ambiguity in Hegel's conception is a reflection of the heterogeneity and richness of the subsequent phenomenological tradition.

The Subject Matter and Scope of Phenomenology

How Hegel understands the subject matter of phenomenology is not so straightforward. This question is bound up with the complex story of the composition of the *Phenomenology of Spirit* itself. It seems that when Hegel originally conceived of the work, it was intended to have only three chapters: "Consciousness," "Self-Consciousness," and "Reason."[6] This original conception has a clear systematic symmetry: first, there is an account of different models of the object sphere; second, an account of the self-conscious subject; and finally, these two spheres of objectivity and subjectivity come together in the "Reason" chapter. This course of analysis demonstrates how the object and the subject are necessarily bound up with one another. Perhaps most important, it is shown how the subject serves to determine objectivity as such. An object is thus always an object "for consciousness," that is, something that appears to the human mind.

However, at some point along the way when writing the *Phenomenology*, Hegel realized that this three-step analysis was inadequate. For a complete account of the spheres of objectivity and subjectivity, a broader analysis was needed that included the spheres of history, religion, and philosophy. How humans conceive the world is bound up with their specific historical period. Similarly, their conceptions of their gods are also a reflection of their conceptions of themselves and the world around them. Thus, Hegel continued to work on the *Phenomenology*, adding long chapters on history (the "Spirit" chapter) and religion. These chapters are disproportionately long in comparison with the "Consciousness" and "Self-Consciousness" chapters at the beginning of the work.[7]

This shift in the conception of the structure and contents of the *Phenomenology of Spirit* is important for our present purposes. Hegel's expansion of the original material seems to imply that the phenomenological method can be extended to many different spheres including history, religion, and art.[8] In other words, if "phenomenology" means primarily an examination of the phenomena of consciousness as they appear, these phenomena can in principle be almost anything that a person experiences and are not confined to the objects that are typically discussed in questions of epistemology. Evidence of Hegel's intention can be found in the fact that he chose to entitle the work the "Phenomenology of Spirit" and not the "Phenomenology of Consciousness" or the "Phenomenology of Self-Consciousness." In other words, Hegel's ideas of, for example, the Greek spirit or world spirit go beyond the exploration of individual conscious or self-conscious agents. This suggests something like a collective self-consciousness. Since the "Spirit" chapter of the *Phenomenology* is dedicated to a treatment of history, the implication is clearly that history and larger social structures can be the subject of phenomenological analysis.

This is an important issue since Hegel's expanded use of phenomenology to include areas such as history, religion, and art anticipates the expansion of phenomenology in recent years into many other fields. Today we find books and articles dedicated to the phenomenology of almost any kind of human experience whatsoever: the phenomenology of intimacy, of food cravings, of pain, of learning, etc. Although some of these works should presumably be taken with a grain of salt since they do not, strictly speaking, follow a phenomenological methodology, the tendency in general is clear and should not be dismissed. On this point, we can see an important point of overlap between Hegel's conception of phenomenology and the modern conception of it. The scope of phenomenological analysis is in both cases conceived very broadly and can be applied to most anything in the rich world of human experience.

Hegel's Description of His Method

Hegel's most detailed account of his phenomenological method can be found in the Introduction to the *Phenomenology of Spirit*.[9] Just as Husserl's phenomenology was a response to the neo-Kantianism of the day, so also Hegel's original account of phenomenology was clearly developed in response to Kant's epistemology. Hegel's phenomenological method can thus be seen as a proposed solution to the paradoxes that resulted from Kant's two-world split between representations and things in themselves. In the *Critique of Pure Reason*, Kant argued that space and time are not things in the world but rather the necessary forms of human perception—in his language, the forms of sensible intuition. We always perceive things in space and time since this is a necessary feature of our sensory apparatus. But it would be an unwarranted assumption to believe that objects themselves exist in space and time on their own as a fact of the world. Similarly, Kant claimed that the so-called categories of the understanding, such as causality and substance, are also a part of the human cognitive capacity and not features of the world itself. These categories spontaneously shape an incoherent set of perceptual data or input into determinate, discrete objects. These are what Kant calls representations (*Vorstellungen*) since they are thought to represent something in the outside world. We know of these external things since we receive sense perceptions from them, but it is our sensory and cognitive apparatus that turns them into determinate objects for us.

Kant consistently reminds his readers that we cannot know how the objects really are in themselves since we are confined to grasping them through our cognitive faculties, which shape them in specific ways in order to create the world of objectivity that we are familiar with. But how these things really are on their own, apart from how our cognitive capacities perceive and conceive them, we can never know since we can never put aside our cognitive faculties. They are our only access to the world around us. This theory represents the core of Kant's idealism. Objects in the world are essentially representations created by the spontaneous functions of the human mind.

For the post-Kantian philosophers, this led to the unfortunate result that we are forever cut off from the world as it is in itself. We want to believe that our representations are correct. When I have a perception of something in the world, I have a need to believe that my perception really corresponds to something outside me, and, moreover, that my perception is an accurate representation of that thing. But on Kant's epistemological model, this is impossible since we can never compare our perceptions with the things in themselves, since the latter are never given to us as objects of perception. They are, alas, forever beyond our reach. Thus, although Kant explained the rules of objectivity, his system can be said to end in an unintended skepticism. While we all perceive the world according to a certain set of common rules, and therefore we all have generally the same perception of reality, we might all be completely wrong.

In the Introduction to the *Phenomenology*, Hegel, without naming Kant, explains the Kantian epistemology that understands cognition as an instrument or a medium that is used to grasp the world. This instrument shapes the incoming perceptions and makes them into discrete objects, or, put differently, the sense data coming from the object must pass through the medium of our cognitive faculties. But this means that the thing, whatever it is, is reshaped in accordance with the nature of the cognitive faculties and thus appears to us in a way that is changed from its original being: "if cognition is the instrument for getting hold of absolute being, it is obvious that the use of an instrument on a thing certainly does not let it be what it is for itself, but rather sets out to reshape and alter it" (PhG 46). Hegel then suggests that the problem might be eliminated if we come to an understanding of the nature of the cognitive faculties in the way Kant had done. If we know how these faculties shape and determine objects, then it would seem to follow that we could just eliminate these changes and end up with the original object prior to transformation by the faculties of the human mind. Thus, we need to imagine an object that is not in space or time and stands outside all categorical determination of substance, causality, etc. But this is of course impossible to grasp, and we cannot imagine anything at all if we abstract from our faculties of cognition. Without them, there would be no object left.

Hegel notes that this model is doomed to failure since it assumes from the start that there is a fundamental difference between the objects of perception and how things are in themselves. Our cognition is in principle different from the truth since our cognitive faculties change the objects as we perceive and think them. If we take the object in itself to be the absolute that we desire to grasp, this is forever cut off from us since our only means of grasping it is through the instrument of our cognition, which changes it. Thus, we can never get hold of the truth on its own but must be satisfied with the way in which we perceive things, never knowing if they correspond accurately to actual things in the world.

Hegel then proposes a methodology that reconceives the basic terms of Kant's epistemology in order to avoid ending in skepticism. Hegel points out that it is no surprise that it is impossible to unify representations and things in themselves since they are conceived at the outset to be fundamentally different and separate. Instead of starting with a dualism, he proposes a model whereby everything is simply an object of consciousness. In other words, our consciousness contains both our perceptions of the world and our more abstract conceptions of things. We can perceive with our senses a specific cat, and we have in our minds the idea or concept of a cat. Both of these are in my consciousness, and so they can be compared with one another. I can compare my perceptions with my ideas and see if they match up. Based on these comparisons, I can correct mistaken views.

Only a little reflection shows that this is something that we do all the time. We have ideas about things and people that we have created due to our experiences with them. I might believe that a given person is kind, just, or intelligent. But we often feel the need to modify these ideas when they are called into question by new experiences. When a person does or says something that surprises us, this surprise is an indication of the fact that the perception has contradicted our idea. It enjoins us to make a modification in order to bring the idea into line with the perception and thus to avoid a contradiction. Sometimes we want to believe certain things about people and try to resist changing our views, but when we perceive certain behaviors repeatedly, the contradiction becomes so striking that we are compelled to do so. This is just a single example about our views of other people, but it can easily be extended to include any given object that we encounter in the world.

Hegel suggests that this approach resolves the problem of skepticism created by Kant's epistemology since there is no external or transcendent element involved. As noted, on the Kantian view, it is impossible to compare our representations with the things in themselves since we cannot get hold of the latter. But we can compare our representations with one another and with our ideas and concepts. This is the key to the phenomenological analysis, which Hegel calls "an investigation and *examination of the reality of cognition*" (PhG 52). As noted, on the Kantian model there is an implicit need to compare the representations with the things in themselves in order to see if the former are true representations. Thus, the idea is that the things in themselves must be what is true and real. They are, for Kant unintentionally, the criterion or benchmark for truth. This was of course not intended by Kant since he adamantly asserted that we cannot know things in themselves. But his talk of representations inevitably gives rise to the idea of common sense that there must be something external that is represented. Hegel's insight is to show that this model contains a misunderstanding and that the true criterion can be found in consciousness itself, namely, in our conceptions of things.

We often have experiences that compel us to correct our views and perceptions. I see what I take to be a cat in the dark, and then when I get a closer look, I realize that it was not a cat but rather a skunk. Our common sense tells us that the first perception was a mistake, and the second was the truth, when I got hold of reality or the thing itself. But this experience can go on indefinitely, and I can continue to correct my perceptions forever with new experiences as they arise. This shows that our different experiences provide us with a sense of the truth without any need to appeal to something beyond experience. As Hegel says, "Consciousness provides its own criterion from within itself, so that the investigation becomes a comparison of consciousness with itself; for the distinction made above falls within it" (PhG 53). This is the key to phenomenology, which consists in coming to terms with the world by strictly insisting on how it appears to us in experience and making no appeal to something beyond experience. Hegel changes the terminology of Kant, which posited a dualism between representation and the thing in itself, by introducing a new term "for consciousness," which encompasses both. Even the thing in itself is an object for consciousness in the sense that it is simply our imagined idea of what a thing would look like if we could *per impossible* abstract from the determinations of our perceptual and cognitive faculties. The key is his idea that what Kant calls the thing in itself is not something unknown behind the curtain of the human mind. Instead, it too is an object of consciousness. Phenomenology is thus an examination of everything that appears for consciousness, or as Hegel says, with his famous formulation, "the science of the *experience of consciousness*" (PhG 56). This corresponds to his description at the very end of the *Phenomenology of Spirit*, where the work is described as "the science of knowing in the sphere of appearance" (PhG 493).

Hegel explains that he wishes to trace a series of different conceptions along these lines using his phenomenological actor, the so-called natural consciousness, as his model (PhG 49).[10] At each given stage, natural consciousness believes a certain thing to be true. But then in the course of its experience with the world, it realizes that it was mistaken. As a result, natural consciousness is compelled to revise its original idea and develop a new, more accurate one. Thus, phenomenology can be conceived as a series of stages, where one conception leads to the next, as different views are discarded to the advantage of what appear to be better ones, which are then in turn discarded. Hegel traces an idealized model of this development with the natural consciousness, and he has been criticized for his claim that this development, some of which appears rather strange and counterintuitive to the reader, is necessary. This is a broader issue that can be discussed, but the key point for our purposes is simply that, for whatever the content of Hegel's specific phenomenological analyses, it will be noted that this procedure is an accurate picture of one aspect of our mental life, since we are constantly revising our views based on new experiences. There is no need to appeal to something beyond consciousness or experience to explain this. This aspect of his theory should be more or less uncontroversial.

Hegel's Use of Phenomenology in the *Encyclopedia*

Hegel also uses the term "phenomenology" in his account in the section "Subjective Spirit" from the third part of the *Encyclopedia of the Philosophical Sciences*.[11] It is conceived here to represent a full-blown science alongside anthropology and psychology. His account covers primarily the material that corresponds to the "Consciousness" and the "Self-Consciousness" chapters of the *Phenomenology*. This is completed by a short section entitled "Reason." His usage of the term "phenomenology" in the *Encyclopedia* thus corresponds to his first conception of it in his original plan for the *Phenomenology of Spirit*, as mentioned in the previous section.

The first stage of Hegel's theory of the mind or spirit is anthropology. This represents the stage of immediacy or "spirit in *nature*."[12] Hegel explains that anthropology is the science that examines human beings in their physical dimension. Humans are a part of nature and have bodies just like animals. At this level, humans are continuous with nature. At first, babies are not able to distinguish themselves from the outside world. The ability to think of oneself as an independent entity presupposes the ability to see oneself from the perspective of the other. Small children must learn to make this leap of abstraction, that is, to abstract from their immediate, natural first-person orientation. This requires them to ignore for a moment their own inward feelings, drives, and desires and see themselves from the outside, which is for them a new perspective that stands in contrast to their intuitive, more immediate one. Moreover, in the course of time, the human spirit begins to develop and to oppose itself to the purely corporeal side of its existence. Through an act of the mind, humans can resist the demands of nature, by, for example, staying awake, fasting, or refraining from sex. In this way, humans become increasingly aware of themselves as something separate from nature and from their purely physical dimension.

Phenomenology is the discipline that follows anthropology. This is the stage of mediation that is relevant as humans distinguish themselves from their immediate relation to nature. Hegel explains, "In phenomenology, the soul, by the negation of its corporeity, raises itself to purely ideal self-identity, becomes *consciousness*, becomes 'I,' is for itself against its other."[13] As in the *Phenomenology of Spirit*, the basic notion of phenomenology here still concerns an examination of the sphere of appearances. Hegel explains, "spirit here is no longer immersed in nature but reflected into itself and in a relation to nature, but it only *appears*, stands only in a relation to actuality, is not yet *actual* mind. Therefore, we call the part of the science in which this form of mind is treated, 'phenomenology.'"[14] At the stage of consciousness, human beings try to determine themselves as a particular individuals, that is, in contrast to other things and people. But in the course of the experience, the individual consciousness realizes that it is necessarily connected with other conscious subjects. This is the level of self-consciousness. With this realization, people are compelled to recognize that, despite their need to determine themselves as individuals, there is a universal element in spirit that they share with everyone else. This universal element does not destroy individuality or subjectivity, but, on the contrary, makes it possible in the first place.

The third stage of Hegel's philosophy of mind is psychology. This represents the unity of objectivity (anthropology) and subjectivity (phenomenology). Here the human subject develops itself to a truly free agent. This is the stage that explores the universal rational element of the human. The individual is able to choose the universal by means of its rational will. This is no longer a part of phenomenology since this, according to Hegel, is no longer an appearance that can change. Instead, this is the truth that has finally been arrived at after a long development. Spirit is neither a simple unity with nature nor a radical separation from it. Instead, it is a higher unity of the individual with the world based on the individual's own reason. Individuals have their own will as something separate from nature (as in the first stage), but this will is not arbitrary and purely subjective (as in the second stage). Rather the individual's will is determined by rationality and thus becomes objective.

This conception in a sense relegates phenomenology to a lower form of knowing since it does not manage to reach the final truth. It remains at the level of a dualism or split between the mind and the world. This critical assessment of phenomenology is made clear in Hegel's association of Kant with it: "The Kantian philosophy may be most accurately described as having viewed the mind as consciousness, and as containing the propositions only of a *phenomenology* (not a *philosophy*) of mind."[15] He cites as a reason for this that the Kantian subject remains a thing in itself, an unknowable presupposition for knowledge.[16] While the true philosophy of mind manages to attain the truth, a phenomenology occupies a stage along the way to this. This view ultimately squares with the conception of phenomenology as something that precedes the level of science itself, the latter of which represents truth. This is the view of the *Phenomenology of Spirit*, which is presented as a kind of introduction to or preparation for true science, which is only reached at the end of the work.

On this account in the *Encyclopedia*, phenomenology plays a considerably more limited role than in the *Phenomenology of Spirit*. After the section on "Subjective Spirit" in the *Encyclopedia* Hegel goes on to treat what he calls "Objective Spirit." Here the spheres of law, morality (*Moralität*), social ethics (*Sittlichkeit*), social-political philosophy, and history make their appearance. Much of what is treated here corresponds to the "Spirit" chapter in the *Phenomenology of Spirit*. But what is important is that in the *Encyclopedia*, none of these things falls under the rubric of "phenomenology," which is confined primarily to the material corresponding to the chapters "Consciousness" and "Self-Consciousness" from the *Phenomenology of Spirit*.

Given all of this, we can say that Hegel seems to have two conceptions of phenomenology, a broad one (from the *Phenomenology of Spirit*) and a narrow one (from the *Encyclopedia of the Philosophical Sciences*). At the time he was writing the *Phenomenology of Spirit*, he was himself unclear about the precise scope of the term, as was discussed in the first section above. This is important since it gives us two different conceptions to use in the comparison with the later school of phenomenology. It might be argued that, with regard to its actual content, the narrow conception corresponds more closely to Husserl's view of phenomenology. By contrast, the broader conception corresponds better to later developments in phenomenology, which apply the method to an increasingly large sphere of phenomena.

Husserl's Critical Assessment of Hegel

Given that the later tradition of phenomenology was founded by Husserl and further developed by a number of other thinkers, it is natural to start with Husserl's understanding of Hegel as the point of departure when addressing the question of Hegel's relation to this tradition. Surprisingly Husserl has very little to say about Hegel. In his published works, he has two important, albeit brief, discussions of Hegel, one in "Phenomenology as Rigorous Science" and the other in *The Crisis of European Sciences and Transcendental Phenomenology*. Although these works are separated by two decades, their basic view is consistent. While Husserl dedicates a couple of pages of continuous text to Hegel in the former work,[17] in the latter it is more a case of a few scattered mentions (C 132, 192, 194, 198, 201).

In the context of a thumbnail overview of the history of philosophy, Husserl gives a brief critical discussion of Hegel at the beginning of his essay "Phenomenology as Rigorous Science." He reads this history as a series of renewed attempts to make philosophy into a strict science. Important breakthroughs can be understood as attempts to reframe the issues and to introduce a new methodology with the goal of giving philosophy a truly scientific foundation. These important episodes in the history of philosophy expose the shortcomings of previous systems by demonstrating their lack of scientific rigor.[18] While Socrates, Descartes, Kant, and Fichte are mentioned as examples of such revolutions in philosophical thought, Husserl singles out Hegel for criticism.[19]

He rebukes Hegel for lacking a critical account of reason and thereby retarding the progress of philosophy as a genuinely scientific undertaking. Despite Hegel's insistence on the term "science," Husserl claims, "his system lacks a critique of reason, which is the foremost prerequisite for being scientific in philosophy."[20] According to this view, Hegel has failed to show the limits of reason so that it is clear what can be known and what cannot. This has led to what Husserl regards as Hegel's exuberant assessment of the powers of human rationality. Hegel's understanding of science as speculative philosophy was quickly rejected by thinkers in the second half of the nineteenth century when naturalism and scientific materialism began to gain traction with the ascendency of the natural sciences.

Husserl is especially critical of the historical element in Hegel's philosophy, according to which ideas are born and develop in specific times. While this was not Hegel's intention, the conclusion that many people drew from this was one of historical relativism. Hegel's account of history culminating in the attainment of full human freedom never gained a following, and his true legacy is one of historical contingency and relativity, which Husserl sees as widespread in his own time. With this interest in history, Hegel—like the German Romantics—veered away from the road of true scientific philosophy.

Husserl's discussion of Hegel in *The Crisis of European Sciences and Transcendental Phenomenology* can also be seen as a part of his attempt to give an account of the development of philosophy, by which he understands the impulse to make philosophy a rigorous science (C 198–203). In this context, Hegel's philosophy is again characterized as a failure despite the fact that it managed to attract a following for a period of time. While there were no mentions of any specific work by Hegel in his previous discussion in "Phenomenology as Rigorous Science," here Husserl parenthetically refers to the *Phenomenology of Spirit*. With reference to the Preface to this work, Husserl unflatteringly describes Hegel's thought as based on "mythical concept-constructions and of world-interpretations based on obscure metaphysical anticipations" (C 201). Husserl's accounts of Hegel in "Phenomenology as Rigorous Science" and *The Crisis of European Sciences and Transcendental Phenomenology* are entirely consistent. Without going into any detail with regard to Hegel's writings, Husserl declares him to be a wrong turn in the history of philosophy. While the truly important thinkers in the tradition strive to attain a rigorous conception of philosophy as a science, Hegel wallows in a subjective conceptual structure that could never endure for long.

The most striking thing about Husserl's mentions of Hegel is that there is no engagement with Hegel's conception of phenomenology as a method. Husserl rejects a certain picture of Hegel's later philosophy as a kind of historical relativism, but this has nothing to do with Hegel as a phenomenologist. This is surprising since we would expect that in Husserl's lifelong attempt to articulate the nature of phenomenology as a field, it would be natural for him to do so by positioning his own undertaking vis-à-vis that of Hegel. Instead, he confines himself to making some rather general remarks about different aspects of Hegel's philosophy and its subsequent reception. Thus, strangely enough, we cannot glean much information about the relation of Husserl's phenomenology to that of Hegel based on Husserl's own comments.

Unfortunately scholars have inferred from these criticisms that Husserl's notion of phenomenology is completely different from that of Hegel. But this is an unwarranted inference based on these criticisms, which have precious little to do with the phenomenological method. Given all this, Spiegelberg's conclusion seems to be correct that "Husserl himself ... does not seem to have studied Hegel more than casually" and inherited a wholly negative picture of Hegelian philosophy from his teacher Brentano.[21] It should also be noted that Hegel's philosophy was generally held in rather low esteem by the generation of Husserl's teachers, and this presumably played a role in his view that any detailed study of it would be a waste of time.

Interestingly, Husserl's student Eugen Fink lectured on Hegel's *Phenomenology of Spirit*, where he focused specifically on the phenomenological method of the work. These lectures were later published under the title, *Hegel. Phänomenologische Interpretationen der "Phänomenologie des Geistes."*[22] This work offers a close reading of the first three chapters of Hegel's text ("Consciousness," "Self-Consciousness," and "Reason") and represents in some respects a valuable guide, although it is informed by certain Heideggerian presuppositions about Hegel's project. Unfortunately, there is no attempt to offer a detailed comparison between Hegel's work and Husserl's phenomenology. In any case, it seems that Fink is more open than Husserl toward the phenomenological direction pioneered by Hegel.

The More Positive Assessment of Hegel in French Phenomenology

The French phenomenologists Jean-Paul Sartre and Maurice Merleau-Ponty are fairly up front about their use of Hegel's phenomenological method. Both men were influenced by the French tradition of Hegel research that was focused primarily on the *Phenomenology of Spirit*. Merleau-Ponty attended Alexandre Kojève's famous lectures on Hegel's *Phenomenology of Spirit* in the 1930s.[23] Both Sartre and Merleau-Ponty were on familiar terms with the Hegel scholar Jean Hyppolite, who produced a French translation of the *Phenomenology* and an extensive commentary on it.[24]

There can be little doubt that Sartre owes a great debt to Hegel in *Being and Nothingness*, which, as is well known, is designated as a phenomenological analysis.[25] Sartre develops in that work a theory of consciousness that draws on Hegel. Just as Hegel sketches the movement of consciousness from one stage to the next, with natural consciousness always being compelled to a new, higher view, so also for Sartre consciousness is fundamentally future oriented. Consciousness is never just a fixed thing like tables and chairs but is always open-ended and always reinterpreting itself. Sartre finds inspiration in Hegel's account of the unhappy consciousness—that is, the idea that human consciousness is internally divided and always struggling.[26] Sartre's account of human relations seems to be based on Hegel's analysis of the lord and the bondsman in the *Phenomenology of Spirit*. My phenomenological experience of myself is always mediated by the look of the other, which tries to impose itself on me. Sartre's objection to Hegel is that there is in the *Phenomenology* a final absolute position of totality, "Absolute Knowing," where the contradictions are ultimately resolved. For Sartre, by contrast, consciousness never attains totality or completeness. Despite this objection, it seems clear that Sartre makes use of Hegel's phenomenological methodology.

In his article "Hegel's Existentialism," Merleau-Ponty tries to sketch important points of continuity between the philosophy of Hegel and the existentialist movement.[27] While his main focus is not explicitly phenomenology, it is clear from the points that he discusses that this is central to his account. He is somewhat dismissive of the later Hegel for falling victim to abstraction, for example, with regard to social-political philosophy and the philosophy of history. However, Merleau-Ponty focuses his analysis on the *Phenomenology of Spirit* as an important work for the existentialist movement. Specifically, he regards Hegel's analysis of history in this work as being in harmony with the phenomenological approach, and he takes this as the point of departure for his comparison of Hegel's philosophy with existentialism.[28] He points out that this implies a broader conception of experience than what is found in Kant's epistemology. This corresponds precisely to Hegel's broadening of the original vision of the *Phenomenology of Spirit* to include an account of history and religion. This perspective is also supported by Merleau-Ponty's article "Marxism and Philosophy," where he ascribes to Marx a phenomenological approach to the social, historical, and economic spheres based on Hegel's method.[29]

Merleau-Ponty sees in Hegel's account of the different stages of consciousness a kind of proto-existentialism. For Hegel individuals are continually having new experiences about the world and themselves, and these experiences constantly enjoin them to rethink their views. Along the lines sketched by Sartre, Merleau-Ponty claims that it lies in the nature of consciousness to surpass itself, and it is impossible remain for long in a static position. Life is thus movement that is accompanied by anxiety and unhappiness, since the individual can never reach a final certainty. Thus, Hegel's notion of the unhappy consciousness is also hailed as an existentialist motif.

The key connection between Hegel's phenomenology and existentialism can be found in the concepts of existence or life. Merleau-Ponty makes the Hegelian point, "all we say about life has to do in reality with consciousness of life, since we who talk about it are conscious of it."[30] He thus seems to suggest that all of the existentialist analyses in the end can be reduced to a kind of phenomenological method. Like Hegel, Merleau-Ponty rejects any appeal to something transcendent or beyond consciousness that might be taken to ground human existence. Merleau-Ponty points to Hegel's analysis in the lordship and bondage dialectic from the *Phenomenology* as the forerunner of the account of death found in Heidegger.[31] It is the fear of death that initially motivates the bondsman. This is a key experience in what makes us fully self-conscious human beings and constitutes a central point in our mental life. This anticipates Heidegger's rich analysis of what he calls being-toward-death.

The French phenomenologists thus seem to have no serious objection to seeing Hegel's methodology as a part of the phenomenological tradition to which they themselves subscribe. Spiegelberg's observation on this is to the point: "while the German phenomenological movement never considered Hegel as a phenomenologist in the full sense, the present French phenomenologists seem to take his inclusion in the phenomenological movement for granted."[32] The French phenomenologists tend to be more in line with Hegel's broader conception of the use of phenomenology in the social and historical sphere, which is what they identified with but what Husserl rejected.

Comparison with the Later Tradition of Phenomenology

How does Hegel's conception of phenomenology match up with later conceptions? Before we address this question directly, we must briefly attend to a methodological problem. Husserl is known as the founder of modern phenomenology, and his work was later developed in very different ways by his student Heidegger. In turn the school of French phenomenology with Sartre and Merleau-Ponty largely drew upon the language and method of Heidegger. In recent years, phenomenology has grown immensely and has found its way into a great many disciplines. One might argue that this has resulted in a devaluation of the term itself, whereby what goes under the heading "phenomenology" can describe quite different things. As with any school of thought, it is therefore difficult to arrive as a single point of continuity that can be said to be the defining feature in such a way that absolutely all of the theorists can ascribe to it. This is illustrated by the fact that there are many disputes among the phenomenologists themselves about who has in fact got it right.

When we wish to compare Hegel's phenomenology with modern phenomenology, we thus find that the latter is something of a moving target. This means that we are compelled to do one of two things. Either we can confine our observations to a comparison of Hegel with specific phenomenologists. This would, however, result in a long book, and not a short chapter. Or we are obliged to speak of "modern phenomenology" in more general terms, all the while being aware that whatever we say about it might fit sometimes better and sometimes worse with any given phenomenologist. In what follows I have tried to combine these approaches by focusing both on general points of contrast between Hegel and phenomenology in the twentieth century and specific points of contrast between Hegel and Husserl.

One way in which modern phenomenology differs from Hegel is that the former does not make use of a single linear movement of thought. It is interested in exploring the vast range of human experiences and is not confined to tracing the strict path of something like Hegel's natural consciousness. In a nutshell, Hegel's phenomenology follows a single line of the development of consciousness, whereas modern phenomenology is more open-ended or, some would say, creative. It is open for almost any analysis of consciousness and its experience and can involve numerous different paths that each could potentially offer new insights. In modern phenomenology, there is no necessary movement of thought from one stage to the next, and the phenomenologist enjoys a degree of freedom in the presentation of the investigation.

The second important point of difference is related to this. In the *Phenomenology of Spirit*, there is a teleology in the development of the movement: "the *goal* is as necessarily fixed for knowledge as the serial progression" (PhG 51). The point of the movement of thought in the *Phenomenology* is to justify what Hegel calls "science." Thus, natural consciousness must overcome its mistaken conceptions and attain the truth that is found in science. The various stages of thought that Hegel traces in the work can thus be seen as "the detailed history of the *education* of consciousness itself to the standpoint of science" (PhG 50). Hegel claims, somewhat enigmatically, that the movement of thought in the *Phenomenology* is necessary. This way of thinking that understands the appearances as a necessary linear sequence aimed toward a specific end seems generally foreign to the later phenomenological school. In this sense, one might say that that there is a critical or normative element in Hegel's phenomenology, whereas modern phenomenology is more purely descriptive. Phenomenological analyses today can take many forms and concern many subjects. There is no necessary connection among them. Nowadays commentators are more inclined to say that Hegel's presentation of the journey of natural consciousness is anything but intuitive and cannot be rightly claimed to be the result of an examination of the contents of consciousness. Rather, Hegel's account seems to be something abstract that is imposed on consciousness in a sense from above, although Hegel claims that philosophical observers are merely looking on and observing how the ideas naturally develop themselves.

The third point of discontinuity between Hegelian phenomenology and the later tradition is related to this. The difference between Hegel and Husserl can be articulated as one of content versus method. Husserl was primarily concerned to develop phenomenology as a rigorous method of science that produced certainties. But complaints are sometimes heard that he did not do as much as one might have liked to apply this method once it was determined.[33] As a result, the content is not as rich as one might have wished. By contrast, Hegel throws himself into his phenomenological analysis with only a fairly schematic account of his method, sketched above. The result is a long book that is full of rich content on a number of subjects. Husserl does not appear particularly interested in history or religion, whereas Hegel devotes long chapters to these fields in the *Phenomenology*. Hegel seems more committed to exploring all of the different spheres of human experience in a systematic manner. By contrast, Husserl is primarily concerned to establish and refine the phenomenological method itself and to leave the analyses of these different spheres to others. However, it should be noted that while this observation holds for the important difference between Hegel and Husserl, it loses its force when it is applied to other phenomenologists who indeed provide a wealth of interesting and insightful analyses using what they regard as some version of the phenomenological method.

As a fourth point of difference, it has also been noted that Hegel's and Husserl's respective approaches to the history of philosophy are quite different.[34] Hegel devotes great effort to understanding the history of philosophy, and this constitutes an important element in his own philosophizing. He sees the movement of philosophical thought as an expression of the development of spirit and freedom. By contrast, Husserl's account of the history of philosophy is much more limited and focused on only a handful of key thinkers. His knowledge of the history of philosophy is less extensive, and his only interest seems to be to document previous attempts to develop philosophy as a scientific enterprise, that is, to trace a lineage leading up to his own understanding of philosophy as a rigorous science. Husserl has no use for Hegel's account of the development of world history.

Fifth, it has also been pointed out that there is nothing corresponding to Husserl's phenomenological reduction in Hegel.[35] According to Husserl, it is necessary to put aside all of our theories and conceptual frameworks and return to our original experience of things in the world. For Hegel, this corresponds to the very first stage of the phenomenological development of the natural consciousness, that he calls "Sense Certainty." This is Hegel's attempt to give an account of the most basic conception of a thing that we can have without any further forms of determination. As is well known from the *Phenomenology of Spirit* and the *Science of Logic*, this is the concept of pure being. But, for Hegel, this is just an initial stage that must be surpassed with further conceptual development. While Husserl believes that the truth can be found in the original experience with the world, once the prejudices of our ways of thinking have been stripped away, this is for Hegel only a single step along the way. Our later theories and conceptual structures also constitute our ways of thinking and need to be explored since they too produce certain object models.

A final point of dissimilarity can be found in the attempt to capture something basic or fundamental about our conscious experience. Spiegelberg rightly asserts that there is nothing in Hegel that resembles Husserl's intuitive method.[36] For Husserl, once we peel away the abstract conceptual structures and prejudices, we can get to intuitive experience. Similarly, Heidegger's account of the experience of objects in the world as ready-to-hand is supposed to strike us as intuitive. In Hegel, the movement is the opposite: our commonsense intuitions are not recovered and vindicated but are proven to be mistaken. Concretely, our naïve common sense believes that what we find in the world is radically different and separate from us. Common sense is dualistic. The point of the long sequence of stages in the *Phenomenology* is to disabuse us of this prejudice and to lead us beyond it to the realm of science, which sees the numerous interconnections between subject and object. Hegel's account of our basic conceptions of the external world in the "Consciousness" chapter is intended to capture our basic intuitions and then to refute them. The intuitive views of common sense are exoteric, whereas the views of science are esoteric.

Perhaps the minority view is that Hegel's phenomenology forms the basis for the later phenomenological tradition or at least minimally is consistent with it.[37] At the most general level, it can be said that Hegel and the later phenomenologists share the basic intuition that philosophy should start with consciousness. They all share the Cartesian conviction that there is something primary about consciousness and our immediate experience that is important for philosophy.

A second, more complex, point of similarity is the reference to phenomenology as a science. This is a point of dogma for Husserl, who is insistent on this. In Hegel, the matter is more ambiguous. As has been seen, in the Introduction to the *Phenomenology of Spirit*, he does refer to phenomenology as a science. This seems to be what is implied in the original title of the work: *System of Science: Part One, The Phenomenology of Spirit*. But Hegel also seems to indicate that the phenomenological analysis is not, strictly speaking, a science in its own right but rather a preparation for science. Here one might recall his reference to the *Phenomenology* as a ladder that one must climb in order to reach the level of science (PhG 14–15; see also EL §25). This is a complicated and disputed issue in Hegel scholarship.[38] In any case, there is somewhere here a common point with Husserl's conception. Husserl is also concerned to see phenomenology as something fundamental that provides the groundwork or foundation for science. Of course, this is just a question of common terminology, but the real issue remains open: How do they understand the word "science"? It is clear that they have quite different views on this matter.

A third basic point of continuity is that both Hegel and the later phenomenologists want to focus on what is given in experience and avoid any talk of what is beyond or outside experience. They see themselves as concerned primarily with appearances and conceive the world as something that is "for consciousness" in contrast to something in itself. Or put differently, whatever is in itself is in itself for consciousness. They thus share a common aim of attaining the truth about reality from the experiences themselves. Spiegelberg's objection that Husserl is concerned with an epistemological problem whereas Hegel is concerned with an ontological one is highly dubious.[39] Commentators have long read the *Phenomenology of Spirit* as a complex epistemology or transcendental philosophy in contrast to the earlier metaphysical readings.[40] There is clearly an epistemological agenda in Hegel's account since the point is to demonstrate, via the experience of the natural consciousness, the necessary relation of subject to object and to reveal the many ways in which objectivity is determined by the subject. It is thus a mistake to conceive of Hegel's phenomenological project as primarily metaphysical.

An objection can be made to Spiegelberg's claim that Hegel, in contrast to Husserl, is not interested in determining the essences of things based on a phenomenological analysis, and in this we can find another point of similarity.[41] Hegel's point is that the individual stages of the *Phenomenology* are intended to represent specific conceptions of objects, that is, their essences. However, this is something that is always changing as natural consciousness progresses. At the stage of consciousness, it is the object sphere that is considered to be the essence or the truth in contrast to what is regarded as mere appearance. By contrast, at the stage of self-consciousness, it is the subject or the human mind that is considered to be the essence.[42] It misses the point to claim that Hegel's specific treatment of the object model as an essence or substance with properties (in the "Perception" chapter) exhausts this concept. Hegel continues to use the term "essence" in his subsequent analyses, and it is clear that he takes this to be something that is common to any theory of epistemology insofar as the goal is to determine what the true nature of things is.

Most works on the topic of the present chapter end with some kind of overview like the one presented here of the similarities and differences between Hegel and the later tradition of phenomenology. As has been seen, these are both numerous and complex. It is thus difficult to come down definitely with an unqualified statement about whether Hegel can be rightly considered a member of the phenomenological tradition or if he was simply doing something else. But at a minimum it can be claimed that his account of phenomenology has enough in common with the basic premises of that tradition that he deserved more careful consideration than Husserl ever gave him.[43]

Notes

1. The term "phenomenology" had been used previously, but it referred to something quite different, namely, a theory of illusion. See Herbert Spiegelberg, *The Phenomenological Movement: A Historical Interpretation*, vols. 1–2, 2nd ed. (The Hague: Martinus Nijhoff, 1976); vols. 1, 11. See also Johannes Hoffmeister's account of the term in the preface to his edition of the *Phenomenology*: *Phänomenologie des Geistes*, ed. Johannes Hoffmeister (Hamburg: Felix Meiner, 1952), vii–xvii.

2. See Frank M. Kirkland, "Husserl and Hegel: A Historical and Religious Encounter," *Journal of the British Society for Phenomenology* 16, no. 1 (1985): 70–87; Alphonse De Waelhens, "Phénoménologie husserlienne et Phénoménologie hégélienne," *Revue Philosophique de Louvain* 52, no. 34 (1954): 234–49; Jean Ladrière, "Hegel, Husserl, and Reason Today," *Modern Schoolman* 37, no. 3 (1959): 171–95; Quentin Lauer, "Phenomenology: Hegel and Husserl," in *Beyond Epistemology: New Studies in the Philosophy of Hegel*, ed. Frederick G. Weiss (The Hague: Martinus Nijhoff, 1975), 174–96; Leo Rauch, "Hegel's *Phenomenology of Spirit* as a Phenomenological Project," *Thought* 56, no. 222 (1981): 328–41; Spiegelberg, *The Phenomenological Movement: A Historical Interpretation*, vols. 1, 12–15; Michael Theunissen, "Begriff und Realität. Hegels Aufhebung des metaphysischen Wahrheitsbegriffs," in *Seminar: Dialektik in der Philosophie Hegels*, ed. Rolf-Peter Horstmann (Frankfurt am Main: Suhrkamp, 1978), 334–37; Dieter Henrich, "Über die Grundlagen von Husserls Kritik der Philosophischen Tradition," *Philosophische Rundschau* 6, nos. 1–2 (1958): 1–26; and Tanja Staehler, *Hegel, Husserl and the Phenomenology of Historical Worlds* (London: Rowman & Littlefield, 2019).

3. See Spiegelberg, *The Phenomenological Movement: A Historical Interpretation*, vol. 1, 13–14; and Quentin Lauer, "Phenomenology: Hegel and Husserl," 174.

4. See David Ciavatta, "Merleau-Ponty and Hegel: Meaning and its Expression in History," in *The Palgrave Handbook of German Idealism and Existentialism*, ed. Jon Stewart (Basingstoke: Palgrave Macmillan, 2020), 473–498; David Ciavatta, "Embodied Meaning in Hegel and Merleau-Ponty," *Hegel Bulletin* 38, no. 1 (2017): 45–66; Bruce Baugh, "Hegel and Sartre: The Search for Totality," in *The Palgrave Handbook of German Idealism and Existentialism*, 499–521; and Christopher M. Fry, *Sartre and Hegel: The Variations of an Enigma in "L'être et le Néant"* (Bonn: Bouvier, 1988).

5. Maurice Merleau-Ponty, "Hegel's Existentialism," in *Sense and Non-Sense*, trans. Hubert Dreyfus and Patricia Allen Dreyfus (Evanston, IL: Northwestern University Press, 1964), 63–70.

6. See Jon Stewart, "The Architectonic of Hegel's *Phenomenology of Spirit*," *Philosophy and Phenomenological Research* 55, no. 4 (1995): 747–76; Theodore Haering, "Entstehungsgeschichte der *Phänomenologie des Geistes*," in *Verhandlungen des III. Internationalen Hegel Kongresses 1933*, ed. Baltus Wigersma

(Haarlem: N/VH.D. Tjeenk Willink & Zn. and Tübingen: J. C. B. Mohr, 1934), 118–36; and Otto Pöggeler, "Die Komposition der *Phänomenologie des Geistes*," in *Hegel-Tage Royaumont 1964. Beiträge zur Phänomenologie des Geistes*, ed. Hans-Georg Gadamer (Bonn: Bouvier, 1966 [*Hegel-Studien*, Beiheft 3]), 27–74.

7. For a detailed overview of the structure of the work, see Jon Stewart, *The Unity of Hegel's Phenomenology of Spirit: A Systematic Interpretation* (Evanston, IL: Northwestern University Press, 2000). See also Jon Stewart, "The Architectonic of Hegel's *Phenomenology of Spirit*," 747–76.

8. Although it might be argued that given his more restricted usage in the *Encyclopedia*, which is the later, more mature work, he in fact did not intend the term "phenomenology" to be applied to these more complex social and historical phenomena.

9. For useful analyses of this text, see Kenneth R. Westphal, "Hegel's Solution to the Dilemma of the Criterion," *History of Philosophy Quarterly* 5, no. 2 (1988): 173–88; Kenley R. Dove, "Hegel's Phenomenological Method," *The Review of Metaphysics* 23, no. 4 (1970): 615–41; Andreas Graeser, *Einleitung zur Phänomenologie des Geistes, Kommentar* (Stuttgart: Reclam, 1988); Hans-Jürgen Krahl, *Erfahrung des Bewußtseins. Kommentare zu Hegels Einleitung der Phänomenologie des Geistes und Exkurse zur materialistischen Erkenntnistheorie* (Frankfurt a.M.: Materialis Verlag, 1979); Gerhard Krüger, "Die dialektische Erfahrung des natürlichen Bewußtseins bei Hegel," in *Hermeneutik und Dialektik*, ed. Rüdiger Bubner, Konrad Cramer, and Reiner Wiehl (Tübingen: Mohr, 1970), 285–303; Werner Marx, *Hegel's Phenomenology of Spirit, Its Point and Purpose: A Commentary on the Preface and Introduction*, trans. Peter Heath (New York: Harper and Row, 1975); Alexis Philonenko, *Lecture de la Phénoménologie de Hegel. Préface—Introduction* (Paris: Librarie Philosophique Joseph Vrin, 1993); Georges Van Riet, "Y-a-t-il un chemin vers la vérite? À propos de l'introduction à la *Phénoménologie de l'esprit* de Hegel," *Revue philosophique de Louvain* 62 (1964): 466–76; and Michael Theunissen, "Begriff und Realität. Hegels Aufhebung des metaphysischen Wahrheitsbegriffs," 324–59.

10. See Heribert Boeder, "Das natürliche Bewußtsein," *Hegel-Studien* 12 (1977): 157–78.

11. See "Phenomenology of Mind: Consciousness," in *Hegel's Philosophy of Mind, Being Part Three of the Encyclopedia of the Philosophical Sciences*, trans. William Wallace and A. V. Miller (Oxford: Clarendon Press, 1971), §§413–439, pp. 153–78.

12. Ibid., §387, p. 25.

13. Ibid., §387, Zusatz, p. 27.

14. Ibid. Translation modified.

15. Ibid., §415, p. 156.

16. Although he does not mention it explicitly, Hegel clearly has in mind Kant's doctrine of the transcendental unity of apperception from the *Critique of Pure*

Reason. According to this view, although we never experience ourselves as a unified subject in experience, we must presuppose such a subject where all of our perceptions are unified since otherwise they would be atomic and disparate, and objectivity would be impossible.

17. Husserl, "Philosophy as Rigorous Science," in *Phenomenology and the Crisis of Philosophy*, trans. Quentin Lauer (New York: Harper, 1965), 76–78.
18. Ibid., 76.
19. Ibid., 76. See also C, 191–92.
20. Husserl, "Philosophy as Rigorous Science," 77.
21. Spiegelberg, *The Phenomenological Movement: A Historical Interpretation*, vol. 1, p. 13.
22. Eugen Fink, *Hegel. Phänomenologische Interpretationen der "Phänomenologie des Geistes,"* ed. Jann Holl (Frankfurt am Main: Vittorio Klostermann, 1977).
23. Later published as Alexandre Kojève, *Introduction à la lecture de Hegel. Leçons sur la Phénoménologie de l'Esprit professées de 1933 à 1939 à l'École des Hautes-Études*, ed. Raymond Queneau (Paris: Gallimard, 1947); translated as *Introduction to the Reading of Hegel: Lectures on the Phenomenology of Spirit*, ed. Allan Bloom, trans. James H. Nichols, Jr. (Ithaca: Cornell University Press, 1980).
24. Jean Hyppolite, *Genése et structure de la Phénoménologie de l'Esprit de Hegel* (Paris: Aubier, 1946); translated as *Genesis and Structure of Hegel's Phenomenology of Spirit*, trans. Samuel Cherniak and John Heckman (Evanston, IL: Northwestern University Press, 1974).
25. See Baugh, "Hegel and Sartre: The Search for Totality," in *The Palgrave Handbook of German Idealism and Existentialism*, 499–521; and Gilles Marmasse, "The Hegelian Legacy in Kojève and Sartre," in *Hegel's Thought in Europe: Currents, Crosscurrents and Undercurrents*, ed. Lisa Herzog (London: Palgrave Macmillan, 2013), 239–49.
26. Here Sartre draws on Jean Wahl's *Le malheur de la conscience dans la philosophie de Hegel* (Paris: Rieder, 1929).
27. Maurice Merleau-Ponty, "Hegel's Existentialism," 63–70.
28. Ibid., 65.
29. Merleau-Ponty, "Marxism and Philosophy," in *Sense and Non-Sense*, 131–33.
30. Merleau-Ponty, "Hegel's Existentialism," 66.
31. Ibid., 67–68.
32. Spiegelberg, *The Phenomenological Movement: A Historical Interpretation*, vol. 1, p. 12.
33. This is an important point in Lauer's "Phenomenology: Hegel and Husserl," 175, 182.
34. Ibid., 176.
35. See Spiegelberg, *The Phenomenological Movement: A Historical Interpretation*, vol. 1, p. 14.
36. See ibid., vol. 1, p. 14.

37. See Rauch, "Hegel's *Phenomenology of Spirit* as a Phenomenological Project," 328–41. A promising recent attempt to see the projects of Hegel and Husserl as complementary can be found in Tanja Staehler's *Hegel, Husserl and the Phenomenology of Historical Worlds.*

38. See, for example, Horst Henning Ottmann, *Das Scheitern einer Einleitung in Hegels Philosophie. Eine Analyse der Phänomenologie des Geistes* (Munich and Salzburg: Verlag Anton Pustet, 1973); and Hans Friedrich Fulda, *Das Problem einer Einleitung in Hegels Wissenschaft der Logik* (Frankfurt a.M.: Klostermann, 1965).

39. See Spiegelberg, *The Phenomenological Movement: A Historical Interpretation,* vol. 1, p. 14.

40. See, for example, Robert B. Pippin, *Hegel's Idealism: The Satisfactions of Self-Consciousness* (Cambridge: Cambridge University Press, 1989); and Jon Stewart, *The Unity of Hegel's Phenomenology of Spirit: A Systematic Interpretation.*

41. Spiegelberg, *The Phenomenological Movement: A Historical Interpretation,* vol. 1, p. 14.

42. E.g., PhS, 59, 67, 81. *Hegel's Philosophy of Mind, Being Part Three of the Encyclopedia of the Philosophical Sciences,* §414, p. 155.

43. This work was produced at the Institute of Philosophy, Slovak Academy of Sciences. It was supported by the Agency VEGA under the project Synergy and Conflict as Sources of Cultural Identity, No. 2/0025/20. This chapter has been improved by the kind help of Jaroslava Vydrová and Hynek Janoušek.

22

On the Mutations of the Concept: Phenomenology, Conceptual Change, and the Persistence of Hegel in Merleau-Ponty's Thought

Stephen H. Watson

Maurice Merleau-Ponty was often occupied with the work of classical German thought—and especially Hegel—throughout his career. In his final writings, those commitments become tempered and transformed by a more expansive investigation of Hegel's post-Kantian predecessors, especially Schelling. Even so, he renewed his interest in Hegel, lecturing on him in his final semester at the Collège de France in 1961.

At the outset Merleau-Ponty interpreted Hegel through the existentialist lenses that characterized French philosophy in the late thirties and forties. He is rightly associated with those like Lacan, Queneau, or Bataille who attended Alexandre Kojève's 1930s lectures on Hegel's *Phenomenology of Spirit*. To this, as is often noted, we should add the general context of Hegel's reception in Paris. This includes, for example, Jean Wahl's study emphasizing Hegel's account of the unhappy consciousness or Alexandre Koyré's early interpretations on Hegel's Jena period or his research detailing the long history of Hegel scholarship in France. In addition, we will need to include Jean Hyppolite's more recent scholarly interpretations. But in Merleau-Ponty's case, we encounter, as will become evident, an even broader range of interpretive strains, not standardly associated with his thought. These include, for

S. H. Watson (✉)
Department of Philosophy, University of Notre Dame, Notre Dame, IN, USA
e-mail: swatson@nd.edu

© The Author(s), under exclusive license to Springer Nature
Switzerland AG 2021
C. D. Coe (eds.), *The Palgrave Handbook of German Idealism and Phenomenology*,
Palgrave Handbooks in German Idealism,
https://doi.org/10.1007/978-3-030-66857-0_22

example, strains as distinct as Breton's surrealist interpretation of Hegel and Marx, or Cassirer's expressionist, neo-Hegelian articulation of the "sublimations" of idealism and empiricism. While Cassirer's influence is important in issues of philosophy of language or scientific rationality, for the latter we would also need to include his teacher, Brunschvicg, or his ongoing dialogue with Bachelard (or later, Canguilhem) whose accounts of experimental scientific dialectic appeared beginning in the thirties. Though at most tacit in his early writing, they would become more explicitly paired with Merleau-Ponty's own "reading" of science, one of the catalysts for the ontological investigations in his final years (N 206).[1] Throughout, or, at least by 1947, when Merleau-Ponty's interest in Hegel had also become intense, Canguilhem, a figure more proximate to Merleau-Ponty than is sometimes thought, could simply assert in an article on "Hegel in France" that "contemporary philosophical thought is dominated by Hegelianism."[2] He did so, however, like many of these interpreters, including Merleau-Ponty, also insisting that we take our distance from Hegel. Yet as thinkers from Brunschvicg to Hyppolite would continually insist, in this he had become to them something of what Aristotle was to the Middle Ages.[3]

This chapter will be devoted to the itinerary of classical German thought, and especially Hegel, in Merleau-Ponty's thought. I begin by examining Merleau-Ponty's initial use of Hegel's systematic and metaphysical ideas in phenomenological analyses of behavior (*comportement*) and perception. Next, I examine Merleau-Ponty's role in controversies regarding the existentialists' interpretation and objections to Hegel's system. I trace his attempts to surmount antinomies between subjectivity and system that emerged in the existentialist's anthropological reading of Hegel. Here Merleau-Ponty focused on linguistics and more general analyses of institution and expression. Finally, I will view the renewed role that classical German philosophy, including Schelling and Hegel, played in his final works. Still reflecting these interests, his writings and lectures engaged in a wide-ranging dialogue with contemporary aesthetics, science, and philosophy, culminating in an attempt to formulate a new ontology.

Beginnings

Merleau-Ponty's initial interest in Hegel is manifest in his first book, *The Structure of Behavior*. Completed in 1938, it already obliquely reveals Merleau-Ponty's initial existentialist commitments. It also reveals, in some respects even more, significant influences of the 1930s on his work, e.g.,

Scheler's account of personal embodiment and its omission in the critical tradition, and would not incorrectly be read as a work of philosophical anthropology in Scheler's vein (which it cites). It moreover reveals a first reference to what would become a lifelong dialogue with Hyppolite. Indeed the persistence of Hegel in Merleau-Ponty's work, as will become evident, is equally facilitated by the persistence of Hyppolite himself. *The Structure of Behavior* cited Hyppolite's 1938 article on life and the consciousness of life that emphasized the dialectic of infinity in Hegel's Jena philosophy, one with portentous consequences for phenomenology's intuitionism. Here Hyppolite claimed, "we witness the subordination (*se subordonner*) of intuition to the concept, the development of a creative consciousness and the realization of the spirit solely through the medium of its own history."[4] Yet, while Hyppolite (like Koyré) had pointed out Hegel's "biological dialectic" in the Jena philosophy of life, he argued that "it is in the cultural sciences that the dialectic remains a fruitful method."[5]

Merleau-Ponty's first work sought to integrate Hegel's dialectic into his analysis of behavior. He claimed that human behavior could not be reduced to a crude reflexology nor could it be sufficiently grasped by a critical philosophy reducing behavior to reflection. Citing Hegel's claim that "the concept is only the interior of nature," Merleau-Ponty argued that life involves increasingly more complicated dialectical articulations of organization and reorganization (SB 162). Early on, as Canguilhem would in his 1943 *The Normal and the Pathological*, Merleau-Ponty criticized causal or behaviorist accounts for being conceptually incoherent; both agreed that the vital order could neither be atomistically reduced to causal reflexes nor projected into a teleologically fixed end. Canguilhem himself (who would appeal to the same authors, especially Goldstein, noting his Hegelian lineage) would speak similarly of a convergence between their accounts—even though he had only been able to read Merleau-Ponty when his own book was in press.[6] Both also integrated recent philosophy into their interpretations; Rabinow, for example, spoke in this regard of Canguilhem's "not so latent existentialism."[7] But Merleau-Ponty did so explicitly in a footnote added when his book was at the printers: "In our opinion, when Watson spoke of behavior he had in mind what others have called *existence*; but the new notion could receive its philosophical status only if causal or mechanical thinking were abandoned for dialectical thinking" (SB 226n3). Watson's "achievement" was to overcome psychology as a science of conscious facts but without being able to grasp it as a structure of behavior itself, i.e., as *meaningful* behavior (SB 4, 182). Consciousness cannot be explained without a body but the body can only be grasped as the phenomenon of this consciousness, "but also without it being anywhere pure idea," i.e., disembodied. This was "the truth of naturalism": hence, the necessity of their dialectical explication (SB 207). This dialectic becomes more and more complicated as the vital and human orders emerge, eluding modern naturalist commitments as much as traditional metaphysics; "Man is not a rational animal" (SB 181). We will need a more concrete account.

Following Goldstein, vital systems are said to equilibrate themselves in respect to given forces of a milieu; the animal organism articulates a relatively stable milieu corresponding to ongoing need and instinct. Here we can also see the early formulations of the pairing of Hegel and Husserl that would become part of Merleau-Ponty's continuing itinerary. For the human dialectic, he chooses the Hegelian word "work" instead of "action" in which humans transform (*transforme*) physical and living nature: "between man and the physico-chemical stimuli, [work] projects 'use objects (*Gebrauchobjekts*)' [now explicitly citing Husserl]—clothing, tables, gardens—and 'cultural objects'—books, musical instruments, language—which constitute the proper milieu of humans and facilitate new cycles of behavior" (SB 162). He also noted the ambiguity at stake, stating that such practices involve "a principle of bondage," a term also not without Hegelian overtones in Kojève's emphasis of the *Phenomenology of Spirit*'s master/slave dialectic: in order "to orient oneself in relation to the possible" the human dialectic "imprisons" itself in the cultural structures in order to acquire meaning if only to reject and surpass it (SB 176). Thus: "For thought, language is at the same time a principle of slavery, since it is interposed between things and thought, and a principle of liberty, since one rids oneself of a prejudice by giving it its name" (SB 245n95). He understood the Freudian account of the libidinal economy similarly as the "pretext" of human action (SB 180). In both cases, what facilitates surpassing the limits in question was, again to speak Husserlian, imaginative variation, the emergence (or not) of "varying points of view" (SB 175).

Still, the ambiguity surrounding such expressive works continues. Language does not exhaust all meaning, even if (as here he references Cassirer's expressivism) it is necessary to the "constitution of the perceived world" (SB 169). In addition, he articulated an extralinguistic experience on the basis of Gestalt psychology—though he claims again that the "notion of 'Gestalt' led us back to its Hegelian meaning, that is, to the concept before it has become conscious of itself" (SB 210). Here he insists, at odds with Hegel's account of the contradictions of sense certainty, precisely because it remained locked in the oppositions of sense and certainty, that perception is more complicated:

The sensible mass in which I live when I stare at a sector of the field without trying to recognize it, the "this" which my consciousness wordlessly intends, is not a signification or an ideal, although subsequently it can serve as base for acts of logical explicitation and verbal expression. Already when I name the perceived *as* a chair or a tree, I substitute the subsumption under a concept for the experience of a fleeting reality (*réalitè fuyante*); even when I pronounce the word "this," I already relate a singular and lived existence to the essence of lived existence. But these acts of expression or reflection intend an original text which cannot be deprived of meaning. (SB 211)

Hegel had identified the concept and reference, sense and sensibility; indeed "*Sinn*" (like "*Aufhebung*") is identified in this respect as a "*Wundebare Wort*" in this speculative facilitation.[8] Unlike logicist or inferentialist interpretations of Hegel, Merleau-Ponty's interpretation of the dialectic is a dialectic of prelogical tensions or "ambiguity," an indeterminate significative wholism (or *Gestalt*) of interdependent terms (e.g., subject and object, body and world). Through the course of the dialectic of experience, to use Hegel's term, their "fluidity" would be explored, further transformed and refined.

The result, he already argued, requires a "reformulation of the notion of consciousness," articulating an intentional experience that is not reducible to reflection: "an intentional network of significative intentions which are sometimes clear to themselves and sometimes, on the contrary lived rather than known" (SB 169, 173). Rather than being reduced to judgment or reflective consciousness, the pre-reflective exploration of the perceived world is thus "unfinished," the rational clarification of its explication, singular and problematic. Moreover, to use Husserl's model that Merleau-Ponty invokes, citing *Ideas I*, it involves a field of profiles or aspects (*Abschattungen*) unfolded through time, the latter "not treated as the degradation of true knowledge which would grasp the totality of the possible aspects of the object all at once" (SB 186). This field of adumbrations provides the hinge between past experience (or cultural setting) and its future unfolding and transformation. The "ecceitas of knowledge by profiles" is thus an experience never exhausted because never fully conceptually possessed or ultimately adequated (SB 214). Here determining reflection never undoes the ambiguity of what Hegel called "positing" and "external or presupposing reflection," a facticity defying the determinacy of strict or intentional correlation.[9] "The perceived is grasped in an indivisible manner and 'in itself' (*en soi*), that is, as gifted with an interior which I will never have finished exploring and as 'for me' (*pour moi*), that is, as given 'in person' through its momentary aspects" (SB 186).

This facticity, the structures of body and culture are thus inescapable but again not ultimately determining; their meaning (*sens*) is inextricably open to interpretation and transformation. Still, while noting that nature can be experienced as devoid of the human, as in itself, indeed he connects such experience to surrealist poetry, he nonetheless posits its anthropocentric reference: "nature is perhaps grasped initially only as the minimum of stage stetting (*mis en scène*) which is necessary for the performance of a human drama (*drame humaine*)" (SB 168). What is left to be grasped is the delineation of these two "histories," articulating what he will ultimately call the bond or "flesh" that binds together nature and culture. And here a final footnote to Husserl's *Formal and Transcendental Logic* in the closing pages states as much:

> Nevertheless, there would be a place for investigating more thoroughly the distinction of our "natural body" which is always already there, already constituted for consciousness, and our "cultural body" which is the sedimentation of its spontaneous acts. The problem is posed by Husserl when he distinguishes "original passivity" and "secondary passivity." (SB 249n54)

This promissory note regarding Husserl would begin to be fulfilled in Merleau-Ponty's second thesis, the 1945 *Phenomenology of Perception*. The lived encounter with the environment explored in *The Structure of Behavior* would now explicitly be articulated as the operative, habitual, sedimented, and historical intentionality that underlies our perceptual being-in-the-world. But again the claim is that perceptions arising out of operative intentionality provide "the original text" that more precise forms of knowledge attempt to translate (PhP lxxxii, 12).

Still, this problem of transcendental genesis rebounds on what he claimed to be Husserl's lingering neo-Kantianism, rendering it further historical. Hyppolite aptly argued in this regard that Merleau-Ponty's *Phenomenology* admitted history into the existentialist account and thus admitted Hegel's truth.[10] But he did so by integrating it with Husserl's account of the sedimented history. At one point, he claimed, against such "intellectualism," that, until phenomenology has become genetic phenomenology, articulating or authenticating its emergence from its milieu, a retreat into causal thought and naturalism would remain justified (PhP 128). Husserl's chief discovery was not static intentional correlation with an object; in Merleau-Ponty's mind, this was largely a Cartesian concept operative throughout modern philosophy. Rather Husserl's account is claimed to have taken up again Kant's extension in the third *Critique*—that is, a broadly phenomenological account of the teleology of consciousness, precisely the one Hegel had also emphasized in the *Differenzschrift*.[11] But Husserl's phenomenological teleology (like Kant's) also articulates a lived pre-reflective milieu, a harmony between myself and the *haecceity* of the other or the sensible "which is without any concept" (PhP lxxv, lxxxi). Here Husserl's account of intentionality merges, for Merleau-Ponty, with Heidegger's analysis of Dasein's being-in-the-world: beyond the correlationism of static intuition, a "phenomenology of genesis" exhibits both the "opacity and transcendence of the world" (PhP lxxxii, lxxv). We require, accordingly, a more radical account of reflection than reflective analysis. Like time itself, genesis is not the act of a subject but "the movement of a life that unfolds and the only way to actualize this life is to live it" (PhP 446). As such, we confront what Canguilhem will call the meaning or "the orig- inality of life," the internal (and undecomposable) relation of the organism to its milieu.[12] For Merleau-Ponty, the task of a radical reflection in relation to it "consists paradoxically in recovering the unreflective experience of the world in order to import the attitude of verification and reflective operations back into this experience…" (PhP 251). Nonetheless, Husserl's intuitionism and what Hyppolite described as Hegel's "subordination of intuition to the concept," accordingly, could not be more at odds.

Significant for Merleau-Ponty's interpretation of Hegel, however, is that he claims that the origin of lived intentionality of Husserl and Heidegger's philosophy is tacitly already at work in Hegel. Phenomenology itself is interpreted as the culmination of a manner of thinking that originates in Hegel's dialectic. Indeed the ultimate articuleme for lived experience in the *Phenomenology* is through Hegel.

[T]he synthesis of the in-itself and the for-itself that brings about Hegelian freedom has its truth. In a sense, it is the very definition of existence; it is accomplished at each moment before our eye in the phenomenon of presence, only it must be immediately started over and does not suppress our finitude. By taking up a present, I again take hold of my past and transform it. (PhP 481–82)

Healthy behavior is not just adaption to milieu but its transformation, in introducing a new or figured meaning (*sens figuré*) into the environment. As Canguilhem will argue, what Goldstein saw was that health is not linked to a single norm but to a plurality, a result of changing demands of the vital environment.[13] In the human order, Merleau-Ponty claimed, such variance is linked to the transformation of work: it involves knowing not only how to follow a norm but when to change it. In *The Structure of Behavior*, this very transformation and its plurality was linked to behavior understood as existence and ultimately to transcendence itself. While as has been seen, tran- scendence was linked to the opacity of the world, ultimately such opacity is overcome by the truth of Hegelian freedom: "'Transcendence' is the name we shall give to this movement by which existence takes up for itself and transforms a de facto situation" (PhP 173). It was the movement by which "chance is transformed into reason" and, as emerging from the milieu of its "de facto situation," never escapes its bonds to facticity and finitude (PhP 173). This was doubtless true of his most explicit early reading of Hegel in *Sense and Non-Sense*, an article entitled "Hegel's Existentialism." Here the dialectic of Hegel's Absolute is transformed into "a way of life (*manière de vivre*)" and is viewed less as a philosophy that "has arrived at a consciousness equal to its spontaneous life" than a "militant philosophy" (SNS 64).

Existentialist Hegel

This writing can also be read as a response to Hyppolite, in particular a discussion of the concept of existence in Hegelian phenomenology. Here again, he begins by delineating the itinerary of modern thought:

> All the great philosophical ideas of the past century—the philosophies of Marx and Nietzsche, phenomenology, German existentialism, and psychoanalysis—had their beginnings in Hegel; it was he who started the attempt to explore the irrational and integrate it into an expanded reason which remains the task of our century. He is the inventor of that Reason, broader than understanding, which can respect the variety and singularity of individual consciousness, civilization, ways of thinking, and historical contingency but which nevertheless does not give up the attempt to master them in order to guide them to their own truth. (SNS 63)

Merleau-Ponty however sought in this expanded sense of reason, one again capable of integrating the variety and dispersion of life and reflection, "a new classicism," indeed an organic civilization, "while maintaining the sharpest sense of subjectivity" (SNS 63). And therein, in the significance of the finite itself, arose the argument concerning the existentialist's appropriation of Hegel. While *The Structure of Behavior* had focused on Hyppolite's account of life, integrating consciousness into nature, here the focus of Hyppolite's own argument concerns the status of individuality itself and, in particular, the existentialist's appropriation of Heidegger's emphasis on the individualization in being-toward-death. Deliberately eschewing the existentialists' account of schism between the in-itself and for-itself, Hyppolite instead focused his analysis on the anxiety of death, hence upon the legacy of Heidegger. He argued that Hegel had transcended this naïve conception of consciousness and life, again, through the infinity of dialectic itself. Hegel did so, on the one hand, by integrating life and death, and on the other hand, the dialectic of consciousness of self and other, in both senses generating a history of the Subject "not limited to the historicity of a particular being."[14] Instead individual existences "are interrelated in the history which they make and which as a concrete universality is what judges them and transcends them."[15] Such a "Subject" transcends individuality and the unconscious in the same moment that it "subordinates intuition." Against Kojève's anthropological emphasis in Hegel, here Hyppolite emphasized the speculative resolution of the relation between immanence and transcendence in philosophy of religion, indeed what he called elsewhere Hegel's "heroic effort to reduce vertical transcendence to horizontal transcendence."[16] But Hyppolite notes further that "this God that dies in man while man raises him to the divine through history that is his judge" may well be, as Kierkegaard thought, "the very contrary of existentialist philosophy."[17]

Merleau-Ponty responded that, unlike Sartre, for whom the unhappy contradictions of the for-itself and the in-itself have no remedy (thus "truncating the dialectic"), Hegel then, on Hyppolite's reading, seemingly "makes possible a Communist philosophy of the party or a philosophy of the Church rather than a philosophy of individual such as existentialism" (SNS 69). Elsewhere, consistent with his more anthropological reading, Merleau-Ponty claimed such teleologies or theodicies must be confronted: Aristotle or St. Thomas with Descartes' or Pascal's blindness or incomprehensibility: "Perhaps in the end the religion of the God-made-man arrives by an unavoidable dialectic at an anthropology and not a theology" (SNS 76). Instead the final word would involve, like the final essay of *Sense and Non-sense*, not death or history but man as its hero (SNS 187).

Hence, his disagreement with Hyppolite: what Merleau-Ponty took to be "the nonsystematic existentialism" of Hegel's *Phenomenology of Mind* culminated not in a Subject that transcends individuality but "in a genuine reconciliation between men" (SNS 65). It was this ultimate reconciliation, this "humanism in extension," understood "as the power of man over nature and reconciliation of man with man" that he also sought in Marx in the concrete realization of praxis (HT 166, 176). This perhaps would be his closest proximity to Kojève's anthropological reading of Hegel. But it remained unclear how the logic of ambiguous or unfinished "extension" in the endless exploration of the world was itself to be reconciled with the language and the *Aufhebung* of such reconciliation itself or, as such, how far Merleau-Ponty's reading of Hegel had moved beyond the more metaphysical Hegel he criticized. Moreover, it remained unclear how Hegel, existentialist or not, could be reconciled with Husserl's pre-predicative or passive synthesis of the lived world, how the transcendence linked to existential freedom, the truth of the in-itself and for-itself was to be linked to the opacity, haecceity, and transcendence of the world. Indeed Hyppolite later suggested that the *Phenomenology of Perception*'s elusive synthesis of Heidegger and Husserl led in two possible directions: one to the truth of perception and the other to the origin of the perceived world.[18] The question seemed to be whether phenomenology or ontology was more fundamental, a question that would increasingly occupy him (and had been pressed by Hyppolite as early as the 1946 defense of Merleau-Ponty's thesis): whether he were inevitably led to questions of totality and "the very being of all meaning" (PP 40). It would become increasingly clear to Merleau-Ponty, too, that the phenomenology of perception seemed to "imply" an ontology, albeit one lacking such totalization (LMS 46).

The Preface to *Sense and Non-Sense* seemed more nuanced—and precisely in alluding to the cultural studies in which Hyppolite claimed Hegel still held effect. Noting again the revolt of life's immediacy against reason," Merleau-Ponty claims, "we need a new idea of reason" (SNS 3). Once more, we would need then to regain the realm of the lived, understood as aspects of reason that are unreflective and "irrational," understood in the sense of the "alogical," to use Scheler's term. But here he now adds that, rather than simply extending the rational to include the lived in order to articulate a new classicism, the situation may be more complex: our classical models for reason may no longer obtain: "Mathematical entities can only be grasped by oblique procedures, improvised methods as opaque as an unknown mineral. Instead of an intelligible world, there are radiant nebulae separated by expanses of darkness. The world of culture is as discontinuous as the other world, and it too has its secret mutations" (SNS 4).

Still, more metaphor than concept at this point, it is not clear what such "mutation" entails. A radio address presented soon thereafter would in fact contrast the modern and classical worlds. Even *The Structure of Behavior* declared that "All the sciences situate themselves in a 'complete' and real world without realizing that perceptual experience is constituting with respect to this world" (SB 219). But modern science has refined this view: "We think of all scientific work as provisional and approximate, whereas Descartes believed he could deduce, once and for all time, the laws governing the collision of bodies from the divine attributes" (WP 197). This might bring Merleau-Ponty more proximate to Bachelard's experimental dialectic—a science, in contrast with a metaphysical dialectic, no longer envisioned simply as a return to origins but in terms of imagination, open extension and continual refinement.[19] Again, Hyppolite thought as much in a later paper describing the confluence of interest in Husserl and Hegel in France, also echoing Bachelard's or Koyrè's terms: "What we have refused in Hegel, was the dialectic as a constructive procedure."[20]

In a 1946 interview Merleau-Ponty similarly speaks of Hegel as already articulating an extended philosophy of the "human situation," but also described Brunschvicg as representing an "open" and non-"dogmatic" philosophy of science (P 66–67). Such of course would be equally true of his associates such as Bachelard, Cavaillès, or Canguilhem. Indeed Merleau-Ponty thought "the French school" of philosophy of science "confirmed" what he called the "primacy of perception," an unfinished "knowledge that cannot be closed in on itself, that is always approximate" (PP 19). Yet while Merleau-Ponty believed that modern science had shorn itself of the metaphysics of classical rationalism, he also insisted that more than modern science was available: modern "painting, poetry and philosophy have forged ahead boldly by presenting us with a very new and characteristically contemporary vision" of our lived world (WP 45). The task now was precisely deriving a philosophy capable of expressing this extension, one that brought the philosophy of language itself to the center of his research for next decade.

The problem this philosophically entailed was twofold. More than simply involving a broadening of reason to include the life anterior to it, he would need to provide the means and a form of philosophy to bring it to expression. He would initially have found this issue in Fink's *Sixth Cartesian Meditation*, which he had read in manuscript, and had met the author in 1939 in Louvain. Fink had stressed the problem of expressing the meaning of the *haecceities* of the lived world, in his terms, the problem of a transcendental language (which could only be analogically related to the natural language).[21] The classic concepts of transcendental philosophy would need to be refigured within phenomenology: "science," "constitution," "consciousness," "worldhood," "foundation," "being," etc., would not mean the same thing in Husserl and his followers as they had been in Kant's. New interpretations, and in some cases new terms, would need to be invented: here, too, meaning would need to be refigured. *Phenomenology of Perception* had devoted a good deal of space to the expressive capacities of language, but less by examining contemporary linguistics (as he had done in the case of psychology) than literary and poetic sources, comparing language (as he had the body's spontaneity) to a work of art (PhP 152). The Preface to the *Sense and Non-Sense* had once more insisted that "we are born into reason as to language," recalling *The Structure of Behavior*'s claim that first we are imprisoned in it.

Consistent with this, however, two projects reciprocally emerge, one outlining our historical dependence on the coherence and constraints of the natural language and one detailing the expressive capacity for linguistic and language-like (*langagière*) practices of creative transformation. By 1951, he declared, accordingly, the philosophy of language to belong to first philosophy (S 84). The first project, outlining our contingent dependence upon language, found its model in Merleau-Ponty's interpretation of Saussurian linguistics, especially in the diacritical account of linguistic terms. This again involved an indeterminate or "thick" holism of interdependent parts, with its distinction of language (*la langue*) and speech (*la parole*). Merleau-Ponty again interpreted this distinction dialectically. Saussure outlines in this regard, he states, the presence of the individual in the institution and of the institution in the individual as evidenced in linguistic change (IPP 55). But as his initial lectures on Saussure evidence, the very concept of institution in this regard renders the origin (*Ursprung*) of language problematic. There is an "Ursprung" only in the sense of springing-forth and surpassing: again, transformation (CAL 80–82). Expression continually reinstitutes the origin of language, but precisely in transforming it. At the same time, as the 1953 inaugural lecture at the *Collège de France* states, this entails "a rationality in the contingent" or "lived logic" that outlined "a conception of historical meaning beyond the opposition of things versus consciousness." In this, Saussure "could have sketched a new philosophy of history" (IPP 54–55). Expression emerges as a response to a world that is inherently intersubjective and a historical symbolism, a truth to be made (AD 200). This rationality conflicts with the totalizing rationality of absolute idealism, but it also conflicts with the constitutive and foundational pretension of the classical transcendental subject: language is constitutive of consciousness (CAL 50). It jibes, moreover, neither with immediacy, "the sharpest sense of subjectivity" of existential individuality, nor the transcendent development of the Hegelian Subject.

At the same time, however, it required an account of linguistic transformation. In 1951, he declared surrealism in this regard to be one of the constants of our time (S 234). Sartre had opposed the surrealists in claiming a strict opposition between the real and the imaginary, sign and signified. Merleau-Ponty had again argued for their dialectic, pointing out, following Blanchot, that surrealism's task was not simply a matter of chaos, but of liberation from linguistic convention, precisely in order to say the unsaid (S 233). In this, it sought a creative language everywhere, and literature in particular sought to transform the literal, drawing upon "the halo of signification words owe to their history and uses" (S 234). Surrealism, that is, is no longer invoked to articulate the "pre-human" world but the "sur-signification," or step-beyond the world of constituted expression (PW 144). The term itself again echoes

Bachelard's account of "surrationality" based again on the dialectical over-coming of the past: in such transformations, both authors sought to remain proximate to surrealism.[22]

Merleau-Ponty again also linked such expression to Kant's third *Critique*: here we depend less on possessed truths or fixed ideas than, like aesthetic monograms, novel meanings capable of generating possible readings, without necessarily rising to ultimately determinate ideas (WP 101). Beyond the determinate, such sur-signification articulates the tacit, unformulated, and nonthematized semantic polysemy upon which literary expression, for example, depends—yet still distinguishing it from non-sense (PW 144). The judgments at stake are "always conceived as an expression or truth of an experience in which the commerce of subjects with one another and with being was previously instituted" (AD 204). The result is a history of trans-formations, a matrix of ideas, or coherent deformations (S 77). Here again knowledge proceeds by "multiplying views"—still proximate to Husserl's imaginary variation—resulting, to use Merleau-Ponty's term, in a "reading" that reveals "conclusions that are provisional, open and justifiable (that is to say conditional)" (AD 10, 18). Moreover, again proximate to Bachelard's account of the rational as rectification of error, Merleau-Ponty states, "At best we rectify errors which occur along the way; but the new scheme is not immune to errors which will have to be rectified anew" (AD 22). But, for Merleau-Ponty, this history includes dialectical facts and adumbrative signifi-cations (once again Husserl's term) (AD 24). Indeed this had led Husserl "to the threshold of dialectical philosophy" (AD 138). Experience is no longer foundational but thoroughly historical and dialectical. Nor is it simply indi-vidual; the dialectic at stake involves an historical "interworld' with "several points of entry" (AD 200–204).

The "Flesh of History": On the Mutations of the Concept

All of this thus seems to have left not only Hegel, but much of Husserl's position behind. Merleau-Ponty already had criticized what he took to be the neo-Kantian and logicist tendencies in Husserl, for the sake of what he identified as his more "existentialism of the final period" (PhP 543n). Nonetheless, he emphasized the dialectical "mutations," previously flagged to be at work in cultural studies, to be at work in Husserl's own evolution. He focused first on Husserl's historical account of constitution or institution or *Stiftung* in the late writings of the *Crisis* period. In the phenomenologist's account of the reconstitution of historical rationality, Merleau-Ponty found another convergence with his reading of Saussure: both, according to Merleau-Ponty, involved the lived transformation of received meaning (S 105–106). Phenomenology was not simply a return to prelinguistic experience, but the exploration of language and institutions itself. *Stiftung* was less a "*fondation*," as he originally translated it, than—consistent with his interpretation of Hegel—a matter of transformation (*Nachstiftung*).[23] Denying that language simply occurs as a matter of chance or destiny, Hegel's "behind the back of consciousness," he read Saussure's model as an account of historically contingent, yet still intentionally motivated expression (CAL 101). Such a dialectic would always contain a double reference, to the "readings" of "mute being" whose experience is interrogated and to the historical tractable (*maniable*) meaning which it is derived from it (IPP 19).

The result however would overturn his hopes to formulate a new classicism. The latter united his "anti-systematic" readings of Hegel with existentialist anthropology, in both respects a kind of immanence his own appeals to the haecceity and transcendence of the world had perhaps belied. If Hyppolite were right that Merleau-Ponty introduced history into phenomenology, here the account would need to find further sufficiency. Now, ironically, the classical was precisely what would need to be surpassed in the account. In 1955, he had argued with respect to "the classical spirit (which reaches its extreme limit in Einstein)" that the problem with the classical idea of reason still possesses its object in advance (S 192–93). This surely also held true of his criticism of Husserl's logicism. The 1960 Preface to *Signs* (still tacitly invoking the account of *sens figuré*) further refines this account by claiming that the classical is precisely what no one takes literally, but rather as "obligatory steps for those who want to go further" (S 10–11). We must abandon such classical views of the literal as if "the 'true' and the 'false' were the only modes of intellectual existence" or its correlationism guaranteed by some miraculous adequation or refutation with an object possessed in advance. "Even in the sciences, an outmoded theoretical framework can be reintegrated into the language of the one which it replaced; it remains significant, keeps its truth" (S 10). Concepts, too, are historical and rationally transformed. As Canguilhem put it in an investigation of the concept of reflex movement, some concepts are "polyvalent," capable of being integrated and transformed across theoretical domains, rectifying the emerging concept of the reflex.[24] The history of science itself belies continuity: it is less about simply correspondence or verification than rectification and ordered transformation through conceptual mutation, varying both the concept's extension and its intelligibility: rather than a dialectic constructed by will of negation, it proceeds by "the power of integration and the freedom of variation."[25] Indeed the commitment to the fertility and rationality of such mutation (a concept originating in Bachelard), became invoked and extended in the "French school" from Koyrè to Canguilhem and beyond.[26]

We can see Merleau-Ponty himself tracing this "mutation of biological concepts" in his extensive lectures on nature from the late fifties (N 140). These lectures not only trace the historical emergence of the concept of nature, but engage the scientists and philosophers of science of his time. For example, returning to a subject of *The Structure of Behavior*, he traces the impact of the introduction of the concepts of information and communication in Watson's understanding of behavior. Both were introduced to renew the conception of the "animal machine" but became charged with a meaning that was no longer simply mechanical. Still, the world itself remained unproblematic in both cases. Both accounts, he claimed, remained in this respect the same, in exhaustively purporting to capture the object by reduction to operationalism (Bridgeman) or experimental activity (Bachelard) without sufficiently interrogating its ontological complex, as Merleau-Ponty's phenomenology demanded (N 203–204).[27]

What is striking is that Merleau-Ponty does not restrict such conceptual mutation to the history of science or even politics, where, for example, he denied that one could invoke events to simply falsify theories. Stepping away from his earlier views on the reconciliation of man to man, Merleau-Ponty glossed Marx, too, as a "classic" now in need of transformation (S 10). The same was true of the architectonics of phenomenological of theory itself, where he argued for a similar conceptual transformation at work in its history. For example, from the outset Merleau-Ponty had been interested in retracing the move from Husserl to Heidegger: both philosophers again were "obligatory steps for those who want to go further" (S 10–11). But this transformation remained complicated for him in precisely the way we have followed: "Are we to say therefore that Husserl refuses to make the passage to ontology in Heidegger's sense? To the problematic of negativity? Naivety: what is at stake is not the recognition of an error—but the mutation of concepts" (HLP 53). In his later work, he argued that such an "ontological mutation" was further required for phenomenology (N 204). After working on the "program" of language and symbolism ("which took us several years"), he then turned to the problem of ontology based initially on the problem of nature (N 220). Here, too, he argued against the limitations of the models of contemporary biology (N 204). But he spoke similarly about the limitation of classical phenomenology, based on the "metaphysics" of the transcendental ego. In both cases, Being is not the static correlate of thought (N 121). Instead: "The idea of a well-behaved world left to us by classical philosophy had to be pushed to the limit—in order to reveal all that was left over: these beings beneath our idealization and objectification which secretly nourish them and in which we have difficulty recognizing noema" (S 180). Again, we will need to reveal the intentional matrix that provides their intertwining, to use Husserl's term, the *Ineinander* of self and world and self and others, which both language and perception presupposed (Themes 108).

Ontologically, this would require articulating both the nature that is in us as well as the nature outside us. To begin, reminiscent of his earlier rejection of the metaphysics of the rational animal, he rejected the view of classical metaphysics that these two natures can be simply determined or identified. They cannot find their "ultimate coherence," for example, in God, "a place where I cannot place myself by definition because I am a human" (N 206). Instead the lectures suggest that we leave behind the ontotheological zigzag between essence and existence and attempt to provide "an explication of what being-natural or being naturally means, while waiting for being-human (*attendant l'être homme*) and the ontology of God" (N 206). He ultimately would further focus on the explication of what "has no name in philosophy," this zero-degree of signification that, like the polysemy of "God," is "neither a class name nor a logical possibility"—but which equally eluded the identity claims of classical metaphysics.[28] *The Visible and the Invisible* articulates not the transcendence of our Divine origin but something more like our common "element" or "flesh" (VI 140). The element of the flesh, that is, would again provide "the formative medium" of subject and object, what he called early on the natural body and the cultural body. Emphasizing Husserl's late texts in which my body or flesh becomes the opening not only onto other carnal things, but others whose flesh is like mine, out of which the intelligible finds its genesis, Merleau-Ponty declares that Husserl "rediscovers sensible being as the universal form of brute being" (S 172cf).[29] The flesh would provide the circular intertwining, the belonging-together and even reciprocity or bond between my body and the world, the visible and the invisible (VI 147).

This articulation is again based on the experience of our embodied being-in-the-world and in this regard is not new. But what motivates the ontological mutation is a radicalization of the horizon itself: precisely the claim that "a philosophy of perspective" is more properly a "philosophy of vertical being" (HLP 74; N 207). As Leibniz fully exemplifies, the metaphysics of classical perspectivism internally maintains its relation with the immanence of infinity, the ontotheological in-itself (VI 223). The elemental labyrinth of the flesh is devoid of such immanence, devoid of the guarantees of preestablished harmony; instead the opening of depth or transcendence itself is *urstiftet* (VI 219). Rather than infinity, there is openness (*Offenheit*), neither tragic nor eleatic, and the intersubjective expressivism of the monads is that of our being-in-the-world (VI 223, 251).[30]

Grasping the theoretical status of this "element" thus becomes critical, especially as it emerges in its divergence from classical German thought. It is clear from Working Notes that Merleau-Ponty is explicitly invoking the term, in the first place, in relation to Bachelard, who, in addition to his experimental dialectic in the philosophy of science, used the term to undertake a phenomenological poetics (VI 245, 267). Recent research has further demonstrated the robust role Bachelard has in the development of Merleau-Ponty's concept of the flesh.[31] For Bachelard, this operative imaginary would supplement scientific rationality with a psychoanalysis and poetics of the elemental or pure images of the senses. Merleau-Ponty would speak similarly of the "facticity" of the flesh (still proximate to Husserl's *Lebenswelt*) as the oneiric power that sustains and nourishes the rational. Hyppolite would not be wrong to compare the dialectic at stake in Bachelard to the external reflection of Fichte's *Wissenschafstlehre* and its account of poetic imagination to Novalis.[32] But as has become apparent, Merleau-Ponty will require that we continually question "the brute being" that the "sedimented-ontic being" of science omits or represses (N 220). For Fichte nature remains pure object, like the body itself, "the tool of reason."[33] But are the extensions of reflection and poetry external to one another: "Is not Fichte's *Ichheit überhaupt* simply Fichte?" (TL 107)?

Merleau-Ponty, instead, seemingly drew closer to Schelling for his analysis.[34] The nature lectures invoked the privilege Schelling granted to nature as a precursor; here, too, beyond merely subjective intuition we require a reflection upon its own emergence: again, an "intuition of intuition" (N 44). The result would be "an intuition capable of radiating out without ceasing to be dispersed" (N 44). We are also not far from the *Phenomenology*'s account of radical reflection, or what *The Visible and the Invisible* will call a hyper-reflection (*sur-refléxion*) that "would not lose sight of the brute thing and the brute perception" (VI 38). A concluding note articulates what are essentially the mutations in the genesis of apperception in phenomenology: stepping beyond the Kantian account of self-contact, as condition of possibility or Husserl's account of psychological immanence, to an account of reflection as emerging from the absolute or primordial flux (VI 49). Such *sur-réflexion* would clearly echo both his commitments to surrealism and Husserl's *Stiftung* account, a reflection that would arise out of the previously instituted, by ontological mutation to articulate the brute world of perception. The *Lebenswelt* itself then becomes "a fresh mutation in the doctrine of the reduction" (Themes 107). But it does so, for Merleau-Ponty, by demonstrating how the reduction leads beyond "alleged transcendental immanence" (VI 172). In such rectifications, the reduction becomes less an experience or a method "defined once and for all than the index of a multitude of problems" (TL 106).

The "radiating" intuition attributed to the idealist's intuition of intuition is still being conceptualized by the Husserlian account of "the rays of the world," opening to reflective attention (VI 241). But: "Reflection cannot 'go beyond' this opening to the world, except by making use of the powers it owes to the opening itself" (S 164). It is in this sense that he referred to it again in Schelling's term, as our "barbarous source": brute or abyssal being (S 178). Indeed it is at this point, he claimed, Schelling and Husserl converged (N 71). Still, for all Merleau-Ponty's proximity to Schelling, as much as he thought Schelling was right against Hegel in going beyond pure logic, in the end he claimed that Hegel's dialectic was right in attacking Schelling's more speculative constructions (N 49). And, as close as he was to Schelling's elevation of art in explaining the "modern world," he likewise claimed that "philosophy does not sublate itself in art" (N 46). He denied further that this ontology could be confused with primitivism or prescientism (VI 182). Indeed, as has been seen (as much as Husserl's seemingly pre-Copernican "the earth does not move") he thought the account moved beyond Einstein's classical theoretical and metaphysical limitations.[35] In both cases, what was at stake was not a condition of possibility but an inextricable dimension or horizon of experience (VI 185).[36]

To fully grasp Merleau-Ponty's final position, we should refer (as do his final lectures on Hegel) to Hyppolite's 1952 *Logic and Existence*, a work that had focused on Hegel's *Logic*, insisting, once more, against the existentialists, on its consistency in relation to the *Phenomenology*. Hyppolite openly cited Hegel's speculative equation of *Sinn*, which, again like that other "wondrous word" "*Aufhebung*" that preserves and surpasses at the same time, equates sense and meaning in one term.[37] In so doing, the concept sublates the sensible world: it is "the sublating and reduction of that material as mere phenomenal appearance to essential, which is manifest only in the Notion (*Begriff*)."[38] For Hegel, it is the concept which is the *element* of logic.[39] In a footnote, Hyppolite further explains this, already anticipating his writings on Bachelard a few years later: "We are taking the word, element, in the Hegelian sense of medium (*milieu*), as when we say the 'element of water.'

When saying 'the self' we want to note, like Hegel, the absolutely reflective character of being itself and of the 'I.'"[40]

Still insisting on the subordination of intuition, Hyppolite claims that Hegel's speculative account of *Sinn* is to be contrasted with the idea of the "mute": the "thought of the sensible does not remain interior and mute," explicitly citing Merleau-Ponty's use of the term.[41] Instead there is no "ontological silence, rather dialectical discourse is a progressive conquest of sense."[42]

Merleau-Ponty invokes Bachelard's account and the poetics of the ancient elements in *The Visible and the Invisible* (and thus seemingly again stands close to Novalis and Schelling). But Hegel remains proximate as well. He will reinvoke Hyppolite's account of the *Begriff* as element in his final lectures on Hegel (PNP 77). But now we also have to grasp, to what extent, in invoking the silent ontology of the "mute" world, Merleau-Ponty is still invoking Husserl's term.

Merleau-Ponty's reading of the element of the flesh involves not the sublation of sensibility in *Sinn*, but the origin of their differentiation between the visible and the invisible, where the invisible or the intelligible reciprocally articulates the visible as its hidden, "other side" or meaning. Hegel's account of reflection is still proximate in positing the outside and the inside are united or intertwined, but the latter is understood not as the infinite or divine logos exhibited in humanity (Hyppolite) but as the opening of the unending exploration of the visible and the invisible itself. It is in just this sense that his final lectures on Hegel still links the Hegelian absolute to the articulemes of the flesh, as reversibility or intertwining chiasm (PNP 58, 61, 64).

> The relation between phenomenology and absolute knowledge (metaphysics) is the relation between perception and the thing: partial perception is not simply reconciled with the thing. In order to be total, it must be partial. This is at least the case if one considers the "vertical," present world—and an "understanding" which is not distinct from our being. (PNP 51)

For Merleau-Ponty, this silent ontology belongs to the unfinished task of the rational. It involves, to use Hyppolite's terms, a "conquest of sense" but also, precisely as the silence or the "halos" of the not yet said; language itself contains its own silence precisely as the not fully adequated and yet to be developed (VI 176). The silence of the perceived world is not the ineffable: indeed the "whole landscape is alive with words" (VI 155). The silence of this opening is "overrun with words" whose articulations never surpass it, nor ultimately possess it (VI 110). For precisely this reason Merleau-Ponty abandoned the Husserlian model of parallel expressive "layers" (between expression and the expressed, concept and intuition). Instead he substituted the idea of dimensions that open on to circular (or reciprocally conditioning) relations between the visible and the invisible: between the sayable and the said, expression and perception, humanity and nature (N 220). As he put it with respect to the thematization of language that emerged from the phenomenology of perception:

> The thematization of language overcomes another stage of naiveté, discloses yet a little more the horizon of *Selbtverstandlichkeiten*—the passage from philosophy to the absolute, to the transcendental field, to the wild and "vertical" being is *by definition* progressive, incomplete. This is to be understood not as an imperfection … but as a philosophical theme: the incompleteness of the reduction ("biological reduction," psychological reduction," "reduction to immanence," and finally "fundamental thought") is not an obstacle to the reduction, it is the reduction itself, the rediscovery of vertical being. (VI 178)

In this "baroque" world, each dimension implicitly opens or radiates on to the other, again "tracing a path through multiple points of a circle" (S 181; see N 44). Yet he insisted both on its evidence and its justification, one that belied relativism, skepticism, and reductions to the ineffable (VI 95). "There is an ordered sequence of steps, but it is without end as it is without beginning" (S 165). Decentered in the reversibility of the visible and the invisible, even the visible loses its founding priority—precisely in losing its independence.[43] That is, emerging from the flesh and the horizons of history itself, the visible is always the visible of some experience, but also some language (or theory), some community, some culture (VI 229).

The latter perhaps is crucial to grasping the conceptual labyrinth of Merleau-Ponty's account. "There are certainly more things in the world and in us than what is perceptible in the narrow sense of the term" (S 171). The *Phenomenology* had already referred to a perception "in the broad sense of knowledge of existences," and, as such, already "implied" an ontology (PhP 42). The ontology is perspectival, unfinished, an exploration of the visible and the invisible, but it is by no means narrowly a perceptual reductionism, that is, simply or univocally perceptual in content; even "sense data," already deemed an abstraction or theoretical construct by the *Phenomenology*, "varied throughout the centuries" (S 48). Instead, ventured between the visible and the invisible, the rational never stops being what it is in perception: historical, adumbrative, unfinished. It is in this sense that the reduction is a *Rücksfrage*, as has become evident, by reinstitution, exploration, theoretical extension, or reimagination—and not simply by remembrance. The latter had been precisely Bachelard's (and others') objection to phenomenology (and classical reason more generally). Such reductions or returns to the given were simply illusion. For Merleau-Ponty, as has become evident, this *Nachstiftung* involves less simply a return than a "mutation of knowledge often the result of a return to the sources or the side-paths neglected by the mainstream, which results in a new interpretation of all that went before" (Themes 115–16).[44]

Accordingly, Merleau-Ponty provided an original reading of Husserl's account of the sensible world through Bachelard's figure of the poetic element. For Bachelard, the result would be a "*diphènomènologie*" of scientific and poetic truth.[45] Merleau-Ponty resisted this easy alliance that would reduce the task of the phenomenologist to a poetics at the margins of scientific truth. As has been seen, instead, his final ontological mutation transformed what Husserl called the depth "poetics" (*Dichtung*) at stake in the history of the rational in the *Crisis* writings.[46]

> Certainly the position of the philosopher is not without risk. As Bachelard saw, what we call "natural" is often only bad theory. But if we are aware of the artificiality of thinking, as Bachelard is, do we need to find a dialectical contrary for it, this opposing entity—if not Nature, at least the perceived? (N 85)

It was precisely this emphasis on nature as "the nonconstructed" or "non-instituted," as what all construction and institution explores, that made it initially a "privileged expression" or propaedeutic for the elemental ontology of the later writings, since it "more clearly shows the necessity of the onto-logical mutation" (N 4, 204). As has been seen, *The Structure of Behavior* had already railed against the idea of science as a complete world. But the early work still anthropologically understood nature (and dialectic) as the correlate of the "human drama." Then perhaps Merleau-Ponty's position becomes clearer: "What resists phenomenology within us—natural being, the 'barbarous' being which Schelling spoke of—cannot remain outside phenomenology" (S 178). But nor can it remain "outside" of science.

What justifies phenomenological description here has become more complex: not simply a correspondence or a correlation that it cannot possess. Surely it remains an experience but, as the Hegel lectures note, "experience is necessary but not sufficient" (PNP 75). The *Phenomenology of Perception* had already rejected both the idea of a pure perception or coincidence: "I cannot identify what I perceive with the thing itself" (PhP 211, 213). Nor can I simply identify my description with the thing itself. Instead its locutions remains always partial, emerging from an unfinished epistemic and concep-tual history, "allucatory"—but precisely out of the attempt to say the unsaid, the attempt to articulate the invisibility of the visible anew (VI 154). It is in this respect that this itinerary explores what remains of the "rhythmics" of the speculative: "the ruins of the spirit" (VI 180). Hence, the complicated status (and the itinerary) of Merleau-Ponty's ontology of the flesh.

Grasping the latter too is crucial. The objection is sometimes made that what he called the "ultimate notion" of the flesh remained illusory, another form of identity philosophy or preestablished harmony (one that still anthropologically privileged vision, consciousness, the human body) (VI 140).[47] True or not, such objections might presume that ultimate notions were unrevisable: that is, unlike, for example, the venture Bachelard found risked in all concepts, that such notions were immune from mutation and rectification.[48] As has become evident this would go against the grain of Merleau-Ponty's reading of both Husserl and Hegel; it presumed that the lacunae or the latency in his account had not itself called for such rectification, as part of its extension or mutation: that is, it presupposes that an ultimate notion, to use Bachelard's term, were a "closed" notion.[49] Indeed that it was not was the very point of his reading of the phenomenological reduction, "the adventures of constitutive analysis"—or more precisely "the adventures of the dialectic" as necessary steps "for those who want to go further."[50]

In a 1957 lecture devoted to phenomenology in Hegel and contemporary French thought, Hyppolite concluded that we are no longer involved "in the great movements of Marxism and Existentialism" but "we surpass them in order to reflect on them in the sense of the Hegelian *Aufhebung*."[51] As has become evident, Merleau-Ponty and Hyppolite ultimately did not disagree here. Still, if Merleau-Ponty himself had turned away from the anthropological rendering of both Marxism and Existentialism, he had not given up on phenomenology—he provided an original reading or discovered a "figured" meaning in it. It is precisely in this respect that he reaffirmed the persistence of Husserl in his final writings: "Husserl had understood: our philosophical problem is to open up the concept without destroying it" (S 138).

Notes

1. I will use the following abbreviations for works by Maurice Merleau-Ponty:

    AD   *Adventures of the Dialectic*, trans. Joseph Bien (Evanston: Northwestern University Press, 1973).

    CAL   *Consciousness and the Acquisition of Language*, trans. Hugh J. Silverman (Evanston: Northwestern University Press, 1973).

    HLP   *Husserl and the Limits of Phenomenology*, ed. Leonard Lawlor and Bettina Bergo (Evanston: Northwestern University Press, 2002).

HT   *Humanism and Terror*, trans. John O'Neill (Boston: Beacon Press, 1969).

IP   *Institution and Passivity: Course Notes from the Collège de France* (1954–55), trans. Leonard Lawler and Heath Massey (Evanston: Northwestern University Press, 2010).

IPP   *In Praise of Philosophy*, trans. James Wild and James M. Edie (Evanston: Northwestern University Press, 1963).

LMS   *Le monde sensible et le monde de l'expression*, ed. Emmanuel de Saint Aubert, Stefan Kristensen (Genève: MetisPresses, 2011).

N   *Nature: Course Notes from the Collège de France*, trans. Robert Vallier (Evanston: Northwestern University Press, 2003).

NC   *Notes de cours 1959–1961*, ed. Stéphanie Ménasè (Paris: Gallimard, 1996).

P   "Le Mouvement Philosophique Moderne" in *Parcours* (Lagrass: Verdier, 1997).

PP   *The Primacy of Perception*, trans. James M. Edie (Evanston: Northwestern University Press, 1964).

PhP   *Phenomenology of Perception*, trans. Donald A. Landes (London: Routledge, 2012).

PNP   "Philosophy and Non-Philosophy since Hegel," trans. Hugh J. Silverman, *Telos* 29 (Fall 1976): 43–105.

PW   *The Prose of the World*, trans. John O'Neill (Evanston: Northwestern University Press, 1973).

S   *Signs*, trans. Richard C. McCleary (Evanston: Northwestern University Press, 1964).

Themes   *Themes from the Lectures at the Collège de France*, trans. John O'Neill (Evanston: Northwestern University Press, 1970).

VI   *The Visible and the Invisible*, trans. Alphonso Lingis (Evanston: Northwestern University Press, 1968).

WP   *The World of Perception*, trans. Oliver Davis (New York: Routledge, 2004).

2. Georges Canguilhem, "Hegel in France," in *Oeuvres completes tome IV* (Paris: Vrin, 2015), 321.
3. See Léon Brunschvicg, *Le progrés de la conscience dans la philosophie occidentale* (Paris: Alcan, 1927), 378; Jean Hyppolite, "La Situation de la Philosophie dans Le Monde Contemporain," in *Figures de la pensée philosophique II* (Paris: Presses Universitaires de France, 1971), 1033.
4. Jean Hyppolite, "The Concept of Life and Consciousness of Life in Hegel's Jena Philosophy," in *Studies on Marx and Hegel*, trans. John O'Neill (New York: Basic Books, 1969), 15.
5. Ibid., 10, 18.
6. Georges Canguilhem, *The Normal and the Pathological*, trans. Carolyn R. Fawcett and Robert S. Cohen (New York: Zone Books, 1989), 30. Canguilhem

claimed that he had not been able to read Merleau-Ponty's *Structure of Behavior* before his manuscript was in press. Still, he acknowledged both the convergence of their views and that he might have found "help" therein. Doubtless Merleau-Ponty could have found similar assistance in Canguilhem since he held at points a view Canguilhem rightly criticized, that of health as statistical average (PhP 177–78; see SB 159). Later his lectures on nature will cite Canguilhem's book for his views on "autoregulatory fluctuation" in again articulating a non-substantialist or dialectical account of life (N 149).

7. Paul Rabinow, "Introduction" to *A Vital Rationalism: Selected Writings of Georges Canguilhem* (New York: Zone Books, 1994), 18.
8. See G. W. F. Hegel, *Aesthetics*, trans. T. M. Knox (Oxford: Clarendon Press, 1975), 128.
9. See G. W. F. Hegel, *Science of Logic*, trans. A. V. Miller (New York: Humanities Press, 1969), 400–8.
10. Jean Hyppolite, *Figures de la pensée philosophique I*, 236–37.
11. See G. W. F. Hegel, *The Difference Between Fichte's and Schelling's System of Philosophy*, trans. H. S. Harris and Walter Cerf (Albany: State University of New York Press, 1977), 163.
12. Canguilhem again would argue for "the originality of life," claiming that life can be "grasped only in a vision and never by division" and suggested that while in mathematics it would suffice that we be angels, in biology "we sometimes need to feel like the beasts themselves." See *Knowledge of Life*, trans. Stefanos Geroulanos and Daniel Ginsburgh (New York: Fordham University Press, 2008), ix–x. Nonetheless, elsewhere Canguilhem denied that Merleau-Ponty's invocation of the body schema in his analysis of radical reflection surmounted "the paradox of a consciousness of self as a body in space." See *Études d'histoire et de philosophie des sciences* (Paris: Vrin, 1983), 408.
13. Canguilhem, *Knowledge of Life*, 132.
14. Jean Hyppolite, "The Concept of Existence in the Hegelian Phenomenology," in *Studies on Marx and Hegel*, 31.
15. Ibid.
16. Hyppolite, *Figures de la pensée philosophique*, I, 241. See Hyppolite, *Genesis and Structure of Hegel's Phenomenology of Spirit*, trans. Samuel Cherniak and John Heckman (Evanston: Northwestern University Press, 1974), 544n.
17. Ibid., 31.
18. Hyppolite, "Sens et Existence dans La Philosophie de Maurice Merleau-Ponty," in *Figures de la pensée philosophique II*, 753.
19. Gaston Bachelard, *The New Scientific Spirit*, trans. Arthur Goldhammer (Boston: Beacon Press, 1984), 1–19.
20. Jean Hyppolite, "L'Intersubjectivité chez Husserl," in *Figures de la pensée philosophique*, I, 501.
21. Eugen Fink, *Sixth Cartesian Meditation*, trans. Ronald Bruzina (Bloomington: Indiana University Press, 1995), 84–99.

22. See Gaston Bachelard, "Surrationalism," trans. Julien Levy, *Arsenal*, vol. 4 (1989): 112–13.

23. See Edmund Husserl, *The Crisis of the European Science and Transcendental Phenomenology*, trans. David Carr (Evanston: Northwestern University Press, 1970), 71. See also HLP 27. Here Merleau-Ponty questioned again whether the *Rücksfrage* could be simply a matter of return or memory.

24. Canguilhem, *A Vital Rationalist*, 181. See Merleau-Ponty's use of this research, criticizing Descartes' account of the automata (and, like Canguilhem himself, Gueroult's conceptual approach) in N 198. On Merleau-Ponty's alternate "history—Dichtung" approach (Husserl's term) to Geuroult's, see VI 177.

25. Gaston Bachelard, *L'activité rationaliste de la physique contemporaine* (Paris: Presses Universitaires de France, 1951), 16. See Canguilhem's discussion of this text in *Études de histoire et de philosophie des sciences* (Paris: Vrin, 1983), 296.

26. See Canguilhem, *Études de histoire et de philosophie des sciences*, 206. Also see Alexandre Koyré, *Galileo Studies*, trans. John Mepham (New Jersey: Humanities Press, 1978), 39n2; and "Galilée et Platon," in *Études d'histoire de la pensée scientifique* (Paris: Gallimard, 1971), 166–95.

27. The extent to which Husserl's *Crisis* had relied on Koyré's analysis of Galileo's "mutation" of the world of classical science and metaphysis has always been controversial; that Merleau-Ponty found them both significant cannot be denied.

28. On the interpretation of nature and ontotheology, especially the account of the divine as "no longer the attribute of a class of beings' as it is in Aristotle," see N 133.

29. A working note at the time explains: "The flesh of the world is not self-sensing (*se sentir*) as is my flesh. It is sensible and not sentient—I call it flesh nonetheless ... in order to say that it is a pregnancy of the possible *Weltmöglichkeit* (the possible world, variants of this world, the world beneath the singular and the plural) that is not an object, that the *blosse Sache* mode of being is but a partial and second expression of it.... It is by the flesh of the world that in the last analysis one can understand the lived body (*corps proper*)" (VI 250).

30. Compare Merleau-Ponty's marginal note: "Tragic-comedy of consciousness and being, unhappy consciousness, becomes, through horizon, not the ruse of being which escapes from consciousness, but *Offenheit*: neither finite nor infinite, nothing justifying finitude (Hegel): open" (HLP 83n88).

31. See for example, Emmanuel de Saint Aubert, *Du lien des êtres aus élément de l'etre: Merleau-Ponty au tournant des années 1945–1951* (Paris: Vrin, 2004), 255–71. As will become evident, Bachelard will be further proximate in Merleau-Ponty's account of the philosophy of science and dialectic.

32. Hyppolite, "Gaston Bachelard ou Le Romantism De L'Intelligence," *Figures de la pensée philosophique* II, 653. Also see "L'épistémologie de Gaston Bachelard," 667.

33. J. G. Fichte, *The System of Ethics*, trans. Daniel Breazeale and Günter Zöller (Cambridge: Cambridge University Press, 2005), 267.

34. Bachelard credited Schelling with "great metaphysical intuition" but claimed in the end it remained "literary." See *The Formation of the Scientific Mind*, trans. Mary McAllester Jones (Manchester: Clinamen Press, 2002), 91, 102.

35. See Edmund Husserl, "Foundational Investigations of the Phenomenological Origin of the Spatiality of Nature," trans. Fred Kersten, in *Husserl: Shorter Works*, ed. Peter McCormich and Frederick Elliston (Notre Dame: University of Notre Dame Press, 1981), 225. Cf. HLP 69. Merleau-Ponty suggested that Husserl's apparent pre-Copernican paradox would have been avoided if he "had not enclosed his own discovery in the "consciousness' of the absolute Ego" (76).

36. See "Einstein and the Crisis of Reason" (S 182–91). While Merleau-Ponty defended Bergson against Einstein, he also invoked (as did Heidegger) Oscar Becker (and Hermann Weyl's account of the continuum) in criticizing Einstein's account. For further discussion of these issues see my "The Symbolic Function and Phenomenological Architectonics: Merleau-Ponty's *Phenomenology of Perception* and the Specter of Cassirer," *Études Phénoménologiques* No. 4 (2020).

37. Jean Hyppolite, *Logic and Existence*, trans. Leonard Lawlor and Amit Sen (Albany: State University of New York Press, 1997), 24.

38. Hegel, *Science of Logic*, 588.

39. Hyppolite, *Logic and Existence*, 60.

40. Ibid., 11n.

41. Ibid., 23–25.

42. Ibid., 21.

43. From the outset Bachelard had objected to the priority given to vision in phenomenology. See for example, *L'Activité rationaliste de la physique contmporaine* (Paris: Presses Universitaires de France, 1951), 2; *Matérialisime rationnel* (Paris: Presses Universitaires de France, 1953), 11. This priority (or the priority of any sense, e.g., touch, as is sometimes argued) has been foregone with the abandonment of the foundational model of expressive layers. *Funderiung* like *Stiftung* becomes "bi-directional" (HLP 54). Instead the account arguably seeks to "rectify" classical transcendental claims regarding perspectivism, where, as Kant claimed in *The Critique of Pure Reason*'s *Dialectic* concepts are horizons, or points of view. But, Merleau-Ponty claimed, it is this that "he seems to forget in the Analytic" (PhP 318), As Hegel realized as much as Husserl, what Kant lacks is an account of genesis. In this respect the notion of the flesh belongs to the legacy of transcendental schematism; the corporeal schema as opening on to the world and to others, as articulated or oriented, "as preliminary *Auffassung als* of the signifier and the signified as separated," is already symbolic (N 211).

44. Thus here too concepts would be polyvalent. Merleau-Ponty's would be different from what he described as "the ontological mutation in Husserl," distinct from the metaphysics of the absolute ego (HLP 74). Moreover it would be equally distinct from the "mutation of concepts" in the "passage to ontology" in Heidegger, which he variously claimed risked falling into mysticism or a metaphysic of destiny, and at risk of losing its link to factuality (HLP 53).

He further criticized Heidegger's account of science based upon the distinction between the ontic and the ontological as "Cartesian," precisely, that is, the account he (and Bachelard et al.) had sought to rectify (N 82).

45. Bachelard, *Matérialism rationnel*, 49.

46. See Husserl, *Crisis*, 394; see Themes, 114.

47. If *The Visible and the Invisible* does indeed suggest that the experience of the flesh emerges "as though it were in a relation of preestablished harmony" (VI 133), this experience had been removed from its ontotheological past and ventured within an *Offenheit* that was not without *caesura* or risk. Moreover, the *Phenomenology* had already questioned the principles of such a metaphysical or preestablished harmony: "But do we know whether complete objectivity can be thought? Whether all perspectives are compossible?" (PhP 228).

48. Bachelard, *Philosophie du non* (Paris: Presses Universitaires de France, 1940), 20. For further discussion of this issue see my "Notes on Bachelard and Merleau-Ponty: Between Phenomenology and Poetics," in *Phenomenology, Institution and History: Writings After Merleau-Ponty II* (New York: Continuum, 2009), chapter four.

49. Put otherwise, it presupposed that the remains or the grammar of the speculative *Satz* were "direct": a simple nominal sentence. See CAL 89.

50. For further discussion of this issue see my "On the Metamorphoses of Transcendental Reduction: Merleau-Ponty and 'the Adventure of Constitutive Analysis'," in *Phenomenology and the Primacy of the Political: Essays in Honor of Jacques Taminiaux*, ed. V. Foti and P. Kontos (Cham: Springer, 2017), 107–24.

51. Hyppolite, "La 'Phènomènologie' de Hegel et La Pensée Française Contemporaine," in *Figures de la pensée philosophique*, *I*, 241.

Part VI

Hermeneutics

23

The Thread of Imagination in Heidegger's Retrieval of Kant: The Play of a Double Hermeneutic

Frank Schalow

At various key points throughout his career, Heidegger engages in a crucial dialogue with his German predecessor, Immanuel Kant. That dialogue not only casts new light on the intricacies of Kant's transcendental philosophy, but also serves as a leaping-off point (*Absprung*) to extend and radicalize Heidegger's inquiry into being (KPM 163).[1] As such, Heidegger's interpretation of Kant plays out on these two fronts. On the one hand, Heidegger dismantles or deconstructs extraneous aspects of Kant's philosophy that remain mired in the metaphysical tradition of rationalism; on the other hand, Heidegger retrieves those elements of transcendental philosophy that align with his own attempt to re-ask the question of being and ground that perennial inquiry upon the problematic of human temporality and finitude. If there is a way of unraveling the complexity of this interpretation, then its thread lies in a single topic interwoven into Heidegger's diverse lectures and writings—namely the power of imagination (*Einbildungskraft*).

The challenge is to outline the trajectory of Heidegger's interpretation as it plays out on these two fronts, and coalesces into a mosaic that comprises something like a "double hermeneutic."[2] In this way, we learn from, but do

F. Schalow (✉)
Department of Philosophy, University of New Orleans, New Orleans, LA, USA
e-mail: fschalow@uno.edu

C. D. Coe (eds.), *The Palgrave Handbook of German Idealism and Phenomenology*, Palgrave Handbooks in German Idealism, https://doi.org/10.1007/978-3-030-66857-0_23

not simply concede, the criticism launched against Heidegger's Kant interpretation from its inception, by his German counterpart, Ernst Cassirer, and, subsequently by one of the leaders in the French Continental tradition, Paul Ricoeur. Both criticize Heidegger for overplaying the importance of the imagination in Kant's writings, and in effect "ontologizing" what is essentially an epistemic notion.[3] We will discover that Heidegger's dialogue with Kant does not simply proceed along a linear path, but in turn follows the curvature of a hermeneutical circle central to all interpretation. Correlatively, the same holds true for unfolding the internal design of Kant's critical philosophy. Through the play of imagination, the third *Critique* implements a figurative mode of expression that shapes the self-reflexivity of Kant's critical enterprise as initiated through the *Critique of Pure Reason*.

In the first part of this chapter, I will formulate the provisional link that Heidegger makes between the cognitive role of imagination (in Kant's sense) and its development as a linguistic prefix or intermediary (in the hermeneutic role) of transliterating what it means "to be" into temporal idioms. In this second part, I will show how Heidegger's retrieval of the imagination leads to deconstructing the rationalist tradition of German idealism, on the one hand, and, on the other, rediscovering in it the catalyst to overcome the metaphysical dichotomies between subject–object, freedom and nature. In this way, Heidegger extends his critical exchange (*Auseinandersetzung*) with Kant into the practical arena of the ethical, not only to recast the question of ethics on a more radical footing than that provided by metaphysics, but also to undertake an inquiry into freedom as a new origin for his ontological project. In the third part of this chapter, I will illustrate how Heidegger's destructive-retrieval of imagination provides a detour around German Idealism in an effort to reclaim the implicit concern for language, which is shrouded in Kant's discussion of art in his *Critique of the Power of Judgment*. Destructive-retrieval is the task of peeling back the layers of assumption that comprise the philosophical tradition, in order to recover a deeper insight otherwise hidden since the inception of Western thought. Despite Heidegger's resistance to German Idealism, there is also some common ground in the attempt to overcome the metaphysical dualisms that have gripped modern philosophy; the difference will lie in the pathway of their overcoming. We will discover that the hermeneutic path of thinking (*Denkweg*) that Heidegger traverses in his dialogue with Kant ruptures the linear sequence of Kant's three *Critiques*. The architectonic of the Kantian system is then supplanted by an ellipsis that interweaves the three major works of his critical philosophy into a hermeneutic mosaic.

The Question of Knowledge: Why Imagination?

Throughout his *magnum opus*, *Being and Time*, Heidegger dismisses many traditional epistemic concerns, including the concern for the enigma of knowing external objects (and other enigmas stemming from "idealism"), as derivative questions resting on a false premise of a subject–object dichotomy. But we would be remiss to assume that he simply conflates ontology and epistemology, at least without also recasting the question of knowledge in a way that directly pertains to his overall task of re-asking the question of being. Instead, Heidegger rejects first and for the most part metaphysical dualisms that obstruct the inquiry into being, including the divisions between mental and physical, subject and object, which compartmentalize concerns for "knowing" into a smaller subset of issues, e.g., the divorce between the theoretical and practical or theory and praxis. If Kant champions these modern dualisms, then he may also provide the clue for subverting them; and, accordingly, from Heidegger's perspective, the subversion of these dichotomies may also point the way for transplanting the perennial philosophical question—which traditionally has been cast under the umbrella of the "problem of metaphysics"—upon a broader, more original, and universal ground.

Insofar as Heidegger's inquiry into being proceeds from a pre-philosophical level of everyday dealings and comportments, then its ultimate aim is to ascend to a "thematic" level, that is, in an effort to determine the "meaning" of what is explicitly inquired into (e.g., "to be"). The so-called meaning of being (*Sinn von Sein*), as he describes it, is to be understood in thematic and philosophical terms, and thereby as articulated in words, rather than merely "intuitively" or mystically apprehended. Yet, following the lead of the nineteenth-century philosopher, Wilhelm Dilthey, Heidegger characterizes understanding as "pre-theoretical," or *Verstehen*, rather than as a theoretical construction of objectivity or *Verstand* (in a Kantian sense).[4] *Verstehen* pertains to the development of self-understanding that is rooted in the individual's lived experience, while *Verstand* involves comprehending the generic determinations of physical objects. Heidegger, then, appeals to a form of understanding that is "disclosive," in such a way as to address what shows itself, or the phenomenon, in its singularity. The corresponding mode of determination on which the possibility of a thematic understanding rests must be aligned with the uniqueness of this manifestation; the manner of articulation and determination must ultimately serve this end of disclosedness (*Erschlossenheit*).

Heidegger then proposes a distinctly new method, namely hermeneutic phenomenology, in order to address this unique dilemma: how can an inquiry ascend to a universal level in order to develop a thematic understanding of "being," and yet do so in such a way as to address the singularity of manifestation pertaining to a distinctive mode of experience (*Erfahrung*)? The disclosedness that we experience in our way of existing as human beings must both illuminate and come to light in the thematic attempt at *philosophical* understanding. In order to address what shows or manifests itself, phenomenology joins with hermeneutics to interweave different levels of meaning: that is, outline on a universal plane the horizon that gathers together the possibilities of human understanding and thereby anchors philosophy in the potential that human beings possess, and which ultimately refers to the constitution (of their "to be") as finite. In mirroring human finitude, the universal horizon of such understanding must be temporally constituted. The ecstatic projection of temporality, in originating from the future, returning from the past, and opening forth into the present, shapes the trajectory by which we can project our understanding "upon" (*Woraufhin*) that universal horizon and thereby express what can be meaningfully understood.

Posed as it is by hermeneutic phenomenology, this dilemma takes an ontological form. Yet, Heidegger also proposed a distinctly philosophical or "productive" logic, which would be equipped to tackle the logical side of the problem.[5] Put simply, such an inquiry seeks to establish a linchpin between the universal and the particular. In this way, we arrive at a uniquely epistemic problem which, in the figure of Immanuel Kant, takes a distinctly "transcendental turn" due to his effort to establish our finitude as a new ground for the possibility (of both the nature and limits of human knowledge). In a revealing passage in the first division of *Being and Time*, Heidegger points to the key thrust of transcendental idealism, which references the cornerstone of any inquiry into the possibility of metaphysics, namely the difference between being and beings or the ontological difference: "If what the term 'idealism' says, amounts to the understanding of being that can never be explained by beings but is already 'transcendental' for every being, then idealism affords the only correct possibility for a philosophical problematic. If so, then Aristotle was no less an idealist than Kant" (BT 251).[6] Kant centers his attention on the *logos* of knowledge, with the unique formulation "how are synthetic *a priori* judgments possible?" He proposes a transcendental logic to couch this question in a way that reassembles that problematic around a new axis, namely the finitude of human knower as the anchor point for delineating the preconditions for knowledge. Kant's celebrated Copernican revolution shifts the coordinates of logic, such that a pre-conformity to the finite conditions of knower dictates the possibility of determining an object through a synthetic *a priori* judgment. With equal economy and simplicity, Kant summarizes this transcendental turn, which transforms the basis of epistemology, with this memorable remark: "Thoughts without content [percepts] are empty; intuitions without concepts are blind" (CPR A52/B75).

To balance this epistemic equation Kant sought an intermediary, which could express the determination of thought in relation to that which is othermost (or what is given in experience), i.e., the object. For Kant, imagination is this intermediary; it is the synthetic power that unifies time by anticipating the future, recovering the past, and holding open the present. Imagination performs the task of schematism, that is, interposing the temporal horizon of our finitude, or time, as the medium through which pure concepts can achieve their determination(s) and acquire the capacity (as predicates) to signify an object. The imagination integrates the three dimensions of time—future, past, and present—and maintains them in a dynamic unity. The schemata of the pure concepts serve as transcendental time-determinations (*als transzendentale Zeit bestimmungen*) (KPM 139).[7] In service of the transcendental power of imagination, time assumes a new, extraordinary role. Time not only exhibits the dynamism of human experience, but also provides the template or blueprint for generating the content for each of the pure concepts, its potential for signification, and even the vocabulary (entailing the predicates) in a synthetic *a priori* judgment: "The schemata of pure concepts of understanding, the categories, are *a priori* time-determinations and as such they are a transcendental product of the pure power of the imagination."[8] The schematic power of imagination illustrates how time can both outline the horizon to understand being and express its meaning in words (e.g., temporal idioms such as permanence and presence). Kant's schematism thereby provides the transition from a metaphysical description of beings in their interconnection with each other to an inquiry into being itself, the possibility of its disclosure as the theme of Heidegger's fundamental ontology. Imagination points to a new philosophical beginning, which usurps the priority of reason (metaphysics) and distinguishes finite temporality as the clue to re-asking the question of being (fundamental ontology). Heidegger can develop a thematic understanding of being, of being as being (*Sein als Sein*)—requisite to developing a science of ontology—in contrast to merely establishing generic determinations of beings in their beingness (*Seiendheit des Seiende*).

With various schematic formulations, Kant provides Heidegger with a clue to how time can provide the cluster of connotations surrounding a single word, "being": "succession in time" (for the pure concept of cause and effect), "permanence in time" for the pure concept of substance, and "presence in time" for the pure concept of existence.[9] In this way, Kant's account of transcendental schematism provides a prototypical demonstration of how temporality, in Heidegger's sense, could unify the manifold ways of what it means "to be." The universality of the concern for being in its potential to be thematized or defined philosophically becomes inextricably interwoven with time. As Heidegger states at the close of his lecture course from the winter semester of 1927/28, *Phenomenological Interpretation of Kant's* Critique of Pure Reason: "*Universality of being and radicality of time are the two titles which together denote the tasks which a further thinking of the possibility of metaphysics calls for.*"[10] In acknowledging the importance that the Kantian clue makes to his own philosophical advancement, he remarks: "When some years ago I studied the *Critique of Pure Reason* anew and read it, as it were, against the background of Husserl's phenomenology, it opened my eyes; and Kant became for me a crucial confirmation of the accuracy of the path which I took in my search."[11]

Thus, Heidegger extends the sense of the "transcendental," which Kant had reserved primarily for addressing the problem of synthetic *a priori* knowledge, so as to elicit determinations of being on a universal plane in a manner congruent with the task of fundamental ontology. "To be sure, this concept of transcendental science does not coincide directly with the Kantian; but we are certainly in a position to explicate by means of the more original concept of transcendence the Kantian idea of the transcendental and of philosophy as transcendental philosophy in their basic tendencies" (BPP 323).[12] Ultimately, the "transcendental" is rooted in the projecting of (and surpassing toward) a horizon for understanding being—that is, the ecstatic trajectory of finite transcendence. Through his extension of the transcendental in this way, Heidegger can retrieve the key insights of Kantian schematism. He can thereby dismantle the (epistemic) barrier of the application of the schematized categories to the regional sphere of beings (designated under the rubric of physical "nature"), and demarcate the finite horizon of the world (*Welt*) in order to supplant the subject–object dichotomy.

Almost forty-five years later (1973), Heidegger summarizes the lasting impact of this breakthrough, in responding to a query raised by Jean Beaufret in a seminar in Zähringen: namely that schematism is "the Kantian way of discussing being and time."[13] Conversely, schematism paves the way for a hermeneutic inquiry into the possibility of finite transcendence, which "is Kant's elementary self-defense against the violation of an external architectonic of formal logic."[14] By "self-defense" Heidegger refers to Kant's attempt to outline the boundary or horizon of human finitude, in opposition to the presumption by rationalism to utilize logic as an unfettered vehicle to know objects outside of possible experience. Imagination reveals the origin of ecstatic temporality, and thereby serves as a hermeneutic intermediary to translate the meaning of being by prioritizing the grammar of its verbal form (i.e., the "to be") through such temporal idioms as "presencing."[15]

Revisiting the Problem of Ethics

In the late 1920s, Heidegger engages in a destructive-retrieval of transcendental philosophy to highlight the internal design of his own project and to transpose it within the wider compass of the philosophical tradition. At the beginning of a new decade, as we will discover, Heidegger radicalizes his inquiry further, uncovering an even deeper foundation than is provided by fundamental ontology. In this case, Heidegger embarks upon an inquiry into a new problematic, that of the origin of human freedom, thereby establishing a hermeneutic foothold by appropriating the practical side of Kant's critical philosophy. Before retracing the steps that led Heidegger upon this new pathway, we need to also consider, by way of contrast, the avenue that he circumvents if not completely forecloses. Indeed, due to a common interest in the concerns for temporality and finitude, it is not an accident that Heidegger engages Kant's thought in order to initiate a conversation with other thinkers of the Western tradition. Among modern thinkers, Kant's philosophy provides a preferential route over his successors in German Idealism, most notably Hegel.[16] This initial disjunction becomes evident in Part IV of *Kant and the Problem of Metaphysics*, when Heidegger remarks:

> What does the struggle against the "thing in itself," which started with German Idealism, mean, other than the growing forgetting of what Kant struggled for: that the inner possibility and necessity of metaphysics ... are at bottom brought forth and preserved through the more original working-out and preservation of the problem of human finitude. (KPM 171)[17]

Following on the heels of his dialogue with Kant, German Idealism reappears, in Heidegger's language, as a *Holwege*, that is, as the reopening of a way that is initially blocked. With his usual subtlety, Heidegger appeals to what is unthought (*das Ungedachte*). While German Idealists present philosophical systems, the writings of the major proponents, Hegeland Schelling, leave behind the trace of a subtext, specifically a logic that seeks to address the dynamic tension between thinking and being, i.e., through a clash of opposites.[18] If knowledge is to be concrete as well as comprehensive, it must be able to mirror this dynamism and elicit its internal logic or bring the tension of opposites to expression. To be sure, Heidegger resists Hegel's dialectical method as the key to unlocking the enigma of being. The major upshot of his retrieval of the imagination has been to overturn the supremacy of reason in mapping out the higher echelons of the Absolute.

For the logic of imagination mirrors a parallel problem in the metaphysics of the dialectic, namely how the possibility of determining "being" hinges on interposing the "not," negativity, and difference.[19] According to Heidegger, ontology becomes possible as a science only when being is differentiated from beings, that is, because of the ontological difference.[20] From the perspective of the inquirer, or *Da-sein*, being appears as the "not" of beings, which is revealed, for example, in the anticipation of death or the prospect of ceasing to be. Heidegger's retrieval of the imagination occupies this intermediary of the "nothing," thereby portending the collapse of the metaphysics of presence and of the symmetry of the Absolute. But how is it possible to think asymmetry as the other side of presence, or absence as such, the differentiation between being and beings? Once again, the Hegelian dialectic proves to be instructive, if only in a reverse or an inverted way.

Herein lies the catalyst to radicalize Heidegger's methodology, or the hermeneutic circle that yields the compass of his inquiry into being. The phenomenon, the given, or being, must be granted more radically, that is, through a circularity in which the theme of the inquiry, or being magnifies its own inscrutability and mystery (*Geheimnis*), addressing "what is" through the veil of the "nothing," that is, as wholly other. The otherness evokes a sense of wonder through which the inquirer recasts the most perennial question of all, *die Seinsfrage*. In retrospect, we can trace these steps more easily, where for Heidegger they appear much more abrupt, precipitating, as it were, a "leap" (*der Sprung*). In section 63 of his *magnum opus*, he had already emphasized the need to "leap" into the hermeneutical circle (BT 363).[21] In his lecture course from the summer semester of 1930 dealing with Kant's practical philosophy, Heidegger enacts a similar move of freedom. He redefines freedom as the uncovering or disclosing of a horizon of possibilities. That is, he recasts the concept of freedom on a *new hermeneutic platform*—in contrast to that provided by Hegel's dialectical method—in order to subvert the metaphysical dichotomy between theory and praxis. Accordingly, Heidegger describes a radical shift in inquiry, thereby transposing the relation between what is inquired into and the inquirer. The initiative or "free reign" of the inquirer does not simply reside as an extant property in us, but rather, in pointing back to the origin of temporality, coincides with the openness of being. Heidegger characterizes this transformation this way: freedom is no longer a "property" of the human being, but instead the human being is a *"possibility of freedom."*[22]

The question of human freedom provides a new platform on which to recast the question of being. As Friedrich-Wilhelm von Herrmann points out, with this 1930 lecture course takes a key step toward developing a new draft of *Being and Time*.[23] As Heidegger states at the conclusion of these lectures: "The question concerning what is ownmost to human freedom is the most basic question of philosophy, *in which even the question of being is rooted.*"[24] Freedom can no longer be described through an exclusively human capacity or exercise of the will. What Heidegger first described as resoluteness (*Entschlossenheit*), or "choosing to choose," must still be enacted within the openness or broader horizon of possibilities. In this way, Heidegger arrives at a groundbreaking insight: freedom has an extra-human source, a power that can only be granted from the side of the otherness of being and its transposition into the openness of being-in-the-world.

Imagination ceases to be only a capacity to extend our knowledge through a synthesis, that is, by combining the manifold of a sensuous intuition. Instead, imagination re-emerges as a creative power, which can draw upon the negativity of absencing, thereby accentuating the play of differentiation in order to traverse the area of the "between" (*Zwischen*). In this way, imagination allows us to construe heterogeneous relations that cannot otherwise be conceptualized. In the Kant book, Heidegger characterizes the imagination as the midpoint (*Mitte*) between spontaneity and receptivity within human knowledge itself. Imagination overcomes such binary oppositions in order to establish the possibility of a receptive–spontaneity and a spontaneous–receptivity as the transcendental linchpin within the finitude of theoretical knowledge. In his 1930 lectures on Kant, Heidegger goes a step further to establish how practical reason can be reconfigured; specifically, he shows how the ultimate instance of the pure spontaneity of noumenal freedom can be generated anew on a finite, temporal plane, that is, from the fact of our being-in-the-world or on the ground of human facticity.

The practical dimension of human freedom arises from the same temporal origin as does the imagination. Correlatively, human praxis does not stem from a disembodied, atemporal source (in the noumenon), but rather from the dispositional character (e.g., as receptive-spontaneity) of the self—for example, in its submission through respect for the moral law. The feeling of respect that Kant had reserved for the practical domain of moral autonomy exhibits a factical origin in affectivity, by which the individual can be awakened to its constraints of its accountability as finite. Heidegger then recasts moral responsibility in a Kantian sense as a mode of responsiveness, which becomes factically concrete when the self heeds the othermost voice of its conscience. The otherness of this "silent" call intervenes to bring the self before and ahead of its potential to be responsible (BT 326).[25] Let us take a simple example.

One of the primary moral requirements that Kant attributes to the categorical imperative is the binding character of a promise (G 4:422).[26] But any such promise reveals a dual dimension, the making of the promise and the upholding of it. Implicitly, a promise not only binds an individual to an agreement made in the present, but also carries forward or extends what is agreed upon into the future. Correlatively, the moral requirement falls upon the self to uphold the promise by reaffirming and renewing a prior commitment (made from the past). The imagination interjects this temporal spacing, as it were, by projecting ahead a possibility into the future and in holding forth an avenue extended from the past for renewing a commitment. The temporal, imaginative play of anticipating the future, returning to the past, and entering the present makes possible a perpetually binding and renewable commitment as the heart of a promise. Through this elasticity of time that the play of imagination creates, the self appropriates freedom as the power to choose, by which an individual can bind him/herself to the moral requirement of a categorical imperative (in this case, a promise). By establishing the imagination as the temporal origin of moral decision-making, Heidegger then translates Kant's dictum of autonomy into the reciprocal response that the human self can exhibit in its finitude. As Heidegger states in the lecture course from the summer semester of 1930, "autonomy is self-responsibility."[27]

In his lecture course on Schelling's philosophy from the summer semester of 1936, Heidegger takes the further step to identify the limitation of the Kantian notion of freedom, which in its mere formality harbors an idealistic premise that Heidegger seeks to overcome:

> The formal concept of freedom is independence as standing within one's essential law. That is what freedom means in the true sense, historically expressed, in the Idealistic sense. Kant's philosophy creates and forms the transitions from the inappropriate to the appropriate concept of freedom. For him, freedom is still mastery over sensuousness, but not this alone, but freedom as independence in one's own ground and self-determination as self-legislation. And yet the determination of the formal essence of human freedom is not completed in Kant's concept of freedom. For Kant places this freedom as autonomy exclusively in man's pure reason.[28]

By seeking an alternative, temporally defined, finite platform on which to base Kant's notion of praxis, Heidegger appeals to imagination as a vessel of freedom, creativity, and play of possibilities. Imagination remerges as an intermediating power that overcomes the phenomenon-noumenon split, the separation between the supersensuous and sensuous realms, and thereby re-establishes new coordinates for moral action through the self's possibilities of being-in-the-world.

According to this destructive-retrieval, imagination provides an entryway into the open expanse of possibilities and hence as exemplifying the power of freedom as "letting-be" (*Sein-lassen*). In *Contributions to Philosophy* (1936–38), Heidegger spells out these coordinates by addressing the play of time–space (*Zeit-Spiel-Raum*). We cannot go into this development here, except to quote a passage from this text in which he summarizes the importance of imagination: "'Imagination' as the occurrence of the *clearing* itself," designating "not only something transcendental (cf. Kant-book)," but also as the granting of being or enowning (*Ereignis*).[29]

Language and the Singularity of Art

Heidegger's destructive-retrieval of imagination also has implications for the development of language beyond its traditional model of predication. Kant's apparent neglect of language provides fuel to his staunchest critics, including Herder and Fichte, who emerge as pioneers in the effort to make linguistic concerns a central topic of philosophy.[30] Because of its scattered discussions of beauty and the sublime, art and nature, as well as their symbolic modes of expression, Kant's *Critique of the Power of Judgment* provides a wealth of unexplored issues. Parallel to the German Idealists, Heidegger's emphasis on addressing that is "unthought" provides an occasion to explore the third *Critique*, even if his explicit remarks about this text remain somewhat muted. "We cannot discuss here the sense in which the pure power of imagination recurs in the *Critique of the Power of Judgment* and above all whether it still recurs in express relationship to the laying of the ground for metaphysics" (KPM 110).[31] Through its capacity for symbolism, imagination points to the figurative use of language beyond its employment in the theoretical knowledge of objects. The power of imagination harbors a creative wellspring by which language can spawn new idioms of expression. The symbolic power of imagination reveals a deeper, pre-predicative origin of language.

The third *Critique* indirectly points back to the issue of language, if only by raising topics that preclude objective determination, on the one hand, and, on the other, by calling for boundaries to mark what can be expressed, or become meaningful on one plane even if unknowable on another. Once again, the imagination comes to the forefront because (1) it corresponds to a reflective judgment, e.g., independently of an object (as in a determinate judgment) and (2) appeals to experiences, e.g., of the sublimity of "nature," which can only be conveyed at the boundaries of what is expressible, primarily in a figurative way. Within this field of figurative meanings and expressions, nature no longer pertains exclusively to the ensemble of physical objects that can be determined by the Newtonian laws of science. The so-called indeterminacy of nature is not merely a drawback, but also provides an invitation to explore a second level of meaning beyond what can be correlated with an objective referent given through our empirical intuition. This further configuration of meaning is opened up through the portals of imagination.

As an expression of the sublime, nature is animated with an overwhelming power which can evoke in us a myriad of responses, including terror and awe. Seen on one level, Kant's third *Critique* can be construed as his attempt to re-establish the intersection, if not union, of the otherwise disparate sides of the supersensuous and the sensuous. Through his ontological inquiry, Heidegger does not seek to overcome this polarity through a higher level of unification and sublation in the form of the Absolute. But his retrieval of freedom outside its disjunction with its opposite (e.g., the physical realm of "nature") has further repercussions with regard to with retrieving the natural realm. As the obverse of his argument in his 1930 lectures on Kant, Heidegger addresses the organic character of nature as rooted in *physis* in the primordial, Greek sense of self-emerging presence. *Physis* in the ancient sense of genesis, growth, and development stands in stark contrast to the modern conception of nature as a mechanistic system based on the principle of cause and effect. Nature is no longer a separate domain with physical laws that ostensibly conflicts with an opposing domain regulated by the self-legislative law of moral freedom. Through his destructive-retrieval of Kant, Heidegger thereby provides an alternative platform to German Idealism for revisiting the key issues of the third *Critique*, even if he does not do so with the detail of exposition that we find elsewhere in his writings.

The openness of imagination also points to the exteriority of our relation to nature. The question of "who we are?" is not simply answered by mental faculties divorced from our capacity for feeling, and the roots of materiality that through our openness exposed us to both to the wonder of nature and our fragility (in the words of Hannah Arendt) as earth-bound creatures.[32] A new play of differentiation becomes possible precisely in wake of overcoming the preceding metaphysical dichotomy. For Heidegger, the tie to our materiality, to our embodiment or incarnality, as set forth on the earth, allows for another opposition of concealment with unconcealment. But the new grounding of nature requires that disclosedness cannot be anchored alone in *Da-sein*'s disclosedness and its manner of being-in-the-world. The incarnality of *Da-sein*, the exposure of its openness, tracks the withdrawal of being into a new configuration of conflict, namely what Heidegger describes as the strife (*Streit*) between world (*Welt*) and earth (*Erde*). The self-occluding and receding of the earth provides the backdrop against which the disclosedness of the world can unfold. But this unfolding still calls upon the activities and endeavors of human beings, and the manner in which they participate in this interplay of earth and world, by becoming a conduit of play itself. Foremost among these endeavors is the work of art itself, and the manner in which human beings become vessels of this mimesis, of art "imitating" the creative power of nature, and, vice versa, how the work of art, e.g., a sculpture, wrenches forth the unconcealment (of world) from the concealment (of earth).

But how does this analysis square with, and direct us back to Kant's portrayal on imagination in the third *Critique* as form of play? Indeed, it is the "free play" of imagination that sets it apart in its aesthetic form. As Kant states:

> Now there belongs to a representation by which can object is given, in order for there to be cognition of it in general, imagination for the composition of the manifold of intuition and understanding for the unity of the concept that unifies the representations. This state of a free play of the faculties of cognition with a representation through an object is given must be able to be universally communicated....The subjective universal communicability of the kind of representation in a judgment of taste, since it is supposed to occur without presupposing a determinate concept, can be nothing other than the state of mind in the free play of the imagination and the understanding (so far as they agree with each other as is requisite for a cognition in general); for we are conscious that this subjective relation suited to cognition in general must be valid for everyone and consequently universally communicable, just as any determinate cognition is, which still always rests on that relation as its subjective condition. (CJ 5:217–218)[33]

No longer constrained by the need to determine an object, imagination (in a reflective judgment) exhibits a "free lawfulness," schematizing without a concept (CJ 5:212–213, 240, 241).[34] In this way, imagination exhibits a playfulness, which activates the interplay or interaction of our cognitive powers. Accordingly, imagination can then allow nature to re-emerge—extending the vistas of disclosedness—in a way that parallels art and allows us to experience both the heights and depths of our ek-sistence (*Ek-sistenz*). Such is the case when Kant describes the experience of the sublime. As Kant remarks:

> The disposition of the mind to the feeling of the sublime requires its receptivity to ideas; for it is precisely in the inadequacy of nature to the latter, thus only under the presupposition of them, and of the effort of the imagination to treat nature as a schema for them, that what is repellent for the sensibility, but which is at the same time attractive for it, consists, because it is a dominion that reason exercises over sensibility only in order to enlarge it in a way suitable for its own proper domain (the practical) and to allow it to look out upon the infinite, which for sensibility is an abyss. (CJ 5:265)[35]

The experience of the sublime stretches the power of language to express what cannot be conceptually represented—in an analogous way to art—thereby summoning the power of imagination to engender figurative patterns of meaning (e.g., as schema-like). Language is a figurative mode of expression, which facilitates the communication of both the experience of the sublime (nature) and the beauty of art. By schematizing without a concept, the free play of imagination points to a deeper enactment of language, through which human expression receives its capacity to address what is singular in our experience and render it meaningful. Just as imagination provides the catalyst to depose the supremacy of reason, so on this deeper level language endows human beings with the capacity to engage in different practices of dialogue and communication. When seen in this light, a more radical treatment of the imagination in the third *Critique* breaks the constraints of predication, thereby following through on the earlier attempt (in the Kant book) to depose the supremacy of reason. The entire enterprise of critical philosophy depends upon the ability of language to sustain the movement of self-reflexivity and the vocabulary that is intimated through an investigation into the preconditions of human experience. The further deployment of Heidegger's destructive-retrieval of the imagination unearths from the third *Critique* an innovative power reserved for language in engendering new meanings and figurative modes of expression.[36]

Conclusion

The basic thrust of Heidegger's dialogue with Kant revolves around an encounter (*Auseinandersetzung*) with the *Critique of Pure Reason*, and, to a lesser degree, with the *Critique of Practical Reason*, in an effort to appropriate the key motifs of his thinking within a new context. In the process, he also provides an alternative platform than that of German Idealism for retrieving the imagination within the aesthetic context of the *Critique of the Power of Judgment*, even without following through all the way on the implications of his approach. Heidegger thereby holds in reserve a further stage of his reciprocal rejoinder (*Erwiderung*) with his German predecessor, which brings to the forefront the overall strategy of that dialogue: the appropriation of Kant's philosophy around the centerpiece of imagination (at the expense of metaphysical dichotomies), and the broader contextualizing of the key motifs of Heidegger's thinking after *Being and Time*. In play, then, is a double hermeneutic by which Heidegger's destructive-retrieval of transcendental philosophy unfolds on these two fronts. When seen within this broader hermeneutic context, the appropriation of Kant's insights into the finite temporality of imagination implies a reciprocal transformation of Heidegger's own project of "being and time." Through his destructive-retrieval of imagination, Heidegger supplants the linear structure of Kant's architectonic with the circularity of a hermeneutics, in which the unthought dimension of language hidden in the third *Critique* comes to the forefront as the ground for his critical enterprise overall.

While developed in contrast to the dialectical method of German Idealism, Heidegger's hermeneutical approach allows for a further layering of understanding that can uncover issues endemic to the idealist movement (of the nineteenth century), including the importance of language. As the guiding thread of his critical exchange with Kant, Heidegger's supplanting of reason in favor of imagination also has implications for his attempt to rediscover language as the presupposition (*Voraussetzung*) of thinking (rather than the reverse), thereby overcoming the rationalist premise of German Idealism. As such, the thinkers who epitomize the tradition of German Idealism, Hegel and Schelling, provide a counterpoint to Heidegger's destructive-retrieval of Kant's transcendental philosophy. On occasion, Heidegger claims that Schelling's thinking surpasses Hegel's,[37] not in terms of its ingenuity and systematic completeness, but by prioritizing the key issues that punctuate Kant's *Critique of the Power of Judgment*: the interdependence of freedom and nature, the fragility and exaltation of the spirit.

A retrospective glance at German Idealism, through the prism of Friedrich Hölderlin's poetry, uncovers a confluence of issues that points back to the first beginning of philosophy and ahead to the inception of another beginning: the interplay of poetry and truth (*poiesis* and *aletheia*), the beauty of art and the unconcealment of being. When seen in this light, Heidegger's dialogue with Kant opens a new frontier of inquiry, which turns toward the discovery of the work of art, away from aesthetics as an independent philosophical discipline, and returns to the earth as the site of poetic dwelling.

Notes

1. Heidegger, *Kant und das Problem der Metaphysik, Gesamtausgabe* 3 (Frankfurt am Main: Vittorio Klostermann, 1991), 223. Hereafter: GA.
2. For an earlier use of this term, see James Risser, "The Disappearance of the Text: Nietzsche's Double Hermeneutic," *Research in Phenomenology*, 15 (1985): 134. Also see Frank Schalow, *The Renewal of the Heidegger-Kant Dialogue: Action, Thought, and Responsibility* (Albany: State University of New York Press, 1992), 306.
3. Ernst Cassirer, "Kant und das Problem der Metaphysik: Bemerkungen zu Martin Heidegger's Kant-Interpretation," *Kant-Studien* 36 (1931): 1–26. Also see Paul Ricoeur, *Fallible Man* (Chicago: Henry Regnery Company, 1965), 66–67. Ricoeur argues that Heidegger's Kant-interpretation succumbed to the "pious wish" of an ontological reductionism, that is, in seeking to derive the pure concepts of the understanding from the temporal schema of the transcendental imagination).
4. See Frank Schalow, "A Diltheyan Loop? The Methodological Side of Heidegger's Kant-Interpretation," *Frontiers of Philosophy in China*, ed. Eric Nelson, 11, no. 3 (Fall 2016): 377–94.
5. Heidegger, *Metaphysische Anfangsgründe der Logik im Ausgang von Leibniz*, GA 26 (Frankfurt am Main: Vittorio Klostermann, 1978), 192. *The Metaphysical Foundations of Logic*, trans. Michael Heim (Bloomington: Indiana University Press, 1984), 152.
6. Heidegger, *Sein und Zeit*, GA 2 (Frankfurt am Main: Vittorio Klostermann, 1976), 275 (translation slightly modified). For further discussion, see Frank Schalow, "The question of the ontological difference in Heidegger's dialogue with Kant," *Heidegger Studies* 35 (2019): 45–60.
7. GA 3, 198.
8. GA 25, 431; tr. 292.
9. See Frank Schalow, "The Language of Time in Kant's Transcendental Schematism," in *The Linguistic Dimension of Kant's Thought: Historical and Critical Essays*, ed. Frank Schalow and Richard Velkley (Evanston: Northwestern University Press, 2014), 53–69 (esp. 56–74).

10. *Phänomenologische Interpretation von Kants Kritik der reinen Vernunft*, GA 25 (Frankfurt am Main: Vittorio Klostermann, 1978), 427; translated as *Phenomenological Interpretation of Kant's Critique of Pure Reason*, trans. Parvis Emad and Kenneth Maly (Bloomington: Indiana University Press, 1995), 289.
11. GA 25, 431; trans. 292.
12. See Heidegger, *Die Grundprobleme der Phänomenologie*, GA 24 (Frankfurt am Main: Vittorio Klostermann, 1975), 461.
13. Heidegger, *Four Seminars*, trans. F. Raffoul and A. Mitchell (Bloomington: Indiana University Press, 2003), 69.
14. Heidegger, GA 25, 430; trans. 292.
15. See Frank Schalow, *Departures: At the Crossroads between Heidegger and Kant* (Berlin: Walter de Gruyter, 2013), 65–69.
16. See Dennis J. Schmidt, *The Ubiquity of the Finite: Hegel, Heidegger, and the Entitlements of Philosophy* (Cambridge, MA: MIT Press, 1988), 207.
17. GA 3, 244.
18. Heidegger, *Hegels Phänomenlogie des Geistes*, GA 32 (Frankfurt am Main: Vittorio Klostermann, 1980), 209–210; translated as *Hegel's Phenomenology of Spirit*, trans. Parvis Emad and Kenneth Maly (Bloomington: Indiana University Press, 1988), 144–45. At the conclusion of this lecture course from the winter semester 1931/32, Heidegger reaffirms his allegiance with Kant as the seminal thinker who brought the issue of "being and time" to the forefront, if only in a provisional manner (212/146–47). For a later context in which Heidegger addresses the limitations of Hegel's dialectical logic, see *What Is Called Thinking*, trans. J. Glenn Gray (New York: Harper Collins, 1968), 239–49.
19. For a comprehensive account of this issue, see John Sallis, *Logic of Imagination: Expanse of the Elemental* (Bloomington: Indiana University Press, 2012), 7–9. See Section C, "Schemata of Imagination" in Chapter 5 ("Schematism").
20. GA 26, 193; trans. 152.
21. GA 2, 418.
22. Heidegger, *Vom Wesen der menschlichen Freiheit: Einleitung der Philosophie*, GA 31 (Frankfurt am Main: Vittorio Klostermann, 1982), 135; translated as *The Essence of Human Freedom: An Introduction to Philosophy*, trans. Ted Sadler (London: Continuum, 2002), 93.
23. Friedrich-Wilhelm von Herrmann, "The Role of Martin Heidegger's Notebooks within the Context of His Oeuvre," in *Reading Heidegger's Black Notebooks 1931–1941*, ed. Ingo Farin and Jeff Malpas (Cambridge, MA: The MIT Press, 2016), 89.
24. GA 31, 300; trans. 203. See Heidegger, *Schelling's Treatise on the Essence of Human Freedom*, trans. Joan Stambaugh (Athens: Ohio University Press, 1985), 9.
25. GA 2, 373. See Schalow, *The Renewal of the Heidegger-Kant Dialogue*, 281–82.
26. This is the second of the four examples that Kant provides to illustrate the universally binding character of the categorical imperative.

27. GA 31, 296; trans. 201.

28. Heidegger, *Schelling's Treatise on the Essence of Human Freedom*, 84.

29. Heidegger, *Beiträge zur Philosophie (Vom Ereignis)*, GA 65 (Frankfurt am Main: Vittorio Klostermann, 1989), 312; translated as *Contributions to Philosophy (From Enowning)*, trans. Parvis Emad and Kenneth Maly (Bloomington: Indiana University Press, 1999), 219.

30. For further discussion, see Jere Paul Surber, *Language and German Idealism: Fichte's Linguistic Philosophy* (Atlantic Highlands, NJ: Humanities Press, 1996), 5–8. Also see Frank Schalow and Richard Velkley, "Introduction: Situating the Problem of Language in Kant's Thought," in *The Linguistic Dimension of Kant's Thought*: 7–9.

31. GA 3, 161. The translation has been modified slightly. See Schalow, *Departures*, 195–204.

32. Hannah Arendt, *Lectures on Kant's Political Philosophy*, ed. Ronald Biener (Chicago: University of Chicago Press, 1982), 4, 27.

33. AA (*Akadamie Ausgabe*) 5, *Critique of the Power of Judgment*, trans. Paul Guyer and Eric Matthews (Cambridge: Cambridge University Press, 2000), 102–03.

34. AA 5, *Critique of the Power of Judgment*, 97–98, 124–25.

35. AA 5, *Critique of the Power of Judgment*, 148.

36. For further discussion, see Schalow, *Departures*, 191–94.

37. See Hans-Georg Gadamer, *Heidegger's Ways*, trans. John Stanley (Albany: State University of New York Press, 1994), 116–17.

24

Gadamer, German Idealism, and the Hermeneutic Turn in Phenomenology

Theodore George

Gadamer's philosophical hermeneutics is important to phenomenology for a number of reasons. Chief among these, perhaps, is that Gadamer describes his philosophical hermeneutics as an attempt to build on and even advance beyond the early Heidegger's break from the transcendental idealism of Husserl's phenomenology. Yet Gadamer's philosophical hermeneutics takes him down a path that diverges from Heidegger's *Denkwege*.

What I wish to show in this chapter is that Gadamer clarifies central tenets of his divergence from Heidegger indirectly, as it were by proxy, in reference to the legacy of German Idealism generally and to Hegel's legacy in particular.[1] As we shall see, Gadamer takes his point of departure from critical concerns about German Idealism. Gadamer suggests that German Idealism has left not only a broader legacy of alienation from art and history but also a philosophical legacy of subjective idealism that haunts even phenomenology. Yet, as Gadamer believes, this legacy of German Idealism does not exhaust the significance of Hegel. As I shall argue, Gadamer turns to Hegel in order to elucidate historico-lingusitic conditions of what the early Heidegger called "facticity." Thus, Gadamer's integration of Hegel's legacy into his philosophical hermeneutics, though often viewed as a retreat from Heidegger's project

T. George (✉)
Texas A&M University, College Station, TX, USA
e-mail: t-george@tamu.edu

C. D. Coe (eds.), *The Palgrave Handbook of German Idealism and Phenomenology*,
Palgrave Handbooks in German Idealism,
https://doi.org/10.1007/978-3-030-66857-0_24

of a "destruction" of metaphysics, in fact proves to be the basis of his attempt to make Heidegger's hermeneutics more radical.

Gadamer on the Hermeneutic Turn in Phenomenology

In his *Reflections on his Philosophical Journey*, Gadamer recalls that his orientation in philosophy and, with it, his orientation toward the legacy of German Idealism, was first formed by his experiences as a student. Gadamer entered university near the end of the First World War, and his studies unfolded with the tumult of the interwar period in Germany. Gadamer experienced these as times of crisis that made it untenable for him to accept the world he had inherited. In this, Gadamer was a child of his times. As Charles Bambach has argued, many of the most important writers of the period "developed a new kind of rhetorical discourse sensitive to the collapse and dissolution of the old order."[2] Gadamer sums up that "in the confusion which the First World War and its end had brought to the whole German scene, to try to mold oneself unquestioningly to the surviving tradition was simply no longer possible."[3] Certainly, for many in Gadamer's generation, the untenability of the world they inherited was experienced in political terms. In this, neither German imperialism nor republicanism in the Western European style retained their credentials. Indeed, as the imperial regime collapsed and an uninspiring republic was installed, Germany saw the rise of revolutionary movements on both the right and left.[4]

Gadamer, for his part, however, saw the untenability of the world first of all as a "perplexity" that provided "an impetus to philosophical questioning."[5] He identified the untenability of the world he inherited not first with the untenability of the old political orders now in question, then, but with the ideals of the philosophical establishment that purported to give legitimacy to those old orders in the first place. He writes,

> In philosophy, too, it was obvious that merely accepting and continuing what the older generation had accomplished was no longer feasible for us in the younger generation. In the First World War's grisly trench warfare and heavy-artillery battles for position, the Neo-Kantianism which had up to then been accorded a truly worldwide acceptance, though not undisputed, was just as thoroughly defeated as was the proud cultural consciousness of that liberal age, with its faith in scientifically based progress.[6]

Gadamer's statement is compressed. But what he first of all has in mind are the ideals of the most influential movements of Neo-Kantianism, the Marburg School and the Baden School, and in particular their claim that self-consciousness, and with this the transcendental subject, provides the only firm foundation for the sciences.[7] He also seems to have in mind, though, the air of legitimacy that Neo-Kantianism had meant to give to the old orders of the previous generation. Gadamer describes that order as a "liberal age," and, while the German liberalism of that period differs from the liberalism of other periods and places, it, too, involved the idea that progress in society would be supported by science, classically, by helping to overcome superstition and scarcity. Neo-Kantianism helped to bolster belief that liberal progress could count on science precisely by clarifying and establishing the validity of the foundations of scientific research. But, if the First World War had taught anything, it taught that science not only helps overcome superstition, but also contributes to nationalistic arms races through the invention of ever more powerful artilleries; and that scientific disciplines, such as chemistry, will not only lead to fertilizers for increased crop production, but also to poison gases for killing soldiers. Gadamer was led by his experience as a student in times of crisis to see the ideals of the Neo-Kantian philosophical establishment, no less than the old orders they were supposed to support, as a house of cards falling down around him.

Gadamer, like many students in his generation, sought an alternative to Neo-Kantianism in the emergence of existentialism on the German philosophical scene. In contrast with mainline Neo-Kantianism, "existentialism dealt with a truth which was supposed to be demonstrated not so much in terms of universally held propositions or knowledge as rather in the immediacy of one's own experience and in the absolute unsubstitutability of own's own existence."[8] As Gadamer has it, the basic approach of Neo-Kantianism is transcendental idealism; it is a legacy of German Idealism. The basic claim of this idealism is that the truth of universal propositions is founded in self-consciousness and depends on the validity of those structures of the transcendental subject on which the propositions are founded in the first place. Indeed, in accord with such a transcendental idealism, not only the truth of universal propositions but also our own individual experience of ourselves, the world, and everything we encounter in the world, are founded in structures of the transcendental subject operative as it were interchangeably in each of us. So, it is perhaps no surprise that proponents of existentialism, in their opposition to the transcendental idealism of Neo-Kantianism, focused on figures such as Kierkegaard, Dostoevsky, and Nietzsche, who questioned whether self-consciousness played as much of a foundational role in our experience as the transcendental-idealist Neo-Kantians believed. Gadamer points to the inspiration of Nietzsche for him and his fellow students in particular: "the gigantic form of Friedrich Nietzsche with his ecstatic critique of everything, including the illusions of self-consciousness."[9]

Gadamer observes that the emergence of existentialism on the German intellectual scene, though inspired by figures such as Nietzsche, coalesced in the early Heidegger's critical response to Husserl's phenomenology. Students taken with existentialism had already turned to Husserl, no doubt in part because of Husserl's characterization of phenomenology as an approach, or even method, that would overturn the naiveté of the modern sciences through a return "to the things themselves!"[10] No doubt for many at the time, this motto would have appeared as a promise for something very much like the break with the philosophical establishment they had sought. The motto made phenomenology sound like a method that answered to more than the demands of science for universal truths, truths which, precisely in their universality, seemed abstract and increasingly disconnected from and irrelevant to the immediacy of experience and individual existence. The motto made phenomenology sound like a method that would get back to the things themselves, *die Sachen*, the things that really mattered, ultimately, the things that mattered concretely, as a matter of fact, for immediate experience and individual existence as such. But, as Gadamer observed, those who heard this possibility to overturn the philosophical establishment in Husserl's motto were quickly disappointed. For as Gadamer observes, he and others soon discovered that "Husserl himself, who with all his analytic genius and inexhaustible descriptive patience that continuously pressed on for final evidence, had envisioned no better philosophical support than a Neo-Kantian transcendental idealism."[11] Husserl, in his call to return to the things themselves, continued to adhere to the transcendental idealism of the Neo-Kantian philosophical establishment. For Gadamer and the other students of his generation around him, Husserl's motto proved to be less of a promise than a mere promissory note, and one that was underwritten by neo-Kantian foundations with about as much remaining value as the *Reichsmark*.

The early Heidegger organizes his critical response to the transcendental idealism of Husserl's phenomenology around a different motto, and indeed, a rather unlikely one: "hermeneutics."[12] Thus, in the crises in Germany between the wars, Gadamer and fellow students found in Heidegger's invocation of "hermeneutics" the possibility of a radical break from the philosophical establishment. To be sure, it is difficult to recognize the radicality of the term "hermeneutics" that Gadamer and the others of his times heard in Heidegger's use of it. "'Hermeneutics' refers" first of all "to the study of understanding and interpretation, and ... focuses on the art, methods and foundations of research in the arts and humanities."[13] Moreover, hermeneutics is thus oftentimes associated with the preservation of the significance of artworks and texts from the past—practically the opposite of a *break* from the past.

Yet the contrast Heidegger draws between the transcendental idealism of Husserl's phenomenology and hermeneutics draws out the subtle radicality at the heart of hermeneutics. Husserl suggests that the transcendental idealism of his phenomenology provides a firm foundation for the sciences. Hermeneutics, by contrast, is for inquiries without firm foundations, for example, inquiries about the meaning of an artwork from the past or from another civilization. Moreover, Husserl suggests that the transcendental idealism of his phenomenology provides a firm foundation because it is based on the apodicticity that attends our self-conscious reflection on the transcendental subject. Hermeneutics, by contrast, is for inquiries that cannot be based on our self-conscious reflection on the transcendental subject, but that rather require us to attend to things that exceed any origins in the transcendental subject at all. For Gadamer and his fellow students, Heidegger's use of the term "hermeneutics" signified more than the study of understanding and interpretation; it resonated with the possibility of a new orientation in philosophy—a radicalization of phenomenology liberated at once from transcendental idealism and the subject.

Heidegger maintains, against Husserl, that phenomenology is bound up with what he calls the "hermeneutics of facticity." Heidegger elucidates what he means by this in his own phenomenological inquiry into the being of human beings, or, as he treats this, *existence*. For him, such phenomenological inquiry into existence reveals that the kind of self-conscious, transcendental subject that Husserl talks about is an abstraction. Accordingly, Heidegger maintains, phenomenological inquiry cannot be founded in such a subject, but, instead, always begins with the *facticity* of our existence, that is, the fact that we find ourselves called to understand and interpret ourselves in the context of situations which we neither created nor control but into which we have nevertheless been thrown. As Gadamer puts it, for Heidegger "phenomenology should be ontologically based on the facticity of Dasein, existence, which cannot be based on or derived from anything else, and not on the pure cogito as the essential constitution of typical universality."[14]

In this, Heidegger introduces a sense of hermeneutics—the study of understanding and interpretation—that concerns something much more originary than an art and method of research in the arts and sciences. In fact, for him, the uses made of understanding and interpretation in the arts and sciences are only possible because human beings are, in their very being, hermeneutical. "*Understanding* is not ... as with Husserl, a last methodological ideal of philosophy in contrast to the naivete of unreflecting life; it is, on the contrary, the *original form of the realization of* Dasein, which is being-in-the-world."[15] To exist: really, this means to engage in understanding and interpretation, or, perhaps better, to enact ourselves through understanding and interpretation. Accordingly, phenomenological inquiry unfolds as the attempt to understand and interpret ourselves that remains conditioned by the facticity of existence. For Heidegger, contra Husserl, then, phenomenology does not really admit of eidetic reduction—that is, a reduction to the *eidoi* or essences of what is *de facto* given in our consciousness. Rather, because phenomenological inquiry is without recourse to any such transcendental basis, it can proceed only hermeneutically, in the self-interpretation of existence made possible and limited by the factically given meanings that comprise the situation we find ourselves in.[16]

Gadamer suggests that Heidegger's hermeneutical intervention against Husserl's phenomenology spoke to his and his fellow students' desire to overturn the philosophical establishment. Yet Gadamer maintains that as Heidegger approached and then made his celebrated "turn," Heidegger himself came to believe that his hermeneutical phenomenology still cleaved too closely to the notion of a transcendental subject.[17] To be sure, this is Gadamer's account of Heidegger's turn. But Gadamer's idea is not difficult to reconstruct. Ironically, the early Heidegger appears to remain closest to the notion of a transcendental subject in ideas that many took to be his most "existential." This irony becomes especially evident in connection with Heidegger's *Being and Time*, for example, in his treatment of what he calls the authentic anticipation of our own death. For Heidegger, such anticipation reveals that this possibility of our own death is, in fact, the "*ownmost*" possibility of our existence, one that individuates us as "*nonrelational*" in regard to the world, things, and others, and that looms as a "*certain ... indefinite and insuperable possibility*."[18] In this, the anticipation of our own death "exhibits a different kind of certainty, and is more primordial than any certainty related to beings encountered in the world or to formal objects."[19] Heidegger, in turn, suggests that such anticipation of our own death therefore frees us for an unmitigated relation to ourselves as the ground of our existence.[20]

Here, in Heidegger's account of the authentic anticipation of our own death, it appears as if existence is no longer bound by the hermeneutics of facticity, but finds a ground of its existence in a kind of pure relation to itself.

To be sure, this self-relation is not a transcendental idealist self-conscious rela-tion to universal structures of the transcendental subject that provide firm foundations for research in the sciences. Rather, authentic anticipation of our own death attests to the singularity of our existence and attests to our possi-bility to take ownership over those possibilities to be that are available in this singular existence. Yet, as Gadamer suggests, notwithstanding all differ-ences between Husserl's and Heidegger's accounts of self-relation, Heidegger, too, appears to uphold authentic anticipation of our own death as a possi-bility of self-relation that is free from all the worldly factical conditions of our attempts to understand and interpret ourselves.

Gadamer's Hermeneutics and the Legacy of German Idealism

Gadamer maintains that the orientation of his philosophical hermeneutics is, at bottom, the same as that of Heidegger's turn; as Gadamer reports, his philosophical hermeneutics, like Heidegger's later *Denkwege*, is an attempt to develop further the break with the transcendental idealism of Husserl's phenomenology that was initiated in those early years. He writes, "The hermeneutics I developed was based upon the finitude of the historical char-acter of Dasein, and it tried also to carry forward Heidegger's turn away from his own transcendental account of himself."[21]

Yet Gadamer's philosophical hermeneutics nevertheless takes him down a path that diverges from Heidegger's paths. The later Heidegger's paths leave hermeneutics behind. He no longer turns to hermeneutics, and the project of a hermeneutics of facticity, as an intervention against the notion of a self-conscious, transcendental subject. Rather, he attempts to clarify the stakes of what he initially intended by facticity in reference to a daunting sweep of figures and themes, though, as Gadamer observes, perhaps espe-cially in reference to "the poetic mythos of Hölderlin."[22] Gadamer's path, by contrast, keeps faith in the power of hermeneutics to break from the notion of a self-conscious, transcendental subject. His philosophical hermeneutics is an attempt to trade on this power of hermeneutics by taking the early Heidegger's hermeneutics of facticity further than Heidegger himself did. In this, Gadamer focuses on historico-lingusitic conditions of facticity that Heidegger's account must entail, but that Heidegger himself appears to ignore in his treatment of motifs such as the authentic anticipation of our own death. Crucially, as I wish to discuss now, Gadamer develops these historico-linguistic conditions of facticity in reference to the legacy of German Idealism generally and Hegel's legacy in particular.

Gadamer's approach begins in a critique of the legacy of German Idealism. In this, Gadamer maintains that "German Idealism and its Romantic traditions" have left us with "inherited forms of consciousness" that not only set the stage for Neo-Kantianism and Husserl's phenomenology, but, moreover, that "represent only alienated forms of our true historical being."[23] For Gadamer, human beings are, in their very being, historical. On his view, this means that to be human is to participate in the historical transmission of meaning. We have been left with forms of consciousness from German Idealism and its Romantic traditions that are alienated, however, in that they treat our consciousness of transmitted meaning not as something in which we *participate*, but, rather, as something we can *possess*, even as a token of status or privilege. He suggests that these alienated forms of consciousness appear, in particular, in "the tranquil distance from which a consciousness conditioned by the usual middle-class education enjoyed its cultural privilege" but remains detached from "how much of *ourselves* must come into play and is at stake when we encounter works of art and studies of history."[24] Such an education maintains "tranquil distance" to the arts in what Gadamer calls "aesthetic consciousness."[25] Here, our encounters with artworks are reduced from participation in the re-enactment of a truth claim passed down in the work to a merely subjective experience produced by an art object—for example, an affective pleasure or other excitation. Likewise, such an education maintains a "tranquil distance" from history in what Gadamer calls "historical consciousness."[26] Here, we no longer experience history as a process of transmission in which we participate, but, instead, subjectively, as a succession of "objects," people, and occurrences, that have passed before us.[27]

Gadamer maintains that the forms of consciousness inherited from German Idealism result in alienation because, like their followers in Neo-Kantianism and Husserlian phenomenology, many in German Idealism sought firm foundations in the self-consciousness of the transcendental subject. Indeed, in some ways, the German Idealist pursuit of firm foundations is even more expansive than that of the Neo-Kantians and Husserlians after them. German Idealism was after firm foundations for the sciences, but they also wished to establish the unity not only of the natural sciences but also the moral sciences, the arts, and history—really, all of human experience. In Kant's transcendental idealism, and with emphasis in the "subjective" idealism of figures such as Fichte, this unity was supposed to be founded in nothing else than the self-consciousness of the transcendental subject. As Gadamer seems to suggest, the alienations we experience today, not only the alienation he associates with Neo-Kantian and Husserlian pursuits of firm foundations in the sciences, but also the alienated aesthetic and historical consciousness that filters through bourgeois education, are a legacy of the German Idealist attempt to found a grand unity in the self-consciousness of the transcendental subject.

Gadamer's critique of the legacy of German Idealism is tempered, however, by his reception of Hegel. He believes that there is more to Hegel's legacy than the role played in his thought by the self-consciousness of a transcendental subject. In fact, Gadamer finds in Hegel an important ally for his and, before him, Heidegger's attempt to break from all philosophers founded in such self-consciousness of a transcendental subject. Certainly, in this, Gadamer's opinion of Hegel differs from Heidegger's. As Richard Palmer notes, Gadamer in fact engaged in a sustained dialogue with Heidegger over this difference that began with a 1965 lecture course, was further carried out in an exchange of letters, and includes Gadamer's essay, "The Heritage of Hegel" (or, as this may also be translated, "Hegel's Legacy").[28] Heidegger, as we recall, sees Hegel as a German Idealist who sought a grand unity in the self-consciousness of the transcendental subject. As Palmer puts it, "for Heidegger, Hegel was another figure against whose absolute idealism he rebelled and in doing so he could profile the originality of his own philosophy."[29] Thus, to Heidegger's mind, Hegel is not an ally in the attempt to break from the legacy of German Idealism but is, instead, an epigone of the history of Western metaphysics from which we are called to twist free. Gadamer disagrees with Heidegger in the starkest of terms. Gadamer writes,

> The path of Hegel's thought, above all, should be newly examined.... Heidegger's *Destruktion* of metaphysics has not, in my view, robbed meta-physics of its importance today. In particular, Hegel's powerful speculative leap beyond the subjectivity of subjective Spirit established this possibility and offered a way of shattering the predominance of subjectivism. Was Hegel's intention not the same as that in Heidegger's turn [*Kehre*]: away from the tran-scendental principle of the self? Was it not Hegel's intention, also, to surpass the orientation of self-consciousness and the subject-object schema of a philosophy of consciousness?[30]

Many philosophers, and among them many critics of Hegel, identify his "absolute" idealism as the pinnacle or high point of the German Idealist movement. Indeed, Hegel himself at times cast his absolute idealism as a completion of the German Idealist movement that superseded previous forms of idealism in the period. Gadamer, however, sees Hegel not so much a highpoint of German Idealism but instead as a counterpoint to the German Idealist pursuit of founding a grand unity on the self-conscious subject.

Gadamer's philosophical hermeneutics is, as we recall, an attempt to develop further the radicality of Heidegger's discovery of the hermeneutics of facticity. In this, Gadamer aims to make good on the promise of hermeneutics to break from the transcendental idealism of not only Husserl'sphenomenology but, as we have seen, Neo-Kantianism and the legacy of German Idealism. It is to this end that Gadamer integrates into his philosophical hermeneutics lessons from Hegel's attempt to "shatter" the pursuit of foundations in the self-consciousness of the transcendental subject. With his integration of Hegel, Gadamer elucidates what he believes are key historico-linguistic conditions of the hermeneutics of facticity.

History

Gadamer turns to Hegel, first, to elucidate the role played in the hermeneutics of facticity by history. For Gadamer, hermeneutical experience concerns the pursuit of self-understanding through our efforts to understand and interpret persons and texts. This pursuit of self-understanding is guided by what he calls "the principle of history of effect."[31] Gadamer, as we shall see, incorporates into his elucidation of this principle lessons from what he calls the "step" Hegel took beyond "the orientation toward self-consciousness" to "objective" spirit.[32] Hegel takes his step beyond the perspective of self-consciousness to "objective" spirit in his *Encyclopedia of Philosophical Sciences* account of the philosophy of spirit. Hegel's account begins with what he calls "subjective" spirit—broadly, the mind grasped in terms of the individual subject. Thus, the topic of Hegel's account of subjective spirit is meant to capture the same matter taken up by subjective idealist accounts of the self-consciousness of a transcendental subject, such as Kant's or Fichte's. Hegel's approach means to show, however, that genuine self-consciousness cannot actually be achieved by subjective spirit in isolation because, in truth, the individual subject's consciousness is dependent on a larger context of meaning. Hegel, in the *Encyclopedia*, associates this larger context with objective spirit, and argues that it is comprised by structures of sociality—roughly, customs, morality, and the law. Hegel scholars observe that Hegel's *Encyclopedia* account of objective spirit is compatible with many of the forms of spirit that he treats in his celebrated *Phenomenology of Spirit*.[33] There, however, he describes the structures of sociality that shape our awareness not first of all as objective spirit, but, instead, as substance. Hegel's main idea, in any case, is that the pursuit of self-consciousness cannot be comprised of reflection on individual consciousness alone. Rather, our attempts to become aware of ourselves require that we come to recognize how our subjective spirit is conditioned by objective spirit, or substance—customs, morality, the law, and, more encompassingly, the traditions that shape our experience.

Gadamer elucidates the hermeneutical significance of history in reference to Hegel's idea. Gadamer, we recall, sees his philosophical hermeneutics as an attempt to make good on the radicality promised by the early Heidegger's hermeneutics of facticity. In this, Gadamer builds on the early Heidegger's claim that the pursuit of self-understanding and self-interpretation cannot be founded in the self-consciousness of the transcendental subject but, instead, begins always with facticity. Now, as we have seen, the early Heidegger appears to believe that the hermeneutics of facticity nevertheless admits of the possibility of something rather like a pure relation to ourselves—for example, in the authentic anticipation of our own death. Gadamer, by contrast, argues that no such pure relation to ourselves is possible. In *Truth and Method*, he elucidates this conviction, first of all, in terms of the "principle of history of effect." By this, he means that if we are genuinely to understand ourselves, we must thus also understand that every attempt of ours to understand, regardless of what we attempt to understand, is "already affected by history."[34] He explains that in all of our attempts to understand and interpret, the efficacy of history "determines in advance both what seems to us worth inquiring about and what will appear as an object of investigation."[35] Thus, neither our self-understanding of ourselves nor of any matter, is ever immediate, not even our anticipation of our own death.

Yet Gadamer maintains that this efficacy of history itself is to be understood with Hegel's notion of objective spirit or substance. Thus, to say that our pursuit of self-understanding is guided by the principle of the history of effect is to indicate that our awareness of ourselves remains conditioned by objective spirit or substance, the tradition that shapes the situations we find ourselves in. Gadamer writes, "all self-knowledge arises from what is historically pregiven, what with Hegel we call 'substance,' because it underlies all subjective intentions and actions..."[36] As Anders Odenstedt observes, in earlier theories of the mind, factors such as custom and tradition "were described ... as an external milieu in which thought more or less contingently happens to occur and which can only superficially enable or obstruct it."[37] In Hegel, by contrast, "Objective Spirit is not an ancillary aid or obstacle to it. Objective Spirit forms part of the very constitution of thought."[38] Hence, Gadamer, building on Hegel, maintains that the pursuit of self-understanding takes shape not through reflection on individual consciousness, but, instead, through our repeated experiences of the "objective" world that slowly allow us to understand how tradition shapes our awareness. Gadamer, then, does not think Hegel's philosophy is fit for *Destruktion*. Rather, he believes that Hegel helps us elucidate that and how our pursuit of self-understanding is referred to the objective spirit around us.

There is a caveat. Gadamer rejects Hegel's belief (if, indeed, Hegel believes this![39]) that we finally attain absolute self-consciousness in conclusion of our repeated experiences of objective spirit. As he puts it in *Truth and Method*, "For Hegel, it is necessary, of course, that conscious experience should lead to a self-knowledge that no longer has anything alien to itself."[40] Hegel, on this reading, claims that our pursuit of self-knowledge results in "absolute" self-consciousness, a scientific knowledge of the infinity, in the sense of a complete *totality*, of the conditions of our experience. Gadamer, by contrast, believes that our pursuit of self-understanding is interminable because facticity, grasped in terms of the principle of the effect of history as objective spirit or substance, remains inexorably back behind all of our attempts to become aware of it. "*To be historically*," as Gadamer famously puts it, "*means that knowledge of oneself can never be complete.*"[41] Accordingly, for Gadamer self-understanding is really nothing else than the understanding that absolute self-consciousness is not possible. Self-understanding is understanding of our finitude, and with this, the acceptance of the fact that our pursuit of self-understanding is and will always remain incomplete. With this, the pursuit of self-understanding is not after a "science" of self-consciousness at all, but an ongoing formation of our characters through experiences that teach us to be "radically undogmatic,"[42] open always and again to the pursuit of further self-understanding through our experience of new and ever different aspects of objective spirit.

Gadamer's caveat, then, leads him to conclude that "we can now understand why applying Hegel's dialectic of history, insofar as he regarded it as part of the absolute self-consciousness of philosophy, does not do justice to hermeneutical consciousness."[43] To bring the point home, Gadamer sometimes asserts that he is an advocate of what Hegel called the "bad infinite."[44] Whereas Hegel claims that our pursuit of self-knowledge results in the absolute, self-conscious science of the infinite, in the sense of complete *totality* of the conditions of our experience, Gadamer suggests that our pursuit of self-understanding yields always only partial insight into the "bad" infinity, that is, the indefinite and indeterminate manifold of conditions of our experience. Of course, as Gadamer's advocacy makes clear, he does not think this infinity is "bad" at all; this "bad" in truth signifies the inexhaustible openness of our experience.

Language

Gadamer turns to Hegel, moreover, to elucidate the role played in the hermeneutics of facticity by language. For Gadamer, as we have seen, the pursuit of self-understanding is guided by the principle of history of effect. Thus, this pursuit requires that we come to understand how objective spirit, substance, or tradition, shape our awareness of ourselves. Gadamer maintains, however, that it is thanks to language that we are able to understand traditions and everything that belongs them. He writes that whenever we come to understand, this "*is actually an achievement of language.*"[45] At one level, Gadamer has in mind a common feature of our attempts to understand ourselves though our encounters with aspects of objective spirit: these attempts take place in conversation with someone about something, even if the conversation is a silent conversation with ourselves about something, or a silent conversation we have when we read a text about something. Whenever we pursue self-understanding through encounters with something, we carry out this pursuit through the enactment of language. For Gadamer, however, this common feature of our attempts to understand ourselves reveals a deeper insight about language. Language is the very "element" of our access to the world as such. Gadamer writes:

> In the linguistic character of our access to the world, we find ourselves implanted in a process of tradition that marks us as historical in essence. Language is not an instrumental setup, a tool that we apply, but the element in which we live and which we can never so objectify that it ceases to surround us.[46]

Our pursuit of self-understanding requires us to make a transition from reflection on our subjective, individual consciousness to objective spirit. But this transition is both made possible by and enacted in language.

Gadamer maintains that, in our pursuit of self-understanding, language concerns the truth of our experience of ourselves, the world, and whatever in it we encounter. In this, Gadamer does not first of all have in mind the experience of truth as a property of a linguistic statement about something, for example, "the vaccine is effective." He believes that this experience of truth, familiar to us no less from the study of formal logic than research in the modern sciences, is a derivative one. This experience of truth as the property of a statement says very little about the being of the matter talked about, in our example, the vaccine; the being of the matter, to the extent it comes into focus at all, is taken simply as an object, or, as Gadamer follows Heidegger, something present-at-hand.[47]

Gadamer, by contrast, is concerned with a more originary experience of truth, one that belongs to the hermeneutical enactment of language in a conversation or interpretation, and not simply to a statement. Here, the enactment of language concerns our experience of the being of the matter itself, what the matter genuinely, or, *truly* is. It is precisely such an experience of truth at issue in Gadamer's celebrated motto, "*being that can be understood is language.*"[48] To be sure, Gadamer rejects the belief, typical of the Western metaphysical tradition, that such an enactment of language discloses the pregiven being of the matter—for example, if such being were ordained by God's creation. Rather, for Gadamer, the enactment of language in a conversation or interpretation is a finite "occurrence"[49] that brings the being of the matter into focus in an original manner. Thus, truth concerns the understanding of the being of something *as* something, but only *as* this comes singularly into view in this conversation or interpretation. Truth, then, is not something that comes into view through transcendental self-reflection; rather, the achievement of truth remains always conditioned by the context of history and the social relations that allow for its transmission. In our example, a conversation or interpretation might reveal the being of the vaccine as—in one case, a testament of the power of modern medicine; in another, a stopgap made necessary by poor public health conditions or poverty; or, in another still, perhaps an expression of the they-self in its attempt to take flight from the *Angst* of existence. It is not difficult to see why Gadamer thinks that the experience of truth as the property of a statement is derivative. In the example, the determination of the truth of the statement "the vaccine is effective" is wholly dependent on the truth about the being of the vaccine that comes out in a conversation or interpretation of it.

Gadamer turns to Hegel's doctrine of the "speculative sentence" to help clarify how the language of a conversation can train itself on the being of whatever is being talked about. On Gadamer's recounting, Hegel maintains that language has a "*speculative element.*"[50] By this, as the etymology of the word "speculative" already suggests, Hegel means that language has the power to mirror itself. In our conversations or interpretations, our words need not only be directed outwards, toward things exterior to language—for example, by making reference to something through predication. Rather, our words can also be directed back upon themselves, and, thereby, to make more explicit the being of what the word refers to. As Gadamer suggests, this possibility of language to mirror itself turns on "a constant substitution of one thing for another."[51] When we direct our words back upon themselves in order to make the being of what they refer to more explicit, we substitute one word for another, one after the other, so that the being of what we refer to comes increasingly into focus. Hegel, then, maintains that a speculative sentence "does not pass over the subject-concept to another concept that is placed in relation to it; it states the truth of the subject in the form of the predicate."[52] In illustration, Gadamer considers the speculative sentence, "God is one."[53] Here, the sentence does not connect the concept of God with something else. Rather, the term "God" mirrors itself in the word "one," such that the being of what "God" refers to comes more fully into focus. To this, we may add that "God is good," or that "God is just." With these sentences, we again do not connect the concept of God to something else; we bring the being of what "God" refers to more and more fully into view.

Gadamer maintains that language, precisely in this speculative element, comprises the most originary condition of the hermeneutics of facticity. On the one hand, this means that our pursuit of self-understanding is made possible by language. In Gadamer's hermeneutics, facticity entails that this pursuit is not founded in the self-conscious, transcendental subject, but rather is only possible through our participation in the "element" of language. At bottom, what makes this pursuit of self-understanding possible is the speculative character of language that allows it to mirror itself, and thereby bring into focus the being of what our words refer to. Yet, on the other hand, to say that language comprises the most originary condition of the hermeneutics of facticity also means that our pursuits of self-understanding cannot escape the element of language. The early Heidegger, as we have said, appears to suggest that the hermeneutics of facticity admits of a kind of pure relation to ourselves—for example, in the authentic anticipation of our own deaths. It is worth adding that Heidegger, in *Being and Time*, goes on to suggest that this pure relation to ourselves is related to our experience of what he describes as a peculiar silence of the call of our conscience.[54] For Gadamer, by contrast, the hermeneutics of facticity means that we remain always within the element of language, no matter how inward, how intimate, our experience of ourselves seems to be.

Notes

1. The purpose of this chapter is to clarify how Gadamer's significance to the phenomenological movement, in particular, is contoured by his relation to German Idealism generally and Hegel in particular. There are, however, important more general studies of Gadamer's relation to German Idealism. See, for example, Kristin Gjesdal, *Gadamer and the Legacy of German Idealism* (Cambridge: Cambridge University Press, 2009); Theodore George, "Gadamer and German Idealism," in *The Blackwell Companion to Hermeneutics*, ed. Niall

Keane and Chris Lawn (Chichester: Wiley Blackwell, 2016), 54–62. See also Robert Pippin, "Gadamer's Hegel," in *Gadamer's Century: Essays in Honor of Hans-Georg Gadamer* (Cambridge, MA: MIT Press, 2002); and James Risser, "In the Shadow of Hegel: Infinite Dialogue in Gadamer's Hermeneutics," *Research in Phenomenology* 32 (2002): 86–102.

2. Charles R. Bambach, *Heidegger, Dilthey, and the Crisis of Historicism* (Ithaca: Cornell University Press, 1995), 37.

3. Hans-Georg Gadamer, "Reflections on My Philosophical Journey," trans. Richard Palmer, in *The Philosophy of Hans-Georg Gadamer*, ed. Lewis Edwin Hahn (Chicago: Open Court, 1997), 3.

4. See Jean Grondin, *Hans-Georg Gadamer: A Biography* (New Haven: Yale University Press, 2003), 55.

5. Gadamer, "Reflections," 3.

6. Ibid., 3–4.

7. For a concise account, see John Protevi (ed.), *A Dictionary of Continental Philosophy* (New Haven: Yale University Press, 2006), 421–22.

8. Gadamer, "Reflections," 6.

9. Ibid.

10. Edmund Husserl, *Logical Investigations*, ed. Dermot Moran, 2nd ed. (London: Routledge, 2001), 168.

11. Gadamer, "Reflections," 7.

12. See Martin Heidegger, *Ontology—The Hermeneutics of Facticity*, trans. John van Buren (Bloomington: Indiana University Press), 1999.

13. David Liakos and Theodore George, "Hermeneutics in Post-War Continental European Philosophy," in *The Cambridge History of Philosophy, 1945–2015* (Cambridge: Cambridge University Press), 399.

14. Hans-Georg Gadamer, *Truth and Method*, trans. Joel Weinsheimer and Donald G. Marshall, 2nd rev. ed. (New York: Continuum, 1995), 254.

15. Ibid., 259.

16. See ibid., 256–57.

17. See Gadamer, "Reflections," 37.

18. Martin Heidegger, *Being and Time*, trans. John Stambaugh and Dennis J. Schmidt (Albany: State University of New York Press, 2010), 248.

19. Ibid., 253–54.

20. Ibid., 254.

21. Hans-Georg Gadamer, "The Heritage of Hegel," in *The Gadamer Reader: A Bouquet of Later Writings*, ed. Richard E. Palmer (Evanston: Northwestern University Press, 2007), 339.

22. Ibid.

23. Gadamer, "Reflections," 27.

24. Ibid.

25. Ibid.

26. Ibid.

27. See also Hans-Georg Gadamer, "The Universality of the Hermeneutical Problem," in *The Gadamer Reader*, 72–89.
28. Richard Palmer, introductory remarks to Gadamer, "The Heritage of Hegel," 322.
29. Ibid.
30. Gadamer, "Reflections," 37.
31. Gadamer, *Truth and Method*, 300.
32. Gadamer, "The Heritage of Hegel," 344.
33. See Paul Reading, "Georg Wilhelm Friedrich Hegel," in *Stanford Encyclopedia of Philosophy* (https://plato.stanford.edu/entries/hegel/), Section 3.2.2.
34. Gadamer, *Truth and Method*, 300.
35. Ibid.
36. Ibid., 302.
37. Anders Odenstedt, *Gadamer on Tradition: Historical Context and the Limits of Reflection* (Cham: Springer, 2017), vii.
38. Ibid.
39. Gadamer himself at times questions this. See, for example, Gadamer, "The Heritage of Hegel," 341.
40. Gadamer, *Truth and Method*, 355.
41. Ibid., 302.
42. Ibid., 355.
43. Ibid.
44. See, for example, Gadamer, "The Heritage of Hegel," 328. See also Gadamer, "Reflections," 44.
45. Gadamer, *Truth and Method*, 378.
46. Gadamer, "The Heritage of Hegel," 335.
47. See, for example, Gadamer, *Truth and Method*, 455.
48. Gadamer, *Truth and Method*, 474.
49. Ibid., 461.
50. Ibid., 465.
51. Ibid., 465–66.
52. Ibid., 466.
53. Ibid.
54. See Heidegger, *Being and Time*, 282–88.

25

Too Many Hegels? Ricoeur's Relation to German Idealism Reconsidered

Robert Piercey

No one could accuse Paul Ricoeur of having too little to say about Hegel. He mentions him often, in texts from every stage of his career, and there are extended discussions of Hegel's thought in works as diverse as *Freud and Philosophy, Oneself as Another*, and *The Course of Recognition*. Ricoeur is also fond of characterizing his own views by placing them into relation with Hegel's. His tendency to call himself a "post-Hegelian Kantian" is a well-known example, but as we shall see, there are plenty of others.[1] The sheer number of references to Hegel in his work might suggest that there can be no mysteries about what Ricoeur thinks of him. Whatever else remains obscure in Ricoeur's work, we might think, his attitude toward Hegel is clear.

The problem is that there is more than one Hegel in Ricoeur's corpus. When he describes an idea as "Hegelian," or alludes to the lessons that Hegel has taught us, he does not always have the same thing, or even the same *sort* of thing, in mind. These terms have several different senses in his writings, and while they sometimes overlap, they are ultimately distinct. If we fail to distinguish these senses, we risk misunderstanding Ricoeur's attitude toward German Idealism. Worse, we might not see that when he claims to reject Hegel's philosophy—as he does in his well-known criticisms of what he calls

R. Piercey (✉)
Campion College, University of Regina, Regina, SK, Canada
e-mail: robert.piercey@uregina.ca

C. D. Coe (eds.), *The Palgrave Handbook of German Idealism and Phenomenology*,
Palgrave Handbooks in German Idealism,
https://doi.org/10.1007/978-3-030-66857-0_25

"the Hegelian temptation"—his target is not Hegelian thinking *tout court*, but one specific form of it.[2] This suggests that in Ricoeur's view, other forms of Hegelianism might remain live options for the contemporary thinker. Indeed, it raises the possibility that in some sense, Ricoeur might himself *be* a Hegelian thinker.

My goal in this chapter is to disentangle the different Hegels discussed in Ricoeur's work. I want to show that in his large and varied corpus, Ricoeur uses the term "Hegel" to name three distinct philosophical outlooks: a *methodology*, an *ontology*, and a *metaphilosophy*. Taken in its methodological sense, Hegelianism is a way of thinking, a procedure for doing philosophy. It is a strategy of thinking dialectically, an attempt to transcend binary oppositions by treating their poles as moments of dynamic processes. Taken in its ontological sense, Hegelianism is the view that concrete particulars are an indispensable element of our account of the real—that although the rational is real, it exists only as instantiated in historically specific forms. Finally, taken in its metaphilosophical sense, Hegelianism is a thesis about what philosophy can and should hope to accomplish. It is the view that philosophy's goal is "total mediation,"[3] a state of closure that "reabsorbs all rationality in the already accomplished meaning."[4] This third sort of Hegelianism, I argue, is the one that Ricoeur has in mind when he claims that "we no longer think in the same way Hegel did."[5] Finally, having distinguished these three senses, I illustrate the dangers of conflating them. I do this through an examination of a text where the risk of such confusion is especially high: the penultimate chapter of *Time and Narrative*, entitled "Should We Renounce Hegel?" The conclusion I draw from all of this is that for Ricoeur, renouncing Hegel does not mean abandoning dialectical thinking. It does not even mean rejecting all Hegelian tendencies in ontology. It is simply a matter of avoiding unrealistic hopes about what dialectical thinking can accomplish. Ricoeur's so-called renunciation of Hegel is thus a rejection of a particular metaphilosophy, and it is far more compatible with Hegel's insights into a range of issues than one might initially think. This suggests that, for those of us who wish to continue Ricoeur's philosophical project, Hegelian thinking remains a powerful resource. To a surprising degree, to think with Ricoeur today is to think with and through Hegel as well.[6]

Hegel Today?

Let me start with a sceptical question: why should we be at all interested in Ricoeur's relation to Hegel? Yes, he mentions Hegel often, but there are quite a few philosophers whom he mentions often. Ricoeur is, as Bernard Dauenhauer puts it, "the exponent of the 'both-and,' and the opponent of the 'either-or,'" someone who "finds instruction not only in both Kant and Hegel but also in both Plato and Aristotle, Augustine and Benedict de Spinoza, and Karl Marx and Freud."[7] That Ricoeur often mentions Hegel does not show that Hegel has any special relevance for his work. So why be interested in the relation between the two?

The answer has to do with the sort of philosopher Ricoeur is, and the sort of project in which he is engaged. In a word, Ricoeur is a *hermeneutical* thinker, someone convinced that "every question concerning any sort of 'being' is a question about the meaning of that 'being,'" someone who therefore thinks that the topics of meaning and interpretation are central to the business of philosophy.[8] Ricoeur did not begin his career as a hermeneutical thinker—though it might be more fitting to say that he did not initially *recognize* that his project was a hermeneutical one. His work from the 1940s and 1950s was most strongly shaped by the traditions of phenomenology, reflective philosophy, and personalism. His most ambitious early work, 1950's *Freedom and Nature*, uses the tools of Husserlian phenomenology to describe experiences of willing and acting.[9] But by the appearance in 1960 of *The Symbolism of Evil*—a work originally conceived as part of a single project that started with *Freedom and Nature*—Ricoeur came to believe that a phenomenology of the will could not be purely descriptive, but required a "transition to philosophical hermeneutics."[10] By its own lights, a phenomenology of the will must take account of failures of willing in the experiences of evil and sin. These experiences, Ricoeur argues, do not lend themselves to direct description. They present themselves obliquely through symbol and myth, figurative discourses whose meanings are obscure and in need of explication. A phenomenology of the will, therefore, must pass over into an interpretation of fault and symbol; more generally, phenomenology can achieve its aims only by becoming a "*hermeneutic phenomenology.*"[11] Phenomenology, Ricoeur came to believe, "cannot carry out its program of *constitution* without constituting itself in the *interpretation* of the experience of the ego."[12]

But what does this have to do with Hegel? Ricoeur came to believe that his journey from Husserlian phenomenology to hermeneutics required him to reckon with Hegel—and perhaps even to think in a "quasi-Hegelian" way. In a 1974 lecture entitled "Hegel aujourd'hui," he put the point like this:

> A certain common project undoubtedly links the task of hermeneutics and Hegelian thought: a philosophy of interpretation is only serious if it is quasi-Hegelian, or in any case always in debate with Hegel. It shares with him the conviction that human experience is meaningful, that we are not in the absurd; also the conviction that the meaning of human experience is made through us, but not by us: we do not dominate the meaning, but the meaning makes us at the same time that we make it. A philosophy of interpretation must conserve this reciprocity that I admire very much in Hegel.... [W]e must continue the task of elevating our images, our myths, our symbols, to the level of the concept, and thereby of gathering together ourselves.[13]

No one familiar with Ricoeur, or with hermeneutical philosophy more generally, will be surprised by this talk of the meaningfulness of human experience. But the most crucial part of this passage is its reference to a meaning "made through us, but not by us." For Ricoeur, Hegel's importance for hermeneutical philosophy does not lie in the mere conviction that experience is meaningful. It does not even lie in his conviction that the philosopher's task is to explicate or reconstruct this meaning. It lies in Hegel's understanding of the *nature* of this meaning: his belief that it involves a distinctive "reciprocity." Hegel's contribution to hermeneutics is to have shown how the meaning of our condition can be shaped by our activity without being a deliberate product of it. He teaches us how to see this meaning as something that is found or uncovered, but without being a brute given that is imposed without a contribution from us. In short, Hegel shows how to grasp the meaning of our condition as something that is not quite made and not quite found, a meaning that emerges in and through a dynamic interaction. In the 1969 essay "Psychoanalysis and the Movement of Contemporary Culture," Ricoeur illustrates this interaction with the example of religion. He criticizes the Freudian approach to religion for its "utter lack of interest for whatever is not a simple repetition of an archaic or infantile form and, in the end, a simple 'return of the repressed.'"[14] The meanings of religious phenomena are not merely waiting to be unearthed by genetic inquiry. But neither are they merely created—for example, by a revisionist thinking that ignores the past and claims to see for the first time what religious phenomena really mean. Retrospection and prospection are both essential. Ricoeur puts it this way:

Who can settle the question, then, of whether religion lies in the *return* of memories bound to the murder of the father of the horde rather than in the innovations by which religion moves away from the primitive model? Is meaning in genesis or in epigenesis? In the return of the repressed or in the rectification of the old by the new? A genetic explanation [such as Freud's] cannot decide this question, for it requires a radical explanation, such as, for example, Hegel's in the *Philosophy of Religion*.[15]

More generally, the emergence of meaning is neither simply the reappearance of something that already exists, nor simply the construction of something without precedent. It is an interaction through which old and new, found and made, reciprocally shape each other. If hermeneutical philosophy is able to understand meaning in this way, it is thanks to Hegel. That is why a philosophy of interpretation must be quasi-Hegelian.[16]

But there are two important qualifications to make. In "Hegel aujourd'hui," after noting these affinities between Hegel and hermeneutics, Ricoeur adds that there is an "irreducible difference" between the two:

Interpretation is always a function of finitude. Because I do not know the whole, it is in the midst of things, in the midst of discourse, that I interpret and try to orient myself. I inhabit a finite point of view on totality. I cannot, like Hegel, place myself at a point where I would see the whole. That way of identifying oneself with the whole seems to me forbidden by philosophical consciousness.[17]

This is obviously a controversial characterization of absolute knowing. Indeed, it is not the characterization that Ricoeur himself always favors. Earlier in this very essay, he suggests that a more fruitful way to understand absolute knowing is to liken it to the rereading of a poem (albeit a "supreme rereading of all that we have noticed along the way"[18]). But it is nevertheless a helpful statement of what Ricoeur accepts and rejects in Hegel. He accepts Hegel's general approach to the meaning of our condition; he rejects what he sees as Hegel's overweening attempt to say the last word about that meaning.

Second, Ricoeur applies this lesson to Hegel's corpus itself. He argues that it does not present a single, entirely unified outlook. It contains multiple and sometimes conflicting strands, strands that must be pulled apart by the interpreter. In particular, Ricoeur claims that there is a "profound divorce" between the "two great Hegelian works," the *Phenomenology of Spirit* and the *Encyclopedia*.[19] It is not clear that the tension between these works can be resolved. Ricoeur asks: "Does the *Encyclopedia* nullify the *Phenomenology*? We would expect so, but why, then, did Hegel insist on reworking his phenomenology with such care? Is the system therefore unrealizable, since it requires that we set out on two different paths, from consciousness and from logic?"[20] Ricoeur voices this worry in other texts, often distinguishing carefully between "the Hegel I accept" and "the Hegel I reject."[21] But simple formulas such as these, and simple distinctions between the *Phenomenology* and the *Encyclopedia*, dramatically understate the variety in Ricoeur's discussions of Hegel. Once we look beyond Ricoeur's programmatic statements about Hegel—statements such as those found in "Hegel aujourd'hui"—and look at his *use* of Hegelian ideas in his own projects, we quickly find tremendous diversity. It is not too much to say that for Ricoeur, "Hegel" names not a single thinker, and not a single outlook, but several very different *sorts* of outlooks—and outlooks that do not always sit together comfortably.

What follows is a survey of the very different outlooks that Ricoeur denotes with the term "Hegel." It draws on a great many texts, from all stages of Ricoeur's career. Like any survey, it is selective and impressionistic. But as we will see, it is hard to ignore the diversity that it discloses—not to mention the tensions among Ricoeur's different Hegels.

A Triad of Hegels

The first thing Ricoeur has in mind when he speaks of Hegel is a methodology. Taken in this sense, "Hegel" names a style of thinking, a distinctive way of posing and answering philosophical questions. This method is marked by its use of dialectic, which Ricoeur defines as "an attempt to use negativity as the dynamic principle of a thought that would no longer be equated with knowledge, where knowledge is understood as a subject–object correlation."[22] Hegelianism in this sense stands opposed to all non-dialectical thinking, but especially to Kantianism. Methodological Hegelianism, as I will call it, starts with the observation that the objects of philosophical inquiry often involve dichotomies and antinomies—binary oppositions of which the subject–object relation is the best example. The self may appear to be both an object in a deterministic nature and a free agent independent of it; the self's actions can appear to involve both the autonomy of self-legislation and the heteronomy of following inclination; and so on. Kantian philosophy ties itself in knots trying to overcome the oppositions in our ideas of self, world, and God. The dialectical thinker tries to grasp these opposed poles as moments of a dynamic process, and thus as not ultimately opposed at all.

It is clear that Ricoeur does not object to methodological Hegelianism. He thinks it can be valuable and even necessary to see that what looks like an unbridgeable opposition is "simply a segment in a larger trajectory," and to grasp that from a higher standpoint, its poles do not contradict.[23] Indeed, Ricoeur practices methodological Hegelianism himself, every time he approaches a problem as what he calls a post-Hegelian Kantian. He does so, for instance, when he criticizes Kant's approach to ethics, arguing that the Kantian dichotomy between duty and inclination vanishes when both are seen as indispensable moments in "the realization of freedom."[24] He does so as well in his many discussions of selfhood, above all in *Oneself as Another*. To non-dialectical thought, Ricoeur argues, the very idea of *other selves* is paradoxical, since the meaning of this idea must be constituted in and by me. The paradoxes vanish when we grasp selfhood dialectically, seeing that "the selfhood of oneself implies otherness to such an intimate degree that one cannot be thought of without the other, that instead one passes into the other, as we might say in Hegelian terms."[25] Being a *pre*-Hegelian Kantian, a Kantian who has not learned to bridge oppositions by grasping their poles dialectically, is not an option for Ricoeur.

This is not to say that dialectical thinking is the only tool in Ricoeur's philosophical toolbox, or the most important one. He is, after all, a post-Hegelian *Kantian*, someone who thinks that "something of Kant has vanquished something of Hegel"[26]—namely that Kant's philosophy of limits, with its refusal to bridge all the dichotomies that confront reason, has vanquished the Hegelian dream of overcoming such oppositions. The point is simply that for Ricoeur, dialectical thinking of a Hegelian sort is not itself objectionable. When he criticizes Hegel's dialectic for being overly "conclusive"[27] or for involving an implausible "total recapitulation,"[28] he is criticizing particular second-order views about what the *outcome* of this method will be—not the method itself. It is one thing to use dialectics as a method; it is something else to assume that this method can solve every problem to which it is applied. So when Ricoeur says we no longer think as Hegel does, he cannot mean that we have abandoned dialectical thinking. At least in principle, methodological Hegelianism remains viable.

Now let me turn to Ricoeur's second Hegel. Hegelianism in this sense is an ontological outlook, a view about what there is. Put negatively, it is the view that the real is not abstract. Ideas and ideals possess reality and intelligibility only to the extent that they are instantiated in concrete, historically specific particulars. Ontological Hegelianism is therefore a rejection of Platonism—not necessarily the thought of Plato himself, but the position attributed to thinkers such as Frege or Iris Murdoch when they speak of abstract entities that transcend the ontic realm.[29] Though it is based on a rejection of abstract entities understood in a Platonic way, ontological Hegelianism is not the same thing as nominalism. It is not the view that only individuals are real or that allegedly abstract entities are illusions. Universals such as freedom and justice are real, but only in so far as they are instantiated in concrete particulars. The distinction between ontological Hegelianism and Platonism can be sharpened through a comparison with Quentin Meillassoux's distinction between *instantiation* and *exemplification*. Meillassoux writes: "An entity is said to be instantiated by an individual when that entity does not exist apart from its individuation; and it is said to be merely exemplified by an individual if one assumes that the entity also exists apart from its individuation."[30] Ontological Hegelianism insists that the relation between universal and particular is one of instantiation. Again, it is not, as nominalism might have it, that the universal is unreal. But it exists only in and through the individual entities that instantiate it.

As with methodological Hegelianism, Ricoeur accepts ontological Hegelianism. In texts from every stage of his career, he rejects Platonism and warns of its dangers; and when he mentions Hegel's approach to this matter, it is always favorably. A good example appears in the first pages of the *Lectures on Ideology and Utopia*. Ricoeur argues there that the most destructive misunderstandings of ideology stem from "the claim that ideas constitute a realm of their own autonomous reality" and thus "provide guides or models or paradigms for construing experience" that can be "separated from the process of life."[31] He suggests that a better approach to ideology is available "within a post-Hegelian framework," since the "Hegelian philosophy emphasized that the rationality of the real is known through its appearance in history, and this is contrary to any Platonic reconstruction of reality according to ideal models. Hegel's philosophy is much more neo-Aristotelian than neo-Platonic."[32] Similar themes appear in Ricoeur's writings on religion. "The naming of God," Ricoeur argues, "is not simple but multiple. It is not a single tone, but polyphonic."[33] It appears in the many and varied forms of "narration that recounts the divine acts, prophecy that speaks in the divine name, prescription that designates God as the source of the imperative, wisdom that seeks God as the meaning of meaning, and the hymn that invokes God in the second person."[34] Such talk recalls Ricoeur's assessment of Hegel's philosophy of religion, which he sees as irreducibly dependent on *Vorstellungen*—ineliminably "pictorial or figurative,"[35] always "relying on founding events, embodied in distinctive symbols, and transmitted by highly institutionalized communities."[36] To say that the idea of God must be approached through specific narratives, symbols, and the like is to insist that this idea can be understood only in and through concrete particulars—which is just what ontological Hegelianism maintains. We also find this outlook in Ricoeur's many favorable discussions of Hegelian ethics. In *The Just*, Ricoeur applauds Hegel for "surpassing the point of view of morality with that of *Sittlichkeit*, of the concrete social morality that brings with it the wisdom of mores, customs, shared beliefs, and institutions that bear the stamp of history."[37]

In saying that Ricoeur embraces ontological Hegelianism, I do not mean he has anything like a developed metaphysical system. He does not, as he makes clear in his essay "Existence and Hermeneutics." In the final sentences of that essay, Ricoeur calls ontology "the promised land for a philosophy that begins with language and reflection"—a land that "the speaking and reflecting subject can only glimpse ... before dying."[38] But despite offering no metaphysical system, Ricoeur has plenty to say about merits and demerits of various approaches to ontological questions. In this domain, Hegel's anti-Platonist tendencies serve as a model.

Finally, let me turn to the third sort of Hegelianism in Ricoeur's work: metaphilosophical Hegelianism. Hegelianism in this sense is a view about what philosophy can achieve, and a corresponding recommendation about what philosophers should *try* to achieve. It is the view that philosophy culminates in "total mediation,"[39] a state of closure that "reabsorbs all rationality in the already accomplished meaning."[40] We have already encountered this view in "Hegel aujourd'hui," with its criticisms of Hegel's alleged spurning of finitude and his desire to "see the whole."[41] But Ricoeur discusses this approach to philosophy in a great many texts—anywhere, in fact, where he wants to contrast the modesty of his own hermeneutical thinking with what he sees as a more totalizing, system-building approach to philosophy. It might be helpful to distinguish between narrower and broader versions of this approach. The narrower version, which Ricoeur discusses at length in *Time and Narrative*, is the attempt to totalize *time*: to assert, in the face of lived temporal experience,[42] "the oneness of time," and to maintain that all particular temporalities make up "a singular collective."[43] Ricoeur calls this project Hegelian because of Hegel's wish to unify world history by imposing a single idea on it: the idea of freedom.[44] This unifying idea is "only understood by someone who has traversed the whole philosophy of the Spirit presented in the *Encyclopedia of the Philosophical Sciences*, that is, by someone who has thought through the conditions that make freedom both rational and real."[45] To have traversed this terrain is to occupy a standpoint for which all of history can be gathered together and made present for reflection. The broader version of this impulse does not restrict itself to totalizing time, but seeks totalizing accounts of other phenomena as well. Ricoeur cites Hegel's philosophy of religion as an example: it claims to have discovered a single thread tying together all appearances of religious consciousness into one teleological progression.[46] Ricoeur identifies a similar impulse in Freud—whom he calls "an inverted image of Hegel"[47]—because of the way Freud "links a thematized archaeology of the unconscious to an unthematized teleology of the process of becoming conscious."[48]

Both the narrower and the broader versions of this sort of Hegelianism involve a claim to something like absolute knowledge—which, as Ricoeur sees it, "does not constitute one more level of knowledge. It is not like a supplement of science, extrinsic to the whole process of thought. It is the ability to recapitulate the process itself in the eternal present."[49] A metaphilosophical Hegelian, as I am using the term, need not think that absolute knowledge has actually been achieved. She need not even think that it *can* be achieved. Someone who thinks absolute knowledge is unattainable in principle might find it intelligible as an ideal, and see it as a worthy standard for assessing the success or failure of philosophical practice. Metaphilosophical Hegelianism is, therefore, simply the view that absolute knowing is an intelligible ideal and an appropriate norm for our thinking. It is more than the use of dialectics as a method; it is a second-order view about what the outcome of dialectical method can be.

Unlike the first two Hegelianisms, this third Hegelianism *is* one that Ricoeur rejects. He claims not to have a compelling argument against it, saying that "the loss of credibility the Hegelian philosophy of history has undergone has the significance of an event in thinking, concerning which we may say neither that we brought it about nor that it simply happened."[50] He even grants that many of the arguments that originally led to this loss of credibility—arguments advanced by Kierkegaard, Feuerbach, and Marx, for example—are palpably bad, and "appear today as a monumental case of misunderstanding and malevolence."[51] But this claim not to have an argument against metaphilosophical Hegelianism is misleading. When we examine Ricoeur's criticisms of this outlook, it becomes apparent that his suspicions of it are more principled. They seem to rest on the claim that, though not itself an ontology, metaphilosophical Hegelianism presupposes an ontology: namely an ontology that privileges *presence*. And as we will see, this ontology of presence is incompatible with the anti-Platonic ontology that Ricoeur admires in Hegel. In *Time and Narrative*, he says that Hegel's assertion of the oneness of time

> gets sublimated into the idea of a "return upon itself" of the Spirit and its concept, by means of which its reality is identical to its presence. Philosophy, it must be said, "is concerned with what is present and real." This equating

of reality and presence marks the abolition of narrativity in the thoughtful consideration of history.[52]

Because the present does *not* exhaust the real, Ricoeur argues that we cannot make sense of a standpoint that recapitulates all times into a single time, all forms of consciousness into a single structure. Though made in the late 1980s, this claim from *Time and Narrative* echoes one that Ricoeur made in the 1960s, when contrasting a present-oriented thinking of "the Greek *logos*"[53] with a future-oriented thinking of "promise" and "superabundance," a Hellenic "logic of repetition" with a Christian logic of "Resurrection."[54] Metaphilosophical Hegelianism requires such a standpoint, and it is ultimately for this reason that Ricoeur rejects it.

In Search of a Higher Unity

We should note two things about these three Hegelianisms. First, they are distinct and, at least to some degree, separable. In particular, methodological Hegelianism can be kept separate from metaphilosophical Hegelianism. Nothing about the use of dialectical thinking as a method requires one to assume that its outcome will be a state of total mediation. If it did, then thinkers as diverse as Adorno and Gadamer would deserve all the same criticisms that Ricoeur directs at Hegel—which they clearly do not. Similarly, ontological Hegelianism can be kept separate from both of the other Hegelianisms. One could reject Platonic ontology and insist that "the rationality of the real is known through its appearance in history"[55] without believing that dialectical thinking is the best way to investigate it—let alone believing that such thinking will culminate in absolute knowing.[56] If these outlooks could not be separated, then Ricoeur's criticisms of Hegel would apply equally to Aristotle, which seems absurd. This does not mean that the three Hegelianisms have nothing to do with each other. At the very least, metaphilosophical Hegelianism seems to involve both of the other two kinds. In order to believe that dialectical thinking is a route to total mediation, one must presumably be committed to dialectical thinking in the first place. Hegelianism as a metaphilosophy presupposes Hegelianism as a method. Likewise, since the ideal of total mediation is presumably one in which universals and particulars are fully adequate to each other, it seems to rest on the assumption that concrete particulars are fully real. If they were not, there would be no need for them to enter into dialectical mediation with universals in the first place. Hegelianism as a metaphilosophy therefore presupposes Hegelianism as an ontology. But neither the method nor the ontology entails the metaphilosophy. One can embrace the first or the second, or both, without embracing the third.

The second thing to note is that not only *can* the three Hegelianisms be separated; they *must* be separated. In particular, metaphilosophical Hegelianism must be kept separate from ontological Hegelianism, since the ontology presupposed by the latter is inconsistent with that of the former. After all, ontological Hegelianism insists that the rational is real only to the extent that it is instantiated in the concrete—in historically specific particulars. And historically specific particulars inhabit time. They do not inhabit an eternal present; they admit only of an "open-ended, incomplete, imperfect mediation" in the sphere of action.[57] When we entertain the possibility of totalizing all such particulars by weaving them into a single story governed by a single idea, we falsify them *as* particulars. This is a point that Ricoeur stresses in the 1980s in *Time and Narrative*, but that has precursors in his earliest writings. In the early essay "The History of Philosophy and Historicity," for example, he writes that "we cannot be Hegelian"—that is, metaphilosophical Hegelians—because while the "absorption of history … into the system" promises "the appearance of meaning," this appearance is actually "a Pyrrhic victory. The triumph of the system or the triumph of coherence and rationality leaves a gigantic loss in its wake: *this loss is precisely history*."[58] Seen in this light, metaphilosophical Hegelianism is a betrayal of ontological Hegelianism. We can have an ontology that gives concreteness its due, or we can have a totalizing philosophy of history. But we cannot have both. "As soon as one grants the system," Ricoeur concludes, "there is no more history."[59]

Thus, the task of determining Ricoeur's attitude toward Hegel is considerably more complicated than it first appears. Not only are there different Hegels in his corpus; they are to some degree incompatible. Embracing one sort of Hegelianism may require rejecting another. This explains, I think, the vehemence in Ricoeur's rejection of Hegelianism as a totalizing metaphilosophy, even as he embraces it as a dialectical method and as an ontology of concreteness. As we have seen, the problem with metaphilosophical Hegelianism is not that we happen to be unable to achieve absolute knowing. It is that absolute knowledge is an unsuitable norm or ideal, since it requires us to occupy a standpoint—that of a spectator who gathers all of history into an eternal present—that is not a possibility for thinkers like us. This makes it all the more urgent to distinguish metaphilosophical Hegelianism from the forms of Hegelian thinking that *are* live options for us.

From this perspective, the criticisms of Hegel advanced in the penultimate chapter of *Time and Narrative* look far less sweeping than they first appear. Despite its provocative title—"Should We Renounce Hegel?"—a close reading of this chapter shows that its criticisms of Hegel do not target dialectical thinking as such, or anti-Platonist ontology as such. All of them concern metaphilosophical Hegelianism. Indeed, all of them concern what I have called its narrow form: the urge to think about history in a totalizing way, to gather all the appearances of the real in history into an eternal present. It is this ambitious totalizing impulse, not a method or an ontology, that Ricoeur attacks in the chapter. He first condemns the impulse in general terms, claiming that the aspect of Hegel we can no longer embrace is "the one that equates with the eternal present the capacity of the actual present to retain the known past and anticipate the future."[60] Again, he claims not to have a definitive argument against the project of seeing all historical time as united in an eternal present, saying simply that our loss of faith in it is "a kind of beginning" or "origin" for us, an "exodus … intimately linked to our way of asking questions."[61] But as we have seen, his rejection of this project is entirely in keeping with his longstanding refusal to privilege presence and his embrace of a logic of promise and superabundance. Next, Ricoeur says that once we stop trying to equate the eternal present and the actual present, "all [Hegel's] other equations also fall apart in a chain reaction."[62] If we do not aspire to grasp all historical time from a single totalizing standpoint, we will no longer seek to "bring together—totalize—all the national spirits in a single world spirit."[63] Nor will we assume that a single "guiding idea" could possibly be used to integrate all the national spirits.[64] Once we abandon the totalizing ambition, Ricoeur argues, the Eurocentrism of Hegel's philosophy of history becomes painfully apparent: it looks like a totalization of "a few leading aspects of the spiritual history of Europe and of its geographical and historical environment, ones that, since that time, have come undone."[65] Even if it were appropriate to integrate all the data of history under a single guiding idea, it would not follow that Hegel had found the right one. Those of us who come after Hegel, Ricoeur says, "are no longer even sure whether the idea of freedom is or should be the focal point of this realization."[66] Nor can we be confident that the actions of individual human beings are the right sort of thing to generate whatever meaning historical developments possess: "the passion of the great men of history no longer seems capable to us of carrying, by itself, the whole weight of meaning, like Atlas. As the emphasis on political history wanes, it is the great anonymous forces of history that hold our attention, fascinate us, and make us uneasy."[67] As we have seen, it does not help to say that the totality of an eternal present is a mere ideal, not something that can actually be achieved. What has become implausible is its intelligibility *as an ideal*—the very idea of a "basis upon which the history of the world may be *thought of* as a completed whole, *even if this realization is taken as inchoative or only present as a seed*."[68] It may well be that the stages of history form a "branching development where difference constantly wins out over identity," a development unified by "family resemblance" rather than an overarching idea.[69]

Ricoeur's critique of the Hegelian temptation contains many targets. What it does not contain is any suggestion that dialectical thinking, or an ontology that gives full weight to concrete particulars, are in themselves problematic. Nor does it contain any suggestion that these outlooks are inseparable from Hegelianism as an overweening metaphilosophy. If anything, it suggests precisely the opposite—as when Ricoeur asks us to imagine a non-totalizing dialectic in which "difference constantly wins out over identity," and an ontology of political life in which the various national spirits never coalesce into a single world spirit. In short, the conclusion we must draw from this chapter is that when Ricoeur asks whether we should renounce Hegel, what he means by "Hegel" is simply "the very project of totalization."[70] He means nothing less, and nothing more, than what I have called metaphilosophical Hegelianism. This is not to deny that Ricoeur's criticisms of metaphilosophical Hegelianism are sincere and powerful. But they should not be seen as his last word on Hegel—as, unfortunately, they sometimes are.[71]

It might sound like I am arguing that Ricoeur simply *is* some sort of idealist philosopher, because two out of three Hegels agree that he is. I am not. It would not be unprecedented to do so; a quarter-century ago, Don Ihde noted a tendency to regard Ricoeur as "a kind of latter-day 'Hegel.'"[72] But Ricoeur presumably had good reasons for not embracing this label—not least the fact that Hegel is only one of the important influences on his enormous body of work. All I am suggesting is that Ricoeur's criticisms of Hegelianism as a metaphilosophy should be viewed in the context of his admiration for other aspects of Hegelian thinking, and his willingness to use Hegelian resources in his own projects. They should be treated not as absolutes, but as moments of a larger trajectory.[73]

Notes

1. There are many examples of this tendency in Ricoeur's writings. See, for example: Paul Ricoeur, "Freedom in the Light of Hope," trans. Robert Sweeney, in *The Conflict of Interpretations*, ed. Don Ihde (Evanston: Northwestern University Press, 1974), 412; Paul Ricoeur, "Practical Reason," in *From Text to*

Action: Essays in Hermeneutics, II, trans. Kathleen Blamey and John Thompson (Evanston: Northwestern University Press, 1991), 200; and Paul Ricoeur, *Time and Narrative*, vol. 3, trans. Kathleen Blamey and David Pellauer (Chicago: University of Chicago Press, 1988), 215.

2. Ibid., 193. Ricoeur also uses the phrase "Hegelian temptation" in the essay "Practical Reason" (200).
3. Ricoeur, *Time and Narrative*, vol. 3, 207.
4. Ricoeur, "Freedom in the Light of Hope," 414.
5. Ricoeur, *Time and Narrative*, vol. 3, 206.
6. Although its title speaks of "Ricoeur's relation to German Idealism," this chapter explores only his relation to Hegel. It does not examine his links to other German Idealists, and in particular, it has nothing to say about his relation to Schelling. This is not because there are no interesting links between the two—on the contrary. While there is little mention of Schelling in Ricoeur's work, several of his writings on symbols and on evil refer approvingly to Schelling's philosophy of myth. In the 1970s, Ricoeur supervised a thesis on Schelling by Miklos Vetö, and served on a committee for a broadly Schellingian thesis by Henri Maldiney. Moreover, as Philippe Grosos has argued, there are intriguing parallels between Schelling's and Ricoeur's approaches to the topics of selfhood and personal identity. Space does not permit me to explore any of these links here; for a fuller discussion of them, see Philippe Grosos, "Schelling, Ricoeur, et l'identité narrative," in *Ricoeur et la philosophie allemande: De Kant à Dilthey*, ed. Gilles Marmasse and Roberta Picardi (Paris: CNRS Éditions, 2019), 203–17. Still, while it would be interesting to explore Ricoeur's links to Schelling in detail, there is every reason to think that reflecting on his links to Hegel can only help in this task. The reason is that when Ricoeur does discuss Schelling and other idealists, his usual strategy is to contrast them with Hegel, depicting their views as alternatives to his. From this perspective, if one wishes to understand Ricoeur's view of Schelling and other idealists, one must first understand his view of Hegel. And if, as I have suggested, Ricoeur's relation to Hegel is less straightforward than one might hope, then clarifying it will be a necessary first step toward understanding his relation to German Idealism more generally.
7. Bernard Dauenhauer, *Paul Ricoeur: The Promise and Risk of Politics* (Lanham, MD: Rowman and Littlefield, 1998), 3.
8. Paul Ricoeur, "Phenomenology and Hermeneutics," in *From Text to Action*, 38.
9. Paul Ricoeur, *Freedom and Nature: The Voluntary and the Involuntary*, trans. Erazim V. Kohák (Evanston: Northwestern University Press, 1966).
10. Paul Ricoeur, *The Symbolism of Evil*, trans. Emerson Buchanan (Boston: Beacon Press, 1967), 354.
11. Ricoeur, "Phenomenology and Hermeneutics," 38.
12. Ibid. Ricoeur's view of the relation between phenomenology and hermeneutics is more complex than this formulation suggests. He sees it as a relation

of *mutual* presupposition: phenomenology rests on a hermeneutical presupposition, but hermeneutics also rests on phenomenological presuppositions. Specifically, hermeneutics presupposes the phenomenological insights that "consciousness of meaning involves ... a distancing from 'lived experience'" (40); that "linguistic meaning [is] derivative" (41); and that "the objectifying and explanatory attitude" is made possible by "the reservoir of meaning" that is the *Lebenswelt* (43).

13. Paul Ricoeur, "Hegel aujourd'hui," *Esprit* 323, no. 3/4 (Mars-Avril 2006): 188–89, my translation. Though not published until 2006, "Hegel aujourd'hui" is the text of a lecture delivered in 1974.

14. Paul Ricoeur, "Psychoanalysis and the Movement of Contemporary Culture," trans. Willis Domingo, in *The Conflict of Interpretations*, 146.

15. Ricoeur, "Psychoanalysis and the Movement of Contemporary Culture," 146–47. Catherine Malabou singles out this passage in her book *Before Tomorrow: Epigenesis and Rationality*, trans. Carolyn Shead (Cambridge: Polity, 2016), 157–60. Malabou praises Ricoeur for his recognition that new meanings are "neither a pure product from outside, nor the revelation of a preformed meaning" (159), even suggesting that Ricoeur can help resolve a debate in Kant scholarship concerning the origin of the categories. Malabou does not, however, note that Ricoeur claims to have found this idea in Hegel.

16. This conception of meaning as not quite made and not quite found is also captured in Ricoeur's well-known slogan, "The symbol gives rise to thought" (Ricoeur, *The Symbolism of Evil*, 348). Meaning is *given* by the symbol; I do not create it. But *what* the symbol gives is a matter *for thought*, something that culminates in my thoughtful explication of it.

17. Ricoeur, "Hegel aujourd'hui," 189, my translation.

18. Ibid., 176, my translation. Dosse notes that the Hegel scholars in Ricoeur's orbit generally admired his "supple" and "humble" interpretation of absolute knowing. Dosse further reports that a lecture Ricoeur gave on the topic in Stuttgart in 1981 was well received, and that Gwendoline Jarczyk admired the "probity in his exposition of absolute knowing." See François Dosse, *Paul Ricoeur: Le sens d'une vie*, 589, my translation.

19. Ricoeur, "Hegel aujourd'hui," 181, my translation.

20. Ibid., my translation.

21. See, for example, Ricoeur, "Freedom in the Light of Hope," 414.

22. Paul Ricoeur, "Evil, a Challenge to Philosophy and Theology," in *Figuring the Sacred: Religion, Narrative, and Imagination*, trans. David Pellauer, ed. Mark Wallace (Minneapolis: Fortress Press, 1995), 256. Matters are more complicated than I have suggested here, since Ricoeur sometimes flirts with the idea that there are non-Hegelian forms of dialectic. In this essay, for instance, he speaks of Hegel's as "the paradigm of a conclusive dialectic, Barth the paradigm of an inconclusive, even a broken dialectic" (256). For reasons that will become clear, however, what Ricoeur calls a "conclusive dialectic" is better described as

a fusion of two distinct positions: methodological Hegelianism and metaphilosophical Hegelianism. It is not just a way of thinking, but the additional (and separable) thesis that dialectical thinking can result in total mediation.

23. Ricoeur, "Freedom in the Light of Hope," 413.
24. Ibid.
25. Paul Ricoeur, *Oneself as Another*, trans. Kathleen Blamey (Chicago: University of Chicago Press, 1992), 3. For a more detailed discussion of the role of Hegelian thinking in this work, see Emilio Brito, "Hegel dans *Soi-même comme un autre* de Paul Ricoeur," *Laval théologique et philosophique* 51, no. 2 (1995): 389–404.
26. Ricoeur, "Freedom in the Light of Hope," 412.
27. Ricoeur, "Evil, a Challenge to Philosophy and Theology," 256.
28. Paul Ricoeur, "Structure and Hermeneutics," in *The Conflict of Interpretations*, 51.
29. Ricoeur's understanding of the relation between Hegelianism and Platonism is more complex than I have suggested here. He does typically describe Hegelianism as having a more palatable ontology than Platonism, because of the former's insistence that ideals have reality only in so far as they are mediated by concrete particulars. But he occasionally depicts Platonism as preferable to Hegelianism on ontological grounds. A notable example appears in the early work *Being, Substance, and Essence in Plato and Aristotle*, trans. David Pellauer and John Starker (Cambridge: Polity, 2013). Noting the "laborious, partial, and incomplete character" of the dialogues, Ricoeur writes that for Platonism, "there is no total system, such that one could say that the vision of the One would entirely be recovered and reabsorbed into the dialectic; there are only dialectical fragments… *but nowhere does one find the complete system; if that were the case, the transcendence of the Good would be equaled by the system itself and Plato's philosophy would be Hegel's philosophy*" (134). Note that what Ricoeur criticizes in Hegel's ontology is the impulse to totalize, and not anything else.
30. Quentin Meillassoux, *After Finitude: An Essay on the Necessity of Contingency*, trans. Ray Brassier (London: Bloomsbury, 2008), 25. Meillassoux goes on to characterize exemplification as a specifically Platonic notion: "in Plato, the entity 'man' is merely exemplified by perceptible individual men since it also exists—and exists above all—as an Idea" (25).
31. Paul Ricoeur, *Lectures on Ideology and Utopia*, ed. George Taylor (New York: Columbia University Press, 1986), 5.
32. Ibid.
33. Paul Ricoeur, "Naming God," in *Figuring the Sacred*, 224.
34. Ibid., 227.
35. Paul Ricoeur, "The Status of *Vorstellung* in Hegel's Philosophy of Religion," in *Meaning, Truth, and God*, ed. Leroy Rouner (Notre Dame, IN: University of Notre Dame Press, 1982), 70.

36. Ibid., 71. For an insightful interpretation of Ricoeur's views on this topic, see Gilles Marmasse, "Ricoeur et le concept hégélien de *Vorstellung* religieuse," in *Ricoeur et la philosophie allemande*, 183–201.

37. Paul Ricoeur, *The Just*, trans. David Pellauer (Chicago: University of Chicago Press, 2000), 33.

38. Paul Ricoeur, "Existence and Hermeneutics," in *The Conflict of Interpretations*, 24.

39. Ricoeur, *Time and Narrative*, vol. 3, 207.

40. Ricoeur, "Freedom in the Light of Hope," 414.

41. Ricoeur, "Hegel aujourd'hui," 189, my translation.

42. By this I mean Ricoeur's claim that the oneness of time is not directly experienced in "lived time;" it is "constructed" through artifacts such as calendars and archives, which form a "bridge ... between lived time and universal time." See Ricoeur, *Time and Narrative*, vol. 3, 105.

43. Ibid., 193.

44. Ibid., 194.

45. Ibid.

46. The unifying thread in question is "the journey of the human spirit from nature to culture, and from culture to the self-disclosure of the absolute" (Ricoeur, "The Status of *Vorstellung*," 72). Ricoeur does, however, complicate this claim when he adds that this self-disclosure "does not proceed in an additive way, part after part, as happens in nature, but ... is present as a whole in each of its moments" (73).

47. Paul Ricoeur, *Freud and Philosophy*, trans. Denis Savage (New Haven: Yale University Press, 1970), 461.

48. Ibid.

49. Ricoeur, "The Status of *Vorstellung*," 86.

50. Ricoeur, *Time and Narrative*, vol. 3, 202.

51. Ibid., 202–3.

52. Ibid., 199.

53. Ricoeur, "Freedom in the Light of Hope," 411.

54. Ibid., 412. That said, Ricoeur argues that "we cannot restrict ourselves to the nondialectical opposition between the promise and the Greek *logos*" (412) but must seek to overcome the antinomy between them.

55. Ricoeur, *Lectures on Ideology and Utopia*, 5.

56. As we have seen, Ricoeur sees Aristotle as someone who does precisely this. See his *Lectures on Ideology and Utopia*, 5.

57. Ricoeur, *Time and Narrative*, vol. 3, 207. Specifically, action links past, present and future in an imperfect "pluralistic unity" (207), the "time of initiative" (208), which draws on the resources of tradition while simultaneously looking forward to a certain "horizon of expectations" (208).

58. Paul Ricoeur, "The History of Philosophy and Historicity," in *History and Truth*, trans. Charles Kelbey (Evanston: Northwestern University Press, 1965), 66.

59. Ibid., 75. He goes on to qualify this claim somewhat: "In the *Phenomenology of Spirit* one still finds a certain history, but it is, however, 'ideal.' But when we move on to Hegel's *Logic*, we no longer find 'forms' but 'categories;' there is no more history at all. The ultimate goal of historical understanding involves, therefore, the suppression of history in the system" (75).

60. Ricoeur, *Time and Narrative*, vol. 3, 204.

61. Ibid., 202.

62. Ibid., 204.

63. Ibid.

64. Ibid.

65. Ibid., 205.

66. Ibid.

67. Ibid.

68. Ibid., emphasis added.

69. Ibid.

70. Ibid.

71. A good example is François Dosse, *Paul Ricoeur: Un philosophe dans son siècle* (Paris: Armand Colin, 2012), which discusses Ricoeur's attitude toward the German philosopher under the heading "Renoncer à Hegel" (207).

72. Don Ihde, "Paul Ricoeur's Place in the Hermeneutic Tradition," in *The Philosophy of Paul Ricoeur*, ed. Lewis Hahn (Chicago: Open Court, 1995), 64.

73. I am grateful to Joel Hubick for his helpful comments on an earlier version of this chapter. A draft of Part II was presented to the Society for Ricoeur Studies in October 2019.

26

Conclusion

Cynthia D. Coe

Philosophers tend to read philosophical ideas outside of the historical contexts in which they arise—perhaps resisting the reduction of such ideas to products of social, political, or economic influences, or reactions to specific historical conditions or events. Although philosophy challenges normalized beliefs, behaviors, and institutions, it is also a cultural product, marked by the circumstances under which it is generated and by the perspectives of those who participate in its conversations. The historical trends that have shaped German Idealism and phenomenology are no exception, as their central ideas react to the rise of the scientific worldview, to the political and economic transformations of modernity, and to the threat of industrialized death in the twentieth century. It seems fitting to conclude this volume examining the intersections between German Idealism and phenomenology by considering their respective historical contexts, and then considering the continuing resonance of those ideas in our own time.

C. D. Coe (✉)
Department of Philosophy and Religious Studies, Central Washington University, Ellensburg, WA, USA
e-mail: cynthia.coe@cwu.edu

© The Author(s), under exclusive license to Springer Nature Switzerland AG 2021
C. D. Coe (eds.), *The Palgrave Handbook of German Idealism and Phenomenology*, Palgrave Handbooks in German Idealism,
https://doi.org/10.1007/978-3-030-66857-0_26

The Historical Context of German Idealism

German Idealism arises in an era that generally glorified the power of individual reason or conscience—whether in Enlightenment philosophy, in empirical investigation, in Protestant concerns about the abuses of religious authority, or in political revolutions that rejected monarchical authority. It is the era of the Scientific Revolution, which prioritized the evidence of the senses and material, causal explanations, as opposed to religious or otherwise metaphysical worldviews. Throughout this period there were of course debates, intellectual conflicts, and minority reports that complicate this picture. But we can read German Idealism as an attempt to preserve the primacy of the autonomous subject in an environment that increasingly located all things in a physical universe and attempted to provide causal explanations for all events. Scientific experimentation is an activity that expresses the powers of the thinking subject, but it becomes such a powerful way of comprehending and controlling the world that it threatens to treat its creator as yet one more natural phenomenon.

Even as German Idealists resist the reduction of the conscious subject to one physical being among others, they also interrogate the account of reason generated by Enlightenment philosophers. Kant's transcendental idealism famously undermines the pretension that human knowledge can capture mind-independent reality, and he describes the ambitions of reason in somewhat tragic terms: theoretical knowledge is limited by how experience is conditioned, but it also yearns to overcome those limits. Even as he critiques dogmatism (materialism and determinism), Fichte acknowledges that reason cannot resolve the conflict between idealism and dogmatism; only practical faith can motivate us to choose one option or the other. Schelling radicalizes this idea by questioning the very capacity of reason to account for its own origins and to comprehend Nature in a totalized narrative. He instead focuses our attention on what exceeds or resists such comprehension. The claim that reason cannot account for its own origins and therefore cannot guarantee an objective representation of reality is then further elaborated by Schopenhauer and Nietzsche. The links between the Romantic movement (both in its philosophical and literary registers), early existentialists, and German Idealism become clearer in this complex re-evaluation of reason.

In positioning themselves against the reductive consequences of the scientific worldview, however, idealists were also generally eager to disavow earlier forms of mystical or metaphysical speculation. In this sense, they built on the work of early modern philosophers to separate philosophical methods from theology, and to establish the knowledge-claims that reason could independently justify—even knowledge-claims about the limits of reason. That emphasis on the self-reflective and dynamic quality of consciousness pervades German Idealism but crystallizes as the core intuition of Hegel's absolute idealism.

We should also note that German Idealism flourishes at a time of contestations over subjectivity at a political level, in the context of European imperialism and the slave trade. Defending the primacy of the subject—a being deserving of respect, possessing inherent rights, and demanding moral obligations—becomes particularly charged when political and social hierarchies are drawn among human beings, hierarchies that separate full subjects from those excluded from that status. Aided by early anthropologists, philosophers such as Kant and Hegel draw on the newly constructed concept of race to frame some subjects as rational persons (at least capable of autonomous agency) and to associate others permanently with a state of nature: primitive, irrational, uncivilized, and animalistic. Those distinctions then could be used to justify various projects of racialized domination: settler colonialism, enslavement, extermination, and cultural genocide. Given the contemporaneous intensity of such projects, German Idealist attempts to protect the concept of self-determining subjectivity should be read against that very real possibility by which subjects can be reduced to objects, or relegated to a political status beneath that of full persons.

The historical events commonly associated with the Enlightenment are the political revolutions—in the American colonies, in France, and in Haiti—against absolutist governments based on traditional authority, which supported deeply inegalitarian political, social, and economic systems. The German Idealists observed those revolutions as contemporary events but also forecasted or witnessed the aftermath of those upheavals, as in Kant's essay "An Answer to the Question: 'What is Enlightenment?'" (1784), when he cautions that one cannot simply remove political and intellectual limits on people who have been discouraged from thinking for themselves: "A revolution may well put an end to autocratic despotism and to rapacious or power-seeking oppression, but it will never produce a true reform in ways of thinking. Instead, new prejudices, like the ones they replaced, will serve as a leash to control the great unthinking mass."[1] Fichte, Schelling, and Hegel all consider the temporal and historical significance of the activity of thinking, and each of them considers the possibility of progress or "perfectibility" (to use Hegel's term) through that activity. As a group, they retain an optimism about the movement of history toward greater justice and rationality, including through political change. The imagery of childhood, education,

and adulthood appears frequently in their discourse, with a teleological implication that humanity as a whole is moving from a state of immaturity into
maturity.

The Historical Context of Classical Phenomenology

That fundamental optimism (even where it is limited in German Idealists'
accounts) belongs to a different historical period than the one in which
phenomenology develops. The experience of two world wars, the Russian
Revolution and its reverberations, cycles of economic upheaval, the pandemic
of the 1918–19 flu, the rise of fascist and communist authoritarianism,
the horrors of the Shoah and other events of mass death (for instance, in
Turkey, China, and Russia), the violent struggles for independence in European colonies, and the increasing industrialization and technologization of
society contribute to a sense of crisis or alienation that pervades twentieth-
century phenomenology. That crisis is framed in various terms—including as
a loss of a sense of rootedness and meaning, as an unwillingness to ask about
the foundations of scientific investigation, as a forgetting of primordial philosophical questions, as an estrangement from our lived experience, and as an
unwillingness to treat ourselves and others as free, self-determining beings.
Husserl writes about the need for renewal, Heidegger about recapturing the
essence of philosophy and our nature as Dasein, Sartre about the need to
avoid bad faith, and Levinas about the ethical as interrupting the tendency to
treat others as merely intentional objects.

Perhaps compounding this overarching pessimism is the fact that
phenomenologists also grappled with the after-effects of the Scientific Revolution, including the impact of technology in how we relate to the natural
world, to ourselves, and to each other. Some phenomenologists explicitly
admire the gains that the sciences had made and either draw philosophical connections to empirical methods or knowledge, or aspire to establish a
philosophical science with equally impressive achievements. Others argue that
philosophy shelters a set of concerns that could not be pursued through scientific methods, and that it needs to preserve a separate domain of reflection
that is central to our humanity. All of these philosophers share a commitment to describing the lived experience of conscious beings, as distinct from
studying human beings objectively (in the sense of treating human beings
as objects or specimens), in which the distance between the observer and
the observed serves as a guarantee of the objectivity of the knowledge-claims.

Despite the many divergences from Husserl that constitute the generations of phenomenology after him, his rejection of naturalism and positivism persists. Phenomenologists generally attempt to overcome the traditional opposition between the knowing subject and the known object that dominates the work of Descartes and Locke, and that forms one of the foundational assumptions of the Scientific Revolution.

That focus on lived experience opens up questions and issues that German Idealists approach quite differently, if they approach them at all: the nature of freedom and determination, the significance of the body, intersubjective experience, political recognition, the centrality of practical activity, the connections between language and thought, and the meaning of temporality and mortality for human existence. The subject that phenomenologists describe is thus much broader than the focus on rational mindedness that occupies Kant, for instance. It is a subject defined and constituted by its relations to other subjects, to a material world, and to its historical context.

This broad set of concerns, paired with an attention to the limitations of reason, produces in phenomenology a great deal more hesitation about establishing a systematic narrative of the meaningful world—a philosophical master narrative. In part as a response to the anti-colonialist, anti-racist, and anti-sexist movements of the twentieth century, recent phenomenologists have tended to recognize the political dangers of assuming a generic human subject, and some (notably Sarah Ahmed, Alia Al-Saji, and Shannon Sullivan) have used the methods of phenomenology to explore how lived experience is shaped by gender, sexuality, and race. That acknowledgment of differentiated lived experience and its implications deepens phenomenological resistance to philosophical system-building or aspirations to establish a philosophical science of the subject.

The Future of These Legacies

The question of how to understand subjectivity continues to resonate in contemporary philosophy, even if the dominant accounts of German Idealism and phenomenology confront new challenges, as we consider whether human existence can be sharply distinguished from animal life or technical functioning, whether there can be such a thing as a generic subject, how we might relate to the natural world more sustainably in a time of climate disaster, and the demand for philosophy that does not merely describe the world but transforms it for the better. Recent decades have seen productive overlaps between phenomenology and philosophy of mind—for instance, in the work of Francisco Varela and David Woodruff Smith. Merleau-Ponty's and Heidegger's work has been prominently drawn into discussions of environmental ethics by a number of scholars, in order to think through the significance of technology and our embodied inhabiting of the natural world.[2] A key concern of German Idealism persists in questions of how to make room for human freedom in an otherwise material and determined world. Fichte's concerns about dogmatism and Husserl's concerns about naturalism help us to navigate questions about the effects of information algorithms on democratic politics, the increasing mechanization of many industries, and ever more labyrinthine interactions between organic life and technology.

I would particularly like to highlight the continuing legacy of German Idealism and phenomenology in education. Fichte argues that one has to have had the right kind of education to turn to idealism, and away from what he called dogmatism, the belief that the world is made up of material entities, and that we are just one material entity among others.[3] Our practical certainty of our own freedom needs to be cultivated by an education that allows us to see ourselves as free beings in relation to other free beings and an external world that opposes our will (or in his terms, objective representations accompanied by the feeling of necessity). It is all too easy for us to become dogmatists, to see ourselves as merely part of larger mechanisms to which we need to adapt in order to successfully live our lives. The right kind of education involves becoming attuned to one's own freedom and creative power as a conscious being, or tracing out the rational implications of that immediate sense of our own freedom. These insights ground Paulo Freire's twentieth-century conception of critical, transformative pedagogy, which blends a phenomenological account of subjectivity with Marxist social critique of the commodification of workers.[4] In Freire's account, education should empower students as thinkers and activists, and create in the classroom a space in which rigid structures of authority are questioned and students weave connections between their personal experiences, theoretical approaches, and their commitments as engaged citizens. In a pedagogical version of Fichte's distinction between dogmatism and idealism, Freire juxtaposes the "banking model of education" with the "problem-posing model of education," in which the former treats students as inert receptacles of information and skills that will train them to be useful, obedient workers—and in which the style of teaching itself habituates students and teachers to an authoritarian dynamic in which questioning, creative thinking, and the live connections between academic ideas and personal experience are discouraged. By contrast, problem-posing education emphasizes the creative and critical power that each human being has, in the role that students play in the class-room as co-creators of meaning, which then prepares those students for the role that they do and will play as co-creators of reality—a reality that is open to transformation. In the last thirty years, Freire's work on teaching has been taken up by a wide variety of educators, including feminist philosophers, critical race theorists, and political activists.[5]

The humanities have traditionally been an academic space in which students are invited to interpret what the world means or to judge what it should be, rather than merely describing or manipulating it. I do not mean to suggest that scientific or vocational education must conform to the banking model of education; indeed, the intellectual curiosity and critical questioning that animate genuine scientific investigation are precisely the attitudes that Freire associates with liberation from the banking model. But to the extent that education is popularly justified as career training—as instrumental to earning a high salary, to achieving social status, to gaining entrance to systems of power—schools and universities will continue to emphasize the "useful-ness" of STEM and vocational fields. Students will also be encouraged to understand themselves (at least in their working lives) in these instrumental terms.

At their best the humanities address a need to inhabit a meaningful world, not merely a comfortable, comprehensible, or manipulable world. That is, literature, history, philosophy, religious studies—whether we encounter them as part of our formal education or not—speak to the irreducibly first-person experience emphasized by German Idealists and phenomenologists. They challenge students not only to study how others have interpreted the world, but also to interpret it for themselves. Although disciplines in the human-ities persistently make the case for their usefulness in terms of transferable skills or preparation for careers, we inhabit a culture in which the sciences and vocational tracks are assumed to be more profitable both for individual students and for institutions. The emphasis on profitability leaves little room for coming to terms with our situation as partially free, partially constrained beings—beings who are mortal, who are self-reflective, who are embodied, who exist in time, whose identity is constituted through complex relations to particular others and in a social world, and who live within particular histor-ical contexts—and who encounter mysteries and paradoxes about all of those aspects of subjectivity.

Devaluing the humanities on the assumption that they do not allow a person to accumulate wealth or prestige—to fit into the existing world successfully—is one more way in which consciousness is treated as "a little tag-end of the world," as Husserl puts it (CM §10). We are called not only to control a world of objects, but to make sense of that world, as living, questioning, striving, and narrative-telling creatures. We are also called upon to relate to other human beings not merely as sources of added value, competitors, consumers, or objects of study, but as persons with meaning-making projects of their own. To what extent will education prepare us for open-ended dialogue and interpretation, for self-critique and self-reflection, in the midst of those projects? That is, to what extent will education encourage us to explore the full range of the powers of subjectivity, and to come to terms with the limits of those powers? By no means should this reading of what is at work in the humanities, and the invocation of German Idealism and phenomenology in that reading, be taken as monolithic hostility toward the sciences—only a caution about a reductive or simplistic reliance on the sciences and the worldviews they have generated to represent and navigate reality as we experience it.

I have dwelt at some length on how we should understand the goals of education and the role that humanities play in that endeavor. These debates are at once highly concrete, in the sense that funding and curricular decisions hinge upon them, and also speak to deeply philosophical questions about how we imagine human flourishing (both individually and collectively) and the methods by which such flourishing can be cultivated. German Idealism and phenomenology give us insight into those issues, by calling attention to how we are engaged with and in the world, and the understanding we forge in the process.

The chapters in this book express the range of ways in which that engagement can be understood—in our experience as embodied beings, as knowing beings, as creative beings, as religious beings, as social beings, as ethical beings, and as political beings—and the contemporary reverberations of the rich dialogue between these two traditions. These careful, diverse readings speak to the intellectual legacy that we have inherited, and invite us not only to situate ourselves in relation to that history, but also to participate in that ongoing conversation.

Notes

1. Immanuel Kant, "An Answer to the Question: 'What is Enlightenment?',", in *Kant: Political Writings*, ed. H. S. Reiss, 2nd ed. (Cambridge: Cambridge University Press, 1991), 55.
2. See, for instance, Ted Toadvine, *Merleau-Ponty's Philosophy of Nature* (Evanston: Northwestern University Press, 2009); and Ruth Irwin, *Heidegger, Politics, and Climate Change: Risking It All* (London: Continuum, 2008).

3. Johann Gottlieb Fichte, *Introductions to the Wissenschaftslehre and Other Writings (1797–1800)*, trans. and ed. Daniel Breazeale (Indianapolis: Hackett, 1994), 20, 92.
4. Paulo Freire, *Pedagogy of the Oppressed*, trans. Myra Bergman Ramos (New York, NY: Continuum, 1970).
5. See, for instance, Renee Smith-Maddox and Daniel G. Solórzano, "Using Critical Race Theory, Paulo Freire's Problem-Posing Method, and Case Study Research to Confront Race and Racism in Education," *Qualitative Inquiry* 8, no. 1 (2002): 66–84; and Kathleen Weiler, "Rereading Paulo Freire," in *Feminist Engagements*, ed. Kathleen Weiler (New York: Routledge, 2001), 67–88.

Select Bibliography

Altman, Meryl. "Beauvoir, Hegel, War." *Hypatia* 22, no. 3 (Summer 2007): 66–91.

Ameriks, Karl, et al., ed. *The Impact of Idealism: The Legacy of Post-Kantian German Thought*. Cambridge: Cambridge University Press, 2013.

Apostolescu, Iulian, and Claudia Serban, ed. *Husserl, Kant, and Transcendental Phenomenology*. Berlin: Walter de Gruyter, 2020.

Baiasu, Sorin. *Kant and Sartre: Re-discovering Critical Ethics*. Basingstoke: Palgrave Macmillan, 2011.

Basterra, Gabriela. *The Subject of Freedom: Kant, Levinas*. New York: Fordham University Press, 2015.

Bauer, Nancy. "Reading Beauvoir Reading Hegel: *Pyrrhus Et Cinéas* and *The Ethics of Ambiguity*." In *Simone De Beauvoir, Philosophy, and Feminism*, 136–71. New York: Columbia University Press, 2015.

Benso, Silvia. "Gestures of Work: Levinas and Hegel." *Continental Philosophy Review* 40, no. 3 (July 2007): 307–30.

Canguilhem, Georges. "Hegel en France." *Revue d'histoire et de philosophie religieuses* 28–29 (1948–49): 282–97.

Chalier, Catherine. *What Ought I to Do?: Morality in Kant and Levinas*. Translated by Jane Marie Todd. Ithaca: Cornell University Press, 2002.

Engelland, Chad. *Heidegger's Shadow: Kant, Husserl, and the Transcendental Turn*. New York: Routledge, 2017.

Findler, Richard S. "Kant's Phenomenological Ethics." *Research in Phenomenology* 27, no. 1 (January 1997): 167–88.

Fisette, Denis. "Phénoménologie et/ou idéalisme? Réflexions critiques sur l'attribution d'une forme ou d'une outre d'idéalisme à la phénoménologie." In

C. D. Coe (eds.), *The Palgrave Handbook of German Idealism and Phenomenology*, Palgrave Handbooks in German Idealism,
https://doi.org/10.1007/978-3-030-66857-0

Idealisme et phénomenologie, ed. Marc Maesschalck, 25–55. Hildesheim: Olms, 2010.

Fry, Christopher M. *Sartre and Hegel: The Variations of an Enigma in "L'etre Et Le Néant."* Bonn: Bouvier Verlag, 1988.

Gardner, Sebastian. "Merleau-Ponty's Phenomenology in the Light of Kant's Third Critique and Schelling's *Real-Idealismus.*" *Continental Philosophy Review* 50, no. 1 (March 2017): 5–25.

Gardner, Sebastian. "Sartre, Intersubjectivity, and German Idealism." *Journal of the History of Philosophy* 43, no. 3 (July 2005): 325–51.

George, Theodore. "Gadamer and German Idealism." In *A Companion to Hermeneutics*, edited by Niall Keane and Chris Lawn, 54–62. Hoboken, NJ: John Wiley, 2015.

Gibbs, Robert. "The Limits of Thought: Rosenzweig, Schelling, and Cohen." *Zeitschrift für philosophische Forschung* 43, no. 4 (October–December 1989): 618–40.

Gjesdal, Kristin. *Gadamer and the Legacy of German Idealism.* Cambridge: Cambridge University Press, 2009.

Hyppolite, Jean. *Genesis and Structure of Hegel's Phenomenology of Spirit.* Translated by Samuel Cherniak and John Heckman. Evanston: Northwestern University Press, 1974.

King, Dennis Keenan. *Hegel and Contemporary Continental Philosophy.* Albany: State University of New York Press, 2004.

Kojève, Alexandre. *Introduction to the Reading of Hegel: Lectures on the* Phenomenology of Spirit. Translated by Raymond Queneau. New York: Basic Books, 1969.

Llewellyn, John. *The Hypocritical Imagination: Between Kant and Levinas.* New York: Routledge, 2000.

Luft, Sebastian. "From Being to Givenness and Back: Some Remarks on the Meaning of Transcendental Idealism in Kant and Husserl." *International Journal of Philosophical Studies* 15, no. 3 (2007): 367–94.

Lumsden, Simon. *Self-Consciousness and the Critique of the Subject: Hegel, Heidegger, and the Post-structuralists.* New York: Columbia University Press, 2014.

Marmasse, Gilles, and Roberta Picardi, ed. *Ricoeur et la philosophie allemande*: De Kant à Dilthey. Paris: CNRS Éditions, 2019.

Moran, Dermot, et al., ed. *Hegel and Phenomenology.* Cham: Springer, 2019.

Moran, Dermot. "Making Sense: Husserl's Phenomenology as Transcendental Idealism." In *From Kant to Davidson: Philosophy and the Idea of the Transcendental*, edited by Jeff Malpas, 48–74. London: Routledge, 2003.

Mussett, Shannon M. "Life and Sexual Difference in Hegel and Beauvoir." *The Journal of Speculative Philosophy* 31, no. 3 (2017): 396–408.

Nuzzo, Angelica. "Merleau-Ponty and Classical German Philosophy: Transcendental Philosophy after Kant." *Chiasmi International* 16 (2014): 151–66.

Pippin, Robert. "Gadamer's Hegel." In *Gadamer's Century: Essays in Honor of Hans-Georg Gadamer*, edited by Jeff Malpas, Ulrich Arnswald, and Jens Kertcher, 217–38. Cambridge, MA: MIT Press, 2002.

Rockmore, Tom. *Heidegger, German Idealism and Neo-Kantianism*. Amherst, NY: Humanity Books, 2000.

Rockmore, Tom. *Kant and Phenomenology*. Chicago: University of Chicago Press, 2011.

Roth, Michael S. *Knowing and History: Appropriations of Hegel in Twentieth-Century France*. Ithaca: Cornell University Press, 1988.

Schalow, Frank. *Departures: At the Crossroads between Heidegger and Kant*. Berlin: Walter de Gruyter, 2013.

Schmidt, Dennis J. *The Ubiquity of the Finite: Hegel, Heidegger, and the Entitlements of Philosophy*. Cambridge, MA: MIT Press, 1988.

Seebohm, Thomas M., and Kockelmans, Joseph J., ed. *Kant and Phenomenology: 1984*. Washington, DC: Center for Advanced Research in Phenomenology, 1984.

Sherover, Charles M. *Heidegger, Kant and Time*. Bloomington: Indiana University Press, 1971.

Spiegelberg, Herbert. *The Phenomenological Movement: A Historical Interpretation*. 2nd ed. The Hague: Martinus Nijhoff, 1976.

Staehler, Tanja. *Hegel, Husserl and the Phenomenology of Historical Worlds*. London: Rowman & Littlefield, 2019.

Stewart, Jon. *Idealism and Existentialism: Hegel and Nineteenth- and Twentieth-Century European Philosophy*. London: Bloomsbury, 2010.

Vallega, Alejandro A. "Unbounded Histories: Hegel, Fanon, and Gabriel García Marquez." *Idealistic Studies* 38, no. 1 (Spring/Summer 2008): 41–54.

Waibel, Violetta L., et al., ed. *Fichte and the Phenomenological Tradition*. Berlin: De Gruyter, 2010.

Westphal, Merold. *Hegel, Freedom, and Modernity*. Albany: State University of New York Press, 1992.

Wirth, Jason M., and Patrick Burke. *The Barbarian Principle: Merleau-Ponty, Schelling, and the Question of Nature*. Albany: State University of New York Press, 2013.

Wyschogrod, Edith. *Spirit in Ashes: Hegel, Heidegger, and Man-Made Mass Death*. New Haven: Yale University Press, 1985.

Young, Julian. "Death and Transfiguration: Kant, Schopenhauer, and Heidegger on the Sublime." *Inquiry* 48, no. 2 (2005): 131–44.

Index

Printed in the United States
by Baker & Taylor Publisher Services